Windows® 2000 Developer's Guide

Windows® 2000 Developer's Guide

Ben Forta

Paul Fonte

Greg Brewer

M&T Books
An imprint of IDG Books Worldwide, Inc.

Foster City, CA ◆ Chicago, IL ◆ Indianapolis, IN ◆ New York, NY

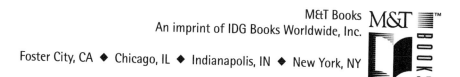

Windows® 2000 Developer's Guide

Published by
M&T Books
An imprint of IDG Books Worldwide, Inc.
919 E. Hillsdale Blvd., Suite 400
Foster City, CA 94404
www.idgbooks.com (IDG Books Worldwide Web site)

Library of Congress Catalog Card Number: 00-100276

ISBN: 0-7645-4653-8

Printed in the United States of America

10 9 8 7 6 5 4 3 2 1

10/SZ/QS/QQ/FC

Distributed in the United States by IDG Books Worldwide, Inc.

Distributed by CDG Books Canada Inc. for Canada; by Transworld Publishers Limited in the United Kingdom; by IDG Norge Books for Norway; by IDG Sweden Books for Sweden; by IDG Books Australia Publishing Corporation Pty. Ltd. for Australia and New Zealand; by TransQuest Publishers Pte Ltd. for Singapore, Malaysia, Thailand, Indonesia, and Hong Kong; by Gotop Information Inc. for Taiwan; by ICG Muse, Inc. for Japan; by Intersoft for South Africa; by Eyrolles for France; by International Thomson Publishing for Germany, Austria and Switzerland; by Distribuidora Cuspide for Argentina; by LR International for Brazil; by Galileo Libros for Chile; by Ediciones ZETA S.C.R. Ltda. for Peru; by WS Computer Publishing Corporation, Inc., for the Philippines; by Contemporanea de Ediciones for Venezuela; by Express Computer Distributors for the Caribbean and West Indies; by Micronesia Media Distributor, Inc. for Micronesia; by Chips Computadoras S.A. de C.V. for Mexico; by Editorial Norma de Panama S.A. for Panama; by American Bookshops for Finland.

For general information on IDG Books Worldwide's books in the U.S., please call our Consumer Customer Service department at 800-762-2974. For reseller information, including discounts and premium sales, please call our Reseller Customer Service department at 800-434-3422.

For information on where to purchase IDG Books Worldwide's books outside the U.S., please contact our International Sales department at 317-596-5530 or fax 317-572-4002.

For consumer information on foreign language translations, please contact our Customer Service department at 800-434-3422, fax 317-572-4002, or e-mail rights@idgbooks.com.

For information on licensing foreign or domestic rights, please phone +1-650-653-7098.

For sales inquiries and special prices for bulk quantities, please contact our Order Services department at 800-434-3422 or write to the address above.

For information on using IDG Books Worldwide's books in the classroom or for ordering examination copies, please contact our Educational Sales department at 800-434-2086 or fax 317-572-4005.

For press review copies, author interviews, or other publicity information, please contact our Public Relations department at 650-655-3000 or fax 650-653-7000.

For authorization to photocopy items for corporate, personal, or educational use, please contact Copyright Clearance Center, 222 Rosewood Drive, Danvers, MA 01923, or fax 978-750-4470.

 is a registered trademark or trademark under exclusive license to IDG Books Worldwide, Inc. from International Data Group, Inc. in the United States and/or other countries.

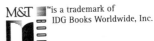 is a trademark of IDG Books Worldwide, Inc.

ABOUT IDG BOOKS WORLDWIDE

Welcome to the world of IDG Books Worldwide.

IDG Books Worldwide, Inc., is a subsidiary of International Data Group, the world's largest publisher of computer-related information and the leading global provider of information services on information technology. IDG was founded more than 30 years ago by Patrick J. McGovern and now employs more than 9,000 people worldwide. IDG publishes more than 290 computer publications in over 75 countries. More than 90 million people read one or more IDG publications each month.

Launched in 1990, IDG Books Worldwide is today the #1 publisher of best-selling computer books in the United States. We are proud to have received eight awards from the Computer Press Association in recognition of editorial excellence and three from Computer Currents' First Annual Readers' Choice Awards. Our best-selling ...For Dummies® series has more than 50 million copies in print with translations in 31 languages. IDG Books Worldwide, through a joint venture with IDG's Hi-Tech Beijing, became the first U.S. publisher to publish a computer book in the People's Republic of China. In record time, IDG Books Worldwide has become the first choice for millions of readers around the world who want to learn how to better manage their businesses.

Our mission is simple: Every one of our books is designed to bring extra value and skill-building instructions to the reader. Our books are written by experts who understand and care about our readers. The knowledge base of our editorial staff comes from years of experience in publishing, education, and journalism — experience we use to produce books to carry us into the new millennium. In short, we care about books, so we attract the best people. We devote special attention to details such as audience, interior design, use of icons, and illustrations. And because we use an efficient process of authoring, editing, and desktop publishing our books electronically, we can spend more time ensuring superior content and less time on the technicalities of making books.

You can count on our commitment to deliver high-quality books at competitive prices on topics you want to read about. At IDG Books Worldwide, we continue in the IDG tradition of delivering quality for more than 30 years. You'll find no better book on a subject than one from IDG Books Worldwide.

John Kilcullen
Chairman and CEO
IDG Books Worldwide, Inc.

Eighth Annual Computer Press Awards ≥1992

Ninth Annual Computer Press Awards ≥1993

Tenth Annual Computer Press Awards ≥1994

Eleventh Annual Computer Press Awards ≥1995

Credits

ACQUISITIONS EDITOR
Debra Williams Cauley

PROJECT EDITOR
Terri Varveris

TECHNICAL EDITORS
Zev Handler
Marion Nalepa

COPY EDITORS
Victoria Lee
Mildred Sanchez

PROJECT COORDINATORS
Linda Marousek
Joe Shines

ILLUSTRATOR
Mary Jo Richards

GRAPHICS AND PRODUCTION SPECIALISTS
Jude Levinson
Dina F Quan
Michael Lewis
Ramses Ramirez
Victor Varela

QUALITY CONTROL SPECIALISTS
Chris Weisbart
Laura Taflinger

BOOK DESIGNER
Jim Donohue

PROOFREADING AND INDEXING
York Production Services

COVER DESIGN
The Stock Market
Photographer: Ryszard Horowitz

About the Author

Ben Forta is Allaire Corporation's Product Evangelist for the ColdFusion product line. He has over 15 years of experience in the computer industry involving product development, support, training, and product marketing. He spent six years as part of the development team responsible for creating OnTime, one of the most successful calendar and group-scheduling products with over 1 million users worldwide. Ben is the author of several best-selling books on Internet application development and on database design, and currently is working on several books focusing on emerging development technologies. He writes regular columns on application development issues, and is a much sought-after speaker and teacher. Born in London, England, and educated in London, New York, and Los Angeles, Ben now lives in Oak Park, Michigan with his wife, Marcy, and their five children. Ben welcomes your e-mail at ben@forta.com, and invites you to visit his own ColdFusion Web site at http://www.forta.com.

Paul Fonte is Principal Software Engineer with Media Station Inc., located in Ann Arbor, Michigan. He has been architecting, designing, and implementing commercial software systems for over 10 years. Paul received engineering degrees from both Purdue University and the University of Michigan. He has worked for OnTime as lead engineer and architect of the enterprise-wide group scheduler for Windows and the Web. He was part of the development team for Open Text LiveLink, an intranet development platform built on Windows NT. With Media Station, he now contributes to the CD-ROM virtual jukebox product called SelectPlay that delivers applications over a high-speed Internet connection to home Windows desktops. When he is not working, Paul relaxes with his family and friends, takes on house projects, and enjoys sports from all angles. Paul welcomes your e-mail correspondence at paul@fonte.com.

Greg Brewer has over 10 years experience developing Windows applications. He is currently working on improving the usability of Windows applications by taking advantage of new Windows 2000 features. Greg welcomes your email at gbrewer@computer.org.

Preface

Welcome to the *Windows 2000 Developer's Guide*. The fact that you are holding this book in your hands indicates that you have an interest in writing applications for Windows 2000. That's a good thing. As you are about to see, Windows 2000 is an exciting and powerful platform on which to develop and deploy all sorts of applications.

But with that power comes complexity. Yes, Windows 2000 is the most powerful and complete operating system yet in the Microsoft Windows family. But leveraging all that power requires a thorough and complete understanding of the Windows 2000 architecture and solid knowledge of the ins and outs of Windows application development.

And that's what this book is designed to provide. Step-by-step, methodically and systematically, this book teaches you all you need to know to develop Windows 2000 applications. Written clearly and concisely, with detailed examples and thorough explanations, the *Windows 2000 Developer's Guide* is the type of book that my co-authors and I wished was available when we first learned Windows application development.

Most of the applications for which you will write code can run on both the Windows 2000 Professional version and the Windows 2000 Server version. Most of the content in this book applies to both versions.

Who This Book Is For

This developer's guide is for anyone who wants to learn Windows 2000 application development. You'll find this book particularly valuable if you

- ◆ Are new to application development and want to be able to take advantage of the most successful operating system in history.

- ◆ Have written code for other platforms or operating systems. Learning to write for Windows 2000 will open the doors to a massive new audience, while increasing your own value as a developer.

- ◆ Are a professional developer who writes Windows applications for a living. If this is the case, then you must be ready to port your code to Windows 2000.

Regardless of the incentive, developing for Windows 2000 requires a good understanding of Windows 2000 architecture coupled with a thorough knowledge of Windows 2000 programming techniques. And that's where this book fits in.

But there are some prerequisites — read on.

What You Need to Know and Have

You can write Windows applications in many languages, but the language of choice for most Windows developers is C or C++. As such, all the code in this book is C based, and prior knowledge of C is a must. This book does not teach you C; however, it does teach you Windows 2000 development in the C programming language.

The C development environment of choice for Windows 2000 is Microsoft's Visual C++ 6 (also known as MSVC). All the code in this book is written to be compiled and linked using MSVC, so you really should have a comfortable working knowledge of the environment. (The appendix at the end of the book explains how to work with and compile the sample applications.)

 If you'd like to learn more about Microsoft Visual C++, you might want to take a look at the "Visual C++ 6 Bible," by Richard C. Leinecker and Tom Archer (ISBN 0-7645-3228-6), published by IDG Books Worldwide, Inc.

A handful of example applications in this book use Microsoft Visual Basic. To use these examples, you also need Microsoft Visual Basic 6 (or Microsoft Visual Studio 6, which includes both MSVC and MSVB).

The only other thing I expect is that you are comfortable using the Windows environment. Of course, being comfortable means having the right tools. To follow along with this book, here's what you need to have:

- ◆ A computer running Windows 2000 (Professional or Server)
- ◆ A copy of Microsoft Visual C++ 6 (with the latest service packs applied)

How to Use This Book

My fellow authors and I designed this book to be used in two ways. You can use it

- ◆ To learn Windows 2000 systematically and methodically
- ◆ As a tutorial and a reference book

To learn Windows 2000 development systematically and methodically, start with Chapter 1 and work your way through the book. Each chapter builds on the technologies and skills learned in prior chapters, and working through each lesson and example provides you with all the knowledge and know-how needed to start writing world-class Windows 2000 applications.

Developers with prior Windows development experience (especially Windows NT development experience) might want to use the book as a tutorial and reference on the new features and technologies in Windows 2000. To aid your use of the book in this way, I include a thorough and comprehensive index. Also, throughout the book, there are cross-references to chapters containing other relevant information. This enables you to pinpoint the information you need when you need it.

What the Icons Mean

Throughout the book, various icons are used to help reference, clarify, exemplify, and describe the material discussed. Specifically, this book contains the following icons:

This icon points out relevant information, such as a concept or important point, to help you master the task at hand. This book also includes this icon to provide additional useful information that might not be an integral part of the core text.

This icon describes tips and tricks that will make your development life much easier. Most of these tips are things my co-authors and I learned the hard way.

This icon warns you of potential headaches as you work with the operating system and the sample code.

This icon, which is used frequently, references other places in the book and in the MSDN where a topic is covered in more detail. (Don't know about the MSDN? I'll tell you all about it in the first chapter.)

How This Book Is Organized

To help organize the contents, this book is divided into five parts made up of a total of 18 chapters and an appendix. The parts contain the following content:

Part 1: The Basics of Windows 2000

This first part introduces Windows programming, concentrating on basic concepts and building blocks. Chapter 1 explains what Windows is, and what Windows 2000 is all about. Chapter 2 introduces Windows architecture and details the basics of the kernel, threads, and other core technologies. This coverage continues in Chapters 3 and 4, with a detailed tutorial on working with kernel objects.

Part II: User Interaction

This part covers working with your application's user interface and the user experience. Chapter 5 explains basic GDI programming and introduces contexts, primitives, and other basic GUI building blocks. Windows 2000 features an extensive range of dialog boxes and controls of which your application should take advantage. Chapters 6 and 7 cover the common controls and common dialogs, respectively. Chapter 8 provides in-depth knowledge of working with Windows (including coverage of newer features such as multiple monitor support). The final chapter, Chapter 9, explains how to interact with the Windows shell.

Part III: Building Applications

This part is one of the most important, and includes coverage of all the major technologies and features that make up your application. Chapter 10 covers working with processes and other fundamental Windows technologies. Chapter 11 introduces services, including how to write and manage these special types of applications. Memory management and file-system management are key components of any application; these two subjects are featured in Chapters 12 and 13 respectively. Chapter 14 covers the user of directory services including the new Active Directory (security and LDAP integration also are covered here). Chapter 15 continues this thread with coverage of other application building blocks (including power management and Internet integration). COM is an extremely important part of Microsoft's application-building strategy; Chapter 16 introduces this technology.

Part IV: The Finishing Touches

The last two chapters of the book cover the bits and pieces needed to complete your application. Chapter 17 details programming best practices and logo compliance, as well as tips and tricks to improve and simplify your development efforts. In Chapter 18, you learn all about debugging, application performance monitoring, and other technologies needed to turn out a world-class application.

Appendix

This book has a single appendix. It explains how to build and work with the sample applications in this book.

 Windows 2000 comprises lots of different technologies, many of which are beyond the scope of this book. The following chapters cover all the basics and fundamentals needed for Windows 2000 application development, and much more. But there are technologies that this book does not cover in detail for they require books unto themselves. When this is the case, this is noted in the text. Also, where appropriate, there are cross-references to reading recommendations.

About the Companion Web Site

This book has a companion Web site that you may visit to

◆ Download the source-code listings in this book

◆ Browse lists of other book that might interest you

◆ Read (or download) the errata (if any errors or typos creep into the final text)

◆ Provide feedback to the authors

The appendix at the end of this book details how to download the source code and work with the code examples in the book. Feel free to drop by my Web site located at the following address:

http://w2kdg.forta.com/

Let Us Know What You Think

I, my fellow authors, and the publisher want your feedback. After you have the chance to use this book, please take a moment to register this book on the http://my2cents.idgbooks.com Web site. (Details are listed on the my2cents page in the back of the book.) Please be honest with your evaluation. Positive or negative, the information you provide can help to shape future versions and editions of this book.

Feel free to send e-mail with specific questions regarding the material in this book. I'll do my best to help you out and answer your questions by return e-mail. You can use the form on the above-listed Web site, or just send an e-mail to

`w2kdg@forta.com`

And with that, good luck, and happy coding!

Acknowledgments

First and foremost, I must thank my coauthors Paul Fonte and Greg Brewer — two highly accomplished developers whom I had the privilege of working with in a prior life. It is Paul and Greg who primarily are responsible for the content in this book. I could not (and probably would not) have done it without them. Thanks to Debra Williams Cauley and Terri Varveris of IDG Books Worldwide for all their help, support, and advice — and most of all for remaining incredibly calm and patient with us all. A special thank you to my technical editors Marion Nalepa and Zev Handler (two other accomplished developers whom I had the privilege of working with in that same prior life) for an awesome job. Thanks to Lisa Swayne for putting this all together. And most importantly, a heartfelt thank you to my wife, Marcy, for working harder than is humanly possible and thereby enabling me to embark on yet another writing project.

Ben Forta

Not to be predictable, but first I would like to thank my gorgeous, loving wife, Nancy. She not only encouraged me to take this on and give it my best effort, but she also gave me the interruption-free hours during the day and the sleep-in hours the next morning that I needed. Along with our three sons, Nancy accepted a heavy loss of attention while I focused on writing this book. She knows that I love projects such as this and chooses to share these projects with me rather than be jealous of them; she is truly special.

It seems that I've been the luckiest engineer ever. My career has taken me through the most remarkable series of mentors that anyone could dream up. Each has taught me a part of what engineering and thinking big are.

Jim Hayes from Spectra Physics taught me that you can be a nerd as long as you want, as long as The Man thinks you want to be like him. Larry DaPrato from Tekmar taught me that engineering requires process and process delivers good results in almost any situation. Anik Ganguly at OnTime gave me the ability to calmly step back and see the bigger picture, not only when looking at the problem, but also when looking at myself. Finally, Tom Steppe at OnTime and Media Station has taught me, and is teaching me, to evaluate my strengths and weaknesses and then to use the gestalt of the team. These wise gentlemen each have shown me the differences between thinking and doing.

Furthermore, I would like to thank some of the peers that I have had over the years who have given me at least one of their skills and encouraged me to develop at least one new skill of my own. Rob Guiher at Sporty's; Al Madden and Ken Rowe at Tekmar; and Ed Driscoll, Mike Foster, Keith Rhodes, Tim Abla, Greg Brewer, and Ben Forta at OnTime. These men have shown me the value of embracing my nerd-dom.

I would like to wrap up by thanking my mom, Lynn, my grandmother, Dolores, my mother-in-law, Linda, and father-in-law, Phil, for their patience as I deprived them of their extended family during this project. Also, thank you to all of the IDG editors who made this possible. I know that I'm not the easiest person to work with, but I think each one of you has been. Finally, thank you to all of the other nerds out there that write great books. I'm a huge bibliophile, and a great number of my best skills have come from your pages — don't stop, ever.

    Paul Fonte

Contents at a Glance

Contents

Part I

The Basics of Windows 2000

IN THIS PART

Chapter 1

An Overview of Windows 2000

THIS CHAPTER PROVIDES AN overview of Windows as an operating system, and of the new Windows 2000 product. It describes the new features in Windows 2000 as well as the reasons why you will want to write code for Windows 2000.

What is Windows?

When most people refer to Windows, they typically refer to the *GUI (graphical user interface)* that they see on the screen. Windows got its name because its interface usually is made up of lots of Windows, each containing a running program (or part thereof).

But there's much more to Windows then a fancy GUI. While it is the GUI that comes to mind for most users who think of Windows, the real magic of the operating system (and most of the features it offers) is buried far beneath the GUI.

Microsoft Windows is an operating system — actually it's the most successful operating system in the history of computing. Since Windows 3 shipped in 1990, more applications have been written and deployed for the Windows platform than any other. And Windows 3.1 (released in 1992), Windows 95 (released in 1995), Windows 98 (released in 1998, second edition released in 1999), and the Windows NT family (version 3.5 released in 1994, version 4 released in 1996) were even more successful. The following sidebar, "Windows vs. Windows NT," explains what Windows NT's purpose is and the differences between it and Windows.

3

Windows versus Windows NT

Windows 95 and Windows 98 were based on prior versions of Windows (which, in turn, has its roots in MS-DOS). Unlike these earlier versions, Windows NT is a brand-new operating system designed from the ground up. While it looks a lot like prior versions of Windows, NT was designed to offer a highly scalable and robust computing environment — one that can take advantage of new hardware technologies.

For a while, there was talk of phasing out Windows and forcing all users to migrate to Windows NT. Obviously this has not happened (and for a good reason: most users and their hardware are not ready for that). Whereas Windows NT is more powerful and reliable than the original Windows (all the way up to Windows 98), thus far it has not been as intuitive to use, not offered as flexible hardware and peripheral support, and its base hardware requirements are considerably higher. So for now, both operating systems exist. However, Microsoft has announced that Windows 2000 Professional is suited for the consumer market (the Windows 98 market), promising a 30 percent performance gain.

As I just explained, Windows is an operating system. As such, it offers all the features we've come to expect from modern operating systems:

◆ **File system:** The basis of any operating system, the file system stores information (in files) on your computer (usually on a hard disk). Different versions of Windows support different file systems.

◆ **Device drivers:** Now, there are more hardware options (and more versions and flavors of each) available than ever before. From video cards and monitors, to pointing devices, printers, scanners and cameras, to modems and storage devices, the list keeps growing. Instead of requiring application developers to write interfaces to each device (each device from each vendor, that is), device drivers create a level of device independence. Application developers write code that interacts with device drivers (which usually are provided by the device vendor), and Windows supports many different types of device drivers.

◆ **User interfaces:** As I mentioned earlier, Windows has a GUI that is distinctly familiar and almost all Windows applications have a common look and feel. This is deliberate and by design. Windows provides support for common screen elements (dialog boxes and controls) and user interface components (fields, menus, and keyboard shortcuts) thereby freeing the developer to write applications without having to reinvent the wheel.

♦ **Security:** Early versions of Windows had no real concept of users or security (which was adequate for that phase of computing). But that has changed, and like every major operating system, Windows provides support for user identification and authentication, as well as the ability to secure individual resources as needed.

♦ **Networking:** Whether you are dealing with a simple *LAN (local area network)*, an enterprise *WAN (wide area network)*, Internet access, or peer-to-peer resources sharing, Windows provides all the technology and components needed to facilitate networking.

As you can see, there is more to Windows than pretty screens with title bars, menus, and mouse controls. Windows has evolved into a family of complete and robust operating systems – and an incredibly successful family at that.

What is Windows 2000?

Windows 2000 is the newest member to the Microsoft Windows family of operating systems. Combining the power and reliability of Windows NT with the graphical interface and usability of Windows 98, Windows 2000 is Microsoft's most ambitious and exciting operating system ever.

Windows 2000 comes in two distinct flavors:

♦ **Windows 2000 Professional** is the client (desktop) version of Windows 2000. This product replaces what previously was known as Windows NT Workstation and primarily is designed for use by end users.

♦ **Windows 2000 Server** is the server version of Windows 2000. This product replaces what previously was known as Windows NT Server and primarily is designed as a file, print, and application server.

There actually are several versions of Windows 2000 Server: Windows 2000 Server, Windows 2000 Advanced Server, and Windows 2000 Datacenter Server. The major difference among these is that Advanced Server features support for high-end scalability technologies (such as enhanced symmetric multiprocessing, clustering, and load balancing), and Datacenter Server extends this with technologies designed for large data warehouses and very high activity hosts (more than 10,000 simultaneous users). And while Windows 2000 Advanced Server and Windows 2000 Datacenter Server both are important new products, most of the development you'll perform does not need to be aware of these differences. For this reason, I do not make a distinction between these versions in this book.

Most of the applications you'll write will run on both Professional and Server, and indeed most of the content in this book applies equally to both versions. If ever this is not the case, I note it.

What's New in Windows 2000?

Windows 2000 is a very important operating system, and one that plays a crucial role in Microsoft's future. Some of the new technologies in Windows 2000 (technologies covered in this book) include

- ◆ A simpler and more intuitive user interface and the ability for you to create the same for your own applications (using new GUI APIs, new common controls, and more)

The new user interface features and options are covered in Chapter 6, "Using the Common Controls," and Chapter 7, "Using the Common Dialogs."

- ◆ Improved and simplified installation wizards, and the ability for you to create the same
- ◆ Sophisticated Web and Internet integration

Refer to Chapter 15, "Additional System Services," for detailed information on Internet services.

- ◆ Active Directory – a next generation Directory Service

Chapter 14, "The Active Directory," features complete information about this directory.

- ◆ Standards-based security structure

Security issues are covered in Chapter 2, "Basic Operating System Programming," and Chapter 3, "Using Kernel Objects."

◆ Support for more processors and memory than ever before

Working with memory is covered in Chapter 12, "Memory Management."

◆ Improved system management
◆ Integrated support for COM+, message queuing, and other application services

COM+ is covered in Chapter 16, "Working with COM+."

◆ Rigid compliance rules to ensure application stability and consistency

Logo compliance is covered in Chapter 17, "Delivering Applications."

The preceding list is only the tip of the iceberg. Windows 2000 offers so much more. In recent years, Microsoft NT has proven to be a solid, reliable, and cost-effective option – both as a client desktop and as a network operating system. Windows 2000 promises to continue this trend, further solidifying Windows' place on the majority of the computers out there.

Why Write for Windows 2000?

Why write for Windows 2000? By now, this should be obvious. Windows (in its various flavors and versions) is the world's most popular operating system. And Windows 2000 is the successor to the Windows throne. There are three primary reasons why you may want to write code for Windows 2000:

1. If you are new to application development, and want to take advantage of the most successful operating system in history, then you must learn to write for Windows 2000.

2. If you have written code for other platforms or operating systems, learning to write for Windows 2000 will open the doors to a massive new audience while increasing your own value as a developer. Using Microsoft's latest compilers and development tools, you'll find that writing production-quality applications for Windows 2000 is easier than you expected.

3. If you are a professional developer who writes Windows applications for a living, then you must be ready to port your code to Windows 2000. The new technologies and features offered by this next-generation operating system will play an increasingly important role in professional and enterprise computing, and clients and customers will come to expect that your applications will leverage this new world of options.

Regardless of the incentive, developing for Windows 2000 requires a good understanding of Windows 2000 architecture coupled with a thorough knowledge of Windows 2000 programming techniques. And that's where this book fits in.

 Throughout this book you'll find useful functions and code snippets that the authors use in their daily development, and you can do the same. Where appropriate, I've noted it with a note like this one.

Basic Concepts for Writing Windows Code

Before you can actually start writing Windows 2000 code, there are some basic concepts that you must be familiar with. If you are an experienced Windows developer, feel free to skip this section.

This is a very high level overview. All of these topics and more are covered extensively throughout this book.

Windows 2000's programs are *executable applications* (files with an *EXE* extension). They may be written in many languages, although the most popular are Microsoft Visual C++ and Microsoft Visual Basic (both of which you'll use with this book). Windows also allows parts of application to reside in external files known as *DLLs* (*Dynamic Link Libraries*). DLLs are also executable applications, but they cannot be executed directly. Rather, they must be executed from within another application. Later in this book, you'll learn how (and why) to create DLLs.

As explained above, Windows 2000 is more than a simple operating system. It also provides all sorts of features and functionality that you can (and should) use within your applications. Using these features requires that you interact with Windows to perform a task (for example, display a dialog, update a registry entry, launch an application), and that interaction occurs via calls to *API* (*Application Programming Interface*) functions. These functions (often referred to as *APIs*) each perform specific tasks. Some are simple functions that may be used in isolation (e.g., the Beep() function, which generates a beeping sound just as its name implies). Others are more complex, taking multiple parameters and designed to be used as part of a group. You'll use hundreds of the APIs while working through this book, but not all of them. The definitive Windows API reference is the help files that come with Microsoft Visual C++.

Many APIs require that you pass special forms of data. These may include information about a window that you want to write text to, font and color information, or details about a memory block that you are using. To simplify working with these types of data, the Windows 2000 APIs define numerous data types, and you'll be introduced to many of these as you work through this book.

Another important concept is that of *events*, or *messages*. If you've ever written code for an application running under DOS, you know that a function named main() gets executed, and from that point on, you have full control over the execution and flow of your application. If you want to respond to the user input, you use functions to retrieve that user input and then you respond to it directly. Windows 2000 works differently. Your applications don't trap and respond to user input directly. Rather, Windows 2000 responds and then notifies you of what the user did, thereby allowing you to respond to it. Windows does this by sending *messages* (yes, they are called *messages*) to applications that notify them of events (e.g., a key being pressed or a menu being selected). Your Windows application contains a message loop, a piece of code that sits in a loop waiting for messages from the operating system. In other words, while DOS-based programs poll the operating system for information, Windows-based programs wait until the operating system reports that an action has occurred. The difference is subtle, but it dramatically impacts how you write your code, as you'll see starting in Chapter 2.

How to Use the Microsoft Developer Network

Throughout this book, you'll see cross-references to the *MSDN*—the *Microsoft Developer Network*. MSDN is Microsoft's primary resource for developers that use Microsoft tools, languages, and operating systems. MSDN comes in several flavors, one or more of which may suit your needs:

◆ **MSDN Online:** This is Microsoft's online repository of news, libraries, knowledge bases, online communities and magazines, image and sound libraries, and more. Membership is required for much of the content. Visit http://msdn.microsoft.com for more information.

◆ **MSDN Subscriptions:** This is an annual membership offering that is designed to ensure that developers have instant access to the latest and greatest that Microsoft offers. Several times a year, Microsoft sends MSDN Subscribers CDs that contain operating system updates, Visual Studio and language enhancements, *SDKs* (*Software Development Kits*), *DDKs* (*Driver Development Kits*), testing tools, and much more. There are several levels of subscription offered. More information is available at http://msdn. microsoft.com/subscriptions.

◆ **Special Programs for ISVs:** The MSDN also offers special programs for *ISVs* (*Independent Software Vendors*) that produce commercial prepackaged applications, user groups, and more. Information on this is available at http://msdn.microsoft.com.

Although I can't tell you which MSDN offering is right for you, I do strongly urge you to visit the MSDN site and browse the options. If you are serious about Windows 2000 development, you must have access to the resources that the MSDN makes available to you.

Summary

Windows 2000 is the latest and greatest addition to the Microsoft Windows family — and one that is going to change the face of desktop and network computing dramatically. Windows 2000 features many new technologies and enhancements. Learning to write Windows 2000 applications can greatly enhance the value of both you and the code you write.

In this chapter, you learned what Windows 2000 is and why you should write for it. I also covered some basic terminology and concepts and introduced the MSDN (which I urge you to take advantage of). Now let's move on to the next chapter of this book. In Chapter 2, you will learn about the basic programming functionality needed to build world-class applications.

Chapter 2

Basic Operating System Programming

IN THIS CHAPTER

- ◆ Architecture of Windows 2000
- ◆ The basics of applications
- ◆ Threads of execution

WINDOWS 2000 PROVIDES YOU with great facilities to build world-class applications atop cutting-edge hardware. Whenever you create an application, you rely on the underlying operating system to provide some basic programming functionality. First, the system must provide easy access to the hardware inputs and outputs through which the user communicates. Next, the system must allow processes to share limited resources (e.g., the network or the display). Finally, you need the system to protect your application from others doing the wrong thing, causing it to crash (and vice-versa). Windows 2000 has all of these qualities of a great operating system.

In this chapter, I show you the basic architecture of Windows 2000 and how your applications fit into it. I also show you how to use the Windows API to create and manipulate processes and threads of execution.

Architecture of Windows 2000

Microsoft built Windows 2000 using the Windows NT architecture; that is, Windows 2000 is a preemptive multitasking operating system. It is a layered micro-kernel, a hybrid design that runs its executive process in kernel mode while most system services and all applications run in user mode. The rest of this section attempts to explain how this works. I try to be as brief as possible since this mostly is background information explaining how programs work and not how to write them (which is the fun part).

The Windows executive

The *executive* is the Windows term for the heart of the operating system, and it is used almost interchangeably with the term *kernel* for this core functionality. This component supplies all system services including thread scheduling and hardware I/O. The executive directs the CPU to run a process's threads and provides a process access to system resources (e.g., I/O, memory, and thread synchronization objects). The executive accomplishes this by owning all access to vital components of the system and forcing all processes to call into it when using them.

The Windows 2000 architecture takes advantage of privilege levels supplied by modern CPUs to segregate processes. The most privileged execution level, called *kernel mode* by Windows 2000, runs the executive. The least privileged execution level, called *user mode* by Windows 2000, is where most system services and all applications run. If you're a hardware nerd, the operating system implements kernel mode as Ring 0 on the Intel x86 processor line and user mode as Ring 3.

The processor allows processes in kernel mode complete access to all instructions and system resources. The processor does not allow processes in user mode to execute all instructions or access all system resources. Windows 2000 uses this separation to insulate the executive from all applications and services as well as those applications and services from one another — it forces everyone outside the executive to play by its rules.

Each time an application desires a service from the system, it must call into the Windows 2000 executive, which requires a transition from user mode to kernel mode. The application executes this transition by passing the execution thread into a system DLL (e.g., `Kernel32.DLL`) that then executes a software exception (a trap). This transition is quite expensive in terms of CPU cycles.

When an application desires a system service that does not exist within the executive, the executive must use a *local procedure call (LPC)* to send the request to a system service process that also is running in user mode. This message passing creates an environment for the application much like the client-server relationship. The requestor makes a call into a local *dynamic link library (DLL)* that executes the LPC, and somewhere a server does the right thing to fulfill that request. The client has no real idea where or how the server accomplished it and neither process can crash the other.

Since the kernel-mode/user-mode transition is very CPU intensive, the design team needed to minimize the number of LPCs typically used while providing the security of the client-server model. They realized this balance with the hybrid nature of the design (the layered part of the layered microkernel design) and placed some of the most commonly used system services in the executive. The executive's local system services typically are broken into the following major categories and all execute in kernel mode:

◆ Object manager: owns the kernel objects that give access to core services for creating Windows 2000 applications.

- Security reference monitor: provides consistent security checking and enforcement for system resources. It is an integral part of the Windows 2000 security system.

- Process manager: manages thread and process lifetime and assumes responsibility for scheduling execution time.

- Local procedure call facility: provides simple message-passing utilities to clients and servers on the same machine. This subsystem provides client-server access to environment subsystems (e.g., Win32 subsystem) for applications.

- Virtual memory manager (VMM): provides each process with its own uniform, private address space. This enables each process to treat all addressable memory as if it owned the space and prevents one process from overwriting another's data.

- I/O manager: supplies access to hardware device drivers, the file systems, and the network for all processes.

- Window manager: creates the interface that you are familiar with and provides processes access to the *graphics device interface (GDI)* that actually controls the display hardware.

The underpinning of the Windows executive is the microkernel and the hardware abstraction layer. I discuss the functionality of these two critical components in the following sections.

MICROKERNEL

Just as the kernel, or executive, is the heart of the system, the heart of the executive is the microkernel. It does most of the work of the operating system such as scheduling threads, managing multiple processors, and handling exceptions. In fact, the microkernel is an operating system unto itself — accessible only to other components of the Windows 2000 executive.

The microkernel uses a prioritization scheme to determine which thread should run when. It attempts to keep the processor, or processors, in the system as utilized as possible (not running the system-idle process). The microkernel does this by pre-empting the execution of one thread and starting the execution of another waiting thread. This enables you to create your process as if it were the only process running on the machine — the microkernel takes care of pausing it then resuming when it needs to, and your code doesn't even notice. Further, when creating a multi-threaded application, you must pay heed to the fact that the system might stop one thread at any point and start another — your code must be thread-safe or reentrant.

Since the executive contains systems that could have existed as user mode processes and the microkernel is a mini operating system, the microkernel provides scheduling and synchronization for them. The microkernel also exposes objects such as events, mutexes, threads, and processes that eventually are propagated out to user mode processes as application services.

Chapter 3, "Using Kernel Objects," and Chapter 4, "Commonly Used Kernel Objects," discuss the user mode versions of the microkernel objects.

HARDWARE ABSTRACTION LAYER

The *hardware abstraction layer (HAL)* is the bottommost layer of the Windows 2000 executive. It allows the microkernel and all other executive components to manipulate the hardware of the current system using a uniform set of interfaces. That is, all components of the executive, including device drivers, access the actual hardware through a single body of code called Hal.DLL.

The HAL prevents executive components from having to access hardware directly and littering their implementation with hardware-specific code. It provides a simple software interface to system hardware that abstracts away differences between low-level hardware interfaces (e.g., DMA controllers, interrupt controllers, and clocks). This makes it easy to write and debug the low-level device drivers and enables manufacturers to supply a custom HAL (i.e., Hal.DLL) when they create new hardware.

Programming at the executive level or below (e.g., the device driver level) is beyond the scope of this text.

Windows protected subsystems

All system services not in the executive by definition are user mode services called protected subsystems. These service processes have properties identical to applications as far as the operating system is concerned. The protected subsystems complete the operating system and enable the designers to extend it.

Examples of the protected subsystems are the environment and integral subsystems. The environment subsystems provide APIs that supply the services specific to an operating system such as POSIX, OS/2, or Win32. An integral subsystem is one that is required by most or all applications, but that can afford the performance hit of a kernel mode to user mode transition. Examples include the security subsystem, the workstation service, and the server service.

The Basics of Applications

Now that I've gone over the basic architecture of the Windows 2000 system and you have an inkling of what code lives where, we can look at creating applications that run within it. The system recognizes applications internally as process objects and provides a variety of facilities for manipulating them. This section first discusses the various application types and then moves on to creating applications and how they are constructed. I then discuss interacting with process objects that are the system realization of your application code.

Application types

I could tell you that Windows 2000 recognizes three types of applications – console applications, GUI applications, and service applications – but that would be misleading. Windows 2000 actually treats all Win32 applications the same; a console application can create GUI, a GUI application can run as a service, and a service can write to its *standard output stream* (stdout). The only important distinction between applications types is the startup method.

First, let's look at the details of application development. When you tell the C++ compiler to build an executable, it compiles the source into an OBJ file, then it links together that OBJ file with its standard libraries, and anything else that you tell it goes into the application.

The resulting EXE file is a collection of loader directives, machine code, and data for the application. A loader directive tells the system where to load the machine code. Another loader directive tells the system where to begin execution of the process's primary thread; this location is the low-level entry point that does some setup then enters the main(), ServiceMain(), or WinMain() function that you've supplied. The machine code is where your control logic goes; it does things such as jump into Windows APIs, make calculations, and write data to disk. This machine code is the principal value that you add – it's your source turned into a useful collection of ones and zeroes. The last part of the executable, the application data, supports the machine code with strings, bitmaps, icons, and so on.

SIMPLE CONSOLE APPLICATIONS

When approaching a new language or platform, tradition in the programming world tells us to create a "Hello, World" application, so let's do it. You can type Listing 2-1 into notepad or use Visual Studio to create a console application project then type it. Once you save the code as Hello.CPP, building it is as simple as using the command line CL Hello.CPP or the Build toolbar tool in Visual Studio. That's it; you now have the executable Hello.EXE, which produces the innocuous line you type in when you run it.

Listing 2-1: Demonstrating a very simple Windows 2000 console application

```
// project hello
#include <iostream>

void main()
{
    std::cout << "Hello, Windows 2000" << std::endl;
}
```

Listing 2-1 and the results shown in Figure 2-1 demonstrate that developing applications for Windows has become simple. I'm sure you've heard horror stories about how very difficult it is to build applications, that handling Windows messages is black magic, that creating "real" applications in *Microsoft foundation classes (MFC)* is confusing, or that *component object model (COM)* will drive you crazy if you try to understand it. These stories have grains of truth, but there's no reason for you to experience them first-hand.

Figure 2-1: The traditional first program implemented as a simple console application

Windows 2000, built on NT technology, gives you the ability to create console applications. These applications behave very much like the old DOS or UNIX applications in that they use the character mode streams, *standard input* (stdin) and *standard output* (stdout), as the principal methods for communication with the user. The Windows 2000 console enables you to create small, focused applications using standard C++ tools such as the iostream library's cout and cin objects.

Chapter 15, "System Services," covers console handling.

GUI APPLICATIONS

You've seen an application that uses the traditional C main() entry point; the Visual Studio C++ compiler knows that when you include this method that it should mark the resulting EXE file as a console application. In Listing 2-2, the C++ compiler creates a GUI application since the code contains the WinMain() method which is the standard entry point for this type of application.

 Again, you can type in the code from Listing 2-2 with Notepad or any text editor, save it, and run CL.EXE from the command line to produce MsgBox.EXE.

Listing 2-2: Demonstrating a simple Windows 2000 GUI application

```
// project msgbox
#include <windows.h>                // standard include

// tell linker to get user32 which contains the MessageBox API
#pragma comment(lib,"user32.lib")

// simple application that pops up a message box and
//  exits
int APIENTRY WinMain(HINSTANCE /*hInstance*/,
                     HINSTANCE /*hPrevInstance*/,
                     LPSTR     /*lpCmdLine*/,
                     int       /*nCmdShow*/)
{
    ::MessageBox(
        NULL,                   // no parent window
        "Hello, Windows 2000",  // box text
        "Greetings",            // box caption
        MB_OK);                 // just an OK button

    // send back zero to tell the system we never got to the
    //  message loop
    return(0);
}
```

The GUI application from Listing 2-2 requires more code than the console application, but it's still small. First, the Windows.H header file is required in order to get the definitions of the data types passed into WinMain() and the MessageBox() API.

Microsoft publishes this header file as part of the Platform SDK and includes it with the Visual Studio compiler for convenience.

The next line of code is rather interesting. It's a `pragma` directive to the compiler/linker to find `User32.LIB` and link it into the resulting EXE file. This enables you to run the simple command line of `CL MsgBox.CPP` to build this application; otherwise the `MessageBox()` API would be unresolved and you would have to find it. This tool is specific to the Visual Studio C++ compiler (all `pragma` statements are compiler-specific). You should use it to make it easy for consumers of your code to get their job done.

Next, the `WinMain()` method is implemented. There are four parameters passed in to you by the actual low-level entry point. The `hInstance` parameter is unique to the EXE file; you use it for loading resources such as icons or bitmaps attached to the code and you can retrieve it at any point using the `GetModuleHandle()` API. The system uses instance handles to indicate to the system where code and initial data are loaded into memory. (The value actually is the base address of the EXE file image – usually 0x00400000.) The next parameter, `hPrevInstance`, exists for backward compatibility, and the system now guarantees it is `NULL`. The application's command line, excluding the name of the program, is the `lpCmdLine` parameter. Additionally, the system tells the application how it should display its main window with the `nCmdShow` parameter (choices include minimized, maximized, and normal).

Finally, the program executes the call to the `MessageBox()` API and quits. The message box, shown in Figure 2-2, has the same message as in Listing 2-1 and waits for acknowledgment at the `OK` button. The system suggests that the program return zero if it ends before entering a main message loop.

Figure 2-2: The traditional first program implemented as a simple GUI application

 Chapter 8, "Working with Windows," covers windowing applications in detail.

SERVICE APPLICATIONS

The final type of application that is important to you is the service application. A Windows 2000 service generally supplies functionality to users of the system whenever the system is running. For example, an *FTP (File Transfer Protocol)* server on Windows 2000 usually is a service application. Windows typically runs services automatically at startup; services do not depend on a user to log on and start them although an administrator can start and stop them manually.

The service application type has neither a `main()` nor a `WinMain()` function; it requires a `ServiceMain()` function that actually gets called by the *service control manager (SCM)*. The SCM is an integral part of the operating system and is responsible for starting the services in response to system boot, direct user control, or a request from another service. It alone is responsible for making the application behave like a service. Typically, services log on to the machine under the special `LocalSystem` account, which has different privileges than the developer creating the services. In addition, services do not interact with the user at the desktop using Windows GUI – although it is possible.

Chapter 11, "Service Applications," covers service applications and the SCM in detail.

Application construction

In the previous section, I briefly cover some of the mechanics of creating applications. The Visual Studio C++ compiler does most of the work for you for simple applications. But for full-blown applications, you need some more tools. Windows enables you to break code up into smaller chunks of code called *dynamic link libraries (DLLs)* that also contain machine code and application data for your application to use.

DLLs are convenient tools for modularizing a large application into small, cohesive packages of services. Windows itself supplies most of its services in the form of DLLs that you link into your application. For example, Listing 2-2 calls out `User32.LIB` as a library to link with when constructing the EXE file; `User32.LIB` actually is an import library that tells the EXE file that it can call into `User32.DLL` when it needs the `MessageBox()` API. The system maps the code from a DLL into the process's address space just like the EXE file – either explicitly through a call to `LoadLibrary()` or implicitly by the system loader. It exposes functionality as a set of function calls (e.g., `MessageBox()`) that get assigned memory locations for the process to jump into when appropriate.

Chapter 10, "Application Building Services," covers DLLs in more detail.

Behind the scenes, the C++ compiler tells the system to start up your application by calling another method that it supplies prior to your main() or WinMain() function. This method takes care of initializing the C++ runtime, which includes calling constructors for static objects and initializing the heap. In addition, when your process returns from its main method, the outer method does the opposite job and terminates the C++ runtime.

Most Windows applications also contain large portions of data called resources. These resources can be string tables, dialog templates, bitmaps and icons, as well as other standard and custom chunks of data. You can attach this data to DLLs or EXEs. Then, using the instance handles discussed earlier, you can ask Windows to retrieve this data so that your application code can use it. Listing 2-3 shows you an example of an EXE pulling strings out of a string table for use in a dialog box.

Listing 2-3: Using data attached to an EXE as a resource

```
// project loadrsrc
#include <windows.h>
#include "resource.h"

// simple application to grab strings attached to the EXE
//   file and display them
int APIENTRY WinMain(HINSTANCE hInstance,
                     HINSTANCE /*hPrevInstance*/,
                     LPSTR     /*lpCmdLine*/,
                     int       /*nCmdShow*/)
{
    // data buffers to hold the strings from the resource
    const int c_nBufSize = 1024;
    TCHAR szCaption[c_nBufSize], szMessage[c_nBufSize];

    // tell Windows to load the two required strings attached
    //   to this EXE
    ::LoadString(
        hInstance,  // handle of image to load from (this EXE)
        IDS_MESSAGE,// ID of string to grab
        szMessage,  // buffer to fill
        c_nBufSize);// size of buffer
    ::LoadString(
        hInstance,  // handle of image to load from (this EXE)
        IDS_CAPTION,// ID of string to grab
        szCaption,  // buffer to fill
        c_nBufSize);// size of buffer

    // just display a simple message box
    ::MessageBox(
```

```
        NULL,          // no parent window, use the desktop
        szMessage,     // body of message to display
        szCaption,     // caption to use for display
        MB_OK);        // only need an OK button

    // send back 0, the system wants it
    return 0;
}
```

In order to build the example in Listing 2-3 and the remaining listings throughout the book, you will need to use the Visual Studio workspace in place of the raw C++ compiler call at the command line.

The appendix, "Using the Examples in This Book," explains where to find and how to build the listings throughout the book.

The application in Listing 2-3 behaves identically to that in Listing 2-2. It simply replaces the hard-coded strings that the message box displays with strings taken from the attached resource. The example does this by calling the LoadString() API – supplying the location of the module to find the string, its ID number, and a buffer into which to copy it.

Listing 2-3 demonstrates a powerful technique that enables you to change the data used and displayed by the application without editing the code. After you create the EXE file, you can open it with Visual Studio as a resource, change the strings, then save it. When you run the application again, it displays the new strings – no recompile is required. Also, the strings are attached to the EXE file in this example, but they just as easily could have come from a DLL, in which case the application would retrieve the instance handle using GetModuleHandle() or some other technique to supply it to the LoadString() API calls.

Process objects

As I stated earlier, the operating system sees applications that currently are running on the system as process objects. You get to interact with process objects using a system-supplied unique number called a HANDLE; this value is valid only in the current process. The example in Listing 2-4 shows a very simple use of the process handle. Any process running in the system can call the GetCurrentProcess() API which returns a handle to identify itself. Then you can use this handle anywhere Windows requires the specification of a process.

Listing 2-4: Getting and using a process handle

```
// project prochandle
#include <windows.h>
#include <iostream>

// simple application to determine its own priority
void main()
{
    // grab a handle to the current process
    HANDLE hProcessThis = ::GetCurrentProcess();

    // ask the kernel for the priority class this process
    //  belongs to
    DWORD dwPriority = ::GetPriorityClass(hProcessThis);

    // emit a message for the user describing the class
    std::cout << "Current process priority: ";
    switch(dwPriority)
    {
        case HIGH_PRIORITY_CLASS:
            std::cout << "High";
            break;
        case NORMAL_PRIORITY_CLASS:
            std::cout << "Normal";
            break;
        case IDLE_PRIORITY_CLASS:
            std::cout << "Idle";
            break;
        case REALTIME_PRIORITY_CLASS:
            std::cout << "Realtime";
            break;
        default:
            std::cout << "<unknown>";
            break;
    }
    std::cout << std::endl;
}
```

The only useful act you can perform on a process handle is to send it back to the system as a parameter in an API call – as the call to the GetPriorityClass() API in Listing 2-4 illustrates. In this call, the system peers inside the process object, determines its priority class, then returns that data to the application.

Listing 2-4 shows you one way to get the handle to a process. The OpenProcess() and CreateProcess() APIs also can be used to fetch a process handle. The former function lets you retrieve the handle to an existing process while the latter makes a new one and gives you a handle to it. Listing 2-5 shows you how to look up all of the currently running processes in the system and how to use the OpenProcess() API to get extended information on each process to which you have access.

Listing 2-5: Looking up detailed information with process handles

```
// project proclist
#define _WIN32_WINNT 0x0500
#define WINVER 0x0500
#include <windows.h>
#include <tlhelp32.h>
#include <iostream>


// helper method to do the 64-bit calculation of time spent
//   in kernel mode when time spent in both user and kernel
//   modes is supplied
DWORD GetKernelModePercentage(const FILETIME& ftKernel,
                              const FILETIME& ftUser)
{
    // turn the filetime structures into 64-bit integers
    ULONGLONG qwKernel =
        (((ULONGLONG)ftKernel.dwHighDateTime) << 32) +
        ftKernel.dwLowDateTime;
    ULONGLONG qwUser =
        (((ULONGLONG)ftUser.dwHighDateTime) << 32) +
        ftUser.dwLowDateTime;

    // sum up the times spent, then find the percentage of
    //   time spent in kernel mode
    ULONGLONG qwTotal = qwKernel + qwUser;
    DWORD dwPct =
        (DWORD)(((ULONGLONG)100 * qwKernel) / qwTotal);

    return(dwPct);
}


// application to dump out currently running process names
//   and percentage of time spent in kernel mode
void main()
{
    // take a snapshot of the current processes in the system
    HANDLE hSnapshot = ::CreateToolhelp32Snapshot(
        TH32CS_SNAPPROCESS, // grab the current processes
        0); // for the current process, ignored
```

```
// initialize the process entry
PROCESSENTRY32 pe;
::ZeroMemory(&pe, sizeof(pe));
pe.dwSize = sizeof(pe);

// loop until we run out of processes
BOOL bMore = ::Process32First(hSnapshot, &pe);
while(bMore)
{
    // attempt to open the process for read
    HANDLE hProcess = ::OpenProcess(
        PROCESS_QUERY_INFORMATION,  // want to get info
        FALSE,  // don't need to inherit this handle
        pe.th32ProcessID);  // process to open
    if(hProcess!=NULL)
    {
        // find the times of the process
        FILETIME ftCreation, ftExit, ftKernelMode,
            ftUserMode;
        ::GetProcessTimes(
            hProcess,   // process of interest
            &ftCreation,// when it was started (absolute)
            &ftExit,    // time it ended (if any)
            &ftKernelMode,  // time spent in kernel mode
            &ftUserMode);   // time spent in user mode

        // find percentage of time spent in kernel mode
        DWORD dwPctKernel = ::GetKernelModePercentage(
            ftKernelMode,   // time spent in kernel mode
            ftUserMode);    // time spent in user mode

        // show the user some information about the process
        std::cout << "Process ID: " << pe.th32ProcessID
            << ", EXE file: " << pe.szExeFile
            << ", % in kernel mode: " << dwPctKernel
            << std::endl;

        // clean up the handle
        ::CloseHandle(hProcess);
    }

    // move on to the next process
    bMore = ::Process32Next(hSnapshot, &pe);
}
}
```

Listing 2-5 shows you some interesting code. First, it uses a brand new feature in Windows 2000, the tool help library, to get a snapshot of the currently running processes. Next, the application walks each process out of the snapshot, getting its characteristics in the form of a PROCESSENTRY32 structure. This structure is used to supply the process ID to the OpenProcess() API. Windows keeps track of various times relevant to each process; the example accesses these using the process handle opened for query and the GetProcessTimes() API. Next, a custom helper function takes a couple of the returned values and determines the percentage of time that the process spent in kernel mode (relative to its entire uptime). The rest of the program is simple; it dumps the information to the user, cleans up the process handle, and continues the loop until it can find no more processes. Figure 2-3 shows the resulting output.

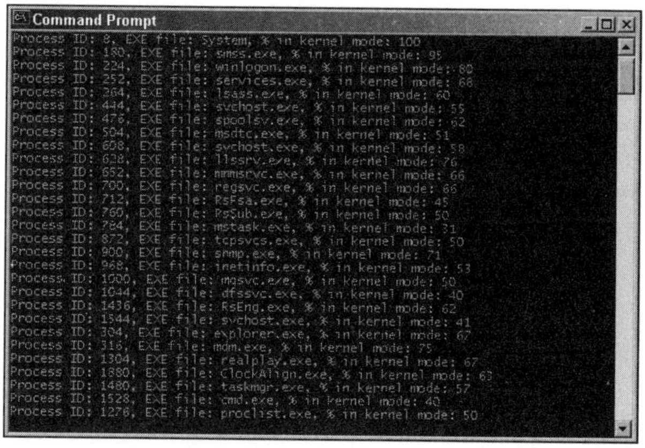

Figure 2-3: The list of processes running in the system along with the time in kernel mode

The process object allows Windows to identify each application running in the system uniquely. Windows associates all system resources in use with that process using the object. This keeps each process from stepping on the resources from another. In addition, when a process terminates and all processes referencing it release the references, Windows can reclaim all of the resources that it used and did not release.

The most important feature that the process object enables Windows to supply is the illusion of the private resources and data space. The Windows executive has the opportunity to determine the current process every time the process makes a user mode to kernel mode transition. This allows the executive to give access only to resources that the calling process has allocated; the system treats all executive-supplied resources, such as memory, disk files, and threads in this fashion. Therefore, each application has the illusion of the full available memory space (4GB on a 32-bit system) since all memory allocation has to travel through the executive's virtual memory manager (VMM) as mentioned earlier.

Chapter 12, "Memory Management," covers virtual memory.

One of the more important resources associated with a process object is the machine code and initial data contained in the EXE file that defines the application. The Windows loader code maps this into the process memory space as part of creating the object. The next section looks at the entire life cycle of a process.

Lastly, like all first-class kernel objects, the process object has an internal Boolean flag called the signaled state in which threads can test and wait. A process object is non-signaled while any threads it owns are running or paused (non-signaled). When the final thread that a process owns transitions to the signaled state, that process object is signaled and the system releases all threads waiting for it to reach that state.

Chapter 3, "Using Kernel Objects," covers the signaled state and waiting for it.

Process life cycle

Each process that Windows creates begins with a call to the `CreateProcess()` API. This method does the work of instantiating a process object in the object manager subsystem of the executive. The process object is highly configurable at creation time and only moderately configurable while alive. Every process ends with a call to either the `ExitProcess()` or the `TerminateProcess()` API. Usually, the application framework will take care of calling the `ExitProcess()` API. In the case of the C++ runtime library, this happens after the application's `main()` function returns.

CREATING PROCESSES

The core parameters to the `CreateProcess()` call are the name of the executable to run and its command line. Table 2-1 details the type and name of each parameter.

The parameter descriptions shown in Table 2-1 are summaries only. For details on legal values, side effects, etc., please see the *Microsoft Developer Network (MSDN)* Platform SDK entry for the function. This is the case for all function parameter and structure member tables I present in this text.

TABLE 2-1 PARAMETERS TO THE CREATEPROCESS() API

Parameter Name	Intention
LPCTSTR lpApplicationName	Fully or partially specified name of the EXE file that contains the code to execute.
LPTSTR lpCommandLine	The parameters to send to the executable.
LPSECURIITY_ATTRIBUTES lpProcessAttributes	Security attributes on the returned process handle. This mainly specifies whether the handle should be inheritable by other child processes.
LPSECURIITY_ATTRIBUTES lpThreadAttributes	Security attributes on the returned handle to the main thread of the process.
BOOL bInheritHandle	Flag that tells the system to allow the new process to inherit handles from the creato.
DWORD dwCreationFlags	Bitmask of special creation flags, such as CREATE_SUSPENDED.
LPVOID lpEnvironment	The set of environment variables to send to the new process; a null value sends the environment of the caller.
LPCTSTR lpCurrentDirectory	The startup directory for the new process.
STARTUPINFO lpStartupInfo	A STARTUPINFO structure that details the input and output configuration for the new process
LPPROCESS_INFORMATION lpProcessInformation	The results block for the call; sends handles and IDs for the process and main thread of the new application.

You can specify the first parameter, the application name, fully, relative to the current process's current directory, or to be found using the search path. The lpCommandLine parameter allows the caller to send data to the new application. The next parameters involve security on the process and its main thread, as well as the returned handles to those objects.

Chapter 3, "Using Kernel Objects," covers security on kernel objects, such as processes and threads, in detail.

The function then takes flags indicating what behavior the system should give to the new process in the dwCreationFlags parameter. An often-used flag is CREATE_SUSPENDED, which tells the main thread to suspend immediately. You should use the ResumeThread() API to start the process when you are ready. Another often-used flag is CREATE_NEW_CONSOLE, which tells the new process to start its own console window rather than use the parent's. This parameter also enables you to set the priority class for the process that indicates to the system how much CPU time to give to this process relative to all others active in the system.

Next, the CreateProcess() call asks for three parameters that often are defaulted. The first parameter, lpEnvironment, is the environment to supply the new process. This is just a list of environment variables as name-value pairs that you should be familiar with from old DOS or UNIX programming. Second, you can send a specific current directory for the new process rather than default to the creator process's current directory with the lpCurrentDirectory parameter. Third, a STARTUPINFO data structure is required. This specifies the appearance of the main window for the new application when appropriate.

The final parameter to CreateProcess() is the return buffer for handles and IDs of the new process object and its main thread. It's important that you call the CloseHandle() API on the returned handles in this PROCESS_INFORMATION data structure since not closing them dangles any unreleased resources until the creator process fully terminates.

Listing 2-6 shows you the basics of creating child processes. The program simply starts itself up again, displaying its system process ID and its position in the list of processes as passed on the command line.

Listing 2-6: Creating child processes

```
// project proccreate
#include <windows.h>
#include <iostream>
#include <stdio.h>

// simple method to create a clone process of the one passed
//  and give it an ID number
void StartClone(int nCloneID)
{
    // fetch the file name for the current executable
    TCHAR szFilename[MAX_PATH];
    ::GetModuleFileName(NULL, szFilename, MAX_PATH);

    // format the command line for the child process, telling
    //  it its EXE file and clone ID
    TCHAR szCmdLine[MAX_PATH];
    ::sprintf(szCmdLine, "\"%s\" %d", szFilename, nCloneID);
```

```
    // startup info for the child
    STARTUPINFO si;
    ::ZeroMemory(reinterpret_cast<void*>(&si), sizeof(si));
    si.cb = sizeof(si); // must be sizeof this struct

    // returned process info for the child
    PROCESS_INFORMATION pi;

    // create the process, using the same executable and a
    //   command line that tells it to be a baby
    BOOL bCreateOK = ::CreateProcess(
        szFilename, // name of the app to spawn (this EXE)
        szCmdLine,  // flag to tell us to behave like a child
        NULL,       // default security for the process
        NULL,       // default security for the thread
        FALSE,      // don't inherit handles
        CREATE_NEW_CONSOLE, // use a new console
        NULL,       // new environment
        NULL,       // current dir
        &si,        // startup info
        &pi);       // returned process info

    // release our references to the child process
    if(bCreateOK)
    {
        ::CloseHandle(pi.hProcess);
        ::CloseHandle(pi.hThread);
    }
}

int main(int argc, char* argv[])
{
    // determine this process's position in the list
    int nClone(0);
    if(argc>1)
    {
        // grab the clone ID from the second param
        ::sscanf(argv[1], "%d", &nClone);
    }

    // display our process position
    std::cout << "Process ID: " << ::GetCurrentProcessId()
        << ", Clone ID: " << nClone
        << std::endl;
```

```
// check for the need to create a child process
const int c_nCloneMax = 25;
if(nClone < c_nCloneMax)
{
    // send the command line and the new process's
    //  clone number
    StartClone(++nClone);
}

// pause a bit (1/2 a sec) before leaving
::Sleep(500);

return 0;
}
```

Listing 2-6 shows a simple use of the CreateProcess() API. First, it constructs a very simple command line, supplying the current, fully specified name of the EXE file and a number that represents its generation of clone. Most parameters are defaulted, but the creation flags parameter tells the new process to allocate its own console with the CREATE_NEW_CONSOLE flag, which causes a bunch of activity in the task bar when you run the example. The clone creator method then closes up the passed-back handles and returns to main(). Before leaving, the main thread of execution for each process pauses to let you see the contents of at least one of the windows (hopefully).

You should notice that creating a new process object also creates its main thread. A process object is distinct from a thread of execution. The previous section explained how the system uses the process object to associate resources with an application instance; a thread of execution is such a resource.

There are additional ways to create processes. Both accomplish this using a system account other than the one running the creator process. These functions enable you to run processes that require another account's security context to perform their functions without logging in as that account. The CreateProcessAsUser() API requires an access token handle which can be passed using the DuplicateHandle() API or created using the LoginUser() API. The CreateProcessWithLogonW() API takes a username, domain, and password of the account under which to create the process. They create the new process without an interactive desktop (the process owner is not logged on to the desktop) so you generally should use them to start non-GUI applications.

 You can find the details of these APIs in the MSDN documentation.

XREF

RUNNING PROCESSES

Each process within the system is "running" when it owns at least one thread of execution. Usually, the process uses the main thread as its lifetime indicator. When the main thread finishes, it tells the system to terminate all other threads it owns that currently are running, ready, or suspended by calling the `ExitProcess()` API. While the process is running, you can view a bunch of its characteristics and modify a few.

The first thing you can view about a process is its system *process identifier (PID)* using the `GetCurrentProcessId()` API. This function, like the `GetCurrentProcess()` API, cannot fail; but unlike the handle returned, the PID returned is usable throughout the system. Other APIs that deliver information about the current process only are `GetStartupInfo()` and `GetProcessShutdownParameters()`, which give you details about the lifetime configuration of the process.

Often, a process desires information about its runtime environment. Some APIs that help are `GetModuleFileName()` and `GetCommandLine()`, which deliver the parameters used in `CreateProcess()` to start up the application. Another API that you may want to use while creating applications is called `IsDebuggerPresent()`. It allows the process to behave differently when being debugged than it does in release mode.

Chapter 18, "Development Support," covers process interaction with the debugger.

You can look at a process's GUI resources using the new API `GetGuiResources()`. It returns either the number of open GDI objects or the number of open USER objects in the specified process. Other performance information about a process is available in the `GetProcessIoCounters()`, `GetProcessPriorityBoost()`, `GetProcessTimes()`, and `GetProcessWorkingSetSize()` APIs. All of these APIs simply require a handle to the process of interest that has `PROCESS_QUERY_INFORMATION` access.

Chapter 3, "Using Kernel Objects," covers access flags for a kernel object.

Yet another process information query API is `GetProcessVersion()`. This API only requires the PID of the process of interest. Listing 2-7 shows this API in action along with `GetVersionEx()`, which determines the version of the system running the process.

Listing 2-7: Using version information from a process and the operating system

```cpp
// project version
#define _WIN32_WINNT 0x0500
#define WINVER 0x0500
#include <windows.h>
#include <iostream>

// simple example of using version information from a process
//   and the operating system
void main()
{
    // grab this process's ID
    DWORD dwIdThis = ::GetCurrentProcessId();

    // fetch the version required for this process and report
    //   could also send 0 to indicate this process
    DWORD dwVerReq = ::GetProcessVersion(dwIdThis);
    WORD wMajorReq = (WORD)(dwVerReq > 16);
    WORD wMinorReq = (WORD)(dwVerReq & 0xffff);
    std::cout << "Process ID: " << dwIdThis
        << ", requires OS: " << wMajorReq << "."
        << wMinorReq << std::endl;

    // set up a version info data structure to hold the version
    //   of the operating system
    OSVERSIONINFOEX osvix;
    ::ZeroMemory(&osvix, sizeof(osvix));
    osvix.dwOSVersionInfoSize = sizeof(osvix);

    // fetch the version information and report
    ::GetVersionEx(reinterpret_cast<LPOSVERSIONINFO>(&osvix));
    std::cout << "Running on OS: " << osvix.dwMajorVersion << "."
        << osvix.dwMinorVersion << std::endl;

    // if this is an NT5 (Windows 2000) system,
    //   boost the priority
    if(osvix.dwPlatformId==VER_PLATFORM_WIN32_NT &&
        osvix.dwMajorVersion>=5)
    {
        // change the priority class
        ::SetPriorityClass(
            ::GetCurrentProcess(),       // use this process
            ABOVE_NORMAL_PRIORITY_CLASS);// change to normal+

        // report to the user
```

```
        std::cout << "Task Manager should now indicate this "
            "process is above normal priority." << std::endl;
    }
}
```

The program in Listing 2-7 shows you how to get the current PID and required version for a process. Notice that this information is reported, but there is no action to take since the system worked out any version incompatibilities in order to run it. Next, the example demonstrates the use of the GetVersionEx() API, retrieving an OSVERSIONINFOEX structure. This block tells you all that you need to know about the version of the operating system. Windows 2000 is stamped as NT version 5.0 in the block.

Chapter 10, "Application Building Services," covers collecting version information in more detail.

The final piece of Listing 2-7 uses the version information from the operating system to make sure we are running Windows 2000. The code then boosts the priority class of the current process from normal priority to above normal priority. Windows 2000 adds the ABOVE_NORMAL_PRIORITY_CLASS class, which is a compromise between HIGH_PRIORITY_CLASS and NORMAL_PRIORITY_CLASS. The Task Manager application should reflect the change immediately when you right-click the process to change its priority from there. Once you see the new priority in the Task Manager, as shown in Figure 2-4, you can change it to another value.

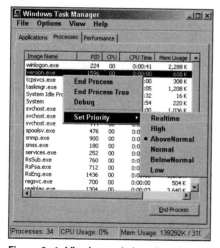

Figure 2-4: Viewing and changing the priority of a process through the Windows Task Manager

In addition to changing a process's priority, you can perform a few other operations on a process while it is running and you have its process handle. The SetProcessAffinityMask() API enables you to map threads to processors, the SetProcessPriorityBoost() API lets you turn off foreground application priority boosting, and the SetProcessWorkingSet() API tunes the size of available non-paged RAM for the process. An API that is only usable on the current process, SetProcessShutdownParameters(), enables you to tell the system how to kill the process.

TERMINATING PROCESSES

As I alluded earlier, all processes end with either a call to the ExitProcess() API or the TerminateProcess() API. The former is preferred over the latter since the process calls the former in the normal course of termination once it completes all of its shutdown responsibilities. An outside process typically calls the latter method and abruptly ends processing, possibly leading to errant behavior since shutdown cannot run its course.

The TerminateProcess() API requires that you open the process object with PROCESS_TERMINATE access. Once you have this, you can kill the process and specify what exit code to send back to the system. This is a brutal way to end a process, but it is necessary sometimes — especially in cases where you don't write the victim application.

When you do get the chance to design both the killer and victim processes, you should create an interprocess communication kernel object — such as a mutex — that the victim simply waits on or periodically tests to understand that it should end. The program shown in Listing 2-8 creates a child process, and then tells it to kill itself by releasing its "suicide pill" mutex.

Listing 2-8: A parent process telling its child to kill itself

```
// project procterm
#include <windows.h>
#include <iostream>
#include <stdio.h>
static LPCTSTR g_szMutexName = "w2kdg.ProcTerm.mutex.Suicide";

// simple method to create a clone process of the current
void StartClone()
{
    // fetch the file name for the current executable
    TCHAR szFilename[MAX_PATH];
    ::GetModuleFileName(NULL, szFilename, MAX_PATH);

    // format the command line for the child process, telling
    //  it its EXE file and that it is a child
    TCHAR szCmdLine[MAX_PATH];
    ::sprintf(szCmdLine, "\"%s\" child", szFilename);
```

```
    // startup info for the child
    STARTUPINFO si;
    ::ZeroMemory(reinterpret_cast<void*>(&si), sizeof(si));
    si.cb = sizeof(si); // must be sizeof this struct

    // returned process info for the child
    PROCESS_INFORMATION pi;

    // create the process, using the same executable and a
    //   command line that tells it to be a baby
    BOOL bCreateOK = ::CreateProcess(
        szFilename,  // name of the app to spawn (this EXE)
        szCmdLine,   // flag to tell us to behave like a child
        NULL,        // default security for the process
        NULL,        // default security for the thread
        FALSE,       // don't inherit handles
        0,           // no special creation flags
        NULL,        // new environment
        NULL,        // current dir
        &si,         // startup info
        &pi);        // returned process info

    // release our references to the child process
    if(bCreateOK)
    {
        ::CloseHandle(pi.hProcess);
        ::CloseHandle(pi.hThread);
    }
}

void Parent()
{
    // create the suicide mutex
    HANDLE hMutexSuicide = ::CreateMutex(
        NULL,            // default security
        TRUE,            // initially own it
        g_szMutexName); // name it
    if(hMutexSuicide!=NULL)
    {
        // create the child process
        std::cout << "Creating the child process."
            << std::endl;
        ::StartClone();

        // pause for awhile
```

```
        ::Sleep(5000);

        // tell the child to kill itself
        std::cout << "Telling the child process to quit."
            << std::endl;
        ::ReleaseMutex(hMutexSuicide);

        // clean up the handle
        ::CloseHandle(hMutexSuicide);
    }
}

void Child()
{
    // open up the suicide mutex
    HANDLE hMutexSuicide = ::OpenMutex(
        SYNCHRONIZE,      // open it for synch
        FALSE,            // don't need to pass it on
        g_szMutexName); // the name
    if(hMutexSuicide!=NULL)
    {
        // report that we are waiting then do it
        std::cout << "Child waiting for suicide instructions."
            << std::endl;
        ::WaitForSingleObject(hMutexSuicide, INFINITE);

        // ready to quit, clean up the handle
        std::cout << "Child quitting." << std::endl;
        ::CloseHandle(hMutexSuicide);
    }
}

int main(int argc, char* argv[])
{
    // decide whether to act as a parent or a child
    if(argc>1 && ::strcmp(argv[1],"child")==0)
    {
        Child();
    }
    else
    {
        Parent();
    }
    return 0;
}
```

The program in Listing 2-8 illustrates the entire life cycle of a process. The first time it executes, it acts as a parent by creating a child process. It does this after creating a mutex kernel object that acts as a suicide pill to the child. Once the child is created, it opens up the mutex and begins doing work in other threads while waiting for the parent to signal the death using the ReleaseMutex() API. The parent goes about doing its business, simulated by the Sleep() API call and, once complete, tells the child to end.

The ExitProcess() API is the preferred method or process termination, but you need to be careful of how you use it. When ExitProcess() is called, all threads in the process are halted and signaled immediately; the call does not return until the system executes the detach method for each DLL used by the process. You should design your application so that the main thread is the thread that calls ExitProcess() after its normal C++ runtime shutdown (this is the default behavior provided by the compiler). Creating a central termination event that each active thread can wait for and stop when it transitions to the signaled state often does this.

During normal end operation, each worker thread in the process terminates and the main thread calls ExitProcess(). Next, the executive releases references to all objects the process added and changes the exit code, found with the GetExitCodeProcess() from STILL_ACTIVE to the value sent in the ExitProcess() call. Finally, the main thread object transitions to the signaled state, as does the process object.

The executive's object manager does not destroy the process object itself until all open handles are closed. There is no method available to take a terminated process object and start it up again. When the process object references a terminated process, a couple of API calls mentioned earlier are still useful. The process can use the exit code to communicate the manner of termination to other processes that call GetExitCodeProcess(). Also, the GetProcessTimes() API delivers the termination time of the process to a caller.

Threads of Execution

In addition to being a preemptive multitasking operating system, Windows 2000 provides native support for multithreaded processes. This enables you to create applications that split apart the work they must accomplish into logical tasks and assign each to its own thread. In order to do this well, you need to know what Windows 2000 thread objects are and how to use them.

Basic multithreading

Windows 2000 is not the only multithreaded operating system. In fact, many engineers have created numerous multithreaded operating systems and applications through the course of computer development. Multithreading is a well-known technique that has generated many theories and best practices regarding its use. Since I don't expect it to be brand new to you, I only briefly cover the basics.

SCHEDULING THREADS

The multithreaded operating system relies on a component at the lowest level to manage the currently executing threads. In Windows 2000, this component is the microkernel. The microkernel is responsible for knowing what threads currently desire and deserve CPU cycles. It consequently gives each one its fair share of execution. The system uses a scheduling policy to dole out its precious cycles.

The microkernel creates a schedule of what thread is run by a CPU at each instant of time and the minimum duration that thread can run. In order to give each thread execution, the microkernel slices up each CPU's schedule into small chunks; usually we refer to each of these chunks as a *quantum*. That is, the microkernel assigns every quantum to a thread, expecting to run forever. To give you a sense of their size, a quantum typically is on the order of tens of milliseconds. The smaller the quantum, the more evenly the CPU can distribute its efforts among the active threads and, therefore, processes. When processes get to execute closer in time together, the user sees very smooth response from each one, as if each one has a CPU dedicated to running it.

The microkernel must implement its schedule by grabbing control of the CPU when a quantum is complete, pausing the running thread, and resuming the scheduled thread. Multithreading theory calls this change in threads a *context switch*. In order to execute a context switch, the microkernel must save all of the CPU's register contents to associate with the pausing thread, and restore the CPU's register contents for the resuming thread. This takes some time and forces the microkernel designer to balance responsiveness against cycles wasted pushing registers around when selecting the quantum size.

Further complicating the scheduling policy is the reality that some processes and threads are more important than other ones. For example, the network server service deserves more CPU cycles than the screen saver. To accommodate this, you can assign the Windows process and thread objects a *priority*. Priorities simply tell the scheduler to run some threads for more quanta than others, and not to run all threads of higher priority before any of lower.

Another complication to the scheduling lies in the difference in effort between intraprocess and interprocess context switches. Switching between processes forces the machine's address translation table to reload for the new process—another time-intensive process.

One of the big features of a thread is its ability to suspend itself or be suspended. This tells the microkernel not to include that thread in the schedule until it resumes. Once a thread transitions from the suspended to the running state, it simply takes its place in the run schedule.

Often, you will break your process up into execution threads that make logical sense and so you end up with some fixed number. There are times however when you can expand the number of threads in a process arbitrarily. In those cases, you should match the number of threads in your application to the number of CPUs in the system. Listing 2-9 shows you how to find this quantity.

Listing 2-9: Determining the number of processors in the system

```
// project numproc
#include <windows.h>
#include <iostream>

// simple app to look up the number of processors in the system
//   and report it.
void main()
{
    // initialize the system_info data structure
    SYSTEM_INFO si;
    ::GetSystemInfo(&si);

    // report the value to the user
    std::cout << "Number of available processors: "
        << si.dwNumberOfProcessors
        << std::endl;

    // check each processor's active state
    for(DWORD dwProc=0;
        dwProc < si.dwNumberOfProcessors;
        ++dwProc)
    {
        // shoot out the processor number
        std::cout << "Processor #" << dwProc;

        // determine if the processor is currently active
        if((si.dwActiveProcessorMask & (1<<dwProc))!=0)
        {
            std::cout << " is active." << std::endl;
        }
        else
        {
            std::cout << " is inactive." << std::endl;
        }
    }
}
```

Finding the processor count is extremely simple: one call to the `GetSystem Info()` API that cannot fail. The program in Listing 2-9 also checks each available processor to determine whether it currently is active and so able to accept a thread. You should do this whenever you can take advantage of more processors in the system.

DANGERS OF MULTITHREADING

Along with the benefits of multithreaded applications come some real dangers. You need to keep problems such as race conditions, starvation, and deadlock in the back of your mind whenever you decide to add an additional thread of execution to your process. I describe these below:

♦ **Multithreaded race condition:** This occurs when two threads of execution access the same resource, the operations they perform are order-dependent, and there is no mechanism to guarantee they happen in that correct order. Since a multithreaded application cannot guarantee the order in which the system executes its threads, it must ensure that the threads synchronize their operations with each other. As an example, a dual-threaded application which reads from one file and writes to another with its threads must make sure that the reading occurs into the buffer before the write from the buffer is attempted.

 Chapter 4,"Commonly Used Kernel Objects," shows you techniques to synchronize threads.

♦ **Multithreaded starvation:** This is one thread depriving access to a shared resource to other threads, thus never satisfying the starving thread's hunger for CPU cycles. This starvation occurs when there is no mechanism present to force a thread to give up its use of the shared resource. For example, a worker thread might grab a mutex indicating it can access an object in the system. Then it can call a long, involved method on the object while the main GUI thread needs brief access to query a value but cannot gain it. This causes the user to see nonresponsive behavior in the GUI thread because the worker thread is starving it. Starvation is a deviant of the race condition problem. In the previous example, there would not have been a problem if the GUI thread had reached the object first. This problem sometimes is lumped in with priority inversion. Both are effectively the same – one thread does not get the CPU cycles that the scheduler would like to give it.

♦ **Deadlock:** This occurs when two or more threads create a circular wait. In a dual-threaded case, thread 1 does not give up its ownership of resource A until it gains ownership of resource B – which currently is owned by thread 2, which does not give up ownership until it gains ownership of resource A. This sounds contrived and doesn't actually happen that often, but you do need to be wary of the order of acquisition and relinquishment for shared resources. Threads should not hold on to ownership of any resource beyond the time that is necessary.

Thread objects

Threads are first-class kernel objects. They originate in the microkernel, and the process that creates them references them through object handles, just as it references any other first-class kernel object. Each thread object represents a set of registers that includes the instruction pointer and the address translation table, which can be loaded into a CPU. An active thread object is non-signaled and is either suspended, ready to run, or running on a CPU.

Chapter 3,"Using Kernel Objects," covers first-class kernel objects.

CREATING THREAD OBJECTS

You've already seen that creating a new process creates that process's main thread. The thread object handle is returned in the PROCESS_INFORMATION output from CreateProcess(). You'll see that the creation of the process object is a superset of the creation of a thread.

To start a new thread of execution, you must use the CreateThread() API, which makes a new entry in the system's list of threads to execute. I detail the parameters to this function in Table 2-2. By comparing this table to Table 2-1, you should see that the CreateProcess() API has enough information to create the main thread of an application with CreateThread(), since it retrieves the main thread's start address, supplies it a null parameter, and defaults the stack size to the application choice.

TABLE 2-2 PARAMETERS TO THE CREATETHREAD() API

Parameter Name	Intention
LPSECURITY_ATTRIBUTES lpThreadAttributes	The security to apply to the new thread. This includes discretionary access and inheritance.
DWORD dwStackSize	The size of the stack the thread will receive; sending 0 uses the default stack size of the process.

Continued

TABLE 2-2 PARAMETERS TO THE CREATETHREAD() API *(Continued)*

`LPTHREAD_START_ROUTINE lpStartAddress`	The address of the function to execute to begin the thread. Once this function exits, the thread will terminate. This function is often called `ThreadProc`.
`LPVOID lpParameter`	The value to pass into the thread procedure at `lpStartAddress`.
`DWORD dwCreationFlags`	Special attributes to grant the thread, only `CREATE_SUSPENDED` is currently available.
`LPDWORD lpThreadID`	A return buffer to hold the system identifier for the new thread.

The `CreateThread()` API first requires a parameter describing security to associate with the new object in the `lpThreadAttributes` parameter. This information tells the system what accounts to allow and deny access to the thread object for modification and synchronization while it exists.

The next three parameters to `CreateThread()` usually are set implicitly by the process object creation procedure. The first, the stack size, is set from the process EXE file through a linker directive, and when setting manually, the process typically accepts the default by setting 0 to the `dwStackSize` parameter. The next parameter is the address of the function for the thread to execute, the `ThreadProc`. When the system loads the EXE file into memory, it sets this value from the result, but when you call the creator function you must pass the address of a real function. Finally, the parameter to the `ThreadProc` has no direct analog during process creation. When creating standalone threads, this parameter allows the creator to give each one its own context information. For example, the process often passes a pointer to a data structure containing initialization information.

The next-to-last parameter is a subset of the acceptable process creation flags. Threads only have one possible value other than zero; that value is `CREATE_SUSPENDED`. Finally, the function passes the system's *thread identifier (TID)* to the caller, which completes the subset of `PROCESS_INFORMATION` applicable to threads.

One good practice to get into when creating a thread is to encapsulate its behavior into a C++ class. This enables you to hide the thread procedure as a static member, passing the object pointer as the parameter, and reducing the thread procedure simply to calling a nonstatic method. Listing 2-10 illustrates this technique along with the use of the `CreateThread()` API.

Listing 2-10: Creating a new thread

```
// project threadcreate
#include <windows.h>
```

```cpp
#include <iostream>

// simple class to encapsulate the creation of a worker thread
class CWorkerThread
{
public:
    CWorkerThread(LPCTSTR szName) :
        m_szName(szName), m_hThread(INVALID_HANDLE_VALUE)
    {
        // create the new thread and let it rip
        m_hThread = ::CreateThread(
            NULL,         // default security
            0,            // default stack
            ThreadProc,   // class-wide thread proc
            reinterpret_cast<LPVOID>(this),
                          // send the 'this' ptr to the proc
            0,            // no special creation flags
            NULL);        // don't need the returned thread ID
    }
    virtual ~CWorkerThread() { ::CloseHandle(m_hThread); }

    // simple method to wait until the thread is complete
    virtual void WaitForCompletion()
    {
        ::WaitForSingleObject(m_hThread, INFINITE);
    }

protected:
    static DWORD WINAPI ThreadProc(LPVOID lpParam)
    {
        // fetch the this pointer from the param and call the
        //   object worker method
        CWorkerThread* pThis =
            reinterpret_cast<CWorkerThread*>(lpParam);
        pThis->DoStuff();

        // exit code from the thread is reasonably uninteresting
        return(0);
    }

    virtual void DoStuff()
    {
        // just emit the ID and name a bunch of times
        for(int n=0;n<1000;++n)
```

```
        {
            std::cout << "Thread " << m_szName
                << " ID: " << ::GetCurrentThreadId()
                << ", count " << n
                << std::endl;
        }
    }
protected:
    HANDLE  m_hThread;   // handle to thread kernel object
    LPCTSTR m_szName;    // name to display for this thread
};

void main()
{
    // create the two threads
    CWorkerThread wtA("A");
    CWorkerThread wtB("B");

    // pause until they are complete
    wtA.WaitForCompletion();
    wtB.WaitForCompletion();

    // report
    std::cout << "Both threads complete." << std::endl;
}
```

The example in Listing 2-10 shows you how to bake a thread procedure right into a class such that instantiating an object of that class starts up a thread to execute the proper work. The object's this pointer is sent to the static thread procedure which then de-references it and calls the DoStuff() method that is the actual worker method. The DoStuff() method then has access to instance variables such as the name of the thread. The class also contains a WaitForCompletion() method that allows the caller to pause until the thread exits the DoStuff() call. The main thread waits for both threads to be complete before it exits since it really doesn't know which one will finish last.

ASSIGNING PRIORITIES TO THREADS

You can assign priorities to different threads in your application. You might want to do this in order to force the system to give more cycles to one part of your process than another part. For example, in a mail reader the thread that checks for new messages on the server is not as important as the GUI thread since you don't want the user to lose responsiveness while checking for mail that may have been delivered 15 minutes ago.

Windows 2000 has a broad range of prioritization for processes and threads. The prioritization boils down to an integer range including 1 to 31, with 1 being the lowest and 31 the highest. *Process prioritization* is logically how important the application is relative to other applications in the system, while *thread prioritization* is how important one thread is relative to others within the process. Process prioritization acts as an offset to the resulting overall prioritization. The terms that Windows assigns to priorities, in increasing priority order, are idle, lowest, below-normal, normal, above-normal, highest, and time-critical.

 Many articles on the MSDN explain how to select priority values. Start with the Platform SDK documentation in the "Base Services" section.

After you create a thread, you can change its priority from the default of normal to something that makes sense for your application. You can do this before execution actually begins if you create the thread suspended, change the priority, then call the ResumeThread() API. Listing 2-11 adds the SetPriority() method to the class from Listing 2-10.

Listing 2-11: Changing a thread's priority

```
// project threadpriority
// ...

// simple class to encapsulate the creation of a worker thread
class CWorkerThread
{
// ...

    // change the priority of the thread
    virtual void SetPriority(int nPriority)
    {
        ::SetThreadPriority(m_hThread, nPriority);
    }

// ...
};

void main()
{
    // create the two threads
    CWorkerThread wtA("A");
```

```
CWorkerThread wtB("B");

// lower the priority of thread A as much as possible
wtA.SetPriority(THREAD_PRIORITY_LOWEST);

// pause until they are complete
wtA.WaitForCompletion();
wtB.WaitForCompletion();

// report
std::cout << "Both threads complete." << std::endl;
}
```

The results of executing Listing 2-11 differ greatly from the results in Listing 2-10. Thread B always finishes first since thread A has its priority reduced as far as possible before execution can complete. Since thread B is still a normal priority thread, it gets many more CPU cycles.

STARTING AND STOPPING THREADS

The example in Listing 2-10 illustrates one way to block the main thread from executing. The main thread calls into the threads' WaitForCompletion() methods after they are constructed. This calls into the WaitForSingleObject() API, which moves the thread out of the scheduler's ready-to-run pool and into its suspended pool. Once the target meets the condition of the waiting function (the thread is complete), the kernel moves the thread back into the ready-to-run pool.

Another action you can take on existing threads is to pause and resume them manually. You can do this in response to program logic if necessary. For example, in the mail reader application, if the user chooses to work disconnected from the network, the mail-checking thread either can be suspended or terminated. The former option seems ideal since the user might connect again at any moment and it is quicker to resume than create a new thread.

The example shown in Listing 2-12 demonstrates the use of both the SuspendThread() and the ResumeThread() APIs. This example enhances Listing 2-11 to allow pause and resumption of execution.

Listing 2-12: Pausing and resuming a thread

```
// project threadpause
// ...

class CWorkerThread
{
// ...
```

```
    // suspend execution
    virtual void Suspend()
    {
        ::SuspendThread(m_hThread);
    }

    // resume execution
    virtual void Resume()
    {
        ::ResumeThread(m_hThread);
    }

// ...
};

void main()
{
    // create the two threads
    CWorkerThread wtA("A");
    CWorkerThread wtB("B");

    // lower the priority of thread A as much as possible
    wtA.SetPriority(THREAD_PRIORITY_LOWEST);

    // stop thread b
    wtB.Suspend();

    // pause until they are complete
    wtA.WaitForCompletion();

    // continue with b
    wtB.Resume();
    wtB.WaitForCompletion();

    // report
    std::cout << "Both threads complete." << std::endl;
}
```

Again, the program has swapped the results from the previous example. Listing 2-12 always ends with thread B even though thread A's priority still is set to the lowest available. The main thread pauses thread B until thread A is complete; then it resumes thread B.

MANAGING THE STATE OF THREADS

Windows 2000 supplies a bunch of APIs that enable you to determine characteristics of a thread. Most of these APIs are analogs of the process APIs that I introduced previously. The `GetCurrentThread()` and `GetCurrentThreadId()` are almost identical to their process counterparts in that they return information about the calling thread.

The `GetThreadTimes()` API is a direct analog of its process counterpart that looks up the passed thread's start time, end time, and time spent in both kernel and user mode. The `GetThreadPriority()` API fetches the current setting for the thread's priority, and the `GetThreadPriorityBoost()` API checks whether the system thinks it can increase the priority when desired. The last two APIs have partner methods — `SetThreadPriority()` and `SetThreadPriorityBoost()` — to change the values.

Finally, the system enables you to manage the processor onto which the scheduler assigns a thread. This feature is useful if you have two threads that you know need to be on different CPUs to provide the desired performance in your application. The first API, `SetThreadIdealProcessor()`, tells the scheduler that the passed thread should run on the supplied CPU (by number) whenever possible. The `SetThreadAffinityMask()` API tells the kernel scheduler which CPU it is allowed to assign the passed thread to. You can also use this function to tell the system that a particular thread cannot run on a certain CPU when, for example, you have assigned another thread to that CPU.

MAKING DATA SPECIFIC TO THREADS

Each thread within a process has access to all of the memory and resources allocated to that process. That is, there are no inherent per-thread barriers to system resources within a process. Threads must take great care when accessing any of the data in their process when more than one of them will be using that data.

Threads do get a private stack for storing automatic variables. Functions that use only automatic variables are termed *reentrant* since no two threads executing concurrently can do harm to the other. Functions that reference process global data often are not reentrant, especially if they modify that data.

There are many tools available to a thread to ensure proper access to data in a process and create reentrant functions: critical sections, mutexes, events, and semaphores. These tools orchestrate the sequence of access to shared resources and data. Sharing data across threads is usually done simply by allocating a block of memory. However, occasionally, more sophisticated tools, such as file I/O, mailslots, or memory mapped files are used.

Chapter 4, "Commonly Used Kernel Objects," covers critical sections, mutexes, events, and semaphores.

The example in Listing 2-10 illustrates the association of instance data with a particular thread using a C++ class. There are times when this data association is not sufficient — for example, when updating old single-threaded C code. Windows supplies the *thread-local storage (TLS)* mechanism to solve this problem.

TLS is a reasonably straightforward subsystem that tells the executive to allocate an array of LPVOIDs, one for every thread in the process. The TlsAlloc() API allocates the array and returns a value that you can consider its handle. You then return this handle to the system when setting the value using the TlsSetValue() API and retrieving it using the TlsGetValue() API. Once you are finished with the array, you call the TlsFree() API to release the array.

Behind the scenes, the system simply looks up the calling thread's ID and accesses the array element for that thread in the TlsGetValue()and TlsSetValue() APIs. Listing 2-13 illustrates a simple use of TLS by creating a zero-parameter C-style API for recording and retrieving the start time of a thread.

Listing 2-13: Using TLS to record and retrieve thread start times

```
// project tls
#include <windows.h>
#include <iostream>

//
// thread start time recording using TLS
//
// the index into TLS that will hold each thread's start time
static DWORD s_dwTlsStart = 0;

void StartTimeInit()
{
    // begin the start time system by allocating a new array
    s_dwTlsStart = ::TlsAlloc();
}

void RecordStartTime()
{
    // grab the current time
    DWORD dwStart = ::GetTickCount();

    // set the time into the slot allocated for it
    ::TlsSetValue(
        s_dwTlsStart,    // slot for start time
        reinterpret_cast<LPVOID>(dwStart)); // value
}

DWORD GetStartTime()
{
```

```
        // look up the start time for the current thread in
        //  the slot allocated for start times
        LPVOID pValue = ::TlsGetValue(s_dwTlsStart);
        DWORD dwStart = reinterpret_cast<DWORD>(pValue);
        return(dwStart);
    }


void StartTimeExit()
{
    // close the start time system by freeing its slot
    ::TlsFree(s_dwTlsStart);
    s_dwTlsStart = 0;
}


// simple class to encapsulate the creation of a worker thread
class CWorkerThread
{
public:
    CWorkerThread(LPCTSTR szName) :
        m_szName(szName), m_hThread(INVALID_HANDLE_VALUE)
    {
        // create the new thread and let it rip
        m_hThread = ::CreateThread(
            NULL,       // default security
            0,          // default stack
            ThreadProc, // class-wide thread proc
            reinterpret_cast<LPVOID>(this),
                        // send the 'this' ptr to the proc
            0,          // no special creation flags
            NULL);      // don't need the returned thread ID
    }
    virtual ~CWorkerThread() { ::CloseHandle(m_hThread); }

    // simple method to wait until the thread is complete
    virtual void WaitForCompletion()
    {
        ::WaitForSingleObject(m_hThread, INFINITE);
    }

protected:
    static DWORD WINAPI ThreadProc(LPVOID lpParam)
    {
        // fetch the this pointer from the param and call the
        //  object worker method
        CWorkerThread* pThis =
```

```
                reinterpret_cast<CWorkerThread*>(lpParam);
        pThis->DoStuff();

        // exit code from the thread is reasonably uninteresting
        return(0);
    }

    virtual void DoStuff()
    {
        // save the start time
        ::RecordStartTime();

        // just emit the TID and name a bunch of times
        for(int n=0;n<1000;++n)
        {
            std::cout << "Thread " << m_szName
                << " ID: " << ::GetCurrentThreadId()
                << ", started: " << ::GetStartTime()
                << ", count " << n
                << std::endl;
        }
    }
protected:
    HANDLE  m_hThread;  // handle to thread kernel object
    LPCTSTR m_szName;   // name to display for this thread
};

void main()
{
    // initialize the start time system
    ::StartTimeInit();

    // create the two threads
    CWorkerThread wtA("A");
    CWorkerThread wtB("B");

    // pause until they are complete
    wtA.WaitForCompletion();
    wtB.WaitForCompletion();

    // report
    std::cout << "Both threads complete." << std::endl;

    // clean up the start time system
    ::StartTimeExit();
}
```

I also based Listing 2-13 on Listing 2-10. The start time recording system is started and shut down using the `StartTimeInit()` and `StartTimeExit()` functions. Each thread simply calls the `RecordStartTime()` function to save its start and then calls the `GetStartTime()` function to retrieve it; Figure 2-5 shows the resulting output. Even though the calling thread never sends identification to these functions, the TLS stores and retrieves the proper times for each thread. In the single-threaded world, a single static variable would back the API, and each time a new thread started it would clobber the value.

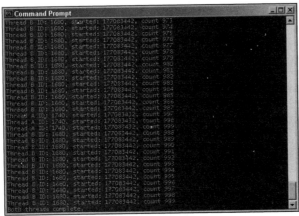

Figure 2-5: Using TLS to report individual thread start times through the same function call

TERMINATING THREADS

Terminating a thread is very similar to terminating a process. The `ExitThread()` API is the preferred method that the system calls for each thread as it exits from the thread procedure. The `TerminateThread()` API abruptly kills the thread without allowing it to clean up any associated resources properly.

Also like the process object, the thread object transitions to the signaled state after the call to the `ExitThread()` or `TerminateThread()` APIs. When the transition occurs, the system releases all other threads waiting for the object.

Fibers

A fiber is another multithreading object that you can use in your applications. It is, in fact, a manually scheduled thread of execution. Rather than allow the executive's scheduler to pick when to run threads within your process, you can do it yourself with fibers. A fiber runs in the context of the thread that created it.

The general life cycle of fibers begins with a thread that you should split up into more discrete execution chunks. The thread allocates fibers that it needs using the

CreateFiber() API, sending them the address of and parameter for a FiberProc, which is much like a thread's ThreadProc.

Once it creates all the required fibers, the thread transforms itself into a fiber using the ConvertThreadToFiber() API. Now, execution can proceed using the SwitchToFiber() API to schedule which task should be accomplished within the thread. To destroy the fibers, one of the fibers calls the DeleteFiber() API on the others. It then exits itself or calls one of the termination APIs described earlier.

Fibers can be useful to save state information within a thread of execution. The example in Listing 2-14 uses two fibers to calculate and display the Fibonacci sequence.

The Fibonacci sequence is a famous mathematical result that originated with the study of how fast rabbits breed and is noted in many other natural phenomena. See your high school algebra book or http://dir.yahoo.com /Science/Mathematics/Numerical_Analysis/Numbers/Fibonacci/ for detailed information.

Listing 2-14: Using fibers to calculate the Fibonacci sequence

```
// project fibofiber
#define _WIN32_WINNT 0x0500
#define WINVER 0x0500
#include <windows.h>
#include <iostream>

// data for the Fibonacci fibers
static DWORD s_dwFiber1 = 1;
static LPVOID s_pFiber1 = NULL;

static DWORD s_dwFiber2 = 1;
static LPVOID s_pFiber2 = NULL;

// simple fiber procedure that calculates the values of the
//  Fibonacci sequence by adding the values of the previous two
//  runs together
void WINAPI FiboProc(LPVOID lpParam)
{
    // grab the fiber number from the parameter
    DWORD dwFiberNum = reinterpret_cast<DWORD>(lpParam);

    // grab the address of the fiber's data
```

```
        DWORD* pdwFiber =
            (dwFiberNum==1) ? (&s_dwFiber1) : (&s_dwFiber2);

        // grab the handle to the other fiber
        LPVOID pFiberOther =
            (dwFiberNum==1) ? (s_pFiber2) : (s_pFiber1);

        // run until the Fibonacci sequence exceeds some reasonable
        //  value
        while(*pdwFiber<100000)
        {
            // report the current value
            std::cout << *pdwFiber << std::endl;

            // calculate the new value
            DWORD dwSeqNew = s_dwFiber1 + s_dwFiber2;

            // store the new value in the current fiber's storage
            *pdwFiber = dwSeqNew;

            // swap to the other fiber
            ::SwitchToFiber(pFiberOther);
        }
    }

void main()
{
    // create two fibers for the Fibonacci sequence
    s_pFiber1 = ::CreateFiber(
        0,              // default stack
        FiboProc,       // use the Fibonacci fiber proc
        reinterpret_cast<LPVOID>(1));    // fiber 1
    s_pFiber2 = ::CreateFiber(
        0,              // default stack
        FiboProc,       // use the Fibonacci fiber proc
        reinterpret_cast<LPVOID>(2));    // fiber 2

    // convert this thread to a fiber and run the first fiber
    ::ConvertThreadToFiber(NULL);
    ::SwitchToFiber(s_pFiber1);

    // clean up the fibers
    ::DeleteFiber(s_pFiber1);
    s_pFiber1 = NULL;
    ::DeleteFiber(s_pFiber2);
```

```
        s_pFiber2 = NULL;
}
```

The program in Listing 2-14 simply creates two fibers to manage the previous and previous-previous values in the Fibonacci sequence. Each fiber calculates the next value in the sequence, saves the value to the location it manages, and then swaps to the other fiber – which does the same. This sequence lasts for about the first 25 values of the sequence while the value is less than 100,000, then each fiber function returns and forces a return from the main thread's `SwitchToFiber()` API call. The resulting calculation is shown in Figure 2-6.

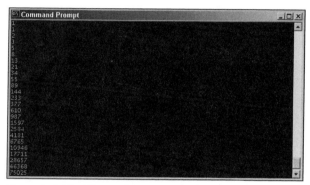

Figure 2-6: The Fibonacci sequence to 100,000 calculated using Windows fibers

Fibers are a clever idea and give you extra control over how your application gets its work done, but they don't allay any of the dangers of multithreading. In fact, fibers are not preemptable to your thread so you must rely on each fiber yielding control to the others in order to ensure that the thread accomplishes its task.

Summary

I've covered a lot of ground in this chapter. I showed you the basics of the Windows 2000 system architecture that delivers a powerful platform for building world-class applications. You've seen the types of applications that Windows enables you to build and how Windows interacts with them through process objects. Finally, you've seen the basics of creating multithreaded applications along with some of the tools for manipulating threads of execution.

As I alluded throughout this chapter, the Windows kernel supplies a number of objects that you will use in your applications to take advantage of system services. The next two chapters introduce the mechanics of using these objects and the properties of the most commonly used ones.

Chapter 3

Using Kernel Objects

IN THIS CHAPTER

- ◆ General use of kernel objects
- ◆ Kernel object security
- ◆ Waiting for the signaled state

THE WINDOWS 2000 KERNEL exposes a small (and growing) set of objects for applications to gain access to the system; these objects are fundamental to all applications. Already you are familiar with the process and thread objects. This chapter introduces you to using other kernel objects. Kernel objects provide your application with the tools to be a good citizen in the Windows 2000 world. Most of the code that implements these objects lives in the `Kernel32.DLL` library within the Windows 2000 `System32` directory.

General Use of Kernel Objects

All kernel objects are reasonably similar in creation, use, and cleanup. This part gives you the tools to approach any kernel object and use it.

What is a kernel object?

You'll often hear the terms "kernel object" or "system object" thrown into a conversation about Windows system-level programming, so let's go over exactly what a kernel object is. Simply put, a kernel object is an association of data and functions owned by the system that enable you to access services critical to creating applications within it. The kernel object, like all objects, contains state information, has well-known behavior, and is identifiably unique.

In the world of C APIs, a common technique to provide object-oriented services is the *handle idiom*. You can think of handles as pointers to data structures of which the client does not know the definition (sometimes they're more complicated than that, but you get the basic idea). This technique allows the server to protect the internals of its data structures and tie methods to data (encapsulation). In Listing 3-1, I show you how to simulate a fortune-telling device as a software object. The behavior of the object is not very important; it is an illustration and simplification of what the kernel does for you when it exposes an object. The library in the example manages the lifetime of a magic eight ball object by exposing a creator and destructor API in addition to a couple of operational APIs that it wants to give the client application.

Listing 3-1: Object-oriented C class example

```
// project handledemo
#include <windows.h>

static int M8BPrognosticate(int nSeed)
{
    return(nSeed+1);
}
static LPTSTR M8BLookupFortune(int /*nFortune*/)
{
    return "Maybe";
}


//
// the client of the object sees the following snippet in
//  a header file
//
#ifdef CLIENT

    // the handle is just a ptr to the client
    typedef void* HMAGIC8BALL;

    // the client code is just passing a void* back and forth
    HMAGIC8BALL CreateMagic8Ball();
    LPTSTR TellFortune(HMAGIC8BALL hBall);
    // ... other APIs (including cleanup)

//
// the server of the object gets to see the following
//  snippet in its implementation
//
#else // SERVER

    // definitions used by object server
    struct Magic8Ball
    {
        // data the client will use, not see
        int nSeed;
```

```
        int nLastFortune;
    };
    typedef Magic8Ball* HMAGIC8BALL;

    // the server knows how to allocate the object and
    //   set up its internal state
    HMAGIC8BALL CreateMagic8Ball()
    {
        HMAGIC8BALL hNew = new Magic8Ball;
        hNew->nSeed = ::GetTickCount();
        hNew->nLastFortune = 0;
        return hNew;
    }

    // to tell a fortune, the server can use the random number
    //   seed and last granted fortune to appear oracular
    LPTSTR TellFortune(HMAGIC8BALL hBall)
    {
        // use the last seed and avoid the
        int nNewFortune = hBall->nLastFortune;
        while(nNewFortune==hBall->nLastFortune)
        {
            // find a candidate fortune
            nNewFortune = M8BPrognosticate(hBall->nSeed);
        }

        // save the new fortune
        hBall->nLastFortune = nNewFortune;

        // look up the string and return it
        return(M8BLookupFortune(nNewFortune));
    }

    // ... other APIs

#endif

// the way this would be done in C++
class CMagic8Ball
{
private:
    int nSeed;
    int nLastFortune;
    CMagic8Ball() : nSeed(::GetTickCount()), nLastFortune(0)
```

```
        {}
public:
    static CMagic8Ball* Create() { return new CMagic8Ball; }
    LPSTR TellFortune()
    {
        // implementation
    }
    // ... other methods
};
```

 The appendix in the back of this book, "Using the Examples in This Book," explains where to find and how to build the listings throughout the book.

The code in Listing 3-1 shows you how to implement a `Magic8Ball` class. The client application can create an instance (object) without ever knowing how you implemented it through the use of the `CreateMagic8Ball()` API, which simply returns an opaque `HMAGIC8BALL` handle. The interesting implementation trick lies in `#ifdef CLIENT`. The header that the client sees treats the handle as a `void*`, while the server gets to treat the handle as a pointer to the actual structure. This opacity prevents the client from being able to use the internals of the object (the seed or last fortune) and enables the server to add new functionality or change the internal structure in the future without breaking existing clients.

Since we used C to create the API, any programming language supported by Windows 2000 can use it. Kernel objects are simply object-oriented C classes like the object shown in Listing 3-1. The principal difference is that the objects from the kernel are much more useful in creating applications.

Basic properties of kernel objects

Kernel objects all originate from the same location (`Kernel32.DLL`) and so are similar to one another. Each kernel object has the following characteristics:

◆ All client code refers to kernel objects using the opaque `HANDLE` type.

◆ When manipulating kernel objects, you must use the Windows 2000 API set; you cannot access the internal data pointed to by the handle.

◆ For some kernel object types, different processes can access the same kernel object simultaneously through unique handles. The kernel is responsible for reference counting and resource management.

◆ Clients can assign unique names to some kernel object types, which facilitates cross-process sharing with other kernel object clients.

◆ Clients can associate permissions to some kernel object types. These permissions grant or deny uses to accounts found on the system.

◆ Each kernel object has a Boolean attribute called *signaled.*

Available kernel objects

The module `Kernel32.DLL` implements at least 20 different kernel objects. You'll find that most of them provide you with very powerful facilities and that Windows 2000 provides APIs to finely control their behavior. Table 3-1 briefly describes the most commonly used objects along with the name of a top-level API you can use to access each object.

You should use the MSDN index (either online or from the MSDN's CD-ROM) to look up the top-level function and access more detailed information.

TABLE 3-1 AVAILABLE KERNEL OBJECTS

Kernel Object Name	Intention	Top-Level API
Access token	Grants permission to accounts for access to other kernel objects	`CreateRestricted Token`
Change notification	Notifies the owner that a change has occurred on a file	`FindFirstChange Notification`
Console I/O	Permits reading from and writing to the character-mode console	`GetStdHandle`
Event	Signals a programmatic occurrence, used for thread synchronization	`CreateEvent`
File	References a generic blob of data, usually located on persistent storage	`CreateFile`

Continued

TABLE 3-1 AVAILABLE KERNEL OBJECTS *(Continued)*

Kernel Object Name	Intention	Top-Level API
File mapping	Associates the contents of a file with a process's address space; a file view realizes contents within memory for direct access	`CreateFileMapping`
Find object (File, Volume, VolumeMountPoint)	Provides centralized searching through system objects	`FindFirstFile`
Heap	Allocates small regions of the process's virtual address space for temporary data	`HeapCreate`
Job	Groups an associated set of processes	`CreateJobObject`
Mailslot	Queues messages sent between threads	`CreateMailslot`
Module	Delivers a body of code and resources that can be mapped into the process's address space for use	`LoadLibrary`
Mutex	Synchronizes access to an inter-thread resource	`CreateMutex`
Pipe	Sends data from one thread to another	`CreateNamedPipe`
Process	Executes a group of one or more threads to perform a task, delivered by an EXE module	`CreateProcess`
Semaphore	Controls access to a resource shared across thread and restricts simultaneous accesses to a specified count	`CreateSemaphore`
Thread	Embodies a scheduled execution path for the OS	`CreateThread`

Kernel Object Name	Intention	Top-Level API
Timer queue	Holds a list of events scheduled to expire at a designated frequency and execute a callback function	`CreateTimerQueue`
Waitable timer	Signals a thread at a designated time or frequency	`CreateWaitable Timer`

Of the objects listed in the table, most are sharable across processes but some are private to the process. For example, the `module`, `heap`, `file mapping`, `file find`, `console input`, and `change notification` objects are accessible only within the calling process.

There is yet another set of objects not exported by `Kernel32.DLL`, which behave very much like kernel objects. These objects originate from `AdvAPI32.DLL` and include registry keys, services, event log entries, critical sections, access control entries (ACEs), security identifiers (SIDs), access control lists (ACLs), and security descriptors (SDs). I call these pseudo-kernel objects.

I discuss some of the above-listed objects later in this chapter.

Kernel object handles

The handles that the kernel returns to a process when it creates or opens an object are special. You need to take special care when using them.

Kernel object handles are specific to each process even if the kernel allows more than one process to share an object. Any process that knows the name of a kernel object and has sufficient access to open it may do so. All processes receive handles that differ in value, even if they refer to the same underlying object. This enables the kernel to trap improper access to the objects. Also, kernel objects are securable. This ensures that applications do not poke holes in the system security by passing a file handle, for instance, that it opened to another process owned by a different account that does not have permission to access the file.

When using handles, you always should initialize them to an invalid state. The preferred value is `INVALID_HANDLE_VALUE` found in `WinBase.H`. Be aware of the return values from kernel APIs though; they sometimes return a value of `NULL` and sometimes return `INVALID_HANDLE_VALUE` when they fail.

In order to minimize the number of resources that your application consumes, you should make sure that every handle the process creates or opens gets closed with a corresponding call to the `CloseHandle()` API. Another good idea is to set the handle back to `INVALID_HANDLE_VALUE` after you close it; this practice helps you avoid problems if you decide to reuse handle variables (as in a loop). Listing 3-2 demonstrates these best practices for using kernel objects. When the kernel terminates a process, it also closes all handles that the process neglected to close – freeing any improperly claimed resources.

Listing 3-2: The correct way to use a kernel handle in C++

```
// project usinghandles
#include <windows.h>

void UseAHandle()
{
    // set up the handle
    HANDLE hEvent = INVALID_HANDLE_VALUE;

    // create an event object
    hEvent = ::CreateEvent(
        NULL,    // default security descriptor
        TRUE,    // manual reset
        FALSE,   // not initially set
        "w2kdg.UsingHandles.event.Dummy");  // unique name
    if(hEvent!=NULL)
    {
        // use the object through the handle
        ::SetEvent(hEvent);

        // clean it up
        ::CloseHandle(hEvent);
        hEvent = INVALID_HANDLE_VALUE;
    }
}

void main()
{
    UseAHandle();
}
```

The important lesson from Listing 3-2 lies in the manner in which I initialize and clean up the handle, `hEvent`. Using `INVALID_HANDLE_VALUE` helps you avoid many bugs that pop up because of complicated logic flows and/or reuse of variables. It is a good habit to develop.

SHARING KERNEL OBJECT HANDLES

When communicating with other processes, your application sometimes wants to pass them handles to kernel objects. In order to share a handle with another process, the kernel provides the `DuplicateHandle()` API. This function creates a new handle that refers to the same object, but one that is valid only in the context of the target process. The recipient is responsible for closing this handle when finished using it.

For a review of threads and processes, see Chapter 2,"Basic Operating System Programming."

Listing 3-3 shows you the basics of using the `DuplicateHandle()` API to get a new handle. The function requires that you send it the handle to the receiving process and the handle you want it to duplicate. It then determines the current process and picks some default parameters for access and inheritance. When complete, it verifies the correctness of the result and returns the new handle to the caller.

Listing 3-3: Duplicating a handle for another process

```
// project usinghandles file duphandle.cpp
#include <windows.h>

HANDLE DupAHandle(HANDLE hProcessNew, HANDLE hParent)
{
    // fetch a handle to the current process
    HANDLE hProcessThis = ::GetCurrentProcess();

    // the result buffer
    HANDLE hClone = INVALID_HANDLE_VALUE;

    // execute the duplication
    if(!::DuplicateHandle(
        hProcessThis,   // the current (source) process
        hParent,        // the handle to duplicate
        hProcessNew,    // the target process
        &hClone,        // the destination handle
        GENERIC_READ,   // desired access (ignored due
                        //  to last param)
        FALSE,          // do not allow this to be inherited
        DUPLICATE_SAME_ACCESS)) // grant identical access
```

```
  {
      // it failed, return a bad handle
      hClone = INVALID_HANDLE_VALUE;
  }
  return(hClone);
}
```

As this example shows, duplicating a handle is quite straightforward – it requires only a simple API call. There is, however, no standard mechanism for sharing the duplicated handle with its destination process. You have to construct your own interprocess communication mechanism to make this happen. This involves writing the handle value to some repository and signaling the receiving process that it is waiting. The receiving process must then retrieve the handle value from the repository and use it.

The handle duplication procedure is sometimes necessary – for example, when the process sending the information terminates before the receiver can use the standard mechanism to share objects across processes (and the target object is destroyed). However, in my opinion, you should avoid this practice and design your processes to properly set up the name and security for the object, share its name, and confirm reception. The kernel provides an elegant, simple mechanism for sharing objects across processes; creating your own is probably a waste of your time.

INHERITING KERNEL OBJECT HANDLES

Often in large applications, one Windows process will create another to carry out part of the original task. This new process is called a *child process*. Sharing object handles with child processes is slightly easier than with peer or parent processes. This mechanism, called *inheritance*, automatically copies all specified handles to the child process. The child is then responsible for closing each handle that it inherits. Further, inheritance requires extra work: the `bInheritHandle` flag must be set in the `SECURITY_ATTRIBUTES` structure when creating the object, or passed when opening a handle to the object. Also, when creating the process, the parent must set the `bInheritHandles` parameter in the `CreateProcess()` API. Finally, the parent process must pass the values of each inherited handle down through the command line or some other interprocess communication.

I detail the `SECURITY_ATTRIBUTES` structure members in Table 3-2 in the Kernel Object Security section of this chapter.

Listing 3-4 shows an example of creating a child process that receives an inherited handle to an *event* object. This code creates both the parent and child processes using the command line to determine the desired behavior and pass the value of the inherited handle. The first (parent) process starts up without any command-line parameters, which causes it to create an event object that the second (child) process will use to signal that the parent should continue processing. This event is available for inheritance. Once the event object is ready, the parent creates a command line of "child N" for its child process where N is the value of the event's handle. It simply creates another instance of its own executable that recognizes that it is the child process from the command line. The parent process waits on the child to allow it to exit with the event object. When the child starts up and recognizes the event handle, it signals the event, closes the handle (the kernel opened it on the child's behalf), and exits. When the event object goes to the signaled state, the parent also exits.

Listing 3-4: Inheriting a handle from a parent process

```
// project inherithandle
#include <windows.h>
#include <stdio.h>

// the handle event to continue on
static HANDLE g_hEventContinue = INVALID_HANDLE_VALUE;

void CreateContinueEvent()
{
    // clean up any leftovers
    if(g_hEventContinue!=INVALID_HANDLE_VALUE)
    {
        ::CloseHandle(g_hEventContinue);
        g_hEventContinue = INVALID_HANDLE_VALUE;
    }

    // set up security so that the child inherits the handle
    SECURITY_ATTRIBUTES sa;
    sa.nLength = sizeof(sa);
    sa.bInheritHandle = TRUE;
    sa.lpSecurityDescriptor = NULL;

    g_hEventContinue = ::CreateEvent(
        &sa,        // our security values
        TRUE,       // manual reset event
        FALSE,      // initially non-signaled
        NULL);      // anonymous
    if(g_hEventContinue==NULL)
    {
        g_hEventContinue = INVALID_HANDLE_VALUE;
    }
```

```
}

BOOL CreateChild(LPTSTR szAppName)
{
    // format the command line for the child process, telling
    //  it that it is the child and handing it the
    //  handle to the continue event
    TCHAR szCmdLine[256];
    ::sprintf(szCmdLine, "child %d",
        reinterpret_cast<int>(g_hEventContinue));

    // startup info for the child
    STARTUPINFO si;
    ::ZeroMemory(reinterpret_cast<void*>(&si), sizeof(si));
    si.cb = sizeof(si); // must be sizeof this struct

    // returned process info for the child
    PROCESS_INFORMATION pi;

    // create the process, using the same executable and a
    //  command line that tells it to be a baby
    BOOL bCreateOK = ::CreateProcess(
        szAppName,   // name of the app to spawn (this exe)
        szCmdLine,   // flag to tell us to behave like a child
        NULL,        // security for the child process handle
        NULL,        // security for the child thread handle
        TRUE,        // inherit all inheritable handles
        0,           // special creation flags
        NULL,        // new environment
        NULL,        // current dir
        &si,         // startup info
        &pi);        // returned process info

    // release our references to the child process
    if(bCreateOK)
    {
        ::CloseHandle(pi.hProcess);
        ::CloseHandle(pi.hThread);
    }

    return(bCreateOK);
}

int main(int argc, char* argv[])
```

```
{
    if(argc<=1 || ::strcmp(argv[0], "child")!=0)
    {
        // we're the parent process, let's create the continue
        //  event and the child process
        CreateContinueEvent();

        if(CreateChild(argv[0]))
        {
            // wait for the child to signal
            ::WaitForSingleObject(g_hEventContinue, INFINITE);
        }

        // cleanup
        ::CloseHandle(g_hEventContinue);
        g_hEventContinue = INVALID_HANDLE_VALUE;
    }
    else
    {
        // we're the child process, let's grab the inherited
        //  event handle from the param list, signal it,
        //  and leave
        LPTSTR szHandle = argv[1];
        ::sscanf(szHandle, "%d",
            reinterpret_cast<int*>(&g_hEventContinue));
        if(g_hEventContinue!=INVALID_HANDLE_VALUE)
        {
            ::SetEvent(g_hEventContinue);

            // we must close the handle, it has been opened
            //  for us by the kernel (our parent could
            //  be gone before we use it)
            ::CloseHandle(g_hEventContinue);
        }
    }
    return 0;
}
```

Again, sharing object handle values does not lead to clean, maintainable code. You should avoid sharing objects by passing handle values when possible.

Kernel object naming

There are two types of kernel objects: *named* and *anonymous*. You generally create named objects when you need to share them across processes and create anonymous objects for use within the process only. Inter-thread synchronization and communication is a typical use of an anonymous kernel object. Listing 3-5 demonstrates a one-time use of a simple system service like a timer. Execution enters the Wait10Sec() function, which creates an anonymous, *waitable timer* object, sets it to expire in 10 seconds, and suspends until expiration. Once the timer expires, the function cleans it up and execution is complete.

Chapter 4, "Commonly Used Kernel Objects," covers thread synchronization.

In Listing 3-5, the preprocessor constants _WIN32_WINNT and WINVER are set to 0x05000 before the inclusion of Windows.H to enable Windows 2000-specific features. The SDK include files assume you want to create an application to run on Windows NT 3.51 or Windows 95, and so they disable many of the newer Windows features unless you direct them otherwise with the definals.

Listing 3-5: An anonymous kernel object for one-time use

```
// project anontimer
#define _WIN32_WINNT 0x0500
#define WINVER 0x0500
#include <windows.h>

void Wait10Sec()
{
    // create the timer, the last
    HANDLE hTimer = ::CreateWaitableTimer(
        NULL,   // no security needed, not shared
        TRUE,   // manual reset timer
        NULL);  // no name needed (anonymous)
    if(hTimer!=NULL)
    {
```

```
// set the due time as 10 seconds from now
//   as a negative 64-bit value
const __int64 c_SECOND = 10000000; // see Q188768
__int64 qwDueTime = -10 * c_SECOND;

// push the relative time into the proper format
LARGE_INTEGER liDueTime;
liDueTime.LowPart  = (DWORD)(qwDueTime & 0xFFFFFFFF);
liDueTime.HighPart = (DWORD)(qwDueTime > 32);

// tell the timer to expire in 10 sec
if(::SetWaitableTimer(
    hTimer,       // the timer
    &liDueTime,   // due time
    0,            // period (once)
    NULL,         // completion callback
    NULL,         // arg to callback
    FALSE))       // power-up
{
    // execute the wait
    ::WaitForSingleObject(hTimer, INFINITE);
}

// clean up
::CloseHandle(hTimer);
hTimer = INVALID_HANDLE_VALUE;
    }
}

void main()
{
    Wait10Sec();
}
```

Listing 3-5 has a mysterious reference to Q188768. This is a Microsoft Knowledge Base (KB) article. To view the article, you should use the search facility of the MSDN and supply the word "Q188768."

There are times when you have kernel objects that you want to assign system-wide names so that other processes can reference them. For example, a service application may wish to expose a signal to other processes that it is actively processing. To accomplish this, it creates an event kernel object with a particular name and sets its state to signaled. Listing 3-6 demonstrates an application that creates an event object to signal peer processes that it is active. This code simply creates an event object that it can use to signal it is actively doing work (of some sort). The event, g_hEventActive, is a manual-reset event so that it can signal and leave it in that state. It creates the event in the signaled state, and names it in a simple, unique, and intelligible fashion. When the process moves to the inactive state, it simply clears the event. It does not destroy it, however, so that client services know that the service is running—just not actively doing its job (for whatever reason). Just before the process exits, it destroys and cleans up the object.

Listing 3-6: A named kernel object for broadcasting state

```
// project namedobj
#include <windows.h>

// the application's signal that it is processing
static HANDLE g_hEventActive = INVALID_HANDLE_VALUE;

// this value would probably come from a header file so that
//   client processes could find it as well
static LPTSTR g_szActiveEventName =
    "w2kdg.NamedObj.event.Active";

// tell the world that we are active
void BroadcastActive()
{
    if(g_hEventActive==INVALID_HANDLE_VALUE)
    {
        // create the event in the signaled state,
        //      giving it a useful name
        g_hEventActive = ::CreateEvent(
            NULL,   // use default security descriptor
            TRUE,   // manual reset
            TRUE,   // initially signaled
            g_szActiveEventName);

        // watch out for failure to create
        if(g_hEventActive==NULL)
        {
            g_hEventActive = INVALID_HANDLE_VALUE;
        }
    }
}

void BroadcastInactive()
```

```
{
    if(g_hEventActive!=INVALID_HANDLE_VALUE)
    {
        // clear the signaled state but do not destroy
        //     the object
        ::ResetEvent(g_hEventActive);
    }
}

void Cleanup()
{
    if(g_hEventActive!=INVALID_HANDLE_VALUE)
    {
        // release our reference to the object and reset
        //     our handle value
        ::CloseHandle(g_hEventActive);
        g_hEventActive = INVALID_HANDLE_VALUE;
    }
}

void main()
{
    // let everyone know we're doing stuff
    BroadcastActive();

    // do stuff
    ::Sleep(1000);

    // let everyone know we're done doing stuff
    BroadcastInactive();

    // release the resources
    Cleanup();
}
```

This example allows clients of its services to know when it is active by simply opening the event object and testing its state. An added responsibility for this service process is that it must share the name of its active event; often it can do this at compile time through header files.

Chapter 4, "Commonly Used Kernel Objects," covers opening an event object. The section on advanced single object waits (later in this chapter) covers how to test a kernel object's signaled state.

When naming kernel objects, you must adhere to the restrictions imposed by the object itself, and you must construct a mechanism for broadcasting the names to the interested parties. In addition, you should pick a convention for naming your objects. I suggest using one similar to the registry in order to avoid cross-application conflicts as shown below:

```
<company name>.<product>.<object type>.<purpose>
```

This scheme enables you to restrict the object's name by the name of your organization (I would just pick the colloquial name), and the product (I would choose the root and not use any versions). After those restrictions, a Hungarian notation type of abbreviation for the object type and the general purpose of the object within the product should give you a universally unique name. Some examples of the use of the above naming convention are shown below:

```
AcmeLabs.GeneSplicer.event.Active
AcmeLabs.GeneSplicer.mmfile.ACTGSequence
```

This goes a long way to help keep your objects unique. It also should make it easier for you to write code since your names should be simple to reconstruct from memory.

Kernel object names are case sensitive, restricted to MAX_PATH (currently 260) characters in length, and cannot contain a backslash. Further, Windows 2000 Terminal Services imposes other restrictions. See the MSDN for details.

Kernel Object Security

Security for kernel objects is a broad topic. This section gives you the tools to use it and understand what you're doing without diving into the low-level details. I first introduce the objects involved in security setting and then show you how to use them.

When creating or using a kernel object, you must pay attention to the Windows 2000 security rules. When creating a new interprocess kernel object, you get to specify how other processes get to use your object. You'll find that Windows 2000 gives you very fine control over the access and that it is necessarily complicated to set up. Most of the time, you simply will accept the default object security (the full meaning of default access depends on the object but always gives full access to the owner-creator). Most of your remaining security settings will be for wide-open security (full access to the world).

Security object types

At the highest level, you specify object security with the SECURITY_ATTRIBUTES structure required by most kernel object creator APIs. This structure's members are shown in Table 3-2. Two of the three members of this structure are very straight-forward. The nLength member is always set to sizeof(SECURITY_ATTRIBUTES) and the bInheritHandle member is set according to whether the handle is passed to child processes (it is typically FALSE).

TABLE **3-2** MEMBERS OF THE SECURITY_ATTRIBUTES STRUCTURE

Member Name	Intention
DWORD nLength	The size of the structure, in bytes
LPVOID lpSecurityDescriptor	Pointer to a security descriptor (SD) object that controls sharing of object
BOOL bInheritHandle	Boolean flag that determines whether the process can send the object's handle to child processes

The final member of the SECURITY_ATTRIBUTES structure, lpSecurity Descriptor, is a pointer to a pseudo-kernel object called a security descriptor (SD). Typically, you set this pointer to NULL to receive the default security. However, in order to allow finer control over who gets access to the object, you have to fill it out; in order to do that, you have to take a look at some other objects: security identifiers (SIDs), access control lists (ACLs), and access control entries (ACEs).

SECURITY IDENTIFIERS

A *security identifier (SID)* is a pseudo-kernel object that describes a user account. You probably will never want to manually construct one using the Allocate AndInitializeSid() function; you likely will use the LookupAccountName() API to get the SID for a particular user or group. The SID is an integral part of the ACE (described later in detail). Listing 3-7 shows you how to look up the SID for an account – in this case, the current account using the GetUserName() and LookupAccountName() APIs. (The latter function might have been better named LookupAccountByName().) The SID is then converted to a semi-readable string using a new API call, `ConvertSidToStringSid()`, and sent to the console output window through `std::cout`. Note that it is the caller's responsibility to clean up the SID string after it is returned with the `LocalFree()` API.

Listing 3-7: Looking up the current user's SID

```
// project sidlookup
#define _WIN32_WINNT 0x0500
#define WINVER 0x0500
#include <windows.h>
#include <sddl.h>
#include <iostream>

void PrintCurrentSID()
{
    // variables to be filled
    const int c_nBufSize = 2048;
    BYTE arSid[c_nBufSize];
    PSID psid = reinterpret_cast<PSID>(arSid);
    DWORD dwSidSize(c_nBufSize);
    TCHAR szUserName[c_nBufSize], szDomainName[c_nBufSize];
    DWORD dwUserSize(c_nBufSize), dwDomainSize(c_nBufSize);
    SID_NAME_USE snu = SidTypeInvalid;

    // find the current user's name
    ::GetUserName(szUserName, &dwUserSize);

    // look up the account
    if(::LookupAccountName(
        NULL,           // system name - use this system
        szUserName,     // the user to look up
        psid,           // the sid we will look up
        &dwSidSize,     // the size of the sid returned
        szDomainName,   // the returned domain name
        &dwDomainSize,  // the size of the domain name
        &snu))          // the type of sid
    {
        // make a human-readable string
        LPTSTR szSid = NULL;
        ::ConvertSidToStringSid(psid, &szSid);

        // simple output
        std::cout << "Found SID " << szSid << " for " << szUserName
            << " in " << szDomainName << " domain." << std::endl;
```

```
        // free up the memory
        ::LocalFree(szSid);
        szSid = NULL;
    }
}

void main()
{
    PrintCurrentSID();
}
```

The application in Listing 3-7 simply finds the SID of the current user and converts it to a string. The resulting string, as shown in Figure 3-1, is not very intelligible to the end-user, but it is useful to Windows, since it uniquely identifies the account running the process.

Figure 3–1: The fetch and display of an SID that uses Listing 3–7

ACCESS CONTROL LISTS

An *access control list (ACL)* is a simple data structure that contains zero or more ACEs. Since it is a pseudo-kernel object, all initialization and manipulation is done through API calls. You must specify a buffer for it and call the InitializeAcl() function. You then can begin adding ACEs (discussed below) for each account that you wish to allow or deny a particular type of access to your kernel object.

ACCESS CONTROL ENTRIES

The kernel object uses an *access control entry (ACE)* psuedo-kernel object to grant or prevent access for a specified SID to execute an operation on the kernel object. Typically, this is done using the AddAccessAllowedAce() and AddAccess DeniedAce() functions. The ACE is composed of a header, the target SID, and an access mask.

The ACE header indicates its type, some type-specific flags, and its size. The SID indicates what account (or group of accounts) the ACE affects. The access mask determines what rights are affected. The access mask consists of standard and object type-specific rights; for example, it may be a bit-wise OR of FILE_MAP_READ and FILE_MAP_WRITE in order to allow full access to a file-mapping object.

Listing 3-8 shows a snippet of adding ACEs to an ACL that then can become a member of the SECURITY_DESCRIPTOR for a kernel object. It uses part of Listing 3-7, which has been grouped into GetCurrentSid(), then creates a new (empty) ACL using the InitalizeAcl() API. Next, the SID is packaged up in an ACE for the ACL using the `AddAccessAllowedAce()` function, with access to all features using the `GENERIC_ALL` mask. In this example, all buffers are allocated as 2K bytes long, which is much larger than required in all cases. When allocating these buffers in production, you should refer to the MSDN for details on allocating just enough space.

Listing 3-8: Creating an ACE and adding it to an ACL

```
// project aceconstruct
#define _WIN32_WINNT 0x0500
#define WINVER 0x0500
#include <windows.h>
#include <sddl.h>
const int c_nBufSize = 2048;

// helper mehod to grab current user's SID
BOOL GetCurrentSid(PSID psid)
{
    // variables to be filled
    DWORD dwSidSize(c_nBufSize);
    TCHAR szUserName[c_nBufSize], szDomainName[c_nBufSize];
    DWORD dwUserSize(c_nBufSize), dwDomainSize(c_nBufSize);
    SID_NAME_USE snu = SidTypeInvalid;

    // find the current user's name
    ::GetUserName(szUserName, &dwUserSize);

    // look up the account
    BOOL bLookupOK = ::LookupAccountName(
        NULL,            // system name - use this system
        szUserName,      // the user to look up
        psid,            // the sid we will look up
        &dwSidSize,      // the size of the sid returned
        szDomainName,    // the returned domain name
        &dwDomainSize,   // the size of the domain name
        &snu);           // the type of sid
    return(bLookupOK);
}

void CreateAce()
{
    BYTE arSid[c_nBufSize];
    PSID psid = reinterpret_cast<PSID>(arSid);
    if(GetCurrentSid(psid))
    {
```

```
    // create a dummy ACL
    BYTE arAcl[c_nBufSize];
    PACL pacl = reinterpret_cast<PACL>(arAcl);
    ::InitializeAcl(
        pacl,           // buffer to hold the resulting ACL
        c_nBufSize,     // size of the buffer
        ACL_REVISION);  // current rev of the ACL (winnt.h)

    // add an access-allowed ACE to it
    ::AddAccessAllowedAce(
        pacl,           // the ACL to add the new ACE to
        ACL_REVISION,   // current rev of the ACL
        GENERIC_ALL,    // as much access as we can get
        psid);          // the sid to grant rights to

    // now, grab the ACE out - this is how we could return
    //  it from the function if requested
    ACCESS_ALLOWED_ACE* pAce = NULL;
    ::GetAce(pacl, 0, reinterpret_cast<LPVOID*>(&pAce));
    }
}

void main()
{
    CreateAce();
}
```

   The application in Listing 3-8 shows you how to create an ACE and make it part of an ACL with the `CreateACE()` function. This function simply takes the current account's SID, creates an ACL that it will eventually throw away, then uses the `AddAccessAllowedAce()` API to create and add it to the ACL. The function then retrieves the ACE with the `GetAce()` API and could return it to the caller if asked.

SECURITY DESCRIPTORS
The *security descriptor (SD)* is a simple data structure that conveys a bunch of information to the system. The SD is the heart of the `SECURITY_ATTRIBUTES` structure that I introduced to you at the beginning of this section. This is data required by all securable kernel objects.
   The security descriptor data structure contains four main pieces of data:

◆ The most important part is the *discretionary access control list (DACL)* – a type of ACL – that contains grants or denials of access to specific SIDs. If this is empty, only the owner-creator of the object is permitted access. If this is `NULL`, the world has full access to the object.

◆ The owner SID that specifies the owner of the object.

◆ A primary group SID that specifies a security group to which this object belongs.

◆ The system access control list (SACL) – another type of ACL – that contains grants or denials of auditing access to the system.

You create a new SD for the security attributes structure, then manipulate it using API calls exclusively. The following example, Listing 3-9, shows you how to go about setting non-default permissions on a file that your process creates. This only works with file systems that support secure files, which means NTFS. First, the example creates a new SD using the InitializeSecurityDescriptor() function; then, it looks up the SID of the current account and sets the owner attribute of the SD with the SetSecurityDescriptorOwner() API. Next, using much of the code from the previous two examples, it creates an ACL that enables the current user (the owner) full access to the object (file). Then, this ACL is placed in the SD as the DACL. Finally, this SD is wrapped up in the security attributes structure, which is sent to the CreateFile() API call.

Listing 3-9: Creating a kernel object with specific permissions

```
// project sdcconstruct
#define _WIN32_WINNT 0x0500
#define WINVER 0x0500
#include <windows.h>
#include <sddl.h>
#include <string>
const int c_nBufSize = 2048;

// helper mehod to grab current user's SID
BOOL GetCurrentSid(PSID psid)
{
    // variables to be filled
    DWORD dwSidSize(c_nBufSize);
    TCHAR szUserName[c_nBufSize], szDomainName[c_nBufSize];
    DWORD dwUserSize(c_nBufSize), dwDomainSize(c_nBufSize);
    SID_NAME_USE snu = SidTypeInvalid;

    // find the current user's name
    ::GetUserName(szUserName, &dwUserSize);

    // look up the account
    BOOL bLookupOK = ::LookupAccountName(
        NULL,              // system name - use this system
        szUserName,        // the user to look up
```

```
        psid,            // the sid we will look up
        &dwSidSize,      // the size of the sid returned
        szDomainName,    // the returned domain name
        &dwDomainSize,   // the size of the domain name
        &snu);           // the type of sid
    return(bLookupOK);
}


// helper method to set the passed DACL to only allow access to
//   the passed SID
BOOL FillDacl(PACL pacl, DWORD dwAclSize, PSID psidPermit)
{
    // clear the current acl
    ::InitializeAcl(
        pacl,            // buffer to hold the resulting ACL
        dwAclSize,       // size of the buffer
        ACL_REVISION);   // current rev of the ACL (winnt.h)

    // add an access-allowed ACE to it
    BOOL bFillOK = ::AddAccessAllowedAce(
        pacl,            // the ACL to add the new ACE to
        ACL_REVISION,    // current rev of the ACL
        GENERIC_ALL,     // as much access as we can get
        psidPermit);     // the sid to grant rights to

    return(bFillOK);
}


// NOTE: this works on NTFS volumes only
void CreatePermissionedFile(const std::string& strFilename)
{
    // set up the security descriptor
    SECURITY_DESCRIPTOR sd;
    ::InitializeSecurityDescriptor(&sd,
        SECURITY_DESCRIPTOR_REVISION);

    // get the SID of the spawning account
    BYTE arSidCurrent[c_nBufSize];
    PSID psidCurrent =
        reinterpret_cast<PSID>(arSidCurrent);
    GetCurrentSid(psidCurrent);

    // set the file owner to the current account
    ::SetSecurityDescriptorOwner(
```

```
    &sd,        // the descriptor to fill
    psidCurrent,// the sid of the current user
    FALSE);     // don't use the default

// fill up our DACL and place it in the SD so that only
//   the current account can access the file
BYTE arAcl[c_nBufSize];
PACL pacl = reinterpret_cast<PACL>(arAcl);
FillDacl(pacl, c_nBufSize, psidCurrent);
::SetSecurityDescriptorDacl(
    &sd,     // the descriptor to fill
    TRUE,    // flag for an ACL present
    pacl,    // the ACL to set
    FALSE);  // flag to use the default

// create a security attributes structure
SECURITY_ATTRIBUTES sa;
sa.nLength = sizeof(sa);
sa.bInheritHandle = FALSE;
sa.lpSecurityDescriptor = &sd;

// create a (0-length) file and close it up
HANDLE hFile = ::CreateFile(
    strFilename.c_str(),    // file to create
    GENERIC_ALL,            // all access to the file
    0,                      // no sharing flags required
    &sa,                    // our security attributes
    CREATE_ALWAYS,          // always create a new file
    FILE_ATTRIBUTE_NORMAL,  // this is a standard file
    NULL);                  // template file
::CloseHandle(hFile);
hFile = NULL;

// you should now use the security properties dialog box
//   to view the permissions
}

void main()
{
    CreatePermissionedFile("c:\\owneronly.txt");
}
```

The application in Listing 3-9 creates a single zero-length file at the root of the
c: drive called OwnerOnly.TXT. The new file will only allow the creator any access.

Figure 3-2 shows the Security page of the shell's Properties dialog box for that new file. In Figure 3-2, you can see that the only permissions listed grant the `Author` account full control over the file; the shell does not show any other account as having any permissions.

You can use the `Advanced...` button on the Security page of the Properties dialog box shown in Figure 3-2 to launch another dialog box that will display the current file's owner.

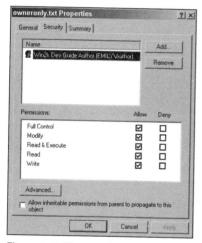

Figure 3-2: The security page of the shell's Properties dialog box

Viewing and adjusting kernel object security information

Windows 2000 provides methods for you to view and adjust the security information on kernel objects. The `GetSecurityInfo()` and `SetSecurityInfo()` functions enable you to modify any part of the security descriptor.

Of course, to modify any part of the security descriptor, your account must have sufficient access rights. The system administrator will assign these access rights in the Local Security Policy snap-in found in the Administrative Tools folder. For more information about this, see the Windows 2000 help file on the Start menu.

Listing 3-10 uses `GetSecurityInfo()` to display the security information attached to a file object. First, the example does something counter-intuitive — it calls `CreateFile()` to open the file. You should think of this API as creating the file handle, not necessarily the backing disk file. As you can see from the parameter list, it simply opens an existing file. The rest is straightforward; it fetches the SID for the owner, converts to a string, prints it, and cleans everything up.

Listing 3-10: Viewing part of the security descriptor on a kernel object

```
// project securinfo
#define _WIN32_WINNT 0x0500
#define WINVER 0x0500
#include <windows.h>
#include <sddl.h>
#include <aclapi.h>
#include <iostream>
#include <string>

void ShowSecureInfo(const std::string& strFilename)
{
    // show the string to the user
    std::cout << "\nSecurity info for file: " << strFilename
        << std::endl;

    // open the file
    HANDLE hFile = ::CreateFile(
        strFilename.c_str(),// file to open
        GENERIC_READ,       // read-only
        FILE_SHARE_READ,    // sharing, read-only
        NULL,               // no security attribs needed
        OPEN_EXISTING,      // open style, it must exist
        0,                  // file flags, ignored
        NULL);              // template file, not used
    if(hFile==INVALID_HANDLE_VALUE)
    {
        std::cout << "\tError: " << ::GetLastError()
            << std::endl;
        return;
    }

    // get the security info
    PSID psidOwner = NULL;
    PSECURITY_DESCRIPTOR psd = NULL;
    DWORD dwResult = ::GetSecurityInfo(
        hFile,              // the object to get info from
```

```
        SE_FILE_OBJECT,         // it's a file
        OWNER_SECURITY_INFORMATION, // let's get the owner SID
        &psidOwner,             // results
        NULL,                   // group SID output, ignored
        NULL,                   // DACL output, ignored
        NULL,                   // SACL output, ignored
        &psd);                  // the security descriptor output
    if(dwResult==ERROR_SUCCESS)
    {
        // make a string out of the SID
        LPTSTR szSid = NULL;
        ::ConvertSidToStringSid(psidOwner, &szSid);

        std::cout << "\tOwner SID: " << szSid << std::endl;

        // find the account and domain name from the SID
        TCHAR szName[MAX_PATH], szDomain[MAX_PATH];
        DWORD dwNameSize(MAX_PATH), dwDomainSize(MAX_PATH);
        SID_NAME_USE nametype(SidTypeUnknown);
        if(::LookupAccountSid(
            NULL,           // use this computer
            psidOwner,      // the SID to lookup
            szName,         // resulting account name
            &dwNameSize,    // size of the account name
            szDomain,       // resulting domain name
            &dwDomainSize,  // size of domain name buffer
            &nametype))     // type of name resulting
        {
            std::cout << "\tOwner Account: "
                << szDomain << "\\" << szName
                << std::endl;
        }

        // cleanup the SID and SD
        ::LocalFree(szSid);
        ::LocalFree(psd);
        psd = NULL;
    }
    else
    {
        std::cout << "\tError: " << ::GetLastError()
            << std::endl;
    }
```

```
    // close up the file handle
    ::CloseHandle(hFile);
    hFile = NULL;
}

void main()
{
    ShowSecureInfo("c:\\ntldr");
    ShowSecureInfo("c:\\owneronly.txt");
}
```

The application in Listing 3-10 illustrates the method of finding security information in Windows. First, it creates a kernel file object around the actual disk file. Next, it calls the `GetSecurityInfo()` API, which returns an SD that contains any or all of the security information that the system has associated with the object. Finally, the example uses the returned SID for the owner (actually just a pointer into the returned SD) to display the SID in string form with the `ConvertSid ToStringSid()` API. In order to make the information meaningful, the application also uses `LookupAccountSid()` to fetch the human-readable name of the account. Figure 3-3 shows the results of running the application. The security information in the figure is produced by Listing 3-10 on a system file and on the file created in Listing 3-9.

Figure 3-3: Security information display produced by Listings 3-10 and 3-9

Typical uses of security tools

You rarely will require most of the tools for setting security that you just learned to use, but you occasionally will run into object security problems for which they are required. Let's look at some commonly used security settings with four examples in Listings 3-11 through 3-14.

The first case, shown in Listing 3-11, introduces the `PrintDacl()` method, which shows you the discretionary access list of the objects created by the examples. The output from `PrintDacl()` actually seems a bit cryptic; it is an example of *security descriptor definition language (SDDL)*.

The MSDN has a full explanation of the SDDL syntax; simply search for the term "SDDL."

Listing 3-11 then creates an empty ACL and sets it to the kernel object's DACL. Setting an empty DACL to a kernel object explicitly tells the kernel that you permit no account access to this object. Therefore, it is private. (Only you, the owner, have permission to access it.) This is much like the example in Listing 3-9, except no call to an `AddAccessXxxAce()` function is made, leaving the ACL empty.

Listing 3-11: An object usable only by the owner

```
// project securex
#define _WIN32_WINNT 0x0500
#define WINVER 0x0500
#include <windows.h>
#include <sddl.h>
#include <iostream>
#include <aclapi.h>
const int c_nBufSize = 2048;

// utility method to produce an SDDL string representing the
//   passed kernel object's DACL
void PrintDacl(HANDLE hTarget)
{
    // fetch the DACL for the target
    PACL pDacl = NULL;
    PSECURITY_DESCRIPTOR psd = NULL;
    if(::GetSecurityInfo(hTarget, SE_KERNEL_OBJECT,
        DACL_SECURITY_INFORMATION, NULL, NULL, &pDacl,
        NULL, &psd)!=ERROR_SUCCESS)
    {
        return;
    }

    // check for a NULL DACL
    if(pDacl==NULL)
    {
        std::cout << "DACL is NULL, all access permitted"
            << std::endl;
        ::LocalFree(psd);
        return;
```

```
    }

    // use an API to create a (semi-)readable string from it
    LPTSTR szSD = NULL;
    if(::ConvertSecurityDescriptorToStringSecurityDescriptor(
        psd, SDDL_REVISION_1,
        DACL_SECURITY_INFORMATION,
        &szSD, NULL))
    {
        // dump the string and clean it up
        std::cout << "DACL: " << szSD << std::endl;

        ::LocalFree(szSD);
        szSD = NULL;
    }

    // clean up the security info
    ::LocalFree(psd);
    pDacl = NULL;
    psd = NULL;
}

//
// passing a security descriptor with an empty DACL
//  allows nobody but the owner access to the object
//
void CreateOwnerEvent()
{
    // create an ACL with no ACEs
    BYTE arDacl[c_nBufSize];
    PACL pDacl = reinterpret_cast<PACL>(arDacl);
    ::InitializeAcl(
        pDacl,          // the ACL
        c_nBufSize,     // size allocated for it
        ACL_REVISION);  // current revision

    // allocate and initialize a security descriptor
    BYTE arSD[SECURITY_DESCRIPTOR_MIN_LENGTH + c_nBufSize];
    PSECURITY_DESCRIPTOR psd =
        reinterpret_cast<PSECURITY_DESCRIPTOR>(arSD);
    ::InitializeSecurityDescriptor(
        psd,                            // the SD
        SECURITY_DESCRIPTOR_REVISION);  // current rev of SD
```

```
    // take the ACL with now ACEs (empty ACL) and place it in
    //  the SD's DACL field to deny all access
    ::SetSecurityDescriptorDacl(
        psd,    // the SD to use
        TRUE,   // a DACL will now be present in the SD
        pDacl,  // the ACL to make the SD's DACL
        FALSE); // do not use the default DACL

    // create the security attributes struct to deliver the SD
    SECURITY_ATTRIBUTES sa;
    sa.nLength = sizeof(sa);
    sa.bInheritHandle = FALSE;
    sa.lpSecurityDescriptor = psd;

    // create a new event
    HANDLE hEvent = ::CreateEvent(
        &sa,    // send a filled-out DACL
        TRUE,   // manual reset
        TRUE,   // initially set
        "w2kdg.SecurEx.event.OwnerOnly");

    // show the dacl
    std::cout << "Owner-only event - ";
    PrintDacl(hEvent);

    // cleanup
    ::CloseHandle(hEvent);
    hEvent = INVALID_HANDLE_VALUE;
}
```

The next example, Listing 3-12, sets a value of NULL to the event's DACL. Setting a null DACL tells the kernel that you are not explicitly denying access to anyone and so it should permit everyone to access it. The best way to remember this is to refer to this line when you need it: *A null DACL means all access; an empty DACL means no access.*

Listing 3–12: An object usable by any process

```
// project securex
//
// passing a security descriptor with a NULL DACL
//  allows everyone all access to the object
//
void CreateWorldWideEvent()
{
```

```
// initialize the SD wrapper object
SECURITY_ATTRIBUTES sa;
sa.nLength = sizeof(sa);
sa.bInheritHandle = FALSE;
sa.lpSecurityDescriptor = NULL;

// allocate an SD and initialize it
BYTE arSD[SECURITY_DESCRIPTOR_MIN_LENGTH];
PSECURITY_DESCRIPTOR psd =
    reinterpret_cast<PSECURITY_DESCRIPTOR>(arSD);
if(::InitializeSecurityDescriptor(
    psd,                              // the SD to init
    SECURITY_DESCRIPTOR_REVISION))    // current rev
{
    // now set a null DACL
    if(::SetSecurityDescriptorDacl(
        psd,    // the SD to use
        TRUE,   // a DACL will now be present in the SD
        NULL,   // the value of the DACL -
                //  NULL means no denial
        FALSE)) // do not use the default DACL
    {
        // set the SD for the object
        sa.lpSecurityDescriptor = psd;
    }
}

// create a new event
HANDLE hEvent = ::CreateEvent(
    &sa,    // send a NULL DACL
    TRUE,   // manual reset
    TRUE,   // initially set
    "w2kdg.SecurEx.event.WorldWide");

// show the dacl
std::cout << "World-wide event - ";
PrintDacl(hEvent);

// cleanup
::CloseHandle(hEvent);
hEvent = INVALID_HANDLE_VALUE;
}
```

Chapter 11, "Service Applications," introduces a C++ class called `CGlobalAccessSA` that delivers an SA with a null DACL without all of the manual work in Listing 3-12.

Listing 3-13 shows perhaps the most commonly used access setting: default access. Simply passing a `NULL` for the security attributes (and hence the SD) tells the kernel that you want the default access for the object. The actual access granted depends on the default DACL of the creator's access token. Generally, this means that the wrong thing is likely to happen when your application runs under another account or communicates with a process that does. When creating objects for inter-account, interprocess communication (for example, service applications) you probably will want to grant worldwide access to your objects or have a solid way of picking the groups that you want to grant access. See that Listing 3-13 simply passes `NULL` where the creator API requested the `SECURITY_ATTRIBUTES` structure.

Listing 3-13: An object with default access

```
// project securex
//
// the default security descriptor is used when you pass a
//  NULL security attributes ptr
//
void CreateDefaultAccessEvent()
{
    // create a new event
    HANDLE hEvent = ::CreateEvent(
        NULL,   // use default security descriptor
        TRUE,   // manual reset
        TRUE,   // initially set
        "w2kdg.SecurEx.event.DefaultAccess");

    // show the dacl
    std::cout << "Process-only event - ";
    PrintDacl(hEvent);

    // cleanup
    ::CloseHandle(hEvent);
    hEvent = INVALID_HANDLE_VALUE;
}
```

The final example of access setting for a kernel object, Listing 3-14, shows you how to grant all access to a specific group of accounts. In particular, this example looks up the SID of the administrators group on the local machine, creates an ACL that grants them all access, sets it as an SD's DACL, then passes it to the creator method for an event. Listing 3-14 is the basic flow of logic you need to follow to grant complex discretionary access to your kernel objects in Windows 2000.

Listing 3-14: Object usable by any process run by a member of the administrators group

```
// project sercurex
//
// passing a security descriptor with specific DACL that
//  allows any "Administrator" account access
//
void CreateAdministratorsEvent()
{
    // look up the Administrators group
    BYTE arSid[c_nBufSize];
    PSID psid = reinterpret_cast<PSID>(arSid);
    DWORD dwSidSize(c_nBufSize);
    TCHAR szDomainName[c_nBufSize];
    DWORD dwDomainSize(c_nBufSize);
    SID_NAME_USE snu = SidTypeInvalid;
    ::LookupAccountName(
        NULL,                // system name - use this system
        "Administrators",    // the user to look up
        psid,                // the sid we will look up
        &dwSidSize,          // the size of the sid returned
        szDomainName,        // the returned domain name
        &dwDomainSize,       // the size of the domain name
        &snu);               // the type of sid

    // create an ACL with a single ACE allowing all access
    //  to the Administrators SID
    BYTE arDacl[c_nBufSize];
    PACL pDacl = reinterpret_cast<PACL>(arDacl);
    ::InitializeAcl(pDacl, c_nBufSize, ACL_REVISION);
    ::AddAccessAllowedAce(pDacl, ACL_REVISION, GENERIC_ALL,
        psid);

    // create a descriptor and push the ACL into the DACL
    BYTE arSD[SECURITY_DESCRIPTOR_MIN_LENGTH + c_nBufSize];
    PSECURITY_DESCRIPTOR psd =
        reinterpret_cast<PSECURITY_DESCRIPTOR>(arSD);
    ::InitializeSecurityDescriptor(psd,
        SECURITY_DESCRIPTOR_REVISION);
    ::SetSecurityDescriptorDacl(psd, TRUE, pDacl, FALSE);
```

```
// create the security attributes struct to deliver the
//  descriptor
SECURITY_ATTRIBUTES sa;
sa.nLength = sizeof(sa);
sa.bInheritHandle = FALSE;
sa.lpSecurityDescriptor = psd;

// create a new event
HANDLE hEvent = ::CreateEvent(
    &sa,    // send a filled-out DACL
    TRUE,   // manual reset
    TRUE,   // initially set
    "w2kdg.SecurEx.event.AdminsOnly");

// show the dacl
std::cout << "Admins-only event - ";
PrintDacl(hEvent);

// cleanup
::CloseHandle(hEvent);
hEvent = INVALID_HANDLE_VALUE;
}
```

From Listing 3-14 we can see a reasonably simple procedure for using the security pseudo-kernel objects. In this case, granting permission to a specific account or group of accounts begins by looking up the SID for the account – usually with the LookupAccountName() API. Next, you initialize an ACL and add an ACE to it granting or denying a set of rights. Once the ACL is ready, you create and initialize an SD and set your ACL to its DACL field. Finally, you wrap up the SD in a SECURITY_ATTRIBUTES structure and send it to the creator API for the kernel object.

The four code snippets in Listings 3-11 through Listing 3-14 show you typical uses of the security tools that you will encounter when writing applications in Windows 2000. You will often come upon a situation that requires an SA structure, but you will not often have to know its inner workings or the details about any of its components. You'll simply have to use one of the examples I just covered. Figure 3-4 shows the results of calling each of the SA setup functions.

Figure 3-4: The results of the PrintDacl() calls in Listings 3-11 through 3-14

Waiting for the Signaled State

Now that you understand the basics of what kernel objects are, and how to construct, secure, and reference them, let's move on to using them. As I indicated earlier in this chapter, all kernel objects have a Boolean attribute called *signaled*. Alone, this value is uninteresting, but the kernel provides a set of *waiting functions* that enable you to suspend thread execution until an object reaches the signaled state.

Why wait for the signaled state?

Waiting on an object to reach the signaled state enables you to build multithreaded applications since it allows threads to enter a suspended state while waiting for an action to occur. This action might originate from another thread within the thread's process or from another process entirely. The important attribute of this suspended state is that it takes almost no CPU cycles away from other applications, allowing them to execute their tasks.

The kernel object types that you can wait on for the signaled state are

◆ Change notification

◆ File (during console input)

◆ Event

◆ Job

◆ Mutex

◆ Process

◆ Semaphore

◆ Thread

◆ Timer queue timer

◆ Waitable timer

As an example of the utility of a suspend state, let's look at the old practice of applications sending data to each other in the form of .INI files. Without the kernel object waiting functions, we'd have to do something like Listing 3-15. This code simply enters a tight polling loop attempting to find the existence of a file with the .INI extension in the temporary files' directory. Since this example is meant to show CPU monopolization, you should just quit it in the debugger once you see it bogging the system down.

Listing 3-15: Polling for a file to show up

```
// project filewait
#include <windows.h>
#include <iostream>

// helper method to check for the presence of an ini file
//   in the temporary directory
BOOL FindIni()
{
    // look up the temp directory
    TCHAR szTempPath[MAX_PATH];
    ::GetTempPath(MAX_PATH, szTempPath);

    // create the wildcard target as all .INIs in the temp
    TCHAR szTargetFile[MAX_PATH];
    ::strcpy(szTargetFile, szTempPath);
    ::strcat(szTempPath, "*.ini");

    // call the kernel's file find method
    WIN32_FIND_DATA fd;
    HANDLE hLocator = ::FindFirstFile(szTargetFile, &fd);

    // check the results
    BOOL bFound = hLocator!=INVALID_HANDLE_VALUE;
    if(bFound)
    {
        // report our find
        std::cout << "Found file: " << fd.cFileName
            << std::endl;

        // clean up the handle
        ::FindClose(hLocator);
        hLocator = INVALID_HANDLE_VALUE;
    }
    return(bFound);
}

void PollForIni()
{
    // continuously loop
    while(!FindIni())
        /*loop*/;
}
```

When you run the polling loop in Listing 3-15, watch it consume 90-100% of CPU usage in the task manager's processes page. The `FindIni()` function uses the `FindFirstFile()` API to create a file find object to sift through all of the files in the target directory. When the `FindIni()` function returns, the `PollForIni()` function simply runs it again; there is not a pause in thread execution unless the system preempts.

The Windows 2000 task manager has added the ability to view additional process statistics in the Processes tab from the `View... Select Columns...` menu choice. While running the examples in this book, you may want to experiment with adding some of the new columns. For example, you may find the `Handles` and `Threads` columns interesting to watch. Figure 3-5 shows this dialog box and the resulting columns in action.

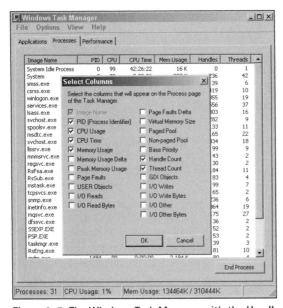

Figure 3-5: The Windows Task Manager with the Handles and Threads columns displayed

Using the file change kernel object and a waiting function, Listing 3-16 improves Listing 3-15 to consume almost no CPU. This new version simply adds a body to the find loop that suspends polling — until there is something new to look at — using the `WaitForSingleObject()` API.

Listing 3-16: Waiting for directory changes and then looking for a file

```
void WaitForIni()
{
    // look up the temp directory
    TCHAR szTempPath[MAX_PATH];
    ::GetTempPath(MAX_PATH, szTempPath);

    // create an object to wait on changes to the dir
    HANDLE hChange = ::FindFirstChangeNotification(
        szTempPath, // the directory to watch
        FALSE,      // do not watch the entire subtree
        FILE_NOTIFY_CHANGE_FILE_NAME);  // any change
    if(hChange!=INVALID_HANDLE_VALUE)
    {
        // loop until we find our target
        while(!FindIni())
        {
            // suspend until someone makes a change to
            //  the directory we're interested in
            ::WaitForSingleObject(hChange, INFINITE);

            // reset the handle
            ::FindNextChangeNotification(hChange);
        }
    }

    // clean up the change handle
    ::FindCloseChangeNotification(hChange);
    hChange = INVALID_HANDLE_VALUE;
}
```

The waiting functions that the kernel supplies come in two main flavors: single and multiple object waits. Listing 3-16 used a single object wait, the `WaitFor SingleObject()` API. Additionally, the kernel supports *asynchronous procedure calls (APCs)* and some advanced wait APIs to support them. The rest of this section explores these topics.

Single object waits

Let's start looking at the waiting methods with the single object waits. These methods simply suspend the current thread until either the specified object reaches the signaled state or the supplied timeout expires. The most commonly used API is called `WaitForSingleObject()`. Listing 3-17 shows you how to wait for a change to the file *Internet cache directory* – a change that occurs just about whenever you visit a Web site.

The code in Listing 3-17 simply looks up the name of the cache directory and creates a change notification object to watch for any changes to the directory tree rooted there. It then begins waiting for the change, timing out if nothing happens for one second. The return code from the wait API indicates what happened. If it's a timeout, a dot is printed and the wait is renewed. If the object reaches the signaled state, you are told. If an error occurs, you can retrieve the error code with the `GetLastError()` API.

Chapter 18, "Development Support," covers the `GetLastError()` API.

Listing 3-17 uses the function `SHGetFolderPath()` to find the Internet cache directory. This is the only recommended way to find folders in the system. Chapter 9, "Shell Services," covers it in detail.

Listing 3-17: Using WaitForSingleObject and handling the return codes

```
// project waitex
#include <windows.h>
#include <iostream>
#include <shlobj.h>

// method to pause until a change happens in the
//   internet cache directory, as soon as a change happens,
//   this method returns
void WaitForChange()
{
    HANDLE hChange = INVALID_HANDLE_VALUE;

    // find the internet cache directory
    TCHAR szInetCache[MAX_PATH];
    if(SUCCEEDED(::SHGetFolderPath(
        NULL,   // parent window for GUI, don't have one
        CSIDL_INTERNET_CACHE,   // id of the cache dir
        NULL,   // use the current user's access token
        SHGFP_TYPE_CURRENT, // fetch the current value
        szInetCache)))
    {
```

```
        // look for changes to the cache dir and below
        hChange = ::FindFirstChangeNotification(
            szInetCache,    // the directory to watch
            TRUE,           // watch the tree
            FILE_NOTIFY_CHANGE_FILE_NAME);  // any change
    }

if(hChange!=INVALID_HANDLE_VALUE)
{
    // loop until we don't timeout
    DWORD dwResult = WAIT_TIMEOUT;
    while(dwResult==WAIT_TIMEOUT)
    {
        // suspend until someone makes a change to
        //  the file system
        dwResult = ::WaitForSingleObject(
            hChange,    // reference to the change object
            1000);      // wait in 1 sec (1000ms) chunks

        // check for a timeout
        if(dwResult==WAIT_TIMEOUT)
        {
            // reset the wait handle
            ::FindNextChangeNotification(hChange);

            // show some activity
            std::cout << ".";
            std::cout.flush();
        }
        // found a change
        else if(dwResult==WAIT_OBJECT_0)
        {
            std::cout << "saw a change to the internet cache."
                << std::endl;
        }
        // something bad has happened
        else if(dwResult==WAIT_FAILED)
        {
            std::cout << "Failed, error: " <<
                ::GetLastError() << std::endl;
        }
    }
}
```

```
    // clean up the change handle
    ::FindCloseChangeNotification(hChange);
    hChange = INVALID_HANDLE_VALUE;
}


void main()
{
    WaitForChange();
}
```

You can see that the new loop in Listing 3-17 takes almost no CPU cycles and reports immediately when something changes. Note that I take a hard look at the return values from WaitForSingleObject() API here. This is recommended practice since you'll find that the result code often points directly at problems when you construct your application.

Advanced single object waits

A special timeout value for the waiting APIs is zero. This instructs the kernel to return immediately after testing the signaled state of the object. This is how you instantly test the signaled state of an object.

There is another special timeout value, INFINITE, that tells the kernel not to wake up the thread unless the watched object is signaled. You should avoid an infinite wait in production applications if possible, since, if things go wrong, the waiting thread will be locked up for the life of the process. In addition, the INFINTIE value causes problems if the thread waiting uses an APC (asynchronous procedure call) somewhere else since the kernel will never release the thread to execute the APC. Windows 2000 provides a solution for this deadlock problem, the WaitFor SingleObjectEx() API.

I discuss the WaitForSingleObjectEx() API later in the section on Waiting and APCs.

You should see that the kernel object can set its signaled value, but it cannot tell how many, if any, threads are waiting for it. Also, the waiting threads have no way of determining if any other threads are ahead in queue for the signaled state or whether the object will ever really reach the signaled state. Signaling decouples the server thread from the client thread.

AVOIDING MISSED SIGNALS

Another cousin of `WaitForSingleObject()` is the `SignalObjectAndWait()` API, which enables you to signal an event, mutex, or semaphore object and immediately enter the wait state for another object. This function is required if you design a thread handshake where the thread immediately must begin waiting on another signal after signaling itself.

The event kernel object has a mode called auto-reset, which forces the object to return to the non-signaled state immediately after releasing all waiting threads. When this mode is used, all threads that might wish to wait on the event must guarantee that they are already in the waiting state whenever this signaling might occur. For example, a client thread might tell the server thread to begin processing with the use of a manual-reset event and wait on the auto-reset event to be signaled before continuing. If the server were to immediately signal finished after the client signaled to begin, the client might reach the waiting state after the server signaled the completion event. Since the system will immediately clear the completion event, the client might wait forever. Closing up the hole is the main purpose of the `SignalObjectAndWait()` API.

Listing 3-18 shows you a snippet in which the thread must begin waiting as soon as an object enters the signaled state. In this example, the pending event must be auto-reset since more than one process may want to signal that it has a request ready. Since the request-ready event might be signaled and non-signaled before a wait function can be entered, the `SignalObjectAndWait()` function is required. This function guarantees that no signaling can occur without the wait ending properly (with code `WAIT_OBJECT_0`), thus preventing a missed request or even a deadlock.

Listing 3-18: Using SignalObjectAndWait() to avoid lost signals

```
// project waitex, file singalandwait.cpp
//
// create an event signaling readiness
HANDLE hEventReady = ::CreateEvent(
    &sa,    // proper security
    TRUE,   // manual-reset event
    FALSE,  // initially unsignaled
    "w2kdg.Waiting.event.Ready");  // unique name

// create an event signaling a pending request
HANDLE hEventPending = ::CreateEvent(
    &sa,    // proper security
    FALSE,  // auto-reset event
    FALSE,  // initially unsignaled
    "w2kdg.Waiting.event.Pending");   // unique name

// as soon as we are ready, a request ready may be
```

```
//  signaled, so we cannot return to this execution
//  thread until that signal without risk of losing it
DWORD dwResult = ::SignalObjectAndWait(
    hEventReady,    // flag that we're ready (set it)
    hEventPending,  // flag that request is ready (wait)
    INFINITE,       // wait forever
    FALSE);         // not alertable, no APC
if(dwResult==WAIT_OBJECT_0)
{
    // clear the ready flag
    ::ResetEvent(hEventReady);

    // handle the request
    // ...
}
```

This example illustrates the code that you need to write when you come upon this situation. This race condition is an easy one to overlook if you've never been exposed to it. Now that you have seen it, hopefully you will catch it.

USING SINGLE OBJECT CALLBACK WAITS

Another way to act on an object's transition to the signaled state is by using a callback method. The RegisterWaitForSingleObject()API enables you to create a method that is called once a kernel object is signaled. The system uses a thread from its working thread pool to execute the callback in the context of your process. This gives you the ability to act as a multithreaded application without creating additional threads.

In Listing 3-19, the main thread sets up a periodic timer, tells the system to use the display callback every time it expires, and goes about counting all files in the windows directory depth-first. The display callback simply queries the value of the counter and dumps it to the standard output stream every tenth-second. Once the calculation is complete, the main thread tells the system to stop calling back into the display function using UnregisterWaitEx() function with the handle returned from the registration API.

This technique enables you to concentrate your effort on making the main worker thread do its job without worrying about how to get a *user interface (UI)* thread to give the user feedback as it happens.

Listing 3-19: Using RegisterWaitForSingleObject() to count files

```
// project regwait
#define _WIN32_WINNT 0x0500
#define WINVER 0x0500
#include <windows.h>
#include <iostream>
```

```
#include <shlobj.h>

HANDLE CreateUITimer()
{
    // create a raw timer
    HANDLE hTimer = ::CreateWaitableTimer(NULL, FALSE, NULL);
    if(hTimer!=NULL)
    {
        // set the due time as quick as possible
        LARGE_INTEGER liDueTime = { 0, 0 };

        // activate the periodic timer
        if(!::SetWaitableTimer(
            hTimer,      // timer object to activate
            &liDueTime,  // 1st expiry in immediately
            100,         // expire every 1/10 sec
            NULL,        // no completion routine
            NULL,        // no arg to completion routine
            FALSE))      // ignore restore power
        {
            hTimer = INVALID_HANDLE_VALUE;
        }
    }
    else
    {
        hTimer = INVALID_HANDLE_VALUE;
    }
    return(hTimer);
}


// this is the UI callback for the file counter
VOID NTAPI CBShowStatus(PVOID lpParameter,
    BOOLEAN bTimerOrWaitFired)
{
    // make sure we are in the timer loop
    if(!bTimerOrWaitFired && lpParameter!=NULL)
    {
        // understand the param
        LONG* pnFileCt = reinterpret_cast<LONG*>(lpParameter);

        // dump the current file count
        std::cout << "thread: " << ::GetCurrentThreadId()
            << " count: " << (*pnFileCt) << std::endl;
    }
```

```
}

HANDLE SetupUICallback(HANDLE hTimer, LONG* pnFileCt)
{
    // the return buffer
    HANDLE hCB = INVALID_HANDLE_VALUE;

    // register our callback with the kernel
    if(!::RegisterWaitForSingleObject(
        &hCB,                   // the calling-back object
        hTimer,                 // the waiting-on object
        ::CBShowStatus,         // the callback fcn
        reinterpret_cast<LPVOID>(pnFileCt),
                                // cb param, value to display
        INFINITE,               // no need to timeout
        WT_EXECUTEDEFAULT))     // nothing fancy
    {
        // we failed, let the caller know
        hCB = INVALID_HANDLE_VALUE;
    }
    return(hCB);
}


void CleanupCallback(HANDLE hCB)
{
    // the unregistration API allows you to wait
    //   synchronously, asynchronously, or not at all
    //   for it to finish
    ::UnregisterWaitEx(hCB, NULL);
}

void CountFiles(LPTSTR szRoot, LONG* pnTotal)
{
    // start looping through all of the files in the dir
    WIN32_FIND_DATA fd;
    HANDLE hFind = ::FindFirstFile(szRoot, &fd);
    while(hFind!=INVALID_HANDLE_VALUE)
    {
        // for directories, count all files there
        if((fd.dwFileAttributes &
            FILE_ATTRIBUTE_DIRECTORY)!=0)
        {
            // don't count the . or .. dirs
            if(fd.cFileName[0]!='.')
```

```
            {
                // create the full path
                TCHAR szDir[MAX_PATH];
                ::strcpy(szDir, szRoot);
                szDir[::strlen(szDir)-1] = '\0';
                ::strcat(szDir, fd.cFileName);
                ::strcat(szDir, "\\*");

                // count the new dir first
                CountFiles(szDir, pnTotal);
            }
        }
        else
        {
            // bump the total count
            ++(*pnTotal);
        }

        // move to the next file
        if(!::FindNextFile(hFind, &fd))
        {
            hFind = INVALID_HANDLE_VALUE;
        }

        // tell the kernel to allow any callbacks to happen
        // (it's ok to preempt this thread)
        ::SleepEx(0, TRUE);
    }
}

void main()
{
    // count of files
    LONG nFileCt(0);

    // set up our UI timer and callback
    HANDLE hTimer = CreateUITimer();
    HANDLE hCB = SetupUICallback(hTimer, &nFileCt);

    // grab the windows directory
    TCHAR szWinDir[MAX_PATH];
    if(FAILED(::SHGetFolderPath(
        NULL,            // no parent window for GUI
        CSIDL_WINDOWS,   // id of the windows dir
```

```
    NULL,              // use the current user's access token
    SHGFP_TYPE_CURRENT, // fetch the current value
    szWinDir)))
{
    *szWinDir = '\0';
}


// do the counting and show the results
if(hCB!=INVALID_HANDLE_VALUE &&
    hTimer!=INVALID_HANDLE_VALUE &&
    *szWinDir!='\0')
{
    // add the wildcard for all files to the dir
    ::strcat(szWinDir, "\\*");
    std::cout << "thread: " << ::GetCurrentThreadId()
        << " counting all files in " << szWinDir
        << std::endl;
    CountFiles(szWinDir, &nFileCt);
    std::cout << "Total files found: " << nFileCt << std::endl;
}

// cleanup
CleanupCallback(hCB);
hCB = INVALID_HANDLE_VALUE;
::CloseHandle(hTimer);
hTimer = INVALID_HANDLE_VALUE;
}
```

The application in Listing 3-19 implements a depth-first-file counter with UI feedback. First, the application creates a timer to generate the feedback with the `CreateUITimer()` function, which creates and starts a *waitable timer* kernel object. Next, the application installs the feedback function with the `SetupUICallback()` helper, which calls the `RegisterWaitForSingleObject()` API to ask the system to call into the local `CBShowStatus()` function every time the waitable timer expires.

Chapter 4, "Commonly Used Kernel Objects," covers waitable timer kernel objects.

After the application in Listing 3-19 has installed the UI feedback mechanism, it begins the counting of files. The application uses the `SHGetFolderPath()` API to find the system folder. It then calls its `CountFiles()` function with that folder name.

Using this callback mechanism on a single-processor machine requires the call to the `SleepEx()` API within the loop. This tells the kernel that it can preempt the current thread and run a thread to execute any registered wait timeouts. As you can see in Figure 3-6, the system calls into the feedback function to display progress at regular intervals, and I did not need to alter the flow of the `CountFiles()` other than to include a yielding statement.

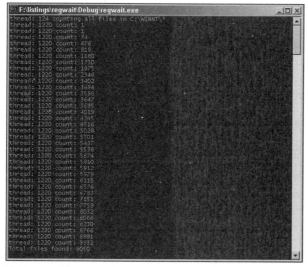

Figure 3-6: The results of counting files in Listing 3-19 with scheduled feedback

Multiple object waits

As soon as you begin mastering waiting for single objects, you're going to want to wait for more than one object at a time. Going back to the file system change wait example, Listing 3-17, you easily can add another directory of interest. As you can see in Listing 3-20, waiting for multiple objects is simply a matter of collecting up the handles to objects you're interested in signaling, then interpreting the return code. The example looks for changes in either the user's Internet cache directory or the *favorites* directory. You can trigger these changes by starting Internet Explorer and going to a new site or adding a site to its `Favorites` menu.

The code simply creates an array of handles, creates change objects for each directory and stores them in the array, then calls the waiting function. The `WaitForMultipleObjects()` API lets you accomplish the pause required in Listing 3-20. The parameters to the function are detailed in Table 3-3.

TABLE **3-3 PARAMETERS OF THE WAITFORMULTIPLEOBJECTS() API**

Parameter Name	Intention
DWORD nCount	The number of kernel object handles supplied in the lpHandles array
CONST HANDLE* lpHandles	An array of handles to kernel objects that the thread wishes to block on until one or more reach the signaled state
BOOL fWaitAll	Flag that determines whether the thread will wait until all passed kernel objects reach the signaled state (TRUE) or any of the objects reach the signaled state (FALSE)
DWORD dwMilliseconds	Maximum duration to pause the thread, in milliseconds, before abandoning the wait

I have taken the example from Listing 3-17 (that waits for changes in a single directory) and produced Listing 3-20 (that waits for changes in two directories). I designed the code shown in Listing 3-20 to allow expansion beyond the directory pair to any number of directories.

Listing 3-20: Using WaitForMultipleObjects() to collect one-of-many signals

```
// project waitmulti
#include <windows.h>
#include <shlobj.h>
#include <iostream>

void WaitForChange()
{
    // allocate and initialize the handles of objects
    //  to wait for
    const int c_nWaitCt = 2;
    HANDLE arHandleChange[c_nWaitCt];
    for(int nHandle=0;nHandle<c_nWaitCt;nHandle++)
    {
        arHandleChange[nHandle] = INVALID_HANDLE_VALUE;
    }

    // find the internet cache directory
    TCHAR szInetCache[MAX_PATH];
```

```
if(SUCCEEDED(::SHGetFolderPath(
    NULL,                      // no parent window for GUI
    CSIDL_INTERNET_CACHE,      // id of the cache dir
    NULL,            // use the current user's access token
    SHGFP_TYPE_CURRENT,        // fetch the current value
    szInetCache)))
{
    // look for changes to the cache dir and below
    arHandleChange[0] = ::FindFirstChangeNotification(
        szInetCache,           // the directory to watch
        TRUE,                  // watch the tree
        FILE_NOTIFY_CHANGE_FILE_NAME);  // any change
}

// find the user's favorites directory
TCHAR szFavorites[MAX_PATH];
if(SUCCEEDED(::SHGetFolderPath(
    NULL,                   // no parent window for GUI
    CSIDL_FAVORITES,        // id of the favorites dir
    NULL,    // use the current user's access token
    SHGFP_TYPE_CURRENT,  // fetch the current value
    szFavorites)))
{
    // look for changes to the favorites dir and below
    arHandleChange[1] = ::FindFirstChangeNotification(
        szFavorites,           // the directory to watch
        TRUE,                  // watch the tree
        FILE_NOTIFY_CHANGE_FILE_NAME);  // any change
}

// make sure all of the handles are ready
BOOL bReady = TRUE;
for(nHandle=0;nHandle<c_nWaitCt && bReady;nHandle++)
{
    bReady = arHandleChange[nHandle]!=
        INVALID_HANDLE_VALUE;
}
if(bReady)
{
    // loop until we don't timeout
    DWORD dwResult = WAIT_TIMEOUT;
    while(dwResult==WAIT_TIMEOUT)
    {
        // suspend until someone makes a change to
```

```
// the one of the directories
dwResult = ::WaitForMultipleObjects(
    c_nWaitCt,       // number of handles we have
    arHandleChange,  // the handle array
    FALSE,           // do not wait for them all to
                     // be signaled, any will do
    1000);           // wait in 1 sec (1000ms) chunks

// check for a timeout
if(dwResult==WAIT_TIMEOUT)
{
    // reset the wait handles
    for(nHandle=0;nHandle<c_nWaitCt;nHandle++)
    {
        ::FindNextChangeNotification(
            arHandleChange[nHandle]);
    }

    // show some activity
    std::cout << ".";
    std::cout.flush();
}
// found a change
else if(WAIT_OBJECT_0<=dwResult &&
    dwResult<=(WAIT_OBJECT_0+c_nWaitCt-1))
{
    std::cout << "saw a change to the filesystem"
        << std::endl;
}
// something bad has happened
else if(dwResult==WAIT_FAILED)
{
    std::cout << "Failed, error: " <<
        ::GetLastError() << std::endl;
}
        }
}

// clean up the change handles
for(nHandle=0;nHandle<c_nWaitCt;nHandle++)
{
    ::FindCloseChangeNotification(
        arHandleChange[nHandle]);
    arHandleChange[nHandle] = INVALID_HANDLE_VALUE;
```

```
    }
}

void main()
{
    WaitForChange();
}
```

The example in Listing 3-20 uses the workhorse function, `WaitForChange()`, to display all changes in the Internet temporary files and favorites directories. The function first creates an array of kernel object handles and file finds notification objects to fill it. The function then simply waits until one of the change notification objects moves to the signaled state. Once notified that an object is in the signaled state, the function resets all of the change notification objects and interprets the return code from the waiting function, displaying the status to the user.

RETURN CODES AND QUEUING

Notice that the return code from `WaitForMultipleObjects()` in Listing 3-20 can be a value in the range `WAIT_OBJECT_0` to (`WAIT_OBJECT_0` + `<count>` - 1). This allows you to tell which object transitioned to the signaled state if waiting for any of the passed objects to do so. When the wait is in the logical `OR` mode, the return value from the function corresponds to the location of the newly signaled object in the handle array you passed the API.

I haven't added handling for the `WAIT_ABANDONED_0` return codes to any of the examples, but they deserve a little explanation. This error code applies only to mutex objects; it tells you that the last thread to own the mutex has terminated without releasing the object. Since the object can never reach the signaled state — the thread is now dead — the kernel tells you to stop waiting for it.

Chapter 4, "Commonly Used Kernel Objects," covers mutex objects.

One of the properties of the waiting mechanism that the kernel guarantees you is the true signal queuing. The first object to signal is the one indicated to you by the system. Further, if another one or more signal while you service the first, the kernel protects their order. The kernel does not allow you to select the prioritization of the queue, nor does it give you intrinsic support for the time that it transitioned to the signaled state. You have to build structures on top of the queue for yourself.

ADVANCED MULTIPLE OBJECT WAITS

When creating threads that have a mixture of signals to wait for and user input or Windows messages to wait for, you must use the `MsgWaitForMultipleObjects()` function (implemented by `User32.DLL`, not `Kernel32.DLL`). This API enables you to pass a handle array, just like `WaitForMultipleObjects()`, then specify on which types of Windows messages you wish to resume using a bitmask.

Waiting and APCs

An asynchronous procedure call (APC) is a function call that your application asks the kernel to have you execute at the appropriate time. This execution is performed by one of your threads in an alertable state. Threads enter the alertable state by setting a flag in the `WaitForSingleObjectEx()`, `SleepEx()`, `WaitForMultiple ObjectsEx()`, `MsgWaitForMultipleObjects()`, or `SignalObjectAndWait()` API calls. Also, thread startup and shutdown executes APCs. Overlapped I/O and wait-able timers use the APC mechanism, but the mechanism is very complicated and of little actual use. I doubt that you will find yourself in a situation that requires the use of APCs; if you do, you should refer to the MSDN.

Summary

Now you should feel comfortable with the nature of kernel objects. You've seen how they expose functionality using opaque handles and how you should use those handles. You've also seen the various types of available kernel objects and some examples of what they can do. Although the security on kernel objects can be quite complicated to set up, you've seen some simple examples of how to get the basics accomplished. Finally, you learned how to use the signaled state of the kernel objects to gently pause execution while you wait for events to happen that are external to your thread. I elaborate on these concepts in the next chapter when I go over the most common kernel objects and how they're used.

Chapter 4

Commonly Used Kernel Objects

IN THIS CHAPTER

- ◆ Objects supplied by the Windows 2000 kernel
- ◆ Core application services
- ◆ Thread synchronization
- ◆ Inter-thread communication

YOU NOW HAVE THE skills needed to create and manipulate any object provided by the Windows 2000 kernel. This chapter covers some of the more common objects supplied by the kernel.

Objects Supplied by the Windows 2000 Kernel

The common objects supplied by the Windows 2000 kernel fall broadly into three categories: core application services, thread synchronization, and inter-thread communication. The categories are described as follows:

1. **Application services:** These give you the tools you need to create great executables that coexist nicely with the system and other processes. Objects in this category include timers, heaps, change notifications, console I/O, file finds, threads, processes, and jobs.

2. **Thread synchronization:** These objects enable you to orchestrate how threads and processes work together to share information and perform actions. Objects in this category include interlocked data, critical sections, events, mutexes, and semaphores.

3. **Inter-thread communication.** These objects allow threads within the same process or across processes to send information to one another. Kernel objects in this category include files, file mappings, mailslots, and named pipes.

This chapter is divided into the three above object types. A section is devoted to each object category.

Core Application Services

The objects I cover in this section provide basic tools to Windows 2000 applications. The application services kernel objects give you some basic facilities that you will find yourself using repeatedly. You will be thankful that you don't have to invent them. You will use these tools to create great executables that coexist nicely with the system and other processes.

This section takes a look at the objects you're most likely to need to write code you use. Your C++ runtime library usually handles the heap and console I/O for you. I already covered threads and processes. Timers (full and lightweight), file finds, change notifications, and jobs are covered here.

Chapter 2, "Basic Operating System Programming," covers threads and processes; Chapter 12, "Memory Management," covers application heaps; and Chapter 15, "System Services," covers consoles.

Timers

Probably the simplest example of a service that you can use in most of your applications is a timer. All operating systems should provide some sort of timer mechanism for applications so that they can execute periodic tasks on behalf of the user. A timer is simply a notification to an execution thread that it should do something. In the world of kernel objects, this notification is reaching the signaled state. Here are some basic properties that the operating system should give to a timer object:

◆ Timers should be simple to create, set up, and use.

◆ A timer should consume no system resources (especially CPU cycles) while a thread is waiting for it to expire.

◆ An application or thread should be able to create and use as many timers as it wants.

◆ A timer should be set to expire at a certain absolute time or a time relative to the current time (e.g., midnight, or five minutes from now).

◆ An application should be able to create a periodic timer.

◆ A timer should be a first-class kernel object – it should be usable across processes and securable.

WAITABLE TIMER

The Windows 2000 *waitable timer* meets all these specifications. To use a waitable timer, you must first create a waitable timer object with the `CreateWaitableTimer()` API. This function requires security attributes, a system-wide unique name, and a flag for manual-reset or auto-reset behavior. Both a manual-reset and an auto-reset waitable timer will transition to the signaled state at expiration time. An auto-reset timer will immediately transition out of the signaled state once any waiting threads have released while a manual -reset timer requires an API call from your application.

Waitable timer objects are first-class, namable, securable kernel objects. Another process can open up your named timer if it has proper access and the name with the `OpenWaitableTimer()` API. With a handle to your timer object, the client process can synchronize its task execution with yours.

 Chapter 3, "Using Kernel Objects," covers kernel object naming and security.

You must activate the newly created waitable timer with the `SetWaitiableTimer()` API to set its initial expiry time and frequency. You then execute tasks on the signaled state, either synchronously with a waiting function or asynchronously with a callback method. To stop a timer from expiring, use the `CancelWaitableTimer()` API, and to destroy the object, call the `CloseHandle()` API.

Typically, an application uses a timer in the synchronous mode by placing a worker thread in suspension until the timer expires – at which time it carries out the required task then terminates or suspends again. The following example, Listing 4-1, shows a simple console application that uses a class, `CCmdlineFeedback`, to create a worker thread that causes feedback to be given to the user periodically. The feedback is simply in the form of dots ('.'s) sent to the standard output stream (through the C++ standard library's `std::cout` object). Just before entering a lengthy operation, the main thread constructs an instance of the feedback class telling it how often to generate feedback. The class constructor saves this period and creates a new worker thread, passing it the `this` pointer to the newly created object. The thread then starts up and creates a timer object, setting it to auto-reset in order to take advantage of periodicity. Once the timer object is ready, it is set to go off at the period asked for by the instance creator and then enters a tight loop waiting for expiration or the stop flag to be set.

In Listing 4-1, when feedback is requested, the class calls the object's virtual `ShowFeedback()` method, which allows derived classes to alter the feedback behavior. This example uses the `Sleep()` API to simulate a long operation in the main thread. The helper thread gives the user confidence that the process is still working by emitting a dot every half-second. You also can extend this class to use a kernel event object to end the feedback stream (using the multiple-objects wait) in place of the m_bContinue member flag. This would allow the thread to terminate properly since it otherwise would likely be in the wait state when the object is destructed and its handle is closed.

Listing 4-1: Creating a feedback dot stream with a waitable timer

```
// project dottimer
#define _WIN32_WINNT 0x0500
#define WINVER 0x0500
#include <windows.h>
#include <iostream>

// class to generate feedback for the user in a command-line
//  application during long processing
class CCmdlineFeedback
{
public:
    // constructor, simply initializes members and starts
    //  the feedback thread
    CCmdlineFeedback(int nPeriodMs) :
        m_hThread(INVALID_HANDLE_VALUE),
        m_nPeriodMs(nPeriodMs),
        m_bContinue(true)
    {
        m_hThread = ::CreateThread(
            NULL,       // default security
            0,          // default stack
            ThreadProc, // class feedback routine
            reinterpret_cast<LPVOID>(this),
                        // value to pass thread proc - current
                        //  'this' ptr
            0,          // no special creation flags
            NULL);      // ignore the returned thread id
    }

    // destructor simply stops feedback timer and cleans up
    virtual ~CCmdlineFeedback()
    {
        Stop();
        ::CloseHandle(m_hThread);
    }

    // simple stop routine sets an internal stop flag
    void Stop(){ m_bContinue = false;}
```

```
protected:
    // the feedback routine, this should be overridden in
    //  derived classes to be more flashy
    virtual void ShowFeedback()
    {
        std::cout << ".";
        std::cout.flush();
    }

    // the class's thread routine, it becomes the object's
    //  thread routine with the passing of the 'this' ptr
    static DWORD WINAPI ThreadProc(LPVOID lPParam)
    {
        // convert the passed param to the this ptr
        CCmdlineFeedback* pThis =
            reinterpret_cast<CCmdlineFeedback*>(lPParam);

        // create the timer object
        HANDLE  hTimer = ::CreateWaitableTimer(
            NULL,   // no security needed, not shared
            FALSE,  // it's an auto-reset timer
            "w2kdg.DotTimer.timer");   // unique name
        if(hTimer!=NULL)
        {
            // first expiration will be immediate
            LARGE_INTEGER liDueTime = {0,0};

            // tell the timer to expire with proper period
            if(::SetWaitableTimer(
                hTimer,     // the timer object
                &liDueTime, // due time
                pThis->m_nPeriodMs, // period
                NULL,       // no completion callback
                NULL,       // and no arg to callback
                FALSE))     // no resume from low-power
            {
                // provide feedback until told to stop
                while(pThis->m_bContinue)
                {
                    // wait for the timer to expire, and
                    //  call the class's feedback method
                    if(::WaitForSingleObject(hTimer,
                        INFINITE)==WAIT_OBJECT_0)
                    {
```

```
                        pThis->ShowFeedback();
                }
            }

            // end the timer
            ::CancelWaitableTimer(hTimer);
            hTimer = INVALID_HANDLE_VALUE;
        }

        // clean up
        ::CloseHandle(hTimer);
        hTimer = INVALID_HANDLE_VALUE;
    }
    // this class will not look at the return value from
    //  this thread (with GetExitCodeThread) so just
    //  send 0 back
    return(0);
    }
protected:
    HANDLE  m_hThread;      // handle to the feedback thread
    int     m_nPeriodMs;    // interval between feedback
    bool    m_bContinue;    // continue giving feedback
};

void main()
{
    std::cout << "Begin";

    // long, complicated work simulated with the sleep API
    //  which suspends the main thread
    {
        // create feedback object that tells the user every
        //  1/2 second that we're still alive
        CCmdlineFeedback fb(500);

        ::Sleep(10000);

        // class destructor will stop feedback and clean up
        //  implementation kernel objects
    }

    std::cout << "End" << std::endl;
}
```

The appendix, "Using the Examples in This Book," explains where to find and how to build the listings throughout the book.

In Listing 4-1, you can see that the creation of the timer object is separate from its configuration and startup. The `SetWaitableTimer()` API must be called to set the timer in motion. The timer can be canceled by any thread that has opened the timer with sufficient access using the `CancelWaitableTimer()` API.

It's likely that you'll find the hardest part of setting up timers to be the specification of the due time. You input the time as a `FILETIME` structure that uses 64 bits to specify the time in 100 nanosecond increments since the first day of the year 1601 (it has a range of over 29 millennia). You often will use helper APIs, such as `SystemTimeToFileTime()`, to calculate the absolute expiry times. However, most timer applications that you will come across do not require absolute times and can use the relative form of the due time, which is simply the number of 100 nanosecond intervals to wait for first expiration negated (0 causes immediate signaling). That is, to wait one microsecond, you would send -10 for the expiration time.

Listing 4-1 shows a timer object used solely in the owning process. In that example, I do not supply a name for the object, nor do I allow child processes to inherit it. This timer could be reconfigured for use across processes.

You can extend the timer object for use across processes by communicating the timer name from the creating (server) process and opening it up in a client process. This provides your application with a simple method to execute tasks on a schedule and to share that schedule with other applications.

Using a waitable timer asynchronously requires a completion routine. This routine is simply a callback that you want your worker thread to call into each time the timer expires. Listing 4-2 shows the feedback timer of Listing 4-1 re-implemented using a completion routine and an event object for ending the callback. (I cover thread-synchronization objects in detail later in this chapter.) This requires the use of the `WaitXxxEx()` method in order to tell the kernel to use its *APC (asynchronous procedure call)* mechanism to call into the function. This is a primitive example of the use of APCs.

Chapter 3, "Using Kernel Objects," discusses APCs.

Listing 4-2: Creating a feedback dot stream with a waitable timer callback

```cpp
// project dotcbtimer
#define _WIN32_WINNT 0x0500
#define WINVER 0x0500
#include <windows.h>
#include <iostream>

// class to generate feedback for the user in a command-line
//  application during long processing
class CCmdlineFeedback
{
public:
    // constructor, simply initializes members and starts
    //  the feedback thread
    CCmdlineFeedback(int nPeriodMs) :
        m_hThread(INVALID_HANDLE_VALUE),
        m_hEventEnd(INVALID_HANDLE_VALUE),
        m_nPeriodMs(nPeriodMs)
    {
        // create and init the end processing event
        m_hEventEnd = ::CreateEvent(
            NULL,   // default security
            TRUE,   // manual-reset
            FALSE,  // initially not signaled
            NULL);  // no name

        // create the timer thread
        m_hThread = ::CreateThread(
            NULL,       // default security
            0,          // default stack
            ThreadProc, // class feedback routine
            reinterpret_cast<LPVOID>(this),
                        // value to pass thread proc -
                        //  current 'this' ptr
            0,          // no special creation flags
            NULL);      // ignore the returned thread id
    }

    // object destructor simply stops the feedback and
    //  cleans up the objects
    virtual ~CCmdlineFeedback()
    {
        Stop();
        ::CloseHandle(m_hEventEnd);
```

```
        ::CloseHandle(m_hThread);
    }

    // simple stop routine signals our end object
    void Stop(){ ::SetEvent(m_hEventEnd); }

protected:
    // the feedback routine, this should be overridden in
    //   derived classes to be more flashy
    virtual void ShowFeedback(const FILETIME& ftExpire)
    {
        std::cout << ".";
        std::cout.flush();
    }

    // the callback method for the timer object, this simply
    //   redirects to the object's virtual feedback method
    static VOID CALLBACK TimerAPCProc(LPVOID lpParam,
        DWORD dwLow, DWORD dwHigh)
    {
        // interpret the params
        CCmdlineFeedback* pThis =
            reinterpret_cast<CCmdlineFeedback*>(lpParam);

        FILETIME ft;
        ft.dwLowDateTime = dwLow;
        ft.dwHighDateTime = dwHigh;

        // call the feedback method with the expiration time
        pThis->ShowFeedback(ft);
    }

    // the class's thread routine, it becomes the object's
    //   thread routine with the passing of the this ptr
    static DWORD WINAPI ThreadProc(LPVOID lpParam)
    {
        // grab the ptr to the instance that called
        CCmdlineFeedback* pThis =
            reinterpret_cast<CCmdlineFeedback*>(lpParam);

        // create the timer object
        HANDLE  hTimer = ::CreateWaitableTimer(
            NULL,   // no security needed, not shared
            FALSE,  // auto-reset timer
```

```
            NULL);  // no name needed (anonymous)
        if(hTimer!=NULL)
        {
            // first expiration will be immediate
            LARGE_INTEGER liDueTime = {0,0};

            // tell the timer to expire with proper period
            if(::SetWaitableTimer(
                hTimer,              // the timer
                &liDueTime,          // due time
                pThis->m_nPeriodMs,  // period
                TimerAPCProc,        // the completion callback
                lpParam,             // arg to callback, 'this'
                FALSE))              // no need to power-up
            {
                // wait until we're told to end (OBJECT_0
                //  is returned)
                DWORD dwResult = WAIT_IO_COMPLETION;
                while(dwResult==WAIT_IO_COMPLETION)
                {
                    // the API will return IO_COMPLETION
                    //   each time the period expires
                    //   unless the end event gets
                    //   signaled
                    dwResult = ::WaitForSingleObjectEx(
                        pThis->m_hEventEnd,// end signal
                        INFINITE,       // wait forever
                        TRUE);          // allow timer to fire
                }

                // end the timer
                ::CancelWaitableTimer(hTimer);
                hTimer = INVALID_HANDLE_VALUE;
            }

            // clean up the timer object
            ::CloseHandle(hTimer);
            hTimer = INVALID_HANDLE_VALUE;
        }
        // the owner will never be looking at the return code
        //  from this thread, just send 0
        return(0);
    }
protected:
```

```
    HANDLE  m_hThread;      // handle to the feedback thread
    HANDLE  m_hEventEnd;    // handle to the end event
    int     m_nPeriodMs;    // interval between feedback
};


// derived feedback class to supply slightly flashier feedback
class CSpinFeedback : public CCmdlineFeedback
{
public:
    // constructor simply sends the period to the base class
    CSpinFeedback(int nPeriodMs) :
      CCmdlineFeedback(nPeriodMs) {}
protected:
    // the flashier feedback method
    virtual void ShowFeedback(const FILETIME& ftExpire)
    {
        // simple rotating line
        static const TCHAR c_arSpinner[] = {'|','/','-','\\'};
        static int s_nPos = 0;

        // move to the next position of the spinner, checking
        //  for return to the beginning
        if(++s_nPos==
            (sizeof(c_arSpinner)/sizeof(c_arSpinner[0])))
        {
            s_nPos = 0;
        }

        // send the character out and flush it
        std::cout << c_arSpinner[s_nPos] << '\r';
        std::cout.flush();
    }
};


void main()
{
    std::cout << "Begin" << std::endl;

    // long, complicated work simulated with the sleep API
    //  which suspends the main thread
    {
        // create feedback object that tells the user every
        //  1/2 second that we're still alive
        CSpinFeedback fb(50);
```

```
    ::Sleep(10000);

    // class destructor will stop feedback and clean up
    //  implementation kernel objects
  }

  std::cout << "End" << std::endl;
}
```

Listing 4-2 creates a class that is identical in use to that of Listing 4-1, but implements the wait using APC. This change produces only small differences in behavior. Chiefly, the worker thread waits using the WaitForSingleObjectEx() API for the class destructor or Stop() method to signal the end event, and when the main thread does so, the worker thread terminates almost immediately. In addition, the callback method gets the time at which the timer object called it so that the method can log it or use it in some other way.

I also demonstrate in Listing 4-2 how to take advantage of the virtual method that I used in the creation of the base class to do the actual feedback. The new class, CSpinFeedback, simply supplies a constructor and a version of the Show Feedback() method that walks through straight-line characters to create the illusion of spinning.

TIMER QUEUE TIMER

Another type of timer object in Windows 2000 kernel is the *timer queue timer*. It simply is a lighter weight version of the full waitable timer object. You cannot name, secure, set an absolute expiration time, or synchronously wait for a timer queue timer object but it has the rest of the desirable timer characteristics that I presented earlier.

Since there are fewer features in the timer queue timer, it's much easier to use. There is no need for a separate thread with a wait or wait-ex function. You simply supply the callback, create a queue for timers, create at least one timer in the queue, and let it run.

To create a timer queue, use the CreateTimerQueue() API which takes no parameters and returns the handle to the object. To begin a timer, you must create a timer within the queue with the CreateTimerQueueTimer() API. This function lets you configure a callback function, the frequency, and first expiration time of a new timer; it returns a handle to the new timer object.

While the timer queue timer is active, it will execute the supplied callback at the supplied frequency until stopped with the DeleteTimerQueueTimer() API. To clean up the timer queue object, use the DeleteTimerQueueEx() API which stops all running timers and releases all resources; no CloseHandle() API call is required.

Listing 4-3 shows the simplified version of our feedback class using timer queue timers. This class has the same interface as the previous two examples – only the implementation has changed.

Listing 4-3: Creating a feedback dot stream with a timer queue timer

```
// project timerq
#define _WIN32_WINNT 0x0500
#define WINVER 0x0500
#include <windows.h>
#include <iostream>

// class to generate feedback for the user in a command-line
//   application during long processing
class CCmdlineFeedback
{
public:
    // constructor, simply initializes members and starts
    //   the feedback thread
    CCmdlineFeedback(int nPeriodMs) :
        m_hTimerQueue(INVALID_HANDLE_VALUE),
        m_hTimer(INVALID_HANDLE_VALUE)
    {
        StartTimer(nPeriodMs);
    }

    // object destructor simply stops the feedback
    virtual ~CCmdlineFeedback() { Stop(); }

    // simple stop routine signals our object
    void Stop(){ StopTimer(); }

protected:
    // the feedback routine, this should be overridden in
    //   derived classes to be more flashy
    virtual void ShowFeedback()
    {
        std::cout << ".";
        std::cout.flush();
    }

    // the callback method for the timer object, this simply
    //   redirects to the object's virtual feedback method
    static VOID NTAPI TimerProc(PVOID lpParam,
        BOOLEAN /*bTimerFired*/)
```

```
{
    // interpret the params
    CCmdlineFeedback* pThis =
        reinterpret_cast<CCmdlineFeedback*>(lpParam);
    pThis->ShowFeedback();
}

// begin the feedback timer
virtual void StartTimer(int nPeriodMs)
{
    // first, stop any current timer
    StopTimer();

    // create the timer queue
    m_hTimerQueue = ::CreateTimerQueue();
    if(m_hTimerQueue!=NULL)
    {
        // create a timer in the queue
        ::CreateTimerQueueTimer(
            &m_hTimer,        // the timer
            m_hTimerQueue,    // the queue
            TimerProc,        // the callback
            reinterpret_cast<LPVOID>(this),// cb arg
            0,                // due time immediate
            nPeriodMs,        // period
            WT_EXECUTEINTIMERTHREAD);
                // flag to indicate short callback
                //   execution should use the timer thread
    }
    else
    {
        m_hTimerQueue = INVALID_HANDLE_VALUE;
    }
}

// shut down timer operation
virtual void StopTimer()
{
    // remove the active timer from the queue
    if(m_hTimer!=INVALID_HANDLE_VALUE)
    {
        ::DeleteTimerQueueTimer(
            m_hTimerQueue,    // queue in which it lived
            m_hTimer,         // the victim timer
            NULL);            // no event to signal complete
```

```
            m_hTimer = INVALID_HANDLE_VALUE;
        }
        // clean up the timer queue
        if(m_hTimerQueue!=INVALID_HANDLE_VALUE)
        {
            ::DeleteTimerQueueEx(
                m_hTimerQueue,  // the victim queue
                NULL);          // no event to signal complete
            m_hTimerQueue = INVALID_HANDLE_VALUE;
        }
    }
protected:
    HANDLE   m_hTimerQueue; // queue in which timer lives
    HANDLE   m_hTimer;      // currently active timer
};


void main()
{
    std::cout << "Begin";

    // long, complicated work simulated with the sleep API
    //   which suspends the main thread
    {
        // create feedback object that tells the user every
        //   1/2 second that we're still alive
        CCmdlineFeedback fb(500);

        ::Sleep(10000);

        // class destructor will stop feedback and clean up
        //   implementation kernel objects
    }

    std::cout << "End" << std::endl;
}
```

In Listing 4-3, you can see that a timer queue object is required for the timer. This queue simply holds all of the timers that you will use in your application; it's created with the CreateTimerQueue() API. In order to actually start a timer up, you must call the CreateTimerQueueTimer() API, supplying the timer queue kernel object you just created. Stopping the timer does not require either the flag technique from Listing 4-1 or the event technique from Listing 4-2. You simply need to remove the timer from the timer queue with the DeleteTimerQueueTimer() API in the class' StopTimer() method.

The code in Listing 4-3 does the identical job that the example from Listing 4-1 does — in fewer lines. The lightweight timers are preferable for application-only, repeating timers because they are so simple to use.

File finds

Enumerating files in a folder is another common task for Windows 2000 applications. The kernel provides the *file find* object to accomplish file searching. This enables you to do wildcard searching for files within a folder. The file find object maintains your place in the list of files and gives you a detailed report on each matching file with the `WIN32_FIND_DATA` structure.

Listing 4-4 shows an example of finding .GIFs in your Internet cache directory. In this example, you can see the procedure for creating a file find object with the `FindFirstFile()` API, iterating through the remaining matches with the `FindNextFile()` API, and cleaning up with the `FindCloseFile()` API.

The API for releasing a reference to a file find object is not the `CloseHandle()` function that most other kernel objects use. You must take care to use the correct reference release API, `FindCloseFile()`, in this case, for each object type.

Listing 4-4: Locating all .GIFs within the Internet cache folder

```
// project findgif
#define _WIN32_WINNT 0x0500
#define WINVER 0x0500
#include <windows.h>
#include <iostream>
#include <shlobj.h>

void RecurseFind(LPCTSTR szRoot, LPCTSTR szWildcard)
{
    //
    // first let's look in the passed directory
    //
    TCHAR szSearch[MAX_PATH];
    ::strcpy(szSearch, szRoot);
    ::strcat(szSearch, "\\");
    ::strcat(szSearch, szWildcard);
```

```
// start looping through all of the files in the dir
WIN32_FIND_DATA fd;
HANDLE hFind = ::FindFirstFile(szSearch, &fd);
while(hFind!=INVALID_HANDLE_VALUE)
{
    std::cout << szRoot << "\\" << fd.cFileName
        << std::endl;

    // move to the next file
    if(!::FindNextFile(hFind, &fd))
    {
        ::FindClose(hFind);
        hFind = INVALID_HANDLE_VALUE;
    }
}


//
// now, look for all subdirs and do the same to them
//
// add the full wildcard to search for all directories
::strcpy(szSearch, szRoot);
::strcat(szSearch, "\\*");

// start looping through all of the files in the dir
hFind = ::FindFirstFile(szSearch, &fd);
while(hFind!=INVALID_HANDLE_VALUE)
{
    // for directories, count all files there
    if((fd.dwFileAttributes &
        FILE_ATTRIBUTE_DIRECTORY)!=0)
    {
        // ignore the . and .. dirs
        if(fd.cFileName[0]!='.')
        {
            // create the full path
            TCHAR szDir[MAX_PATH];
            ::strcpy(szDir, szRoot);
            ::strcat(szDir, "\\");
            ::strcat(szDir, fd.cFileName);

            // count the new dir first
            RecurseFind(szDir, szWildcard);
        }
    }
```

```
        // move to the next file
        if(!::FindNextFile(hFind, &fd))
        {
            ::FindClose(hFind);
            hFind = INVALID_HANDLE_VALUE;
        }
    }
}

void main()
{
    // grab the Internet cache directory
    TCHAR szCacheDir[MAX_PATH];
    if(SUCCEEDED(::SHGetFolderPath(
        NULL,                     // no parent window for GUI
        CSIDL_INTERNET_CACHE,     // ID of the cache dir
        NULL,                     // current user's access token
        SHGFP_TYPE_CURRENT,       // fetch the current value
        szCacheDir)))             // destination
    {
        // find everything ending in gif
        RecurseFind(szCacheDir,"*gif");
    }
}
```

Listing 4-4 creates a general purpose RecurseFind() function that takes in a
root directory name, finds all of the files in that folder matching the passed wildcard, then grabs all of the subdirectories in the folder and passes them back to the
same function. Since the program is searching for all files matching the wildcard
and all directories, the loops run until FindNextFile() returns FALSE, at which
time it will call FindCloseFile() to complete our use of the file find object.

While the RecurseFind() function in Listing 4-4 is descending the subdirectories of the directory it is passed, it maintains an open file find object. Once the subdirectory is examined, the function uses this open object to move on to the next
subdirectory. This illustrates that the file find object is simply a pointer to a search
results set for that directory. It shows some of the output from the program after
visiting http://msdn.microsoft.com/.

The kernel exposes other "find" facilities for locating other objects in the system.
Table 4-1 contains a short summary of these facilities and the name of an API that
you can look up in the MSDN for more information. Other system components,
such as the WinSpool.DLL and WinInet.DLL libraries, expose find methods for the
objects they provide.

Figure 4-1: Contents of the Internet cache directory (.GIFs only)

TABLE 4-1 KERNEL OBJECT FIND FACILITIES

Kernel Object Name	Top-Level Find API
File	`FindFirstFile()`
Change notification	`FindFirstChangeNotification()`
Volume	`FindFirstVolume()`
Volume mount point	`FindFirstVolumeMountPoint()`
Access control entry (ACE)	`FindFirstFreeAce()`

Chapter 13, "The File System," covers file system volumes and mount points.

Change notifications

It's common to write applications that need to monitor some portion of the file system for changes. For example, almost any application that stores data for the user as files will want to respond to a change in the contents of any of the currently open files (perhaps another application edited a configuration file for your program). You can do this gracefully using the kernel's `FindFirstChangeNotification()` and `FindNextChange Notification()` APIs. These functions manage a *change notification* kernel object that simply transitions to the signaled state once a change that it is configured to watch for occurs.

Typically, you create a worker thread that owns a change notification kernel object that watches all of the folders that contain files your application thinks are interesting. When a change happens to a file in one of the folders, the change notification object for that folder goes to the signaled state and the worker thread communicates that information back to the main thread.

Listing 3-17 in Chapter 3, "Using Kernel Objects," shows a simplified example where the only thread in the application watches for all changes to a folder. In this listing, the change notification object must be reset manually to the non-signaled state after each use using the `FindNextChangeNotification()` function.

The function used to close the change notification object handle is not the typical `CloseHandle()` API used for most other kernel objects; it is the `FindCloseChangeNotification()` API.

Listing 4-5 combines the change notification and the file find objects to create a directory change logger for the `.GIF`s in Listing 4-4. The example simply creates a change notification object on the cache directory and waits for signaling. Whenever the system signals the change object, execution enters the method to recurse the folder and find any files that are newer than the latest from before the wait began. When you start up this program and your browser, you should see many new `.GIF`s logged to the console window as you surf the Web.

Listing 4-5: Creating a directory change logger for Internet cache .GIFs

```
// project loggifs
#define _WIN32_WINNT 0x0500
#define WINVER 0x0500
#include <windows.h>
#include <iostream>
#include <shlobj.h>

// helper data for an initial file time
static const FILETIME g_ftNull = { 0, 0 };

// worker method to find all files matching the passed wildcard
```

```
//  in the passed root folder and below that have been created
//  after the passed time stamp
FILETIME RecurseFindLater(LPCTSTR szRoot, LPCTSTR szWildcard,
    const FILETIME& ftLatest = g_ftNull)
{
    // initialize the latest time stamp
    FILETIME ftNewLatest(ftLatest);

    //
    // first let's look in the passed directory
    //
    TCHAR szSearch[MAX_PATH];
    ::strcpy(szSearch, szRoot);
    ::strcat(szSearch, "\\");
    ::strcat(szSearch, szWildcard);

    // start looping through all of the files in the dir
    WIN32_FIND_DATA fd;
    HANDLE hFind = ::FindFirstFile(szSearch, &fd);
    while(hFind!=INVALID_HANDLE_VALUE)
    {
        // look at the creation time
        FILETIME ftNew = fd.ftCreationTime;
        if(::CompareFileTime(&ftNew, &ftLatest)>0)
        {
            std::cout << szRoot << "\\" << fd.cFileName
                << std::endl;

            // see if we've found a new latest time
            if(::CompareFileTime(&ftNew, &ftNewLatest)>0)
            {
                ftNewLatest = ftNew;
            }
        }

        // move to the next file or close up
        if(!::FindNextFile(hFind, &fd))
        {
            ::FindClose(hFind);
            hFind = INVALID_HANDLE_VALUE;
        }
    }

    //
```

```
    // now, look for all subdirs and do the same to them
    //
    // add the full wildcard to search for all directories
    ::strcpy(szSearch, szRoot);
    ::strcat(szSearch, "\\*");

    // start looping through all of the files in the dir
    hFind = ::FindFirstFile(szSearch, &fd);
    while(hFind!=INVALID_HANDLE_VALUE)
    {
        // for directories, count all files there
        if((fd.dwFileAttributes &
            FILE_ATTRIBUTE_DIRECTORY)!=0)
        {
            // ignore the . and .. dirs
            if(fd.cFileName[0]!='.')
            {
                // create the full path
                TCHAR szDir[MAX_PATH];
                ::strcpy(szDir, szRoot);
                ::strcat(szDir, "\\");
                ::strcat(szDir, fd.cFileName);

                // look at the new dir
                FILETIME ftSubLatest = RecurseFindLater(
                    szDir, szWildcard, ftLatest);

                // watch for a new latest time
                if(::CompareFileTime(&ftSubLatest,
                    &ftNewLatest)>0)
                {
                    ftNewLatest = ftSubLatest;
                }
            }
        }

        // move to the next file or close up
        if(!::FindNextFile(hFind, &fd))
        {
            ::FindClose(hFind);
            hFind = INVALID_HANDLE_VALUE;
        }
    }
    return(ftNewLatest);
```

```
}

void main()
{
    // grab the Internet cache directory
    TCHAR szCacheDir[MAX_PATH];
    if(FAILED(::SHGetFolderPath(
        NULL,                    // no parent window for GUI
        CSIDL_INTERNET_CACHE,    // ID of the cache dir
        NULL,                    // current user's access token
        SHGFP_TYPE_CURRENT,      // fetch the current value
        szCacheDir)))            // destination
    {
        *szCacheDir = '\0';
    }

    // create a change notification object
    HANDLE hChange = ::FindFirstChangeNotification(
        szCacheDir, // watch the cache dir
        TRUE,       // include all sub folders
        FILE_NOTIFY_CHANGE_LAST_WRITE|  // grab writes
        FILE_NOTIFY_CHANGE_FILE_NAME);  // grab creations

    if(*szCacheDir!='\0' && hChange!=INVALID_HANDLE_VALUE)
    {
        // get the starting set and the latest create time
        FILETIME ftLatest = ::RecurseFindLater(szCacheDir,
            "*gif");
        while(true)
        {
            // every time there's a change, find anything
            //  later than the late watermark
            if(::WaitForSingleObject(hChange, INFINITE)==
                WAIT_OBJECT_0)
            {
                ftLatest = ::RecurseFindLater(szCacheDir,
                    "*gif", ftLatest);
            }

            // reset the change notification object
            ::FindNextChangeNotification(hChange);
        }
    }
}
```

```
// cleanup
::FindCloseChangeNotification(hChange);
hChange = INVALID_HANDLE_VALUE;
}
```

The code in Listing 4-5 became a little more complicated when I added the ability to log changes to the directory. In order to accomplish this, the program needed to save the latest time the user created a file in the directory tree. This last save time gets passed into our RecurseFindLater() method whenever a change occurs in the directory tree. The lookup method displays all files found with a later time stamp than the one passed in, sends the name to std::cout, and returns the new latest time. The while loop in the main() function watches for changes but never exits, so you'll have to break execution of this program manually (press Ctrl-C).

Jobs

The Windows 2000 operating system lets you control the behavior of related groups of process with the *job* kernel object. This object enables you to create a group of one or more processes that collectively (hopefully) perform a single job. You will want to do this in order to assign uniform security, resource limits, priority, and so on to a set of processes that perform a task for you.

Jobs are very much like superprocess objects — you treat them almost identically. The key benefits are the resource limit setting and the ability to name, secure, share, and terminate multiple processes as a single group. As you might expect, the CreateJob Object() API kicks off the procedure of using a job. You then assign processes that you create suspended to the job with the AssignProcessToJobObject() API. Next, you set any limits you want (CPU usage, memory, end time, and so on) on the job with the SetInformationJobObject() API.

To begin the job, you must call the ResumeThread() API on each of the main threads of each process in the job. Unlike the thread and process objects, the job object does not transition to the signaled state when complete. It transitions to the signaled state when its time limit (set with the SetInformationJobObject() API) expires. Windows also terminates all processes within the job when they use up the CPU time limit. Whenever you want to prematurely kill all of the processes in a job, you can use TerminateJobObject() API, which stops all threads of all processes that are still executing. When finished with the job object, use the CloseHandle() API to free all remaining resources.

Listing 4-6 shows an example of a process that follows this outline by creating three infinite counting processes (each of which identifies itself), waiting some time, then killing them all simultaneously. The same executable supplies the job creator process and the worker process by interpreting the command line differently. The example does not demonstrate limit setting on the job with the use of the SetInformationJobObject() API.

You should see the MSDN for details on possible limits that you can set on the job object as the system executes its processes. Simply find the `SetInformationJobObject()` API reference.

Listing 4-6: Creating a short-lived, multiprocess job

```
// project jobs
#define _WIN32_WINNT 0x0500
#define WINVER 0x0500
#include <windows.h>
#include <iostream>

// this helper method will create a worker process for the job
PROCESS_INFORMATION CreateWorker(LPTSTR szAppName)
{
    // startup info for the child
    STARTUPINFO si;
    ::ZeroMemory(reinterpret_cast<void*>(&si), sizeof(si));
    si.cb = sizeof(si); // must be sizeof this struct

    // returned process info for the child
    const PROCESS_INFORMATION c_piInvalid =
        { INVALID_HANDLE_VALUE, INVALID_HANDLE_VALUE, 0, 0};
    PROCESS_INFORMATION pi = c_piInvalid;

    // create the process, using the same executable and a
    //   command line that tells it to be a baby
    if(!::CreateProcess(
        szAppName,   // name of the app to spawn (this exe)
        "child",     // flag to tell us to behave like a child
        NULL,        // security for the child process handle
        NULL,        // security for the child thread handle
        FALSE,       // inherit no inheritable handles
        CREATE_SUSPENDED,   // leave it suspended for now
        NULL,        // new environment
        NULL,        // current dir
        &si,         // startup info
        &pi))        // returned process info
    {
        pi = c_piInvalid;
    }
    return(pi);
```

```
}

// this helper method will create the job and set its
//   processes in motion
HANDLE StartJob(LPTSTR szAppName)
{
    // create a job to hold the processes
    HANDLE hJob = ::CreateJobObject(
        NULL,    // default security
        NULL);   // anonymous job
    if(hJob!=NULL)
    {
        // first, create a few processes to be part of the job
        PROCESS_INFORMATION pi1 = CreateWorker(szAppName);
        PROCESS_INFORMATION pi2 = CreateWorker(szAppName);
        PROCESS_INFORMATION pi3 = CreateWorker(szAppName);

        // assign the processes into the job
        ::AssignProcessToJobObject(hJob, pi1.hProcess);
        ::AssignProcessToJobObject(hJob, pi2.hProcess);
        ::AssignProcessToJobObject(hJob, pi3.hProcess);

        // start up all of the processes
        ::ResumeThread(pi1.hThread);
        ::ResumeThread(pi2.hThread);
        ::ResumeThread(pi3.hThread);
    }
    else
    {
        hJob = INVALID_HANDLE_VALUE;
    }
    return(hJob);
}

int main(int argc, char* argv[])
{
    // check for being the job creator process
    if(::strcmp(argv[0], "child")!=0)
    {
        // create the job and start it in motion
        HANDLE hJob = ::StartJob(argv[0]);
        if(hJob!=INVALID_HANDLE_VALUE)
        {
            // let the job run for 10 sec, then
```

```
            // kill it (and all processes)
            ::Sleep(10000);
            ::TerminateJobObject(
                hJob,   // the victim
                0);     // exit code for all running threads

            // clean up the object
            ::CloseHandle(hJob);
            hJob = INVALID_HANDLE_VALUE;
        }
    }
    else
    {
        // we're one of the job's processes, let's just do
        //  some counting with our ID, the job will take
        //  care of terminating us
        int nValue = 0;
        while(TRUE)
        {
            std::cout << ::GetCurrentProcessId() << ": " <<
                ++nValue << std::endl;
            ::Sleep(100);
        }
    }

    // note that the job is done before leaving the process
    std::cout << "Job is done." << std::endl;
    return 0;
}
```

Listing 4-6 begins by creating a job kernel object with the StartJob() function. When starting the job, the example uses the local CreateWorker() function to pass child as a command line flag to a new copy of the same executable three times, forcing each process to run as part of the job. The child processes simply write to the output stream continuously. The example creates each worker process instance in the suspended state and adds it to the job object. Once they are all added, the parent process starts each child process's main thread and simply waits around a while (10 seconds), then kills them all simultaneously.

In this section, I've shown you five very different kernel objects that provide core services for your Windows 2000 applications. The waitable and timer queue timers allow you to take actions on a schedule. The file find and change notification objects allow you to examine and respond to the file system, and the job object allows you to logically group your processes.

Thread Synchronization

The topic of thread synchronization is vast and consumes many texts in theoretical computer science due to its complexity. I am going to stick to the basics of what you will need to construct multithreaded applications or to orchestrate multiprocess access to shared resources.

One essential leap that you must make when moving to multithreaded programming is to protect all shared resources from different threads attempting to modify them simultaneously. Tools that can help you gate the access to shared resources are the interlocked functions (not objects at all), critical sections (not kernel objects), and mutexes.

Another essential piece of multithreaded programming is orchestrating threads' efforts to complete the task of the application. In order to get threads to work simultaneously on the same problem, use event objects from the kernel and semaphores so that they can signal each other when they complete a portion of their work. These objects, along with mutexes, are first-class kernel objects that are nameable and securable so that you can share them across processes.

Interlocked functions

The kernel provides the interlocked functions to enable you to share data in the form of 32-bit signed data (a LONG) across threads and access it without the possibility of being preempted by another thread that could compromise the value of the data. For example, a reference count to a multithreaded COM object needs to make sure that the value being incremented in one thread is not in the process of being decremented in another. The *interlocked APIs* available to you are summarized in Table 4-2. All of these functions provide atomic operations to the data of interest — that is, the executing thread cannot be preempted until the function completes.

TABLE **4-2 INTERLOCKED DATA ACCESS APIS**

API Name	Description
InterlockedIncrement()	Adds one to the LONG value referenced by the passed pointer.
InterlockedDecrement()	Subtracts one from the LONG value referenced by the passed pointer.
InterlockedExchangeAdd()	Adds a passed signed value to the LONG value referenced by the passed pointer.

API Name	Description
InterlockedExchangePointer()	Replaces the LONG value referenced by the passed pointer with the passed value; returns the previous value.
InterlockedCompareExchangePointer()	Performs the same value exchange as InterlockedExchangePointer(). Also compares the previous value to a passed value and returns the result.

Listing 4-7 shows how to use the interlocked functions in a dual-threaded process that attempts to increment and decrement two variables, one with raw C++ and the other with the interlocked functions. At the end of the process, both values should end up at zero, but only the one managed by the interlocked functions can guarantee this. I have created a slightly contrived example since it pauses and writes the value to the output stream before saving the incremented value back to the raw location, giving Windows the opportunity to preempt the thread. We need to do this for all of the single-processor machines that want to see this problem; a multiprocessor system might assign each thread to its own CPU and show the problem with little effort.

Listing 4-7: Demonstrating count up/count down with and without interlocked functions

```cpp
// project interlock
#include <windows.h>
#include <iostream>

// this class takes pointers to two counter locations and a step
//   value then increments the counters a fixed number of times
//   in a thread-safe and a thread-dangerous manner
//   respectively
class CCountUpDown
{
public:
    // constructor simply creates a thread to increment values
    //    using plain C++ code and the interlocked functions
    CCountUpDown(LPLONG pnProtectedValue, LPLONG pnRawValue,
        int nIncrement) :
        m_pnProtectedValue(pnProtectedValue),
        m_pnRawValue(pnRawValue),
        m_nIncrement(nIncrement),
        m_hThread(INVALID_HANDLE_VALUE)
```

```cpp
    {
        m_hThread = ::CreateThread(
            NULL,       // default security
            0,          // default stack
            ThreadProc, // class thread proc
            reinterpret_cast<LPVOID>(this), // thread arg
            0,          // no special flags
            NULL);      // ignore returned ID
    }

    // destructor simply releases our reference to the thread
    virtual ~CCountUpDown() { ::CloseHandle(m_hThread); }

    // simple waiting method that will pause the caller until
    //  the thread ends
    virtual void WaitForCompletion()
    {
        if(m_hThread!=INVALID_HANDLE_VALUE)
        {
            ::WaitForSingleObject(m_hThread, INFINITE);
        }
    }

protected:

    virtual void DoCounting()
    {
        // loop through some number of times so that other
        //  threads have the chance to interfere with our
        //  values
        for(int nCount=0; nCount < 10000; nCount++)
        {
            // increment the raw value, sending it to the output
            //  before reassigning it, this will give Windows
            //  a chance to swap threads
            LONG nRawPlus = *m_pnRawValue + m_nIncrement;
            std::cout << nRawPlus << std::endl;
            *m_pnRawValue = nRawPlus;

            // increment the protected value
            ::InterlockedExchangeAdd(m_pnProtectedValue,
                m_nIncrement);
        }
    }
```

```
    static DWORD WINAPI ThreadProc(LPVOID lpParam)
    {
        // interpret the param as the 'this' ptr
        CCountUpDown* pThis =
            reinterpret_cast<CCountUpDown*>(lpParam);

        // call the object's counting method and return a
        //   simple success value
        pThis->DoCounting();
        return(0);
    }
protected:
    LPLONG   m_pnProtectedValue;  // thread-safe counter ref
    LPLONG   m_pnRawValue;    // thread-unsafe counter ref
    int      m_nIncrement;    // step value
    HANDLE   m_hThread;       // counting thread
};

void main()
{
    // create two reference counts to count up and down,
    //   the raw one will be preemptable, the protected one will
    //   use the interlocked functions
    LONG nRaw(0);
    LONG nProtected(0);

    // create the threads (they will begin immediately)
    CCountUpDown ud1(&nProtected, &nRaw, +2);
    CCountUpDown ud2(&nProtected, &nRaw, -2);

    // make sure all of the threads have ended (it will
    //   be almost simultaneous)
    ud1.WaitForCompletion();
    ud2.WaitForCompletion();

    // print the results
    std::cout << "Raw value: " << nRaw << std::endl;
    std::cout << "Protected value: " << nProtected << std::endl;
}
```

The class, CCountUpDown, created in Listing 4-7 simply takes references to two memory locations in its constructor and uses a thread-safe and a thread-unsafe method of marching each of the values. The constructor also takes an increment to count up or down the values at the passed references. The unsafe method grabs the value while incrementing it, sends it to the output stream, then writes it back. The time between the increment and write are exaggerated to increase the chances that another thread can write to the location. This preempting thread's change is lost once the first thread is restarted.

The safe counting method uses the interlocked function, `Interlocked ExchangeAdd()`, to ensure that another thread cannot modify the value while it is executing the modification. The program simply creates two of these counter objects and waits for them to do their business simultaneously. You can see in Figure 4-2 that the protected value always comes down to zero and the unprotected (raw) value never does. One value in the figure is protected by an interlocked function, and one value is not protected.

Figure 4-2: The end of the counting in Listing 4-7

Keep in mind that you cannot use the interlocked functions to protect data that your thread shares with another process. The interlocked functions are lightweight kernel APIs. They are optimized for size and speed, and they do not have the implementation mechanics to communicate with another process.

Critical sections

The interlocked functions enable you to make atomic (and hence thread-safe) a simple, often used operation – the modification of a data value. Often you have larger operations that you need to make thread-safe. For example, sharing a linked list across threads means that you need to keep a thread that is inserting into the list locked out until a thread that is deleting from the list completes. This is where critical sections help you.

A critical section is actually not a kernel object (the code lives in `NtDll.DLL`), but the kernel does supply the methods to use it. The critical section enables you to wall off portions of your code with calls to the `EnterCriticalSection()` and `LeaveCriticalSection()` APIs. Windows suspends all other threads (within the same process) attempting to enter the section until the thread currently executing in the section finishes.

To use a critical section, you simply create a cross-thread instance of the CRITI-CAL_SECTION data structure, and initialize it with InitializeCriticalSection(). All access to the critical code should be guarded with the calls to enter and leave already described. When you're finished guarding your code (the threads are about to terminate), you should use DeleteCriticalSection() to free the resources allocated by the object.

Listing 4-8 shows the class from the previous example, modified to succeed by placing a critical section around the raw C++ modification of the data. As you'll see in the example, the critical section object allows you to make code thread-safe by simply adding API calls before and after important code; you need not change any logic.

Listing 4-8: Demonstrating count up/count down guarded by a critical section

```
// project critsec
#include <windows.h>
#include <iostream>

// this class takes pointers to two counter locations and a step
//   value then increments the counters a fixed number of times
//   in a thread-safe manner
class CCountUpDown
{
public:
    // constructor simply creates a thread to increment values
    //     using plain C code and the interlocked functions
    CCountUpDown(LPLONG pnProtectedValue, LPLONG pnRawValue,
        int nIncrement) :
        m_pnProtectedValue(pnProtectedValue),
        m_pnRawValue(pnRawValue),
        m_nIncrement(nIncrement),
        m_hThread(INVALID_HANDLE_VALUE)
    {

        if(m_pCritsec==NULL)
        {
            m_pCritsec = new CRITICAL_SECTION;
            ::InitializeCriticalSection(m_pCritsec);
        }
        m_hThread = ::CreateThread(
            NULL,          // default security
            0,             // default stack
```

```cpp
            ThreadProc, // class thread proc
            reinterpret_cast<LPVOID>(this), // thread arg
            0,          // no special flags
            NULL);      // ignore returned ID
    }

    // destructor simply releases our reference to the thread
    //  then destroys the critical section
    virtual ~CCountUpDown()
    {
        ::CloseHandle(m_hThread);
        ::DeleteCriticalSection(m_pCritsec);
        delete m_pCritsec;
    }

    // simple waiting method that will pause the caller until
    //    the thread ends
    virtual void WaitForCompletion()
    {
        if(m_hThread!=INVALID_HANDLE_VALUE)
        {
            ::WaitForSingleObject(m_hThread, INFINITE);
        }
    }

protected:

    virtual void DoCounting()
    {
        // loop through some number of times so that other
        //  threads have the chance to interfere with our
        //  values
        for(int nCount=0; nCount < 10000; nCount++)
        {
            // increment the raw value, sending it to the output
            //  before reassigning it, this will give Windows
            //  a chance to swap threads
            ::EnterCriticalSection(m_pCritsec);

            LONG nRawPlus = *m_pnRawValue + m_nIncrement;
            std::cout << nRawPlus << std::endl;
            *m_pnRawValue = nRawPlus;

            ::LeaveCriticalSection(m_pCritsec);
```

```
                // increment the protected value
                ::InterlockedExchangeAdd(m_pnProtectedValue,
                    m_nIncrement);
            }
        }

    static DWORD WINAPI ThreadProc(LPVOID lpParam)
    {
        // interpret the param as the 'this' ptr
        CCountUpDown* pThis =
            reinterpret_cast<CCountUpDown*>(lpParam);

        // call the object's counting method and return a
        //  simple
        pThis->DoCounting();
        return(0);
    }
protected:
    LPLONG  m_pnProtectedValue; // thread-safe counter ref
    LPLONG  m_pnRawValue;   // thread-dangerous counter ref
    int     m_nIncrement;   // step value
    HANDLE  m_hThread;  // counting thread
    static LPCRITICAL_SECTION   m_pCritsec; // raw counting prot
};
LPCRITICAL_SECTION CCountUpDown::m_pCritsec = NULL;

void main()
{
    // create two reference counts to count up and down,
    //  the raw one will be preemptable, the protected one will
    //  use the interlocked functions
    LONG nRaw(0);
    LONG nProtected(0);

    // create the threads (they will begin immediately)
    CCountUpDown ud1(&nProtected, &nRaw, +2);
    CCountUpDown ud2(&nProtected, &nRaw, -2);

    // make sure all of the threads have ended (it will
    //  be almost simultaneous()
    ud1.WaitForCompletion();
    ud2.WaitForCompletion();
```

```
// print the results
std::cout << "Raw value: " << nRaw << std::endl;
std::cout << "Protected value: " << nProtected
    << std::endl;
}
```

The results of the program are now quite different as shown in Figure 4-3. Now, both values are properly protected – even though Windows still switches threads before the write-back of the raw value, the other thread simply cannot enter the dangerous section of code until the original has exited. The figure shows one value protected by the interlocked functions and one value protected by a critical section.

Figure 4-3: The end of the counting in Listing 4-8

Under the covers, the critical section normally uses the interlocked functions to check for another thread in the code section – this is normally very fast. However, when the kernel denies access to the thread, the critical section logic uses an event object (covered later in this section) and a waiting function to pause the thread. This long-term waiting is expensive in terms of CPU cycles to get started.

An enhancement to the critical section object is the addition of a *spin count*. To use this, the thread attempting to gain entry to a critical section "spins" in a loop a set number of times before settling down to the waiting function. This spin count only makes sense for very tight sections of code that won't delay the new thread for very long and only works on multiprocessor machines since it's unlikely that Windows would preempt the waiting thread while it is in the spin loop in order to exit the critical section. To take advantage of spin counts, use the `InitalizeCriticalSectionAndSpinCount()` and `SetCriticalSectionSpinCount()` APIs to setup the critical section. The other critical section APIs will work with the returned handle. The critical section APIs are listed in Table 4-3.

TABLE 4-3 CRITICAL SECTION APIS

API Name	Description
InitializeCriticalSection()	Sets up a CRITICAL_SECTION structure passed by a pointer so that it is ready for use.
InitializeCriticalSection AndSpinCount()	Sets up a CRITICAL_SECTION structure passed by a pointer with a passed spin count so that it is ready for use.
EnterCriticalSection()	Attempts to gain exclusive access to a passed CRITICAL_SECTION structure, blocking the calling thread indefinitely until it can.
TryEnterCriticalSection()	Attempts to gain exclusive access to a passed CRITICAL_SECTION structure. The function will return immediately whether it can or cannot gain ownership, the return value indicates the success.
LeaveCriticalSection()	Releases exclusive access to a passed CRITICAL_SECTION structure, allowing another thread to gain access.
DeleteCriticalSection()	Cleans up the resources used by the passed critical section object.
SetCriticalSectionSpinCount()	Changes the spin count for the critical section object passed by pointer.

Critical section objects are simple to use and incur little runtime penalty. Table 4-3 sums up the APIs you will need to use them. Like the interlocked functions, you cannot use critical sections to protect your data from another process's thread – they are neither namable nor securable. You need to use the more heavyweight objects – events, mutexes, and semaphores – to protect data from other processes.

Events

Perhaps the most convenient way to synchronize threads within and across processes is by using the *event* object. This kernel object simply allows a thread to have direct control over its signaled state. That makes these objects the simplest means for one thread to inform another about a binary state. The event kernel object is simply an artifact that lets you to manually broadcast to threads in the same or other processes that something has occurred.

Using an event is simple; you use the CreateEvent() API to produce an instance handle. Events are securable and namable like most first-class kernel objects, plus they come in two flavors: manual-reset and auto-reset. To change the manual-reset event to signaled state, use the SetEvent() API and the ResetEvent() API to clear it. You move an auto-reset event to the signaled state using the PulseEvent() API, which releases all threads in the wait state and immediately returns it to non-signaled before any additional waits can be started.

Within a process, you can simply share the handle to an event object but when another process needs access to the event object. This process must create a reference using the OpenEvent() API. The OpenEvent() API requires the name of the event object and the calling account must possess sufficient security to access the event. All references to an event object need to be cleaned up using the CloseHandle() API. Table 4-4 sums up the APIs used to manage an event object.

TABLE 4-4 EVENT OBJECT APIS

API Name	Description
CreateEvent()	Creates a new event object in the kernel. The API allows specification of a name, detailed security settings, a flag for manual-reset or auto-reset, and a flag marking it as initially signaled or not initially signaled.
OpenEvent()	Creates a reference to an already-existing event object. The API requires the name, a flag for inheritability, and the desired access level.
SetEvent()	Transitions a manual-reset event object to the signaled state.
ResetEvent()	Transitions a manual-reset event object out of the signaled state.
PulseEvent()	Transitions an auto-reset event object into the signaled state. It will immediately transition out of that state once the system releases all threads waiting on it.

The example in Listing 4-9 shows you how to use events between processes. The parent process starts up; creates a named, sharable event with the CreateEvent() API and a child process; then waits for the child process to signal the event and terminate the parent. When created, the child process opens the event object by name with the OpenEvent() API and calls the SetEvent() API to move it to the signaled state. Both processes should end almost immediately after the signaling.

Listing 4-9: Creating and opening event objects to signal between processes

```
// project event
#include <windows.h>
#include <iostream>

// the handle event to continue on, in real life this would
//   likely be communicated using a shared include file
static LPCTSTR g_szContinueEvent =
    "w2kdg.EventDemo.event.Continue";

// this method simply creates a replicate process that acts
//   in child mode (specified by the command line)
BOOL CreateChild(LPCTSTR szAppName)
{
    // startup info for the child
    STARTUPINFO si;
    ::ZeroMemory(reinterpret_cast<void*>(&si), sizeof(si));
    si.cb = sizeof(si); // must be sizeof this struct

    // returned process info for the child
    PROCESS_INFORMATION pi;

    // create the process, using the same executable and a
    //   command line that tells it to be a baby
    BOOL bCreateOK = ::CreateProcess(
        szAppName,   // name of the app to spawn (this exe)
        "child",     // flag to tell us to behave like a child
        NULL,        // security for the child process handle
        NULL,        // security for the child thread handle
        FALSE,       // don't inherit handles
        0,           // special creation flags
        NULL,        // new environment
        NULL,        // current dir
        &si,         // startup info
        &pi);        // returned process info

    // release our references to the child process
    if(bCreateOK)
    {
        ::CloseHandle(pi.hProcess);
        ::CloseHandle(pi.hThread);
    }
    return(bCreateOK);
}
```

```
// this method simply creates an event and a child process, then
//  waits for the child process to signal the event before
//  returning
void WaitForChild(LPCTSTR szAppName)
{
    // create a new event object for the child process
    //  to use when releasing this process
    HANDLE hEventContinue = ::CreateEvent(
        NULL,   // default security, child process will
                //  have access
        TRUE,   // manual-reset event
        FALSE,  // initially non-signaled
        g_szContinueEvent); // our name
    if(hEventContinue!=NULL)
    {
        // create the child process
        if(::CreateChild(szAppName))
        {
            // wait until the child signals
            ::WaitForSingleObject(hEventContinue, INFINITE);
        }

        // clean up the handle
        ::CloseHandle(hEventContinue);
        hEventContinue = INVALID_HANDLE_VALUE;
    }
}


// this method gets called in child mode and simply signals the
//  parent process to terminate
void SignalParent()
{
    // try opening the handle
    HANDLE hEventContinue = ::OpenEvent(
        EVENT_MODIFY_STATE, // desired access, least possible
        FALSE,              // not an inheritable handle
        g_szContinueEvent); // the name of the event
    if(hEventContinue!=NULL)
    {
        ::SetEvent(hEventContinue);
    }

    // clean up the handle
    ::CloseHandle(hEventContinue);
```

```
      hEventContinue = INVALID_HANDLE_VALUE;
}

int main(int argc, char* argv[])
{
    // check for parent or child process startup
    if(::strcmp(argv[0], "child")!=0)
    {
        // create an event and wait for the child to signal it
        std::cout << "Parent waiting on child." << std::endl;
        ::WaitForChild(argv[0]);
        std::cout << "Parent released." << std::endl;
    }
    else
    {
        // signal the event created by the parent
        ::SignalParent();
    }
    return 0;
}
```

You can see that our example uses the executable-sharing trick that I first introduced in Listing 2-8 (in Chapter 2) where the process starts out as a parent then creates a replicate that acts in child mode. The heart of this sharing is found in the `main()` function of Listing 4-6 when it examines the command line for the `child` parameter. This technique enables me to simulate two applications communicating using a shared, named kernel object.

Chapter 3, "Using Kernel Objects," introduces the naming convention used by the event name to make it unique.

Mutexes

A *mutex* is another first-class, nameable, securable kernel object. Its main purpose is to gate access to a shared resource. A mutex is much like a baton in a relay race; a thread that wants to run should wait for the current runner to pass the baton. The thread that owns a single-access resource creates a mutex. All threads that want access to that resource should acquire the mutex before actually performing the operation and should release the mutex as soon as they are done, allowing the next waiting thread to acquire it and proceed.

Mutexes sound a lot like the critical section objects I presented earlier in this section, but these objects have a couple of major differences:

◆ First, they can coordinate access across processes.

◆ Second, they do not guarantee that threads from other processes will do the right thing, since the resource owner does not necessarily write the client code. A thread can choose to access the shared resource without mutex ownership (like running without the baton), but this causes bad things to happen.

Much like the event object, the mutex is simple to create or open, use, and clean up. Creation is done with the `CreateMutex()` API, which allows the standard security and name specification. In addition, you can specify an initial ownership flag during creation that, for example, allows the creator thread to release the mutex only when it's finished all initialization of the resource.

In order to acquire the mutex, the thread that wants access calls first uses the `OpenMutex()` API to acquire a handle to the object. It then supplies this handle to one of the waiting functions. When the kernel signals the mutex object to the waiting thread, it indicates that the thread now has "ownership" of the mutex. While a thread has ownership, the thread monopolizes access to a shared resource – it should make every effort to give it up as soon as possible. Giving up the shared resource means calling the `ReleaseMutex()` API on the object. Then the system is responsible for giving the mutex ownership to the next thread in line (ordered by arrival time).

The counter class, CCountUpDown, shown in Listing 4-10 uses a mutex to guard accesses to a single value between two threads. Each thread attempts to gain control and change the value and then write that value to the stream. The constructor actually creates the mutex object, and the counting method executes the wait and releases required to cooperatively use the mutex (and hence the resource).

Listing 4-10: Using a mutex to protect a shared resource

```
// project mutex
#include <windows.h>
#include <iostream>


// example of a class that uses a mutex to guard a shared
//   resource from simultaneous access
class CCountUpDown
{
public:
    // constructor creates 2 threads to access the shared
    //   value
    CCountUpDown(int nAccesses) :
```

```
    m_hThreadInc(INVALID_HANDLE_VALUE),
    m_hThreadDec(INVALID_HANDLE_VALUE),
    m_hMutexValue(INVALID_HANDLE_VALUE),
    m_nValue(0),
    m_nAccess(nAccesses)
{
    // create a mutex for access to the value
    m_hMutexValue = ::CreateMutex(
        NULL,   // default security
        TRUE,   // own initially, will release
                // after all init complete
        NULL);  // anonymous
    m_hThreadInc = ::CreateThread(
        NULL,   // default security
        0,      // default stack
        IncThreadProc, // class thread proc
        reinterpret_cast<LPVOID>(this), // thread arg
        0,      // no special flags
        NULL);  // ignore returned id
    m_hThreadDec = ::CreateThread(
        NULL,   // default security
        0,      // default stack
        DecThreadProc, // class thread proc
        reinterpret_cast<LPVOID>(this), // thread arg
        0,      // no special flags
        NULL);  // ignore returned id

    // allow the mutex to be acquired by the threads
    ::ReleaseMutex(m_hMutexValue);
}

// destructor simply releases our reference to the objects
virtual ~CCountUpDown()
{
    ::CloseHandle(m_hThreadInc);
    ::CloseHandle(m_hThreadDec);
    ::CloseHandle(m_hMutexValue);
}

// simple waiting method that will pause the caller until
//     both threads end
virtual void WaitForCompletion()
{
    // make sure all of the objects are ready
```

```
        if(m_hThreadInc!=INVALID_HANDLE_VALUE &&
            m_hThreadDec!=INVALID_HANDLE_VALUE)
        {
            // wait for both to complete (order not important)
            ::WaitForSingleObject(m_hThreadInc, INFINITE);
            ::WaitForSingleObject(m_hThreadDec, INFINITE);
        }
    }

protected:

    // simple method to change the shared resource
    virtual void DoCount(int nStep)
    {
        // loop until all accesses have been accomplished
        while(m_nAccess>0)
        {
            // wait for access to the value
            ::WaitForSingleObject(m_hMutexValue, INFINITE);

            // change and show the value
            m_nValue += nStep;
            std::cout << "thread: " << ::GetCurrentThreadId()
                << " value: " << m_nValue
                << " access: " << m_nAccess << std::endl;

            // signal the access and allow the threads to switch
            --m_nAccess;
            ::Sleep(1);

            // release access to the value
            ::ReleaseMutex(m_hMutexValue);
        }
    }
    static DWORD WINAPI IncThreadProc(LPVOID lpParam)
    {
        // interpret the param as the 'this' ptr
        CCountUpDown* pThis =
            reinterpret_cast<CCountUpDown*>(lpParam);

        // call the object's incrementing method and return a
        //  simple value
        pThis->DoCount(+1);
        return(0);
    }
```

```
    static DWORD WINAPI DecThreadProc(LPVOID lpParam)
    {
        // interpret the param as the 'this' ptr
        CCountUpDown* pThis =
            reinterpret_cast<CCountUpDown*>(lpParam);

        // call the object's decrementing method and return a
        //  simple value
        pThis->DoCount(-1);
        return(0);
    }
protected:
    HANDLE  m_hThreadInc;
    HANDLE  m_hThreadDec;
    HANDLE  m_hMutexValue;
    int     m_nValue;
    int     m_nAccess;
};

void main()
{
    CCountUpDown ud(100);
    ud.WaitForCompletion();
}
```

You should see in the output in Figure 4-4 that the threads alternate (thanks to the Sleep() API, which allows Windows to swap threads). The value should return to the initial value (zero) after each run since the writing thread becomes the last in line after each run, and the kernel guarantees that it will not run again before the other thread does.

Figure 4-4: The results of two threads cooperatively accessing a resource through a mutex

The fact that a particular thread owns a mutex object causes the problem Windows terms *abandonment*. This problem occurs when a thread that is in control of a mutex terminates unexpectedly. Since the owning thread has died, Windows 2000 must tell anyone waiting on the object to release; Windows does this using the WAIT_OBJECT_ABANDONED return value from the waiting functions. When this return is sent back, the waiting thread knows to stop waiting on that mutex and take whatever corrective action it can.

Semaphores

A *semaphore* is the last thread synchronization object to discuss. As previously mentioned, semaphores are namable and securable. The semaphore object is probably the most infrequently used object, since its main purpose is to create a mutex that allows an arbitrary number of objects access to a shared resource simultaneously – a situation the just doesn't occur very often.

A semaphore behaves like the door attendant at your favorite bar. It starts out with a maximum number of threads that can have access to the resource and the current number of openings (the maximum minus the current census). Each time another thread desires access to the resource, the thread calls a kernel waiting function that causes the semaphore to check its count again. If there is an opening, it signals to enter; if not, the thread is suspended at the door. As threads finish using the resource, they notify the semaphore, which tells the door attendant he can let in another thread.

To create a semaphore object, the CreateSemaphore() API requires the standard security and naming as well as a maximum and initial free count. The semaphore remains signaled until the current count of threads using the resource reaches zero. Each thread that attempts to wait on the signaled object decrements its free count. When the thread is finished using the resource, it must call the Release Semaphore() API, which allows the thread to indicate it consumed more than one free slot and check the previous number of free slots.

Semaphore objects frequently are used across processes – much like the event and mutex objects. To use a semaphore from a client process, you will call the OpenSemaphore() API and supply the system-wide unique name of the object and the access that you require (usually by supplying the SYNCHRONIZE constant).

Since the owners of the resource might not engineer the client processes, those processes might choose not to go through the semaphore to access the resource (like sneaking in the side door). If they choose to do this, bad things may happen.

Once the kernel suspends threads waiting for access to the resource using the semaphore, it guarantees that the next to gain access is the one that got in line first (order of appearance). Also, a semaphore with a maximum count of one is identical in behavior to a mutex but they are not interchangeable – do not pass mutex handles to semaphore APIs or vice-versa.

The example shown in Listing 4-11 uses a semaphore to keep the number of active threads in the application restricted to a small number. The application simply attempts to start up 100 threads but uses the semaphore to restrict the active count to five. You can see the output window display each thread's creation and termination in Figure 4-5 and watch the task manager's threads column on the Processes tab to ensure the thread count never exceeds six (add one for the main thread).

Listing 4-11: Using a semaphore to restrict the number of active threads

```
// project semaphore
#include <windows.h>
#include <iostream>

// semaphore to control number of active threads (protects
//   threading shared resource)
HANDLE g_hSemThreads = INVALID_HANDLE_VALUE;

// simple thread proc that pauses, releases the semaphore
//   and tells the operator
static DWORD WINAPI ThreadProc(LPVOID lpParam)
{
    // interpret the param as a long
    LONG nPauseMs = reinterpret_cast<LONG>(lpParam);

    // pause
    ::Sleep(nPauseMs);

    // release the semaphore
    if(g_hSemThreads!=INVALID_HANDLE_VALUE)
    {
        LONG nPrevCt(0);
        if(::ReleaseSemaphore(
            g_hSemThreads,  // semaphore to release
            1,  // let go of a single slot
            &nPrevCt))
        {
            // show the destruction
            std::cout << nPauseMs
                << " msec thread ended, slots left: "
```

```
                        << nPrevCt + 1
                        << std::endl;
        }
    }
    return(0);
}


void main()
{
    // create a semaphore to allow 5 threads at once to live
    g_hSemThreads = ::CreateSemaphore(
        NULL,    // default security
        5,       // begin with 5 open slots
        5,       // allow only 5 slots
        NULL);   // anonymous object

    // create 100 threads all together, the semaphore will only
    //   allow 5 to be active at once
    for(int nTotal=100; nTotal > 0; --nTotal)
    {
        // wait until we have room to create a new thread
        ::WaitForSingleObject(g_hSemThreads, INFINITE);

        // pause time for the new thread
        LONG nPauseMs = nTotal * 5;

        // start the thread
        HANDLE hThread = ::CreateThread(
            NULL,    // default security
            0,       // default stack
            ThreadProc, // thread fcn
            reinterpret_cast<LPVOID>(nPauseMs), // lifetime
            0,       // no special creation flags
            NULL);   // ignore the thread id

        // show the new creation
        std::cout << nPauseMs << " msec thread created"
            << std::endl;

        // release our handle to the thread
        ::CloseHandle(hThread);
        hThread = INVALID_HANDLE_VALUE;
    }
```

```
    // close up the semaphore
    ::CloseHandle(g_hSemThreads);
    g_hSemThreads = INVALID_HANDLE_VALUE;
}
```

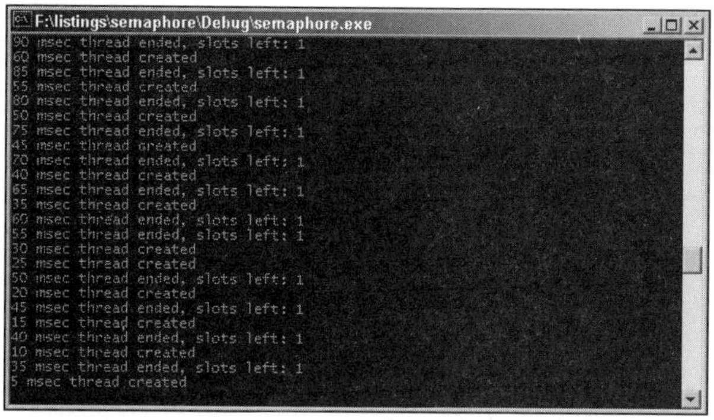

Figure 4-5: Keeping the active thread count to five using a semaphore

The application in Listing 4-11 starts up by creating an anonymous semaphore object with the CreateSemaphore() API to restrict the number of concurrently executing threads to five. It then tries to create 100 threads, making sure to have semaphore permission with the WaitForSingleObject() call. Each new thread that the main() function creates owns a reference to the thread count semaphore. The thread simply waits for a set amount of time, releases its semaphore reference, and exits. Every time a thread releases its semaphore reference, the main thread creates a new one until it has created the 100 that I required from it.

Listing 4-11 protects the system against having 100 threads in operation at once by forcing each thread creation and destruction to go through the semaphore door attendant. You probably won't find a whole lot of uses for semaphores, but when you do, their use is very straightforward.

Inter-Thread Communication

The final category of kernel objects is inter-thread communications objects. The most often used of these objects are files and file mappings. They allow one thread to easily send information to another within the same process or across processes.

   ◆ File object: This is the traditional element of persistent storage with which you are very familiar. Treating a file as a kernel object gives you some additional, powerful capabilities above and beyond the standard set of C++ file operations.

◆ File mapping object: This is a region of a persistent or temporary file object allocated in virtual memory that you can treat as a binary data block. It gives you direct, in-memory access to the contents of a file as opposed to the traditional, sequential reads and writes.

Both the mailslot and named pipe objects also provide inter-thread communication. Chapter 15, "System Services," discusses them.

Files

The kernel enables you to create file objects that represent persistent chunks of data from a system device or network. These file objects are the lowest-level accessors to persistent data; all files that you open with the C++ runtime or anywhere else eventually become calls to the `CreateFile()` API.

The `CreateFile()` function allocates a kernel object to represent a persistent file. This API is called when creating a new file on disk or when opening an existing one. Its parameters are summarized in Table 4-5. The create call is much more complicated than the creation of events, mutexes, or semaphores. First, the name of the object must be specified in `lpFilename` and point to a location on a file system to which you have access. Next, you must supply the desired access level with `dwDesiredAccess`, just as in an open call for a mutex or semaphore.

TABLE 4-5 PARAMETERS OF THE CREATEFILE() API

Parameter Name	Intention
LPCTSTR lpFileName	The name of the file to open or create.
DWORD dwDesiredAccess	Desired access to the file; a bitmask including `GENERIC_READ` or `GENERIC_WRITE`.
DWORD dwShareMode	Specifies type of file sharing with other processes, if any.
LPSECURITY_ATTRIBUTES lpSecurityAttributes	The security to be associated with the backing file object when supported by the filesystem.
DWORD dwCreationDisposition	Type of action to take at the file system level, such as the creation of a new file or the opening of an existing one.

Parameter Name	Intention
DWORD dwFlagsAndAttributes	File system attributes for the file such as read-only or hidden. Also, attributes for the file object such as buffered writing.
HANDLE hTemplateFile	Handle to another file object that will be used to supply attributes for a newly created file.

The sharing mode parameter, dwShareMode, required by the create function enables you to specify what happens if another process attempts to access the data simultaneously. Like all other first-class kernel objects, you can specify the security attributes of the object you create with lpSecurityAttributes. Next, you tell the create function how to behave if the data already exists or does not exist already on the persistent storage with the supplied name through the dwCreation Disposition parameter.

You specify the attributes of a file (e.g., read-only) and determine the behavior of the read/write operations that you perform on the data with the dwFlagsAnd Attributes parameter. Finally, the last parameter, hTemplateFile, enables you to specify another file object to use as a template to copy attributes and extended attributes for a newly created file.

You should be aware of the deprecated OpenFile() method that is provided for backward compatibility with 16-bit Windows applications. This function returns an HFILE that is incompatible with the HANDLE returned by CreateFile(). The API functions _lread(), _llseek(), and _lwrite() all use this old-style handle and hence also should not be used in new development.

Usually, you use the ReadFile() and WriteFile() APIs to move data between the persistent storage and your application through the file object. These functions are very straightforward since the creation call wraps up most of the complexity of the object. These functions simply take the handle of the file object to exchange data with, a pointer to an in-memory data buffer, and a count of bytes to move. In addition, these functions enable you to execute *overlapped I/O*, which is asynchronous data transfer meant for moving large quantities of data, since it does not block the main thread.

For details on overlapped I/O, see the MSDN; begin with the documentation on the `ReadFileEx()` API. Chapter 15, "System Services," discusses both consoles and named pipes.

In addition to standard persistent files, the `CreateFile()` method enables you to access console input and output as well as data from named pipes.

The system includes many file object utility functions. Table 4-6 summarizes the APIs that you will require when working with file objects. The `GetFileType()` API tells you the underlying structure of the file handle that you are working with. In addition to that helper, the kernel supplies the `GetFileSize()`, `GetFileTime()`, and `GetFileInformationByHandle()` APIs for getting details on the underlying data. Other utility functions for changing data in the file include the `LockFile()`, `SetFilePointer()`, and `SetEndOfFile()` APIs.

In addition to these handle-based APIs, the kernel offers a bunch of utilities that operate directly on files by name. Since those APIs do not operate on file objects, they are beyond the scope of this chapter.

Chapter 13, "The File System," covers files in much more detail.

TABLE 4-6 FILE OBJECT APIS

API Name	Description
CreateFile()	Creates a file kernel object that represents a new or existing chunk of data in the file system.

API Name	Description
ReadFile()	Extracts data from a file in the file system, referenced through a file object handle. Reading begins at the current file pointer position and increments that position with each byte read.
WriteFile()	Sends data to a file in the file system, referenced through a file object handle. Writing begins at the current file pointer position and increments that position with each byte written.
SetFilePointer()	Changes the position of the current file pointer a relative or absolute distance into the file.
SetEndOfFile()	Moves the end-of-file marker for the file to the current file pointer position.
LockFile()	Prevents other processes from accessing a region of the passed file.
GetFileType()	Determines if the passed handle refers to a disk file, console, or named pipe.
GetFileSizeEx()	Fetches the 64-bit size of the file.
GetFileTime()	Retrieves the times that the file was created, last accessed, and last modified.
GetFileInformationByHandle()	Fills a BY_HANDLE_FILE_INFORMATION structure with detailed information on the passed file.

When you're finished using the file object, you should clean it up with the CloseHandle() API just like all other first-class kernel objects. The code in Listing 4-12 shows you how threads send data to each other on persistent storage through the file object. The program simply fires up and begins creating thread after thread. Each thread reads data out of the specified file, increments it by a value sent to it during creation, then writes that new value back to the file.

Listing 4-12: Demonstrating threads sending data through a file object

```
// project fileobj
#include <windows.h>
#include <iostream>

// filename to use
static LPCTSTR g_szFilename = "w2kdg.FileObj.file.data.txt";

// simple thread to read the current data in the data file,
//  add the value passed to the thread and write it back
//  to the data file
static DWORD WINAPI ThreadProc(LPVOID lpParam)
{
    // interpret the param as a long
    LONG nAdd = reinterpret_cast<LONG>(lpParam);

    // construct the fully specified file name
    TCHAR szFullName[MAX_PATH];
    ::GetTempPath(MAX_PATH, szFullName);
    ::strcat(szFullName, g_szFilename);

    // open up the file object
    HANDLE hFile = ::CreateFile(
        szFullName,                 // full name of the file
        GENERIC_READ | GENERIC_WRITE,// all access
        FILE_SHARE_READ,            // allow others to read
        NULL,                       // default security
        OPEN_ALWAYS,                // create or open the file
        FILE_ATTRIBUTE_NORMAL,      // generic file
        NULL);                      // no template file
    if(hFile!=INVALID_HANDLE_VALUE)
    {
        // read the current data
        LONG nValue(0);
        DWORD dwXfer(0);
        ::ReadFile(
            hFile,                  // file to read from
            reinterpret_cast<LPVOID>(&nValue),  // buffer
            sizeof(nValue),         // buffer size
            &dwXfer,                // count of bytes read
            NULL);                  // no overlapped i/o
        if(dwXfer==sizeof(nValue))
        {
            // show the current
```

```
            std::cout << "read: " << nValue << std::endl;
        }

        // increment the value
        nValue += nAdd;

        // write it back to the persistent storage
        ::SetFilePointer(hFile, 0, NULL, FILE_BEGIN);
        ::WriteFile(
            hFile,              // file to write to
            reinterpret_cast<LPCVOID>(&nValue),// data
            sizeof(nValue), // buffer size
            &dwXfer,            // count of bytes written
            NULL);              // no overlapped i/o
        if(dwXfer==sizeof(nValue))
        {
            std::cout << "wrote: " << nValue << std::endl;
        }

        // clean up the file
        ::CloseHandle(hFile);
        hFile = INVALID_HANDLE_VALUE;
    }
    return(0);
}


void main()
{
    // create 100 threads to read and write from the file
    for(int nTotal=100; nTotal > 0; --nTotal)
    {
        // start the thread
        HANDLE hThread = ::CreateThread(
            NULL,       // default security
            0,          // default stack
            ThreadProc, // thread fcn
            reinterpret_cast<LPVOID>(1), // increment
            0,          // no special creation flags
            NULL);      // ignore the thread id

        // wait for the thread to complete
        ::WaitForSingleObject(hThread, INFINITE);

        // release our handle to the thread
        ::CloseHandle(hThread);
```

```
        hThread = INVALID_HANDLE_VALUE;
    }
}
```

Listing 4-12 starts 100 individual read-write threads, waiting for each to complete. The thread routine creates or opens a file in the Windows temporary directory uniquely named for the application using the CreateFile() API. Next, the thread reads the first 32-bits with the ReadFile() API, interprets the value as a long, increments it, and finally writes it back to the beginning of the file with the WriteFile() API. The thread then exits having left its value for the next one.

You can watch each thread in Listing 4-12 take the data from the previous thread and add to it every time you run the process; the value in the file continues to increment. This example is a very simple communication mechanism. You can use it as a simple template for writing your own file read/write code. The only interesting code is the reset of the file pointer before the write occurs. Resetting the file pointer is necessary since it will rest after the first four bytes once the read is complete and that same pointer is used for writing to the file. If the function wrote the new value there, the next time the process ran, it would only read the original value.

File mappings

Reading and writing data through file objects using the ReadFile() and WriteFile() APIs can be cumbersome. Windows 2000 has supplied a simple way to manipulate data in a file called a memory-mapped file (also called a file mapping). A *file mapping* object simply takes a region of the file (up to and including the entire file if possible) and enables you to access it as though it were simply a data buffer within your application.

This file-mapping object provides you with a powerful mechanism for scanning through data from a file without having to monkey with moving file pointers. This is especially helpful for multithreaded read operations since each thread might want to move the read pointer to a different location – which would require you to protect the file using some thread synchronization mechanism.

A new file-mapping object requires a persistent file object (from CreateFile()) in the CreateFileMapping() API. The method takes the standard security and naming parameters, as well as a protection flag for allowable operations (e.g., read-only) and a maximum size of the mapping. The mapping then can be used from other threads or processes from the OpenFileMapping() API – which is very similar to the open methods for events and mutexes.

Another powerful use of the memory-mapped file object asks the system to create a temporary file that backs the mapping. The temporary file provides a scratch area for threads or processes to send large chunks of data to each other without having to create and secure an on-disk file. You create this temporary memory-mapped file by sending INVALID_HANDLE_VALUE to the creation function in place of a real file handle; this tells the kernel to use the system page file to construct a temporary data region of maximum size to back the mapping.

Chapter 12, "Memory Management," covers virtual memory issues such as the system page file.

In order to use the file mapping object, the process must map a view of the file into its memory space. That is, you should think of the file-mapping object as the first step of the process; it attaches security and naming to the shared data while the view actually allows you access to the data. Getting a pointer to the memory region requires a call to the MapViewOfFile() API, which takes the file-mapping object handle as its prime parameter. The viewing method also takes a desired access level (e.g., read-write) and an offset within the file to start the view and the size of the view. The function returns to you a pointer to memory within your process that you can use however you like (within limits of your access level).

When you're finished with the file-mapping view, you must call the UnmapViewOfFile() API on the pointer you received and then call the CloseHandle() API on the mapping object to clean it up.

The program in Listing 4-13 shows a file mapping backed by the page file in use across threads. This example is a simple enhancement of Listing 4-12 that shows the simplicity of using a memory-mapped file over a file object resident on disk. The processes use a mutex to arbitrate access to the file-mapping object; then when each thread is released, it maps a view onto the file and increments the data.

Listing 4-13: Demonstrating threads that use a memory mapped file to exchange data

```
// project mappings
#include <windows.h>
#include <iostream>

// mutex to arbitrate access
static HANDLE g_hMutexMapping = INVALID_HANDLE_VALUE;

// simple thread to increment the value in the shared memory
static DWORD WINAPI ThreadProc(LPVOID lpParam)
{
    // interpret the param as a handle
    HANDLE hMapping = reinterpret_cast<HANDLE>(lpParam);

    // wait for access to the file
    ::WaitForSingleObject(g_hMutexMapping, INFINITE);

    // map a view
    LPVOID pFile = ::MapViewOfFile(
        hMapping,          // the object holding the file
```

```
                    FILE_MAP_ALL_ACCESS,// gain read and write access
                    0, // begin at the beginning of file (high 32bits)
                    0, // ...(low 32bits)
                    0);// map the entire file
            if(pFile!=NULL)
            {
                // interpret the data as a long
                LONG* pnData = reinterpret_cast<LONG*>(pFile);

                // bump the data
                ++(*pnData);

                // show the new value
                std::cout << "thread: " << ::GetCurrentThreadId()
                    << " value: " << (*pnData) << std::endl;

                // release the view of the file
                ::UnmapViewOfFile(pFile);
                pFile = NULL;
            }

            // release access to the file
            ::ReleaseMutex(g_hMutexMapping);

            return(0);
        }


        // create a shared data space
        HANDLE MakeSharedFile()
        {
            // create a file mapping object
            HANDLE hMapping = ::CreateFileMapping(
                INVALID_HANDLE_VALUE,   // use the pagefile temp file
                NULL,                   // default security
                PAGE_READWRITE,         // read-write access
                0,                      // max size (high 32bits)
                sizeof(LONG),           // ... (low 32bits)
                NULL);                  // anonymous
            if(hMapping!=INVALID_HANDLE_VALUE)
            {
                // create a view onto the file mapping
                LPVOID pData = ::MapViewOfFile(
                    hMapping,           // the object holding the file
                    FILE_MAP_ALL_ACCESS,// gain read and write access
```

```
            0,  // begin at the beginning of file (high 32bits)
            0,  // ...(low 32bits)
            0); // map the entire file
        if(pData!=NULL)
        {
            ::ZeroMemory(pData, sizeof(LONG));
        }

        // close up the file view
        ::UnmapViewOfFile(pData);
    }
    return(hMapping);
}


void main()
{
    // create a data file
    HANDLE hMapping = ::MakeSharedFile();

    // create the arbitrator mutex
    g_hMutexMapping = ::CreateMutex(NULL, FALSE, NULL);

    // create 100 threads to read and write from the file
    for(int nTotal=100; nTotal > 0; --nTotal)
    {
        // start the thread
        HANDLE hThread = ::CreateThread(
            NULL,       // default security
            0,          // default stack
            ThreadProc, // thread fcn
            reinterpret_cast<LPVOID>(hMapping), //
            0,          // no special creation flags
            NULL);      // ignore the thread id

        // wait for the last thread to release
        if(nTotal==1)
        {
            std::cout << "all threads created, waiting..."
                << std::endl;
            ::WaitForSingleObject(hThread, INFINITE);
        }

        // release our handle to the thread
        ::CloseHandle(hThread);
```

```
        hThread = INVALID_HANDLE_VALUE;
    }

    // close up the objects
    ::CloseHandle(hMapping);
    hMapping = INVALID_HANDLE_VALUE;

    ::CloseHandle(g_hMutexMapping);
    g_hMutexMapping = INVALID_HANDLE_VALUE;
}
```

Listing 4-13 begins by creating a small file-mapping object initialized to zero and a mutex to guard its use. Next, the application creates 100 threads that will each follow the same procedure: gain access through the mutex, map a view to the file, treat the first 32 bits as a signed integer, and increment it while showing the new value at the console. Each thread cleans up its view to the file and releases the mutex just before exiting. Once all threads are complete, the application cleans up and exits. The beginning of the program's execution is shown in Figure 4-6.

Figure 4-6: Threads communicating using a memory-mapped file

The program in Listing 4-13 shows you that accessing the data in the memory-mapped file is done with simple C++ pointer operations. This enables you to do something like sort data in a file without needing the overhead of reading it into an array, passing it to the sort method, and writing it back out. The memory-mapped file is the array and the results are written back out when you clean up the view.

You should be able to see how easily this example can be used across processes and not just across threads. Simply naming the mutex and mapping objects, then assigning them security allows each client process to acquire the mutex and modify the data appropriately. This example illustrates how kernel objects enable you to orchestrate work among threads to accomplish a task.

Summary

You have seen the basics of the commonly used kernel objects. You've seen the basic application services objects that are available to add simple value to your application. Further, I showed you how to use the thread synchronization objects to coordinate efforts between threads and even between processes. Finally, you discovered how to use inter-thread communication objects to send data between threads and processes.

In addition to these objects, the kernel provides some other services that you can take advantage of in your applications. I cover memory management in Chapter 12, the file system in Chapter 13, and all of the remaining services in Chapter 15.

Next up for you is some fun stuff: programming with the graphics portions of the Windows 2000 system. This enables you to add some flash to your applications by taking advantage of the wide variety of GUI services available.

Part II

User Interaction

IN THIS PART

Chapter 5

The GDI API

IN THIS CHAPTER

- ◆ GDI API overview
- ◆ Device contexts
- ◆ Handling screen updates in your applications
- ◆ Displaying text on the screen
- ◆ Displaying bitmaps on the screen
- ◆ Regions and paths
- ◆ Clipping regions
- ◆ Enhanced metafiles

THIS CHAPTER REVIEWS some of the basic functionality the Graphics Device Interface (GDI) API provides and covers the new features that Windows 2000 introduces. Windows has introduced many new graphic libraries for specialized operations (for example, DirectX and OpenGL). However, most general Windows applications still use the GDI library to provide output. Almost all of the GDI API calls are included in the GDI.dll, but some of the newer Windows 98 and 2000 APIs have been added to a new DLL, msimg32.dll.

GDI API Overview

The Graphics Device Interface (GDI) API is an API that provides device independent graphic output. Your application makes GDI API calls to display its output on a device, and the GDI layer makes calls to the device driver for that device. This allows your application to concentrate on generating the graphic output.

The GDI layer provides a structure to represent a device, called a device context (DC). When the application needs to display graphic output on a device, it obtains a handle to a device context for that device and calls the GDI API functions using this device context. The device context structure describes the current graphic objects selected to draw on the device context as well as the currently selected graphic modes used to control the graphic output.

The GDI API provides many functions for manipulating and directing output on a device context. These functions provide facilities for displaying text and bitmaps on a device context, creating regions and paths, setting the clipping region, and creating and playing back enhanced metafiles.

Device Contexts

A *device context* is the fundamental structure used by Windows applications to achieve output device independence. Using device contexts, applications do not have to worry about where they direct their output. The device context is intimately aware of the capabilities of the output device's driver and works with it to produce the required output. The device context structure defines the graphic objects and graphic modes that an application uses to draw on the device. Your application never accesses the device context directly but uses the GDI API to manipulate it.

Device context drawing objects and modes

Windows provides seven *graphic objects* that you can select into a device context. Table 5-1 provides a brief description of these objects. I will cover them in more detail later in the chapter. When your application acquires a device context, Windows automatically selects default objects for most of these objects. However, there is no default bitmap and path object. Your application can use these default objects or create new objects and use them by selecting them into a device context using the `SelectObject()` API. If you select an object into a device context, you should restore the default object as soon as you are finished using your object to prevent your application from leaking resources. Once you are finished with an object that you created, free the resources it uses by calling the `DeleteObject()` API. You must ensure that the graphic object is not selected into a device context when you call `DeleteObject()`.

TABLE 5-1 WINDOWS GRAPHIC OBJECTS

Object	Description
Bitmap	Used to manipulate images
Brush	Used to fill the interior of shapes
Palette	Used to manage color
Font	Used to display text
Path	Used to create complex shapes
Pen	Used to draw the outline of shapes

Object	Description
Region	Used to create complex shapes from a combination of rectangle, polygon, and ellipses

Windows also provides *stock graphic objects* that your application can use without you having to create them. You obtain a handle to these object using the `GetStockObject()` API. Once you have a handle to the stock object, you can select it into a device context and use it. You do not have to call the `DeleteObject()` API when using a stock object. Table 5-2 provides a list and description of the stock objects that Windows provides. By using these stock objects, you can reduce the number of graphic objects your application needs to create and manage. You can set the color of the pen and the brush using the `SetDCPenColor()` and `SetDCBrushColor()` APIs respectively.

TABLE 5-2 STOCK OBJECTS

Stock Object	Description
BLACK_BRUSH	A black brush
DKGRAY_BRUSH	A dark gray brush
DC_BRUSH	A solid color brush (new in Windows 2000)
GRAY_BRUSH	A gray brush
HOLLOW_BRUSH	A hollow brush, same as NULL_BRUSH
LTGRAY_BRUSH	A light gray brush
NULL_BRUSH	A Null brush, same as HOLLOW_BRUSH
WHITE_BRUSH	A white brush
BLACK_PEN	A black pen
DC_PEN	A solid color pen (new in Windows 2000)
WHITE_PEN	A white pen
ANSI_FIXED_FONT	A fixed-pitch system font
ANSI_VAR_FONT	A variable-pitch system font
DEVICE_DEFAULT_FONT	Device dependant font (new in Windows 2000)

Continued

TABLE 5-2 STOCK OBJECTS *(continued)*

Stock Object	Description
DEFAULT_GUI_FONT	Default font for menus and dialog boxes
OEM_FIXED_FONT	Original equipment manufacture dependant fixed-pitch font
SYSTEM_FONT	System font, default device context font
SYSTEM_FIXED_FONT	Fixed-pitch system font, used for compatibility with pre-Windows 3.0 applications
DEFAULT_PALETTE	Static system colors

The DC_PEN and the DC_BRUSH stock objects are new to Windows 98 and 2000.

Windows provides structure to represent information about the graphic object for the Bitmap, Pen, Brush, and Font graphic objects. These structures can be retrieved from a handle to the graphic object using the GetObject() API. Table 5-3 shows the corresponding structure for each graphic object.

TABLE 5-3 GRAPHIC OBJECT STRUCTURES

Graphic Objects	Structure
Pen	LOGPEN
Pen created with ExtCreatePen()	EXTLOGPEN
Brush	LOGBRUSH
Font	LOGFONT
Bitmap	BITMAP
Device Independent Bitmap	DIBSECTION

Windows also provides five graphic modes to allow an application to modify how Windows handles certain GDI calls. Table 5-4 lists and describes the graphic modes.

TABLE 5-4 GRAPHIC MODES

Graphic Mode	Description
Background	Tells Windows how to draw the background for text, hatched brushes, and nonsolid lines
Drawing	Tells Windows how to combine pens and brushes with existing pixels
Mapping	Tells Windows the unit of measure for coordinates
Polygon Fill	Tells Windows how to fill the inside of a polygon
Stretching Mode	Tells Windows how to combine a bitmap with existing pixels when stretching a bitmap

The background mode is set using the SetBkMode() API. Windows uses the background mode when displaying text, hatched brushes, and nonsolid lines. There are two background modes. The OPAQUE mode fills the background with the current background color before the graphic is drawn. The TRANSPARENT mode leaves the background unchanged.

The drawing mode is set using the SetROP2() API. The drawing mode specifies how colors from pens and brushes mix with the exiting pixels. There is a drawing mode for every possible logical (AND, OR, and XOR) combination of values.

The mapping mode defines the unit of measure for a device context. To set the mapping mode you use the SetMapMode() API. The default mapping mode is MM_TEXT, in which each device pixel is mapped to a logical pixel, x increases to the right, and y increases down. Other mapping modes include MM_HIENGLISH (0.001 inch), MM_HIMETRIC (0.01 mm), MM_LOENGLISH (0.01 inch), MM_LOMETRIC (0.1 mm), and MM_TWIPS (1/1440 inch). For all of these mapping modes, x increases to the right and y increases up. The remaining two mapping modes — MM_ANISOTROPIC and MM_ISOTROPIC — use arbitrary units and allow an application to define the units, orientation, and scaling.

You can set the polygon fill mode to one of two values using the SetPolyFillMode() API. The ALTERNATE mode fills the area between the odd and even number sides of the polygon. The WINDING mode fills any region with a nonzero winding value. The winding value is determined by the number of times a pen goes around the region.

The stretching mode defines how existing pixels mix with a bitmap. You use the SetStretchBltMode() API to set the mode. Using this API, you can logically AND the color values of the existing pixels with the image pixels using STRETCH_ANDSCANS, OR the values using STRETCH_ORSCANS, eliminate the existing pixels using STRETCH_DELETESCANS, or average the color values using STRETCH_HALFTONE. The STRETCH_ANDSCANS and STRETCH_ORSCANS modes are most useful when using monochrome bitmaps, with the STRETCH_ANDSCANS mode preserving the black pixels and the STRETCH_ORSCANS mode preserving the white pixels. The STRETCH_HALFTONE is much slower and uses more processing time, but generally produces higher quality images. When using this mode, you must call the SetBrushModeEx() API to set the brush origin; otherwise, the brush will be misaligned.

Acquiring a device context

Applications use one of several API calls to acquire a device context for the device to which they wish to direct their output. The application then calls various GDI APIs using the acquired device context. The most common scenario in which an application acquires a device context is in response to a WM_PAINT message. Listing 5-1 shows how an application acquires a device context using the BeginPaint() API call.

Listing 5-1: Acquiring a device context in response to a WM_PAINT message

```
. . .
PAINTSTRUCT ps;
. . .
    case WM_PAINT:
        hdc = BeginPaint(hWnd, &ps);

        // put drawing code here

        EndPaint(hWnd, &ps);
    break;
```

The BeginPaint() API call takes the handle of the window to prepare for printing and a PAINTSTRUCT to fill with information about the painting as input. It returns a display device context handle for the specified window. The PAINTSTRUCT structure contains the device context handle, a flag indicating whether the application needs to erase the background, and the rectangle of the painting region and a couple of system reserved members. BeginPaint() sets the clip region to the invalidated region of the window, and sends a WM_ERASEBKGND message if the update region needs to be erased. Windows uses the clip region to prevent drawing in regions of the window that have not changed. Each call to BeginPaint() needs to match with a call to EndPaint(). EndPaint() is used to signal the operating system that the application is finished painting. You should call the `BeginPaint()` API only in response to the `WM_PAINT` message.

If you need to acquire a display device context for a window outside of a `WM_PAINT` message, you can use the `GetDC()`, `GetDCEx()`, or `GetWindowDC()` API calls. The `GetDC()` API retrieves a display device context for the specified window. `GetDCEx()` enables you to control how the clipping is applied to the window. The `GetWindowDC()` API returns a device context for the entire window – not just the client area. This enables you to modify the non-client area of a window.

For Windows 2000 and Window 98, if you specify a `NULL` window handle for these functions, Windows returns a device context for the primary display monitor.

Drawing on a device context

Once your application acquires a device context, you can begin drawing on it using the GDI API. Listing 5-2 draws a rectangle in the middle of the client area of the application's window. It is outlined with a three-pixel-wide blue pen and filled with a red brush. Figure 5-1 shows the output from this listing.

Figure 5-1: Drawing a rectangle on the device context

Listing 5-2: Drawing a rectangle on the device context

```
//
// OnPaint:  handles the painting for the window
//
void OnPaint(HWND hWnd)
{
    // Begin painting
    PAINTSTRUCT ps;
    HDC hDC = BeginPaint(hWnd, &ps);

    // get the client window's rectangle
    RECT rectClient;
    GetClientRect(hWnd, &rectClient);
```

```
// create a blue pen and a red brush
HPEN hPenRect = CreatePen(PS_SOLID, 3, RGB(0, 0, 255));
HBRUSH hBrushRect = CreateSolidBrush(RGB(255, 0, 0));

// select the pen and brush
HPEN hPenOld = (HPEN)SelectObject(hDC, hPenRect);
HBRUSH hBrushOld = (HBRUSH)SelectObject(hDC, hBrushRect);

// find the center of the client window
int xCenter = rectClient.right / 2;
int yCenter = rectClient.bottom / 2;

// draw a 100 x 100 pixel rectangle
RECT rectPen;
rectPen.left = xCenter - 50;
rectPen.right = xCenter + 50;
rectPen.top = yCenter - 50;
rectPen.bottom = yCenter + 50;
Rectangle(hDC, rectPen.left, rectPen.top,
    rectPen.right, rectPen.bottom);

// restore the dc to its original state
SelectObject(hDC, hBrushOld);
SelectObject(hDC, hPenOld);

// clean up created objects
DeleteObject(hBrushRect);
DeleteObject(hPenRect);

EndPaint(hWnd, &ps);
}
```

To begin painting, the OnPaint() function calls the BeginPaint() API to acquire a device context for the window. Then it creates a blue pen, three pixels wide, and a solid red brush. After these drawing objects are created, the OnPaint() function selects them into the device context and saves the previous objects to restore later. Then it calculates the position of the rectangle based on the client area of the window and calls the Rectangle() GDI API to draw the rectangle. When finished drawing, the original pen and brush are restored in the device context. It is important to make sure that any object that you create is not selected into a device context when you clean up the object because this leads to resource leaks. After the OnPaint() function selects the original objects, it cleans up the pen and brush it created. Finally, the OnPaint() function calls the EndPaint() API to finish the drawing.

Handling Screen Updates in Your Application

An application should do as much drawing as it can in response to the WM_PAINT message. This allows Windows to handle screen updates efficiently. Windows maintains an update region for each window in the system. It accumulates the invalid region for each window and generates a WM_PAINT message when no other messages exist for the window. This allows your application to remain responsive to user input while enabling it to process multiple screen updates at once. You can draw at other times; however, if you do, it prevents Windows from performing this optimization and can lead to sluggish screen updates.

You can manage the update region for your window by using the InvalidateRect(), InvalidateRgn(), ValidateRect(), and ValidateRgn() API calls. To instruct Windows that an area of your application needs painting, use the InvalidateRect() and InvalidateRgn() APIs. If you need to remove an area from the update region – for example, if your application has updated the screen already – use the ValidateRect() and ValidateRgn() APIs.

Usually an application waits to receive a WM_PAINT message when the system posts the message to the applications message queue. However, if you need to update the screen immediately, you can call either the UpdateWindow() or RedrawWindow() API. Both of these APIs send a WM_PAINT message directly to the window specified, bypassing the application queue. You should use these APIs carefully, since it can affect your application's responsiveness to user input dramatically. The RedrawWindow() allows your application more flexibility in updating the window; it enables you to specify either an update rectangle or region, as well as flags that control how the window is updated.

Displaying Text on the Screen

Applications must display text on the screen frequently. The GDI API provides almost 50 functions to work with fonts and text. However, most applications typically use a small subset of these functions. In order to display text on the screen, the application first has to create a font object to display the text and then select it into a device context.

You can create four different types of fonts in an application. You can create *raster, vector, TrueType,* or *OpenType* fonts. Each of these types of fonts differs in the way they store glyph definitions for their characters. A *raster* font stores its glyph definitions as bitmaps, while a *vector* font stores its glyph definitions as a series of line segments. A *TrueType* font stores its glyph definitions as a series of line and curve commands. In addition, TrueType fonts store a collection of hints that the system uses to provide smooth scaling. An *OpenType* font is the same as a

TrueType font except that it allows for *PostScript glyph definitions* in addition to *TrueType glyph definitions.* OpenType fonts are new in Windows 2000.

You can use either the `CreateFont()`, the `CreateFontIndirect()`, or the `CreateFontIndirectEx()` API to create a font. The `CreateFont()` and `CreateFontIndirect()` APIs use the same information to create a font, they just receive the information a different way. The `CreateFontIndirect()` API takes a pointer to a `LOGFONT` structure that describes the characteristics of the font, while the `CreateFont()` API receives these characteristics as individual parameters. The `CreateFontIndirectEx()` API is new to Windows 2000. This API permits an application to create OpenType fonts.

An OpenType font is the same as a TrueType font except that it allows for PostScript glyph definitions in addition to TrueType glyph definitions.

After the application creates the font and selects it into a device context, it can display the text using one of the six text output functions. Table 5-5 lists and describes these output functions.

 For more information on these functions, refer to the MSDN.

TABLE 5-5 TEXT OUTPUT API FUNCTIONS

Text Output API	Description
DrawText	Draws formatted text in a specific rectangle
DrawTextEx	Draws formatted text in a specific rectangle and extends `DrawText` by providing a pointer to a DRAWTEXTPARAMS structure that enables you to specify the tab size, the left and right margins, and returns the number characters drawn
TabbedTextOut	Draws formatted text, expanding tabs to specified locations
TextOut	Draws text at a specified location
ExtTextOut	Draws text at a specified location, optionally specifying clipping regions, and styles
PolyTextOut	Draws multiple strings at once

Listing 5-3 shows how to create a font and display a text string on the screen. This function creates an Arial font and draws a bounding rectangle around the text. Figure 5-2 shows the output from this function.

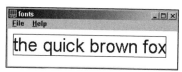

Figure 5-2: Creating a font and displaying text on the screen

Listing 5-3: Creating a font object and displaying text on the screen

```
//
// OnPaint:  handles the painting for the window
//
void OnPaint(HWND hWnd)
{
    // Begin painting
    PAINTSTRUCT ps;
    HDC hDC = BeginPaint(hWnd, &ps);

    // set the background mode to transparent
    SetBkMode(hDC, TRANSPARENT);

    // create a font
    LOGFONT lf;
    memset(&lf, 0x00, sizeof(lf));

    // lf.lfHeight is negative because I want to use character
    // height, not the cell height
    lf.lfHeight = -36;
    strncpy(lf.lfFaceName, _T("Arial"), 32);
    lf.lfWeight = FW_NORMAL;
    HFONT hFont = CreateFontIndirect(&lf);

    HFONT hFontOld = (HFONT)SelectObject(hDC, hFont);

    TCHAR szText[] = _T("the quick brown fox");
    RECT rectDraw;

    // get the extent of the text and draw a rectangle
    // to place the text in
    SIZE size;
    GetTextExtentPoint32(hDC, szText, strlen(szText), &size);
```

```
rectDraw.left = 10;
rectDraw.top = 10;
rectDraw.right = rectDraw.left + size.cx;
rectDraw.bottom = rectDraw.top + size.cy;

Rectangle(hDC, rectDraw.left, rectDraw.top,
    rectDraw.right, rectDraw.bottom);

// set the text color to blue
SetTextColor(hDC, RGB(0,0,255));

// display the text in the rectangle
DrawText(hDC, szText, -1, &rectDraw, DT_LEFT);

SelectObject(hDC, hFontOld);

EndPaint(hWnd, &ps);
}
```

The `OnPaint()` function first acquires a device context for the main window. After obtaining the device context, it sets the background mode to TRANSPARENT to prevent the text from overwriting the rectangle. A font object is created using the `CreateFontIndirect()` API and then selected into the device context. The size of the rectangle required to display the text is calculated using the `GetText-ExtentPoint32()` API. The function then draws a rectangle using this rectangle outlined with the default pen and filled with the default brush. The text color is set to blue and the text is drawn using the `DrawText()` API.

Displaying Bitmaps on the Screen

Another task that applications have to perform frequently is displaying a bitmap on the screen. You may think that you can select a bitmap into a device context and call an API such as `DrawBitmap()` to display the bitmap. Unfortunately, there is no `DrawBitmap()` API. Instead, you have to use APIs such as `BitBlt()`, `StretchBlt()`, or similar functions. These APIs copy bits from one device context to another. Listing 5-4 shows the painting code for displaying a bitmap centered in the client area of the window. Figure 5-3 shows the results of the function.

Figure 5-3: Displaying a bitmap in the client area of a window

Listing 5-4: Displaying a bitmap in the client area of the window

```
//
// OnPaint:  handles the painting for the window
//
void OnPaint(HWND hWnd)
{
    PAINTSTRUCT ps;

    HDC hDC = BeginPaint(hWnd, &ps);

    // create a compatible memory dc
    HDC hDCMem = CreateCompatibleDC(hDC);

    // load the bitmap
    HBITMAP hBitmap = LoadBitmap(
        hInst, MAKEINTRESOURCE(IDB_BITMAP));

    // set the bitmap into the memory dc
    HBITMAP hBitmapOld = (HBITMAP)SelectObject(hDCMem, hBitmap);

    // get the dimension of the bitmap so we can center
    // it in the window
    BITMAP bitmap;
```

```
GetObject(hBitmap, sizeof(bitmap), &bitmap);

RECT rectClient;
GetClientRect(hWnd, &rectClient);

int nLeft = (rectClient.right / 2) - (bitmap.bmWidth / 2);
int nTop = (rectClient.bottom / 2) - (bitmap.bmHeight / 2);

// display the bitmap
BitBlt(hDC, nLeft, nTop, bitmap.bmWidth, bitmap.bmHeight,
    hDCMem, 0, 0, SRCCOPY);

SelectObject(hDCMem, hBitmapOld);

EndPaint(hWnd, &ps);
}
```

First, the `OnPaint()` function gets the device context for the window by calling the `BeginPaint()` API. It then creates a memory device context compatible with the window's device context using the `CreateCompatibleDC()` API. The bitmap is loaded from the applications resources into the device context. It then calculates where to display the bitmap based on the dimensions of the bitmap and the size of the client area. The `GetObject()` API returns information about the GDI object specified; the type of information returned depends on the GDI object. Then the `BitBlt()` API is used to display the bitmap starting at the coordinates specified. By default, bitmaps are displayed in their original sizes. If you want to scale the bitmap to fit in a specified rectangle, you can use the `StretchBlt()` API. When using the `StretchBlt()` API or similar APIs, the stretching mode of the device context is used to determine how the existing pixels should merge with the pixels from the bitmap.

Windows 2000 and Windows 98 provide two new APIs to help in displaying transparent bitmaps. Transparent bitmaps allow the background to show through parts of the bitmap. The `TransparentBlt()` API enables you to display a bitmap treating all of the bits with the specified color as transparent. The `AlphaBlend()` API enables you to display alpha bitmaps with semitransparent and transparent pixels. An alpha bitmap has an alpha channel in addition to the normal red, green, and blue channels. This channel represents the transparency level of the pixel—usually the alpha channel has the same depth as the color channels.

The code in Listing 5-5 uses the code from Listing 5-4 to display a background bitmap, and then it displays a transparent bitmap over the top. The transparent bitmap consists of a black rectangle filled with transparent pixels, which allows the background bitmap to show through.

Figure 5-4: Displaying a background bitmap and a transparent bitmap

Listing 5-5: Displaying a background bitmap and a transparent bitmap

```
//
// OnPaint:  handles the painting for the window
//
void OnPaint(HWND hWnd)
{
    PAINTSTRUCT ps;
    HBITMAP hBitmapOld(NULL);

    HDC hDC = BeginPaint(hWnd, &ps);

    // get the client rect
    RECT rectClient;
    GetClientRect(hWnd, &rectClient);

    // create a compatible memory dc
    HDC hDCMem = CreateCompatibleDC(hDC);

    //
    // draw the background image in the middle of the screen
    //

    // load the background bitmap
    HBITMAP hBitmapBackground = LoadBitmap(
        hInst, MAKEINTRESOURCE(IDB_BACKGROUNDBITMAP));
```

```
// select the bitmap into the memory dc
hBitmapOld = (HBITMAP)SelectObject(
    hDCMem, hBitmapBackground);

// get the dimension of the bitmap so we can center
// it in the window
BITMAP bitmapBackground;
GetObject(hBitmapBackground,
    sizeof(bitmapBackground), &bitmapBackground);

int nLeftBackground =
    (rectClient.right / 2) - (bitmapBackground.bmWidth / 2);
int nTopBackground =
    (rectClient.bottom / 2) - (bitmapBackground.bmHeight / 2);

// draw the background bitmap
BitBlt(hDC, nLeftBackground, nTopBackground,
    bitmapBackground.bmWidth, bitmapBackground.bmHeight,
    hDCMem, 0, 0, SRCCOPY);

//
// Draw a transparent bitmap over the background bitmap
//

// load the transparent bitmap
HBITMAP hBitmapTransparent = LoadBitmap(
    hInst, MAKEINTRESOURCE(IDB_TRANSPARENT));

// select the transparent bitmap into the memory dc
SelectObject(hDCMem, hBitmapTransparent);

// get the dimension of the bitmap so we can center
// it in the window
BITMAP bitmapTransparent;
GetObject(hBitmapTransparent,
    sizeof(bitmapTransparent), &bitmapTransparent);

int nLeft =
    (rectClient.right / 2) - (bitmapTransparent.bmWidth / 2);
int nTop =
    (rectClient.bottom / 2) - (bitmapTransparent.bmHeight / 2);

// draw the transparent bitmap
TransparentBlt(hDC, nLeft, nTop,
```

```
                bitmapTransparent.bmWidth, bitmapTransparent.bmHeight,
                hDCMem, 0, 0,
                bitmapTransparent.bmWidth, bitmapTransparent.bmHeight,
                RGB(0,0,255));

        // Select the old bitmap
        SelectObject(hDCMem, hBitmapOld);

        DeleteObject(hBitmapBackground);
        DeleteObject(hBitmapTransparent);

        EndPaint(hWnd, &ps);
}
```

The code first draws the background bitmap using code similar to that of Listing 5-4. It then loads and selects the transparent bitmap into the memory DC. Then the code centers the transparent bitmap and calls the `TransparentBlt()` API with the transparent color set to the color of the transparent pixels in the bitmap (blue in this case). Unlike the `BitBlt()` API, the `TransparentBlt()` API enables you to scale the bitmap to fit within a specified rectangle. The `SetStretchBltMode()` API can be used to set the stretch mode; however, the `TransparentBlt()` API does not support the `STRETCH_ANDSCANS` and `STRETCH_ORSCANS` modes; they are converted to the `STRETCH_DELETESCANS` mode if they are specified.

Regions and Paths

Regions and *paths* allow an application to create, manipulate, and display complicated shapes. The GDI API provides several functions for creating and manipulating regions and paths. You generally use regions to define nonrectangular shapes for clipping, hit testing, or painting. You can use paths to define irregular shapes for filling, outlining, or creating a complicated clipping region. Paths can be used to generate more complicated shapes than regions; however, they are limited in the operations that you may perform on them. You can convert a path to a region using the `PathToRegion()` API. This API enables you to perform region operations on a path.

Creating regions

The application in Listing 5-6 shows how to create polygon regions. It also shows how to perform hit testing within a region. When the user clicks the left mouse button, the `OnLButtonDown()` function is called, which tests if the click was within a region; if it was, then the function inverts the region. Figure 5-5 shows the output from the application.

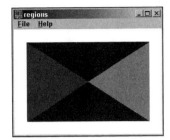

Figure 5-5: Creating polygon regions and performing hit testing

Listing 5-6: Creating polygon regions and performing hit testing

```cpp
// regions.cpp : Defines the entry point for the application.
//

#include "stdafx.h"
#include "resource.h"

#define MAX_LOADSTRING 100

// Global Variables:

...

HRGN g_hRegion1 = NULL;
HRGN g_hRegion2 = NULL;
HRGN g_hRegion3 = NULL;

HBRUSH g_hBrushRed = NULL;
HBRUSH g_hBrushGreen = NULL;
HBRUSH g_hBrushBlue = NULL;

...

//
// InitInstance: creates the window
//
BOOL InitInstance(HINSTANCE hInstance, int nCmdShow)
{
    BOOL bReturn(FALSE);
    HWND hWnd;

    // Store instance handle in our global variable
    hInst = hInstance;
```

```
        hWnd = CreateWindow(szWindowClass, szTitle, WS_OVERLAPPEDWINDOW,
            CW_USEDEFAULT, 0, CW_USEDEFAULT, 0, NULL, NULL, hInstance,
            NULL);
        if (hWnd)
        {
            // create the brushes
            g_hBrushRed = CreateSolidBrush(RGB(255,0,0));
            g_hBrushGreen = CreateSolidBrush(RGB(0,255,0));
            g_hBrushBlue = CreateSolidBrush(RGB(0,0,255));

            ShowWindow(hWnd, nCmdShow);
            UpdateWindow(hWnd);
            bReturn = TRUE;
        }

    return bReturn;
}


//
// ExitInstance: cleans up the resources created
//
void ExitInstance()
{
    // delete the brushes
    DeleteObject(g_hBrushRed);
    DeleteObject(g_hBrushGreen);
    DeleteObject(g_hBrushBlue);

    // delete the regions
    DeleteObject(g_hRegion1);
    DeleteObject(g_hRegion2);
    DeleteObject(g_hRegion3);
}


//
// OnPaint:  handles the painting for the window
//
void OnPaint(HWND hWnd)
{
    PAINTSTRUCT ps;

    HDC hDC = BeginPaint(hWnd, &ps);

    // fill the regions with the brushes
    FillRgn(hDC, g_hRegion1, g_hBrushRed);
```

```
        FillRgn(hDC, g_hRegion2, g_hBrushGreen);
        FillRgn(hDC, g_hRegion3, g_hBrushBlue);

        EndPaint(hWnd, &ps);
}


//
// UpdatesRegions: called to create regions based on the
//  size of the client area
//
BOOL UpdateRegions(HWND hWnd)
{
    BOOL bReturn(TRUE);

    // delete the regions if they already exist
    if (g_hRegion1 != NULL)
    {
        DeleteObject(g_hRegion1);
        g_hRegion1 = NULL;
    }

    if (g_hRegion2 != NULL)
    {
        DeleteObject(g_hRegion2);
        g_hRegion2 = NULL;
    }

    if (g_hRegion3 != NULL)
    {
        DeleteObject(g_hRegion3);
        g_hRegion3 = NULL;
    }

    // calculate the size and position of the rectangle
    RECT rectClient;
    GetClientRect(hWnd, &rectClient);
    InflateRect(&rectClient, -25, -25);

    int xCenter =
        ((rectClient.right - rectClient.left) / 2)
            + rectClient.left;
    int yCenter =
        ((rectClient.bottom - rectClient.top) / 2)
            + rectClient.top;
```

```
// create the regions
POINT arPoints[6];
int arPolyPoints[2];

// create a triangular region from the top, left to
// the center point and then to the left, bottom
arPoints[0].x = rectClient.left;
arPoints[0].y = rectClient.top;
arPoints[1].x = xCenter;
arPoints[1].y = yCenter;
arPoints[2].x = rectClient.left;
arPoints[2].y = rectClient.bottom;
g_hRegion1 = CreatePolygonRgn(arPoints, 3, ALTERNATE);
if (g_hRegion1 != NULL)
{
    // invalidate the region
    InvalidateRgn(hWnd, g_hRegion1, FALSE);
}

// create a triangular region from the right, left to
// the center point and then to the right, bottom
arPoints[0].x = rectClient.right;
arPoints[0].y = rectClient.top;
arPoints[1].x = xCenter;
arPoints[1].y = yCenter;
arPoints[2].x = rectClient.right;
arPoints[2].y = rectClient.bottom;
g_hRegion2 = CreatePolygonRgn(
    arPoints, 3, ALTERNATE);
if (g_hRegion2 != NULL)
{
    // invalidate the region
    InvalidateRgn(hWnd, g_hRegion2, FALSE);
}

// create a region, consisting of two triangular regions
// from the top and bottom of the rectangle
arPoints[0].x = rectClient.left;
arPoints[0].y = rectClient.top;
arPoints[1].x = xCenter;
arPoints[1].y = yCenter;
arPoints[2].x = rectClient.right;
arPoints[2].y = rectClient.top;
arPoints[3].x = rectClient.left;
arPoints[3].y = rectClient.bottom;
```

```
        arPoints[4].x = xCenter;
        arPoints[4].y = yCenter;
        arPoints[5].x = rectClient.right;
        arPoints[5].y = rectClient.bottom;

        arPolyPoints[0] = 3;
        arPolyPoints[1] = 3;
        g_hRegion3 = CreatePolyPolygonRgn(
            arPoints, arPolyPoints, 2, ALTERNATE);
        if (g_hRegion3 != NULL)
        {
            // invalidate the region
            InvalidateRgn(hWnd, g_hRegion3, FALSE);
        }

        return bReturn;
    }


    //
    // OnLButtonDown: inverts a region if the mouse is
    //   clicked within the region
    //
    void OnLButtonDown(HWND hWnd, POINT& pt)
    {
        HRGN hRegion(NULL);

        // find which region if any the mouse was
        //   clicked in
        if (PtInRegion(g_hRegion1, pt.x, pt.y))
        {
            hRegion = g_hRegion1;
        }
        else if (PtInRegion(g_hRegion2, pt.x, pt.y))
        {
            hRegion = g_hRegion2;
        }
        else if (PtInRegion(g_hRegion3, pt.x, pt.y))
        {
            hRegion = g_hRegion3;
        }

        // invert the region
        if (hRegion != NULL)
        {
            HDC hDC = GetDC(hWnd);
```

```
        InvertRgn(hDC, hRegion);
        ReleaseDC(hWnd, hDC);
    }
}
```

The application creates the red, green, and blue brushes that it will use in the
InitInstance() function and cleans up the brushes and regions that are created
by the application in the ExitInstance() function.

The application calls the UpdateRegions() function in response to the WM_SIZE
message. UpdateRegions() first deletes any existing regions. Then it calculates a
rectangle just inside of the main window and calculates the center of the rectangle.
UpdateRegions() uses these coordinates to divide the area into three regions. First
UpdateRegions() calls the CreatePolygonRgn() API twice to create two triangular regions. The first region starts from the top, left of the rectangle, moving to the
center of the rectangle, and then to the bottom, left. The second region starts at the
top, right of the rectangle, moves to the center, and then to the bottom, right. The
CreatePolygonRgn() API takes the array of points, the number of elements in the
array, and the polygon fill mode to use. UpdateRegions() then calls the
CreatePolyPolygon() API to create a region consisting of two triangular areas,
starting from the top, left of the rectangle moving to the center, then to the top,
right and moving to the bottom, left of the rectangle, moving to the center, then to
the bottom right.

The OnPaint() function fills the three regions created by the UpdateRegions()
function. The OnLButtonDown() function is called to process the WM_LBUTTONDOWN
message. It determines which region the user clicks using the PtInRegion() API. If
the user clicks a region, the function inverts the region using the InvertRgn() API.

Creating paths

The code in Listing 5-7 shows how to create, outline, and fill a path. The
DefinePath() function creates a path consisting of two ellipses, one just inside of
the other. The OnPaint() function then outlines and fills this path. Figure 5-6
shows the resulting output from these functions.

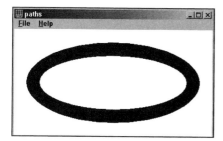

Figure 5-6: Creating, outlining, and filling a path

Listing 5-7: Creating, outlining, and filling a path

```
//
//  DefinePath: defines a path consisting of an ellipse
//       within an ellipse
//
BOOL DefinePath(HWND hWnd, HDC hDC)
{
    BOOL bReturn(FALSE);

    // begin the path
    bReturn = BeginPath(hDC);
    if (bReturn)
    {
        // get the client rect
        RECT rectClient;
        GetClientRect(hWnd, &rectClient);

        // create an ellipse 25 x 25 inside the client area
        InflateRect(&rectClient, -25, -25);
        Ellipse(hDC, rectClient.left, rectClient.top,
            rectClient.right, rectClient.bottom);

        // deflate the rect 25 x 25 and draw another ellipse
        InflateRect(&rectClient, -25, -25);
        Ellipse(hDC, rectClient.left, rectClient.top,
            rectClient.right, rectClient.bottom);

        // end the path
        EndPath(hDC);
    }

    return bReturn;
}

//
// OnPaint:  handles the painting for the window
//
void OnPaint(HWND hWnd)
{
    PAINTSTRUCT ps;
    HDC hDC = BeginPaint(hWnd, &ps);

    // define a path
    DefinePath(hWnd, hDC);
```

```
// get the stock objects
HPEN hPen = (HPEN)GetStockObject(DC_PEN);
HBRUSH hBrush = (HBRUSH)GetStockObject(DC_BRUSH);

// set the default pen and brush color
SetDCPenColor(hDC, RGB(0,0,0));
SetDCBrushColor(hDC, RGB(0,0,255));

// select the pen and brush
HPEN hPenOld = (HPEN)SelectObject(hDC, hPen);
HBRUSH hBrushOld = (HBRUSH)SelectObject(hDC, hBrush);

// fill the path
StrokeAndFillPath(hDC);

// restore the old objects
SelectObject(hDC, hPenOld);
SelectObject(hDC, hBrushOld);

EndPaint(hWnd, &ps);
}
```

The DefinePath() function defines a path by first calling the BeginPath() API to open a path bracket. After the path is open, use the GDI API to define a path. Table 5-6 lists the APIs you can use to define a path.

TABLE 5-6 GDI APIS YOU CAN USE TO DEFINE A PATH

GDI API	Description
MoveToEx()	Moves the current position to the specified point and returns the previous point.
LineTo()	Draws a line from the current position up to the specified point.
Polyline()	Draws a series of lines, by connecting a series of points.
PolylineTo()	Draws multiple lines using the specified array of points.
PolyPolyline()	Draws multiple series of lines connecting a series of points.
Rectangle()	Draws a rectangle at the specified coordinates.
RoundRect()	Draws a rectangle with rounded corners at the specified coordinates.

Continued

TABLE 5-6 GDI APIS YOU CAN USE TO DEFINE A PATH *(continued)*

GDI API	Description
Ellipse()	Draws an ellipse centered around the specified coordinates.
Polygon()	Draws a polygon using the specified array of points.
PolyPolygon()	Draws a series of polygons using the specified array of points and number of points in each polygon.
TextOut()	Draws text at the specified point.
ExtTextOut()	Draws text in a specified rectangle.
Arc()	Draws an arc, at the specified rectangle and two radial points.
ArcTo()	Draws an arc and updates the current position.
AngleArc()	Draws a line segment and an arc. The line is drawn from the current position to the beginning of an arc. The arc is drawn around the specified center point and radius, the length of the arc is specified by the start angle and sweep angle.
Pie()	Draws a pie-shaped wedge specified by the intersection of a rectangle and two radial points.
Chord()	Draws a region created by the intersection of an ellipse and a line.
PolyBezier()	Draws multiple Bezier curves using the specified array of end and control points.
PolyBezierTo()	Draws multiple Bezier curves and updates the current position.
PolyDraw()	Draws a set of lines and Bezier curves using the specified array of points and array of end and control points.
CloseFigure()	Closes an open figure in a path.

After the path is opened, the function adds two ellipses to the path using the Ellipse() API and then calls the EndPath() API to close the path and select the path into the device context.

The OnPaint() function calls the DefinePath() function to create the path and select it into the device context. It then obtains the stock DC_BRUSH and DC_PEN objects using the GetStockObject() API. Then it sets the color of these objects using the SetDCPenColor() and SetDCBrushColor() APIs, and selects these objects into the device context. Finally, it uses these objects to outline and fill the path using the StrokeAndFillPath() API.

Clipping Regions

Regions and paths are often used to clip the display area. Your application can select a *clipping region* or *clipping path* to restrict the area that is available to display output. When you specify a clipping region or path, Windows prevents any areas outside of this area from being overwritten. This enables you to simplify your drawing logic, because you don't without Windows actually updating the screen. However, you want to be careful, because you do not want to waste time drawing objects that lie completely outside of the clipping region. You can use the RectVisible() and PtVisible() API functions to determine if any part of an object lies within the clipping area of a window.

Windows keeps track of the invalid area for a window and when you call the BeginPaint() API, the device text already contains a rectangular clipping region representing the invalid area. Listing 5-8 uses the code from Listing 5-5, the TransparentBlt() API example, but creates a clipping region the size and position of the transparent bitmap. Figure 5-7 shows the output from this listing.

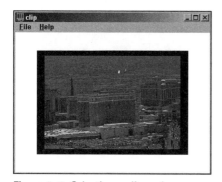

Figure 5-7: Selecting a clip region

Listing 5-8: Selecting a clip region

```
//
// OnPaint:  handles the painting for the window
//
void OnPaint(HWND hWnd)
{
    PAINTSTRUCT ps;
    HBITMAP hBitmapOld(NULL);

    HDC hDC = BeginPaint(hWnd, &ps);

    // get the client rect
    RECT rectClient;
```

```
GetClientRect(hWnd, &rectClient);

// load the transparent bitmap
HBITMAP hBitmapTransparent = LoadBitmap(
    hInst, MAKEINTRESOURCE(IDB_TRANSPARENT));

// get the dimension of the transparent bitmap so we can
// center the window and create a clipping region
BITMAP bitmapTransparent;
GetObject(hBitmapTransparent,
    sizeof(bitmapTransparent), &bitmapTransparent);

int nLeft =
    (rectClient.right / 2) - (bitmapTransparent.bmWidth / 2);
int nTop =
    (rectClient.bottom / 2) - (bitmapTransparent.bmHeight / 2);

// set the clipping region to the size and position of the
//  transparent bitmap
HRGN hrgnClip = CreateRectRgn(
    nLeft, nTop,
    nLeft + bitmapTransparent.bmWidth,
    nTop + bitmapTransparent.bmHeight);

// select the clip region
SelectClipRgn(hDC, hrgnClip);

// delete the region
DeleteObject(hrgnClip);

// create a compatible memory dc
HDC hDCMem = CreateCompatibleDC(hDC);

//
// draw the background image in the middle of the screen
//

...

//
// Draw a transparent bitmap over the background bitmap
//

...
```

```
    EndPaint(hWnd, &ps);
}
```

After acquiring the DC using the BeginPaint() API, the application loads the transparent bitmap so that it can calculate the size and position of the clipping region. It then creates a rectangular region using the CreateRectRgn() API and uses the SelectClipRgn() API to select the region into the DC. The SelectClipRgn() API makes a copy of the region, so after selecting the clipping region, the function frees the region. The remainder of the code is the same as Listing 5-5.

Listing 5-9 uses the code from Listing 5-7 to define a path and then uses the SelectClipPath() API to select the current path as the clipping region and display a bitmap clipped to the path (also see Figure 5-8).

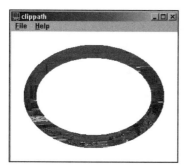

Figure 5-8: Selecting a path for a clipping region

Listing 5-9: Selecting a path for a clipping region

```
//
// OnPaint:  handles the painting for the window
//
void OnPaint(HWND hWnd)
{
    // make sure our clipping region is large enough to set
    // our clipping area since an application cannot grow
    // a clipping area using SelectClipPath or SelectClipRgn
    RECT rectClient;
    GetClientRect(hWnd, &rectClient);

    InflateRect(&rectClient, -25, -25);
    InvalidateRect(hWnd, &rectClient, FALSE);

    PAINTSTRUCT ps;
    HDC hDC = BeginPaint(hWnd, &ps);
```

```
// select clip path
DefinePath(hWnd, hDC);
SelectClipPath(hDC, RGN_COPY);

// load the bitmap
HBITMAP hBitmap = LoadBitmap(
    hInst, MAKEINTRESOURCE(IDB_BITMAP));

// create a compatible memory dc
HDC hDCMem = CreateCompatibleDC(hDC);

// set the bitamp into the memory dc
HBITMAP hBitmapOld = (HBITMAP)SelectObject(hDCMem, hBitmap);

// get the dimension of the bitmap so we can center
// it in the window
BITMAP bitmap;
GetObject(hBitmap, sizeof(bitmap), &bitmap);

int nLeft = (rectClient.right / 2) - (bitmap.bmWidth / 2);
int nTop =  (rectClient.bottom / 2) - (bitmap.bmHeight / 2);

// display the bitmap
BitBlt(hDC, nLeft, nTop, bitmap.bmWidth, bitmap.bmHeight,
    hDCMem, 0, 0, SRCCOPY);

SelectObject(hDCMem, hBitmapOld);

EndPaint(hWnd, &ps);
}
```

The OnPaint() function first ensures that the clipping region is large enough to accommodate the clipping region we are going to set. An application cannot use SelectClipRgn() and SelectClipPath() to increase the size of the clipping region after calling BeginPaint(). You must do this before calling the BeginPaint() API since BeginPaint() sets the clipping region, and calling the InvalidateRect() API between the BeginPaint and EndPaint() calls will cause another WM_PAINT message to be sent.

After the invalid region is updated, the function calls the BeginPaint() API to acquire the device context. Then it calls the DefinePath() function to define a path and uses the SelectClipPath() API to select the path as the clipping area. The DefinePath() function is identical to the DefinePath() function in Listing 5-7. The SelectClipPath() API uses the path selected into the device context and combines it with the current clipping region. The clipping mode parameter controls how the path is combined with the current region. Table 5-7 shows the possible values for the clipping mode parameter and describes the resulting clipping region.

TABLE 5-7 CLIPPING MODES FOR THE SELECTCLIPPATH() API

Clipping Mode	Resulting Clipping Region
RGN_AND	The intersection between the current clipping region and the current path
RGN_COPY	The current path
RGN_DIFF	The current clipping region with the areas of the path excluded
RGN_OR	The union of the current clipping region and the current path
RGN_XOR	The union of the current clipping region and the current path excluding overlapping areas

Enhanced Metafiles

Enhanced metafiles provide a standard, device-independent way to display an image. They consist of a series of variable-length metafile records. The first records describe the characteristics of the device where the metafile was created. The remaining records describe the GDI calls that make up the metafile image. Because these records are standardized, Win32 applications can exchange metafiles. After an application acquires a metafile handle, it can play back the entire metafile to an output device using the PlayEnhMetafile() API or it can go through the metafile records one at a time using the EnumEnhMetaFile() API.

For more information on using enhanced metafiles in your application, refer to the MSDN.

Listing 5-10 shows how to create a metafile and play it back using the PlayEnhMetafile() API. It creates a metafile consisting of an ellipse with a dark gray border, filled with a light gray brush and framed with a rectangle drawn with a dotted red pen. Figure 5-9 shows the results of the playback of the metafile.

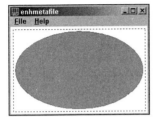

Figure 5-9: Creating and displaying an enhanced metafile

Listing 5-10: Creating and displaying an enhanced metafile

```
//
// InitInstance: creates the window
//
BOOL InitInstance(HINSTANCE hInstance, int nCmdShow)
{
    BOOL bReturn(FALSE);

    // Store instance handle in our global variable
    hInst = hInstance;

    HWND hWnd = CreateWindow(szWindowClass, szTitle,
        WS_OVERLAPPEDWINDOW, CW_USEDEFAULT, 0, CW_USEDEFAULT,
        0, NULL, NULL, hInstance, NULL);
    if (hWnd)
    {
        g_hMetaFile = CreateEnhMetaFile(hWnd);

        ShowWindow(hWnd, nCmdShow);
        UpdateWindow(hWnd);
        bReturn = TRUE;
    }

    return bReturn;
}


//
// ExitInstance: cleans up the resources created
//
void ExitInstance()
{
    if (g_hMetaFile != NULL)
    {
        DeleteEnhMetaFile(g_hMetaFile);
```

```
    }
}

//
//   CreateEnhMetaFile: creates a metafile
//
HENHMETAFILE CreateEnhMetaFile(HWND hWnd)
{
    HENHMETAFILE hMetaFile(NULL);

    // get a dc for the window
    HDC hDC = GetDC(hWnd);

    // set the mapping mode to himetric since metafiles
    // are created in .01 mm units
    int mapmodeOld = SetMapMode(hDC, MM_HIMETRIC);

    // get the client rect and convert to logical units
    RECT rectClientDC;
    GetClientRect(hWnd, &rectClientDC);
    DPtoLP(hDC, (LPPOINT)&rectClientDC, 2);

    // normalize rect, the bottom coordinate will be negative
    // in the himetric mapping mode
    rectClientDC.bottom *= -1;

    // restore the mapping mode
    SetMapMode(hDC, mapmodeOld);

    // create the enhanced metafile
    HDC hDCMeta = CreateEnhMetaFile(hDC, NULL, &rectClientDC, NULL);
    if (hDCMeta != NULL)
    {
        // get the metafile client window
        RECT rectClientMeta;
        GetClientRect(hWnd, &rectClientMeta);
        DPtoLP(hDCMeta, (LPPOINT)&rectClientMeta, 2);

        // draw a red line around the border
        HPEN hPenRedDot = CreatePen(PS_DOT, 1, RGB(255,0,0));
        HPEN hPenOld = (HPEN)SelectObject(hDCMeta, hPenRedDot);

        InflateRect(&rectClientMeta, -10, -10);
        Rectangle(hDCMeta, rectClientMeta.left, rectClientMeta.top,
```

```
                    rectClientMeta.right, rectClientMeta.bottom);

        // draw an ellipse just inside the border with a dark
        // gray border and filled with a light gray brush
        InflateRect(&rectClientMeta, -10, -10);

        HPEN hPenGrey = CreatePen(PS_SOLID, 3, RGB(172,172,172));
        HBRUSH hBrush = (HBRUSH)GetStockObject(DC_BRUSH);
        SetDCBrushColor(hDCMeta, RGB(128,128,128));

        // select objects
        SelectObject(hDCMeta, hPenGrey);
        HBRUSH hBrushOld = (HBRUSH)SelectObject(hDCMeta, hBrush);

        // draw the ellipse
        Ellipse(hDCMeta, rectClientMeta.left, rectClientMeta.top,
            rectClientMeta.right, rectClientMeta.bottom);

        // select original objects
        SelectObject(hDCMeta, hBrushOld);
        SelectObject(hDCMeta, hPenOld);

        // close the metafile
        hMetaFile = CloseEnhMetaFile(hDCMeta);
    }

    ReleaseDC(hWnd, hDC);

    return hMetaFile;
}


//
// OnPaint:  handles the painting for the window
//
void OnPaint(HWND hWnd)
{
    PAINTSTRUCT ps;
    HDC hDC = BeginPaint(hWnd, &ps);

    if (g_hMetaFile != NULL)
    {
        RECT rectClient;

        GetClientRect(hWnd, &rectClient);
```

```
        PlayEnhMetaFile(hDC, g_hMetaFile, &rectClient);
    }

    EndPaint(hWnd, &ps);
}
```

In the `InitInstance()` function, the application calls the `CreateEnhMetaFile()` function to create the metafile. The `ExitInstance()` function cleans up the metafile.

The `CreateEnhMetaFile()` function firsts gets the client area of the window in .01 millimeter units. It then creates a metafile using the `CreateEnhMetaFile()` API. The metafile consists of a dotted red line outlining the client area and an ellipse outlined with a dark-gray pen and filled with a light-gray brush. Then the metafile is closed using the `CloseEnhMetaFile()` API, which returns a handle to the created metafile.

The `OnPaint()` function plays the metafile into the window's client area using the `PlayEnhMetaFile()` API.

Listing 5-11 shows how to examine the individual metafile records using the `EnumEnhMetaFile()` API. This allows an application to modify the playback of specific records or to perform some other action if so desired. Figure 5-10 shows the results of the enumerated metafile. The results are identical to the previous example.

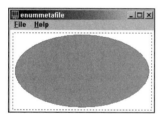

Figure 5-10: Enumerating metafile records

Listing 5-11: Enumerating metafile records

```
//
// OnPaint:  handles the painting for the window
//
void OnPaint(HWND hWnd)
{
    PAINTSTRUCT ps;
    HDC hDC = BeginPaint(hWnd, &ps);

    if (g_hMetaFile != NULL)
    {
        RECT rectClient;
        GetClientRect(hWnd, &rectClient);
```

```
        EnumEnhMetaFile(hDC, g_hMetaFile,
            &PlayMetaFileRecordProc, NULL, &rectClient);
    }

    EndPaint(hWnd, &ps);
}


//
// PlayMetaFileRecordProc:  play the metafile record
//
int CALLBACK PlayMetaFileRecordProc
(
    HDC hDC
    ,HANDLETABLE* phTable
    ,const ENHMETARECORD* pRecord
    ,int numObjects
    ,LPARAM /*lpClientData*/
)
{
    switch (pRecord->iType)
    {
        case EMR_ELLIPSE:
        case EMR_RECTANGLE:
        case EMR_CREATEPEN:
        case EMR_CREATEBRUSHINDIRECT:
        default:
            PlayEnhMetaFileRecord(
                hDC, phTable, pRecord, numObjects);
        break;
    }

    return 1;
}
```

The code in Listing 5-11 is identical to the code in Listing 5-10 except, instead of calling the PlayEnhMetaFile() API to play back the metafile, it uses the EnumEnhMetaFile() API to enumerate through each record in the metafile. For each record, the PlayMetaFileRecordProc() function is called to process the record. The PlayEnhMetaFileRecord() API is used to play the metafile record to the specified device context. You can examine the ENHMETARECORD and alter the playback of the record if you desire.

Summary

In this chapter, I reviewed some of the basic GDI APIs and covered the new functionality introduced in Window 2000. I described how using device contexts the GDI layer provides applications with a device-independent way to produce graphic output. I covered how an application can direct text and bitmaps to a device context. I also showed how to create and use regions and paths to build complex shapes. Additionally, I described how to use regions and paths to define the clipping region for a window. Finally, I covered how to create, play back, and enumerate enhanced metafiles. These objects and techniques will enable you to produce most of the graphic output required by most applications.

The next chapter covers the Common Control Library. The Common Control Library provides a common set of controls that applications can use to provide input and output. This allows applications to have a consistent look and feel with other Windows applications.

Chapter 6

Using the Common Controls

IN THIS CHAPTER

- ◆ The Common Control Library
- ◆ General use of the Common Control Library
- ◆ The common controls

IN THIS CHAPTER, I describe how you can use the controls provided in the Common Control Library to provide your users with a familiar, consistent user interface. Windows 2000 provides a new version of the Common Control Library that contains many new features and enhancements to the existing controls.

The Common Control Library

The common control library provides numerous control windows that an application can use to provide input and output. Using these controls ensures a level of consistency between Windows applications, while saving developers from having to reinvent the same wheels over and over. The Common Control Library includes tree and list controls, date and time pickers, animation controls, and more.

For each control, the Common Control Library provides a set of styles that you can use to control the look and functionality of the control. The Common Control Library also provides control specific messages that you can use to work with the control. In addition to these messages, the Common Control Library defines notification codes that some controls send to their parent windows to notify them when a control-specific event has occurred.

Each new version of Windows and Internet Explorer has shipped with a new version of the Common Control and Shell libraries. Windows 2000 ships with the newest version of `ComCtl32.DLL`, `ShLWApi.DLL`, and `Shell32.DLL`. Table 6-1 provides a history of the common control and shell libraries that have shipped with the various versions of Windows and Internet Explorer.

Chapter 9, "Shell Services," covers the facilities provided by the Windows shell through ShLWApi.DLL and Shell32.DLL.

TABLE 6-1 A HISTORY OF THE COMMON CONTROL AND SHELL LIBRARIES

Platform	ComCtl32.DLL Version	ShLWApi.DLL Version	Shell32.DLL Version
Windows 95 and Windows NT 4.0	4.00	Not shipped	4.00
Internet Explorer 3.x	4.70	Not shipped	4.00
Internet Explorer 4.0	4.71	4.71	4.71
Internet Explorer 4.01 and Windows 98	4.72	4.72	4.72
Internet Explorer 5.0	5.80	5.00	Not shipped
Windows 2000	5.81	5.00	5.00

General Use of the Common Control Library

To use a common control, you call the InitCommonControlsEx() API specifying which controls should be initialized. This ensures that the control you want to use is loaded and registered. You then create the window specifying the common control's window class name in the CreateWindowEx() API or in the dialog box template and the control styles that you want applied to the control. Each control provides control-specific styles, messages, and notification codes that can be used to modify the look and behavior of the controls. Some of the common controls provide macros to simplify using the messages.

The Common Control Library provides some APIs, styles, messages, and notification codes that apply to every common control. These general facilities of the Common Control Library are described in this section, as well as a discussion of the sample application that this chapter will use to demonstrate each of the common controls.

General facilities

The Common Control Library provides several APIs that you can use with any of the common controls. Table 6-2 describes these APIs.

TABLE 6-2 COMMON CONTROL LIBRARY GENERAL APIS

API	Description
GetEffectiveClientRect()	Calculates a bounding rectangle for the specified controls
GetMUILanguage()	Returns the language used by the common controls in the calling process
InitCommonControlsEx()	Registers the specified common control window class
InitMUILanguage()	Specifies the language that the common controls use instead of the system language
ShowHideMenuCtl()	Specifies that the specified menu items check mark be set or cleared and shows or hides the corresponding control

The Common Control Library provides a set of styles that can be applied to header, toolbar, and status bar controls. Table 6-3 describes these general styles.

TABLE 6-3 COMMON CONTROL LIBRARY GENERAL STYLES

Style	Description
CCS_ADJUSTABLE	Specifies that a toolbar should enable its built-in customization features. (I will describe these features in detail in the Toolbar control section later in this chapter.)
CCS_BOTTOM	Specifies that the control be located at the bottom of its parent window (Default style for status bar controls)
CCS_LEFT	Specifies that the control be displayed vertically on the left side of its parent window

Continued

TABLE **6-3** COMMON CONTROL LIBRARY GENERAL STYLES *(Continued)*

Style	Description
CCS_NODIVIDER	Specifies that the top border not have a two pixel highlight
CCS_NOMOVEX	Specifies that the control not allow itself to move or resize horizontally
CCS_NOMOVEY	Specifies that the control not allow itself to move or resize vertically
CCS_NOPARENTALIGN	Specifies that the control not automatically position itself in its parent window
CCS_NORESIZE	Specifies that the control not use the default width and height when being initially displayed, but should use the specified width and height
CCS_RIGHT	Specifies that the control should be displayed vertically on the right side of its parent window
CCS_TOP	Specifies that the control be located at the top of its parent window (Default style for toolbar controls)
CCS_VERT	Specifies that the control be displayed vertically

Table 6-4 describes the common messages that the Common Control Library makes available. These messages apply to all common controls.

TABLE **6-4** COMMON CONTROL LIBRARY GENERAL MESSAGES

Message	Description
CCM_GETVERSION, CCM_SETVERSION	Used to retrieve or set the version number for a control (New in version 5.80)
WM_NOTIFY	Used to notify the parent window of a common control that a control-specific event has occurred
WM_NOTIFYFORMAT	Used to identify if a window uses ANSI or Unicode structures

You can send the CCM_GETVERSION message to get the version that was set with your the last call to CCM_SETVERSION. The CCM_SETVERSION and CCM_GETVERSION messages only apply to the controls to which you send them.

The Common Control Library provides a number of general notification codes that controls will send to their parent windows. Table 6-5 describes these notification codes.

TABLE 6-5 COMMON CONTROL LIBRARY GENERAL NOTIFICATION CODES

Notification	Description
NM_CHAR	A character key message was processed
NM_CLICK	The left mouse button was clicked in the control
NM_DBLCLK	The left mouse button was double-clicked in the control
NM_HOVER	The mouse is hovering above the item
NM_KEYDOWN	A key was pressed
NM_KILLFOCUS	The control lost focus
NM_NCHITTEST	A WM_NCHITEST message was received by the control
NM_OUTOFMEMORY	The control could not complete an operation because it was out of memory
NM_RCLICK	The right mouse button was clicked in the control
NM_RDBLCLK	The right mouse button was double-clicked in the control
NM_RELEASEDCAPTURE	The control has released the mouse capture
NM_RETURN	The return key was pressed
NM_SETCURSOR	The control is setting the cursor
NM_SETFOCUS	The control has received focus
NM_TOOLTIPSCREATED	The control has created a tooltip window

All of the controls explained in this chapter have unique styles, messages, and notification codes (similar to those shown in Tables 6.3, 6.4, and 6.5 above). Please refer to the MSVC online help or the MSDN for details on control specific information.

The CommonControls sample application

All of the controls demonstrated in this chapter with the exception of the Toolbar control are displayed by the CommonControls sample application. This application provides a dialog menu that allows you to display any of the dialogs that contains the common control. There is one dialog per control.

The CommonControls sample application links to the Common Control Library with the use of the ComCtl32.LIB import library. This file links in all the Common Control Library APIs. For all of the new Windows 2000 functionality to be included, the application includes the CommCtrl.H file from the Windows 2000 Platform Software Development Kit (SDK) include file directory (typically C:\MSSDK\include). To enable the new functionality, the StdAfx.H header file defines the WINVER macro to 0x0500. The standard control macros that are included in the WindowsX.H header file are also being used.

The dialogs for each control are implemented similarly. Each dialog is implemented using a C++ class. This class exposes a DoModal() method that is called in response to a menu selection. The following code shows an example of the DoModal() method.

```
// DoModal: called to create and display the dialog
int CAnimateDialog::DoModal(HWND hWnd)
{
    s_pDlg = this;
    int nReturn = DialogBox(
        g_hInst, MAKEINTRESOURCE(IDD_ANIMATE), hWnd,
        reinterpret_cast<DLGPROC>(DialogProc));

    return nReturn;
}
```

The DoModal() method first saves a pointer to the dialog class in a static variable to be used by the DialogProc() function. It then calls the DialogBox() API to create and display the dialog.

The dialog box procedures for each of the samples also follow the same pattern. A sample DialogProc() is shown below:

```
// DialogProc: called to process the messages for the dialog
BOOL CALLBACK CAnimateDialog::DialogProc(HWND hwndDlg, UINT uMsg,
    WPARAM wParam,LPARAM /*lParam*/)
{
    BOOL bReturn(FALSE);

    switch (uMsg)
    {
```

```
case WM_INITDIALOG:
    bReturn = s_pDlg->OnInitDialog(hwndDlg);
break;

case WM_COMMAND:
    switch (LOWORD(wParam))
    {
        case IDOK:
        case IDCANCEL:
            EndDialog(hwndDlg, LOWORD(wParam));
            bReturn = TRUE;
        break;

        case IDC_PLAY:
            bReturn = s_pDlg->OnPlay(hwndDlg);
        break;

        case IDC_STOP:
            bReturn = s_pDlg->OnStop(hwndDlg);
        break;
    }
    break;
}
return bReturn;
}
```

The `DialogProc()` receives the messages and the parses the message. For most messages the `DialogProc()` function calls a member function of the dialog class, using the static dialog pointer saved in the `DoModal()` function.

 Any exceptions to this template are noted in the text. For example the progress bar control is displayed in a modeless dialog. That sample uses a slightly different method to display the dialog.

The Common Controls

In this section, I will describe each of the common controls that are shipped with Windows 2000. For each control, I provide an overview, and, for most controls, I also provide an example that demonstrates its use.

Animation control

The *Animation control* allows an application to show a small *AVI (Audio Video Interleaved) clip*. This control can be very useful in providing the user with feedback during a long operation.

Figure 6-1 shows a dialog with an animation control and buttons that start and stop the AVI clip. Listing 6-1 shows the code that implements the dialog.

Figure 6-1: The Animation control

Listing 6-1: Displaying a dialog with an animation control

```
// project CommonControls, file dlgAnimate.h
class CAnimateDialog
{
public:
    CAnimateDialog() {}
    virtual ~CAnimateDialog() {}

// operations
public:
    int DoModal(HWND hWnd);

// implementation
protected:
    BOOL OnInitDialog(HWND hDlg);
    BOOL OnPlay(HWND hDlg);
    BOOL OnStop(HWND hDlg);

    static BOOL CALLBACK DialogProc(HWND hwndDlg, UINT uMsg,
        WPARAM wParam, LPARAM lParam);
    static CAnimateDialog* s_pDlg;
};

// project CommonControls, file dlgAnimate.cpp
#include "stdafx.h"
#include "resource.h"
#include "dlgAnimate.h"
```

```
extern HINSTANCE g_hInst;
CAnimateDialog* CAnimateDialog::s_pDlg = NULL;

// DoModal: called to create and display the dialog
int CAnimateDialog::DoModal(HWND hWnd)
{
    s_pDlg = this;
    int nReturn = DialogBox(
        g_hInst, MAKEINTRESOURCE(IDD_ANIMATE), hWnd,
        reinterpret_cast<DLGPROC>(DialogProc));

    return nReturn;
}


// OnInitDialog: called to initialize the dialog
BOOL CAnimateDialog::OnInitDialog(HWND hDlg)
{
    // open the animation file from the resource
    HWND hctrlAnimate = ::GetDlgItem(hDlg, IDC_ANIMATE);
    (void)Animate_OpenEx(hctrlAnimate, g_hInst,
        MAKEINTRESOURCE(IDR_AVI));

    return TRUE;
}


// OnPlay: called to play the avi clip
BOOL CAnimateDialog::OnPlay(HWND hDlg)
{
    // play the avi file, start at the beginning,
    // play until the end, and keep on playing
    HWND hctrlAnimate = ::GetDlgItem(hDlg, IDC_ANIMATE);
    (void)Animate_Play(hctrlAnimate, 0, (UINT)-1, (UINT)-1);

    return TRUE;
}


// OnStop: called to stop playing the avi clip
BOOL CAnimateDialog::OnStop(HWND hDlg)
{
    // stop playing the avi file
    HWND hctrlAnimate = ::GetDlgItem(hDlg, IDC_ANIMATE);
    (void)Animate_Stop(hctrlAnimate);

    return TRUE;
```

```
}

// DialogProc: called to process the messages for the dialog
BOOL CALLBACK CAnimateDialog::DialogProc(HWND hwndDlg, UINT uMsg,
    WPARAM wParam, LPARAM /*lParam*/)
{
    BOOL bReturn(FALSE);

    switch (uMsg)
    {
        case WM_INITDIALOG:
            bReturn = s_pDlg->OnInitDialog(hwndDlg);
            break;

        case WM_COMMAND:
            switch (LOWORD(wParam))
            {
                case IDOK:
                case IDCANCEL:
                    EndDialog(hwndDlg, LOWORD(wParam));
                    bReturn = TRUE;
                    break;

                case IDC_PLAY:
                    bReturn = s_pDlg->OnPlay(hwndDlg);
                    break;

                case IDC_STOP:
                    bReturn = s_pDlg->OnStop(hwndDlg);
                    break;
            }
            break;
    }
    return bReturn;
}
```

The dialog template for this sample creates an animation control with the ACS_TRANSPARENT style. This style specifies that the background of the AVI clip should be transparent.

The OnInitDialog() method uses the Animate_OpenEx() macro to send an ACM_OPEN message to the animation control specifying the resource instance handle and ID of the AVI resource. The ACM_OPEN message causes the animation control to open the AVI clip and display its first frame.

In the `OnPlay()` method, the application uses the `Animate_Play()` macro to begin playing the AVI clip. The `Animate_Play()` macro sends the `ACM_PLAY` message to the control and allows you to specify the frame to start playing the clip, the frame to stop playing the clip, and the number of times to repeat the clip. In this example, the control is playing the clip from start to finish and repeating it indefinitely (or until it is manually stopped).

The `OnStop()` method uses the `Animate_Stop()` macro to stop playing the AVI clip. The `Animate_Stop()` macro simply sends the `ACM_STOP` message to the control.

ComboBoxEx control

The *Extended Combo Box (ComboBoxEx) control* extends the traditional Windows ComboBox control by providing support for item images. You can assign a separate image for the normal and selected item states. You can use this control to provide a more polished interface for your user.

Figure 6-2 shows an example of a ComboBoxEx control with different images for the selected and normal items. Listing 6-2 shows the code that implements the dialog.

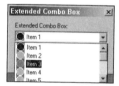

Figure 6-2: The ComboBoxEx control

Listing 6-2: Initializing and setting selection state images for in a ComboBoxEx control

```
// project CommonControls, file dlgExtendedComboBox.h
class CExtendedComboBoxDialog
{
public:
    CExtendedComboBoxDialog() {}
    virtual ~CExtendedComboBoxDialog() {}

// operations
public:
    int DoModal(HWND hWnd);

// implementations
protected:
    BOOL OnInitDialog(HWND hDlg);
```

```cpp
    static BOOL CALLBACK DialogProc(HWND hwndDlg, UINT uMsg,
        WPARAM wParam, LPARAM lParam);
    static CExtendedComboBoxDialog* s_pDlg;

// members
protected:
    HIMAGELIST m_imagelist;
};

// project CommonControls, file dlgExtendedComboBox.cpp
#include "stdafx.h"
#include "resource.h"
#include "dlgExtendedComboBox.h"

extern HINSTANCE g_hInst;
CExtendedComboBoxDialog* CExtendedComboBoxDialog::s_pDlg = NULL;

// DoModal: called to create and display the dialog
int CExtendedComboBoxDialog::DoModal(HWND hWnd)
{
    s_pDlg = this;
    int nReturn = DialogBoxParam(
        g_hInst, MAKEINTRESOURCE(IDD_COMBOBOXEX), hWnd,
        reinterpret_cast<DLGPROC>(DialogProc),
        reinterpret_cast<LPARAM>(this));

    return nReturn;
}

// OnInitDialog: called to initialize the dialog
BOOL CExtendedComboBoxDialog::OnInitDialog(HWND hDlg)
{
    // create the image list
    m_imagelist = ImageList_Create(16, 16, ILC_COLOR4, 2, 2);

    HBITMAP hBitmap = LoadBitmap(g_hInst, MAKEINTRESOURCE(IDB_BITMAP1));
    ImageList_Add(m_imagelist, hBitmap, NULL);
    hBitmap = LoadBitmap(g_hInst, MAKEINTRESOURCE(IDB_BITMAP2));
    ImageList_Add(m_imagelist, hBitmap, NULL);

    // set the image list
    HWND hctrlComboBox = ::GetDlgItem(hDlg, IDC_COMBOBOXEX);
    ::SendMessage(hctrlComboBox, CBEM_SETIMAGELIST, 0,
        (LPARAM)m_imagelist);
```

```
    // add items to combo box
    LPTSTR arItems[] =
    {
        _T("Item 1"), _T("Item 2"), _T("Item 3"), _T("Item 4"), _T("Item 5")
        ,_T("Item 6"), _T("Item 7"), _T("Item 8"), _T("Item 9"), _T("Item 10")
    };

    COMBOBOXEXITEM item;
    item.mask = CBEIF_TEXT | CBEIF_INDENT | CBEIF_IMAGE |
        CBEIF_SELECTEDIMAGE;

    for (int nIndex = 0; nIndex < sizeof(arItems) /
        sizeof(arItems[0]); ++nIndex)
    {
        item.iItem         = nIndex;
        item.pszText       = arItems[nIndex];
        item.cchTextMax    = sizeof(item.pszText);
        item.iImage        = 1;
        item.iSelectedImage = 0;
        item.iIndent       = 0;

        // add sendmessage
        ::SendMessage(hctrlComboBox, CBEM_INSERTITEM, 0, (LPARAM)&item);
    }

    // set the initial select to the first item
    ComboBox_SetCurSel(hctrlComboBox, 0);

    return TRUE;
}


// DialogProc: called to process the messages for the dialog
BOOL CALLBACK CExtendedComboBoxDialog::DialogProc(HWND hwndDlg, UINT uMsg,
    WPARAM wParam, LPARAM /*lParam*/)
{
    BOOL bReturn(FALSE);

    switch (uMsg)
    {
        case WM_INITDIALOG:
            bReturn = s_pDlg->OnInitDialog(hwndDlg);
        break;
```

```
        case WM_COMMAND:
            if (LOWORD(wParam) == IDOK ||
                LOWORD(wParam) == IDCANCEL)
            {
                EndDialog(hwndDlg, LOWORD(wParam));
                bReturn = TRUE;
            }
        break;
    }
    return bReturn;
}
```

The dialog template for this dialog creates the combo box using the CBS_DROPDOWN and CBS_SORT ComboBox styles. The ComboBoxEx control supports all of the ComboBox styles. In addition to the ComboBox styles, the ComboBoxEx control supports several extended styles providing greater flexibility.

In the OnInitDialog() method, the application creates an image list with an image for the normal and selected states of an item using the ImageList_Create() and ImageList_Add() macros. It then sends the CBEM_SETIMAGELIST message to set the image list of the ComboBoxEx control. The function sends the CBEM_INSERTITEM message to add items to the control, specifying the normal and selected images from the image list. Finally, the OnInitDialog() method selects the first item in the combo box using the ComboBox's ComboBox_SetCurSel() macro. You can use any of the ComboBox's messages and macros with the ComboBoxEx control, and there are some additional ones as well.

Date and Time Picker controls

The *Date* and *Time Picker controls* provide users with a common interface to select dates and times. These controls allow a user to easily specify a date or time value and allow the application to easily retrieve this information.

Figure 6-3 shows an example of dialog with both a date picker control and a time picker control. The user has dropped down the date control's month calendar control to select October 26, 1999. The dropped-down month calendar mostly obscures the time picker control. Listing 6-3 shows how to initialize the date time controls, how to process the selection change notification, and how to retrieve the selected date and time.

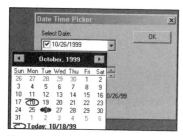

Figure 6-3: The Date Picker control

Listing 6-3: Initializing and processing Date and Time Picker controls

```
// project CommonControls, file dlgDateTimePicker.h
class CDateTimePickerDialog
{
public:
    CDateTimePickerDialog() {}
    virtual ~CDateTimePickerDialog() {}

// access functions
public:
    SYSTEMTIME GetSelectedDate();
    SYSTEMTIME GetSelectedTime();

// operations
public:
    int DoModal(HWND hWnd);

// implementations
protected:
    BOOL OnInitDialog(HWND hDlg);
    BOOL OnNotify(HWND hDlg, LPNMHDR lpNMHDR);
    BOOL OnOK(HWND hWnd);

    static BOOL CALLBACK DialogProc(HWND hwndDlg, UINT uMsg,
        WPARAM wParam, LPARAM lParam);
    static CDateTimePickerDialog* s_pDlg;

    SYSTEMTIME m_sysDate;
    SYSTEMTIME m_sysTime;
};

// project CommonControls, file dlgDateTimePicker.cpp
#include "stdafx.h"
```

```cpp
#include "resource.h"
#include "dlgDateTimePicker.h"

extern HINSTANCE g_hInst;
CDateTimePickerDialog* CDateTimePickerDialog::s_pDlg = NULL;

// DoModal: called to create and display the dialog
int CDateTimePickerDialog::DoModal(HWND hWnd)
{
    s_pDlg = this;

    int nReturn = DialogBox(
        g_hInst, MAKEINTRESOURCE(IDD_DATETIMEPICKER), hWnd,
        reinterpret_cast<DLGPROC>(DialogProc));

    return nReturn;
}

// GetSelectedDate: called to return the selected date
SYSTEMTIME CDateTimePickerDialog::GetSelectedDate()
{
    return m_sysDate;
}

// GetSelectedTime: called to return the selected time
SYSTEMTIME CDateTimePickerDialog::GetSelectedTime()
{
    return m_sysTime;
}

// OnInitDialog: called to initialize the dialog
BOOL CDateTimePickerDialog::OnInitDialog(HWND hDlg)
{
    // add the style to the short date century format
    HWND hwndDate = ::GetDlgItem(hDlg, IDC_DATEPICKER);
    DWORD dwStyle = GetWindowLong(hwndDate, GWL_STYLE);
    dwStyle |= DTS_SHORTDATECENTURYFORMAT;
    SetWindowLong(hwndDate, GWL_STYLE, dwStyle);

    HWND hwndTime = ::GetDlgItem(hDlg, IDC_TIMEPICKER);

    // set the date and time to the current date and time
    GetSystemTime(&m_sysDate);
    m_sysTime = m_sysDate;
```

```
    DateTime_SetSystemtime(hwndDate, GDT_VALID, &m_sysDate);
    DateTime_SetSystemtime(hwndTime, GDT_VALID, &m_sysTime);

    return TRUE;
}


// OnNotify: called to handle the notification messages
BOOL CDateTimePickerDialog::OnNotify(HWND hDlg, LPNMHDR lpNMHDR)
{
    BOOL bResult(FALSE);

    const int BUFFER_SIZE = 255;
    TCHAR szOut[BUFFER_SIZE+1];

    switch(lpNMHDR->code)
    {
        //
        // the date or time changed
        //
        case DTN_DATETIMECHANGE:
        {
            LPNMDATETIMECHANGE lpChange =
                reinterpret_cast<LPNMDATETIMECHANGE>(lpNMHDR);

            if (lpChange->dwFlags == GDT_VALID)
            {
                // the date or time is valid

                if (lpNMHDR->idFrom == IDC_DATEPICKER)
                {
                    // the date changed
                    TCHAR szDate[128];
                    GetDateFormat(LOCALE_USER_DEFAULT,
                        DATE_SHORTDATE, &(lpChange->st), NULL,
                        szDate, 128);

                    wsprintf(szOut, _T("The date was changed to %s"),
                        szDate);
                }
                else
                {
                    // the time changed
                    TCHAR szTime[128];
                    GetTimeFormat(LOCALE_USER_DEFAULT, 0,
```

```
                              &(lpChange->st), NULL, szTime, 128);

                    wsprintf(szOut, _T("The time was changed to %s"),
                        szTime);
                }
            }
            else
            {
                // the date or time is set to no selection

                if (lpNMHDR->idFrom == IDC_DATEPICKER)
                {
                    // the date was set to no date
                    strncpy(szOut,
                        _T("The date was changed to No Selected Date"),
                        BUFFER_SIZE);
                    szOut[BUFFER_SIZE] = 0x00;
                }
                else
                {
                    // the time was set to no time
                    strncpy(szOut,
                        _T("The time was changed to No Selected Time"),
                        BUFFER_SIZE);
                    szOut[BUFFER_SIZE] = 0x00;
                }
            }

            // update the notification text
            HWND hctrlEdit = ::GetDlgItem(hDlg, IDC_NOTIFY_MESSAGE);
            Edit_SetText(hctrlEdit, szOut);
        }
        break;
    }

    return bResult;
}

// OnOK: called when the user presses OK
BOOL CDateTimePickerDialog::OnOK(HWND hWnd)
{
    // update the selected date
    HWND hwndDate = ::GetDlgItem(hWnd, IDC_DATEPICKER);
    DateTime_GetSystemtime(hwndDate, &m_sysDate);
```

```
    // update the selected time
    HWND hwndTime = ::GetDlgItem(hWnd, IDC_TIMEPICKER);
    DateTime_GetSystemtime(hwndTime, &m_sysTime);

    BOOL bReturn = EndDialog(hWnd, IDOK);
    return bReturn;
}


// DialogProc: called to process the messages for the dialog
BOOL CALLBACK CDateTimePickerDialog::DialogProc(HWND hwndDlg, UINT uMsg,
    WPARAM wParam, LPARAM lParam)
{
    BOOL bReturn(FALSE);

    switch (uMsg)
    {
        case WM_INITDIALOG:
            bReturn = s_pDlg->OnInitDialog(hwndDlg);
        break;

        case WM_COMMAND:
            if (LOWORD(wParam) == IDOK ||
                    LOWORD(wParam) == IDCANCEL)
            {
                    bReturn = s_pDlg->OnOK(hwndDlg);
            }
        break;

        case WM_NOTIFY:
            bReturn = s_pDlg->OnNotify(hwndDlg,
                reinterpret_cast<LPNMHDR>(lParam));
        break;
    }
    return bReturn;
}
```

The dialog template for the dialog box in Listing 6-3 creates a date picker control with the DTS_RIGHTALIGN and DTS_SHOWNONE styles and a Time Picker control with the DTS_RIGHTALIGN, DTS_UPDOWN, and DTS_SHOWNONE styles.

In the OnInitDialog() method, the application sets up the style of the date control and initializes the date and time to the current date and time. The function adds the DTS_SHORTDATECENTURYFORMAT style to the Date control.

Th `DTS_SHORTDATECENTURYFORMAT` style is new to version 5.80 of the Common Control Library and is not yet (as of this printing) implemented in the VC 6.0 dialog editor.

The function uses the `DateTime_SetSystemTime()` macro to initialize the date and time control. This macro sends a `DTM_SETSYSTEMTIME` message to the control.

The `OnNotify()` function handles the `DTN_DATETIMECHANGE` notification code and displays the new date or time formatted with the use of the current user's default locale. You can use this notification to validate the date and time the user selects or to update other controls on the dialog box.

When the user presses the OK button, the `OnOK()` method retrieves the selected date and time with the use of the `DateTime_GetSystemTime()` macro and stores the data in the dialog class members. The dialog class provides the `GetSelected Date()` and `GetSelectedTime()` methods to retrieve these values.

Month Calendar control

An application can use the *Month Calendar control* to provide the user with a very familiar interface to select a date or range of dates. The Month Calendar control also provides an easy way for the application to retrieve these dates.

Figure 6-4 shows an example dialog that displays a month calendar. In this figure, the user has selected a date range from October 11, 1999 to October 15, 1999. Listing 6-4 shows the code for this dialog.

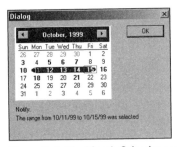

Figure 6-4: The Month Calendar control

Listing 6-4: Selecting a Date or Month Calendar control

```
// project CommonControls, file dlgMonthCalendar.h
class CMonthCalendarDialog
{
public:
    CMonthCalendarDialog() {}
```

```
        virtual ~CMonthCalendarDialog() {}

// operations
public:
    int DoModal(HWND hWnd);

// implementation
protected:
    BOOL OnInitDialog(HWND hDlg);
    BOOL OnNotify(HWND hDlg, LPNMHDR lpNMHDR);

    static BOOL CALLBACK DialogProc(HWND hwndDlg, UINT uMsg,
        WPARAM wParam, LPARAM lParam);
    static CMonthCalendarDialog* s_pDlg;
};

// project CommonControls, file dlgMonthCalendar.cpp
#include "stdafx.h"
#include "resource.h"
#include "dlgMonthCalendar.h"

extern HINSTANCE g_hInst;
CMonthCalendarDialog* CMonthCalendarDialog::s_pDlg = NULL;

// DoModal: called to create and display the dialog
int CMonthCalendarDialog::DoModal(HWND hWnd)
{
    s_pDlg = this;
    int nReturn = DialogBox(
        g_hInst, MAKEINTRESOURCE(IDD_MONTHCALENDAR), hWnd,
        reinterpret_cast<DLGPROC>(DialogProc));

    return nReturn;
}

// OnInitDialog: called to initialize the dialog
BOOL CMonthCalendarDialog::OnInitDialog(HWND hDlg)
{
    // set the selection to the first day of the month
    HWND hctrlMonthCal = ::GetDlgItem(hDlg, IDC_MONTHCALENDAR);

    // set starting and ending time to the first day of the current month
    SYSTEMTIME sysTime[2];
    GetSystemTime(&sysTime[0]);
```

```
        sysTime[0].wDay = 1;

        sysTime[1] = sysTime[0];

        (void)MonthCal_SetSelRange(hctrlMonthCal, &sysTime);

        return TRUE;
}

// OnNotify: called to handle the notification messages
BOOL CMonthCalendarDialog::OnNotify(HWND hDlg, LPNMHDR lpNMHDR)
{
    BOOL bResult(FALSE);

    TCHAR szOut[1024];
    switch(lpNMHDR->code)
    {
        // the selection has changed
        case MCN_SELCHANGE:
        {
            NMSELCHANGE* pSelChange =
                reinterpret_cast<NMSELCHANGE*>(lpNMHDR);

            // format date
            TCHAR szStartDate[128];
            TCHAR szEndDate[128];

            GetDateFormat(LOCALE_USER_DEFAULT, DATE_SHORTDATE,
                &(pSelChange->stSelStart), NULL, szStartDate, 128);
            GetDateFormat(LOCALE_USER_DEFAULT, DATE_SHORTDATE,
                &(pSelChange->stSelEnd), NULL, szEndDate, 128);

            wsprintf(szOut, _T("The range from %s to %s was selected"),
                szStartDate, szEndDate);

            // update the notification text
            HWND hctrlEdit = ::GetDlgItem(hDlg, IDC_NOTIFY_MESSAGE);
            Edit_SetText(hctrlEdit, szOut);
        }
        break;

        // a new date range has been selected
        case MCN_SELECT:
        {
```

```
                NMSELCHANGE* pSelChange =
                    reinterpret_cast<NMSELCHANGE*>(lpNMHDR);

                // format date
                TCHAR szStartDate[128];
                TCHAR szEndDate[128];

                GetDateFormat(LOCALE_USER_DEFAULT, DATE_SHORTDATE,
                    &(pSelChange->stSelStart), NULL, szStartDate, 128);
                GetDateFormat(LOCALE_USER_DEFAULT, DATE_SHORTDATE,
                    &(pSelChange->stSelEnd), NULL, szEndDate, 128);

                // update the notification text
                HWND hctrlMonthCal = ::GetDlgItem(hDlg,
                    IDC_NOTIFY_MESSAGE);
                wsprintf(szOut, _T("The user selected from %s to %s"),
                    szStartDate, szEndDate);
                Edit_SetText(hctrlMonthCal, szOut);
            }
        break;
    }
    return bResult;
}


// DialogProc: called to process the messages for the dialog
BOOL CALLBACK CMonthCalendarDialog::DialogProc(HWND hwndDlg, UINT uMsg,
    WPARAM wParam, LPARAM lParam)
{
    BOOL bReturn(FALSE);

    switch (uMsg)
    {
        case WM_INITDIALOG:
            bReturn = s_pDlg->OnInitDialog(hwndDlg);
        break;

        case WM_COMMAND:
            if (LOWORD(wParam) == IDOK ||
                LOWORD(wParam) == IDCANCEL)
            {
                EndDialog(hwndDlg, LOWORD(wParam));
                bReturn = TRUE;
            }
        break;
```

```
        case WM_NOTIFY:
            bReturn = s_pDlg->OnNotify(hwndDlg,
                reinterpret_cast<LPNMHDR>(lParam));
        break;
    }
    return bReturn;
}
```

The resource for the dialog box in Listing 6-4 creates a Month Calendar with the MCS_MULTISELECT and MCS_NOTODAY styles set. Other styles may be used to further fine-tune control apperance, including displaying or hiding week numbers. The OnInitDialog() method sets the starting and ending dates for the selected range to the first day of the current month. The function uses the GetSystemTime() API to retrieve the current date and time. Since the control allows the user to select a range of dates, the MonthCal_SetSelRange() macro is used to set the initial selected range instead of the MonthCal_SetCurSel() macro. If the control only allowed a single date to be selected, you would use the MonthCal_SetCurSel() macro.

 Chapter 10, "Application Building Services," covers Windows 2000 time support as delivered by the GetSystemTime() API.

The MonthCal_SetSelRange() sends a MCM_SETSELRANGE message to the control, while the MonthCal_SetCurSel() macro sends a MCM_SETCURSEL message. The OnNotify() method handles the MCN_SELCHANGE and the MCN_SELECT notification codes. In this example, the OnNotify() method just updates the IDC_NOTIFY_MESSAGE edit control to display the new dates that were selected. However you can use these notifications to update or validate other controls in response to the users selection.

Drag List Box control

The *Drag List Box control* provide a mechanism to enable a user to reorder the items in a list box. Figure 6-5 shows an example of a drag list box. The user is dragging "Item 5" between "Item 2" and "Item 3." You create and handle notifications for a drag list box a little differently from most common controls. Listing 6-5 shows how to create a drag list box and handle the drag list box notifications.

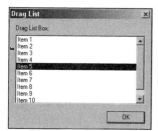

Figure 6-5: The Drag List Box control

Example 6-5: Creating a Drag List Box control

```
// project CommonControls, file dlgDragList.h
class CDragListDialog
{
public:
    CDragListDialog() {}
    virtual ~CDragListDialog() {}

// operations
public:
    int DoModal(HWND hWnd);

// implementations
protected:
    BOOL OnInitDialog(HWND hDlg);
    BOOL OnDragMessage(HWND hDlg, DRAGLISTINFO* lpDragListInfo);

    static BOOL CALLBACK DialogProc(HWND hwndDlg, UINT uMsg,
        WPARAM wParam, LPARAM lParam);
    static CDragListDialog* s_pDlg;

    static const UINT s_DragMessage;

// members
protected:
    UINT m_itemDrag;
};

// project CommonControls, file dlgDragList.cpp
#include "stdafx.h"
#include "resource.h"
#include "dlgDragList.h"
```

```
extern HINSTANCE g_hInst;
CDragListDialog* CDragListDialog::s_pDlg = NULL;

// get the drag list box registered message
const UINT CDragListDialog::s_DragMessage =
    RegisterWindowMessage(DRAGLISTMSGSTRING);

// DoModal: called to create and display the dialog
//
int CDragListDialog::DoModal(HWND hWnd)
{
    s_pDlg = this;
    int nReturn = DialogBoxParam(
        g_hInst, MAKEINTRESOURCE(IDD_DRAGLIST), hWnd,
        reinterpret_cast<DLGPROC>(DialogProc),
        reinterpret_cast<LPARAM>(this));

    return nReturn;
}

// OnInitDialog: called to initialize the dialog
BOOL CDragListDialog::OnInitDialog(HWND hDlg)
{
    LPTSTR arItems[] =
    {
        _T("Item 1"), _T("Item 2"), _T("Item 3"), _T("Item 4"), _T("Item 5")
        ,_T("Item 6"), _T("Item 7"), _T("Item 8"), _T("Item 9"), _T("Item 10")
    };

    // make the list box a drag list box
    HWND hwndDragList = ::GetDlgItem(hDlg, IDC_DRAGLIST);
    MakeDragList(hwndDragList);

    // add items to the list box
    for (int nIndex = 0;
        nIndex < sizeof(arItems) / sizeof(arItems[0]);
        ++nIndex)
    {
        ListBox_AddString(hwndDragList, arItems[nIndex]);
    }

    // set the initial select to the first item
    ListBox_SetCurSel(hwndDragList, 0);
```

```
        return TRUE;
}


// OnDragMessage: called to handle the drag messages
BOOL CDragListDialog::OnDragMessage(HWND hDlg, DRAGLISTINFO* lpDragListInfo)
{
    BOOL bResult(FALSE);

    HWND hwndDragList = ::GetDlgItem(hDlg, IDC_DRAGLIST);

    switch(lpDragListInfo->uNotification)
    {
        // The user clicked an item. Get the item from the point sent with the
        //  message and set the result to TRUE
        case DL_BEGINDRAG:
            m_itemDrag = LBItemFromPt(
                hwndDragList, lpDragListInfo->ptCursor, FALSE);
            if (m_itemDrag != -1)
            {
                SetWindowLong(hDlg, DWL_MSGRESULT, TRUE);
                bResult = TRUE;
            }
        break;

        // The user canceled the drag, reset drag item
        case DL_CANCELDRAG:
            m_itemDrag = (DWORD)-1;
        break;

        // The user is dragging the item get item that the mouse is over. If
        //  the mouse is over an item, draw the insert indicator set the return
        //  value to the Move cursor
        case DL_DRAGGING:
        {
            if (m_itemDrag != -1)
            {
                UINT nItem = LBItemFromPt(
                    hwndDragList, lpDragListInfo->ptCursor, TRUE);
                if (nItem != -1)
                {
                    DrawInsert(hDlg, hwndDragList, nItem);
                }

                SetWindowLong(hDlg, DWL_MSGRESULT, DL_MOVECURSOR);
```

```
                    bResult = TRUE;
            }
        }
        break;

        // The user dropped the item: clear the insert indicator and get the
        //  item dragged over. If the item is dropped on an item, move the item
        //  after the item the mouse is over
        case DL_DROPPED:
        {
            DrawInsert(hDlg, hwndDragList, -1);

            if (m_itemDrag != -1)
            {
                UINT nItem = LBItemFromPt(
                    hwndDragList, lpDragListInfo->ptCursor, FALSE);

                if (nItem != -1)
                {
                    TCHAR szOut[256];
                    ListBox_GetText(hwndDragList, m_itemDrag, szOut);
                    ListBox_DeleteString(hwndDragList, m_itemDrag);
                    ListBox_InsertString(hwndDragList, nItem, szOut);

                    ListBox_SetCurSel(hwndDragList, nItem);
                }
            }
        }
        break;
    }
    return bResult;
}

// DialogProc: called to process the messages for the dialog
BOOL CALLBACK CDragListDialog::DialogProc(HWND hwndDlg, UINT uMsg,
    WPARAM wParam, LPARAM lParam)
{
    BOOL bReturn(FALSE);

    if (uMsg == s_DragMessage)
    {
        bReturn = s_pDlg->OnDragMessage(hwndDlg, (DRAGLISTINFO*)lParam);
    }
    else if (uMsg == WM_INITDIALOG)
```

```
    {
        bReturn = s_pDlg->OnInitDialog(hwndDlg);
    }
    else if (uMsg == WM_COMMAND)
    {
        if (LOWORD(wParam) == IDOK ||
            LOWORD(wParam) == IDCANCEL)
        {
            EndDialog(hwndDlg, LOWORD(wParam));
            bReturn = TRUE;
        }
    }
    return bReturn;
}
```

In Listing 6-5, to create a drag list box, the `OnInitDialog()` method calls the `MakeDragList()` API to make the list control on the dialog box a drag list box. It then adds some items to the list control the use of the list box control's `ListBox_AddString()` macro and sets the initial selection to the first item in the list using the `ListBox_SetCurSel()` macro. Since the Drag List Box control is a list control, you can use the same styles, messages, and macros that you can with a list control, as well as several additional ones.

Drag list boxes send notification messages to their parent window with the "`commctrl_DragListMsg`" registered message. The Common Control Library header file, `ComCtl32.H`, defines the `DRAGLISTMSGSTRING` preprocessor macro as this string to make registering the message easier. The `OnDragMessage()` method processes these notifications to move an item in response to the user dragging an item.

The `OnDragMessage()` method handles the `DL_BEGINDRAG` notification by storing the index of the item being dragged. The index of the item being dragged is retrieved with the use of the `LBItemFromPt()` API. The `DL_CANCELED` drag notification is handled by simply resetting the index of the item being dragged to -1. (This indicates that no item is currently being dragged.) In response to the `DL_DRAGGING` notification, the method retrieves the item index that the cursor is currently over with the use of the `LBItemFromPt()` API and passes this index to the `DrawInsert()` API to draw the insert indicator.

The method handles the `DL_DROPPED` notification by removing the insert indicator, by passing –1 for the index to the `DrawInsert()` API. It then gets the index that the item was dropped on, removes the string being dragged, and inserts it at the new index. The function then sets the selected item to the dropped item.

List View control

The *List View control* provides an interface for displaying items similar to the right-hand pane that you are used to seeing in Windows Explorer. It can provide four different views of the items it contains: the large icon view, the small icon view, the list view, and the report view.

Figure 6-6 shows an example of a List View control in a dialog. The dialog allows you to switch the view of the List View control. Listing 6-6 shows the code for the dialog. It illustrates how to add items to a List View control, switch between views, and retrieve the selected items from the control.

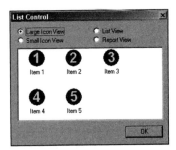

Figure 6-6: The List View control

Listing 6-6: Inserting items into a List View control

```
// project CommonControls, file dlgListControl.h
class CListControlDialog
{
public:
    CListControlDialog() {}
    virtual ~CListControlDialog() {}

// operations
public:
    int DoModal(HWND hWnd);

// implementation
protected:
    BOOL OnInitDialog(HWND hDlg);
    BOOL OnButtonPressed(HWND hDlg, UINT idControl);

    static BOOL CALLBACK DialogProc(HWND hwndDlg, UINT uMsg,
        WPARAM wParam, LPARAM lParam);
    static CListControlDialog* s_pDlg;

// members
protected:
    HIMAGELIST m_imagelistLarge;
    HIMAGELIST m_imagelistSmall;
```

```
};

// project CommonControls, file dlgListControl.cpp
#include "stdafx.h"
#include "resource.h"
#include "dlgListControl.h"

extern HINSTANCE g_hInst;
CListControlDialog* CListControlDialog::s_pDlg = NULL;

// DoModal: called to create and display the dialog
int CListControlDialog::DoModal(HWND hWnd)
{
    s_pDlg = this;
    int nReturn = DialogBox(
        g_hInst, MAKEINTRESOURCE(IDD_LISTCONTROL), hWnd,
        reinterpret_cast<DLGPROC>(DialogProc));

    return nReturn;
}


// OnInitDialog: called to initialize the dialog
BOOL CListControlDialog::OnInitDialog(HWND hDlg)
{
    HWND hwndList = ::GetDlgItem(hDlg, IDC_LISTCONTROL);

    // create the large and small image list
    m_imagelistLarge = ImageList_Create(32, 32, ILC_COLOR4, 5, 0);
    HBITMAP hBitmap = LoadBitmap(g_hInst,
        MAKEINTRESOURCE(IDB_LISTCONTROL_LARGE_BITMAP));
    ImageList_Add(m_imagelistLarge, hBitmap, NULL);
    DeleteObject(hBitmap);

    m_imagelistSmall = ImageList_Create(16, 16, ILC_COLOR4, 5, 0);
    hBitmap = LoadBitmap(g_hInst,
        MAKEINTRESOURCE(IDB_LISTCONTROL_SMALL_BITMAP));
    ImageList_Add(m_imagelistSmall, hBitmap, NULL);
    DeleteObject(hBitmap);

    // set image lists
    ListView_SetImageList(hwndList, m_imagelistLarge, LVSIL_NORMAL);
    ListView_SetImageList(hwndList, m_imagelistSmall, LVSIL_SMALL);

    // add two columns
```

```
LVCOLUMN colInfo;
colInfo.mask = LVCF_TEXT | LVCF_WIDTH | LVCF_SUBITEM;
colInfo.fmt = LVCFMT_CENTER;
colInfo.pszText = _T("Column 1");
colInfo.cx = 120;
colInfo.iSubItem = 0;
ListView_InsertColumn(hwndList, 0, &colInfo);

colInfo.iSubItem = 1;
colInfo.pszText = _T("Column 2");
ListView_InsertColumn(hwndList, 1, &colInfo);

// insert items into the list
int nItem = 0;
LVITEM itemInfo;
itemInfo.mask = LVIF_TEXT | LVIF_IMAGE;

TCHAR szItem[32];
TCHAR szSubItem[32];

for (int nIndex = 1; nIndex <= 5; ++nIndex)
{
    wsprintf(szItem, _T("Item %d"), nIndex);
    wsprintf(szSubItem, _T("SubItem %d"), nIndex);

    itemInfo.iItem = 0;
    itemInfo.iSubItem = 0;
    itemInfo.pszText = szItem;
    itemInfo.iImage = nIndex - 1;
    nItem = ListView_InsertItem(hwndList, &itemInfo);

    itemInfo.iItem = nItem;
    itemInfo.iSubItem = 1;
    itemInfo.pszText = szSubItem;
    itemInfo.iImage = nIndex - 1;
    ListView_SetItem(hwndList, &itemInfo);
}

// set the initial view to the large icon view
HWND hwndLargeIcon = GetDlgItem(hDlg, IDC_LARGE_ICON);
SendMessage(hwndLargeIcon, BM_CLICK, 0, 0);

return TRUE;
}
```

```
// OnButtonPressed: called when the user presses on the radion buttons to select
//   the view the list control should display
BOOL CListControlDialog::OnButtonPressed(HWND hDlg, UINT idControl)
{
    BOOL bReturn(TRUE);

    HWND hwndList = ::GetDlgItem(hDlg, IDC_LISTCONTROL);

    // get and remove the list control view
    DWORD dwStyle = GetWindowLong(hwndList, GWL_STYLE);
    dwStyle &= ~LVS_TYPEMASK;

    switch(idControl)
    {
        case IDOK:
        {
            // determine what items were selected:
            int numItems = ListView_GetItemCount(hwndList);
            for (int nIndex = 0; nIndex < numItems; ++nIndex)
            {
                UINT state = ListView_GetItemState(
                    hwndList, nIndex, LVIS_SELECTED);

                if (state == LVIS_SELECTED)
                {
                    // item is selected
                }
            }

            EndDialog(hDlg, IDOK);
        }
        break;

        // set the style of the list control when the user selects
        // one of the radio buttons
        case IDC_LARGE_ICON:
            SetWindowLong(hwndList, GWL_STYLE, dwStyle | LVS_ICON);
        break;

        case IDC_SMALL_ICON:
            SetWindowLong(hwndList, GWL_STYLE, dwStyle | LVS_SMALLICON);
        break;
```

```
        case IDC_LIST:
            SetWindowLong(hwndList, GWL_STYLE, dwStyle | LVS_LIST);
        break;

        case IDC_REPORT:
            SetWindowLong(hwndList, GWL_STYLE, dwStyle | LVS_REPORT);
        break;

        default:
            bReturn = FALSE;
        break;
    }
    return bReturn;
}

// DialogProc: called to process the messages for the dialog
BOOL CALLBACK CListControlDialog::DialogProc(HWND hwndDlg, UINT uMsg,
    WPARAM wParam, LPARAM /*lParam*/)
{
    BOOL bReturn(FALSE);

    switch (uMsg)
    {
        case WM_INITDIALOG:
            bReturn = s_pDlg->OnInitDialog(hwndDlg);
        break;

        case WM_COMMAND:
            if (HIWORD(wParam) == BN_CLICKED)
            {
                bReturn = s_pDlg->OnButtonPressed(hwndDlg,
                    LOWORD(wParam));
            }
        break;
    }
    return bReturn;
}
```

The dialog resource for the dialog box in Listing 6-6 creates a List View control with the LVS_SORTASCENDING style set. Many other styles are available, including the ability to manage sorting, scrolling, and wrapping.

The `OnInitDialog()` method firsts creates two image lists to use with the control. One provides the 32x32 pixel images to use for the large icon view and the other provides 16x16 pixel images to use with the other views. The function then uses the `ListView_SetImageList()` macro to attach these images lists to the control. The `OnInitDialog()` method adds two columns to the List View control with the use of the `ListView_InsertColumn()` macro. It also adds five items to the List View using the `ListView_InsertItem()` macro. After populating the list view control, the function sets the initial view of the control to the large icon view.

The `OnButtonPressed()` method in Listing 6-6 handles the view radio buttons, as well as the "OK" and "Cancel" buttons. In response to the "OK" button, the method determines what items are selected. The method uses the `ListView_GetItemCount()` to find out how many items are in the control and loops through them to find the items that are selected using the `ListView_GetItemState()` macro. This process could be optimized by using the `ListView_GetSelectedCount()` and `ListView_GetSelectionMark()` macros or corresponding messages.

In response the "Cancel" button, the method simply dismisses the dialog. To handle the view radio buttons, the function determines which button the user selected and sets the corresponding style in the control, using the `SetWindowLong()` API.

Version 5.80 of the Common Control Library provides the `LVM_SORTITEMEX` message, which allows for more flexibility when sorting items. The `LVM_SORTITEMEX` message is similar to the `LVM_SORITEM` message, except that the comparison function uses the current indexes of the items instead of the `lParam` values. You can use the `LVM_GETITEM` or the `LVM_GETITEMTEXT` message to get additional information about the items.

Before the `LVM_SORTITEMEX` message, you had to add some form of item data to the control in order to be able to sort. Now, you can use the information that already exists in the control – the text of the item or subitem for example.

Header control

The *Header control* provides a common interface for defining columns. The control can be divided into multiple sections, and each section can have a label. The report view of the List View control uses a Header control in the report view.

Version 5.80 of the Common Control Library adds filter bars to the Header control. Filter bars provide a common user interface that allows the user to filter the contents of a list that the Header control is managing. Figure 6-7 shows an example of using filter bars with a header control and a List View control. Listing 6-7 shows the code for this dialog. It illustrates how to add a filter bar to a List View control and how to handle the filter bar notifications.

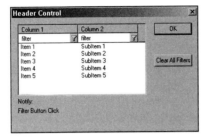

Figure 6-7: Header Control filter bar

Listing 6-7: Adding a filter bar to a list control and handling its notifications

```cpp
// project CommonControls, file dlgListHeader.h
class CListHeaderDialog
{
public:
    CListHeaderDialog() {}
    virtual ~CListHeaderDialog() {}

// operations
public:
    int DoModal(HWND hWnd);

// implementation
protected:
    BOOL OnInitDialog(HWND hDlg);
    BOOL OnNotify(HWND hDlg, LPNMHDR lpNMHDR);

    static BOOL CALLBACK DialogProc(HWND hwndDlg, UINT uMsg,
        WPARAM wParam, LPARAM lParam);
    static CListHeaderDialog* s_pDlg;
};

// project CommonControls, file dlgListHeader.cpp
#include "stdafx.h"
#include "resource.h"
#include "dlgListHeader.h"

extern HINSTANCE g_hInst;
CListHeaderDialog* CListHeaderDialog::s_pDlg = NULL;

// DoModal: called to create and display the dialog
int CListHeaderDialog::DoModal(HWND hWnd)
{
```

```
    s_pDlg = this;
    int nReturn = DialogBox(
        g_hInst, MAKEINTRESOURCE(IDD_HEADERLIST), hWnd,
        reinterpret_cast<DLGPROC>(DialogProc));

    return nReturn;
}


// OnInitDialog: called to initialize the dialog
BOOL CListHeaderDialog::OnInitDialog(HWND hDlg)
{
    HWND hwndList = ::GetDlgItem(hDlg, IDC_LISTCONTROL);
    HWND hwndHeader = ListView_GetHeader(hwndList);

    // add the filter bar style to the header control
    DWORD dwStyle = GetWindowLong(hwndHeader, GWL_STYLE);
    dwStyle |= HDS_FILTERBAR;
    SetWindowLong(hwndHeader, GWL_STYLE, dwStyle);

    // add columns
    LVCOLUMN colInfo;
    colInfo.mask = LVCF_TEXT | LVCF_WIDTH | LVCF_SUBITEM;
    colInfo.fmt = LVCFMT_CENTER;
    colInfo.pszText = _T("Column 1");
    colInfo.cx = 120;
    colInfo.iSubItem = 0;
    ListView_InsertColumn(hwndList, 0, &colInfo);

    colInfo.iSubItem = 1;
    colInfo.pszText = _T("Column 2");
    ListView_InsertColumn(hwndList, 1, &colInfo);

    // insert items into the list
    int nItem = 0;
    LVITEM itemInfo;
    itemInfo.mask = LVIF_TEXT | LVIF_IMAGE;

    TCHAR szItem[32];
    TCHAR szSubItem[32];

    for (int nIndex = 1; nIndex <= 5; ++nIndex)
    {
        wsprintf(szItem, _T("Item %d"), nIndex);
        wsprintf(szSubItem, _T("SubItem %d"), nIndex);
```

```
            itemInfo.iItem = 0;
            itemInfo.iSubItem = 0;
            itemInfo.pszText = szItem;
            nItem = ListView_InsertItem(hwndList, &itemInfo);

            itemInfo.iItem = nItem;
            itemInfo.iSubItem = 1;
            itemInfo.pszText = szSubItem;
            ListView_SetItem(hwndList, &itemInfo);
        }
        return TRUE;
    }


// OnNotify: called to handle the notification messages
BOOL CListHeaderDialog::OnNotify(HWND hDlg, LPNMHDR lpNMHDR)
{
    BOOL bResult(FALSE);

    switch(lpNMHDR->code)
    {
        case HDN_FILTERCHANGE:
        {
            HWND hctrlEdit = ::GetDlgItem(hDlg, IDC_NOTIFY_MESSAGE);
            Edit_SetText(hctrlEdit, _T("Filter Change"));
        }
        break;

        case HDN_FILTERBTNCLICK:
        {
            HWND hctrlEdit = ::GetDlgItem(hDlg, IDC_NOTIFY_MESSAGE);
            Edit_SetText(hctrlEdit, _T("Filter Button Click"));
        }
        break;

        default:
        break;
    }
    return bResult;
}

// DialogProc: called to process the messages for the dialog
BOOL CListHeaderDialog::OnButtonPressed(HWND hDlg, UINT idControl)
{
```

```
    BOOL bReturn(TRUE);

    HWND hwndList = ::GetDlgItem(hDlg, IDC_LISTCONTROL);

    switch(idControl)
    {
        case IDOK:
            EndDialog(hDlg, IDOK);
        break;

        case IDC_CLEAR_ALL_FILTERS:
        {
            // clear all filters
            HWND hwndHeader = ListView_GetHeader(hwndList);
            Header_ClearFilter(hwndHeader, -1);
        }
        break;

        default:
            bReturn = FALSE;
        break;
    }

    return bReturn;
}


// DialogProc: called to process the messages for the dialog
BOOL CALLBACK CListHeaderDialog::DialogProc(HWND hwndDlg, UINT uMsg,
    WPARAM wParam, LPARAM lParam)
{
    BOOL bReturn(FALSE);

    switch (uMsg)
    {
        case WM_INITDIALOG:
            bReturn = s_pDlg->OnInitDialog(hwndDlg);
        break;

        case WM_COMMAND:
            bReturn = s_pDlg->OnButtonPressed(
                hwndDlg, LOWORD(wParam));
        break;

        case WM_NOTIFY:
```

```
                bReturn = s_pDlg->OnNotify(
                    hwndDlg, reinterpret_cast<LPNMHDR>(lParam));
            break;
        }
        return bReturn;
}
```

The resource for this dialog creates a List View control with the LVS_REPORT and LVS_SORTASCENDING styles set. The LVS_REPORT style specifies that the list control should display the report view, which contains a Header control.

The OnInitDialog() method first retrieves the Header control from the List View control using the ListView_GetHeader() macro. It then adds the HDS_FILTERBAR style to the control. This specifies that the filter bars should be displayed.

After adding the filter bars, the OnInitDialog() method adds two columns to the List View control and populates the list with five items. This is the same code used in Listing 6-6.

The OnNotify() method handles the HDN_FILTERCHANGE and the HDN_FILTER BTNCLICK notification codes. In this example, the OnNotify() method just updates the IDC_NOTIFY_MESSAGE edit control to display the notification codes received; however, you can use these notification messages to update the lists contexts.

The OnButtonPressed() method handles the "Clear All Filters" button as well as the "OK" and "Cancel" buttons. This method handles the "Clear All Filters" button using the Header_ClearFilter() macro. The "OK" and "Cancel" buttons just dismiss the dialog.

Tree View control

The *Tree View control* provides an application with a common way to display hierarchical data, like the left pane of Windows Explorer. Hierarchical views on data provide a way to organize large amounts of data in a logical manner. They also allow users to navigate quickly through this data, if it is properly organized.

Figure 6-8 shows an example of an expanded Tree View control. Listing 6-8 demonstrates how to add items to a Tree View control and how to handle some of the notification codes.

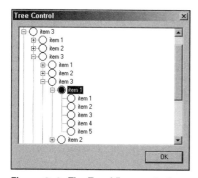

Figure 6-8: The Tree View control

Listing 6-8: Adding items to a Tree View control

```
// project CommonControls, file dlgTreeControl.h
class CTreeControlDialog
{
public:
    CTreeControlDialog();
    virtual ~CTreeControlDialog();

// operations
public:
    int DoModal(HWND hWnd);

// implementation
protected:
    BOOL OnInitDialog(HWND hDlg);
    BOOL OnNotify(HWND hDlg, LPNMHDR lpNMHDR);

    void InsertItems(
        HWND hDlg, int numItems, HTREEITEM hParent, int nLevels);

    static BOOL CALLBACK DialogProc(HWND hwndDlg, UINT uMsg,
        WPARAM wParam, LPARAM lParam);
    static CTreeControlDialog* s_pDlg;

// members
protected:
    HIMAGELIST m_imagelist;
};

// project CommonControls, file dlgTreeControl.cpp
#include "stdafx.h"
```

```
#include "resource.h"
#include "dlgTreeControl.h"

extern HINSTANCE g_hInst;
CTreeControlDialog* CTreeControlDialog::s_pDlg = NULL;

// DoModal: called to create and display the dialog
int CTreeControlDialog::DoModal(HWND hWnd)
{
    s_pDlg = this;
    int nReturn = DialogBox(
        g_hInst, MAKEINTRESOURCE(IDD_TREECONTROL), hWnd,
        reinterpret_cast<DLGPROC>(DialogProc));

    return nReturn;
}

// OnInitDialog: called to initialize the dialog
BOOL CTreeControlDialog::OnInitDialog(HWND hDlg)
{
    HWND hwndTree = ::GetDlgItem(hDlg, IDC_TREECONTROL);

    // create the image list
    m_imagelist = ImageList_Create(16, 16, ILC_COLOR4, 5, 0);
    HBITMAP hBitmap = LoadBitmap(
        g_hInst, MAKEINTRESOURCE(IDB_TREE_CONTROL));
    ImageList_Add(m_imagelist, hBitmap, NULL);
    DeleteObject(hBitmap);

    // set image list
    TreeView_SetImageList(hwndTree, m_imagelist, LVSIL_NORMAL);

    // insert items
    InsertItems(hDlg, 5, TVI_ROOT, 4);

    return TRUE;
}

// OnNotify: called to handle the notification messages
BOOL CTreeControlDialog::OnNotify(HWND /*hDlg*/, LPNMHDR /*lpNMHDR*/)
{
    BOOL bResult(FALSE);
    // handle lpNMHDR->code: TVN_SELCHANGED, TVN_SELCHANGING, TVN_ITEMEXPANDED,
    //   and/or TVN_ITEMEXPANDING
```

```
        return bResult;
}


// InsertItems: Called to recursively insert items into the list
void CTreeControlDialog::InsertItems(HWND hDlg, int numItems,
    HTREEITEM hParent, int nLevels)
{
    HWND hwndTree = ::GetDlgItem(hDlg, IDC_TREECONTROL);

    // set up the insert struct
    TCHAR szOut[32];
    HTREEITEM hItem = NULL;
    TVINSERTSTRUCT insertItem;
    insertItem.itemex.mask = TVIF_CHILDREN | TVIF_IMAGE |
        TVIF_SELECTEDIMAGE | TVIF_TEXT;

    for (int nIndex = 1; nIndex <= numItems; ++nIndex)
    {
        // set up the item
        insertItem.hParent = hParent;
        insertItem.hInsertAfter = TVI_LAST;

        wsprintf(szOut, "item %d", nIndex);
        insertItem.itemex.pszText = szOut;
        insertItem.itemex.iImage  = 0;
        insertItem.itemex.iSelectedImage = 1;
        insertItem.itemex.cChildren = nLevels > 0 ? 1 : 0;
        hItem = TreeView_InsertItem(hwndTree, &insertItem);

        // if the number of levels is greater than 0
        // then call ourselves with one less level
        if (nLevels > 0)
        {
            InsertItems(hDlg, numItems, hItem, nLevels - 1);
        }
    }
}


// DialogProc: called to process the messages for the dialog
BOOL CALLBACK CTreeControlDialog::DialogProc(HWND hwndDlg, UINT uMsg,
    WPARAM wParam, LPARAM lParam)
{
    BOOL bReturn(FALSE);
```

```
switch (uMsg)
{
    case WM_INITDIALOG:
        bReturn = s_pDlg->OnInitDialog(hwndDlg);
    break;

    case WM_COMMAND:
        if (LOWORD(wParam) == IDOK)
        {
            EndDialog(hwndDlg, LOWORD(wParam));
            bReturn = TRUE;
        }
    break;

    case WM_NOTIFY:
        bReturn = s_pDlg->OnNotify(
            hwndDlg, reinterpret_cast<LPNMHDR>(lParam));
    break;
    }
    return bReturn;
}
```

The dialog resource for the dialog box in Listing 6-8 creates a Tree View control with the TVS_HASBUTTONS, TVS_HASLINES, TVS_LINESATROOT, TVS_EDITLABELS, and TVS_INFOTIP styles. Other styles may be used to control buttons, tooltips, and additional options.

The OnInitDialog() method firsts creates an image list to use for the control. This image list consists of a normal image and a selected image. The method attaches the image list to the Tree View control using the TreeView_SetImage List() macro. It then calls the InsertItems() method to populate the Tree View control.

The InsertItems() method is a simple function that quickly populates a tree view with a number of items. It adds the specified number of items to the specified parent node, using the TreeView_InsertItem() macro. It calls itself recursively for each item it adds to add the specified depth to the tree.

The OnNotify() method in Listing 6-8 is simply a placeholder to process some of the notification codes provided by the Tree View control. This exmple does nothing with them; however, you can use them to take some kind of action. For example, you can check access rights to the data before allowing an item to be expanded.

Hot Key control

The *Hot Key control* provides an interface for users to define hot keys for an application to use. Hot keys are a combination of keystrokes that let a user perform an operation quickly. When the Hot Key control has focus and a user presses a key combination, the Hot Key control displays the text that represents the key combination.

Figure 6-9 shows an example of using the hot key control in a dialog. In this example, the user has pressed **Ctrl+X** for the hot key. Listing 6-9 shows how you can use the Hot Key control to define a hot key for the main window of the application.

Figure 6-9: The Hot Key control

Listing 6-9: Defining a hot key for the main window of an application

```
// project CommonControls, file dlgHotKey.h
class CHotKeyDialog
{
public:
    CHotKeyDialog() {}
    virtual ~CHotKeyDialog() {}

// operations
public:
    int DoModal(HWND hWnd);

// implementation
protected:
    BOOL OnInitDialog(HWND hDlg);

    static BOOL CALLBACK DialogProc(HWND hwndDlg, UINT uMsg,
        WPARAM wParam, LPARAM lParam);
    static CHotKeyDialog* s_pDlg;
};

// project CommonControls, file dlgHotKey.cpp
#include "stdafx.h"
#include "resource.h"
```

```
#include "dlgHotKey.h"

extern HINSTANCE g_hInst;
CHotKeyDialog* CHotKeyDialog::s_pDlg = NULL;

// DoModal: called to create and display the dialog
//
// OnInitDialog: called to initialize the dialog
BOOL CHotKeyDialog::OnInitDialog(HWND hDlg)
{
    HWND hctrlHotKey = ::GetDlgItem(hDlg, IDC_HOTKEY);

    // don't allow unmodified keys, if the user presses an
    // unmodified key, add the ctrl key to the key pressed
    SendMessage(hctrlHotKey, HKM_SETRULES, HKCOMB_NONE,
        MAKELPARAM(HOTKEYF_CONTROL , 0));

    // set the initial hot key to 'Ctrl+X'
    SendMessage(hctrlHotKey, HKM_SETHOTKEY,
        MAKEWORD(0x58, HOTKEYF_CONTROL), 0);

    return TRUE;
}


// DialogProc: called to process the messages for the dialog
BOOL CALLBACK CHotKeyDialog::DialogProc(HWND hwndDlg, UINT uMsg,
    WPARAM wParam, LPARAM /*lParam*/)
{
    BOOL bReturn(FALSE);

    switch (uMsg)
    {
        case WM_INITDIALOG:
            bReturn = s_pDlg->OnInitDialog(hwndDlg);
        break;
```

```
case WM_COMMAND:
    switch (LOWORD(wParam))
    {
        case IDOK:
            // get the hot key
            HWND hctrlHotKey = ::GetDlgItem(hwndDlg,
                IDC_HOTKEY);
            LRESULT lHotkey = SendMessage(
                hctrlHotKey, HKM_GETHOTKEY, 0, 0);

            // use the hot key retrieved in your application
            // in this application we send the WM_SETHOTKEY
            // to the parent
            HWND hParent = GetParent(hwndDlg);
            SendMessage(hParent, WM_SETHOTKEY, lHotkey, 0);

            EndDialog(hwndDlg, LOWORD(wParam));
            bReturn = TRUE;
            break;
        }
        break;
    }
    return bReturn;
}
```

The dialog template for the dialog box in Listing 6-9 creates a Hot Key control with the WS_BRODER and WS_TABSTOP styles. There are no control-specific styles for the Hot Key control.

The OnInitDialog() method sends the HKM_SETRULES message to the control, which indicates that it should not allow unmodified keys. In this example, this message tells the hot key control that when the user presses an unmodified key, it should prefix the Ctrl key to the selection. The function then sets the initial hot key combination to Ctrl+X, using the HKM_SETHOTKEY message.

In the DialogProc() method, when the user click the "OK" button, the function retrieves the hot key combination from the control, using the WM_GETHOTKEY message. It then sets the hot key combination to the main window, using the WM_SETHOTKEY message. Now if you switch to another application and then press the hot key combination, the sample application will be activated.

IP Address control

The *IP Address control* allows an application to provide a user with a common method for entering an *Internet Protocol (IP)* address. It also provides a convenient way for the application to retrieve the address.

The control allows the user to enter the four sets of numbers (each consisting of one to three digits) that make up an IP address. The control automatically moves between the fields, if the user enters all three digits in a field. Otherwise, the user can use the arrow keys to navigate through the fields.

Figure 6-10 shows an example of an IP Address control in a dialog. In this example, the user entered a value of 185.25.10.36 for the IP address. Listing 6-10 shows how you can set up the allowable ranges for the IP control and how to retrieve an IP address from the control.

Figure 6-10: The IP Address control

Listing 6-10: Setting the allowable ranges for an IP Address control and retrieving the selected address

```
// project CommonControls, file dlgIPAddress.h
class CIPAddressDialog
{
public:
    CIPAddressDialog() :
      m_byFirst(0), m_bySecond(0), m_byThird(0), m_byFourth(0) {}
    virtual ~CIPAddressDialog() {}

// access functions
public:
    BOOL GetFirstIPAddressValue() { return m_byFirst; }
    BOOL GetSecondIPAddressValue() { return m_bySecond; }
    BOOL GetThirdIPAddressValue() { return m_byThird; }
    BOOL GetFourthIPAddressValue() { return m_byFourth; }

// operations
public:
    int DoModal(HWND hWnd);

// implementation
```

```
protected:
    BOOL OnInitDialog(HWND hDlg);
    BOOL OnOK(HWND hDlg);

    static BOOL CALLBACK DialogProc(HWND hwndDlg, UINT uMsg,
        WPARAM wParam, LPARAM lParam);
    static CIPAddressDialog* s_pDlg;

// members
protected:
    BYTE m_byFirst;
    BYTE m_bySecond;
    BYTE m_byThird;
    BYTE m_byFourth;
};

// project CommonControls, file dlgIPAddress.cpp
#include "stdafx.h"
#include "resource.h"
#include "dlgIPAddress.h"

extern HINSTANCE g_hInst;
CIPAddressDialog* CIPAddressDialog::s_pDlg = NULL;

// DoModal: called to create and display the dialog
int CIPAddressDialog::DoModal(HWND hWnd)
{
    s_pDlg = this;
    int nReturn = DialogBox(
        g_hInst, MAKEINTRESOURCE(IDD_IPADDRESS), hWnd,
        reinterpret_cast<DLGPROC>(DialogProc));

    return nReturn;
}

// OnInitDialog: called to initialize the dialog
BOOL CIPAddressDialog::OnInitDialog(HWND hDlg)
{
    HWND hctrlPAddress = ::GetDlgItem(hDlg, IDC_IPADDRESS);

    // set the range of the addresses
    SendMessage(hctrlPAddress, IPM_SETRANGE,
        0, MAKEIPRANGE(180, 190));
    SendMessage(hctrlPAddress, IPM_SETRANGE,
```

```
                1, MAKEIPRANGE(0, 50));
        SendMessage(hctrlPAddress, IPM_SETRANGE,
                2, MAKEIPRANGE(0, 50));
        SendMessage(hctrlPAddress, IPM_SETRANGE,
                3, MAKEIPRANGE(0, 255));

        // set the initial IP address
        LPARAM lparamIPAddress = MAKEIPADDRESS(185, 25, 10, 36);
        SendMessage(hctrlPAddress, IPM_SETADDRESS, 0, lparamIPAddress);

        return TRUE;
}


// OnOK: called to handle the OK button
BOOL CIPAddressDialog::OnOK(HWND hDlg)
{
        BOOL bReturn(TRUE);

        // get the selected IP address
        HWND hctrlPAddress = ::GetDlgItem(hDlg, IDC_IPADDRESS);

        DWORD dwAddress(0);
        SendMessage(
                hctrlPAddress, IPM_GETADDRESS, 0, (LPARAM)&dwAddress);
        m_byFirst = (BYTE)FIRST_IPADDRESS(dwAddress);
        m_bySecond = (BYTE)SECOND_IPADDRESS(dwAddress);
        m_byThird = (BYTE)THIRD_IPADDRESS(dwAddress);
        m_byFourth = (BYTE)FOURTH_IPADDRESS(dwAddress);

        EndDialog(hDlg, IDOK);

        return bReturn;
}


// DialogProc: called to process the messages for the dialog
BOOL CALLBACK CIPAddressDialog::DialogProc(HWND hwndDlg, UINT uMsg,
        WPARAM wParam, LPARAM /*lParam*/)
{
        BOOL bReturn(FALSE);

        switch (uMsg)
        {
            case WM_INITDIALOG:
                bReturn = s_pDlg->OnInitDialog(hwndDlg);
```

```
        break;

    case WM_COMMAND:
        switch (LOWORD(wParam))
        {
            case IDOK:
                s_pDlg->OnOK(hwndDlg);
                break;
        }
        break;
    }

    return bReturn;
}
```

The dialog resource for the dialog box in Listing 6-10 simply creates the IP address control with the WS_TABSTOP style. There are no control specific styles for the IP Address control.

The OnInitDialog() method sets the range of allowable values for each field of the IP Address control, using the IPM_SETRANGE macro. In this example, the first three fields are restricted to small ranges (180 to 190, 0 to 50, and 0 to 50, respectively) while the fourth field accepts any legal value (0 to 255). There are no macros defined that send the messages for the control.

The OnInitDialog() function then sets the initial IP address displayed in the control as 185.25.10.36 with the use of the IPM_SETADDRESS message. The function uses the MAKEIPADDRESS macro to pack these values into an LPARAM value. The Common Control Library provides several macros for working with the fields of an IP address.The OnOK() method retrieves the IP address from the control using the IPM_GETADDRESS message. It then saves each file of the address in a class data member. These member variables are used by the GetFirstIPAddressField(), GetSecondIPAddressField(), GetThirdIPAddressField(), and GetFourthIP AddressField() methods to return the correct IP address field value.

The Common Control Library also provides the IPN_FIELDCHANGED notification code for the IP Address control that indicates the user has changed a field in the control or moved between fields. The IP Address control also sends some edit control notifications with the use of the WM_COMMAND message.

Trackbar control

The *Trackbar control* allows the user to use a slider button to select a value. The Trackbar control allows you to specify the number of values from which the user can select. Trackbars are often used when allowing the selection of a range of values (e.g., a quantity field or a volume control).

As a user slides the slider button in the trackbar, the control sends either the WM_HSCROLL or WM_VSCROLL message, depending on the orientation of the Trackbar control. Along with this message, the trackbar sends a notification code in the low word of the `wParam` parameter. This value identifies who generated the scroll notification.

Listing 6-11 shows how to initialize the range and value of a trackbar control. It also shows how to process the `WM_HSCROLL` message.

Listing 6-11: Initializing a Trackbar control and processing the WM_HSCROLL message

```
// project CommonControls, file dlgTrackbar.h
class CTrackbarDialog
{
public:
    CTrackbarDialog() : m_nPosition(0) {}
    virtual ~CTrackbarDialog() {}

// access functions
public:
    int GetPosition();
    void SetPosition(int nPosition);

// operations
public:
    int DoModal(HWND hWnd);

// implementation
protected:
    BOOL OnInitDialog(HWND hDlg);
    BOOL OnPositionChanged(HWND hDlg);

    static BOOL CALLBACK DialogProc(HWND hwndDlg, UINT uMsg,
        WPARAM wParam, LPARAM lParam);
    static CTrackbarDialog* s_pDlg;

// members
protected:
    int m_nPosition;
};

// project CommonControls, file dlgTrackbar.cpp
#include "stdafx.h"
#include "resource.h"
#include "dlgTrackbar.h"

extern HINSTANCE g_hInst;
CTrackbarDialog* CTrackbarDialog::s_pDlg = NULL;
```

```
// GetPosition: called to get the selected position of the trackbar
int CTrackbarDialog::GetPosition()
{
    return m_nPosition;
}


// SetPosition: called to set the initial position of the trackbar
void CTrackbarDialog::SetPosition(int nPosition)
{
    m_nPosition = nPosition;
}


// DoModal: called to create and display the dialog
int CTrackbarDialog::DoModal(HWND hWnd)
{
    s_pDlg = this;
    int nReturn = DialogBox(
        g_hInst, MAKEINTRESOURCE(IDD_TRACKBAR), hWnd,
        reinterpret_cast<DLGPROC>(DialogProc));

    return nReturn;
}


// OnInitDialog: called to initialize the dialog
BOOL CTrackbarDialog::OnInitDialog(HWND hDlg)
{
    HWND hctrlTrackbar = ::GetDlgItem(hDlg, IDC_TRACKBAR);

    // open set the range for the track bar
    SendMessage(hctrlTrackbar, TBM_SETRANGE, TRUE, MAKELONG(0, 10));

    // set the intial position
    SendMessage(hctrlTrackbar, TBM_SETPOS, TRUE, m_nPosition);

    return TRUE;
}


// OnPositionChanged: called to handle the WM_HSCROLL notification
BOOL CTrackbarDialog::OnPositionChanged(HWND hDlg)
{
    HWND hctrlTrackbar = ::GetDlgItem(hDlg, IDC_TRACKBAR);
    m_nPosition = SendMessage(hctrlTrackbar, TBM_GETPOS, 0, 0);
```

```
        return TRUE;
}


// DialogProc: called to process the messages for the dialog
BOOL CALLBACK CTrackbarDialog::DialogProc(HWND hwndDlg, UINT uMsg,
    WPARAM wParam, LPARAM /*lParam*/)
{
    BOOL bReturn(FALSE);

    switch (uMsg)
    {
        case WM_INITDIALOG:
            bReturn = s_pDlg->OnInitDialog(hwndDlg);
        break;

        case WM_COMMAND:
            switch (LOWORD(wParam))
            {
                case IDOK:
                case IDCANCEL:
                    EndDialog(hwndDlg, LOWORD(wParam));
                    bReturn = TRUE;
                break;
            }
        break;

        case WM_HSCROLL:
            s_pDlg->OnPositionChanged(hwndDlg);
        break;
    }
    return bReturn;
}
```

The dialog resource for the dialog box in Listing 6-11 creates the Trackbar control with the `TBS_AUTOTICKS` and `TBS_TOOLTIPS` styles. Other styles may be used to specify horizontal versus vertical orientation, as well as other options. The `OnInitDialog()` method in Listing 6-11 sets the initial range for the trackbar using the `TBM_SETRANGE` message. It uses the `TBM_SETPOS` message to set the initial selected position.

The `OnPositionChanged()` method handles the `WM_HSCROLL` message that is sent when the user moves the slider control. The function uses the `TBM_GETPOS` message to get the current position of the Trackbar control. It saves this position in the `m_nPosition` data member. Along with this message, the trackbar sends a notification code in the low word of the `wParam` parameter. The `GetPosition()` and

`SetPosition()` methods expose the position of the track bar for the sample application. The `GetPosition()` method obtains the value that the user selected. The `SetPosition()` method initializes the starting value for the Trackbar control.

Progress Bar control

The *Progress Bar control* allows an application to show the user the status of a long operation. This provides the user with some assurance that program is actually doing something and has not stopped responding. The Progress Bar control allows you to set the range of the progress bar; this value represents the length of the operation. Once you have set the range of the control, you can set the current position to represent the progress of the operation.

When updating the current position of a progress bar, it is important to try to be as accurate as possible as to the time of the operation. For example, if your application is displaying a progress bar for an operation that consists of ten steps, with the tenth step taking ten times longer to complete than the first nine steps combined, you should not divide the progress bar into ten steps and update it when each step in complete. This will mislead the user into believing that the operation is almost done when it really has just begun. Instead, you might break the progress into 100 steps and update the progress bar intermittently while processing the tenth step. This will provide you users with a better indication of the true status of the operation.

Figure 6-11 shows the example of a progress bar in a dialog. This dialog allows the user to cancel the operation by clicking on the "Cancel" button. Listing 6-12 shows the code that implements the dialog.

Figure 6-11: The Progress Bar control

Listing 6-12: Implementing the Progress Bar control

```
// project CommonControls, file dlgProgressBar.h
class CProgressBarDialog
{
public:
    CProgressBarDialog();
    virtual ~CProgressBarDialog();

// operations
public:
```

```
    int Create(HWND hWnd);
    void IncrementProgress();

    BOOL Canceled();

// implementation
protected:
    BOOL OnInitDialog(HWND hDlg);
    BOOL Cancel(HWND hDlg);

    static BOOL CALLBACK DialogProc(HWND hwndDlg, UINT uMsg,
        WPARAM wParam, LPARAM lParam);
    static CProgressBarDialog* s_pDlg;

// members
protected:
    HWND m_hDlg;
    BOOL m_bCanceled;
};

// project CommonControls, file dlgProgressBar.cpp
#include "stdafx.h"
#include "resource.h"
#include "dlgProgressBar.h"

extern HINSTANCE g_hInst;
CProgressBarDialog* CProgressBarDialog::s_pDlg = NULL;

// CProgressBarDialog: default constructor
CProgressBarDialog::CProgressBarDialog()
:    m_hDlg(NULL)
,    m_bCanceled(FALSE)
{
}

// ~CProgressBarDialog: destructor
CProgressBarDialog::~CProgressBarDialog()
{
    if (m_hDlg != NULL)
    {
        DestroyWindow(m_hDlg);
    }
}
```

```
// Create: called to create and display the modeless create dialog
int CProgressBarDialog::Create(HWND hWnd)
{
    s_pDlg = this;

    m_hDlg = CreateDialog(
        g_hInst, MAKEINTRESOURCE(IDD_PROGRESSBAR), hWnd,
        reinterpret_cast<DLGPROC>(DialogProc));

    return 0;
}


// IncrementProgress: called to increment the progress control
void CProgressBarDialog::IncrementProgress()
{
    HWND hctrlProgress = ::GetDlgItem(m_hDlg, IDC_PROGRESSBAR);
    if (hctrlProgress != 0)
    {
        SendMessage(hctrlProgress, PBM_STEPIT, 0, 0);
    }
}


// Canceled: called to determine if the user has canceled the operation
BOOL CProgressBarDialog::Canceled()
{
    // handle any messages
    MSG msg;
    while(PeekMessage (&msg, NULL, 0, 0, PM_REMOVE))
    {
        TranslateMessage(&msg);
        DispatchMessage(&msg);
    }
    return m_bCanceled;
}


// OnInitDialog: called to initialize the dialog
BOOL CProgressBarDialog::OnInitDialog(HWND hDlg)
{
    // open the animation file from the resource
    HWND hctrlProgress = ::GetDlgItem(hDlg, IDC_PROGRESSBAR);

    // set the range from 0 to 100000
    SendMessage(hctrlProgress, PBM_SETRANGE32, 0, 100000);
```

```
    // set each step to 1
    SendMessage(hctrlProgress, PBM_SETSTEP, 1, 0);

    return TRUE;
}


// Cancel: called when the user cancels the operation
BOOL CProgressBarDialog::Cancel(HWND hDlg)
{
    m_bCanceled = TRUE;
    DestroyWindow(hDlg);
    m_hDlg = NULL;
    return TRUE;
}


// DialogProc: called to process the messages for the dialog
BOOL CALLBACK CProgressBarDialog::DialogProc(HWND hwndDlg, UINT uMsg,
    WPARAM wParam, LPARAM /*lParam*/)
{
    BOOL bReturn(FALSE);

    switch (uMsg)
    {
        case WM_INITDIALOG:
            bReturn = s_pDlg->OnInitDialog(hwndDlg);
            break;

        case WM_COMMAND:
            switch (LOWORD(wParam))
            {

                case IDCANCEL:
                    bReturn = s_pDlg->Cancel(hwndDlg);
                    break;
            }
            break;

        case WM_DESTROY:
            s_pDlg->m_hDlg = NULL;
            break;
    }
    return bReturn;
}
```

The code in Listing 6-12 is a little different from the previous listings in this chapter. The Progress Bar control dialog is a modeless dialog box; the previous dialogs were modal dialog boxes. Therefore, this example uses a `Create()` function instead of a `DoModal()` function to display the dialog. The `Create()` function uses the `CreateDialog()` API to create and display the dialog.

Chapter 8, "Working with Windows," describes modal and modeless dialogs in more detail.

The dialog resource for this dialog creates the Progress Bar control with just the `WS_BORDER` style. Progress Bar controls support additional styles such as a smooth bar, `PBS_SMOOTH`, or a bar displayed vertically, `PBS_VERTICAL`.

The `OnInitDialog()` method sets the range of the progress control from 0 to 100,000, using the `PBM_SETRANGE32` message. It then sets the step increment to one with the use of the `PBM_SETSTEP` message. There are no notification codes or message macros provided for the Progress Bar control.

The `Cancel()` method in Listing 6-12 sets the `m_bCanceled` flag to `TRUE` to indicate that the user canceled the dialog. It then destroys the dialog window.

The progress dialog implements a couple of functions that are used by the `CommonControls` sample application to update the progress control. The `IncrementProgress()` method uses the `PBM_STEPIT` message to increment the current position of the progress bar. The `Canceled()` method is called to determine if a user has canceled the operation.

The `Canceled()` method first uses a message loop to handle any messages that have been added to the queue. It then returns the state of the `m_bCanceled` flag. By processing the message loop in the `Canceled()` function, it provides an easy way for the `CommonControls` sample application to be responsive to the "Cancel" button. If the application never processed the message queue during a long operation, the user will be unable to cancel the operation, since the button click message will never be processed.

Because this dialog is modeless, the `CommonControls` sample application uses this dialog differently than the previous dialogs. Listing 6-13 shows the global `OnProgress()` function that creates and updates the Progress Bar control dialog.

Listing 6-13: Creating and updating the Progress Bar control dialog

```
// project CommonControls, file CommonControls.cpp
//
// OnProgressBar: called to display the progress bar dialog
void OnProgressBar(HWND hWnd)
{
```

```
// create and display the dialog
CProgressBarDialog dlg;
dlg.Create(hWnd);

BOOL bCanceled(FALSE);

// perform a long operation
for (int nIndex = 0; nIndex < 100000; ++nIndex)
{
    // check to see if the user canceled the operation
    bCanceled = dlg.Canceled();
    if (bCanceled)
    {
        // stop the operation if he did
        break;
    }

    // increment the progress
    dlg.IncrementProgress();
}
}
```

The OnProgressBar() function firsts creates and displays the progress dialog. It then starts a long operation. In this example, it loops from 0 to 100,000. During this loop, the function calls the progress dialog's Canceled() function to check to see if the user canceled the operation. It then calls the IncrementProgess() function to update the progress bar.

Pager control

The *Pager control* provides an interface widget that enables a user to scroll a portion of the window that is not visible. To allow the Pager control to manage a window, you assign the window to the pager control. The Pager control will then let the users scroll the contained window to access the parts that are not visible.

When you create a Pager control, you can specify the PGS_HORZ or the PGS_VERT style to create a horizontal or vertical pager control. There are additional pager control styles: PGS_DRAGNDROP allows Windows drag-and-drop operations and PGS_AUTOSCROLL scrolls when the user hovers the mouse over a scroll button.

Once you create a Pager control, you can assign a window to it using the PGM_SETCHILD message. This message allows the Pager control to manage the specified window.

In order for the Pager control to know the ideal size for the contained window, you must process the PGN_CALCSIZE notification code. If you do not process this message, the trackbar will not display its scroll arrows, since it does not know the size of the contained window.

Rebar control

The *Rebar control* provides an interface for containing other child windows. A common use is to create a rebar control that contains one or more toolbars. Each Rebar control can contain multiple bands; however, each band can contain only one child window. The bands within the Rebar control can be repositioned by the user. As the bands are moved and resized, the Rebar control manages the layout of the contained child window. An example of the rebar control in use is the toolbars in Microsoft Internet Explorer. The toolbars in Internet Explorer are contained within a rebar control.

When you create a Rebar control, you can specify several styles to control how the rebar control behaves. Once you create a Pager control, you can add bands to it using the RB_INSERTBAND message. When you insert the bands, you assign a child window to the band. The rebar control sends notification codes to its parent window when it is being resized, moved, or deleted.

The RB_PUSHCHEVRON message and RBN_CHEVRONPUSHED notification code are new in version 5.80 of the Common Control Library. The Rebar control now will display a chevron ">" control when part of a band is obscured. When the parent window receives the RBN_CHEVERONPUSHED notification the parent should display a menu item with items for the obscured controls.

Toolbar control

In the recent past, toolbars have become an expected part of a Windows application. The Toolbar control provides a common user interface for managing toolbars. Toolbar controls provide a shortcut for an application's commonly used menu items. The toolbar provides a bitmap picture that represents a command the user can select.

CREATING A SIMPLE TOOLBAR CONTROL

Listing 6-14 shows a simple example of creating a Toolbar control. This is a portion of the toolbar1 sample application. The rest of the examples in this section are based on this application. It creates a toolbar with file new, file open, file save, edit copy, edit cut, edit paste, and about buttons.

Listing 6-14: Creating a simple toolbar

```
// project toolbar1, file toolbar1.cpp
// ...
// Global Variables:
HINSTANCE hInst = NULL;              // current instance
HWND hwndToolbar = NULL;            // toolbar

// menu IDs
#define ID_FILE_NEW                  200
```

```
#define ID_FILE_OPEN              201
#define ID_FILE_SAVE              202
#define ID_EDIT_COPY              203
#define ID_EDIT_CUT               204
#define ID_EDIT_PASTE             205


// ...
// InitInstance: called to create the main window and toolbar
BOOL InitInstance(HINSTANCE hInstance, int nCmdShow)
{
    BOOL bReturn(FALSE);

    HWND hWnd;

    // Store instance handle in our global variable
    hInst = hInstance;

    INITCOMMONCONTROLSEX initControls;
    initControls.dwSize = sizeof(initControls);
    initControls.dwICC = ICC_BAR_CLASSES;
    InitCommonControlsEx(&initControls);

    hWnd = CreateWindow(szWindowClass, szTitle,
        WS_OVERLAPPEDWINDOW, CW_USEDEFAULT, 0,
        CW_USEDEFAULT, 0, NULL, NULL, hInstance, NULL);

    if (hWnd)
    {
        // create toolbar
        TBBUTTON arButtons[] =
        {
            { 0, ID_FILE_NEW, TBSTATE_ENABLED, BTNS_BUTTON, 0, 0 }
            ,{ 1, ID_FILE_OPEN, TBSTATE_ENABLED, BTNS_BUTTON, 0, 0 }
            ,{ 2, ID_FILE_SAVE, TBSTATE_ENABLED, BTNS_BUTTON, 0, 0 }
            ,{ -1, 202, TBSTATE_ENABLED, BTNS_SEP, 0, 0 }
            ,{ 3, ID_EDIT_COPY, TBSTATE_ENABLED, BTNS_BUTTON, 0, 0 }
            ,{ 4, ID_EDIT_CUT, TBSTATE_ENABLED, BTNS_BUTTON, 0, 0 }
            ,{ 5, ID_EDIT_PASTE, TBSTATE_ENABLED, BTNS_BUTTON, 0, 0 }
            ,{ -1, 202, TBSTATE_ENABLED, BTNS_SEP, 0, 0 }
            ,{ 6, IDM_ABOUT, TBSTATE_ENABLED, BTNS_BUTTON, 0, 0 }
        };

        hwndToolbar = CreateToolbarEx(hWnd, WS_CHILD | WS_VISIBLE,
            100, 7, hInst, IDR_TOOLBAR, arButtons,
```

```
            9, 16, 15, 16, 15, sizeof(TBBUTTON));

        ShowWindow(hWnd, nCmdShow);
        UpdateWindow(hWnd);

        bReturn = TRUE;
    }
    return bReturn;
}


// WndProc: handle the message for the window
LRESULT CALLBACK WndProc(HWND hWnd, UINT message, WPARAM wParam, LPARAM lParam)
{
    int wmId, wmEvent;

    // ...

    switch (message)
    {
        case WM_COMMAND:
            wmId    = LOWORD(wParam);
            wmEvent = HIWORD(wParam);

            // Parse the menu selections:
            switch (wmId)
            {
                case ID_FILE_NEW:
                case ID_FILE_OPEN:
                case ID_FILE_SAVE:
                case ID_EDIT_COPY:
                case ID_EDIT_CUT:
                case ID_EDIT_PASTE:
                {
                    TCHAR szOut[256];
                    wsprintf(szOut,
                        _T("The Toolbar button %d was pressed"),
                        wmId);
                    MessageBox(hWnd, szOut, _T("Toolbar"), MB_OK);
                }
                break;

                case IDM_ABOUT:
                    DialogBox(hInst, (LPCTSTR)IDD_ABOUTBOX,
                        hWnd, (DLGPROC)About);
```

```
            break;

            ...

            default:
                return DefWindowProc(
                    hWnd, message, wParam, lParam);
        }
        break;

    // ...

    default:
        return DefWindowProc(hWnd, message, wParam, lParam);
    }
    return 0;
}
```

The `InitInstance()` method in Listing 6-14 first saves the module instance in a module static variable. It calls the `InitCommonControlsEx()` API to initialize the toolbar classes. It then creates the main application window. Once the main window is created successfully, the method creates the toolbar.

The `arButtons` array defines the buttons that will be dispalyed in the toolbar. The values specify the members of the `TBBUTTION` structure.

The method then uses the `CreateToolbarEx()` API to create the bitmap. The toolbar is created with the `WS_CHILD` and `WS_VISIBLE` styles. These are the minimum styles that you can specify. The Common Control Library defines some control specific styles that you can use with the Toolbar control. The `InitInstance()` method completes by showing the main application window.

The `WndProc()` function in Listing 6-14 handles the messages for the window. In the listing, I have removed the code that does not pertain to handling the toolbar buttons for clarity. The toolbar buttons are handled identically to menu item. They send a `WM_COMMAND` message with the low-order word of the `wParam` parameter set to the ID of the toolbar button. In this example, for every button except the "About" button, the function just displays the ID of the button pressed in a message box. For the "About" button, the function displays the About dialog box.

CUSTOMIZING A TOOLBAR CONTROL

The toolbar control provides a customization dialog box that allows a user to add, remove, or rearrange the buttons on the toolbar. It also provides support for allowing the user to drag buttons around on the toolbar.

Figure 6-12 shows an example of the toolbar customization dialog box. Listing 6-15 shows how you can add the ability to allow users to customize their toolbars. This code builds on the code presented in Listing 6-14.

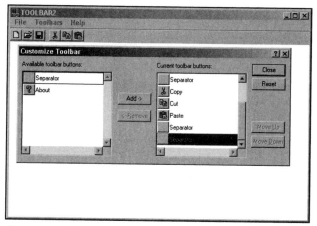

Figure 6-12: The toolbar customization dialog

Listing 6-15: Customizing a Toolbar control

```
// project toolbar2, file toolbar2.cpp
// ...
// toolbar buttons
TBBUTTON arButtons[] =
{
    { 0, ID_FILE_NEW, TBSTATE_ENABLED, BTNS_BUTTON, 0, 0 }
   ,{ 1, ID_FILE_OPEN, TBSTATE_ENABLED, BTNS_BUTTON, 0, 0 }
   ,{ 2, ID_FILE_SAVE, TBSTATE_ENABLED, BTNS_BUTTON, 0, 0 }
   ,{ -1, -1, TBSTATE_ENABLED, BTNS_SEP, 0, 0 }
   ,{ 3, ID_EDIT_COPY, TBSTATE_ENABLED, BTNS_BUTTON, 0, 0 }
   ,{ 4, ID_EDIT_CUT, TBSTATE_ENABLED, BTNS_BUTTON, 0, 0 }
   ,{ 5, ID_EDIT_PASTE, TBSTATE_ENABLED, BTNS_BUTTON, 0, 0 }
   ,{ -1, -1, TBSTATE_ENABLED, BTNS_SEP, 0, 0 }
   ,{ 6, IDM_ABOUT, TBSTATE_ENABLED, BTNS_BUTTON, 0, 0 }
};

// ...
//
// InitInstance: called to create the main window and toolbar
BOOL InitInstance(HINSTANCE hInstance, int nCmdShow)
{
    BOOL bReturn(FALSE);

    HWND hWnd;

    hInst = hInstance;
```

```
INITCOMMONCONTROLSEX initControls;
initControls.dwSize = sizeof(initControls);
initControls.dwICC = ICC_BAR_CLASSES | ICC_COOL_CLASSES;
InitCommonControlsEx(&initControls);

hWnd = CreateWindow(szWindowClass, szTitle,
    WS_OVERLAPPEDWINDOW, CW_USEDEFAULT, 0,
    CW_USEDEFAULT, 0, NULL, NULL, hInstance, NULL);

if (hWnd)
{
    // create toolbar
    DWORD dwStyle = WS_CHILD | WS_VISIBLE | CCS_ADJUSTABLE;
    hwndToolbar = CreateToolbarEx(hWnd, dwStyle,
        1000, 9, hInst, IDR_TOOLBAR, arButtons,
        9, 16, 15, 16, 15, sizeof(TBBUTTON));

    ShowWindow(hWnd, nCmdShow);
    UpdateWindow(hWnd);

    bReturn = TRUE;
}
return bReturn;
}

// OnNotify: called to process the toolbar customization messages.
BOOL OnNotify(int idCtrl, LPARAM lParam)
{
    BOOL bReturn(FALSE);

    LPNMHDR lpNMHDR = reinterpret_cast<LPNMHDR>(lParam);
    LPNMTOOLBAR lpnmToolbar = NULL;

    switch(lpNMHDR->code)
    {
        case TBN_INITCUSTOMIZE:
            bReturn = TRUE;
        break;

        case TBN_GETBUTTONINFO:
        {
            lpnmToolbar =
                reinterpret_cast<LPNMTOOLBAR>(lParam);
```

```
                    if (lpnmToolbar->iItem <
                        sizeof(arButtons) / sizeof(arButtons[0]))
                    {
                        TBBUTTON& buttonInfo =
                            arButtons[lpnmToolbar->iItem];
                        if (buttonInfo.idCommand != -1)
                        {
                            lpnmToolbar->tbButton = buttonInfo;
                            (void)LoadString(hInst, buttonInfo.idCommand,
                                lpnmToolbar->pszText, lpnmToolbar->cchText);
                        }

                        bReturn = TRUE;
                    }
                }
                break;

            case TBN_QUERYINSERT:
            case TBN_QUERYDELETE:
                bReturn = TRUE;
                break;

            case TBN_TOOLBARCHANGE:
                SendMessage(hwndToolbar, TB_AUTOSIZE, 0, 0);
                break;
        }
    return bReturn;
}


// WndProc: handle the message for the window
LRESULT CALLBACK WndProc(HWND hWnd, UINT message, WPARAM wParam, LPARAM lParam)
{
    int wmId, wmEvent;

    // ...

    switch (message)
    {
        case WM_COMMAND:
            wmId    = LOWORD(wParam);
            wmEvent = HIWORD(wParam);

            // Parse the menu selections:
            switch (wmId)
```

```
    {
        case ID_FILE_NEW:
        case ID_FILE_OPEN:
        case ID_FILE_SAVE:
        case ID_EDIT_COPY:
        case ID_EDIT_CUT:
        case ID_EDIT_PASTE:
        {
            TCHAR szOut[256];
            wsprintf(szOut,
                _T("The Toolbar button %d was pressed"),
                wmId);
            MessageBox(hWnd, szOut, _T("Toolbar"), MB_OK);
        }
        break;

        case ID_TOOLBARS_CUSTOMIZE:
        {
            SendMessage(hwndToolbar, TB_CUSTOMIZE, 0, 0);
        }
        break;


        case IDM_ABOUT:
            DialogBox(hInst, (LPCTSTR)IDD_ABOUTBOX,
                hWnd, (DLGPROC)About);
        break;

        // ...

        default:
            return DefWindowProc(
                hWnd, message, wParam, lParam);
    }
    break;

// ...

case WM_NOTIFY:
    bReturn = OnNotify((int)wParam, lParam);
break;


default:
```

```
            return DefWindowProc(hWnd, message, wParam, lParam);
    }
    return 0;
}
```

The `InitInstance()` method in Listing 6-15 is identical to the one in Listing 6-14, except the array of `TBBUTTON` structures has been moved to a module static array, so that it is available outside of the `InitInstance()` method. Also when the `CreateToolbarEx()` API is called, the `CCS_ADJUSTABLE` style is added to the toolbar control. This style enables the toolbar control customization features.

The `OnNotfiy()` method is provided to process the toolbar customization notifications. The function handles the `TBN_INITCUSTOMIZE`, `TBN_GETBUTTONINFO`, `TBN_QUERYINSERT` and `TBN_QUERYDELETE` notifications codes. The `OnNotify()` method returns `TRUE` in response to the `TBN_INITCUSTOMIZE` notification. This notification is used to notify the parent window that the toolbar customization process has begun.

The `TBN_GETBUTTONINFO` notification requests information for a toolbar button to be used in the toolbar customization dialog. The `OnNotify()` method determines the identifier of the button that information is requested and retrieves the information from the static `TBBUTTON` array. The `TBN_QUERYYINSET` and `TBN_QUERYDELETE` notification codes are used to request permission to insert or delete a toolbar button. The `OnNotify()` method returns `TRUE` for both of these messages. You can return `FALSE` if you want to prevent a button from being inserted or deleted.

The `WndProc()` function in Listing 6-15 is identical to the one in Listing 6-14. except that handlers for `ID_TOOLBARS_CUSTOMIZE` menu item and the `WM_NOTIFY` messages are added. The handler for the `WM_NOTIFY` message simply calls the `OnNotify()` function.

In response to the `ID_TOOLBARS_CUSTOMIZE` menu item, the `WndProc()` function sends the `TB_CUSTOMIZE` message to the Toolbar control. This causes the Toolbar control to display the customization dialog box.

Status Bar control

The *Status Bar control* allows an application to display status information to the user. An application can divide the status bar into segments with each showing different information.

You create a Status Bar control with the `CreateStatusWindow()` API. When creating the status window various styles may be used to control its appearance.

Once the Status Bar control is created, you can add segments to the Status Bar control with the use of `SB_SETPARTS` message. You can obtain information about the segments in the Status Bar control with the use of the `SB_GETPARTS` message.

To set the text in a segment of the status bar, you use the `SB_SETTEXT` message. This message draws the string in the specified segment.

Tooltip control

The *Tooltip control* provides a way for an application to display additional information about a control or item that the application normally does not have ample space to display or wants to hide, since it would clutter the display. One common use for this is for a tooltip to appear when the mouse pauses or *hovers* over a button or control in a toolbar or dialog box.

Listing 6-16 shows the how to create a Tooltip control. It also shows how to add tools to the Tootip control.

Listing 6-16: Creating a Tooltip control and adding tools to it

```
// project CommonControls, file dlgTrackbar.h
class CTooltipDialog
{
public:
    CTooltipDialog() : m_hwndTip(NULL) {}
    virtual ~CTooltipDialog() {}

// operations
public:
    int DoModal(HWND hWnd);

// implementations
protected:
    BOOL OnInitDialog(HWND hDlg);
    BOOL OnNotify(HWND hDlg, LPNMHDR lpNMHDR);
    BOOL OnOK(HWND hWnd);

    static BOOL CALLBACK DialogProc(HWND hwndDlg, UINT uMsg,
        WPARAM wParam, LPARAM lParam);
    static CTooltipDialog* s_pDlg;

    HWND m_hwndTip;
};

// project CommonControls, file dlgTrackbar.cpp
#include "stdafx.h"
#include "resource.h"
#include "dlgTooltip.h"

extern HINSTANCE g_hInst;
CTooltipDialog* CTooltipDialog::s_pDlg = NULL;

// DoModal: called to create and display the dialog
```

```
int CTooltipDialog::DoModal(HWND hWnd)
{
    s_pDlg = this;

    int nReturn = DialogBox(
        g_hInst, MAKEINTRESOURCE(IDD_TOOLTIP), hWnd,
        reinterpret_cast<DLGPROC>(DialogProc));

    return nReturn;
}

// OnInitDialog: called to initialize the dialog
BOOL CTooltipDialog::OnInitDialog(HWND hDlg)
{
    // create the tool tip window
    m_hwndTip = CreateWindowEx(NULL, TOOLTIPS_CLASS, NULL,
        WS_POPUP | TTS_NOPREFIX | TTS_ALWAYSTIP | TTS_BALLOON,
        CW_USEDEFAULT, CW_USEDEFAULT, CW_USEDEFAULT, CW_USEDEFAULT,
        hDlg, NULL, g_hInst, NULL);
    SetWindowPos(m_hwndTip, HWND_TOPMOST,0, 0, 0, 0,
            SWP_NOMOVE | SWP_NOSIZE | SWP_NOACTIVATE);

    TOOLINFO toolinfo;

    // add tool tip for the edit control
    toolinfo.cbSize = sizeof(TOOLINFO);
    toolinfo.uFlags = TTF_IDISHWND | TTF_SUBCLASS;
    toolinfo.hwnd = hDlg;
    toolinfo.uId = (UINT)GetDlgItem(hDlg, IDC_EDIT);
    toolinfo.hinst = g_hInst;
    toolinfo.lpszText = MAKEINTRESOURCE(IDS_EDIT);
    toolinfo.lParam = 0;
    SendMessage(
        m_hwndTip, TTM_ADDTOOL, 0, (LPARAM) (LPTOOLINFO) &toolinfo);

    // add tool tip for OK button
    toolinfo.cbSize = sizeof(TOOLINFO);
    toolinfo.uFlags = TTF_IDISHWND | TTF_SUBCLASS;
    toolinfo.hwnd = hDlg;
    toolinfo.uId = (UINT)GetDlgItem(hDlg, IDOK);
    toolinfo.hinst = g_hInst;
    toolinfo.lpszText = MAKEINTRESOURCE(IDS_OK);
    toolinfo.lParam = 0;
    SendMessage(
```

```
            m_hwndTip, TTM_ADDTOOL, 0, (LPARAM) (LPTOOLINFO) &toolinfo);

    // add tooltip for Cancel button
    toolinfo.cbSize = sizeof(TOOLINFO);
    toolinfo.uFlags = TTF_IDISHWND | TTF_SUBCLASS;
    toolinfo.hwnd = hDlg;
    toolinfo.uId = (UINT)GetDlgItem(hDlg, IDCANCEL);
    toolinfo.hinst = g_hInst;
    toolinfo.lpszText = MAKEINTRESOURCE(IDS_CANCEL);
    toolinfo.lParam = 0;
    SendMessage(
            m_hwndTip, TTM_ADDTOOL, 0, (LPARAM) (LPTOOLINFO) &toolinfo);

    return TRUE;
}


// OnOK: called to process the OK button
BOOL CTooltipDialog::OnOK(HWND hWnd)
{
    if (m_hwndTip != NULL)
    {
        ::DestroyWindow(m_hwndTip);
        m_hwndTip = NULL;
    }

    BOOL bReturn = EndDialog(hWnd, IDOK);
    return bReturn;
}


// DialogProc: called to process the messages for the dialog
BOOL CALLBACK CTooltipDialog::DialogProc(HWND hwndDlg, UINT uMsg,
    WPARAM wParam, LPARAM /*lParam*/)
{
    BOOL bReturn(FALSE);

    switch (uMsg)
    {
        case WM_INITDIALOG:
            bReturn = s_pDlg->OnInitDialog(hwndDlg);
        break;

        case WM_COMMAND:
            if (LOWORD(wParam) == IDOK ||
                LOWORD(wParam) == IDCANCEL)
```

```
                {
                    bReturn = s_pDlg->OnOK(hwndDlg);
                }
            break;
        }
        return bReturn;
    }
```

The `OnInitDialog()` method in Listing 6-16 first creates a Tooltip control with the use of the `CreateWindowEx()` API. The Tooltip control is created with the `TTS_NOPREFIX`, `TTS_ALWAYSTIP`, and `TTS_BALLOON` styles.

After the `OnInitDialog()` method creates the Tooltip control, it adds the `IDS_EDIT` control, the `IDOK` button, and the `IDCANCEL` button to the Tooltip control with the use of the `TTM_ADDTOOL` message. There are no macros defined for sending the messages for the control.

The Common Control Library defines some notification codes for the Tooltip control. However, this example does not handle any of the tooltip notification codes.

Up-Down control

The *Up-Down control* enables the user to increase or decrease a value, often in another control. The user can modify the value of the Up-Down control by clicking on one of the arrow buttons that the Up-Down control provides. If the Up-Down control is controlling another window, as is often the case, the associated window is called a buddy window.

Listing 6-17 shows how to initialize the range of an Up-Down control. It also shows how to process the `UDN_DELTAPOS` notification code.

Listing 6-17: Initializing an Up-Down control and handling the UDN_DELTAPOS notification

```
// project CommonControls, file dlgUpDown.h
class CUpDownDialog
{
public:
    CUpDownDialog() {}
    virtual ~CUpDownDialog() {}

// operations
public:
    int DoModal(HWND hWnd);

// implementations
protected:
    BOOL OnInitDialog(HWND hDlg);
```

```
    BOOL OnNotify(HWND hDlg, LPNMHDR lpNMHDR);
    BOOL OnOK(HWND hWnd);

    static BOOL CALLBACK DialogProc(HWND hwndDlg, UINT uMsg,
        WPARAM wParam, LPARAM lParam);
    static CUpDownDialog* s_pDlg;
};

// project CommonControls, file dlgUpDown.cpp
#include "stdafx.h"
#include "resource.h"
#include "dlgUpDown.h"

extern HINSTANCE g_hInst;
CUpDownDialog* CUpDownDialog::s_pDlg = NULL;

// DoModal: called to create and display the dialog
int CUpDownDialog::DoModal(HWND hWnd)
{
    s_pDlg = this;

    int nReturn = DialogBox(
        g_hInst, MAKEINTRESOURCE(IDD_UPDOWN), hWnd,
        reinterpret_cast<DLGPROC>(DialogProc));

    return nReturn;
}

// OnInitDialog: called to initialize the dialog
BOOL CUpDownDialog::OnInitDialog(HWND hDlg)
{
    HWND hwndSpin = ::GetDlgItem(hDlg, IDC_SPIN);
    SendMessage(hwndSpin, UDM_SETRANGE32, 0, 100);

    return TRUE;
}

// OnNotify: called to handle the notification messages
BOOL CUpDownDialog::OnNotify(HWND hDlg, LPNMHDR lpNMHDR)
{
    BOOL bResult(FALSE);

    const int BUFFER_SIZE = 255;
    TCHAR szOut[BUFFER_SIZE+1];
```

```
    switch(lpNMHDR->code)
    {
        case UDN_DELTAPOS:
        {
            LPNMUPDOWN lpnmud = (LPNMUPDOWN)lpNMHDR;
            if (lpnmud->hdr.idFrom == IDC_SPIN_SCROLL)
            {
                wsprintf(szOut,
                    "The spin control was clicked: Current pos %d, delta %d",
                    lpnmud->iPos, lpnmud->iDelta);

                SetDlgItemText(hDlg, IDC_NOTIFY, szOut);
            }
        }
        break;
    }
    return bResult;
}


// OnOK: called to process the OK button
BOOL CUpDownDialog::OnOK(HWND hWnd)
{
    BOOL bReturn = EndDialog(hWnd, IDOK);
    return bReturn;
}


// DialogProc: called to process the messages for the dialog
BOOL CALLBACK CUpDownDialog::DialogProc(HWND hwndDlg, UINT uMsg,
    WPARAM wParam, LPARAM lParam)
{
    BOOL bReturn(FALSE);

    switch (uMsg)
    {
        case WM_INITDIALOG:
            bReturn = s_pDlg->OnInitDialog(hwndDlg);
            break;

        case WM_COMMAND:
            if (LOWORD(wParam) == IDOK ||
                LOWORD(wParam) == IDCANCEL)
            {
                bReturn = s_pDlg->OnOK(hwndDlg);
```

```
        }
    break;

    case WM_NOTIFY:
        bReturn = s_pDlg->OnNotify(hwndDlg,
            reinterpret_cast<LPNMHDR>(lParam));
    break;
    }

    return bReturn;
}
```

The dialog resource for the dialog box in Listing 6-17 creates two up-down controls. The first control has the UDS_SETBUDDYINT, UDS_ALIGNRIGHT, UDS_ AUTOBUDDY, UDS_ARROWKEYS, and UDS_HOTTRACK styles while the second has the UDS_ARROWKEYS and UDS_HORZ styles.

The OnInitDialog() method sets the range of allowable values for vertical up-down control with the use of the UDM_SETRANGE32 message. There are no macros defined sending the messages for the control.

The OnNotify() method handles the UDN_DELTAPOS notification code. This message is sent by the control when the control is about to change values. If you return zero in response to this notification, the value changes; if you return non-zero from the method, the control's value does not change. The OnNotify() method in Listing 6-17 examines this notification, and, if it is from the horizontal spin control, updates the notification message control.

Tab control

The *Tab control* allows an application to display information in logical groups. The Tab control provides an interface for allowing an application to define pages for the same area of a dialog. By using this interface, an application can use the same control to represent the properties for different objects. Tab controls are often used for property or configuration dialogs.

Figure 6-13 shows an example of a Tab control in a dialog. In this example, the Tab control is positioned above a static text label and a static text control that is updated with the selected tab information. Listing 6-18 shows how to insert tabs into the tab control and how to react to events such as when the user clicks a tab.

Figure 6-13: The Tab control

Listing 6-18: Inserting items into a Tab control and processing tab selections

```
// project CommonControls, file dlgTabControl.h
class CTabControlDialog
{
public:
    CTabControlDialog() {}
    virtual ~CTabControlDialog() {}

// operations
public:
    int DoModal(HWND hWnd);

// implementation
protected:
    BOOL OnInitDialog(HWND hDlg);
    BOOL OnNotify(HWND hDlg, LPNMHDR lpNMHDR);

    void UpdateTabControls(HWND hDlg, HWND hTab);

    static BOOL CALLBACK DialogProc(HWND hwndDlg, UINT uMsg,
        WPARAM wParam, LPARAM lParam);
    static CTabControlDialog* s_pDlg;
};

// project CommonControls, file dlgTabControl.cpp
#include "stdafx.h"
#include "resource.h"
#include "dlgTabControl.h"

extern HINSTANCE g_hInst;
CTabControlDialog* CTabControlDialog::s_pDlg = NULL;

// DoModal: called to create and display the dialog
int CTabControlDialog::DoModal(HWND hWnd)
```

```
{
    s_pDlg = this;
    int nReturn = DialogBox(
        g_hInst, MAKEINTRESOURCE(IDD_TABCONTROL), hWnd,
        reinterpret_cast<DLGPROC>(DialogProc));
    return nReturn;
}


// OnInitDialog: called to initialize the dialog
BOOL CTabControlDialog::OnInitDialog(HWND hDlg)
{
    // open the animation file from the resource
    HWND hctrlTabControl = ::GetDlgItem(hDlg, IDC_TABCONTROL);

    // add tabs
    TCITEM item;
    item.mask = TCIF_TEXT;
    item.pszText = _T("Tab 1");
    TabCtrl_InsertItem(hctrlTabControl, 0, &item);

    item.pszText = _T("Tab 2");
    TabCtrl_InsertItem(hctrlTabControl, 1, &item);

    item.pszText = _T("Tab 3");
    TabCtrl_InsertItem(hctrlTabControl, 2, &item);

    item.pszText = _T("Tab 4");
    TabCtrl_InsertItem(hctrlTabControl, 3, &item);

    UpdateTabControls(hDlg, hctrlTabControl);

    return TRUE;
}


// OnNotify: called to handle the notification messages
BOOL CTabControlDialog::OnNotify(HWND hDlg, LPNMHDR lpNMHDR)
{
    BOOL bResult(FALSE);

    switch(lpNMHDR->code)
    {
        case TCN_SELCHANGE:
        {
            UpdateTabControls(hDlg, lpNMHDR->hwndFrom);
```

```
        }
        break;
    }
    return bResult;
}


// UpdateTabControls: called to update the controls with information for the
//   specified tab
void CTabControlDialog::UpdateTabControls(HWND hDlg, HWND hTab)
{
    int nTab = TabCtrl_GetCurSel(hTab);

    TCHAR szTabName[33];
    TCITEM item;
    item.mask = TCIF_TEXT;
    item.pszText = szTabName;
    item.cchTextMax = 32;
    TabCtrl_GetItem(hTab, nTab, &item);

    TCHAR szOut[256];
    wsprintf(szOut, "%s selected", szTabName);
    HWND hwndText = GetDlgItem(hDlg, IDC_TEXT);
    SetWindowText(hwndText, szOut);
}


// DialogProc: called to process the messages for the dialog
BOOL CALLBACK CTabControlDialog::DialogProc(HWND hwndDlg, UINT uMsg,
    WPARAM wParam, LPARAM lParam)
{
    BOOL bReturn(FALSE);

    switch (uMsg)
    {
        case WM_INITDIALOG:
            bReturn = s_pDlg->OnInitDialog(hwndDlg);
            break;

        case WM_COMMAND:
            switch (LOWORD(wParam))
            {
                case IDOK:
                case IDCANCEL:
                    EndDialog(hwndDlg, LOWORD(wParam));
                    bReturn = TRUE;
```

```
                    break;
            }
        break;

        case WM_NOTIFY:
            bReturn = s_pDlg->OnNotify(
                hwndDlg, reinterpret_cast<LPNMHDR>(lParam));
            break;
    }
    return bReturn;
}
```

The dialog resource for the dialog in Listing 6-18 creates a Tab control with the TCS_HOTRACK style. Other options can be used to control buttons placement, icon positioning, and more.

The OnInitDialog() method uses the TabCtrl_InsertItem() macro to insert four tabs into the Tab control. It then calls the UpdateTabControls() function to update the dialog's IDC_EDIT field with information about the selected tab.

The OnNotify() method processes the TCN_SELCHANGE notification code sent when the user selects a tab. The OnNotify() method calls the UpdateTab Controls() method to update the dialog's IDC_EDIT field with information about the selected tab.

The UpdateTabControls() method is called to update the dialog's IDC_EDIT field for the selected tab. It first gets the selected tab using the TabCtrl_Get CurSel() macro. It then gets the name of the tab using the TabCtrl_GetItem() macro. The UpdateTabControls() function finally updates the text with the selected tab Control name, with the use of the SetWindowText() API.

Property Sheet control

The *Property sheet* control is often used to display the properties of an object. The control is also used to display a large amount of related information, such as the options for an application.

In addition, the Property Sheet control can create wizards. Wizards allow you to display a sequential set of pages and are often used to simplify performing complicated operations.

PROPERTY SHEETS

Each property sheet contains a set of one or more pages of controls called *property pages*. A property sheet usually contains more than one property page, all relating to the single purpose of the property sheet.

A property page contains controls that relate to the information the page presents. For example, the spelling options for an application typically are grouped on a single property page. Figure 6-14 shows an example of a Property Sheet control, containing three property pages. Listing 6-19 shows how to create the property sheet and add the three pages.

Figure 6-14: The Property Sheet control

Listing 6-19: Creating a property sheet with three pages

```cpp
// project CommonControls, file propertysheet.h
class CPropertySheet
{
public:
    CPropertySheet() {}
    virtual ~CPropertySheet() {}

// operations
public:
    int DoModal(HWND hWnd);

// implementation
protected:
    HPROPSHEETPAGE CreatePropertyPage1();
    HPROPSHEETPAGE CreatePropertyPage2();
    HPROPSHEETPAGE CreatePropertyPage3();

    static BOOL CALLBACK PageProc(HWND hwndDlg, UINT uMsg,
        WPARAM wParam, LPARAM lParam);
};


// project CommonControls, file propertysheet.cpp
#include "stdafx.h"
#include "resource.h"
#include "PropertySheet.h"
```

```
extern HINSTANCE g_hInst;

// DoModal: called to create and display the property sheet
int CPropertySheet::DoModal(HWND hWnd)
{
    int nReturn(-1);

    // create property pages
    HPROPSHEETPAGE arPropertyPages[3];
    arPropertyPages[0] = CreatePropertyPage1();
    arPropertyPages[1] = CreatePropertyPage2();
    arPropertyPages[2] = CreatePropertyPage3();

    // initialize the property sheet structure
    PROPSHEETHEADER propSheet;
    propSheet.dwSize = sizeof(PROPSHEETHEADER);
    propSheet.dwFlags = PSH_DEFAULT | PSH_NOAPPLYNOW | PSH_NOCONTEXTHELP;
    propSheet.hwndParent = hWnd;
    propSheet.hInstance = g_hInst;
    propSheet.hIcon = NULL;
    propSheet.pszCaption = MAKEINTRESOURCE(IDS_PROPERTYSHEET);
    propSheet.nPages = sizeof(arPropertyPages) / sizeof(arPropertyPages[0]);
    propSheet.nStartPage = 0;
    propSheet.phpage = arPropertyPages;
    propSheet.pfnCallback = NULL;
    propSheet.hbmWatermark = NULL;
    propSheet.hplWatermark = NULL;
    propSheet.hbmHeader = NULL;

    // display the property sheet
    nReturn = PropertySheet(&propSheet);

    return nReturn;
}

// CreatePropertyPage1: called to create the first property page
HPROPSHEETPAGE CPropertySheet::CreatePropertyPage1()
{
    PROPSHEETPAGE proppage;
    proppage.dwSize = sizeof(PROPSHEETPAGE);
    proppage.dwFlags = PSP_DEFAULT;
    proppage.hInstance = g_hInst;
    proppage.pszTemplate = MAKEINTRESOURCE(IDD_PROPPAGE1);
```

```
    proppage.hIcon = NULL;
    proppage.pszTitle = _T("Page 1");
    proppage.pfnDlgProc = &PageProc;
    proppage.lParam = 0;
    proppage.pfnCallback = NULL;
    proppage.pcRefParent = NULL;
    proppage.pszHeaderTitle = NULL;
    proppage.pszHeaderSubTitle = NULL;

    HPROPSHEETPAGE page1 = CreatePropertySheetPage(&proppage);
    return page1;
}


// CreatePropertyPage2: called to create the second property page
HPROPSHEETPAGE CPropertySheet::CreatePropertyPage2()
{
    PROPSHEETPAGE proppage;
    proppage.dwSize = sizeof(PROPSHEETPAGE);
    proppage.dwFlags = PSP_DEFAULT;
    proppage.hInstance = g_hInst;
    proppage.pszTemplate = MAKEINTRESOURCE(IDD_PROPPAGE2);
    proppage.hIcon = NULL;
    proppage.pszTitle = _T("Page 2");
    proppage.pfnDlgProc = &PageProc;
    proppage.lParam = 0;
    proppage.pfnCallback = NULL;
    proppage.pcRefParent = NULL;
    proppage.pszHeaderTitle = NULL;
    proppage.pszHeaderSubTitle = NULL;

    HPROPSHEETPAGE page2 = CreatePropertySheetPage(&proppage);
    return page2;
}


// CreatePropertyPage3: called to create the third property page
HPROPSHEETPAGE CPropertySheet::CreatePropertyPage3()
{
    PROPSHEETPAGE proppage;
    proppage.dwSize = sizeof(PROPSHEETPAGE);
    proppage.dwFlags = PSP_DEFAULT;
    proppage.hInstance = g_hInst;
    proppage.pszTemplate = MAKEINTRESOURCE(IDD_PROPPAGE3);
    proppage.hIcon = NULL;
    proppage.pszTitle = _T("Page 3");
```

```
        proppage.pfnDlgProc = &PageProc;
        proppage.lParam = 0;
        proppage.pfnCallback = NULL;
        proppage.pcRefParent = NULL;
        proppage.pszHeaderTitle = NULL;
        proppage.pszHeaderSubTitle = NULL;

        HPROPSHEETPAGE page3 = CreatePropertySheetPage(&proppage);
        return page3;
}


// PageProc: called to process the messages for the property page
BOOL CALLBACK CPropertySheet::PageProc(HWND /*hwndDlg*/, UINT uMsg,
    WPARAM wParam, LPARAM lParam)
{
    BOOL bReturn(FALSE);

    // for WM_NOTIFY messages, the LPARAM is a NMHDR*, this object's
    //   code member (pNmhdr->code) can be PSN_SETACTIVE or PSN_KILLACTIVE
    //   handle these notifications here

    return bReturn;
}
```

The DoModal() method in Listing 6-19 first creates the three property pages that the property sheet will contain, using the CreatePropertyPageX() function. It then creates and initializes a PROPSHEETHEADER structure. This structure defines the characteristics of the property sheet.

The DoModal() method sets the dwSize member to the size of the PROPSHEET-HEADER structure. The dwFlags member is set to PSH_DEFAULT, PSH_NOAPPLYNOW, and PSH_NOCONTEXTHELP.The hwndParent member is set to the handle of the window passed to the DoModal() function. The hInstance member is set to the global module instance handle. This member is used to find any resource specified by other members. The hIcon member is set to NULL. You could use this member to specify an icon to display in the title bar of the property sheet. The pszCaption member is set to the string resource IDS_PROPERTYSHEET; this member is used for the title of the dialog.

The nPages member is set to the size of the array that specifies the property pages we are going to add. The nStartPage member is set to zero to specify that the first property page should be displayed. This member is used to specify which property page the property sheet will initially display. The phpage member is set to the array of property pages that will be displayed in the property sheet.

The pfnCallback member is set to NULL, since this example does not use call-back functions. You can use this member to specify a callback function that will be called when the Property Sheet control is initialized. The hbmWatermark, hplWatermark, and hbmHeader members are all set to NULL. These members only apply to wizards. These members are discussed in the next section on wizards.

The DoModal() method then calls the PropertySheet() API to create and display the Property Sheet control. The Common Control Library provides several APIs for working with property sheet controls. Table 6-6 describes these APIs. The Common Control Library also provides specific messages and macros for you to use with the Property Sheet control.

TABLE 6-6 PROPERTY SHEET CONTROL APIS

API	Description
CreatePropertySheetPage()	Creates a property page
DestroyPropertySheetPage()	Deletes a property page
PropertySheet()	Creates and displays a property sheet or wizard

The CreatePropertySheet1(), CreatePropertySheet2() and CreateProperty Sheet3() methods create the three property pages that the Property Sheet control displays. They first create and initialize a PROPERTYPAGE structure. They are identical except for the dialog template and title that they specify.

They first set the dwSize member to the size of the PROPSHEETPAGE structure and the dwFlags member to PSP_DEFAULT.

They first set the dwSize member to the size of the PROPSHEETPAGE structure and the dwFlags member to PSP_DEFAULT. The pszTemplate is set to the dialog template to use for the page. This member is set to the respective dialog template in each function. The hIcon member is set to NULL. You can use this member to specify an icon to display on the tab for the page. The pszTitle member is set to the title for the tab. This value overrides the name in the dialog template.

The pfnDlgProc member is set to the address of the PageProc() function. The PageProc() function is used to handle the messages for all three of these dialogs. In general, though, you will specify a dialog box procedure for each property page that you implement.

The lParam member is set to zero. It is used to specify application-specific information to the page's dialog box procedure. When the property sheet is created, a copy of the PROPERTYPAGE structure is sent to the page's dialog box procedure with the WM_INITDIALOG message.

The pfnCallback member is set to NULL, since this example does not use call-back functions. Had it been specified, the callback function would have been called when the page is created and destroyed.

The pcRefParent member is set to NULL. This member is used to specify the address of a reference count variable for the page. The system will increment the value pointed to by this member when the page is created and decrement the value when the page is destroyed.

The pszHeaderTitle and pszHeaderSubTitle members are set to NULL. These members only apply to wizards.(They are discussed in the next section on wizards.) Each of the CreatePropertyPageX() functions then call the CreateProperty SheetPage() API to create the page and return a handle to the created page.

The PageProc() function is used by all three property pages to process their messages. It explains how to catch the PSN_SETACTIVE and PSN_KILLACTIVE notification codes. You can use these notifications to perform actions when the page is activated or deactivated.

WIZARDS

Wizards provide a way for you to prompt a user through a series of steps to accomplish a specific task. They can provide a way to simplify complicated tasks for your users.

 Version 5.80 of the Common Control Library provides support for the Wizard 97 specification. The Wizard 97 specification updates the guidelines for developing wizards for applications and provides guidelines for the graphic design and content of wizards.

 For more information on the Wizard 97 specification, please refer to the "Wizard 97 Specifications and Development FAQ" topic on the MSDN.

Figures 6-15 through 6-19 show examples of each page from a wizard that follows the Wizard 97 style specification. Listing 6-20 shows the code that was used to create these individual wizard pages.

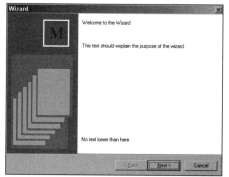
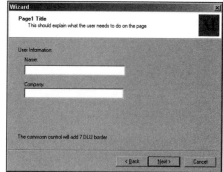

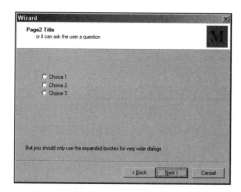
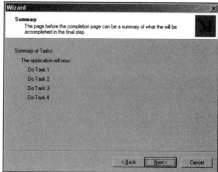

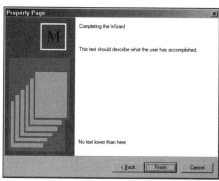

Figure 6-15-19: Examples of each page from a Wizard 97 style wizard

Listing 6-20: Creating the wizard pages

```
// project CommonControls, file wizard.h
class CWizard
{
public:
    CWizard() {}
    virtual ~CWizard() {}
```

```cpp
// operations
public:
    int Show(HWND hWnd);

// implementation
protected:
    HPROPSHEETPAGE CreateStartPage();
    HPROPSHEETPAGE CreatePage1();
    HPROPSHEETPAGE CreatePage2();
    HPROPSHEETPAGE CreatePage3();
    HPROPSHEETPAGE CreateCompletionPage();

    static BOOL CALLBACK StartPageProc(HWND hwndDlg, UINT uMsg,
        WPARAM wParam, LPARAM lParam);
    static BOOL CALLBACK Page1Proc(HWND hwndDlg, UINT uMsg,
        WPARAM wParam, LPARAM lParam);
    static BOOL CALLBACK Page2Proc(HWND hwndDlg, UINT uMsg,
        WPARAM wParam, LPARAM lParam);
    static BOOL CALLBACK Page3Proc(HWND hwndDlg, UINT uMsg,
        WPARAM wParam, LPARAM lParam);
    static BOOL CALLBACK CompletionPageProc(HWND hwndDlg, UINT uMsg,
        WPARAM wParam, LPARAM lParam);
};

// project CommonControls, file wizard.cpp
#include "stdafx.h"
#include "resource.h"
#include "Wizard.h"

extern HINSTANCE g_hInst;

// Show: called to create and display the wizard
int CWizard::Show(HWND hWnd)
{
    int nReturn(-1);

    HPROPSHEETPAGE arWizardPages[5];

    // create the pages
    arWizardPages[0] = CreateStartPage();
    arWizardPages[1] = CreatePage1();
    arWizardPages[2] = CreatePage2();
    arWizardPages[3] = CreatePage3();
    arWizardPages[4] = CreateCompletionPage();
```

```
    // create and show the wizard
    PROPSHEETHEADER wizard;
    wizard.dwSize = sizeof(wizard);
    wizard.dwFlags = PSH_DEFAULT | PSH_NOAPPLYNOW |
        PSH_NOCONTEXTHELP | PSH_WIZARD97 | PSH_WATERMARK | PSH_HEADER;
    wizard.hwndParent = hWnd;
    wizard.hInstance = g_hInst;
    wizard.hIcon = NULL;
    wizard.pszCaption = MAKEINTRESOURCE(IDS_PROPERTYSHEET);
    wizard.nPages = sizeof(arWizardPages) / sizeof(arWizardPages[0]);
    wizard.nStartPage = 0;
    wizard.phpage = arWizardPages;
    wizard.pfnCallback = NULL;
    wizard.pszbmWatermark = MAKEINTRESOURCE(IDB_WATERMARK);;
    wizard.hplWatermark = NULL;
    wizard.pszbmHeader = MAKEINTRESOURCE(IDB_HEADER);

    nReturn = PropertySheet(&wizard);

    return 0;
}


// CreateStartPage: called to create the intial page for the wizard
HPROPSHEETPAGE CWizard::CreateStartPage()
{
    PROPSHEETPAGE wizPage;
    wizPage.dwSize = sizeof(wizPage);
    wizPage.dwFlags = PSP_DEFAULT | PSP_HIDEHEADER | PSP_USETITLE;
    wizPage.hInstance = g_hInst;
    wizPage.pszTemplate = MAKEINTRESOURCE(IDD_WIZARD_START);
    wizPage.hIcon = NULL;
    wizPage.pszTitle = _T("Wizard");
    wizPage.pfnDlgProc = &StartPageProc;
    wizPage.lParam = 0;
    wizPage.pfnCallback = NULL;
    wizPage.pcRefParent = NULL;
    wizPage.pszHeaderTitle = NULL;
    wizPage.pszHeaderSubTitle = NULL;

    HPROPSHEETPAGE page = CreatePropertySheetPage(&wizPage);
    return page;
}


// CreatePage: called to create the first interior page
HPROPSHEETPAGE CWizard::CreatePage1()
{
```

```
    PROPSHEETPAGE wizPage;
    wizPage.dwSize = sizeof(wizPage);
    wizPage.dwFlags = PSP_DEFAULT | PSP_USEHEADERTITLE |
        PSP_USEHEADERSUBTITLE | PSP_USETITLE;
    wizPage.hInstance = g_hInst;
    wizPage.pszTemplate = MAKEINTRESOURCE(IDD_WIZARD1);
    wizPage.hIcon = NULL;
    wizPage.pszTitle = _T("Wizard");
    wizPage.pfnDlgProc = &Page1Proc;
    wizPage.lParam = 0;
    wizPage.pfnCallback = NULL;
    wizPage.pcRefParent = NULL;
    wizPage.pszHeaderTitle = _T("Page1 Title");;
    wizPage.pszHeaderSubTitle = _T("This should explain what "
        "the user needs to do on the page");

    HPROPSHEETPAGE page = CreatePropertySheetPage(&wizPage);
    return page;
}


// CreatePage2: called to create the second interior page
HPROPSHEETPAGE CWizard::CreatePage2()
{
    PROPSHEETPAGE wizPage;
    wizPage.dwSize = sizeof(wizPage);
    wizPage.dwFlags = PSP_DEFAULT | PSP_USEHEADERTITLE |
        PSP_USEHEADERSUBTITLE | PSP_USETITLE;
    wizPage.hInstance = g_hInst;
    wizPage.pszTemplate = MAKEINTRESOURCE(IDD_WIZARD2);
    wizPage.hIcon = NULL;
    wizPage.pszTitle = _T("Wizard");
    wizPage.pfnDlgProc = &Page2Proc;
    wizPage.lParam = 0;
    wizPage.pfnCallback = NULL;
    wizPage.pcRefParent = NULL;
    wizPage.pszHeaderTitle = _T("Page2 Title");;
    wizPage.pszHeaderSubTitle = _T("or it can ask the user a question");

    HPROPSHEETPAGE page = CreatePropertySheetPage(&wizPage);
    return page;
}


// CreatePage3: called to create the summary page
HPROPSHEETPAGE CWizard::CreatePage3()
{
```

```
    PROPSHEETPAGE wizPage;
    wizPage.dwSize = sizeof(wizPage);
    wizPage.dwFlags = PSP_DEFAULT | PSP_USEHEADERTITLE |
        PSP_USEHEADERSUBTITLE | PSP_USETITLE;
    wizPage.hInstance = g_hInst;
    wizPage.pszTemplate = MAKEINTRESOURCE(IDD_WIZARD3);
    wizPage.hIcon = NULL;
    wizPage.pszTitle = _T("Wizard");
    wizPage.pfnDlgProc = &Page3Proc;
    wizPage.lParam = 0;
    wizPage.pfnCallback = NULL;
    wizPage.pcRefParent = NULL;
    wizPage.pszHeaderTitle = _T("Summary");;
    wizPage.pszHeaderSubTitle = _T("The page before the completion "
        "page can be a summary of what will be accomplished in "
        "the final step");

    HPROPSHEETPAGE page = CreatePropertySheetPage(&wizPage);
    return page;
}


// CreateCompletionPage: called to create the final page for the wizard
HPROPSHEETPAGE CWizard::CreateCompletionPage()
{
    PROPSHEETPAGE wizPage;
    wizPage.dwSize = sizeof(wizPage);
    wizPage.dwFlags = PSP_DEFAULT | PSP_HIDEHEADER ;
    wizPage.hInstance = g_hInst;
    wizPage.pszTemplate = MAKEINTRESOURCE(IDD_WIZARD_COMPLETION);
    wizPage.hIcon = NULL;
    wizPage.pszTitle = _T("Wizard");
    wizPage.pfnDlgProc = &CompletionPageProc;
    wizPage.lParam = 0;
    wizPage.pfnCallback = NULL;
    wizPage.pcRefParent = NULL;
    wizPage.pszHeaderTitle = NULL;
    wizPage.pszHeaderSubTitle = NULL;

    HPROPSHEETPAGE page = CreatePropertySheetPage(&wizPage);
    return page;
}


// StartPageProc: called to process the messages for the start page
BOOL CALLBACK CWizard::StartPageProc(HWND hwndDlg, UINT uMsg,
    WPARAM wParam, LPARAM lParam)
```

```
{
    BOOL bReturn(FALSE);

    switch (uMsg)
    {
        case WM_NOTIFY:
        {
            NMHDR* pNmhdr = reinterpret_cast<NMHDR*>(lParam);
            switch(pNmhdr->code)
            {
                case PSN_SETACTIVE:
                {
                    // handle page activation
                    HWND hWndParent = GetParent(hwndDlg);
                    PropSheet_SetWizButtons(hWndParent, PSWIZB_NEXT);
                }
                break;
            }
        }
        break;
    }
    return bReturn;
}

// Page1Proc: called to process the messages for the first interior page
BOOL CALLBACK CWizard::Page1Proc(HWND hwndDlg, UINT uMsg,
    WPARAM wParam, LPARAM lParam)
{
    BOOL bReturn(FALSE);

    switch (uMsg)
    {
        case WM_NOTIFY:
        {
            NMHDR* pNmhdr = reinterpret_cast<NMHDR*>(lParam);
            switch(pNmhdr->code)
            {
                case PSN_SETACTIVE:
                {
                    // handle page activation
                    HWND hWndParent = GetParent(hwndDlg);
                    PropSheet_SetWizButtons(
                        hWndParent, PSWIZB_BACK | PSWIZB_NEXT);
                }
                break;
            }
```

```cpp
        }
        break;
    }
    return bReturn;
}


// Page2Proc: called to process the messages for the second interior page
BOOL CALLBACK CWizard::Page2Proc(HWND hwndDlg, UINT uMsg,
    WPARAM wParam, LPARAM lParam)
{
    BOOL bReturn(FALSE);

    switch (uMsg)
    {
        case WM_NOTIFY:
        {
            NMHDR* pNmhdr = reinterpret_cast<NMHDR*>(lParam);
            switch(pNmhdr->code)
            {
                case PSN_SETACTIVE:
                {
                    // handle page activation
                    HWND hWndParent = GetParent(hwndDlg);
                    PropSheet_SetWizButtons(
                        hWndParent, PSWIZB_BACK | PSWIZB_NEXT);
                }
                break;
            }
        }
        break;
    }
    return bReturn;
}


// Page3Proc: called to process the messages for the third interior page
BOOL CALLBACK CWizard::Page3Proc(HWND hwndDlg, UINT uMsg,
    WPARAM wParam, LPARAM lParam)
{
    BOOL bReturn(FALSE);

    switch (uMsg)
    {
        case WM_NOTIFY:
        {
            NMHDR* pNmhdr = reinterpret_cast<NMHDR*>(lParam);
            switch(pNmhdr->code)
```

```
            {
                case PSN_SETACTIVE:
                {
                    // handle page activation
                    HWND hWndParent = GetParent(hwndDlg);
                    PropSheet_SetWizButtons(
                        hWndParent, PSWIZB_BACK | PSWIZB_NEXT);
                }
                break;
            }
        }
        break;
    }
    return bReturn;
}


// CompletionPageProc: called to process the messages for the third interior
//    page
BOOL CALLBACK CWizard::CompletionPageProc(HWND hwndDlg, UINT uMsg,
    WPARAM wParam, LPARAM lParam)
{
    BOOL bReturn(FALSE);

    switch (uMsg)
    {
        case WM_NOTIFY:
        {
            NMHDR* pNmhdr = reinterpret_cast<NMHDR*>(lParam);
            switch(pNmhdr->code)
            {
                case PSN_SETACTIVE:
                {
                    // handle page activation
                    HWND hWndParent = GetParent(hwndDlg);
                    PropSheet_SetWizButtons(
                        hWndParent, PSWIZB_BACK | PSWIZB_FINISH);
                }
                break;
            }
        }
        break;
    }
    return bReturn;
}
```

The Show() method of the wizard in Listing 6-20 first creates the pages for the wizard. It then creates and initializes a PROPERTYSHEETHEADER structure. This structure was described in detail in the "Property Sheets" section. I cover only the members that are used differently for the wizard here. In this section, I also list the styles, messages, and notifications that are specific to wizards.

The dwFlags member is set to PSH_DEFAULT, PSH_NOAPPLYNOW, PSH_NOCONT EXTHELP, PSH_WIZARD97, PSH_WATERMARK, and PSH_HEADER styles. The pszbm Watermark is set to the identifier for the bitmap to use as the watermark bitmap. A watermark bitmap is the bitmap that is displayed on the left-hand side of the wizard. The hplWatermark member is set to NULL. This member is used to specify a palette for the watermark bitmap. The pszbmHeader member is set to the identifier of the bitmap to use in the header of the interior property pages.

The functions that create the property pages for the wizard are very similar to the functions used to create the property pages for the property sheet in the "Property Sheets" section. They are as follows:

◆ The start and completion pages use the PSP_HIDE header style to hide the header bitmap. This flag specifies that the watermark bitmap be displayed instead of the header bitmap.

◆ The interior pages use the PSP_USEHEADERTITLE and PSP_USEHEADERS UBTITLE flags, and specify strings in the pszHeaderTitle and pszHeaderSubTitle members. The wizard displays these stings in the header of the wizard page.

◆ The dialog box procedures for the pages process the PSN_SETACTIVE notification code. They set the appropriate wizard buttons with the use of the PropSheet_SetWizButtons() macro.

Summary

This chapter described the Common Control Library in detail. I described how you could use the controls provided by the library to present your users with a familiar and consistent user interface. I introduced the new features and improvements that Windows 2000 provides for the controls.

In the next chapter, I will describe how you can use the Common Dialog Library to provide your users with familiar, consistent dialogs for performing common tasks. Windows 2000 has made some minor improvements to some of the common dialogs and introduced a new dialog.

Chapter 7

Using the Common Dialogs

IN THIS CHAPTER

◆ The Common Dialog Library

◆ The common dialogs

THIS CHAPTER DESCRIBES how you can use the Common Dialog Library to provide your users with a familiar, consistent user interface for performing common tasks. Windows 2000 makes some minor enhancements to some of the common dialogs and introduces the Print Property Sheet.

For each common dialog, I provide an overview of the control, describing any Windows 2000 enhancements. I then provide an example of how to use the dialog to perform some common operations.

The Common Dialog Library

The Common Dialog Library allows an application to provide a consistent and familiar user interface for performing many common tasks. The Common Dialog Library provides many dialogs that allow the user to perform common operations. Included in the library are file open and save, print, search and replace dialog boxes, and more.

Windows 2000 provides new features for the Open and Save As dialog boxes and adds a new common dialog box: the Print Property Sheet. I describe the various dialogs in the next section.

This chapter builds upon the following CommonDialogs sample application, which provides a menu that allows you to display each of the common dialogs. Listing 7-1 highlights the overall structure of the sample application. The WndProc() function for the application's main window is shown in Listing 7-1.

Listing 7-1: The WndProc function for the CommonDialogs sample application

```
//
// WndProc: called to process messages for the main window.
//
LRESULT CALLBACK WndProc
(
    HWND hWnd
```

```
        ,UINT message
        ,WPARAM wParam
        ,LPARAM lParam
    )
    {
        BOOL bResult(FALSE);

        int wmId, wmEvent;
        PAINTSTRUCT ps;
        HDC hdc;

        if (message == s_msgFindReplace)
        {
            LPFINDREPLACE lpFindReplace = (LPFINDREPLACE)lParam;
            bResult = HandleFindReplaceMessage(lpFindReplace);
        }
        else
        {
            switch (message)
            {
                case WM_COMMAND:
                    wmId    = LOWORD(wParam);
                    wmEvent = HIWORD(wParam);

                    // Parse the menu selections:
                    switch (wmId)
                    {
                        case IDM_ABOUT:
                            DialogBox(g_hInst, (LPCTSTR)IDD_ABOUTBOX,
                                hWnd, (DLGPROC)About);
                        break;

                        case IDM_EXIT:
                            DestroyWindow(hWnd);
                        break;

                        case ID_FILE_COLORDIALOG:
                            OnColorDialog(hWnd);
                        break;

                        case ID_FILE_FONTDIALOG:
                            OnFontDialog(hWnd);
                        break;

                        case ID_FILE_FINDTEXTDIALOG:
```

```
                              OnFindTextDialog(hWnd);
                          break;

                          case ID_FILE_REPLACETEXTDIALOG:
                              OnReplaceTextDialog(hWnd);
                          break;

                          case ID_FILE_OPENDIALOG:
                              OnOpenDialog(hWnd);
                          break;

                          case ID_FILE_PAGESETUPDIALOG:
                              OnPageSetupDialog(hWnd);
                          break;

                          case ID_FILE_PRINTDIALOG:
                              OnPrintDialog(hWnd);
                          break;

                          case ID_FILE_PRINTPROPERTYPAGE:
                              OnPrintPropertyPage(hWnd);
                          break;

                          default:
                              return DefWindowProc(hWnd, message, wParam,
                          lParam);
                              break;
                      }

              case WM_PAINT:
                  hdc = BeginPaint(hWnd, &ps);
                  EndPaint(hWnd, &ps);
              break;

              case WM_DESTROY:
                  PostQuitMessage(0);
              break;

              default:
                  return DefWindowProc(hWnd, message, wParam, lParam);
          }
      }

      return bResult;
  }
```

The `WndProc()` function first checks to see if the message is for the find or replace common dialogs. If it is, it passes it to the `HandleFindReplaceMessage()` function.

I cover the `HandleFindReplaceMessage()` function in detail in the section on the Find and Replace Text dialogs.

The function then processes any other messages it receives. The `WM_COMMAND` messages are parsed and for each menu selection the appropriate common dialog is displayed. If the `Exit` command is selected, the main window is destroyed. The remainder of the function is pretty standard. It handles the `WM_PAINT` and `WM_DESTORY` messages and passes any other messages to the default window procedure.

In order to build the sample application, the `WINVER` and `_WIN32_WINNT` macros are defined as 0x500 in the `stdafx.h` header file. These macros enable the new Windows 2000 functionality in the Windows include files.

You also must reference the Windows 2000 Software Development Kit (SDK) include files, instead of the Visual C++ files.

The Common Dialogs

This section describes the dialogs that the Common Dialog Library provides. For each dialog, I provide an overview of the functionality of the dialog, highlighting any new features that Windows 2000 introduces. I follow this discussion with sample code that shows how to use the dialog. The following dialogs are described in this section:

◆ Color

◆ Font

◆ Find and Replace

◆ Open and Save As

◆ Page Setup

◆ Print

◆ Print Property Sheet (new in Windows 2000)

Color dialog box

The Color dialog box provides a common interface for allowing users to select a color. This dialog allows a user to select from a set of colors determined by the display driver, and you can also allow the user to define their own custom colors. Figure 7-1 shows an example of the Color dialog box.

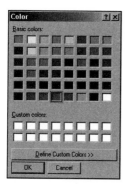

Figure 7-1: The Color dialog box

To create and display the Color dialog, you create and initialize an instance of the CHOOSECOLOR structure and pass a pointer to the ChooseColor() API. If the user selects a color and clicks the OK button, the ChooseColor() API returns TRUE and returns the selected color in the CHOOSECOLOR structure. If the user cancels the dialog or an error occurs, ChooseColor() returns FALSE. You can use the CommDlgExtendedError() API to get more detailed information about the error. Listing 7-2 shows how to create and display a Color dialog that remembers the last selected color and any custom colors selected by the user.

Listing 7-2: Creating and displaying a Color dialog box

```
#include "stdafx.h"
#include "colordialog.h"


//
// static color value used to initialize and hold the selected color
//
static COLORREF s_rgbColor = RGB(128, 128, 128);

//
// static array used to initialize and hold custom colors
//
static COLORREF s_arCustomColors[] =
{
```

```
    RGB (255,255,255)
   ,RGB(255,255,255)
   ,RGB(255,255,255)
   ,RGB(255,255,255)
   ,RGB(255,255,255)
   ,RGB(255,255,255)
   ,RGB(255,255,255)
   ,RGB(255,255,255)
   ,RGB(255,255,255)
   ,RGB(255,255,255)
   ,RGB(255,255,255)
   ,RGB(255,255,255)
   ,RGB(255,255,255)
   ,RGB(255,255,255)
   ,RGB(255,255,255)
   ,RGB(255,255,255)
};


//
//    OnColorDialog: Called to display a color dialog
//
void OnColorDialog(HWND hWnd)
{
    // initalize the dialog structure
    CHOOSECOLOR dlgColor;
    dlgColor.lStructSize = sizeof(CHOOSECOLOR);
    dlgColor.hwndOwner = hWnd;
    dlgColor.hInstance = NULL;
    dlgColor.lpTemplateName = NULL;
    dlgColor.rgbResult = s_rgbColor;
    dlgColor.lpCustColors = s_arCustomColors;
    dlgColor.Flags = CC_ANYCOLOR | CC_RGBINIT;
    dlgColor.lCustData = 0;
    dlgColor.lpfnHook = NULL;


    // display the color dialog
    BOOL bResult = ChooseColor(&dlgColor);
    if (bResult)
    {
        // the user selected a color
        s_rgbColor = dlgColor.rgbResult;
    }
}
```

The `OnColorDialog()` function takes a handle to a window as a parameter. This handle is used as the owner of the color dialog. First, the function creates an instance of the `CHOOSECOLOR` structure. It then initializes this structure with information that the Common Dialog Library uses to initialize the dialog box.

First, the function sets the `lStructSize` member to the size of the `CHOOSECOLOR` structure. The `hwndOwner` member is set to the handle of the window passed as a parameter to the function. The `hInstance` and `lpTemplateName` members are set to `NULL`, since a customized dialog template is not provided. If you want to customize the dialog template of the color dialog, you can use this parameter to tell the Common Dialog Library where to find the custom dialog template.

The `rgbResult` member is set to the `s_rgbColor` static variable to initialize the dialog to the previous selected color. On return, the `ChooseColor()` API sets this member to the color value that the user selects. The `lpCustColors` member is set to the static array of `RGB` values, `s_arCustomColors`. The `ChooseColor()` API updates this array with any custom colors that the user creates.

The `Flags` member is set to the `CC_ANYCOLOR` and `CC_RGBINIT`. The `CC_ANYCOLOR` flag allows the dialog to display all of the basic colors, and the `CC_RGBINIT` flag initializes the selected color to value provided in the `rgbResult` member. Table 7-1 shows the available values for the `Flags` member.

The `lCustData` member is set to zero. This value is passed to the custom hook procedure if you specify one. The `lpfnHook` member is set to `NULL`, since no hook procedure is provided. If you want to provide a hook function that can be used to customize the behavior of the dialog, set this member to your hook function.

You can refer to the MSDN library for more information on custom hook procedures.

TABLE 7-1 CHOOSECOLOR FLAG VALUES

Flag	Description
CC_ANYCOLOR	Specifies that the dialog shows all the available basic colors
CC_ENABLEHOOK	Specifies that the hook function specified in the `lpfnHook` member should be activated
CC_ENABLETEMPLATE	Specifies that the `hInstance` and the `lpTemplate` members contain the information to find the custom dialog template

Continued

TABLE **7-1** **CHOOSECOLOR FLAG VALUES** *(Continued)*

Flag	Description
CC_ENABLETEMPLATEHANDLE	Specifies that the hInstance member contains a data block containing the custom dialog template
CC_FULLOPEN	Specifies that the dialog initially displays the custom color controls
CC_PREVENTFULLOPEN	Creates the dialog with the "Define Custom Colors" button disabled
CC_RGBINIT	Creates the dialog with the initially selected color set to the rgbResult member
CC_SHOWHELP	Creates the dialog with a help button
CC_SOLIDCOLOR	Specifies the dialog only displays solid colors

After initializing the CHOOSECOLOR structure, the function calls the ChooseColor() API to create and display the dialog. If the user selects a color, the value is returned in the rgbResult member and saved in the s_rgbColor static variable.

Font dialog box

The Font dialog box provides a common interface for allowing a user to select properties of a font. The user can choose the fonts family, style, size, and color. Figure 7-2 shows an example of the Font dialog box.

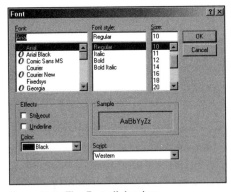

Figure 7-2: The Font dialog box

To create and display a font dialog box, you create and initialize an instance of the CHOOSEFONT structure and pass a pointer to the structure to the ChooseFont() API. If the user clicks the OK button, the ChooseFont() API returns TRUE and returns the selected font properties in the CHOOSEFONT structure. If the user cancels the dialog or an error occurs, ChooseFont() returns FALSE. You can use the CommDlgExtendedError() API to get more detailed information about the error. Listing 7-3 shows how to create and display a font dialog and remembers the previous font selected.

Listing 7-3: Creating and displaying a Font dialog box

```
#include "stdafx.h"
#include "fontdialog.h"


static LOGFONT s_lfSelected;

//
// OnFontDialog:  called to display the font dialog box
//
void OnFontDialog(HWND hWnd)
{
    // initialize the dialog structure
    CHOOSEFONT dlgFont;
    dlgFont.lStructSize = sizeof(CHOOSEFONT);
    dlgFont.hwndOwner = hWnd;
    dlgFont.hDC = NULL;
    dlgFont.lpLogFont = &s_lfSelected;
    dlgFont.iPointSize = 0;
    dlgFont.Flags = CF_SCREENFONTS | CF_EFFECTS;
    dlgFont.rgbColors = RGB(0,0,0);
    dlgFont.lCustData = 0;
    dlgFont.lpfnHook = NULL;
    dlgFont.lpTemplateName = NULL;
    dlgFont.hInstance = NULL;
    dlgFont.lpszStyle = NULL;
    dlgFont.nTypeFont = 0;
    dlgFont.nSizeMin = 0;
    dlgFont.nSizeMax = 0;

    // display the font dialog
    BOOL bResult = ChooseFont(&dlgFont);
    if (bResult)
    {
        // the user selected a font, the selected font properties
```

```
      // are stored in the s_lfSelected static variable.


   }
}
```

The OnFontDialog() function takes a handle to a window as a parameter. This handle is used as the owner of the font dialog. First, the function creates an instance of the CHOOSEFONT structure. It then initializes this structure with information that the Common Dialog Library uses to initialize the dialog box.

First, the function sets the lStructSize member to the size of the CHOOSEFONT structure. It sets the hwndOwner member to the handle of the window passed as a parameter to the function. The hDC member is set to NULL, since printer fonts are not used in this example. The dialog uses this member to specify a device context for the printer whose fonts are listed in the dialog.

The lpLogFont member is set to the static s_lfSelected variable to initialize font properties. If the ChooseFont() API succeeds, it returns the selected font properties in this member. The iPointSize member is initialized to zero. If ChooseFont() is successful, it returns the size of the selected font in units of 1/10 of a point in this member.

The Flags member is set to the CF_SCREENFONTS and CF_EFFECTS. The CF_SCREEN FONTS flag allows the user to select from the fonts available on the screen. The CF_ EFFECTS allows users to specify strikeout, underline, and text color properties. Table 7-2 lists the possible values for the Flags member.

TABLE 7-2 CHOOSEFONT FLAG VALUES

Flags	Description
CF_APPLY	Creates the dialog with an "Apply" button. Provides a hook procedure to handle the apply button.
CF_BOTH	Specifies that both screen fonts and printer fonts are listed.
CF_TTONLY	Specifies that only TrueType fonts are listed.
CF_EFFECTS	Creates the dialog with the strikeout, underline, and text color controls visible.
CF_ENABLEHOOK	Specifies that the hook function in the lpfnHook member be activated.
CF_ENABLETEMPALTE	Specifies the hInstance and the lpTemplate members contain the information to find the custom dialog template.

Flags	Description
CF_ENABLETEMPLATEHANDLE	Specifies that the hInstance member contains a data block that contains the custom dialog template.
CF_FIXEDPITCHONLY	Specifies that only fixed-pitch fonts are listed.
CF_FORCEFONTEXIST	Specifies the users cannot select a font that doesn't exist.
CF_INITTOLOGFONTSTRUCT	Specifies the dialog should be initialized with the properties specified by the lpLogFont member.
CF_LIMITSIZE	Specifies that the dialog only shows font sizes between the nSizeMin and nSizeMax members.
CF_NOOEMFONTS	Specifies that the dialog does not list vector fonts. Same as CF_NOVECTORFONTS.
CF_NOFACESEL	Specifies that the face name control should not be initialized from the lpLogFont member.
CF_NOCRIPTSEL	Created the dialog with the script combo box disabled.
CF_NOSTYLESEL	Specifies that the style combo box should not be initialized from the lpLogFont member.
CF_NOSIZESEL	Specifies that the size combo box should not be initialized from the lpLogFont member.
CF_NOSIMULATIONS	Specifies that the dialog should not allow GDI font simulations.
CF_NOVECTORFONTS	Specifies that the dialog not list vector fonts. Same as CF_NOOEMFONTS.
CF_NOVERTFONTS	Specifies that only horizontally oriented fonts are listed.
CF_PRINTERFONTS	Specifies that only printer fonts for the device context specified in the hDC member are listed.
CF_SCALABLEONLY	Specifies that only scalable fonts are listed.
CF_SCREENFONTS	Specifies that only fonts supported by the screen are listed.
CF_SCRIPTSONLY	Specifies that only fonts that are not part of the OEM and Symbol character sets are listed.

Continued

TABLE 7-2 **CHOOSEFONT FLAG VALUES** *(Continued)*

Flags	Description
CF_SELECTSCRIPT	Specifies that only fonts with the character set identified in the lpLogFont are listed. The user is not allowed to change the script combo box.
CF_SHOWHELP	Creates the dialog with a help button.
CF_USESTYLE	Specifies that the dialog returns the style data in the buffer specified by the lpszStyle member.
CF_WYSIWYG	Specifies that only fonts that are available on both the printer and screen are listed.

The rgbColors member is set to RGB(0,0,0), which is black. This member is used to specify the initial color of the text. If ChooseFont() is successful, it sets this member to the selected text color.

The lCustData member is set to zero. This value is passed to the hook procedure, if one is provided. The lpfnHook member is set to NULL, since the sample does not provide a hook procedure. If you want to provide a hook function that can be used to customize the behavior of the dialog, you set this member to your hook function.

Refer to the MSDN library for more information on custom hook procedures.

The lpTemplateName member is set to NULL. You can use this member to specify a custom template resource. The hInstance member is set to NULL, since a customized dialog template is not provided. If you want to customize the dialog template of the color dialog, you can use this parameter to tell the Common Dialog Library where to find the custom dialog template.

The lpszStyle member is initialized to NULL. This member is used to return style data for the selected font. ChoosFont() fills in this member upon success, if the CF_USESTYLE is specified. The nFontType member is initialized to zero. This member is used to return the type of the selected font. The function initializes the nSizeMin and nSizeMax to zero. You can use these members to restrict the size of the fonts the user can select if the CF_LIMITSIZE flag is specified.

After initializing the CHOOSEFONT structure, the function calls the ChooseFont() API to create and display the dialog. If the user selects a font, the s_lfSelected static variable is updated with the new information.

Find and Replace Text dialog boxes

The Find and Replace Text dialog boxes provide a common interface for searching and replacing text in a document. The Find Text dialog allows a user to enter a string to search for and to specify options to control the search. The Replace Text dialog allows the user to enter the string to search for as well as the string to replace the search string with and options to control the search. Figure 7-3 shows an example of the Find Text dialog box.

Figure 7–3: The Find Text dialog box

To create and display a Find or Replace Text dialog box, you create and initialize an instance of the FINDREPLACE structure and pass a pointer to the structure to the ChooseFont() API. Unlike the other common dialogs, the Find and Replace Text dialog boxes are modeless. This means you must ensure that the FINDREPLACE structure remains around for the lifetime of the dialog. You must create the structure as a static variable, on the heap, or use some other means to ensure the structure lives as long as the dialog.

If the FindText() and ReplaceText() APIs succeed, they return a handle to the new dialog. If they fail, they return NULL. You can use the CommDlgExtendedError() API to get more detailed information about the error. Listing 7-4 shows how to create and display a Find Text dialog and a Replace Text dialog box.

Listing 7–4: Find and Rreplace Text dialog box

```
#include "stdafx.h"
#include "findtextdialog.h"


TCHAR s_lpstrFindWhat[256];
TCHAR s_lpstrReplaceWith[256];

extern HWND g_hwndFind;
extern HWND g_hwndReplace;
FINDREPLACE s_dlgFind;
FINDREPLACE s_dlgReplace;

//
// OnFindTextDialog: called to display the Find Text common dialog
```

```
//
void OnFindTextDialog(HWND hWnd)
{

    s_dlgFind.lStructSize = sizeof(FINDREPLACE);
    s_dlgFind.hwndOwner = hWnd;
    s_dlgFind.hInstance = NULL;
    s_dlgFind.lpTemplateName = NULL;
    s_dlgFind.Flags = FR_DOWN;
    s_dlgFind.lpstrFindWhat = s_lpstrFindWhat;
    s_dlgFind.lpstrReplaceWith = NULL;
    s_dlgFind.wFindWhatLen = 256;
    s_dlgFind.wReplaceWithLen = 0;
    s_dlgFind.lCustData = 0;
    s_dlgFind.lpfnHook = NULL;

    g_hwndFind = FindText(&s_dlgFind);
}


//
// OnReplaceTextDialog: called to display the Replace Text common dialog
//
void OnReplaceTextDialog(HWND hWnd)
{

    s_dlgReplace.lStructSize = sizeof(FINDREPLACE);
    s_dlgReplace.hwndOwner = hWnd;
    s_dlgReplace.hInstance = NULL;
    s_dlgReplace.lpTemplateName = NULL;
    s_dlgReplace.Flags = FR_DOWN;
    s_dlgReplace.lpstrFindWhat = s_lpstrFindWhat;
    s_dlgReplace.lpstrReplaceWith = s_lpstrReplaceWith;
    s_dlgReplace.wFindWhatLen = 256;
    s_dlgReplace.wReplaceWithLen = 256;
    s_dlgReplace.lCustData = 0;
    s_dlgReplace.lpfnHook = NULL;


    g_hwndReplace = ReplaceText(&s_dlgReplace);
}

//
// HandleFindReplaceMessage: called to handle the find replace messages
//
BOOL HandleFindReplaceMessage(LPFINDREPLACE lpFindReplace)
```

```
{
    BOOL bReturn(FALSE);

    TCHAR szOut[128];

    if ((lpFindReplace->Flags & FR_DIALOGTERM) == FR_DIALOGTERM)
    {
        // the dialog is being dismissed
        g_hwndFind = NULL;
        g_hwndReplace = NULL;

        bReturn = TRUE;
    }
    else if ((lpFindReplace->Flags & FR_FINDNEXT) == FR_FINDNEXT)
    {
wsprintf(szOut, _T("Find the next occurrence of %s"),
            lpFindReplace->lpstrFindWhat);
        ::MessageBox(NULL, szOut, _T("Find Next"), MB_OK);
        bReturn = TRUE;
    }
    else if ((lpFindReplace->Flags & FR_REPLACEALL) == FR_REPLACEALL)
    {
        wsprintf(szOut, _T("Replace all occurrences of %s\r\nWith %s"),
            lpFindReplace->lpstrFindWhat, lpFindReplace->lpstrReplaceWith );
        ::MessageBox(NULL, szOut, _T("Replace All"), MB_OK);
        bReturn = TRUE;
    }
    else if (lpFindReplace->Flags & FR_REPLACE == FR_REPLACE)
    {
        wsprintf(szOut, _T("Replace the next occurrence of %s\r\nWith %s"),
            lpFindReplace->lpstrFindWhat, lpFindReplace->lpstrReplaceWith );
        ::MessageBox(NULL, szOut, _T("Replace"), MB_OK);
        bReturn = TRUE;
    }

    return bReturn;
}
```

The `OnFindTextDialog()` function takes a handle to a window as a parameter. This handle is used as the owner of the find text dialog. First, the function initializes the static `FINDREPLACE` structure with information that the Common Dialog Library uses to initialize the dialog box.

The function first sets the lStructSize member to the size of the FINDREPLACE structure. The hwndOwner member is set to the handle of the window passed as a parameter to the function. The hInstance and lpTemplateName members are set to NULL, since this sample does not provide a customized dialog template.

The Flags member is set to FR_DOWN to initialize the down direction radio button on the dialog. Table 7-3 lists all of the possible values for the Flags member.

The function sets lpstrFindWhat to the static variable s_lpstrFindWhat and the lpstrReplace to NULL. These values are used to initialize the find and replace text values in the dialog. The lpstrReplace member is ignored by the FindText() API. The wFindWhatLen is set to 256 and the wReplaceWithLen to zero. These members specify the length of the buffers in the lpstrFindWhat and lpstrReplace members.

The lCustData member is set to zero and the lpfnHook members are set to NULL since this sample does not use a hook procedure. If you want to provide a hook function that can be used to customize the behavior of the dialog, you use these members to specify your hook procedure and the application data passed to it.

 Refer to the MSDN library for more information on custom hook procedures.

TABLE 7-3 FINDREPLACE FLAG VALUES

Flag	Description
FR_DIALOGTERM	Specifies that the dialog is closing. Used with the FINDMSGSTRING registered message.
FR_DOWN	Specifies that the "Down" search direction radio button is selected.
FR_ENABLEHOOK	Specifies that the hook function specified in the lpfnHook member should be activated.
FR_ENABLETEMPLATE	Specifies that the hInstance and the lpTemplate members contain the information to find the custom dialog template.
FR_ENABLETEMPLATEHANDLE	Specifies that the hInstance member contains a data block containing the custom dialog template.
FR_FINDNEXT	Specifies that the user clicked the "Find Next" button. Used with the FINDMSGSTRING registered message.
FR_HIDEUPDOWN	Creates the dialog with the search direction radio buttons hidden.

Flag	Description
FR_HIDEMATCHCASE	Creates the dialog with the Match Case control hidden.
FR_HIDEWHOLEWORD	Creates the dialog with the Whole Word control hidden.
FR_MATCHCASE	Specifes that match case is selected.
FR_NOMATCHCASE	Creates the dialog with the Match Case control disabled.
FR_NOUPDOWN	Creates the dialog with the search direction radio buttons disabled.
FR_NOWHOLEWORD	Creates the dialog with the "Whole Word" control disabled.
FR_REPLACE	Specifies that the user clicked the "Replace" button. Used with the FINDMSGSTRING registered message.
FR_REPLACEALL	Specifies that the user clicked the "Replace All" button. Used with the FINDMSGSTRING registered message.
FR_SHOWHELP	Creates the dialog with a help button.
FR_WHOLEWORD	Specifies that whole word is selected.

The function then calls the FindText() API and saves the resulting handle in the g_hwndFind global variable. The OnReplaceTextDialog() is very similar to the OnFindTextDialog() function, except it initializes the lpstrReplaceWith member to the static variable s_lpstrReplaceWith and the wReplaceWithLen to 256. It then calls the ReplaceText() API instead of the FindText() API and saves the handle in the g_hwndReplace global variable.

Since the find text and replace text dialogs are modeless, you need to call the IsDialogMessage() API in you main windows message loop, so that the dialog keystrokes are handled properly. The following message loop from the applications WinMain() function shows an example of this:

```
int APIENTRY WinMain(...)
{
    ...

    // Main message loop:
    while (GetMessage(&msg, NULL, 0, 0))
    {
```

```
if ((g_hwndFind == NULL || !IsDialogMessage(g_hwndFind, &msg)) &&
    (g_hwndReplace == NULL || !IsDialogMessage(g_hwndReplace, &msg)) &&
    (!TranslateAccelerator(msg.hwnd, hAccelTable, &msg)))
{

    TranslateMessage(&msg);
    DispatchMessage(&msg);

}
}

...
}
```

When the user selects the "Find Next," "Replace," "Replace All," or dismisses the dialog, the Common Control library sends the FINDMSGSTRING registered message passing an updated FINDREPLACE structure with it. The sample application handles this message in its WndProc() function, extracts the FINDREPALCE structure, and calls the HandleFindReplaceMessage() function.

The HandleFindReplaceMessage() function examines the Flags parameter bits to determine what action to take. If the user is dismissing the dialog, it resets the dialog handles to NULL. If the user clicked an action button, this sample displays a message box describing the actions. In your application, you examine the members of the FINDREPLACE structure and perform the specified action.

Open File and File Save As dialog boxes

The Open File and Save As dialog boxes provides a common interface for allowing users to select what files to open or where to save a file. The Open File dialog box allows a user to navigate the directory structure and select what files to open. The File Save As dialog box allows the user to specify the directory and the name of the file to save.

 Windows 2000 has added some new features to the open and save dialog boxes. By default in Windows 2000, these dialogs display a "places" icon bar. This icon bar includes icons for commonly used folders such as "My Documents" and "My Computer." In addition, you can now apply your own custom filter criteria to each item in a newly opened folder. You can also prevent selected files from appearing in the recently used document system folder. Figure 7-4 shows an example of the new open file dialog.

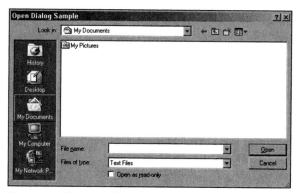

Figure 7-4: The Open File dialog box

To create and display an Open File or Save As dialog box, you create and initialize an instance of the OPENFILENAME structure and pass a pointer to the GetOpenFileName() or the GetSaveFileName() APIs. If the user selects a color and clicks the OK button the GetOpenFileName() and GetSaveFileName() APIs return TRUE and update the OPENFILENAME structure with the information the user selected. If the user cancels the dialog or an error occurs, these APIs return FALSE. You can use the CommDlgExtendedError() API to get more detailed information about the error. Listing 7-5 shows how to create and display an Open File dialog box.

Listing 7-5: Creating and displaying a simple Open File dialog box

```
#include "stdafx.h"

#include "opensavedialog.h"


extern HINSTANCE g_hInst;


TCHAR s_szFileNames[1024];
TCHAR s_lpstrCustomFilter[256];
int s_nFilterIndex = 1;

//
// OnOpenDialog: called to display the Open File dialog
//
void OnOpenDialog(HWND hWnd)
{
    // initialize the OPENFILENAME structure
    s_szFileNames[0] = NULL;
```

```
OPENFILENAME openfile;
openfile.lStructSize = sizeof(OPENFILENAME);
openfile.hwndOwner = hWnd;
openfile.hInstance = NULL;
openfile.lpTemplateName = NULL;
openfile.lpstrFilter = "Text Files\0*.txt\0All Files\0*.*\0\0";
openfile.lpstrCustomFilter = s_lpstrCustomFilter;
openfile.nMaxCustFilter = sizeof(s_lpstrCustomFilter);
openfile.nFilterIndex = s_nFilterIndex;
openfile.lpstrFile = s_szFileNames;
openfile.nMaxFile = sizeof(s_szFileNames);
openfile.lpstrFileTitle = NULL;
openfile.nMaxFileTitle = 0;
openfile.lpstrInitialDir = NULL;
openfile.lpstrTitle = _T("Open Dialog Sample");
openfile.Flags = OFN_ALLOWMULTISELECT | OFN_DONTADDTORECENT |
    OFN_ENABLESIZING | OFN_EXPLORER;
openfile.nFileOffset = 0;
openfile.nFileExtension = 0;
openfile.lpstrDefExt = NULL;
openfile.lCustData = 0;
openfile.lpfnHook = NULL;

openfile. pvReserved= NULL;
openfile. dwReserved= 0;
openfile.FlagsEx = 0;

// display the open dialog
BOOL bReturn = GetOpenFileName(&openfile);
if (bReturn)
{
    // get the selected files
    LPTSTR lpstrFiles = openfile.lpstrFile;

    // retrieve the directroy from the file list
    // it is the first stringTCHAR strDirectory[MAX_PATH+1];
    strncpy(strDirectory, lpstrFiles, MAX_PATH);
    strDirectory[MAX_PATH] = 0x00;

    // copy the directory to the strFile Name so we can
    // find the first file name.
    TCHAR strName[MAX_PATH+1];
    strncpy(strName, strDirectory, MAX_PATH);
    strName[MAX_PATH] = 0x00;
```

```
TCHAR szOut[MAX_PATH*2];

// retrieve and display all of the selected file names
BOOL bDone(FALSE);
while (!bDone)
{
    // get the position of the next file name
    int nLength = strlen(strName);
    lpstrFiles += nLength + 1;

    // if we still have a string
    if (strlen(lpstrFiles) > 0)
    {
        // display the name
        strncpy(strName, lpstrFiles, MAX_PATH);
        strName[MAX_PATH] = 0x00;

        wsprintf(szOut, "%s\\%s", strDirectory, strName);

        MessageBox(hWnd, szOut, _T("Selected Files"),
        MB_OK);
    }
    else
    {
        bDone = TRUE;
    }
}
}
}
```

The `OnOpenDialog()` function takes a handle to a window as a parameter. This handle is used as the owner of the open file dialog. First, the function initializes the `OPENFILENAME` structure with information that the Common Dialog Library uses to initialize the dailog box.

The function first sets the `lStructSize` member to the size of the `OPENFILENAME` structure. The `hwndOwner` member is set to the handle of the window passed as a parameter to the function. The `hInstance` and `lpTemplateName` members are set to NULL, since the sample does not provide a customized dialog template.

The `lpstrFilter` member is set to provide filters for text files (*.txt) and all files (*.*) The format for this string is the file description, followed by a NULL character, followed by the wildcard pattern. The string is terminated by two NULL characters. The `lpstrCustomFilter` member is set to the static `s_lpstrCustomFilter` and the `nMaxCustFilter` is set to the size of the `s_lpstrCustomFilter` buffer. The `lpstr CustomFilter` member is used to store the filter that the user selects. The `nFilterIndex` is initialized to the `s_nFilterIndex` static variable. This value specifies the index of the currently selected filter.

The lpstrFile member is initialized to the s_szFileNames static variable and the nMaxFile member is initialized to the size of the s_szFileName buffer. The lpstrFile member is used to specify the file initially selected. When the GetOpen FileName() API or the GetSaveFileName() API returns this value, it contains the selected files. If the user selected multiple files, this buffer contains the current directory followed by NULL separated file names. The lpstrFileTitle member is initialized to NULL and the nMaxFileTitle member is initialized to zero. You can use these members to specify the selected file's title, the file name without the path and extension. This sample does not use these values.

The lpstrIntialDirectory is set to NULL. This member allows you to specify the initial directory. If this member is not specified, Windows 2000 searches much harder for an appropriate initial directory than did the previous version of Windows. If the lpstrFile member contains a path, that path is used as the initial directory. If the lpstrFile member does not contain a path, the lpstrInitialDirectory member is used as the initial directory. If initial directory is specified and the current directory contains files of the specified filter, the current directory is used as the initial directory. If no files of the specified filter exist, the dialog checks the LastVisited registry value (under HKEY_CLASSES_ROOT\Applications\<APPNAME.EXE>\LastVisited). If this value contains a path then it is used for the initial directory. If no value is found, then the current user's personal files directory is used. Finally, if no other folder has been found, the desktop folder is used.

The lpstrTitle member is set to the text value, "Open Dialog Sample." This member is used for the caption of the dialog. The Flags member is set to OFN_ALLOW MULTISELECT, OFN_DONTADDTORECENT, OFN_ENABLESIZING and OFN_EXPLORER. The OFN_ALLOWMULTISELECT flag specifies that the user can select multiple files. The OFN_DONTADDTORECENT flag specifies that a link to the selected files should not be added to the recent files system folder. The OFN_ENABLESIZING flag specifies that the user can resize the open file dialog. And the OFN_EXPLORER specifies that the dialog should use the Explorer look and feel. Table 7-4 lists all of the possible values for the Flags member.

TABLE 7-4 OPENFILENAME FLAG VALUES

Flag	Description
OFN_ALLOWMULTISELECT	Specifies that the user can select multiple files.
OFN_CREATEPROMPT	Specifies that if the user specifies a file that does not exist, the dialog asks the user if they want to create the file.
OFN_DONTADDTORECENT	Specifies that a link to the selected files should not be added to the recently used system folder. (New in Windows 2000)

Flag	Description
OFN_ENABLEHOOK	Specifies that the hook function specified in the lpfnHook member should be activated.
OFN_ENABLEINCLUDENOTIFY	Specifies that the dialog box should send the CDN_INCLUDEITEM notification message to your hook function for each item in a newly opened folder. (New in Windows 2000)
OFN_ENABLESIZING	Specifies that the Explorer style dialog can be resized by the user. (New in Windows 98 and Windows 2000)
OFN_ENABLETEMPLATE	Specifies the hInstance and the lpTemplate members contain the information to find the custom dialog template.
OFN_ENABLETEMPLATEHANDLE	Specifies that the hInstance member contains a data block containing the custom dialog template.
OFN_EXPLORER	Specifies that the Explorer style customization be used.
OFN_EXTENSIONDIFFERENT	Specifies that the user selected a file extension that is different from the default file extension.
OFN_FILEMUSTEXIST	Specifies that the user can only select files that already exist.
OFN_FORCESHOWHIDDEN	Specifies that hidden and system files always be shown regardless of the user setting.
OFN_HIDEREADONLY	Creates the dialog with the "Read Only" control hidden.
OFN_LONGNAMES	Specifies that old-style dialogs should use long file names. Explorer-style dialogs always use long file names.
OFN_NOCHANGEDIR	Specifies that the current directory should be resorted to its original value, if the user changed the directory.
OFN_NODEREFERENCELINKS	Specifies that the path and file name for any selected shortcut files be returned instead of the files that they reference.
OFN_NOLONGNAMES	Specifies that old-style dialogs use short (8.3) file names. Explorer-style dialogs always use long file names.

Continued

TABLE 7-4 OPENFILENAME FLAG VALUES *(Continued)*

Flag	Description
OFN_NONETWORKBUTTON	Creates the dialog with the "Network" control hidden.
OFN_NOREADONLYRETURN	Specifies that the read only control is not selected and the selected directory is not write protected.
OFN_NOTESTFILECREATE	Specifies that the file should not be created before the dialog is closed.
OFN_NOVALIDATE	Specifies that invalid characters can be returned in the file name.
OFN_OVERWRITEPROMPT	Specifies that the user be asked if they wish to overwrite a file, if they select an existing file.
OFN_PATHMUSTEXIST	Specifies that the user can only select valid paths and file names.
OFN_READONLY	Specifies that the read only check box is selected.
OFN_SHAREAWARE	Specifies that the dialog not display a warning message if an operation fails for an network sharing violation.
OFN_SHOWHELP	Creates the dialog with a help button.

The function initializes the nFileOffset and nExtOffset members to zero. When the GetOpenFileName() API or the GetSaveFileName() API returns, these values contain the offset from the lpstrFile member to the file name and extension, respectively. The lpstrDefExt member is set to NULL. It is used to specify an extension if the user does not provide an extension.

The lCustData member is set to zero and the lpfnHook members are set to NULL since this sample does not use a hook procedure. If you want to provide a hook function that can be used to customize the behavior of the dialog, you use these members to specify your hook procedure and the application data passed to it. Please refer to the MSDN library for more information on custom hook procedures.

The pvReserved and dwReserved members are reserved for future use and should be set to NULL and zero. The FlagsEx member is set to zero. Currently the only possible value for this flag is OFN_EX_NOPLACESBAR. This flag tells the dialog to not display the places bar.

The Windows 2000 Open and Save dialog boxes can be modified by settings in the registry. Under the `HKEY_CURRENT_USERS\Software\Windows\Current Version \Policies\Comdlg32`, the places bar is hidden if the `NoPlaces` value is set to 1. If the `NoFileMRU` value is set to 1, the most recently used list is hidden; if the `NoBackButton` value is set to 1, the back button is hidden. The contents of the places bar are determined by the `HKEY_CURRENT_USERS\Software\Windows\ CurrentVersion \Policies\Comdlg32\Placesbar`. This key can contain a `DWORD` value representing a `CSIDL` value for a folder or a `REG_SZ` or `REG_EXPAND_SZ` containing a null terminated string with a valid path.

CSIDL values are described in Chapter 9, "Shell Services."

After initializing the `OPENFILE` structure, the function calls the `GetOpenFileName()` API to create and display the dialog. If the `GetOpenFileName()` API succeeds the function retrieves the selected directory and then loops through the selected files and displays each file name in a message box.

Page Setup dialog box

The Page Setup dialog box provides a common interface that allows the user to set the properties for a printed page. The user can select the type of paper, the paper source, the orientation of the page, and the page margins. Figure 7-5 shows an example of the Page Setup dialog box.

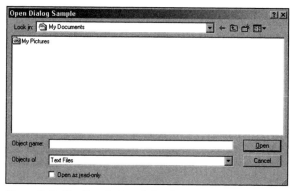

Figure 7-5: The Page Setup dialog box

To create and display the Page Setup dialog box, you create and initialize an instance of the `PAGESETUPDLG` structure and pass a pointer to the structure to the `PageSetupDlg()` API. If the user clicks the OK button, the `PageSetupDlg()` API returns `TRUE` and updates the page properties members of the `PAGESETUPDLG` structure. If the user cancels the dialog or an error occurs `PageSetupDlg()` returns `FALSE`. Listing 7-6 shows how to create display a Page Setup dialog.

 You can use the `CommDlgExtendedError()` API to get more detailed information about the error.

Listing 7-6: The Page Setup dialog box

```
#include "stdafx.h"
#include "pagesetupdialog.h"

extern HINSTANCE hInst;

HGLOBAL s_hDevMode = NULL;
HGLOBAL s_hDevNames = NULL;

//
// OnPageSetupDialog: Called to display the page setup dialog
//
void OnPageSetupDialog(HWND hWnd)
{
    // initialize the dialog structure
    PAGESETUPDLG dlgPageSetup;

    dlgPageSetup.lStructSize = sizeof(PAGESETUPDLG);
    dlgPageSetup.hwndOwner = hWnd;
    dlgPageSetup.hDevMode = s_hDevMode;
    dlgPageSetup.hDevNames = s_hDevNames;
    dlgPageSetup.Flags = PSD_INTHOUSANDTHSOFINCHES | PSD_MARGINS |
        PSD_ENABLEPAGEPAINTHOOK;
    dlgPageSetup.ptPaperSize.x = 0;
    dlgPageSetup.ptPaperSize.y = 0;
    dlgPageSetup.rtMinMargin.top = 50;
    dlgPageSetup.rtMinMargin.left = 50;
    dlgPageSetup.rtMinMargin.right = 50;
    dlgPageSetup.rtMinMargin.bottom = 50;
    dlgPageSetup.rtMargin.top = 1000;
```

```
    dlgPageSetup.rtMargin.left = 1000;
    dlgPageSetup.rtMargin.right = 1000;
    dlgPageSetup.rtMargin.bottom = 1000;
    dlgPageSetup.hInstance= NULL;
    dlgPageSetup.lpPageSetupTemplateName = NULL;
    dlgPageSetup.hPageSetupTemplate = NULL;
    dlgPageSetup.lCustData = 0;
    dlgPageSetup.lpfnPageSetupHook = NULL;
    dlgPageSetup.lpfnPagePaintHook = PagePaintHook;

//
    BOOL bReturn = PageSetupDlg(&dlgPageSetup);
    if (bReturn)
    {
        // the user click OK, you can use the values in the dlgPageDetup

        }

}


//
// PagePaintHook:  Used to paint the page.
//
UINT CALLBACK PagePaintHook
(
    HWND hwndDlg
    ,UINT uMsg
    ,WPARAM wParam
    ,LPARAM lParam
)
{
    BOOL bReturn(FALSE);

switch (uMsg)
    {
        // Drawing the margin rectangle.
        case WM_PSD_MARGINRECT:
        {
            // get the
            HDC hdc = (HDC) wParam;
            LPRECT lprc = (LPRECT) lParam;

            // Get the system highlight color.
            COLORREF crMargRect = GetSysColor(COLOR_HIGHLIGHT);
```

```
                    // Create a dash-dot pen of the system highlight color and
                    // select it into the DC of the sample page.
                    HPEN hPen = (HPEN)SelectObject(hdc, CreatePen(PS_DASHDOT, 1,
                        crMargRect));

                    // Draw the margin rectangle.
                    Rectangle(hdc, lprc->left, lprc->top, lprc->right,
                        lprc->bottom);

                    // Restore the previous pen to the DC.
                    SelectObject(hdc, hPen);
                    bReturn = TRUE;
                }
                break;

                default:
                {
                    bReturn = FALSE;
                }
                break;
        }

        return bReturn;
}
//
// InitPrintSettings: called to get the default devmode settings
//
void InitPrintSettings()
{
        PRINTDLG dlgPrint;

        // Initialize PRINTDLG
        dlgPrint.lStructSize = sizeof(PRINTDLG);
        dlgPrint.hwndOwner = NULL;
        dlgPrint.hDevMode = NULL;
        dlgPrint.hDevNames = NULL;
        dlgPrint.hDC = NULL;
        dlgPrint.Flags = PD_RETURNDEFAULT;
        dlgPrint.nFromPage = 0xFFFF;
        dlgPrint.nToPage = 0xFFFF;
        dlgPrint.nMinPage = 1;
        dlgPrint.nMaxPage = 0xFFFF;
        dlgPrint.nCopies = 1;
        dlgPrint.hInstance = NULL;
        dlgPrint.lCustData = NULL;
```

```
dlgPrint.lpfnPrintHook = NULL;
dlgPrint.lpfnSetupHook = NULL;
dlgPrint.lpPrintTemplateName = NULL;
dlgPrint.lpSetupTemplateName = NULL;
dlgPrint.hPrintTemplate = NULL;
dlgPrint.hSetupTemplate = NULL;

BOOL bReturn = PrintDlg(&dlgPrint);
if (bReturn)
{
    // Allocate a global handle for DEVMODE and copy DEVMODE data.
    DEVMODE* pDefaultDevMode = (DEVMODE*)GlobalLock(dlgPrint.hDevMode);
    s_hDevMode = GlobalAlloc(GHND, GlobalSize(dlgPrint.hDevMode));
    DEVMODE* pDevMode = (DEVMODE*)GlobalLock(s_hDevMode);
    memcpy(pDevMode, pDefaultDevMode, GlobalSize(dlgPrint.hDevMode));
    GlobalUnlock(s_hDevMode);
    GlobalUnlock(dlgPrint.hDevMode);
}
else
{
    DWORD dwError = CommDlgExtendedError();
}
}
```

The `OnPageSetupDialog ()` function takes a handle to a window as a parameter. This handle is used as the owner of the Page Setup dialog. First, the function creates an instance of the `PAGESETUPDLG` structure. It then initializes this structure with information that the Common Dialog Library uses to initialize the dialog box.

First, the function sets the `lStructSize` member to the size of the `PAGESETUPDLG` structure. The `hwndOwner` member is set to the handle of the window passed as a paramter to the function. The `hDevMode` and `hDevNames` members are set to the static s_hDevMode and s_hDevNames variables which are initialized by the application using the `InitPrintSettings()` function described later in this section. If the `PageSetupDlg()` function succeeds it updates the members with the information the user selected.

The function sets the `Flags` member to `PSD_INTHOUSANDTHSOFINCHES`, `PSD_MARGINS`, and `PSD_ENABLEPAGEPAINTHOOK`. The `PSD_INTHOUSANDTHSOFINCHES` flag indicates that the margin and paper size members are in units of thousandths of inches. The `PSD_MARGINS` flag tells the common dialog library to use the `rtMargin` member for the initial margin values. The `PSD_ENABLEPAGEPAINTHOOK` enables the `PagePaintHook()` procedure specified in the `lpfnPageSetupHook` member. Table 7-5 lists all of the possible values for the `Flags` member.

TABLE 7-5 PAGESETUPDLG FLAGS VALUES

Flag	Description
PSD_DEFAULTMINMARGINS	Specifies that the dialog uses the minimum margins for the specified printer as the minimum allowable margins instead of the rtMinMargins member
PSD_DISABLEMARGINS	Creates the dialog with the margin controls disabled
PSD_DISABLEORIENTATION	Creates the dialog with the page orientation controls disabled
PSD_DISABLEPAGEPRINTING	Specifies that the sample page should not be drawn
PSD_DISABLEPAPER	Creates the dialog with the paper controls disabled
PSD_DISABLEPRINTER	Creates the dialog with the "Printer" button disabled
PSD_ENABLEPAGEPAINTHOOK	Specifies that the page painting hook procedure specified by the lpfnPagePaintHook member be enabled
PSD_ENABLEPAGESETUPHOOK	Specifies that the hook procedure specified by the lpfnPageSetupHook member be enabled
PSD_ENABLEPAGESETUPTEMPLATE	Specifies that the hInstance and the lpPageSetupTemplateName members contain the information to find the custom dialog template
PSD_ENABLEPAGESETUPTEMPLATEHANDLE	Specifies that the hPageSetupTemplate member contains a data block containing the custom dialog template
PSD_INHUNDREDTHSOFMILLIMETERS	Specifies that all measurements are in hundreds of millimeters
PSD_INTHOUSANDTHSOFINCHES	Specifies that that all measurements are in thousandths of inches
PSD_MARGINS	Specifies that the rtMargin member is used to initialize the initial margins

Flag	Description
PSD_MINMARGINS	Specifies that the rtMinMargin member is used to set the minimum allowable margins
PSD_NONETWORKBUTTON	Creates the dialog without the "Network" button
PSD_NOWARNING	Specifies that the no default printer dialog message is not displayed
PSD_RETURNDEFAULT	Specifies that the dialog should not be shown, but the hDevNames and hDevMode members are filled with the system default printer information
PSD_SHOWHELP	Creates the dialog with a help button

The ptPaperSize member is initialized to zero. When the PageSetupDlg() API succeeds, this member is filled in with the paper size. The rtMinMargin member is initialized to fifty thousands of an inch for all margins. This value specifies the minimum widths for the margins. The rtMargin member is initialized to one inch for each of the margins. These values are used for the initial margin values.

The hInstance member is set to NULL, since we are not providing a customized dialog template. If you want to customize the dialog template of the color dialog, you can use this parameter to tell the Common Dialog Library where to find the custom dialog template. The lpPageSetupTemplateName and hPageSetupTemplate members are set to NULL; you can use one or the other of these members to specify a custom template resource.

The lCustData member is set to zero. This value is passed to the hook procedure if one is provided. The lpfnPageSetupHook member is set to NULL, since the sample does use a hook procedure. If you want to provide a hook function that can be used to customize the behavior of the dialog, you set this member to your hook function. This function handles the painting of the sample page.

Refer to the MSDN library for more information on custom hook procedures. The lpfnPagePaintHook member is set to the PagePaintHook () function.

After initializing the PAGESETUPDLG structure, the function calls the PageSetupDlg () API to create and display the dialog. If PageSetupDlg() returns TRUE, the values in the PAGESETUPDLG are updated with the values the user selected.

The `PagePaintHook()` function is a page paint hook procedure used to draw the sample page. The Common Dialog Library sends messages to this procedure to allow you to customize the drawing of the sample page. Table 7-6 list the messages sent to the page print hook procedure. The messages are sent in the order they are listed in the table.

TABLE 7-6 PAGEPAINTHOOK() MESSAGES

Message	Description
WM_PSD_PAGESETUPLG	Sent when the dialog box is about to draw the sample page. The wParam identifies the paper size and paper orientation. The lParam points to a PAGESETUPDLG structure.
WM_PSD_FULLPAGERECT	Sent when the dialog box is about to draw the sample page. The wParam identifies the device context for the sample page. The lParam points to a RECT structure containing the coordinates of the sample page.
WM_PSD_MINMARGINRECT	Sent when the dialog box is about to draw the sample page. The wParam identifies the device context for the sample page. The lParam points to a RECT structure containing the coordinates of the minimum margins.
WM_PSD_MARGINRECT	Sent when the dialog box is about to draw the sample page. The wParam identifies the device context for the sample page. The lParam points to a RECT structure containing the coordinates of the margins.
WM_PSD_GREEKTEXTRECT	Sent when the dialog box is about to draw the partial (greek) text inside the margin rectangle. The wParam identifies the device context for the sample page. The lParam points to a RECT structure containing the coordinates of the Greek text rectangle.
WM_PSD_ENVSTAMPRECT	Sent when the dialog box is about to draw the envelope stamp rectangle of the envelope. The wParam identifies the device context for the sample page. The lParam points to a RECT structure containing the coordinates of the envelope stamp rectangle.
WM_PSD_YAFULLPAGERECT	Sent when the dialog box is about to draw the return address of the envelope. The wParam identifies the device context for the sample page. The lParam points to a RECT structure containing the coordinates of the return address of the envelope.

The hook procedure returns TRUE to indicate that it has handled the message and the Common Dialog Library does not need to process the message. If the procedure returns FALSE, the library processes the message. If the hook function returns TRUE for any of the first three messages (WM_PSD_PAGESETUPLG, WM_PSD_FULLPAGERECT, or WM_PSD_MINMARGINRECT), the library does not send any of the other messages.

The PagePaintHook() function handles the WM_PSD_MARGINRECT message to customize the drawing of the margin rectangle. Once the function receives the WM_PSD_MARGINRECT message, the function gets the device context and rectangle from the wParam and lParam function parameter. It then gets the COLOR_HIGHLIGHT system color using the GetSysColor() API. Then it creates and selects a pen into the sample window device context, using the PS_DASHDOT style and the highlight color. It the draws the margin rectangle using the Rectangle() API and selects the previous pen back into the device context. It then sets the return value to TRUE to indicate that the dialog should not draw the margin. For all other messages the function returns FALSE, indicating that the dialog should draw these components.

The InitPrintSettings() function is called when the sample application is started. It is used to initialize the s_hDevMode static variable to the default printer information. It creates an instance of a PRINTDLG structure. It initializes all of the members to dummy values, except for the Flags member which is set to PD_RETURNDEFAULT, which tells the PrintDlg() API to return the default printer information in the hDevMode and hDevNames members. The function then calls the PrintDlg() API and copies the return DEVMODE structure to the s_hDevMode static variable.

Print dialog box

The Print dialog box provides a common interface for allowing the user to select the options for a print job. The user can select the printer to use for the print job, the page range to print, the number of copies, and printer specific options. The Print dialog has a new tabbed look in Windows 2000. Figure 7-6 shows an example of the new Print dialog box.

To create and display the Print dialog box, you create and initialize an instance of the PRINTDLG structure and pass a pointer to the structure to the PrintDlg() API. If the user clicks the OK button, the PrintDlg () API returns TRUE and updates the print settings in the PRINTDLG structure. If the user cancels the dialog or an error occurs PrintDlg() returns FALSE. You can use the CommDlgExtendedError() API to get more detailed information about the error. Listing 7-7 shows how to create and display a Print dialog box.

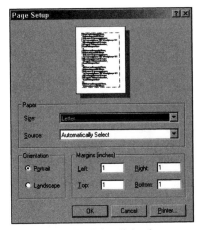

Figure 7-6: The Print dialog box

Listing 7-7: Creating and displaying a Print dialog box

```
#include "stdafx.h"
#include "printdialog.h"

extern HINSTANCE hInst;

//
// OnPrintDialog() called to display a print dialog.
//
void OnPrintDialog(HWND hWnd)
{
    PRINTDLG dlgPrint;

    // Initialize PRINTDLG
    dlgPrint.lStructSize = sizeof(PRINTDLG);
    dlgPrint.hwndOwner = hWnd;
    dlgPrint.hDevMode = NULL;
    dlgPrint.hDevNames = NULL;
    dlgPrint.hDC = NULL;
    dlgPrint.Flags = PD_USEDEVMODECOPIESANDCOLLATE | PD_RETURNDC;
    dlgPrint.nFromPage = 0xFFFF;
    dlgPrint.nToPage = 0xFFFF;
    dlgPrint.nMinPage = 1;
    dlgPrint.nMaxPage = 0xFFFF;
    dlgPrint.nCopies = 1;
    dlgPrint.hInstance = NULL;
    dlgPrint.lCustData = NULL;
    dlgPrint.lpfnPrintHook = NULL;
```

```
dlgPrint.lpfnSetupHook = NULL;
dlgPrint.lpPrintTemplateName = NULL;
dlgPrint.lpSetupTemplateName = NULL;
dlgPrint.hPrintTemplate = NULL;
dlgPrint.hSetupTemplate = NULL;

BOOL bReturn = PrintDlg(&dlgPrint);
if (bReturn)
{
    // GDI calls to render output.

    // Delete DC when done.
    DeleteDC(dlgPrint.hDC);
}
}
```

The OnPrintDialog() function takes a handle to a window as a parameter. This handle is used as the owner of the Print dialog. First, the function creates an instance of the PRINTDLG structure. It then initializes this structure with information that the Common Dialog Library uses to initialize the dialog box.

First, the function sets the lStructSize member to the size of the PRINTDLG structure. The hwndOwner member is set to the handle of the window passed as a parameter to the function. The hDevMode and hDevNames members are set to NULL. If the PrintDlg() API succeeds, these members are updated with the information the user selected. The hDC member is set to NULL if the PD_RETURNDC or the PD_RETURNIC flags are set. This member is updated with a device context handle to the selected printer.

The Flags member is set to PD_USEDEVMODECOPIESANDCOLLATE and PD_RETURNDC. The PD_USEDEVMODECOPIESANDCOLLATE flag specifies that printer driver should handle the copies and collate selections. The PD_RETURNDC flag specifies that a device context representing the selected printer should be returned in the hDC member. Table 7-7 lists all of the possible values for the Flags member.

TABLE 7-7 PRINTDLG FLAGS VALUE

Flag	Description
PD_ALLPAGES	Specifies that the "All" radio button is selected as the page range
PD_COLLATE	Specifies that the "Collate" check box is selected
PD_DISABLEPRINTTOFILE	Creates the dialog with the "Print to File" control disabled

Continued

TABLE **7-7 PRINTDLG FLAGS VALUE** *(Continued)*

Flag	Description
PD_ENABLEPRINTHOOK	Specifies that the hook procedure specified by the lpfnPrintHook member should be enabled
PD_ENABLEPRINTTEMPLATE	Specifies that the hInstance and the lpPrintTemplateName members contains the information to find the custom dialog template
PD_ENABLEPRINTTEMPLATE HANDLE	Specifies that the hPrintTemplate member contains a data block containing the custom dialog template
PD_ENABLESETUPHOOK	Specifies that the hook procedure specified by the lpfnSetupHook member should be enabled
PD_ENABLESETUPTEMPLATE	Specifies the hInstance and the lpSetupTemplateName members contains the information to find the custom dialog template
PD_ENABLESETUPTEMPLATE HANDLE	Specifies that the hSetupTemplate member contains a data block containing the custom dialog template
PD_HIDEPRINTTOFILE	Creates the dialog with the "Print To File" button hidden
PD_NONETWORKBUTTON	Creates the dialog with the "Network" button hidden
PD_NOPAGENUMS	Creates the dialog with the page controls disabled
PD_NOSELECTION	Creates the dialog with the "Selection" button disabled
PD_NOWARNING	Specifes that the no default printer dialog message is not displayed
PD_PAGENUMS	Specifies that the "Pages" radio button is selected
PD_PRINTSETUP	Specifies that the Print Setup Dialog should be displayed instead of the Print Dialog Box
PD_PRINTTOFILE	Specifies that the "Print to File" option is selected
PD_RETURNDC	Specifies that the hDC member contains a device context representing the selected printer if the PrintDlg() API succeeds
PD_RETURNDEFAULT	Specifies that the dialog should not be shown, but the hDevNames and hDevMode members are filled with the system default printer information

Flag	Description
PD_RETURNIC	Specifies that the hDC member contains an information context representing the selected printer if the PrintDlg() API succeeds
PD_SELECTION	Specifies that the "Selection" radio button is selected
PD_SHOWHELP	Creates the dialog with a help button
PD_USEDEVMODECOPIES	Same as PD_USEDEVMODECOPIES-ANDCOLLATE
PD_USEDEVMODECOPIES ANDCOLLATE	Specifies that printer driver should handle the copies and collate selections

For this sample, the nFromPage and nToPage members are set to 0xFFFF; the dialog uses these values to set the initial values for the starting and ending page controls. The nMinPage and nMaxPage values are set to one and 0xFFFF respectively, these values are used to restrict the values in the starting and ending page controls. The nCopies member is initialized to one; this member is used to initialize the dialogs copies control if the hDevMode member is NULL, otherwise the dmCopies member of the DEVMODE structure is used to initialize the copies control.

The hInstance member is set to NULL, since a customized dialog template is not provided. If you want to customize the dialog template of the Print dialog, you can use this parameter to tell the common dialog library where to find the custom dialog template. The lCustData member is set to zero, this value is passed to the print hook or setup hook procedure if one is provided. The lpfnPrintHook and lpfnSetupHook members are set to NULL, since this sample does not use any hook procedures. Similarly the lpPrintTemplateName, lpSetupTemplateName, hPrintTemplate, and hSetupTemplate members are set to NULL, as this sample does not provide custom dialog templates.

After initializing the PRINTDLG structure, the function calls the PrintDlg () API to create and display the dialog. If PrintDlg () returns TRUE, the values in the PRINTDLG are updated with the values the user selected.

Print Property Sheet dialog box

The Print Property Sheet is a new common dialog box that provides an improved user interface for print settings. The Print Property Sheet enables you to add your own application-specific property page, customize the general page by providing a dialog box template for the lower portion of the page, and customize the behavior of the page by providing a callback object. Figure 7-7 shows an example of the Print Property Sheet.

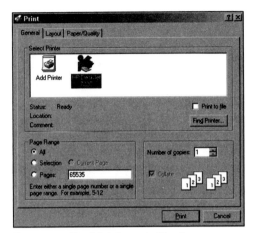

Figure 7-7: The Print Property Sheet

To create and display the print property sheet, you create and initialize an instance of the PRINTDLGEX structure and pass a pointer to the structure to the PrintDlgEx() API. If the call to PrintDlgEx() succeeds, the return value is S_OK and the dwResultAction member is set to either PD_RESULT_PRINT, PD_RESULT_CANCEL, or PD_RESULT_APPLY.

The PD_RESULT_PRINT return value specifies that the user selected the "Print" button, and the PRINTDLGEX structure has been updated with the information the user selected. The PD_RESULT_CANCEL value specifies that the user cancel the print property sheet. The PRINTDLGEX structure does not change. The PD_RESULT_APPLY value indicates that the user pressed the "Apply" button and then the "Cancel" button. This specifies that the information the user selected should be updated, but nothing should be printed. The PRINTDLGEX structure has been updated. Listing 7-8 shows how to add your own property pages to the Print Property Sheet.

Listing 7-8: Adding your own property pages to the Print Property Sheet

```
#include "stdafx.h"
#include "printpropertypage.h"

extern HINSTANCE hInst;
extern HWND s_hWndMain;

//
// OnPrintPropertyPage: called to display a print property page
//
void OnPrintPropertyPage(HWND hWnd)
{
```

```
HDC hDC(NULL);
PRINTPAGERANGE lpPrintPageRange[10];
HPROPSHEETPAGE lphPropertyPages[2];

lphPropertyPages[0] = CreatePropertyPage1();
lphPropertyPages[1] = CreatePropertyPage2();

PRINTDLGEX printData;
printData.lStructSize = sizeof(printData);
printData.hwndOwner = hWnd;
printData.hDevMode = NULL;
printData.hDevNames = NULL;
printData.hDC = hDC;
printData.Flags = PD_ALLPAGES | PD_RETURNDC |
    PD_USELARGETEMPLATE;
printData.Flags2 = 0;
printData.ExclusionFlags = PD_EXCL_COPIESANDCOLLATE;
printData.nPageRanges = 0;
printData.nMaxPageRanges = 10;
printData.lpPageRanges = lpPrintPageRange;
printData.nMinPage = 1;
printData.nMaxPage = 99;
printData.nCopies = 1;
printData.hInstance = NULL;
printData.lpPrintTemplateName = NULL;
printData.lpCallback = NULL;
printData.nPropertyPages = 2;
printData.lphPropertyPages = lphPropertyPages;
printData.nStartPage = START_PAGE_GENERAL;
printData.dwResultAction = 0;

HRESULT hr = PrintDlgEx(&printData);

if (SUCCEEDED(hr) && printData.dwResultAction ==
    PD_RESULT_PRINT)
{
    // The PrintDlgEx was successful and the user selected print
    // so use the info in printData to print
}

if (printData.hDC != NULL)
{
    DeleteDC(printData.hDC);
}
```

```
    if (printData.hDevMode != NULL)
    {
        GlobalFree(printData.hDevMode);
    }

    if (printData.hDevNames != NULL)
    {
        GlobalFree(printData.hDevNames);
    }
}


//
// CreatePropertyPage1: called to create the first property page
//
HPROPSHEETPAGE CreatePropertyPage1()
{
    PROPSHEETPAGE proppage;
    proppage.dwSize = sizeof(proppage);
    proppage.dwFlags = PSP_DEFAULT;
    proppage.hInstance = hInst;
    proppage.pszTemplate = MAKEINTRESOURCE(IDD_PAGE1);
    proppage.hIcon = NULL;
    proppage.pszTitle = "test print";
    proppage.pfnDlgProc = &DialogProc;
    proppage.lParam = 0;
    proppage.pfnCallback = NULL;
    proppage.pcRefParent = NULL;
    proppage.pszHeaderTitle = NULL;
    proppage.pszHeaderSubTitle = NULL;

    HPROPSHEETPAGE page1 = CreatePropertySheetPage(&proppage);
    return page1;
}


//
// CreatePropertyPage2: called to create the second property page
//
HPROPSHEETPAGE CreatePropertyPage2()
{
    PROPSHEETPAGE proppage;
    proppage.dwSize = sizeof(proppage);
    proppage.dwFlags = PSP_DEFAULT;
    proppage.hInstance = hInst;
    proppage.pszTemplate = MAKEINTRESOURCE(IDD_PAGE2);
    proppage.hIcon = NULL;
```

```
    proppage.pszTitle = "test print";
    proppage.pfnDlgProc = &DialogProc;
    proppage.lParam = 0;
    proppage.pfnCallback = NULL;
    proppage.pcRefParent = NULL;
    proppage.pszHeaderTitle = NULL;
    proppage.pszHeaderSubTitle = NULL;

    HPROPSHEETPAGE page2 = CreatePropertySheetPage(&proppage);
    return page2;
}


//
// DialogProc: the window procedure used for the property pages
//
BOOL CALLBACK DialogProc
(
    HWND /*hwndDlg*/     // handle to dialog box
    ,UINT /*uMsg*/        // message
    ,WPARAM /*wParam*/    // first message parameter
    ,LPARAM /*lParam*/    // second message parameter
)
{

    return FALSE;

}
```

The OnPrintPropertySheet () function takes a handle to a window as a parameter. This handle is used as the owner of the Print Property Sheet. The OnPrint PropertySheet() function first creates two property pages using the Create PropertyPage1() and CreatePropertyPage2() functions. These functions create a property page that is added to the Print Property Sheet.

The function then creates and initializes the PRINTDLGEX structure. The lStructSize member is set to the size of the printData variable. The hwndOwner member is set to the handle of the window passed as a parameter to the function. The hDevMode and hDevNames members are set to NULL. If the PrintDlg() API succeeds, these members are updated with the information the user selected. The hDC member is set to the hDC local variable, which is initialized to NULL. If the PD_ RETURNDC or the PD_RETURNIC flags are set, this member is updated with a device context handle to the selected printer.

The Flags member is set to PD_ALLPAGES, PD_RETURNDC, and PD_USELARGE TEMPALTE. The PD_ALLPAGES flag specifies that the "All" radio button is initially selected. The PD_RETURNDC flag specifies that the hDC member should be updated with a device context for the selected printer. The PD_USELARGETEMPLATE flag specifies that a larger template should be used for the general page. This allows you more room to customize the dialog. Table 7-8 lists all of the possible values for the Flags member.

TABLE 7-8 PRINTDLGEX FLAGS VALUES

Flag	Description
PD_ALLPAGES	Specifies that the "All" radio button is selected as the page range
PD_COLLATE	Specifies that the "Collate" check box is selected
PD_CURRENTPAGE	Specifies that the "Current page" radio button is selected
PD_DISABLEPRINTTOFILE	Creates the dialog with the "Print to File" control disabled
PD_ENABLEPRINTTEMPLATE	Specifies that the hInstance and the lpPrintTemplateName members contain the information to find the custom template for the lower portion of the general page
PD_ENABLEPRINTTEMPLATE HANDLE	Specifies that the hInstance member contains a data block containing the custom template for the lower portion of the general page
PD_EXCLUSIONFLAGS	Specifies that the ExclusionFlags member identifies items to be excluded
PD_HIDEPRINTTOFILE	Creates the dialog with the "Print To File" button hidden
PD_NOCURRENTPAGE	Creates the dialog with the "Current page" dialog disabled
PD_NOPAGENUMS	Creates the dialog with the page controls disabled
PD_NOSELECTION	Creates the dialog with the "Selection" button disabled
PD_NOWARNING	Specifies that the no default printer dialog message is not displayed
PD_PAGENUMS	Specifies that the "Pages" radio button is selected
PD_PRINTTOFILE	Specifies that the "Print to File" option is selected
PD_RETURNDC	Specifies that the hDC member contains a device context representing the selected printer if the PrintDlg() API succeeds
PD_RETURNDEFAULT	Specifies that the dialog should not be shown, but the hDevNames and hDevMode members be filled with the system default printer information

Flag	Description
PD_RETURNIC	Specifies that the hDC member contains an information context that represents the selected printer if the PrintDlg() API succeeds
PD_SELECTION	Specifies that the "Selection" radio button is selected
PD_USEDEVMODECOPIES	Same as PD_USEDEVMODECOPIES-ANDCOLLATE
PD_USEDEVMODECOPIES ANDCOLLATE	Specifies that the printer driver handle the copies and collate selections
PD_USELARGETEMPLATE	Creates the property sheet using a large template; this allows for more space for customization

The Flags2 member is reserved for now and must be set to zero. The Exclusion Flags member is set to PD_EXCL_COPIESANDCOLLATE. This flag specifies that the copies and collate controls should be excluded from the printer specific pages. This flag should be set if you are using the default lower portion of the general tab, as these controls are part of this area. The PD_EXCL_COPIESANDCOLLATE is currently the only value allowed for the ExclusionFlags member.

The nPageRanges member is set to zero; this member is used to specify the initial number of PRINTPAGERANGE structures specified in the lpPageRanges member. Upon return from the PrintDlgEx() API this member is updated with the number of page range structures the user specified. The nMaxPageRanges member is set to 10; this is the size of the lpPrintPageRange array used to store the page ranges. The lpPageRanges is set to the lpPrintPageRange array; this member is used to initialize the page range controls and to return the user-selected page ranges. In this sample, the nMinPage and nMaxPage members are arbitrarily set to 1 and 99. These members specify the minimum and maximum values for the page ranges values. The nCopies member is initialized to one. This member is used to initialize the dialogs copies control if the hDevMode member is NULL, otherwise the dmCopies member of the DEVMODE structure is used to initialize the copies control.

The hInstance, lpPrintTemplateName, and lpCallback members are set to NULL, since a customized dialog template is not provided for the lower portion of the general page. If you want to customize the general page, you can use the hInstance and lpPrintTemplateName members to tell the common dialog library where to find the custom dialog template. The lpCallback member is set to NULL since the sample does not provide a callback object. You can use this member to provide a callback object that implements the IPrintDialogCallback and IObjectWithSite COM interfaces. These interfaces allow you to interact with your custom template. Please see the Windows 2000 SDK documentation or the MSDN library for more information on customizing the lower portion of the general tab.

The nPropertyPages member is set to two, which is the number of property pages that we are adding to the property sheet. The lphPropertyPages identify the pages that are added to the property sheet. The lphPropertyPages variable is the array of HPROPSHEETPAGE structure that were created in the CreateProperty Page1() and CreatePropertyPage2() functions. The nStartPage member is set to the START_PAGE_GENERAL, which tells the dialog that the general tab should be the initially selected tab. The dwResultAction member is used to return the action the user took.

The application then calls the PrintDialogEx() API to display the property sheet. After the property is closed, the application checks the dwResultAction member to see if the user selected the print button. If print was selected, the application can use the PRINTDLGEX members to print. The application then frees the DC and memory allocated by the PrintDlgEx() API.

Summary

In this chapter, I described how you can use the Common Dialog Library to provide your users with a familiar, consistent user interface for performing common tasks. Windows 2000 has made some minor improvements to some of the common dialogs and introduced the new Print property sheet.

In the next chapter, I describe the basics of how to work with windows, as well as cover the new functionality that Windows 2000 has provided. Windows 2000 adds several new types of windows and styles for the existing window type that you can use to produce a nicer look and feel for your applications.

Chapter 8

Working with Windows

THIS CHAPTER covers the basics of working with windows. It covers the different types of windows that you can use in your application. I also describe Window Classes, which are used to define the properties for a specific type of window. The chapter then describes how to create a window and how it processes messages with a window procedure. I also describe two new window types that Windows 2000 introduces: the message only window and the layered window.

The chapter also describes the changes in window activation, as well as the new techniques for providing animation when hiding or showing a window. The chapter concludes by describing the multiple monitor support in Windows 2000.

The Windows in Windows

A *window* is the primary means by which an application interacts with a user. The window is where the application displays its output and requests input from the user. There are various types of windows and each window is a member of a Window Class.

Types of windows

Windows provides several types of windows for you to use in your application. The following list describes these windows:

◆ Desktop windows – system-defined windows that occupy the entire screen.

◆ Application windows – provide the user with an interface to interact with the application. Usually includes a title bar, a menu bar, a window menu (formerly known as the system menu), restore, close, minimize and maximize buttons, a resizing border, a client area, and scroll bars.

◆ Dialog boxes – used to request additional information from the user.

◆ Control windows – specialized windows used to perform input or output of a specific type of data.

◆ Message boxes – used to display informational, warning, or error messages to the user.

Window Classes

Each window is a member of a Window Class. A *Window Class* defines the properties for all windows of a specific type. Before you can create a window of a particular class, you need to register the class using the RegisterWindowEx() API.

When your application closes, you usually need not unregister Window Classes explicitly as the system automatically unregisters any classes registered by an application. However, if you register a Window Class in a DLL, you need to call the UnregisterClass() API to unregister the class.

The Window Class specifies the class style, window procedure, extra class bytes, extra window instance bytes, instance handle, large icon, small icon, window cursor, background brush, class menu, and class name. The class name, instance handle, and window procedure are required; all the other values are optional. Every window created with this Window Class automatically has these characteristics. Table 8-1 describes each of these elements.

TABLE 8-1 WINDOW CLASS ELEMENTS

Element	Description
Class style	Specifies the style for the windows of a class. The possible values are described in Table 8-2.
Window procedure	Specifies the function to process all of the messages that are sent to all windows in the class.
Extra class bytes	Specifies the number of bytes that the system allocates for the class. Every window in the class shares these bytes.
Extra window instance bytes	Specifies the number of bytes that the system allocates for each window in the class.
Instance handle	Specifies the module that registered the class.

Element	Description
Large icon	Specifies the large icon for the window.
Small icon	Specifies the small icon for the window.
Window cursor	Specifies the cursor the system will display when it is over any window in the class.
Background brush	Specifies the brush and color the system uses to paint the client area of any window in the class.
Class menu	Specifies the menu for windows of the class that do not define their own menus.
Class name	Specifies an identifier for the registered Window Class.

Windows provides many Window Class styles to control the behavior of all the windows of a class. Table 8-2 describes each of these styles.

TABLE 8-2 WINDOW CLASS STYLES

Style	Description
CS_BYTEALIGNCLIENT	Specifies that the system aligns the windows client area on a byte boundary.
CS_BYTEALIGNWINDOW	Specifies that the system aligns the window on a byte boundary.
CS_CLASSDC	Specifies that the system only allocates one device context for all windows in the class.
CS_DBLCLKS	Specifies that the system sends double-click messages to windows of the class.
CS_GLOBALCLASS	Specifies that the Window Class is available to all modules within a process.
CS_HREDRAW	Specifies that the system redraws the entire window if the width of the client area changes.
CS_NOCLOSE	Specifies that the Close control does not appear on the window menu

Continued

TABLE 8-2 WINDOW CLASS STYLES *(Continued)*

Style	Description
CS_OWNDC	Specifies that the system allocates a device context for each window of the class.
CS_PARENTDC	Specifies that the system sets the clipping rectangle of a child window to the clipping rectangle of its parent window. This allows the child window to draw on its parent.
CS_SAVEBITS	Specifies that the system save a bitmap of any obscured parts of a window. The system uses this bitmap to restore the image without sending a WM_PAINT message to the window, if no changes have invalidated the obscured portions of the window.
CS_VREDRAW	Specifies that the system redraw the entire window, if the height of the client area changes.

Windows 2000 registers several system Window Classes automatically the first time a process calls a USER or GDI API function. These Window Classes specify the default behavior for system windows, such as the window controls and the MDI client window. These classes are available for use in all applications. Table 8-3 describes these Window Classes.

TABLE 8-3 SYSTEM WINDOW CLASSES

Window Class	Description
Button	The Window Class for the button control
ComboBox	The Window Class for the combo box control
Edit	The Window Class for the edit control
ListBox	The Window Class for the list box control
MDIClient	The Window Class for the MDI client window
ScrollBar	The Window Class for the scroll bar control
Static	The Window Class for the static control

Listing 8-1 shows how to register a Window Class. The `MyRegisterClass()` function uses the `RegisterClassEx()` API to register the window classes defined with the `WNDCLASSEX` structure. It returns an `ATOM` that identifies the registered Window Class.

Listing 8-1: Registering a Window Class

```
//
// MyRegisterClass: registers the window class
//
ATOM MyRegisterClass(HINSTANCE hInstance)
{
    WNDCLASSEX wcex;

    wcex.cbSize = sizeof(WNDCLASSEX);

    wcex.style = CS_HREDRAW | CS_VREDRAW;
    wcex.lpfnWndProc = (WNDPROC)WndProc;
    wcex.cbClsExtra = 0;
    wcex.cbWndExtra = 0;
    wcex.hInstance = hInstance;
    wcex.hIcon = LoadIcon(
        hInstance, MAKEINTRESOURCE(IDI_WINDOWDIALOG));
    wcex.hCursor = LoadCursor(NULL, IDC_ARROW);
    wcex.hbrBackground = (HBRUSH)(COLOR_WINDOW+1);
    wcex.lpszMenuName = MAKEINTRESOURCE(IDC_WINDOWDIALOG);
    wcex.lpszClassName = szWindowClass;
    wcex.hIconSm = LoadIcon(
        wcex.hInstance, MAKEINTRESOURCE(IDI_SMALL));

    return RegisterClassEx(&wcex);
}
```

The `MyRegisterClass()` function registers a Window Class for the application. It first creates an instance of a `WNDCLASSEX` structure and initializes the size of the structure. The function then sets the style to `CS_HREDRAW` and `CS_VREDRAW`. This tells the window to redraw the window if the width or height of the window changes. The application does not require any additional class or window instance information so it sets these member values to zero. The `hInstance` member is set to the instance handle of the application. It loads the large icon, cursor, menu, and small icons from the application's resource file. The function uses the `MAKEINTRESOURCE` macro to convert resource identifiers to valid string values. It then calls the `RegisterClassEx()` API to register the Window Class and return an `ATOM` that represents the Window Class.

An ATOM is a 16-bit integer used to reference a string in the system-defined ATOM table. The atom table maps these integers to string values. You typically use ATOMS for sharing memory between applications that use DDE.

How to Create and Manipulate Windows

Applications create their windows using the CreateWindowEx() or CreateWindow() APIs. The CreateWindow() API should be used only to provide backwards compatibility for older applications. It simply calls the CreateWindowEx() API with the extended styles set to a default value of zero.

 Your application also can use the DialogBox(), CreateDialog(), and MessageBox() APIs to create modal dialog boxes, modeless dialog boxes, and message boxes, respectively. The DialogBox() and CreateDialog() APIs are discussed later in this chapter.

The CreateWindowEx() API enables an application to specify window characteristics when the window is created. To use this API, you must specify the window's class name, window name, style, extended style, initial screen coordinates as x and y positions, initial width and height, parent window, menu, instance handle, and a pointer to application-defined data. Table 8-4 describes the parameters to the CreateWindowEx() API, in the order they are passed to the function.

TABLE 8-4 CREATEWINDOWEX() PARAMETERS

Parameter	Description
DWORD dwExStyle	Specifies the extended window styles for the window. Table 8-6 describes the extended styles that are available.
LPCTSTR lpClassName	Specifies the Window Class name or a class atom that represents the class name.
LPCTSTR lpWindowName	Specifies the window's name. The system uses this value for the window caption if the window has a title bar. For controls, the string specifies the contents of the control.

Parameter	Description
DWORD dwStyle	Specifies the style of the window. Table 8-5 describes the available styles.
int x	Specifies the horizontal position of the window. For child windows, this parameter is relative to the client area of its parent. For other windows, this parameter is in screen coordinates. If this parameter is set to CW_USEDEFAULT, the system determines the position of the window.
int y	Specifies the vertical position of the window. For child windows, this parameter is relative to the client area of its parent. For other windows, this parameter is in screen coordinates. If the x parameter is set to CW_USEDEFUALT, this value is ignored.
int nWidth	Specifies the width of the window in device units. If this parameter is set to CW_USEDEFAULT, the system determines the width and height of the window.
int nHeight	Specifies the height of the window. If the nWidth parameter is set to CW_USEDEFAULT, this parameter is ignored.
HWND hWndParent	Specifies the parent window for the window. If this member is set to HWND_MESSAGE, the system creates a message-only window. Message-only windows are new in Windows 2000.
HMENU hMenu	Specifies the menu for the window. For child windows, this member is used to specify the child window identifier.
HINSTANCE hInstance	This parameter is ignored in Windows 2000. In Windows 95 and 98, this parameter is used to identify the module that created the window.
LPVOID lpParam	Specifies a parameter that will be passed to with the WM_CREATE message.

The window's class name must be a class name or *class atom* previously registered with either the RegisterClass() or RegisterClassEx() APIs. If the window has a title bar, the window name is used as the window's caption. You can set the initial x position and/or the initial width to CW_USEDEFAULT. If you create overlapped windows, the system determines the position and/or size of the window. If you specify CW_USEDEFAULT for non-overlapped windows, the system sets the position or size values to zero.

Windows 2000 also enables you to create message-only windows to allow an application to create a window that only processes messages. I cover message-only windows later in the chapter. You can use these windows when you need to communicate between two modules that use windows messages, but have no need for a visible window.

The style and extended-style parameters enable you to specify the characteristics of a window. To change and retrieve styles and extended styles after a window is created, you can use the SetWindowLongPtr() and GetWindowLongPtr() APIs. These APIs supercede the SetWindowLong() and GetWindowLong() APIs and allow your code to work on both 32-bit and 64-bit versions of Windows. The style values can be one or more of the values specified in Table 8-5.

TABLE **8-5** WINDOW STYLES

Window Style	Window Characteristic
WS_CAPTION	Creates a caption for the window (includes WS_BORDER).
WS_SYSMENU	Creates a system menu for the window. You also must specify WS_CAPTION.
WS_MAXIMIZEBOX, WS_MINIMIZEBOX	Specifies a maximize or minimize button on the caption bar of the window. You also must specify WS_CAPTION.
WS_SIZEBOX, WS_THICKFRAME	Specifies that the window has a resizing border.
WS_BORDER	Creates a thin border for the window.
WS_DLGFRAME	Creates a dialog box style border for the window.
WS_CLIPCHILDREN	Specifies that painting is not allowed in the area occupied by the window's children.
WS_CLIPSIBLINGS	Specifies that for child windows, the system does not draw in the area occupied by overlapping child windows.
WS_DISABLED	Creates a disabled window.
WS_VISIBLE	Creates a window that is initially visible.
WS_GROUP	Specifies to start a group of controls. You generally use this with groups of radio or check box controls.

Window Style	Window Characteristic
WS_TABSTOP	Specifies input focus that the window can receive.
WS_HSCROLL, WS_VSCROLL	Creates a horizontal or vertical scroll bar for the window.
WS_ICONIC, WS_MINIMIZE	Creates a window that is initially minimized.
WS_MAXIMIZE	Creates a window that is initially maximized.
WS_CHILD, WS_CHILDWINDOW	Creates a child window.
WS_OVERLAPPED, WS_TILED	Creates an overlapped window with a caption and border.
WS_OVERLAPPEDWINDOW, WS_TILEDWINDOW	Creates an overlapped window; includes WS_OVERLAPPED, WS_CAPTION, WS_MINIMIZEBOX, WS_MAXIMIZEBOX, WS_SYSMENU, and WS_THICKFRAME.
WS_POPUP	Creates a popup window.
WS_POPUPWINDOW	Creates a popup window; includes WS_BORDER, WS_POPUP and WS_SYSMENU.

The extended styles provide even more control over the window characteristics. The extended styles can be a combination of the values in Table 8-6.

TABLE 8-6 WINDOW EXTENDED STYLES

Window Extended Style	Window Characteristic
WS_EX_ACCEPTFILES	Specifies the window can accept dropped files.
WS_EX_TRANSPARENT	Specifies the window is not to be painted until its sibling windows are painted.
WS_EX_APPWINDOW	Displays the window on the task bar.
WS_EX_NOACTIVATE	Specifies the window should not become active when the user clicks the window (New to Windows 2000).

Continued

TABLE **8-6 WINDOW EXTENDED STYLES** *(Continued)*

Window Extended Style	Window Characteristic
WS_EX_NOINHERITLAYOUT	Specifies the child windows should not inherit the layout of the window (New to Windows 2000).
WS_EX_NOPARENTNOTIFY	Specifies the window does not send a WM_PARENTNOTIFY message to its parent when it is created or destroyed.
WS_EX_CONTEXTHELP	Specifies the caption of the window will include a question mark button.
WS_EX_TOPMOST	Specifies the window is placed above all non-topmost windows and will stay above them.
WS_EX_CLIENTEDGE	Specifies the window has a sunken edge.
WS_EX_STATICEDGE	Specifies the window has a three-dimensional border, used to represent windows that do not accept input.
WS_EX_WINDOWEDGE	Creates a window with a raised edge.
WS_EX_OVERLAPPEDWINDOW	Specifies the window has both the WS_EX_CLIENTEDGE and WS_EX_WINDOWEDGE.
WS_EX_DLGMODALFRAME	Creates a window with a double border. You can specify the WS_CAPTION window style.
WS_EX_CONTROLPARENT	Specifies that the window contains child windows that should be part of the tab order of the dialog box.
WS_EX_LAYERED	Creates a layered window (New to Windows 2000).
WS_EX_MDICHILD	Creates an MDI child window.
WS_EX_PALETTEWINDOW	Creates a palette window; includes the WS_EX_TOOLWINDOW, WS_EX_WINDOWEDGE, and WS_EX_TOPMOST.
WS_EX_TOOLWINDOW	Creates a floating window, with a shorter caption bar than a normal caption.
WS_EX_LAYOUTRTL	Creates a window with the horizontal origin on the right edge of the window.
WS_EX_LEFT, WS_EX_RIGHT	Specifies the window is right- or left-aligned. Left-aligned is the default.
WS_EX_LEFTSCROLLBAR,	

Window Extended Style	Window Characteristic
WS_EX_RIGHTSCROLLBAR	Specifies the scroll bar is on the left or right of the window. The WS_EX_LEFTSCROLLBAR style only applies when the shell language supports reading order alignment.
WS_EX_LTRREADING, WS_EX_RTLREADING	Specifies the text is displayed left to right or right to left. Left to right is the default.

Listing 8-2 shows an example of using the CreateWindowEx() API to create a window. The InitInstance() function creates an overlapped window and displays it on the screen. Figure 8-1 shows the window that is created by this code.

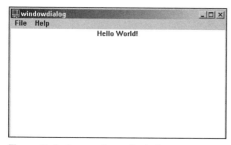

Figure 8-1: An overlapped window

Listing 8-2: Creating a window using the CreateWindowEx() API

```
//
// InitInstance: creates the window
//
BOOL InitInstance(HINSTANCE hInstance, int nCmdShow)
{
    BOOL bReturn(FALSE);
    HWND hWnd;

    // Store instance handle in our global variable
    hInst = hInstance;

    // create the main application window
    hWnd = CreateWindowEx(0, szWindowClass, szTitle,
```

```
        WS_OVERLAPPEDWINDOW, CW_USEDEFAULT, 0, CW_USEDEFAULT, 0,
        NULL, NULL, hInstance, NULL);
    if (hWnd)
    {
        ShowWindow(hWnd, nCmdShow);
        UpdateWindow(hWnd);
        bReturn = TRUE;
    }

    return bReturn;
}
```

The `InitInstance()` function uses the `CreateWindowEX()` API to create the main application window. The main window is an overlapped window; the function specifies that the system itself should determine the initial position and size of the window. If the `CreateWindowEx()` API successfully creates the window, the function shows the window and makes sure it is painted fully.

Window procedures

Windows applications are usually event-driven applications, meaning that they wait for input to be directed to them. The operating system directs this input to an application's windows with the use of messages. The system sends messages for user-generated events, such as mouse movements or keystrokes. The system also generates messages in response to actions that the application performs, such as resizing or moving a window. An application can also generate its own messages. These generated messages are routed to a window's window procedure through message queues. I describe message queues in detail in the Message Routing section later in this chapter.

Every window has a window procedure which processes the messages sent to the window. The Window class for the window defines the default window procedure for all windows of the class. You can override the default window procedure by subclassing the window using the `SetWindowLongPtr()` API.

A Window Procedure function takes a handle to the window whose messages it is to process, a message identifier, and two message data parameters. It returns a 32-bit, signed integer value that varies based on the message being processed. Similarly, the procedure's message parameters vary based on the message being processed.

Many messages pack multiple parameters into the `WPARAM` and `LPARAM` parameters. This can lead to a lot of repetitive template code to unpack these parameters that just serve to complicate your code. The `windowsx.h` header file provides message cracker macros to help in processing these messages. These macros enable you to greatly simplify your code.

Refer to the MSDN and the WindowsX.H header file for more information on the message crackers.

Listing 8-3 shows a window procedure that uses message crackers to help process the messages. This window procedure processes the WM_COMMAND, WM_PAINT, and WM_DESTORY messages.

Listing 8-3: A window procedure using message crackers

```
// command handlers
void OnCommand(HWND hWnd, int id, HWND hwndCtl, UINT codeNotify);
void OnPaint(HWND hWnd);
void OnDestroy(HWND hWnd);


...


//
//  WndProc: main window window procedure
//
LRESULT CALLBACK WndProc
(
    HWND hWnd
    ,UINT message
    ,WPARAM wParam
    ,LPARAM lParam
)
{
    switch (message)
    {
        HANDLE_MSG(hWnd, WM_COMMAND, OnCommand);
        HANDLE_MSG(hWnd, WM_PAINT, OnPaint);
        HANDLE_MSG(hWnd, WM_DESTROY, OnDestroy);

        default:
            return DefWindowProc(hWnd, message, wParam, lParam);
    }
    return 0;
}


//
// OnCommand: process WM_COMMAND messages
//
```

```
void OnCommand
(
    HWND hWnd
  ,int id
  ,HWND /*hwndCtl*/
  ,UINT /*codeNotify*/
)
{
    switch (id)
    {
        case IDM_ABOUT:
           DialogBox(hInst, (LPCTSTR)IDD_ABOUTBOX,
               hWnd, (DLGPROC)About);
        break;

        case IDM_EXIT:
           DestroyWindow(hWnd);
        break;
    }
}


//
// OnPaint: handle the WM_PAINT message
//
void OnPaint(HWND hWnd)
{
    PAINTSTRUCT ps;
    HDC hdc;

    TCHAR szHello[MAX_LOADSTRING];
    LoadString(hInst, IDS_HELLO, szHello, MAX_LOADSTRING);

    hdc = BeginPaint(hWnd, &ps);
    RECT rt;
    GetClientRect(hWnd, &rt);
    DrawText(hdc, szHello, strlen(szHello), &rt, DT_CENTER);
    EndPaint(hWnd, &ps);
}


//
// OnDestroy: handle the WM_DESTORY message
//
void OnDestroy(HWND /*hWnd*/)
{
```

```
    PostQuitMessage(0);
}
```

The WndProc() function processes the messages sent to the application's main window using the HANDLE_MSG macro. This macro expands into a case statement for the message identifier specified. The macro then calls the appropriate function, unpacking the parameters as appropriate for the message. Refer to the windowsx.h file in your compiler's include directory for more information.

The HANDLE_MSG(hWnd, WM_COMMAND, OnCommand) macro unpacks the wParam into the notification code and item identifier for you and calls the OnCommand() function. The HANDLE_MSG(hWnd, WM_PAINT, OnPaint) and HANDLE_MSG(hWnd, WM_DESTROY, OnDestroy) macros just call their respective functions as there are no WPARAM or LPARAM parameters for these messages.

For all other messages, this function calls the DefWindowProc() API. This API provides default processing for messages that your window procedure is not interested in. You need to call this API for any message you do not explicitly process to ensure that all messages are processed.

Dialog boxes

You can use dialog boxes within your windows to request information from the user or display information to the user. Windows provides two types of dialog boxes: *modal dialog boxes* and *modeless dialog boxes*. A modal dialog box requires the user to respond to the dialog box before continuing with the application, while a modeless dialog box allows the user to continue working with the application while the dialog box is visible. When you require information from the user, and want to restrict other operations until that information is provided, you should use a modal dialog box. If the user needs to interact with the application while using the dialog box, you should use a modeless dialog box.

To display a dialog box, first you create a dialog box template that contains the layout of the controls displayed in the dialog box. Usually, the dialog box template is stored in the applications resource file. However, you also can create a template on the fly. Once you define a dialog box template, your application can use one of the CreateDialog() or DialogBox() APIs to create and display the dialog box. Windows provides the CreateDialog(), CreateDialogParam(), CreateDialogIndirect(), and CreateDialogIndirectParam() APIs to create modeless dialog boxes. It also provides the DialogBox(), DialogBoxParam(), DialogBoxIndirect(), and DialogBoxIndirectParam() APIs to create modal dialog boxes.

The Indirect APIs create a dialog box from a template loaded in memory, while all of the others create one from a resource template. These APIs enable you to modify a template programmatically. The Param APIs enable you to specify a 32-bit value that the system passes to the dialog box in the LPARAM parameter of the WM_INITDIALOG message. You can use this value to initialize the control in the dialog box.

Every dialog box has a dialog procedure associated with it to process messages for the dialog box. This dialog procedure is similar to a window procedure, except instead of calling the DefWindowProc() API to process messages the dialog box does not handle, you simply return FALSE from the dialog procedure.

Listing 8-4 shows a simple dialog procedure for a modal dialog box that displays an about dialog box. It handles the WM_INITDIALOG and WM_COMMAND messages. Figure 8-2 shows a typical about dialog that would use this procedure.

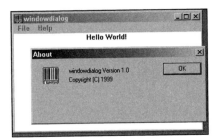

Figure 8-2: Modal about dialog box

Listing 8-4: A Simple modal dialog box procedure

```
//
// Messsage handler for about box.
//
LRESULT CALLBACK About
(
    HWND hDlg
    ,UINT message
    ,WPARAM wParam
    ,LPARAM /*lParam*/
)
{
    switch (message)
    {
        case WM_INITDIALOG:
            return TRUE;

        case WM_COMMAND:
            if (LOWORD(wParam) == IDOK ||
                LOWORD(wParam) == IDCANCEL)
            {
                EndDialog(hDlg, LOWORD(wParam));
                return TRUE;
            }
```

```
      break;
   }

   return FALSE;
}
```

A dialog box procedure – like a window procedure – takes the window the message is intended for, the message identifier, and two data parameters. The About() dialog box procedure handles the WM_INITDIALOG and WM_COMMAND messages; it returns FALSE for all other messages. The WM_INITDIALOG message enables you to initialize the controls on the dialog box. You return TRUE to allow the system to set the focus and FALSE if you set the focus to a control on the dialog box. The procedure handles the WM_COMMAND message to process the OK and CANCEL buttons.

Message-only windows

Windows 2000 provides message-only windows to allow an application to create a window just to process messages. A message-only window is not visible, does not show up in the window list, and does not receive broadcast messages. You use a message-only window when you need a window to communicate between threads or objects, but do not need all of the functionality of a window. For example, if you create a worker thread in your application, you could create a message-only window in this thread to receive messages from the main thread. This way you could communicate with the worker thread and use windows messages without having to create a full-blown window to process them. Prior to Windows 2000, you had to create a hidden window with all the overhead of a window to handle these messages.

You create a message-only window by specifying either HWND_MESSAGE value or a handle to an existing message-only as the parent window in a call to the CreateWindowEx() API. You also can convert an existing window by calling the SetParent() API with the parent window handle set to HWND_MESSAGE. Once your application creates the window, you can post or send messages to it just like a normal window.

Layered windows

Windows 2000 enables you to create a new type of window called a *layered window*; the layered window enables you to create transparent or semitransparent windows. Windows knows how to handle the painting of these windows efficiently and eliminate much of the flickering normally associated with transparent windows. Transparent windows allow the screen beneath the window to show through the window. A semitransparent window blends the underlying screen with the windows contents. Transparent windows are useful for creating irregular-shaped windows.

You create a layered window by specifying the WS_EX_LAYERED flag when calling the CreateWindowEx() API. You also can convert an existing window to a layered window by using the SetWindowLongPtr() API. Once the window is created, you can set the transparent properties of the window using the SetLayeredWindowAttributes () API. This API enables you to set the color of the transparent pixels and the alpha value of the window. The alpha value specifies the transparency level of the window. An alpha value of 0 specifies that the window is completely transparent, while a value of 255 specifies that the window is opaque. For values in between, the contents of the screen underneath the window are blended with the contents of the window. This process is called alpha blending because it is based on the alpha value. The system handles the painting for the window that was specified in the SetLayered WindowAttributes() API. The system also redirects any painting for the window into an offscreen memory DC to eliminate any flickering.

If you want even more control over how the layered window is displayed, you can use the UpdateLayeredWindow() API. This API enables you to change the shape, position, and size of the window. It also allows you to provide a structure to control how the alpha blending will be performed for the window. Once an application calls the SetLayeredWindowAttributes() API for a window, any UpdateLayeredWindow () API call to that window will fail until the layered style is cleared and reset.

Listing 8-5 creates a blue ring, popup layered window on top of all other windows. When the user clicks the ring, the application ends. Figure 8-3 shows the window overlapping a Wordpad document.

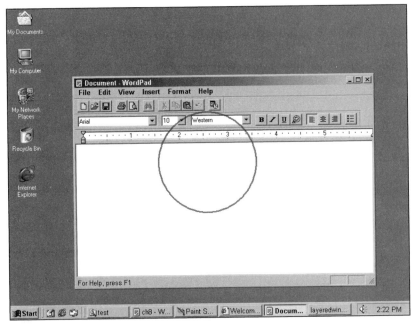

Figure 8-3: A layered window

Listing 8-5: Creating a popup layered window

```
//
// InitInstance: creates the window
//
BOOL InitInstance(HINSTANCE hInstance, int nCmdShow)
{
    BOOL bReturn(FALSE);
    HWND hWnd;

    // Store instance handle in our global variable
    hInst = hInstance;

    // find the center of the screen
    int xCenter = GetSystemMetrics(SM_CXSCREEN) / 2;;
    int yCenter = GetSystemMetrics(SM_CYSCREEN) / 2;

    // create the layered window, on top off all windows
    hWnd = CreateWindowEx(WS_EX_LAYERED | WS_EX_TOPMOST,
        szWindowClass, szTitle, WS_POPUP,
        xCenter - 100, yCenter - 100, 200, 200,
        NULL, NULL, hInstance, NULL);
    if (hWnd)
    {
        // set the background pixels to transparent and set the
        // transparency level to the middle (128)
        COLORREF rgbWindow = GetSysColor(COLOR_WINDOW);
        SetLayeredWindowAttributes(hWnd, rgbWindow,
            128, LWA_COLORKEY | LWA_ALPHA);

        // create the blue pen
        s_hPen = CreatePen(PS_SOLID, 3, RGB(0,0,255));

        // show the window
        ShowWindow(hWnd, nCmdShow);
        UpdateWindow(hWnd);
        bReturn = TRUE;
    }

    return bReturn;
}
//
// OnPaint: handle the WM_PAINT message
//
void OnPaint(HWND hWnd)
{
```

```
PAINTSTRUCT ps;
HDC hDC = BeginPaint(hWnd, &ps);

HPEN hPenOld = (HPEN)SelectObject(hDC, s_hPen);

RECT rect;
GetClientRect(hWnd, &rect);
InflateRect(&rect, -3, -3);
Ellipse(hDC, rect.left, rect.top, rect.right, rect.bottom);

SelectObject(hDC, hPenOld);

EndPaint(hWnd, &ps);
}
```

This code creates a popup layered window using the `CreateWindowEx()` API. It specifies the `WS_EX_LAYERED` flag to create the layered window. It also specifies the `WS_EX_TOPMOST` extended style to keep the window on top of other windows. After the window is created, the application calls the `SetLayeredWindowAttributes()` API specifying the window color (the color of the background brush) as the transparent color. It also makes the window semitransparent by specifying an alpha value of 128.

The `OnPaint()` function draws an ellipse just inside the client rectangle of the window. It does not have to worry about any of the transparency issues of the window; the system handles all of the details for you.

Message Routing

To handle the messages that the system and applications send to windows, Windows uses message queues. The system creates a system-wide message queue and a message queue for each user interface thread. Messages almost always are placed at the end of a message queue. This ensures that the window receives the messages in the order that they are sent. One exception is the `WM_PAINT` message in which the system holds the message until there are no other messages in the window's queue. The system combines multiple paint messages into one message in order to reduce the number of window updates. This helps prevent unnecessary painting that would occur if multiple paint messages were queued.

In addition to the message queues, the system sends some messages directly to the window procedure. Typically, these messages are used to notify windows about events that affect it. For example when a window position is changed, the system sends a `WM_WINDWOWPOSCHANGED` message to the window.

Retrieving messages

To retrieve messages from a message queue, you use either the GetMessage() or PeekMessage() APIs. The GetMessage() API retrieves a message from a specified window. The retrieved message is placed into an MSG structure. Table 8-7 describes the contexts of the MSG structure.

TABLE 8-7 THE MSG STRUCTURE MEMBERS

Member	Description
HWND hwnd	Specifies the handle for the window the message is intended
UNIT message	Specifies the message identifier
WPARAM wParam	Specifies message specific information
LPARAM lParam	Specifies additional information about the message
DWORD time	Specifies the time the message was posted
POINT pt	Specifies the cursor position when the message was posted

The GetMessage() API waits until the system places a message in the queue before returning. The PeekMessage() API, on the other hand, does not wait for a message before returning. The PeekMessage() API allows you to determine if any messages exist in the queue, without removing them. Once you retrieve a message from the queue, you can dispatch the message using the DispatchMessage() API. This API calls the window procedure for the window.

Listing 8-6 shows a simple message loop. This message loop uses the Get Message() API to retrieve messages from all windows in a thread.

Listing 8-6: Retrieving a message

```
MSG msg;
while (GetMessage(&msg, NULL, 0, 0))
{
    TranslateMessage(&msg);
    DispatchMessage(&msg);
}
```

This code calls the GetMessage() API with a NULL hWnd parameter to retrieve messages for all windows in the thread and any thread messages posted using the PostThreadMessage() API. The code waits until a message is placed in the message queue and then uses the `TranslateMessage()` and `DispatchMessage()` APIs to dispatch the message to the message queue. The `TranslateMessage()` API needs to be called if the window is going to receive keyboard input. This API translates the `WM_KEYDOWN` and `WM_KEYUP` messages into `WM_CHAR` messages.

Posting and sending messages

You also can post and send messages to windows using one of the `PostMessage()` or `SendMessage()` APIs. The `PostMessage()`, `PostThreadMessage()`, and `Post QuitMessage()` APIs add messages to a message queue. Table 8-8 describes these APIs.

TABLE 8-8 POSTMESSAGE() APIS

API	Description
`PostMessage()`	Adds a message to the thread queue that created the specified window
`PostThreadMessage()`	Adds a message to the specifed threads message queue
`PostQuitMessage()`	Posts a `WM_QUIT` message to the calling threads message queue

You can use one of the following APIs to send a message to a window: `Send Message()`, `SendDlgItemMessage()`, `BroadcastSystemMessage()`, `SendMessage Callback()`, `SendMessageTimeout()`,and `SendNotifyMessage()`. Table 8-9 describes these APIs.

TABLE 8-9 SENDMESSAGE() APIS

API	Description
`SendMessage()`	Sends a message directly to the specified window's window procedure.
`SendDlgItemMessage()`	Sends a message directly to a dialog box control, using its identifier instead of a handle to the window.
`BroadcastSystem Message()`	Sends a message to system components.

API	Description
SendMessageCallback()	Sends a message to the specified window and returns immediately. An application defined callback function is called after the message is processed.
SendMessageTimeout()	Sends a message to the specified window. If the message is not processed in the specified timeout, then the function returns.
SendNotifyMessage()	Sends a message asynchronously to a window created in another thread.

Window Activation

Windows can be *active* (selected) or *inactive*. Window activation changed in Windows 2000 (and Windows 98). The system now prevents an application from interrupting users while they are working with another application. In addition, the system now only allows a process to set the foreground window if it is the active application by calling the SetForegroundWindow() function. If a call to SetForegroundWindow() fails, the system instead calls SetActiveWindow() and FlashWindowEx() to indicate to the user that the window wants attention.

See the documentation for SetForegroundWindow() on the MSDN or Platform SDK for more information on the exact conditions.

In Windows 2000, if you want to make sure that your application remains the active application, you can use the LockSetForegroundWindow() API. You call this API with LSFW_LOCK flag to prevent other applications from calling the SetForegroundWidow() API, and with the LSFW_UNLOCK flag to enable calls to the SetForegroundWindow() API. You also can allow another process to set the foreground window by calling the AllowSetForegroundWindow() API. You specify the process ID of the process for which you want to set the foreground window. If you specify the ASFW_ANY flag, then any process is able to set the foreground window.

You should be careful when setting the foreground window. Users tend to become irate when one application interrupts them while they are working with another. In general, your application should force only one of its windows to become the active window if the user has to act, so as not to suffer some form of data loss. If you are not sure if an interruption is acceptable or not, your best bet is to allow the user to decide.

Window animation enables you to add a little showmanship to hiding and showing a window. Using the `AnimateWindow()` API, you can roll, slide, or fade a window open or closed. While the animation is playing, you may need to handle the `WM_PRINT` and `WM_PRINTCLIENT` messages. Dialog Boxes, controls, and common controls handle the `WM_PRINTCLIENT` for you already, and the default window procedure handles the `WM_PRINT` message. The system sends the `WM_PRINT` message to render the window in the specified device context.

Listing 8-7 is an example of window animation. It shows how to call the `AnimateWindow()` API and how to process the `WM_PRINT` message. This sample allows you to choose a method of animation and then animates the hiding and showing of the window, using the selected animation method. Figures 8-4 through 8-7 show examples of hiding a window using center animation at various stages of the process.

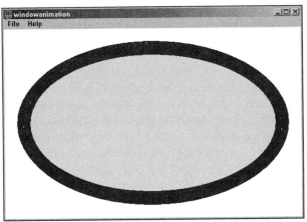

Figure 8-4: Hiding a window using center animation — before animation starts

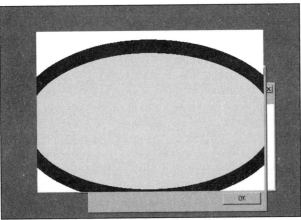

Figure 8-5: Hiding a window using center animation — just starting to hide the window

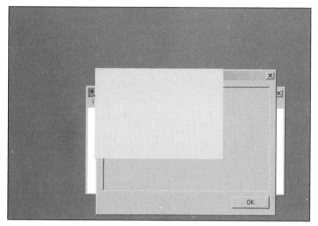

Figure 8-6: Hiding a window using center animation — about halfway closed

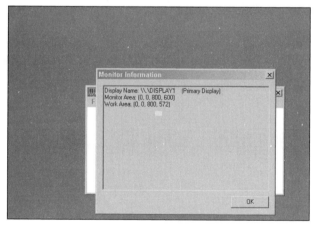

Figure 8-7: Hiding a window using center animation — almost closed

Listing 8-7: Animating a window

```
//
//   WndProc: main window window procedure
//
LRESULT CALLBACK WndProc
(
    HWND hWnd
    ,UINT message
    ,WPARAM wParam
    ,LPARAM lParam
)
{
```

```
int wmId, wmEvent;
switch (message)
{
    case WM_COMMAND:
        wmId    = LOWORD(wParam);
        wmEvent = HIWORD(wParam);

        // Parse the menu selections:
        switch (wmId)
        {
            case ID_FILE_ANIMATE_ROLLLEFT:
            {
                AnimateWindow(hWnd, 5000,
                    AW_HIDE | AW_HOR_POSITIVE);
                AnimateWindow(hWnd, 5000,
                    AW_ACTIVATE | AW_HOR_NEGATIVE);
            }
            break;

            case ID_FILE_ANIMATE_ROLLDIAGONALLY:
            {
                AnimateWindow(hWnd, 5000,
                    AW_HIDE | AW_HOR_NEGATIVE |
                    AW_VER_POSITIVE);
                AnimateWindow(hWnd, 5000,
                    AW_ACTIVATE | AW_HOR_POSITIVE |
                    AW_VER_NEGATIVE);
            }
            break;

            case ID_FILE_ANIMATE_SLIDE:
            {
                AnimateWindow(hWnd, 5000,
                    AW_HIDE | AW_SLIDE | AW_VER_POSITIVE);
                AnimateWindow(hWnd, 5000,
                    AW_ACTIVATE | AW_SLIDE | AW_VER_NEGATIVE);
            }
            break;

            case ID_FILE_ANIMATE_SLIDEDIAGONALLY:
            {
                AnimateWindow(hWnd, 5000,
                    AW_HIDE | AW_SLIDE |
                    AW_HOR_POSITIVE | AW_VER_POSITIVE);
                AnimateWindow(hWnd, 5000,
```

```
                    AW_ACTIVATE | AW_SLIDE |
                    AW_HOR_NEGATIVE | AW_VER_NEGATIVE );
        }
        break;

        case ID_FILE_ANIMATE_CENTER:
        {
            AnimateWindow(
                hWnd, 5000, AW_HIDE | AW_CENTER);
            AnimateWindow(
                hWnd, 5000, AW_ACTIVATE | AW_CENTER);
        }
        break;

        case ID_FILE_ANIMATE_ALPHABLEND:
        {
            AnimateWindow(
                hWnd, 2000, AW_HIDE | AW_BLEND);
            AnimateWindow(
                hWnd, 2000, AW_BLEND);
        }
        break;

        ...

        default:
            return DefWindowProc(
                hWnd, message, wParam, lParam);
    }
    break;

case WM_PAINT:
{
    PAINTSTRUCT ps;
    HDC hDC = BeginPaint(hWnd, &ps);
    Draw(hWnd, hDC);
    EndPaint(hWnd, &ps);
}
break;

case WM_PRINTCLIENT:
{
    HDC hDC = (HDC)wParam;
    Draw(hWnd, hDC);
}
```

```
        break;

        ...

        default:
            return DefWindowProc(
                hWnd, message, wParam, lParam);
    }

    return 0;
}
//
//  Draw: draws the client area
//
void Draw(HWND hWnd, HDC hDC)
{
...
}
```

This code uses the `AnimateWindow()` API in response to the user selecting one of the animate menu items. The first parameter is the handle of the window to be animated. The second parameter is the duration of the animation in milliseconds. Typical animation takes 200 milliseconds to play. I use 5 seconds here to exaggerate the effect. The `AW_HIDE` flag specifies that the window should be hidden. If this flag is not specified, the window is shown. The `AW_ACTIVATE` flag activates the window after the window is shown. You should not use this flag with the `AW_FLAG` flag. The `AW_HOR_POSITIVE`, `AW_HOR_NEGATIVE`, `AW_VER_POSITIVE`, `AW_VER_NEGATIVE`, and `AW_CENTER` flags control the direction of the animation. You can specify roll, slide, or fade animation. By default, roll animation is used. You can use the `AW_SLIDE` or `AW_BLEND` flags to specify slide animation or alpha-blend fading.

The system sends `WM_PRINT` messages to render the window during the animation. The default window procedure handles this message and sends a `WM_PRINTCLIENT` message if the client area of the window needs to be painted. The application handles the `WM_PRINTCLIENT` message by calling the `Draw()` function. The application uses this same function for the `WM_PAINT` message. If you do not handle the `WM_PRINT CLIENT` message, the window is not drawn during the animation.

Multiple Monitor Support

Windows 2000 (and Window 98) enables users to install multiple monitors on their systems. If the system has multiple monitors, users can configure them in a variety of ways. One of the important configuration settings is the *primary display monitor*. The primary monitor contains the (0,0) point – the top left of the screen. However, since other monitors can exist to the left of the primary monitor, applications must be able to handle negative coordinates. (A negative value likely indicates a monitor to the left of the primary display.) This also means that developers cannot rely on the popular trick of moving a window to negative coordinates or coordinates greater than SM_CXSCREEN and SM_CYSCREEN to hide a window. Doing so now can cause your window to end up on another monitor.

It is worth noting that as many of the coordinates passed in messages can be negative, you always should use the GET_X_LPARAM and GET_Y_LPARAM macros to unpack the coordinates.

Your application does not do anything special to run on a machine with multiple monitors. However, the systems provide some new APIs and extensions to existing APIs that you can use to make your application multiple monitor friendly. The Platform Software Development Kit (SDK) provides the file multimon.h to enable your application to call these new APIs on systems that do not support them. I'll explain the use of this include in a moment. The GetSystemMetrics() API has been extended to enable you to retrieve multiple monitor settings. Table 8-10 describes the new indexes that have been added to support multiple monitors.

TABLE 8-10 GETSYSTEMMETRICS() MULTIPLE MONITOR INDEXES

Index	Description
SM_CMONITORS	Determines the number of monitors installed on the system
SM_XVIRTUALSCREEN	Determines the left side of the virtual display
SM_YVIRTUALSCREEN	Determines the top of the virtual display
SM_CXVIRTUALSCREEN	Determines the width of the virtual display
SM_CYVIRTUALSCREEN	Determines the height of the virtual display
SM_SAMEDISPLAYFORMAT	Determines if all the monitors installed on the system have the same color format

To optimally paint a window across multiple monitors or to obtain information about the monitors installed on the system, you use the EnumDisplayMonitors() API. As you specify a callback function, the system calls for each monitor that intersects the specified clipping area. The callback function receives a device context for the enumerated monitor. You can use this DC to optimize drawing for the specified monitor. The callback function also receives an HMONTIOR handle that you can use to obtain information about the monitor using the GetMonitorInfo() API. You also can obtain an HMONITOR handle using the MonitorFromPoint(), MonitorFromRect(), or MonitorFromWindow() APIs.

Listing 8-8 shows how to obtain information about the monitors installed on the system. It displays the monitor information in an edit control in the dialog. Figure 8-8 shows an example of this information.

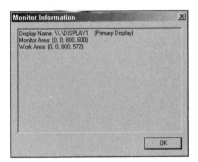

Figure 8-8: Multiple monitor information example

Listing 8-8: Enumerating the windows on the system

```
// dlginfo.h
//
#include <multimon.h>

LRESULT CALLBACK MultiMonitorInfo(HWND hDlg, UINT message,
    WPARAM wParam, LPARAM /*lParam*/);

BOOL OnInitDialog(HWND hDlg);

BOOL CALLBACK MonitorEnumProc(HMONITOR hMonitor, HDC hdcMonitor,
    LPRECT lprcMonitor, LPARAM dwData);




// dlginfo.cpp : Defines the entry point for the application.
//

#include "stdafx.h"

#define COMPILE_MULTIMON_STUBS

#include "resource.h"
#include "dlginfo.h"

const TCHAR c_szPrimaryDisplay[] = _T("(Primary Display)");
```

```
//
// Message handler for monitor info dialog box
//
LRESULT CALLBACK MultiMoniorInfo
(
    HWND hDlg
    ,UINT message
    ,WPARAM wParam
    ,LPARAM /*lParam*/
)
{
    switch (message)
    {
        case WM_INITDIALOG:
            return OnInitDialog(hDlg);
        break;

        case WM_COMMAND:
            if (LOWORD(wParam) == IDOK ||
                LOWORD(wParam) == IDCANCEL)
            {
                EndDialog(hDlg, LOWORD(wParam));
                return TRUE;
            }
        break;
    }

    return FALSE;
}


//
// OnInitDialog: initialize the dialog
//
BOOL OnInitDialog(HWND hDlg)
{
    TCHAR szOut[4096];
    szOut[0] = 0x00;

    // enumerate the display monitors
    EnumDisplayMonitors(NULL, NULL, MonitorEnumProc, (LPARAM)szOut);

    // update the output text
    HWND hEdit = GetDlgItem(hDlg, IDC_EDIT_INFO);
    SetWindowText(hEdit, szOut);
```

```
        return TRUE:
}


//
//  MonitorEnumProc: enum callback function
//
BOOL CALLBACK MonitorEnumProc
(
    HMONITOR hMonitor          // handle to display monitor
    ,HDC /*hdcMonitor*/        // handle to monitor-appropriate device context
    ,LPRECT /*lprcMonitor*/    // pointer to monitor intersection rectangle
    ,LPARAM dwData             // data passed from EnumDisplayMonitors
)
{
    LPTSTR szOut = (LPTSTR)dwData;

    // get extended monitor information
    MONITORINFOEX monitorInfo;
    monitorInfo.cbSize = sizeof(monitorInfo);
    GetMonitorInfo(hMonitor, &monitorInfo);

    // determine if we are the primary display monitor
    LPSTR szPrimary = NULL;
    if (monitorInfo.dwFlags & MONITORINFOF_PRIMARY ==
        MONITORINFOF_PRIMARY)
    {
        szPrimary = (LPTSTR)c_szPrimaryDisplay;
    }

    // format the output
    TCHAR szInfo[1024];
    wsprintf(szInfo, "Display Name: %s     %s\r\n"
        "Monitor Area: (%d, %d, %d, %d)\r\n"
        "Work Area: (%d, %d, %d, %d)\r\n\r\n",
        monitorInfo.szDevice, szPrimary,
        monitorInfo.rcMonitor.left,
        monitorInfo.rcMonitor.top,
        monitorInfo.rcMonitor.right,
        monitorInfo.rcMonitor.bottom,
        monitorInfo.rcWork.left,
        monitorInfo.rcWork.top,
        monitorInfo.rcWork.right,
        monitorInfo.rcWork.bottom);
```

```
    strcat(szOut, szInfo);

    // continue the enumeration
    return TRUE;
}
```

The `dlgInfo.h` file includes the `multimon.h` file to allow the code to work on systems that do not support the multiple monitor calls. To implement these stub functions, you need to define the `COMPILE_MULTIMON_STUBS` once in your code.

The `OnInitDialog()` function calls the `EnumDisplayMonitors()` API with `NULL` for the device context and clipping rectangle to enumerate all of the monitors in the system. If you specify a device context and/or a clipping rectangle, the enumeration is limited to the monitors that intersect the specified values. The function uses the `dwData` parameter to pass a string to the `MonitorEnumProc()` function that holds the monitor information.

The `MonitorEnumProc()` function is called by the system for each monitor installed that meets the criteria specified by a call to the `EnumDisplayMonitors()` API. In this case, the system calls the function for each monitor in the system. The `hMonitor` parameter contains a handle identifying the monitor. The `hdcMonitor` parameter contains a device context with attributes specific to the monitor if you specify a device context in the `EnumDisplayMonitor()` call. If the `hdcMonitor` parameter is not `NULL`, then the `lprcMonitor` parameter contains the clipping area of the device context that is contained on the monitor. If the `hdcMonitor` parameter is `NULL`, this parameter contains the monitor rectangle. The `dwData` parameter contains the value you specify in the call to the `EnumDisplayMonitor()` API.

The function uses the `hMonitor` handle to obtain additional information about the monitor, using the `GetMonitorInfo()` API. The `GetMonitorInfo()` API returns either a `MONITORINFO` structure or an `MONITORINFOEX` structure depending on the size you pass to the API. The `MONITORINFO` structure contains the size of the monitor display area, the size of the work area, and a flag that identifies the primary display. The `MONITORINFOEX` structure provides all of the information the `MONITORINFO` structure provides – plus the display monitor name. Most of the time, you will not care about the display name and simply can use the `MONITORINFO` structure. However in Listing 8-8, I am using the `MONITOR-INFOEX` structure because I want to display the names of the monitors. The function formats this information and adds it to the monitor information string. It then returns `TRUE` to continue the enumeration.

Summary

In this chapter you learned the basics of creating windows and how they process messages. You also learned about the new Windows 2000 window types, as well as the new support for window animation and multiple monitor support.

The next chapter describes how you can use the services the Windows 2000 shell provides. It describes the architecture of the Windows 2000 shell. It also covers the shell API and the COM interfaces it exposes.

Chapter 9

Shell Services

IN THIS CHAPTER

- ◆ What is a shell?
- ◆ Shell components
- ◆ Shell functions
- ◆ Shell interfaces
- ◆ Lightweight APIs

THIS CHAPTER COVERS THE basics of the Windows 2000 shell and how to use some of the many services it provides from within your applications to make them great. This chapter gives you a thorough overview of the shell capabilities built into Windows 2000. I introduce you to the architecture of the Windows shell, the API functions that you have available to work with it, and some of the Component Object Model (COM) interfaces that it exposes. I wrap up the discussion of the Windows shell by showing you some bonus utility functions that the shell supplies in its Lightweight API.

What is a Shell?

Before I begin, you are entitled to a definition for the term *shell*. An operating system's core, typically called a *kernel*, is responsible for providing basic services to applications. In order to interact with a user, the operating system must provide an application that is the starting point to launch other applications. We normally call this starting point the shell. The shell makes up most of what the user sees and uses to organize and launch other applications.

Chapter 2, "Basic Operating System Programming," discusses the kernel in detail.

For the programmer, the shell is distinct from the GDI, USER, and KERNEL subsystems. The shell generally is associated with explorer application – both the Windows Explorer and the Internet Explorer (IE). Almost every release of a Windows 2000 service pack or of IE will incorporate changes to the Windows shell. This subsystem exposes many COM interfaces and simple APIs for manipulating objects within the system. I will show you these throughout the rest of this chapter.

Chapter 10, "Application Building Services," covers creating and using COM interfaces.

Shell Components

To start things off, let's look at the main *user interface (UI)* components that make up the Windows shell. First, and most important, is the desktop. The desktop is the root of all user interaction. The user must pass through the desktop in order to use any applications or any system services. Next is the Windows task bar. This shell component is the opaque strip usually found at the bottom of the desktop with the Start button and status area. This section will explore both desktop and task bar components of the Window shell.

Desktop

The desktop that you see when you log on to Windows 2000 is the heart of the shell. The desktop is not exactly what it seems at first blush; it usually is not visible. The *Windows Client-Server Runtime Subsystem* (found in CSRSS.EXE) creates the root desktop window, which in turn runs the Windows explorer (found in EXPLORER.EXE) to create the desktop and task bar that you use. It turns out that most of the user interaction with Windows 2000 actually occurs with the explorer, and the desktop actually seen is simply a special view of the explorer.

The explorer presents a simple view of the computing universe as your computer sees it – the *namespace*. You can think of the explorer namespace the same way you think of a file system – a hierarchical arrangement of folders and files. The explorer namespace root is the desktop; you can find all objects in the system by navigating down the hierarchy from the desktop. Additionally, the explorer namespace is heterogeneous; it contains items such as the disk hierarchy of My Computer, other computers in My Network Places, and the World Wide Web in Internet Explorer.

Figure 9-1 shows you a sample explorer root and part of the desktop it represents. The Folders pane of the explorer shows the namespace rooted at the desktop with five top-level folders that are identical to the five icons to the left of the explorer main window. You should notice that items in the namespace often are different from one another; this allows the explorer namespace to reach content that you might need.

TIP If you have a keyboard with a Windows button, you can start the explorer browser from the keyboard quickly by holding down the Windows key (it has the Windows icon like the Start button) and pressing the E key (**Windows+E**).

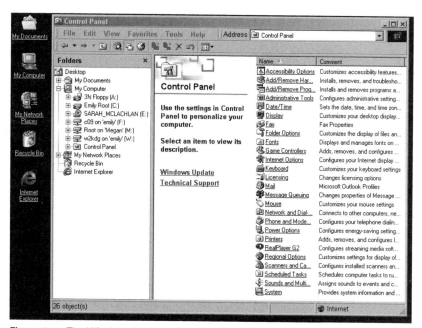

Figure 9-1: The Windows Explorer browser shows the namespace root on the desktop.

It should now be obvious that Windows Explorer is not only a tool that navigates the namespace containing all of the data and services available to you, but it also creates and manages that namespace. The explorer *is* the Windows shell, and all operations that users perform on the system first pass through the explorer.

Since one of the chief responsibilities of the shell is to enable users to launch applications, the first shell API you need to learn is ShellExecuteEx(). This call takes a single parameter, the SHELLEXECUTEINFO structure, and carries out the embedded command if possible. Listing 9-1 shows a very simple use of the API by opening up a ReadMe.TXT file.

Listing 9-1: Calling the shell to open up a text file

```
// project shellexec
#include <windows.h>

// simple program to mimic (double-)clicking a file
//   in the explorer browser
void main()
{
    // create the execute info struct
    SHELLEXECUTEINFO sei;
    ::ZeroMemory(&sei, sizeof(sei));
    sei.cbSize = sizeof(sei);

    // ask the shell to open the readme.txt in the current
    //   directory
    sei.lpVerb = "open";
    sei.lpFile = "readme.txt";
    sei.nShow = SW_SHOW;

    // send the command
    ::ShellExecuteEx(&sei);
}
```

Listing 9-1 shows the simple setup for the structure, which contains many more fields than I used – I defaulted them all to zero. The verb field of the structure corresponds very closely to the menu of actions that the explorer browser gives you when you right-click an object: open, edit, explore, print, and properties are valid verbs. The nShow field controls the manner in which the system displays the new instance of NotePad.EXE. I set it to a value of SW_SHOW for a normal, visible window. By sending the shell a valid file name with the open verb, the application has the same effect as a user double-clicking the file from the explorer browser.

You may wonder about the location of the real desktop window. You can see it by killing off the Explorer.EXE process in the task manager. Try it; you'll see that the desktop icons and the task bar go away, giving you a blank screen with the name of the operating system and the build number in the lower-right corner. This base desktop window is the same one that you see behind the login prompt or when you press **Ctrl+Alt+Delete**. To get back your regular desktop, run Explorer.EXE from the task manager – you should be right back where you started.

TIP

Like Windows+E, the Windows keyboard sequence Windows+D minimizes all current windows and brings the explorer desktop to the foreground.

To restart the shell from an application, you must tell the explorer process to end. The simplest way to do this is to find the main window of the process and send it the WM_QUIT Windows message. For backward compatibility, the main desktop window is still a member of the window class Progman, a name that refers back to the early 16-bit Program Manager application. Listing 9-2 is a quick application that shuts down the current shell and restarts it for you from an application.

Listing 9-2: Shutting down and restarting the system shell

```
// project explrestart
#include <windows.h>

// quick program to reboot the Windows shell
void main()
{
    // find the desktop window, called Progman since Win3.x
    HWND hwndProgman = ::FindWindow("Progman", NULL);
    if(hwndProgman!=NULL)
    {
        // tell the Program Manager to quit, ending the
        // desktop
        if(::PostMessage(hwndProgman, WM_QUIT, 0, 0))
        {
            // create the execute info struct
            SHELLEXECUTEINFO sei;
            ::ZeroMemory(&sei, sizeof(sei));
            sei.cbSize = sizeof(sei);

            // rerun the explorer
            sei.lpFile = "explorer.exe";
            sei.nShow = SW_SHOW;

            // send the command
            ::ShellExecuteEx(&sei);
        }
    }
}
```

As Listing 9-2 shows you, stopping and starting the shell is simple. The program grabs the handle to the main window with the FindWindow() API, then tells it to stop with the PostMessage() API. Restarting the explorer with the ShellExecuteEx() API sends explorer through the same startup procedure it uses when you log on and execute the startup applications from the registry and startup folders.

You should keep Listing 9-2 handy for restarting the shell when you work with shell extensions. I keep a shortcut to it on (of course) my desktop.

You gain programmatic access to the desktop (and shell) through two main conduits: shell APIs and shell COM interfaces. The APIs give you access to a shell pseudo-object that, unlike kernel objects, you do not need to create or destroy – it always exists for you. The shell's COM interfaces simplify programming the shell by reducing the set of APIs you need to wade through; in addition, the shell enables you to deliver your own functionality to the user by implementing the same interfaces that it uses internally.

I mentioned earlier that the explorer namespace contains two types of objects: folders and files. The folder objects are nodes of the namespace tree and can be *real* (such as a disk directory) or *virtual* (such as the control panel). Similarly, the file objects are the leaf nodes of the tree and can be real (such as a disk file) or virtual (such as a control panel applet). Later in this chapter, I will show you how to add virtual nodes to the namespace.

Task bar

The next portion of the shell that you use is the task bar. This control strip usually lives at the bottom of the desktop containing the Start button. In addition to the Start button and menu, the task bar has a status area called the *system tray*, a quick-launch toolbar, and an iconic list of the currently active tasks that you can bring to the foreground or minimize. This task list contains the icons and titles for each main window currently available.

The task bar is a peer of the desktop, also owned by the explorer process, that is actually an instance of an *application desktop toolbar*. Another application desktop toolbar is the Microsoft Office shortcut bar. These windows, also called *appbars* – very similar to toolbars – are anchored to one side of the desktop. You can place any number of appbars on the desktop at once. The shell exposes a simple API to configure them – the SHAppBarMessage() function.

A couple of the SHAppBarMessage() messages actually are useful to the desktop task bar. The first message, ABM_GETTASKBARPOS, tells you where the task bar lives on the desktop – which screen edge it attaches to and its main window rectangle. The task bar supports an auto-hide style in which it disappears when the mouse leaves its client area, as well as an always-on-top style in which no other applications on the desktop can cover its client area. The ABM_GETSTATE message determines the current state of the auto-hide and always-on-top flags for the task bar.

You also can treat the task bar like another desktop window in some ways by grabbing its window handle from the system. Like the desktop, it has a well-known window class name: Shell_TrayWnd. Listing 9-3 shows you how to use the task manager through the described APIs.

Listing 9-3: Getting the current state of the task bar and making it disappear

```cpp
// project taskbarprop
#define _WIN32_WINNT 0x0500
#define WINVER 0x0500
#include <windows.h>
#include <iostream>

void main()
{
    // create a structure for grabbing the current task bar
    //  state
    APPBARDATA abd;
    ::ZeroMemory(&abd, sizeof(abd));
    abd.cbSize = sizeof(abd);

    // fetch the window handle for the task bar in order to
    //  move it to a new position
    HWND hwndTaskbar = ::FindWindow("Shell_TrayWnd", NULL);
    abd.hWnd = hwndTaskbar;

    // fetch the current state
    UINT nState = ::SHAppBarMessage(ABM_GETSTATE, &abd);
    ::SHAppBarMessage(ABM_GETTASKBARPOS, &abd);

    // report it to the user
    std::cout << " Task bar current special flags: ";
    if((nState & ABS_ALWAYSONTOP)!=0)
    {
        std::cout << "always-on-top ";
    }
    if((nState & ABS_AUTOHIDE)!=0)
    {
        std::cout << "auto-hide";
    }
    switch(abd.uEdge)
    {
    case ABE_TOP: std::cout << "top-edge "; break;
    case ABE_BOTTOM: std::cout << "bottom-edge "; break;
    case ABE_LEFT: std::cout << "left-edge "; break;
    case ABE_RIGHT: std::cout << "right-edge "; break;
    }
    std::cout << std::endl;

    // hide the task bar then show it again
    ::ShowWindow(abd.hWnd, SW_HIDE);
```

```
  ::Sleep(500);
  ::ShowWindow(abd.hWnd, SW_SHOW);
}
```

The short program in Listing 9-3 simply exercises the message-based API to fetch the current state of the task bar and report the results to the user. It also grabs the handle of the task bar near the beginning and uses it to hide and show the task bar.

The task bar also adds a COM interface, ITaskbarList, for modifying the current contents of the task list as indicated by the icons. (I don't show this in Listing 9-3.) The last, most useful, interface to the task bar is the system tray, which I discuss in detail in the next section.

Shell Functions

The shell is a singleton object that you never have to instantiate or destroy. As far as your applications are concerned, the shell always exists. Since you don't have to manage its lifetime, none of its APIs require an object handle like other object types in the system.

PIDL functions

In order to identify an object in the shell namespace uniquely, the shell offers the *pointer to identifier lists (PIDL)*. PIDLs are used everywhere within the shell to locate folders and files. They are more general than a fully qualified name from the file system because they need to refer to non-file system objects.

PIDLs are, however, similar in construction to universal path names. A PIDL can be fully specified or relative to another PIDL. The PIDL is a list of identifiers, each specifically identifying a folder in the parent folder until the last, which might identify a file. The actual data structures used by Windows are SHITEMID and LPIMTEMIDLIST. The former is the identifier, composed of freeform binary data, while the latter is a pointer to the identifier.

The SHITEMID structure first contains a two-byte length code that describes the length of the identifier, including itself. The rest of each SHITEMID is the data; its format depends solely on the parent folder. For example, in a PIDL to a file, the data is a string. In a PIDL to the Recycle Bin, the data can be a binary GUID. The identifier is only meaningful to the parent folder, as the parent folder's identifier is only meaningful to its parent.

FETCHING AND DISPLAYING PIDLS

The PIDL is a contiguous block of data that must be allocated using the shell's allocator—an IMalloc COM interface retrieved with the SHGetMalloc() API. You can use the IMalloc pointer to access the Alloc() method to grab the block of memory and the Free() method to free that block. You must use the Release() method to clean up your reference to the IMalloc object. The shell's allocator is described in detail in the sidebar, "The Shell's Allocator."

The Shell's Allocator

The Windows shell process (`Explorer.EXE`) exposes a memory allocator for you to use when supplying data to the shell or releasing data that the shell sends your application. This allocator is a COM object that exposes the `IMalloc` interface.

To retrieve a reference to this allocator, simply use the `SHGetMalloc()` API. It will return a pointer to its `IMalloc` interface after adding an object reference for you. When you are finished using the allocator, simply call its `Release()` method and throw away the pointer's value. The following table describes the members of this COM interface.

Method	Description
`QueryInterface()`	Retrieves a pointer to another interface on the COM object
`AddRef()`	Increments the reference count to the underlying COM object
`Release()`	Decrements the reference count to the COM object, possibly destroying it
`Alloc()`	Reserves a chunk of memory from the heap, simply requires a count of bytes to allocate and returns a pointer
`Realloc()`	Changes the size of a reserved chunk of memory, requires the previous pointer and a new size
`Free()`	Returns a chunk of memory to the heap
`GetSize()`	Determines the size of a chunk of memory previously allocated through the interface
`DidAlloc()`	Determines whether the COM object was responsible for allocating the passed chunk of memory through this interface
`HeapMinimize()`	Reduces the resources used by the heap as much as possible

As you can see from the methods available in the `IMalloc` interface, allocating memory is as simple as calling the standard C runtime `malloc()` and `free()` functions. The most powerful part of this interface is that the shell exposes it for all processes to use, allowing you to share data with Windows and other applications.

The SHGetFolderLocation() API fetches PIDLs for well-known locations in the system. The program in Listing 9-4 shows how to use the API to grab PIDLs from the well-known system locations, walk the individual identifiers, and display the contents.

Listing 9-4: Displaying the PIDLs of some well-known system locations

```
// project viewpidl
#define _WIN32_WINNT 0x0500
#define WINVER 0x0500
#include <windows.h>
#include <iostream>
#include <shlobj.h>

// helper method to display a block of memory
void ShowBlock(LPCTSTR pbStart, size_t nCount)
{
    std::cout << " data: ";

    // display every byte if it is printable
    for(int nShow=0; nShow<nCount ; ++nShow)
    {
        TCHAR chShow = pbStart[nShow];
        std::cout << (isprint(chShow)? chShow : '.');
    }
    std::cout << std::endl;
}

// helper method to show each item in the ID list
void ShowItems(LPCITEMIDLIST pidl)
{
    // show each ID in the list (if possible)
    int nCount(0);
    const SHITEMID* pID =
        reinterpret_cast<const SHITEMID*>(pidl);
    while(pID->cb>0)
    {
        // grab the size of the item
        int nItemSize = pID->cb;

        // show the ID to the user
        std::cout << "\tITEM #" << ++nCount
            << " size: " << nItemSize;

        // show the user
```

```
        ::ShowBlock(reinterpret_cast<LPCTSTR>(pID->abID),
            nItemSize);

        // advance the pointer by the shown byte count
        pID = reinterpret_cast<const SHITEMID*>(
            reinterpret_cast<const BYTE*>(pID) + nItemSize);
    }
}

// helper method to display a PIDL to the user
void ShowPidl(LPCITEMIDLIST pidl)
{
    // use the shell allocator to grab the size of the PIDL
    ULONG nSize(0);
    IMalloc* pMalloc = NULL;
    if(SUCCEEDED(::SHGetMalloc(&pMalloc)))
    {
        // fetch the size
        nSize = pMalloc->GetSize((void*)pidl);

        // clean up the allocator
        pMalloc->Release();
        pMalloc = NULL;
    }
    std::cout << "PIDL size: " << nSize << std::endl;

    ::ShowItems(pidl);
}

// display the PIDL for a passed CSIDL
void ShowCSIDL(int CSIDL)
{
    // fetch the PIDL for the passed folder (by CSIDL)
    LPITEMIDLIST pidl = NULL;
    if(SUCCEEDED(::SHGetFolderLocation(
        NULL,   // desktop is parent for dialup prompt
        CSIDL,  // pass the sent CSIDL
        NULL,   // use token of logged in user
        0,      // must be 0 (reserved)
        &pidl)))// returned PIDL
    {
        // display the PIDL to the user
        ::ShowPidl(pidl);
```

```
        // find the allocator to destroy the PIDL
        IMalloc* pMalloc = NULL;
        ::SHGetMalloc(&pMalloc);

        // clean up the PIDL
        pMalloc->Free(pidl);
        pidl = NULL;

        // clean up the allocator
        pMalloc->Release();
        pMalloc = NULL;
    }
}

void main()
{
    std::cout << "System folder: ";
    ::ShowCSIDL(CSIDL_SYSTEM);
    std::cout << "Program files: ";
    ::ShowCSIDL(CSIDL_PROGRAM_FILES);
    std::cout << "Recycle bin: ";
    ::ShowCSIDL(CSIDL_BITBUCKET);
    std::cout << "Internet cache: ";
    ::ShowCSIDL(CSIDL_INTERNET_CACHE);
}
```

Listing 9-4 shows the simple use of the SHGetFolderLocation() API to fetch a PIDL for a system location. The local function ShowCSIDL() takes an identifier of a well-known folder (program files, system, and so on), fetches its PIDL, and sends it to our local ShowPidl() function. With the PIDL, the program gets the shell's IMalloc to report the block's total size. Then it begins looping through each SHITEMID in the PIDL, displaying its size and contents using the ShowBlock() local method to make all the non-ANSI characters visible. Note that a zero-length SHITEMID denotes the end of the PIDL.

The shell supplies a helper method that translates a PIDL to a path for file system names. The SHGetPathFromIDList() API requires a fully specified PIDL (beginning at the desktop) and a buffer to hold the resulting path name.

DISPLAYING EXTENDED INFORMATION

Another helper method that the shell supplies is the SHGetDataFromIDList() API. This API enables you to take a PIDL and retrieve file system, networking, or shell-extended data about the object. Listing 9-5 uses this function to augment the example from Listing 9-4 with extended information.

Listing 9-5: Displaying the extended information using PIDLs

```cpp
// project viewpidlex
//
// ... local ShowBlock(), ShowItems(), and ShowPidl() functions
//  from Listing 9-4 removed for clarity ...
//
// helper method to show more data about the item in the PIDL
void ShowPidlEx(LPCITEMIDLIST pidl)
{
    // first, get the parent's IShellFolder
    IShellFolder* psfParent = NULL;
    LPCITEMIDLIST pidlRelative = NULL;
    if(SUCCEEDED(::SHBindToParent(
        pidl,                    // child PIDL
        IID_IShellFolder,        // get the IShellFolder
        (void **)&psfParent,     // buffer for the sf ptr
        &pidlRelative)))         // holder of the relative PIDL
    {
        // show the relative PIDL
        std::cout << "\t(relative)";
        ::ShowItems(pidlRelative);

        // fetch extended data
        SHDESCRIPTIONID di;
        if(SUCCEEDED(::SHGetDataFromIDList(
            psfParent,           // parent shell folder interface
            pidlRelative,        // child of interest
            SHGDFIL_DESCRIPTIONID,  // get a description
            &di,                 // data structure to fill
            sizeof(di))))        // buffer size
        {
            // show the description
            switch(di.dwDescriptionId)
            {
            case SHDID_ROOT_REGITEM:
                std::cout << "\tDesktop item"; break;
            case SHDID_FS_DIRECTORY:
                std::cout << "\tFilesystem folder"; break;
            default:
                std::cout << "\tType: " << di.dwDescriptionId;
                break;
            }
            std::cout << std::endl;
        }
```

```
            // clean up the parent interface
            psfParent->Release();
            psfParent = NULL;
        }
    }


// display the PIDL for a passed CSIDL
void ShowCSIDL(int CSIDL)
{
    // fetch the PIDL for the passed folder (by CSIDL)
    LPITEMIDLIST pidl = NULL;
    if(SUCCEEDED(::SHGetFolderLocation(
        NULL,   // desktop is parent for dialup prompt
        CSIDL,  // pass the sent CSIDL
        NULL,   // use token of logged in user
        0,      // must be 0 (reserved)
        &pidl)))// returned PIDL
    {
        // display the PIDL to the user
        ::ShowPidl(pidl);
        ::ShowPidlEx(pidl);

        // find the allocator to destroy the PIDL
        IMalloc* pMalloc = NULL;
        ::SHGetMalloc(&pMalloc);

        // clean up the PIDL
        pMalloc->Free(pidl);
        pidl = NULL;

        // clean up the allocator
        pMalloc->Release();
        pMalloc = NULL;
    }
}

void main()
{
    std::cout << "System folder: ";
    ::ShowCSIDL(CSIDL_SYSTEM);
    std::cout << "Program files: ";
    ::ShowCSIDL(CSIDL_PROGRAM_FILES);
    std::cout << "Recycle bin: ";
    ::ShowCSIDL(CSIDL_BITBUCKET);
```

```
    std::cout << "Internet cache: ";
    ::ShowCSIDL(CSIDL_INTERNET_CACHE);
}
```

Listing 9-5 shows you that in order to get the extended information about a PIDL, you must get the IShellFolder interface from its immediate parent first. To do this, use the SHBindToParent() API. The SHGetDataFromIDList() API can retrieve description data, as in the example. It also can retrieve the WIN32_FIND_DATA about the object (like the FindFirstFile() API) when applicable, as well as data specific to network resources in the NETRESOURCE structure when applicable.

Chapter 4, "Commonly Used Kernel Objects," covers the file find kernel object that is accessed through the FindFirstFile() API.

File object functions

Now that you have the internal data structure for the shell's items under your belt, let's look at manipulating objects with the shell. In particular, let's look at APIs specific to file objects.

The first function is the SHGetFileInfo() API. This method retrieves detailed information about a fully specified file or folder in the system – or even a nonexistent file object. The function enables you to specify the shell object by string name or by PIDL, and it does its best to find the information you need. In particular, you can find all of the attributes the system knows about a file, its display name, details about associated icons, and even the loaded icon. Listing 9-6 shows a quick use of the API to fetch details about the HTML file type.

Listing 9-6: Getting information about a type of file

```
// project fileinfo
#include <windows.h>
#include <shlobj.h>
#include <iostream>
#include <fstream>

void main()
{
    // allocate a buffer and call the API
    SHFILEINFO fi;
    if(::SHGetFileInfo(
```

```
    ".htm",                 // interest (any HTML file)
    0,                      // no file attributes to send
    &fi,                    // return buffer
    sizeof(fi),             // size of buffer
    SHGFI_TYPENAME|         // fetch the type of file
    SHGFI_SYSICONINDEX))// its icon's index in system list
{
    // show the type name and its icon's index
    std::cout << "Type: " << fi.szTypeName
        << "\nIcon index: " << fi.iIcon
        << std::endl;
}

// create a dummy HTML file
LPCTSTR szFilename = "dummy.htm";
{
    std::ofstream ofDummy(szFilename);
    ofDummy << "<html></html>";
}

// find the executable for the file
TCHAR szExe[MAX_PATH];
if((DWORD)::FindExecutable(szFilename, NULL, szExe)>=32)
{
    std::cout << "Exe: " << szExe << std::endl;
}

// delete the new dummy file
{
    SHFILEOPSTRUCT fileop;
    ::ZeroMemory(&fileop, sizeof(fileop));

    fileop.wFunc = FO_DELETE;    // delete the dummy
    fileop.pFrom = szFilename;   // its name
    fileop.fFlags = FOF_NOCONFIRMATION; // be silent

    ::SHFileOperation(&fileop);
}
}
```

The example in Listing 9-6 asks the shell what it knows about files with the .HTM extension. The shell returns the long description for this type of file and the index for the files' icon in the system image list.

You also can ask the shell to locate the executable associated with a document file. This operation is a subset of the ShellExecuteEx() API; the shell exposes it with the FindExecutable() API. This API searches through the Windows registry for an application that has been registered to operate on files with the associated filename extension. Listing 9-6 shows an example of using this function on a newly created, dummy HTML file.

The final API demonstrated in Listing 9-6 is another complicated one: the SHFileOperation() API. This function gives you access to more of the shell browser's functionality. In particular, the API enables you to copy, delete, move, and rename file system objects. This function takes a single parameter, the SHFILEOPSTRUCT detailed in Table 9-1, and returns a simple success flag. The structure enables you to select files by name or wildcard for source or destination names, as well as finely tune the operation and even the GUI that the shell displays during the operation. When you move, copy, or rename files, you can ask the API to return an array of name translations in SHNAMEMAPPING structures. When you are finished with the array, you need to use the SHFreeNameMappings() API to release the memory.

TABLE 9-1 MEMBERS OF THE SHFILEOPSTRUCT

Member	Intention
HWND hWnd	Window to parent any pop-up dialogs that the shell may wish to display; NULL indicates it should use the desktop window.
UINT wFunc	Function to perform; valid values are FO_COPY, FO_DELETE, FO_MOVE, and FO_RENAME.
LPCTSTR pFrom	A null-string terminated list of null-terminated strings that may include wildcards and indicate the names of files on which to perform the passed operation.
LPCTSTR pTo	The names of the resulting files, in the same format as the pFrom member.
FILEOP_FLAGS fFlags	A bitmask of flags that control the behavior of the shell during the operation. An example is the FOF_SILENT flag that suppresses any progress dialog.
BOOL fAnyOperationsAborted	Set by the shell, this flag indicates that the user aborted before completing the operation.

Continued

TABLE 9-1 MEMBERS OF THE SHFILEOPSTRUCT *(Continued)*

Member	Intention
LPVOID hNameMappings	The resulting mapping from source to destination of all of the files on which the shell operated. This requires that the fFlags member has FOF_WANTMAPPINGS set.
LPCTSTR lpszProgressTitle	String to display in the shell's progress dialog box during the operation; valid only when the fFlags member has FOF_SIMPLEPROGRESS set.

Another file operation that you should use is the SHAddToRecentDocs() API. This API accepts a fully qualified path name or PIDL and adds the document path to the recent documents folder that is reflected in the Start menu and Office places. Your application should call this method whenever the user opens a new file. To retrieve the list of recently opened documents, enumerate the shell links found in the CSIDL_RECENT folder (from the SHGetFolderPath() API).

Folder object functions

The other main object in the shell is the *folder object*. All file objects actually have folder objects as their parent. Like file objects, you can manipulate folder objects using their own unique set of shell APIs. Let's begin at the first folder – the desktop. You can access this folder using the intuitive SHGetDesktopFolder() API. This function retrieves the IShellFolder interface for the root node in the shell namespace. I cover the IShellFolder interface later in this chapter, but I should mention now that all folders in the namespace expose this interface. It enables you to enumerate all objects in the system (yes, all of them).

FINDING SPECIAL SHELL FOLDERS

The shell maintains a set of specially named folders, such as the system folder or the control panel. Each of these folders is relative to the currently logged in user. For example, the special My Documents folder typically is located at C:\Documents and Settings\<username>\My Documents where <username> is replaced by the login name of the current user. I use these folders throughout the book in various examples, and each time I call the SHGetFolderPath() API. This is the recommended way to find these folders. You should never assume that Windows is installed in C:\WinNT; call SHGetFolderPath() for CSIDL_WINDOWS instead.

The SHGetFolderPath() API is straightforward. It requires an owner window handle that typically is null, a handle to a token object that typically is null to specify the logged in user, a switch to get the current or default value, a buffer of MAX_PATH length to hold the result, and a CSIDL cookie. The CSIDL actually is an integer value that comes from ShlObj.H and describes the folder of interest, e.g., CSIDL_SYSTEM. You can tell SHGetFolderPath() to create the requested folder if it does not exist by OR-ing the CSIDL_FLAG_CREATE value into the parameter. This API returns a HRESULT rather than a BOOL.

There are CSIDLs for objects in the system that are not members of the file system, e.g., CSIDL_NETHOOD. The SHGetFolderPath() API cannot help you locate these shell objects. The SHGetFolderLocation() API is very similar, but returns a PIDL. You are responsible for releasing the PIDL when you're finished with it. Listings 9-4 and 9-5 show you how to use this API; Listing 9-7 shows you the SHGetFolderPath() API in action.

Listing 9-7: Finding special folders in the shell

```
// project specfolder
#define _WIN32_WINNT 0x0500
#define WINVER 0x0500
#include <windows.h>
#include <iostream>
#include <shlobj.h>

void main()
{
    // loop through all of the available CSIDLs
    // Note that this is for demonstration only, I looked at
    // the values in ShlObj.H and they are consecutive
    // between the bounds in the loop. You should never look
    // at the values for constants in system header files and
    // make any code rely on them.
    for(int nCsidl=CSIDL_DESKTOP;
        nCsidl<=CSIDL_CONNECTIONS;
        ++nCsidl)
    {
        // try looking up the location
        TCHAR szPath[MAX_PATH];
        if(SUCCEEDED(::SHGetFolderPath(
            NULL,       // use the desktop for the owner window
            nCsidl,     // current CSIDL to look up
            NULL,       // use the token of the logged in user
            SHGFP_TYPE_CURRENT, // get the current value
            szPath)))   // the buffer to hold the path
        {
            // dump it out for the user, note that a couple of
            //  paths get returned in DBCS, they won't be
```

```
                    //  displayed
                    std::cout << "CSIDL: " << nCsidl
                        << " Path: " << szPath
                        << std::endl;
                }
            }
        }
```

Listing 9-7 simply runs through the CSIDL values published by the shell and looks up their paths. The code contains warnings about inspecting the values of constants published by the system; you should heed them (it's bad form).

One of the special folders in the shell is the Recycle Bin folder, which holds file and folder objects that you delete with the Windows explorer. The shell exposes specialty methods for dealing with the Recycle Bin objects: the SHQueryRecycleBin() API gives you statistics about the bit bucket on a specified drive, and the SHEmptyRecycleBin() API enables you to empty a bin. SHQueryRecycleBin() takes a drive parameter and a structure to hold 64-bit wide counts of the items and the total size of the Recycle Bin on that drive. The latter API also requires a drive parameter, then enables you to specify whether the shell displays any GUI during the operation.

FINDING A SHELL FOLDER

The shell gives you the opportunity to enable the user to find a folder in the shell with the SHBrowseForFolder() API. This API takes a single parameter – the BROW-SEINFO structure that lets you configure the GUI in detail – and returns the PIDL, which you must free when you're finished with it. Listing 9-8 shows you a quick example of the dialog box.

Listing 9-8: Using the shell folder browser

```
// project browsefolder
#define _WIN32_WINNT 0x0500
#define WINVER 0x0500
#include <windows.h>
#include <iostream>
#include <shlobj.h>

void main()
{
    // clear out the browsing struct
    BROWSEINFO bi;
    ::ZeroMemory(&bi, sizeof(bi));

    // set up the selected path structure
```

```
TCHAR szSelPath[MAX_PATH];
bi.pszDisplayName = szSelPath;

// send detailed instructions to the user
bi.lpszTitle = "Select a folder or file, note the resize "
    "grip in the lower-right, the New Folder button, "
    "and the edit box.";

// set up the UI flags
bi.ulFlags =
    BIF_BROWSEINCLUDEFILES |// allow file selection
    BIF_EDITBOX |           // user can type name
    BIF_RETURNFSANCESTORS | // must be part of file system
    BIF_STATUSTEXT |        // show status area
    BIF_VALIDATE |          // make sure entered name is valid
    BIF_USENEWUI ;          // use the newest UI

// now fetch the list
LPITEMIDLIST pidl = ::SHBrowseForFolder(&bi);
if(pidl!=NULL)
{
    // reflect the selection
    std::cout << "Selected: " << szSelPath
        << std::endl;

    // fetch the allocator
    IMalloc* pMalloc = NULL;
    ::SHGetMalloc(&pMalloc);

    // free the PIDL
    pMalloc->Free(pidl);
    pidl = NULL;

    // clean up the allocator
    pMalloc->Release();
    pMalloc = NULL;
}
}
```

Listing 9-8 shows how simple it is to set up and use the folder browser dialog box. I turned on most of the available UI widgets; you can see the results in Figure 9-2. The figure shows the full-blown Browse For Folder dialog box that is displayed when using the SHBrowseForFolder() API.

In Listing 9-8, I fetch the shell's allocator to release the PIDL by the SHBrowseForFolder() API. You should be careful to release all resources the shell hands back to you. Other applications want them, too.

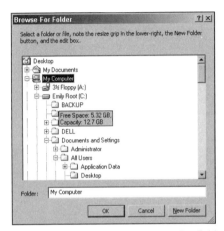

Figure 9-2: The full-blown Browse For Folder dialog box

System tray APIs

On one end of the shell's task bar (which I discussed earlier in this chapter) is the famous Start button. On the other end is an area known as the *system tray*. This area contains a clock and status or notification information from applications in the form of icons. The system tray icons communicate to the user both through the graphic of the icon and with a caption that pops up during a mouse-over. For example, when you run the task manager application (by right-clicking the taskbar and selecting the Task Manager... menu pick), that application installs a CPU usage meter. The CPU usage meter graphically indicates how loaded the processor is at any time (using bright green on top of dark green in the icon) and gives you a precise value when you mouse over it. Figure 9-3 shows you a typical system tray.

Figure 9-3: The system tray area showing the task manager icon and its tool tip in action

You use a single API to modify the system tray, Shell_NotifyIcon(). This API takes only two parameters: an action value and a NOTIFYICONDATA structure. The actions you can perform on the status area are add, delete, modify, and set focus. The second parameter to the API contains data used to configure the tray icon when performing add and modify operations.

Looking closer at the NOTIFYICONDATA structure, as I summarize it in Table 9-2, you can see that Windows supports an application placing more than one icon in the status tray. It has fields for an ID and a window handle that receive notifications from the icon. The system passes messages to the specified window from the user's mouse when over the tray icon. This enables you to display a pop-up menu for a right-click, or take an action for a left-click. The system also enables you to send a tool tip that it displays when the user hovers the mouse over your icon.

TABLE 9-2 MEMBERS OF THE NOTIFYICONDATA STRUCTURE

Member Name	Intention
HWND hWnd	Window to receive notification messages from the tray icon
UINT uID	Application-specific identifier to the tray icon; important when the application places more than one icon in the tray
UINT uFlags	A bitmask of flags that indicate what fields in the remaining structure have valid data
UINT uCallbackMessage	Notification message from the icon (the command identifier)
HICON hIcon	Handle to the Windows icon that will be added, modified, or deleted in the Shell_NotifyIcon() call
TCHAR szTip[128]	Tooltip that the taskbar will display when the user hovers the mouse over the icon
DWORD dwState	Sets the current state of the icon; valid states are: NIS_HIDDEN and NIS_SHAREDICON
DWORD dwStateMask	Mask of states to modify with the function call
UINT uTimeout	Time to wait after showing the tooltip before removing it, in milliseconds

Continued

TABLE **9-2 MEMBERS OF THE NOTIFYICONDATA STRUCTURE** *(Continued)*

Member Name	Intention
UINT uVersion	Flag to use balloon-style tooltips (with a title and icon). Valid values are 0 or NOTIFYICON_VERSION
TCHAR szInfoTitle[64]	Title to the tooltip, displayed in boldface above the description from the szTip field
DWORD dwInfoFlags	Icon to be displayed next to the tooltip when the user hovers the mouse on the icon; valid values are: NIIF_WARNING, NIIF_ERROR, and NIIF_INFO

In order to get messages from the system tray, the application needs to construct a window to receive them. The simplest method for doing this is to create a modeless dialog box and never show it. The example in Listing 9-9 shows a very simple application that inserts an icon into the system tray and responds to commands from the user.

Listing 9-9: Placing an icon in the system tray and responding to commands

```
// project trayicon
#include <windows.h>
#include "resource.h"

// helper data
const UINT g_nMsgIcon =
    ::RegisterWindowMessage("W2kDG.TrayIcon.Notify");
static HICON g_hIconTray = NULL;
static HWND  g_hWndMessages = NULL;
static HMENU g_hMenuTop = NULL;

// helper methods
BOOL CALLBACK TrayProc(HWND hwnd, UINT nMsg, WPARAM wParam,
    LPARAM lParam);
HWND CreateMessageWindow(HINSTANCE hInstance);
void ShowCommandMenu(HWND hwnd);
BOOL CommandTray(UINT nAction);

// main work for the application
void RunTray(HINSTANCE hInstance)
{
```

```
    // the icon (retrieved from the EXE file)
    g_hIconTray = ::LoadIcon(hInstance,
        MAKEINTRESOURCE(IDI_BOOK));

    // the message window
    g_hWndMessages = ::CreateMessageWindow(hInstance);

    // set up the popup menu
    g_hMenuTop = ::LoadMenu(hInstance,
        MAKEINTRESOURCE(IDM_TRAYPOPUP));

    // add the icon to the tray
    if(CommandTray(NIM_ADD))
    {
        // simple message loop that dispatches until user quits
        MSG msg;
        while (::GetMessage(&msg, NULL, 0, 0))
        {
            //  make sure to let the dialog message loop handle
            //  tray messages
            if(!::IsDialogMessage(g_hWndMessages, &msg))
            {
                ::TranslateMessage(&msg);
                ::DispatchMessage(&msg);
            }
        }
    }

    // clean up our resources
    ::DestroyWindow(g_hWndMessages);
    g_hWndMessages = NULL;
    ::DestroyIcon(g_hIconTray);
    g_hIconTray = NULL;
    ::DestroyMenu(g_hMenuTop);
    g_hMenuTop = NULL;
}

// helper method to send commands to the system tray for this
//  application (uses module statics)
BOOL CommandTray(UINT nAction)
{
    // start filling the icon data
    NOTIFYICONDATA nid;
    ::ZeroMemory(&nid, sizeof(nid));
```

```cpp
    nid.cbSize = sizeof(nid);   // size of struct
    nid.hWnd = g_hWndMessages;  // window to get messages
    nid.uCallbackMessage = g_nMsgIcon;  // message ID from icon
    nid.hIcon = g_hIconTray;    // icon to place in the tray
    nid.uID = 1;                // ID of icon
    ::strcpy(nid.szTip, "Simple tray icon from W2KDG."); // tip
    nid.uFlags = NIF_ICON|NIF_TIP|NIF_MESSAGE;  // valid fields

    return(::Shell_NotifyIcon(nAction, &nid));
}


// the callback method for handling tray notifications
BOOL CALLBACK TrayProc(HWND hwnd, UINT nMsg,
                            WPARAM wParam, LPARAM lParam)
{
    // check for our notification messages
    if(nMsg==g_nMsgIcon)
    {
        if(lParam==WM_RBUTTONUP)
        {
            // display the context menu
            ShowCommandMenu(hwnd);
        }
        else if(lParam==WM_LBUTTONDBLCLK)
        {
            ::PostQuitMessage(0);
        }
    }
    // check for messages from the menu
    else if(nMsg==WM_COMMAND)
    {
        if(LOWORD(wParam)==ID_ICON_QUIT)
        {
            ::PostQuitMessage(0);
        }
        else if(LOWORD(wParam)==ID_ICON_ABOUT)
        {
            ::MessageBox(hwnd, "Win2000 Developer's Guide "
                "Status Tray Icon Demo", "About Tray Icon",
                MB_OK);
        }
        // else... handle other messages
    }
    return(FALSE);
}
```

```
// display the menu of commands from the icon
void ShowCommandMenu(HWND hwnd)
{
    // load the top-level menu and fetch the first
    //   submenu, then destroy it
    HMENU hmenu = ::GetSubMenu(g_hMenuTop, 0);

    // make sure the Quit pick is highlighted as the
    //   default
    ::SetMenuDefaultItem(
        hmenu,            // menu to affect
        ID_ICON_QUIT,     // ID to make default
        FALSE);           // not by position, by ID

    // make current window foreground, required to fix
    //   Q135788 from MSDN
    ::SetForegroundWindow(hwnd);

    // grab the point of right-click and pop up the menu
    POINT pt;
    ::GetCursorPos(&pt);
    if(::TrackPopupMenu(
        hmenu,            // menu to pop up
        TPM_RIGHTALIGN,   // align the popup
        pt.x, pt.y,       // point to popup menu from
        0,                // must be 0
        hwnd,             // owner
        NULL))            // ignored
    {
        // force task switch to owner application, from Q135788
        ::PostMessage(hwnd, WM_USER, 0, 0);
    }
}

// helper to create the new window
HWND CreateMessageWindow(HINSTANCE hInstance)
{
    // create a simple dialog-based window to handle the
    //   messages from the tray
    HWND hwndMessage = ::CreateDialog(
        hInstance, // instance of the application
        MAKEINTRESOURCE(IDD_MESSAGE), // dialog template
        NULL,       // parent to the desktop
        TrayProc);  // our message handling
```

```
    return(hwndMessage);
}

// simple entry point, just runs the tray application
int APIENTRY WinMain(HINSTANCE hInstance,
    HINSTANCE hPrevInstance, LPSTR lpCmdLine, int nCmdShow)
{
    // start the tray icon and leave when it tells us to
    RunTray(hInstance);
    return 0;
}
```

 Listing 9-9 refers to MSDN Knowledge Base (KB) article Q135788. To view the detailed text, simply point to the MSDN library and search for 'Q135788.'

The example in Listing 9-9 usurps the `WinMain()` method and runs the local `RunTray()` function. This function simply initializes some useful resources (a window for handling messages, an icon, and a pop-up menu parent), adds an icon to the tray, then simply waits until the user tells it to end while operating a standard Windows message loop. To manipulate the system tray, a helper function called `CommandTray()` takes the action code, creates a `NOTIFYICONDATA` structure from the supporting data, and calls the `Shell_NotifyIcon()` API.

The simple `CreateMessageWindow()` helper method creates a modeless dialog box and points it at the `TrayProc()` method to handle Windows messages. The `TrayProc()` function responds to Windows message destined to its icon. This simple example has the default action of quitting (a double-click). When the user right-clicks the icon, it displays a short popup menu using the `ShowCommandMenu()` helper. This helper simply looks up the popup menu and enables the user to select actions.

Internal functions

When integrating your application with the shell, you sometimes need access to the shell's internal workings. For example, I have used examples throughout this chapter that call shell APIs, which return a chunk of memory that you must free with the shell's `IMalloc` interface. The shell allocator is retrieved with the `SHGetMalloc()` API; you must clean up the pointer with its own `Release()` method.

When using the Active Template Library (ATL), I use a class to retrieve and release the shell's allocator easily. I show the `CSHMallocPtr` class later this chapter, in Listing 9-13.

The shell provides the `SHGetSettings()` API to reflect the current UI setup of the explorer. This API takes a bitmask of the values to query and returns a structure containing Boolean flags, such as the Recycle Bin asking for confirmation on delete.

As I showed you in Chapter 3, the Windows executive allows applications to gather notifications of changes to the file system. The shell is an application on top of the kernel, just like your application, and the only notifications it receives from the kernel about changes to the shell are file system changes. However, it needs more. The `SHChangeNotify()` API enables you to tell the shell about changes that have nothing to do with the file system. The first parameter to this API is the type of change that occurred. For example, the `SHCNE_MEDIAINSERTED` type tells the shell that the user inserted new storage media into a drive so that it can take an action, such as looking up the `AutoRun.INF` and executing the startup application. The API also takes three more parameters that provide extended information for each type of notification, such as a path to the drive of the new media.

For details on the parameters to the `SHChangeNotify()` API, see the Microsoft Developer Network (MSDN) library; look up "SHChangeNotify" in the index.

Your application should use the `SHChangeNotify()` API whenever it does something to the system that might affect an open explorer window. For example, when you insert a new CD into the system CD-ROM drive, the explorer displays the new disk title and may play it automatically; this requires the `SCHNE_MEDIAINSERTED` notification.

Various helper APIs

The shell is a very broad application on top of the Windows kernel; it has many dimensions and provides many facilities that you can leverage in your applications. Among these useful facilities are a simple About box, a convenience function for disk space, and a method to send commands to system printers. I briefly cover these facilities in this section.

ABOUT BOX

One of the facilities that the shell offers your application is the simple construction of an About dialog box. The ShellAbout() method takes a parent window, a caption, an extended description, and even an icon to show in the dialog box. The example in Listing 9-10 starts up and shows the About box for an application.

Listing 9-10: Starting up and displaying the system-supplied About box

```
// project about
#include <windows.h>

void main()
{
    // create and display the About box
    ::ShellAbout(
        NULL,                            // no parent window
        "Windows 2000 Developer's Guide",        // caption
        "Project 'About'. This is the original "
        "version of this text from IDG Books.", // extra text
        NULL);                     // no icon
}
```

The code in Listing 9-10 just pops up and shows the About box with a simplistic caption and helper description. The dialog box reports the current version of Windows, the license information, and the available physical RAM. Figure 9-4 shows the results of running this application on my system running the Windows 2000 Server Release Candidate 3 (RC3).

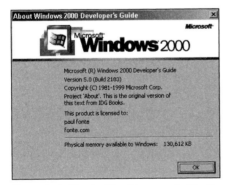

Figure 9-4: Simple About box created by the system

DISK SPACE AND PRINTER STARTUP

Another helper method that the shell provides is the SHGetDiskFreeSpace() API. This function simply requires the name of the volume of interest and returns the total free space, the free space available to the caller, and the total size of the disk. Each value returned from this API is a 64-bit integer, supporting a 16+ million-terabyte disk.

Finally, the SHInvokePrinterCommand() API enables you to start up the shell's printer management functions. You can open the status box or properties for a printer, install a new printer, print a test page, and access a few other operations. The example in Listing 9-11 shows how simple it is to open up the current status window for a printer that I have attached to my system.

Listing 9–11: Opening the printer status window

```
// project printercmd
#define _WIN32_WINNT 0x0500
#define WINVER 0x0500
#include <windows.h>

void main()
{
    // send the printer a simple command
    ::SHInvokePrinterCommand(
        NULL,                   // no parent window
        PRINTACTION_OPEN,       // open the printer's status
        "HP LaserJet 4L",       // name of the printer
        NULL,                   // ignored
        TRUE);                  // modal
}
```

 To lookup the printers attached to the system that runs your application, use the EnumPrinters() API from the WinSpool.DLL library. See the MSDN documentation, *Printing and Print Spooler*, for more information.

The example shows a hard-coded name to my printer, but the point of Listing 9-11 is that the shell enables you to run its printer management through a single, simple API. You can use the SHInvokePrinterCommand() API whenever you need to let users reconfigure their printer setup.

Shell Interfaces

So far, in this chapter, I've shown you how to use the services provided by the Windows shell using mostly plain, vanilla C API calls. The shell, however, is built on COM. It exposes many interfaces for using components and extending the user experience. This section will cover the core interfaces to shell objects and the COM objects required to extend the shell's namespace.

Core interfaces

The root of the Windows shell is the desktop folder. In the previous section on the folder object APIs, I glossed over the return value from the SHGetDesktopFolder() API – an IShellFoler interface. The IShellFolder is the primary interface to the shell, and I detail its methods in Table 9-3. It exposes methods to enumerate each child of the folder and get its IShellFolder interface, enabling you to recurse the entire namespace.

TABLE 9-3 METHODS OF THE ISHELLFOLDER INTERFACE

Method	Description
QueryInterface()	Retrieves a pointer to another interface on the COM object
AddRef()	Increments the reference count to the underlying COM object
Release()	Decrements the reference count to the COM object, possibly destroying it
BindToObject()	Fetches the IShellFolder interface to a subfolder of the current object
CompareIDs()	Fetches the relative order of two objects in the folder using the PIDL of each
CreateViewObject()	Creates a view for the folder; the explorer will display this view
EnumObjects()	Creates an enumerator list for the objects in the folder, returning an IEnumIDList interface to the list
GetAttributesOf()	Fetches the shell attributes of the object passed by PIDL; values such as SFGAO_FOLDER and SFGAO_READONLY are possible
GetDisplayNameOf()	Gets the string that should be displayed to the user for the folder's object passed by PIDL

Method	Description
GetUIObjectOf()	Retrieves an interface to a user interface widget for an object in the folder passed by PIDL; interfaces such as IContextMenu may be returned
ParseDisplayName()	Translates a display name of an object in the folder into a PIDL
SetNameOf()	Modifies the display name of the passed object by PIDL

To enumerate child items with the IShellFolder interface, use the EnumObjects() method, which returns an IEnumIDList interface. To fetch items from the IEnumIDList, call the Next() method, which returns their PIDLs. The example in Listing 9-12 illustrates how to walk child items.

Listing 9-12: Enumerating child objects from a folder

```
// project enumchild
#define _WIN32_WINNT 0x0500
#define WINVER 0x0500
#include <windows.h>
#include <atlbase.h>
#include <shlobj.h>
#include <shlwapi.h>
#include <iostream>

void main()
{
    // look up the shell's allocator for cleaning up
    CComPtr<IMalloc> spMalloc;
    ::SHGetMalloc(&spMalloc);

    // fetch the desktop's ShellFolder interface
    CComPtr<IShellFolder> spsfDesktop;
    ::SHGetDesktopFolder(&spsfDesktop);

    // fetch the PIDL to the cookie jar
    LPITEMIDLIST pidlJar = NULL;
    if(SUCCEEDED(::SHGetFolderLocation(
        NULL,        // no parent window
        CSIDL_COOKIES, // cookie folder's ID
        NULL,        // use the current user security
```

```
                0,              // must be 0
            &pidlJar)))
    {
        // fetch the ShellFolder interface of the cookie jar
        CComPtr<IShellFolder> spsfJar;
        if(SUCCEEDED(spsfDesktop->BindToObject(
            pidlJar,              // PIDL of subfolder
            NULL,                 // must be NULL
            IID_IShellFolder,     // want ShellFolder
            reinterpret_cast<LPVOID*>(&spsfJar))))  // buffer
        {
            // get the enumerator
            CComPtr<IEnumIDList> spenumJar;
            if(SUCCEEDED(spsfJar->EnumObjects(
                NULL,                 // parent window
                SHCONTF_NONFOLDERS, // just get non-folders
                &spenumJar)))         // buffer
            {
                // fetch each PIDL
                LPITEMIDLIST pidlCookie = NULL;
                while(spenumJar->Next(1, &pidlCookie, NULL)
                    ==NOERROR)
                {
                    // look up the display name
                    STRRET strName;
                    spsfJar->GetDisplayNameOf(
                        pidlCookie,     // cookie PIDL
                        SHGDN_NORMAL,   // full name of object
                        &strName);      // return buffer

                    // convert the special return buffer to
                    //   a flat C string
                    LPTSTR szDisplayName;
                    ::StrRetToStr(&strName, pidlCookie,
                        &szDisplayName);

                    // display the results
                    std::cout << "Found Cookie: "
                        << szDisplayName << std::endl;

                    // clean up the name and the PIDL
                    ::CoTaskMemFree(szDisplayName);
                    szDisplayName = NULL;
                    spMalloc->Free(pidlCookie);
```

```
                pidlCookie = NULL;
            }
        }
    }

    // release the cookie jar's PIDL
    spMalloc->Free(pidlJar);
    pidlJar = NULL;
    }
}
```

The item enumerator in Listing 9-12 uses the ATL `CComPtr` class to make sure the shell interfaces are released properly. These smart pointers are used pretty much the same way that normal C (dumb) pointers are used, but they automatically call the `Release()` method on the object as they go out of scope. The first two interfaces the example needs are the desktop's `IShellFolder` and the shell's `IMalloc`. Next, the program fetches the PIDL to the cookie folder using the `SHGetFolderLocation()` API demonstrated earlier.

The `BindToObject()` API of `IShellFolder` requires a PIDL relative to the parent folder; because the cookie folder's PIDL is absolute, it must be relative to the desktop folder. Therefore, the program can use the desktop's `IShellFolder` to find the `IShellFolder` of the cookie folder. With the cookie folder, Listing 9-12 next gets an enumerator interface with the `EnumObjects()` method. The example then loops through the list of child objects with the `Next()` method, fetching the display name of each using the `GetDisplayNameOf()` method on the returned PIDL. Finally, it shows the results to the operator. You also should note the use of the `StrRetToStr()` API to convert the `STRRET` structure to a standard C string; the returned string is freed with a call to the `CoTaskMemFree()` API.

The `StrRetToStr()` API comes from the `ShLWApi.DLL` library that I cover later in this chapter.

If you have an absolute PIDL, you sometimes will want to get to the `IShellFolder` for its parent. The shell supplies a simple helper API, `SHBindToParent()`, for just this purpose. This API takes a fully qualified PIDL and returns the `IShellFolder` interface of its parent. `SHBindToParent()` often is useful for fetching the display name or other attributes of a shell object when all you have is its PIDL.

Another central interface that the shell exposes to you is `IActiveDesktop`. This interface enables you to manipulate the UI presented by the Windows desktop. The desktop UI is simply a view of the desktop folder. This interface enables you to add a desktop item or change the background wallpaper. To fetch the interface, simply use the COM `CoCreateInstance()` API (easily accomplished with the `CComPtr` class). One of the principal items you can add and manipulate on the desktop is termed a *desktop component*. The `COMPONENT` structure wraps this object that can consist of an HTML document, an image, a URL, or an ActiveX control.

Namespace functions

When creating a great application, one goal is to make it appear as if it is part of Windows. In other words, you want the user to transition from another task into your application seamlessly. The Windows shell namespace-extension mechanism enables you to do this.

You've seen PIDLs used throughout this chapter to uniquely identify an object accessible through the shell. A namespace extension places a PIDL somewhere in the desktop's tree that begins your application, or a specific part of it. Additionally, you've seen that the primary COM interface used in the shell is `IShellFolder`, when you fetch one of these using the `BindToObject()` method on the desktop's interface. Exposing an `IShellFolder` from your application enables you to place it in the namespace and enables users to navigate to it using the Windows explorer.

This is slightly more complicated than just implementing `IShellFolder`. You also need to design how your application appears in the shell. You can look at examples of other namespaces to get ideas for your application. One such example is the *cabinet file (CAB)* viewer namespace extension that Microsoft supplies as part of its Power Tools package. This extension enables you to browse into a CAB archive as if it were a folder in the file system. Another example is the Recycle Bin application that caches deleted files from the file system. The former is an example of a non-rooted extension; it shows up dynamically within the shell namespace. The latter is an example of a rooted extension; it shows up in a permanent location (as a first-level child of the desktop node) in the namespace.

MANIPULATING PIDLS

When constructing a namespace, you write lots of code to deal with PIDLs. I have created some stock code that I use for manipulating PIDLs, as shown in Listing 9-13.

Listing 9-13: Manipulating PIDLs with helper classes

```
// project procview, file enumidl.h
#include <windows.h>
#include <tlhelp32.h>
class CShellFolder;

#include <shlobj.h>
#include <atlbase.h>

//
// Helper class to manage the shell's IMalloc interface
//
```

```
class CSHMallocPtr : public CComPtr<IMalloc>
{
public:
    CSHMallocPtr() { ::SHGetMalloc(&p);}
};


//
// Helper class to manage PIDLs
//
class PIDL
{
public:
    //
    // Iteration functions (item independent)
    //
    static LPITEMIDLIST GetNextItem(LPCITEMIDLIST pidl)
    {
        // first get a byte-wise pointer, then add the size of
        //  the whole PIDL to find the next
        PBYTE pStart = (PBYTE)pidl;
        LPITEMIDLIST pidlNext = reinterpret_cast<LPITEMIDLIST>
            (pStart + pidl->mkid.cb);
        return(pidlNext);
    }


    static LPCITEMIDLIST GetLastItem(LPCITEMIDLIST pidl)
    {
        LPCITEMIDLIST pidlLast = pidl;
        while(pidl->mkid.cb>0)
        {
            pidlLast = pidl;
            pidl = GetNextItem(pidl);
        }
        return(pidlLast);
    }


    // determining the total size of a PIDL
    static ULONG GetSize(LPCITEMIDLIST pidl)
    {
        ULONG nTotal(0);
        if(pidl!=NULL)
        {
            nTotal += sizeof(ITEMIDLIST);
            while(pidl->mkid.cb>0)
            {
```

```
            nTotal += pidl->mkid.cb;
            pidl = GetNextItem(pidl);
        }
    }
    return(nTotal);
}

// create a new PIDL from the original
static LPITEMIDLIST Copy(LPCITEMIDLIST pidlSrc)
{
    ULONG nSize = GetSize(pidlSrc);
    LPITEMIDLIST pidl = NULL;
    if(nSize>0)
    {
        CSHMallocPtr spMalloc;
        pidl = (LPITEMIDLIST)spMalloc->Alloc(nSize);
        ::CopyMemory(pidl, pidlSrc, nSize);
    }
    return(pidl);
}

// release a PIDL (and clean up its reference)
static void Free(LPCITEMIDLIST& pidl)
{
    CSHMallocPtr spMalloc;
    if(pidl!=NULL)
    {
        spMalloc->Free((void*)pidl);
    }
    pidl = NULL;
}

// add two PIDLs together
static LPITEMIDLIST Concatenate(LPCITEMIDLIST pidl1,
    LPCITEMIDLIST pidl2)
{
    ULONG nSize1 = GetSize(pidl1);
    ULONG nSize2 = GetSize(pidl2);
    LPITEMIDLIST pidlTotal = NULL;
    if((nSize1 + nSize2)>0)
    {
        // allocate a new PIDL
        CSHMallocPtr spMalloc;
        pidlTotal = (LPITEMIDLIST)spMalloc->
            Alloc(nSize1 + nSize2 -sizeof(ITEMIDLIST));
```

```
            // copy the lists
            ::CopyMemory(pidlTotal, pidl1, nSize1);
            nSize1 -= sizeof(ITEMIDLIST);
            ::CopyMemory((PBYTE)pidlTotal + nSize1, pidl2,
                nSize2);
        }
        return(pidlTotal);
    }
};
```

The class presented in Listing 9-13 — named PIDL — consists simply of a set of static helper methods for adding, destroying, copying, and iterating through PIDLs. The PIDL structure is reasonably simple to use and it appears that every namespace effort writes it. (We'll use it later to construct a custom PIDL for an example application.) You also should note the CSHMallocPtr class near the beginning of the example. It wraps the calls to SHGetMalloc() with an ATL CComPtr so that you can use the shell's IMalloc simply by instantiating an object of that class.

CREATING A NAMESPACE EXTENSION

When creating a namespace extension, there are two main pieces: the data and the UI. The shell asks for both pieces from your application through its IShellFolder interface. This handshake starts when the user browses the folder containing your rooted namespace extension or browses into an item associated with your non-rooted namespace extension.

Let's begin by looking at the design of the extension's data. The shell expects the data to be hierarchical (although a hierarchy one level deep is acceptable) and accesses it through the EnumObjects() method of IShellFolder. EnumObjects() returns a new object that exposes the IEnumIDList interface demonstrated in Listing 9-12. Each PIDL returned from the Next() method of the interface needs to be atomic. The shell can take that PIDL and return it to the IShellFolder interface with the GetAttributesOf(), GetDisplayNameOf(), or GetUIObjectOf() methods. None of these methods takes the IEnumIDList interface, so the PIDL must contain all of the information to uniquely identify the object in the current folder.

I'm going to show you a very basic namespace example that I constructed using a namespace AppWizard from an article by Krishna Kotipalli entitled, "Shell Namespace Extensions" in the March 1999 issue of *Microsoft Internet Developer (MIND)*. The namespace simply enumerates the currently running processes in the system using the Windows ToolHelp32 API and displays each EXE file name, process ID, and currently running thread count.

 You can find the code and part of the Kotipalli article from MIND online at http://www.microsoft.com/mind.

To implement the IEnumIDList for the ProcView namespace, I simply designed the PIDL to own a unique copy of the PROCESSENTRY32 structure that the process iterator APIs return. Listing 9-14 shows the implementation of the PROCITEM class, which backs the PIDLs; it also shows the CEnumIDList class, which exposes the IEnumIDList for the folder.

Listing 9-14: Implementing PIDL and enumerator classes for the ProcView namespace

```
// project procview, file enumidl.h
//
// Item in the PIDL, it simply contains a PROCESSENTRY32
//   object for describing the process
//
class PROCITEM : PIDL
{
public:
    // the process entry
    PROCITEM(PROCESSENTRY32 procentry) : m_procentry(procentry){}

    // the data member
    PROCESSENTRY32 m_procentry;

    //
    // to & from PIDL
    //
    LPITEMIDLIST Create()
    {
        // each PIDL is SHITEM(PROCITEM):SHITEM(NULL)
        size_t nSize = 2*sizeof(ITEMIDLIST) + sizeof(PROCITEM);

        // allocate one, set its size, and copy the data
        CSHMallocPtr spMalloc;
        LPITEMIDLIST pidl = reinterpret_cast<LPITEMIDLIST>
            (spMalloc->Alloc(nSize));
        pidl->mkid.cb = sizeof(ITEMIDLIST) + sizeof(PROCITEM);
        PROCITEM* pProc = reinterpret_cast<PROCITEM*>
            (pidl->mkid.abID);
        pProc->m_procentry = m_procentry;

        // move to the terminator and null it out
        LPITEMIDLIST pidlNull = GetNextItem(pidl);
        ::ZeroMemory(pidlNull, sizeof(ITEMIDLIST));

        return (pidl);
    }
```

```
    static PROCITEM FromPidl(LPCITEMIDLIST pidl)
    {
        // the PROCITEM
        LPCITEMIDLIST pidlLast = GetLastItem(pidl);
        PROCITEM* pProc = (PROCITEM*)(pidlLast->mkid.abID);
        return(*pProc);
    }

};

class CEnumIDList  : public IEnumIDList
{
public:
    CEnumIDList(CShellFolder *, LPCITEMIDLIST pidl,
        DWORD dwFlags);
    ~CEnumIDList();

    //IUnknown methods
    STDMETHOD (QueryInterface)(REFIID, LPVOID*);
    STDMETHOD_ (DWORD, AddRef)();
    STDMETHOD_ (DWORD, Release)();

    //IEnumIDList
    STDMETHOD(Next)  (THIS_ ULONG celt,
                      LPITEMIDLIST *rgelt,
                      ULONG *pceltFetched)
    {
        // begin with a 0 count
        *pceltFetched = 0;
        HRESULT hr = S_OK;

        // loop as long as we have room and we've found
        //   another process for the array
        for(ULONG nFetch=0;nFetch<celt && hr==S_OK;++nFetch)
        {
            PROCESSENTRY32 pe;
            if(Next(pe))
            {
                // create a PIDL and set it into the array
                PROCITEM pi(pe);
                rgelt[nFetch] = pi.Create();

                // bump the return count
                ++(*pceltFetched);
```

```
                }
                else
                {
                    hr = S_FALSE;
                }

            }
            return(S_OK);
        }
        STDMETHOD(Skip)  (THIS_ ULONG celt)
        {
            BOOL bFound(TRUE);
            for(ULONG nVictim=0;nVictim<celt && bFound;++nVictim)
            {
                PROCESSENTRY32 pe;
                bFound = Next(pe);
            }
            return(bFound ? S_OK : S_FALSE);
        }
        STDMETHOD(Reset) (THIS)
        {
            Init();
            return(S_OK);
        }
        STDMETHOD(Clone) (THIS_ IEnumIDList **ppenum)
        {
            return E_NOTIMPL;
        }

        //
        // IUnknown implementation
        //
protected:
    DWORD m_dwRefCount;

        //
        // IEnumIDList implementation
        //
protected:
    HANDLE  m_hSnapshot;

    BOOL Next(PROCESSENTRY32& pe)
    {
        // initialize the process entry struct
```

```
    ::ZeroMemory(&pe, sizeof(pe));
    pe.dwSize = sizeof(pe);

    // grab the process entry if possible
    BOOL bFound(FALSE);
    if(m_hSnapshot==NULL)
    {
        Init();
        bFound = ::Process32First(m_hSnapshot, &pe);
    }
    else
    {
        bFound = ::Process32Next(m_hSnapshot, &pe);
    }
    return(bFound);
}

void Cleanup()
{
    if(m_hSnapshot!=NULL)
    {
        ::CloseHandle(m_hSnapshot);
        m_hSnapshot = NULL;
    }
}

void Init()
{
    // clear ourselves out
    Cleanup();

    // fetch a snapshot of the current processes
    m_hSnapshot = ::CreateToolhelp32Snapshot(
        TH32CS_SNAPPROCESS, // get process information
        0);                 // ignored for process snap
}

// construction parameters (from IShellFolder::EnumObjects)
private:
    CShellFolder* m_pSF;
    DWORD         m_dwFlags;
};
```

The PROCITEM class simply wraps a PROCESSENTRY32 structure and provides methods to create a PIDL from it or create it from a PIDL. Additionally, the PROCITEM inherits all of the functionality from the PIDL class defined in Listing 9-13. The implementation of CEnumIDList shows the implementation methods Init(), Next(), and Cleanup() that implement the actual iteration. The m_hSnapshot handle holds the state of the iteration. This handle references a pseudo-kernel object containing information about all of the processes running when it was constructed. The Next() public method uses the internal Next() to create PIDLs for the requestor (usually the explorer browser) around results from calls to the Process32First() and Process32Next() APIs.

The rest of the code for the namespace implements the UI that is displayed in the righthand pane of the explorer browser. The primary COM interface for this is IShellView, supplied by an object created in the CreateViewObject() method of IShellFolder. For the sample ProcView namespace, I simply use most of the code provided by the AppWizard, which creates a ListView window to display our contents. I'll leave it to you to examine the code – it's very straightforward. Figure 9-5 shows you the namespace in action.

To examine the code that implements the ProcView namespace view, see the appendix in the back of this book, "Using the Examples in This Book."

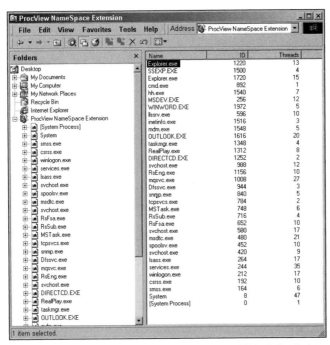

Figure 9-5: The Process Viewer namespace as a child of the desktop

IDENTIFYING AND CUSTOMIZING NAMESPACES

To get the system to recognize your namespace, you must provide what Windows calls a *junction point*. A junction point can be an associated file as in the CAB file viewer, an entry in the registry's HKLM\...\Explorer\Desktop\NameSpace\ key, a simple text file called desktop.ini within a folder, or a folder specially named to have the *class identifier (CLSID)* of your shell folder COM object as its extension. The ProcView namespace uses the registry key to place itself on the desktop (a first-level child of the desktop node).

For more information on junction points, please see the MSDN article entitled *Namespace Extensions* in the Platform SDK's User Interface Services documentation.

Windows also enables your namespace extensions to customize the UI of the explorer when the user browses into it. The IShellBrowser interface of the explorer browser is a parameter to each explorer view instantiation. This interface enables you to modify the status field, menu, and toolbar of the explorer. Please see the documentation on this interface for uses. Also, you can control the context (right-click) menu, supply a tool tip, supply a special icon, or even make items within the folder support drag-and-drop through the GetUIObjectOf() method on the IShellFolder interface.

Lightweight APIs

Before concluding the discussion of Windows shell services, you should know about the shell's *lightweight APIs*. Most of these services originate in the ShLWApi.DLL library. They enable you to manipulate strings, file system paths, URLs, and the registry quickly and easily. In addition, there is another library closely related to the Windows shell called WinInet.DLL that handles Internet-related operations and exposes some helpful APIs for you to use.

Chapter 14, "System Services," covers the WinInet.DLL library in more detail.

To use the ShLWApi.DLL library, you must supply its import library to the Visual C++ linker. I prefer to do this explicitly in the code by adding the line:
#pragma comment(lib, "shlwapi.lib").

String helpers

Windows exposes many string manipulation APIs — such as CharNext(), lstrlen(), and wsprintf() — which also are supplied by most C runtime libraries. As a bit of commentary, I prefer using the std::basic_string class from the C++ *Standard Template Library (STL)* and the C runtime functions when necessary. (They won't change over time, and they enable me to share my code with those on other platforms.) Table 9-4 shows the string helpers that do not have analogs in the STL std::basic_string class.

TABLE 9-4 SHLWAPI STRING HELPERS

API	Intention
StrFormatByteSize()	Takes a count and converts it to a string that represents the byte count — e.g., 10240 becomes "10.0KB". There is also a StrFormatByteSize64() and StrFormatKBSize().
StrFromTimeInterval()	Takes a millisecond interval and returns a string that represents it — e.g., 1000 becomes "1 sec."
StrRetToStr()	Converts the shell's STRRET structure to a useful string. Also StrRetToBuf().

Pathing helpers

File system paths are system specific, and there is no class in the STL or any other library I know of that abstracts them. In addition, file system paths are notoriously painful to manipulate — especially in the age of long file names that contain spaces. The pathing helpers from ShLWApi are a very welcome addition for any of us who have had to munge paths. Table 9-5 briefly covers the pathing functions for you. They should whet your appetite.

TABLE 9-5 SHLWAPI PATHING HELPERS

API	Intention
PathAddBackslash(), PathRemoveBackslash()	Ensures a trailing backslash exists, or does not exist, on the passed buffer for specifying a folder.

API	Intention
`PathAddExtension()`, `PathRemoveExtension()`, `PathRenameExtension()`, `PathCombine()`	These functions are similar to the C runtime `_makepath()` function supplied by Visual C++. They construct a path from its various components.
`PathBuildRoot()`, `PathGetDriveNumber()`	Creates a drive name for the passed integer representing the drive — e.g., 0 maps to `A:\`. The second function is the inverse.
`PathCanonicalize()`	Fixes up included "." and ".." folders within the path — e.g., `A:\.\ReadMe.TXT` becomes `A:\ReadMe.Txt`.
`PathCommonPrefix()`, `PathIsSameRoot()`, `PathRelativePathTo()`	The first is a nifty little function that finds the greatest-depth folder that both passed paths share. The second checks for the same drive. The last joins the two with a common path via a relative path.
`PathCompactPath()`, `PathCompactPathEx()`, `PathSetDlgItemPath()`	Used when writing text directly to a window, they clip the passed path name to fit within the passed width by replacing folders with ellipses when required. They attempt to keep the root and file name — e.g., `C:\...\Hosts.TXT`.
`PathCreateFromUrl()`	Interprets a URL with the `file://` protocol as a file system path.
`PathFileExists()`, `PathIsDirectory()`	These functions have been sorely needed for years. They simply tell you whether the passed file name or directory already exists in the system, they replace your calls to the `_access()` function from the C runtime.
`PathFindExtension()`, `PathFindFileName()`, `PathFindNextComponent()`, `PathRemoveFileSpec()`, `PathSkipRoot()`, `PathStripPath()`, `PathStripToRoot()`	These functions are similar to the C runtime `_splitpath()` function. They decompose a passed path into its components.
`PathFindOnPath()`	Looks in the file system for a named file existing on the passed search path or the default from the `PATH` environment variable.

Continued

TABLE 9-5 SHLWAPI PATHING HELPERS *(Continued)*

API	Intention
PathFindSuffixArray()	Tests a passed file name's extension for inclusion in a passed array of extensions (case-sensitive).
PathGetArgs(), PathRemoveArgs()	Takes a command line with arguments and splits out the file name; useful when dealing with long file names.
PathGetCharType()	Tests a character for inclusion in a path name. Use this to validate user input of paths.
PathIsContentType(), PathIsHTMLFile()	Determines if the passed path points to a specific type of content.
PathIsDirectoryEmpty()	Takes a path name, checks the folder in the file system, and tells you whether it is currently empty.
PathIsFileSpec(), PathIsPrefix(), PathIsLFNFileSpec(), PathIsRoot(), PathIsUNC(), PathIsURL()	Determines the current state of the passed path's specification (root, UNC, and so on).
PathIsNetworkPath(), PathIsSystemFolder(), PathIsUNCServer(), PathIsUNCServerShare()	Determines whether the passed path points to a known type of resource.
PathMakePretty()	Converts characters in the passed path to be uniform (lowercase).
PathMakeSystemFolder(), PathUnmakeSystemFolder()	Marks the passed directory as a system folder (the System attribute is set).
PathMatchSpec()	Determines if the passed path satisfies the passed wildcard — e.g., c:\boot.ini does satisfy *.ini.
PathQuoteSpaces(), PathUnquoteSpaces()	Takes a long file name and wraps it in quotes if it contains spaces, or vice-versa.
PathSearchAndQualify()	Takes a relative path, validates it, and creates a fully qualified path.
PathUnExpandEnvString(), DoEnvironmentSubst()	These methods replace environment variables in a string such as %SystemRoot% with the fully qualified name for the logged in user, or the opposite.

See the MSDN's Shell Lightweight Utility APIs documentation for more details about the pathing functions.

URL helpers

Since *Uniform Resource Locators (URLs)* are now so very much a part of the name-space, the shell exposes a bunch of utility functions for constructing and using them. The original reference for URL specification is RFC 1738. Table 9-6 lists the URL*Xxx*() APIs from ShLWApi.DLL.

You can look up the details of the Internet Request For Comments (RFC) 1738 and others at `http://www.cis.ohio-state.edu/hypertext/information/rfc.html`.

TABLE 9-6 SHLWAPI URL HELPERS

API	Intention
UrlApplyScheme()	Finds the appropriate scheme for the passed path to a file system resource and creates a canonical URL for it
UrlCanonicalize(), UrlEscape(), UrlEscapeSpaces()	Converts the passed URL to canonical form, with a valid scheme, — no "." folders, and no URL-unsafe characters
UrlCombine()	Takes a base scheme, machine, path, and a relative URL, then adds them and canonicalizes the result
UrlCompare()	Sorting of the two passed URLs, like the C `strcmp()` function
UrlCreateFromPath()	Takes a file system path and creates a canonical URL for it
UrlGetLocation(), UrlGetPath(), UrlGetPart()	Breaks the passed URL into its component parts

Continued

TABLE 9-6 SHLWAPI URL HELPERS *(Continued)*

API	Intention
`UrlIs()`, `UrlIsFileUrl()`, `UrlIsNoHistory()`, `UrlIsOpaque()`	Determines whether the passed URL fits into a specific, interesting category
`UrlUnEscape()`, `UrlUnEscapeInPlace()`	Replaces escape sequences within the URL with the ASCII characters

Registry helpers

In the next chapter, I introduce you to the Windows registry and its fully configurable, native APIs for access. The Windows shell simplifies access to the registry and adds APIs that you would have to write a bunch of code to duplicate. Before I even tell you what the registry is and how to access it, I'll show you Table 9-7 with these easy APIs so you can refer back here when you need them.

 Chapter 10, "Application Building Services," introduces and details the Windows registry and its use.

You can see that these functions are very helpful because you do not have to go through the construction and destruction of registry objects. The shell registry helper APIs enable you to name the subkey or value you're interested in and operate on it.

TABLE 9-7 SHLWAPI REGISTRY HELPERS

API	Intention
`SHCopyKey()`	Recursively copies a subkey and all of its subkeys and values to another key
`SHDeleteKey()`, `SHDeleteEmptyKey()`	Removes a key, by name, from the registry — including all of its values and subkeys
`SHDeleteValue()`	Removes the value from its subkey parent by name

API	Intention
SHEnumKeyEx(), SHEnumValue()	Iterates through the names of subkeys or values in the names key
SHGetValue()	Fetches the data for a named value
SHQueryInfoKey(), SHQueryValueEx()	Fetches data about the named subkey or value in the registry
SHRegGetPath(), SHRegSetPath()	Reads or writes values with environment strings to the registry, replacing the strings with fully qualified values from the current environment

Summary

I covered a lot of ground in this chapter. You learned exactly what the Windows shell is constructed from and how it all fits together. You also saw how to access the shell directly from your applications using plain C APIs. Then I showed you some of the COM interfaces that the shell uses internally and how to leverage them by creating a namespace extension to glue your application into the Windows shell. Finally, I showed you some simple services that the Windows shell gives you to help you write great applications.

The next thing you need to know is how to construct applications using the facilities that Windows gives you to access system data and share code with other applications. Chapter 10 will walk you through how to take advantage of the array of application services that Windows provides you to make great applications.

Part III

Building Applications

IN THIS PART

Chapter 10

Application Building Services

IN THIS CHAPTER

+ Software sharing services

+ Programming services

+ System services

I HAVE SHOWN YOU some of the tools such as kernel objects, the GDI, and the Windows shell that Windows 2000 gives you to create great applications that users love to use. This chapter covers some of the essential services that Windows 2000 provides you, the developer, to assemble and use these tools. I break these services into three categories: software sharing services, programming services, and system services.

The first group of services includes tools to consume and share software components with other developers. They let you use the work of others and let others use your work. These software-sharing services include Windows 2000 DLLs (dynamic link libraries) and COM (Component Object Model) objects.

Next, I discuss some programming services that Windows 2000 offers you to make it easy to create great applications. Services in this category include support for large (64-bit) integers, a system clock, file time stamping, and fine-grained real-time timers.

Finally, I cover items that I term system services since they let your application fuse itself into the heart of the Windows 2000 system tightly. Services in this category include the registry, facilities to determine the hardware and software configuration of the system, and APIs to log off the current user or shut the system down.

Software Sharing Services

Here's a quick assertion for you: Using someone else's work to add value to your own - rather than reinvent it - makes you more valuable. There's no doubt that the software you develop on Windows 2000 is unique. However, the building blocks that you use to construct it need not be. In fact, using existing components should give you less code to debug as well as shrink your development time.

Windows 2000 has two built-in mechanisms for sharing runtime code: the *DLL (dynamic link library)* and the *COM (Component Object Model)* object. There are other ways to share runtime code as well as ways to share source code and compiled code. These are discussed in the sidebar. This section looks at DLLs and COM objects, leaving other software sharing services to the compiler and software vendors.

Other Ways to Share Code

There are other ways to share code in addition to using DLLs and COM objects. First, you must choose the level within the software production process that you want to share. You can share code at the source (uncompiled) level, at the binary but undelivered level, or the binary and delivered level.

Sharing code at the source level is as simple as copying the code from one project into another. This level of code sharing is only effective within an organization, does not leverage the compilation effort from other groups, and requires a complex configuration management system.

Sharing software at the binary but undelivered level typically occurs using object code libraries. An object code library delivers compiled versions of code that is linked directly into your EXE or DLL. This level of code sharing can be effective across organizations, does leverage the compilation effort of others, and does not require so complex a configuration management as sharing at the source level. However, in order to share code at this level, you must decide before delivering your software the final versions of other vendor's software that you require – you cannot make the decision at runtime and you cannot take advantage of a new version of the shared components without upgrading your application.

Sharing software at the binary and delivered level is what you do with DLLs and COM objects. This sharing happens at runtime through system services. Dynamic binary code sharing allows you to share across organizations, leverage the build and delivery efforts of others, use an uncomplicated configuration management system, decide at runtime exactly what components to consume, and replace components in the field without upgrading your application.

Other examples of dynamic binary code sharing frameworks are *Enterprise Java Beans (EJB)* and the *Common Object Request Broker Architecture (CORBA)*. Both of these services are available for Windows through third-party vendors and both provide easy access to software components for your Windows applications.

The EJB framework, primarily intended for Web applications, delivers Java objects for runtime binding in the Java Virtual Machine (JVM); see `http://java.sun.com/products/ejb/` for more information. The CORBA framework delivers a distributed binary object architecture in which the objects are implemented in any language, reside on any machine of almost any platform visible to the network, and are dynamically consumed by client applications; see `http://www.omg.org/` for more information.

Dynamic link libraries

In Chapter 2, I briefly introduced you to DLLs and told you that they can help you break up your code into smaller and more manageable pieces. You will notice that most Windows programs use DLLs extensively; for example, nearly every Windows application consumes the `Kernel32.DLL` and `User32.DLL` libraries through the C++ runtime. A DLL is a package of software services that contains machine code and data that any Windows application with the correct knowledge can use.

DLL files are very similar to EXE files; in fact, they have the same format, the *Portable Executable (PE)* file format. The principal difference between the two files is that the EXE has a starting point for execution (the `main()`, `WinMain()`, or `ServiceMain()` function, depending on the application type) while the DLL does not.

The DLL supplies executable code to an application delivered by an EXE file. This DLL code simply joins the code of the EXE in-process. That is, when the application uses a service from the DLL, its thread of execution passes through the DLL's code. Since the application has loaded this code into its process, there is almost no performance overhead to use it. The major disadvantage of executing a DLL's code in your process is that if the DLL has a bug that stops execution, it stops the calling process.

For more information on the PE file format, see the MSDN documentation; search for the term "Portable Executable."

This section covers how to create DLLs. Once you create a DLL, you can link it into your application implicitly or use it explicitly.

CREATING DLLS

As with most software development, the design and implementation of the value-adding logic will be the most difficult part in creating a DLL. Deciding what to put into the library and going through the steps of packaging it are comparatively simple. Only a few steps are required to construct a DLL:

1. You must implement a `DllMain()` function for the system to call when loading and unloading the DLL.

2. You must tell Windows which functions are available publicly in your DLL.

3. You must publish the definitions of the available functions and types for consumers.

The functions that a DLL exposes through its *entry points* are typically C-style. This C-style calling convention specifies how parameter values are delivered to the function, how the function returns its results, and how the thread's *stack* is set up and cleaned up before and after the call. You can create a DLL using many different tools; the fact that C is the standard interface should not dissuade you from using a modern C++ compiler or even Visual Basic.

The DllMain() function is the first chance that you get to add code to a DLL. The actual entry point to the DLL – supplied by the compiler, much like the actual entry point of an executable – is the _DllMainCRTStartup() function. It takes care of initializing the C++ runtime before it calls DllMain(). This call to DllMain() sends you two useful parameters. The first parameter is the instance handle for the DLL; you should save this value in order to access resources attached to the DLL. The second parameter tells you why the system is calling DllMain().

Windows calls DllMain() when it loads the DLL into memory, sending DLL_PROCESS_ATTACH as its reason code. During attachment, the DLL should take care of any initialization it needs to accomplish before the using application begins calling functions. Each time the process creates a new thread, the system calls into the DllMain() of every DLL that the process has loaded with DLL_THREAD_ATTACH as the reason code. This signaling of new threads gives your DLL the chance to initialize data in thread local storage (TLS) or do anything else that it needs to do for each new thread. Likewise, each time a thread terminates in the process, the system sends DLL_THREAD_DETACH to each DLL's DllMain() so that it can clean up TLS. Finally, the system calls DllMain() when the process ends and sends DLL_PROCESS_DETACH as the reason, at which point the DLL should clean up any resources it allocated.

Chapter 2,"Basic Operating System Programming," covers TLS.

Listing 10-1 shows you a full implementation of the DllMain() function. This example is the beginning of a DLL to export the *magic eight ball (M8B)* oracle (originally shown in Listing 3-1). This listing demonstrates full use of the reasons the system will call into your DllMain() function; typical implementations (in your applications) don't need all of these mechanics.

Listing 10-1: Setting up the DLL entry point for the M8B library

```cpp
// project m8ball, file m8ball.cpp
#include <windows.h>
#define M8B_INTERNAL
#include "m8ball.h"


// DllMain must be exported by all DLLs (although the compiler
// will supply a default one if you don't create your own).
// It will be called when the DLL is loaded by and unloaded
// from the process as well each time a thread is created or
// destroyed in the process.
BOOL APIENTRY DllMain( HANDLE hInstDll,
                       DWORD  nReasonCode,
                       LPVOID lpReserved)
{
    BOOL bReturn(FALSE);

    // take action appropriate to the exit code
    switch(nReasonCode)
    {
        case DLL_PROCESS_ATTACH:
        {
            // call the local initialization
            bReturn = ::m8bInitDll(hInstDll);
            break;
        }
        case DLL_THREAD_ATTACH:
        {
            // call the thread initialization
            bReturn = ::m8bInitThread();
            break;
        }
        case DLL_THREAD_DETACH:
        {
            // call the thread exit
            bReturn = ::m8bExitThread();
            break;
        }
        case DLL_PROCESS_DETACH:
        {
            // call the local shutdown
            bReturn = ::m8bExitDll();
```

```
                break;
            }
            default:
                break;
        }
    return(bReturn);
}


// data for DLL management
static HANDLE g_hInstDll = INVALID_HANDLE_VALUE;
static DWORD  g_dwTlsHandle = 0;


// helper method to fetch the stored module handle for the DLL
HANDLE m8bGetModuleHandle()
{
    return(g_hInstDll);
}


// function to retrieve the start time of the calling thread
DWORD m8bGetThreadStart()
{
    // fetch the value out of TLS
    LPVOID value = ::TlsGetValue(g_dwTlsHandle);
    DWORD dwTick = reinterpret_cast<DWORD>(value);
    return(dwTick);
}


// the following four function respond to DllMain events:
//   InitDll for DLL_PROCESS_ATTACH, InitThread for
//   DLL_THREAD_ATTACH, ExitThread for DLL_THREAD_DETACH, and
//   ExitDll for DLL_PROCESS_DETACH
BOOL m8bInitDll(HANDLE hInstDll)
{
    // save the instance handle
    g_hInstDll = hInstDll;

    // allocate TLS for the start times
    g_dwTlsHandle = ::TlsAlloc();

    // prepare the main thread's storage
    BOOL bInitOK = ::m8bInitThread();
    return(bInitOK);
}
```

```
BOOL m8bInitThread()
{
    // store the start time of the thread
    DWORD dwStart = ::GetTickCount();
    LPVOID value = reinterpret_cast<LPVOID>(dwStart);
    BOOL bInitOK = ::TlsSetValue(g_dwTlsHandle, value);

    // seed the random number generator
    ::srand(dwStart);

    return(bInitOK);
}


BOOL m8bExitThread()
{
    // clean out the TLS
    ::TlsSetValue(g_dwTlsHandle, NULL);

    // cannot fail the exit
    return(TRUE);
}


BOOL m8bExitDll()
{
    // exit the main thread
    ::m8bExitThread();

    // clean up the TLS
    ::TlsFree(g_dwTlsHandle);
    g_dwTlsHandle = 0;

    // clean up the DLL instance handle
    g_hInstDll = INVALID_HANDLE_VALUE;

    // cannot fail the exit
    return(TRUE);
}
```

The DLL setup code in Listing 10-1 takes the DllMain() function and creates a helper function for each call that it might receive (one for each possible reason code). Typically, your DllMain() implementations will be much shorter since per-thread initialization is a reasonably rare requirement. Since each process attach or detach operation also implies the attachment or detachment of the main thread, notice that the DLL-wide routines must call into the thread-specific attach and detach routines.

I have placed m8b prefixes on some of the functions in Listing 10-1. This is an old object-oriented C convention that marks functions as part of a class, and lowercase marks them as internal or private.

The next thing to do for the M8B library is to implement the oracle, which is shown in Listing 10-2. There are only four public functions to construct: M8BCreate(), M8BTellFortune(), M8BRateLastFortune(), and M8BDestroy(). The first and last functions manage the lifetime of the object, while the middle two functions give the consumer functionality. Once these are constructed, you need to let the system know that you want to make them available to clients.

The Visual Studio C++ compiler has a built-in flag to mark functions for export, __declspec(dllexport), that you must prefix to the function implementations. I wrap this flag in a macro called M8B_API shown used in Listing 10-2 and defined in Listing 10-3.

Listing 10-2: Implementing the M8B object and exposing its public APIs

```
// project m8ball, file m8ball.cpp
// ...
// DLL setup code from Listing 10-1, removed for clarity
// ...


//
// Implementation
//

// the fortune array and the number of fortunes
static LPCTSTR s_arFortune[] =
{
    "My sources say No.","My reply is No.",
    "Don't count on it.","Outlook not so good.",
    "Better not tell you now.","Reply hazy, try again.",
    "Cannot predict now.","Concentrate and ask again.",
    "Ask again later.","Outlook good.","Signs point to Yes.",
    "As I see it, Yes.","It is decidedly so.","Most likely.",
    "Without a doubt.","You may rely on it.","It is certain.",
    "Yes, definitely.","Yes."
};
static const s_nFortuneCt =
    sizeof(s_arFortune)/sizeof(s_arFortune[0]);

LPCTSTR m8bLookupFortune(int nFortune)
{
```

```
    LPCTSTR szFortune = NULL;

    // make sure the passed number is in-bounds
    if(0<=nFortune && nFortune<s_nFortuneCt)
    {
        // interpret the fortune from the index
        szFortune = s_arFortune[nFortune];
    }
    return(szFortune);
}


int m8bPrognosticate(int /*nSeed*/)
{
    // just call the random number generator, ignore the
    //  passed seed for now
    int nFortune = (int)(::rand() * s_nFortuneCt / RAND_MAX);
    return(nFortune);
}


//
// Public API
//

// allocate the object and set up its internal state
extern "C" M8B_API HMAGIC8BALL M8BCreate()
{
    HMAGIC8BALL hNew = new Magic8Ball;
    hNew->nSeed = ::GetTickCount();
    hNew->nLastFortune = 0;
    return hNew;
}


// to tell a fortune, the server can use the random number
// seed and last granted fortune to appear oracular
extern "C" M8B_API LPCTSTR M8BTellFortune(HMAGIC8BALL hBall)
{
    // use the last fortune to avoid repeats
    int nNewFortune = hBall->nLastFortune;
    while(nNewFortune==hBall->nLastFortune)
    {
        // find a candidate fortune
        nNewFortune = m8bPrognosticate(hBall->nSeed);
    }
```

```
    // save the new fortune
    hBall->nLastFortune = nNewFortune;

    // look up the string and return it
    return(m8bLookupFortune(nNewFortune));
}

// create a simple rating system, 0=No, 1=Yes
extern "C" M8B_API double M8BRateLastFortune(HMAGIC8BALL hBall)
{
    double dblRating =
        (double)hBall->nLastFortune / (s_nFortuneCt - 1);
    return(dblRating);
}

// simple cleanup routine
extern "C" M8B_API void M8BDestroy(HMAGIC8BALL hBall)
{
    delete hBall;
}
```

The implementation in Listing 10-2 prefixes external functions with `extern "C"` `M8B_API`, telling the complier and linker to export the functions prefixed by `M8B` for use by DLL clients. The guts of the code are very similar to the implementation I showed you in Listing 3-1.

The last step to create a full-functioning DLL is to publish the function definitions for consumers. Listing 10-3 shows the header for building and consuming the M8B object, which is called `M8Ball.H`. You will need to publish this header file along with the DLL so that clients know the functions and types that you supply in the library. While developing the library, you should also use the same header file as the primary include file in your implementation modules.

Listing 10-3: Publishing the interface to the M8B library

```
// project m8ball, file m8ball.h
#pragma once    // only parse this header once

//
// API setup definitions, one set for internal,
//  one for the public
//
#ifndef M8B_INTERNAL

    // the handle is just a ptr to the client
    typedef void* HMAGIC8BALL;
```

```
    // since this is a client, it imports the M8B API
    #define M8B_API __declspec(dllimport)

#else   // M8B_INTERNAL

    // internal use means this is the server,
    //   it exports the M8B API
    #define M8B_API __declspec(dllexport)

    // definitions used by object server
    struct Magic8Ball
    {
        // data the client will use, not see
        int nSeed;
        int nLastFortune;
    };
    typedef Magic8Ball* HMAGIC8BALL;

    // DLL management methods
    BOOL m8bInitDll(HANDLE hInstDll);
    BOOL m8bExitDll();
    BOOL m8bInitThread();
    BOOL m8bExitThread();

    HANDLE m8bGetModuleHandle();
    DWORD m8bGetThreadStart();

    // internals
    int m8bPrognosticate(int nSeed);
    LPCTSTR m8bLookupFortune(int nFortune);

#endif

// Public API
extern "C"
{
    // lifetime management
    M8B_API HMAGIC8BALL M8BCreate();
    M8B_API void M8BDestroy(HMAGIC8BALL);

    // functions for consumption
    M8B_API LPCTSTR M8BTellFortune(HMAGIC8BALL);
    M8B_API double M8BRateLastFortune(HMAGIC8BALL);
```

```
// typedefs for explicit linking
typedef HMAGIC8BALL (*M8BCREATEPROC)();
typedef void (*M8BDESTROYPROC)(HMAGIC8BALL);
typedef LPCTSTR (*M8BTELLPROC)(HMAGIC8BALL);
typedef double (*M8BRATEPROC)(HMAGIC8BALL);
}
```

In the header shown in Listing 10-3, the setup block at the top defines the handle and the M8B_API macro. I define the macro as dllexport when constructing the DLL, and as dllimport when consuming the DLL. To let the header know that it is used for construction, I simply define the preprocessor symbol M8B_INTERNAL before including the file, as seen in Listing 10-2. In M8Ball.H I also define the handle as a pointer to the structure when constructing the DLL and as void* when consuming it.

Any client now can consume the DLL. It has all of the specified functionality, and the system knows how to attach it to a process. The object construction and export mechanics illustrated in these examples are almost identical to what Windows supplies in its system DLLs.

IMPLICITLY USING DLLS

Now that we have a functioning DLL, let's use it. The simplest technique for using a DLL is *implicit linking*. Implicit linking adds instructions to the EXE file of your application that it needs a particular DLL, M8Ball.DLL in this case. When the Windows loader maps your EXE module into memory, it notices that it must also map a number of DLLs so it attempts to find them in the file system and do so.

Linking your application with the library's *import library* triggers this implicit use of a DLL through the loader. The build of a DLL generates an import library that is usually named with the same root named as the DLL and a .LIB extension. The import library does not contain any code. The linker simply marks that the application needs the DLL at load time if the application references any entry points found in the import library. The Windows loader does the hard work of dynamically connecting your application to the DLL at run time. Listing 10-4 is a simple application that implicitly links to the magic eight ball library and uses an instance to get a positive response.

Listing 10-4: Client application of the M8B object using implicit linking

```
// project m8ball2
#include <windows.h>
#include <iostream>

// get the m8b object definitions and link to its import library
#include "..\\m8ball\\m8ball.h"
#pragma comment(lib, "m8ball.lib")

void main()
{
```

```
// make ourselves an 8ball
HMAGIC8BALL hBall = ::M8BCreate();

// get fortunes until we find a good one
int nRating = 0;
while(nRating < 50)
{
    // get the text and rating
    LPCTSTR szFortune = ::M8BTellFortune(hBall);
    nRating = (int)(::M8BRateLastFortune(hBall) * 100);

    // report it
    std::cout << "The 8 ball says: " << szFortune
        << " (probability " << nRating << "%)"
        << std::endl;
}

// clean up the object
::M8BDestroy(hBall);
hBall = NULL;
}
```

In order to build the project in Listing 10-4, you must point Visual Studio to the header file, M8Ball.H, and the import library file, M8Ball.LIB. In order to run this application, the DLL, M8Ball.DLL, must be available in the path. I accomplish this by publishing the files to a publishing directory (usually c:\pub) and modify my Windows path and Visual Studio directories to include it.

The appendix in the back of this book, "Using the Examples in This Book," covers the special publishing folder.

The inclusion of the import library tells the Visual Studio linker that the EXE file does not need to create the M8B functions; but in order to run, the system must attach the M8Ball.DLL to the process. This is implicit use of the DLL. The EXE file tells Windows that it must load the file and replace all of the placeholders to M8B calls with real function addresses.

The code in Listing 10-4 treats the M8B object APIs just like Windows APIs or C++ runtime functions – they are simple function calls. The program first creates an M8B object with a call into the M8BCreate() API then begins asking it for predictions with the M8BTellFortune() API until it finds a positive one (probability of at least 50%). Each time Listing 10-4 gets a prediction, it writes the results to the console; when finished, the application cleans up the M8B object with the M8BDestroy() API. Figure 10-1 exemplifies implicit linking with the M8B DLL.

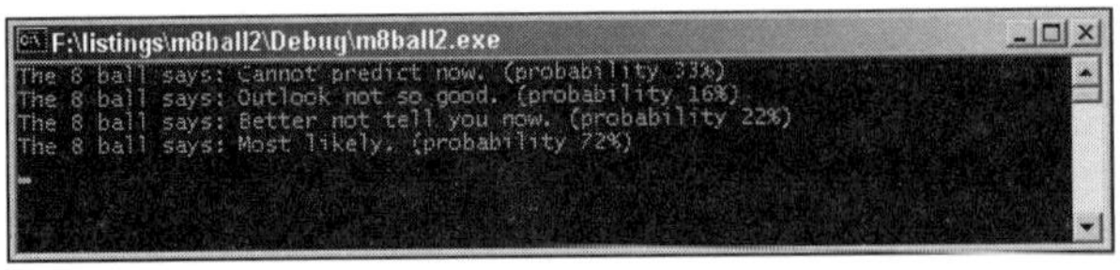

Figure 10-1: Implicitly linking with the M8B DLL to generate a positive response

EXPLICITLY USING DLLS

Another method for using DLLs is *explicit linking*. In this case, the client must load the DLL into memory manually, find the desired entry point or entry points, call them, and then unload the DLL from memory. You will want to use explicit linking when you have a number of libraries that you might chose from at runtime based on the host environment or user preferences. For example, if there were another M8B-like DLL that gave only positive fortunes, the application might chose to load that one or the original based on how optimistic the user wanted the program to be.

The LoadLibrary() API is responsible for bringing a DLL into memory. This function simply takes the file name of the DLL that you want to load. The file name can either be the fully specified path to the DLL or be the root name and rely on the system to search for the DLL. This API creates a kernel object when it succeeds and returns a handle to the object – this handle is not sharable with other processes.

To actually find the function that you wish to call, use the GetProcAddress() API. This function requires the handle to the module and the string name of the function, or its *ordinal value*. Ordinals are another method to export functions from DLLs; an ordinal replaces the entry point name with an integer. The return from GetProcAddress() is a simple function pointer that must be cast to the actual type that you need before you can use it.

> To use ordinals to export functions from DLLs, see the MSDN for detailed documentation; begin with the documentation for the GetProcAddress() API.

When your application completes the work that requires the DLL, you should release it using the FreeLibrary() API. The system reference counts the module object for you, just as it does every other kernel object, so a second call to LoadLibrary() does not necessarily incur the expense of actually going to disk to fetch the code – it just bumps the reference count. Each call to LoadLibrary(), however, should have a matching call to FreeLibrary().

We can accomplish the same task as in Listing 10-4 using explicit dynamic linking. Listing 10-5 shows the work that goes into explicitly linking to, and using functions from, a DLL.

Listing 10-5: Client application of the M8B object using explicit linking

```
// project m8ball3
#include <windows.h>
#include <iostream>

// typedefs of M8B functions and handles
#include "..\\m8ball\\m8ball.h"

void main()
{
    // load the M8B DLL
    HINSTANCE hInstM8B = ::LoadLibrary("m8ball.dll");
    if(hInstM8B!=NULL)
    {
        // get the addresses of each one of the APIs that we
        //  need
        M8BCREATEPROC pfnCreate =
            reinterpret_cast<M8BCREATEPROC>(::GetProcAddress(
                hInstM8B, "M8BCreate"));
        M8BTELLPROC pfnTell =
            reinterpret_cast<M8BTELLPROC>(::GetProcAddress(
                hInstM8B, "M8BTellFortune"));
        M8BRATEPROC pfnRate =
            reinterpret_cast<M8BRATEPROC>(::GetProcAddress(
                hInstM8B, "M8BRateLastFortune"));
        M8BDESTROYPROC pfnDestroy =
            reinterpret_cast<M8BDESTROYPROC>(::GetProcAddress(
                hInstM8B, "M8BDestroy"));

        // create a new M8B object
        HMAGIC8BALL hBall = (*pfnCreate)();

        // get fortunes until we find a good one
        int nRating = 0;
        while(nRating < 50)
        {
            // get the text and rating
            LPCTSTR szFortune = (*pfnTell)(hBall);
            nRating = (int)((*pfnRate)(hBall) * 100);
```

```
                                    // report it
                                    std::cout << "The 8 ball says: " << szFortune
                                        << " (probability " << nRating << "%)"
                                        << std::endl;
                            }

                            // clean up the object
                            (*pfnDestroy)(hBall);

                            // release the module from memory
                            ::FreeLibrary(hInstM8B);
                            hInstM8B = NULL;
                    }
                    else
                    {
                            std::cout << "Could not locate the Oracle."
                                << std::endl;
                    }
            }
```

Listing 10-5 shows the mechanics of loading and freeing a DLL. It also shows that you have to locate and interpret the function pointers. Interpreting the function pointers means casting them to the proper signature for calling into with your code – which requires that the library publish a function pointer C++ `typedef` for each entry point. You can see the application do just this near the beginning of the `main()` function after the `LoadLibrary()` API succeeds.

 In Listing 10-3, I show the header file, `M8Ball.H`, with the function `type-defs` for using the DLL's entry points explicitly.

The logic of Listing 10-5 is identical to the implicit linking example of Listing 10-4. All of the same functions are called from the DLL. They just take more setup, and the DLL must be manually loaded and unloaded with calls to the `LoadLibrary()` and `FreeLibrary()` APIs, respectively.

Although the explicit linking procedure is lengthy, it allows the application to handle error situations gracefully – such as an unavailable DLL. Further, it enables you to select flavors or versions of DLLs at runtime by simply changing the name supplied to `LoadLibrary()`.

For details on the procedure that Windows follows for searching a DLL when you call `LoadLibrary()` without the fully specified path, see the MSDN documentation on the `LoadLibrary()` API.

When explicitly linking to a DLL, you may wish to make sure you have found the correct version of the module before you use it. Windows supplies a standard mechanism of adding version information that you can access. See the MSDN documentation, beginning with the `GetFileVersionInfo()` API, for more information.

COM objects

COM is another method for sharing code, and it generally is preferred over the raw DLL method that I presented in the previous section. The principle player in the world of COM is the COM *object*. COM object providers specify each object by its interfaces using the COM-specific *interface definition language (IDL)*. Orchestrating the instantiation and use of these objects is the main purpose of the Windows COM subsystem.

If you are interested in learning COM from the ground up, you should pick up a copy of the book *Essential COM* by Don Box. This is one of the best introductions to the complex world of COM that you can find.

To create a COM object, a developer first specifies an interface in IDL and assigns that interface a *globally unique identifier (GUID)* to keep it distinct from all other interfaces in the world. The developer then takes that interface, a standard base-level interface called `IUnknown`, and any other interfaces he needs and implements them using a common tool such as Visual C++ or Visual Basic and packages the code in a DLL or EXE.

Implementing COM interfaces is very similar to implementing C++ classes – you wrap instance data together with function calls. The `IUnknown` interface that all objects must have manages the lifetime of the object much like a C++ constructor/destructor pair. All calls into methods from your interface are through an instance pointer and give you the object's context.

Once you have implemented your object as a DLL or EXE, you must register that module with the COM subsystem. This registration lets you advertise what interfaces you expose (by GUID) and where your DLL or EXE lives on the system. When a client application desires an instance of your object, it asks the COM subsystem to find your DLL or EXE, and create one through the CoCreateInstance() API.

You can generate GUIDs for other uses programmatically with the COM CoCreateGuid() API or manually with the GuidGen.EXE application from the Platform SDK.

The object construction, interface advertisement, and component registration are the heart of COM. There are many extensions, such as object aggregation, threading support, and transactioning as in COM+. For this section, we are only interested in the core of COM for its software sharing services.

Chapter 16, "Working with COM+," covers COM+ in detail.

Let's look at a small part of the COM subsystem – the part that enables you to create simple components that you register with the system so that applications can use their services. COM used in this manner provides a standard object wrapper for a set of services and registers the DLL or EXE that contains the code for all applications in the system to use.

CREATING COM SERVERS

The current best way to create a COM object is with the *Active Template Library (ATL)* supplied in Visual Studio. This library is a set of C++ templates that quickly construct a DLL or EXE that adheres to the COM specification and exposes those objects. The resulting DLL or EXE is called a *COM server,* since it serves up one or more COM objects for client applications to consume.

This section will use the Visual Studio ATL COM AppWizard to create a COM server that exposes the oracle exemplified in the previous listings. To begin with, you must create a new project in Visual Studio and choose an ATL COM AppWizard project. The application will present you with a dialog as shown in Figure 10-2. I will be creating a DLL here to serve up the M8B COM object, and I do not need any of the special options near the bottom of the page.

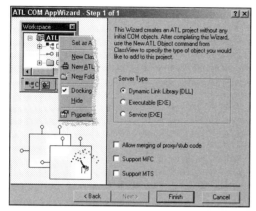

Figure 10-2: Initial dialog for creating a COM object
project to expose the M8B

Once the AppWizard creates the project, it will be a simple DLL with no COM objects. To add the M8B COM object, use the Visual Studio menu and select `Insert... New ATL Object...` and choose to insert a `Simple Object`. This will prompt you with the dialog shown in Figure 10-3. I filled it in as shown for this example.

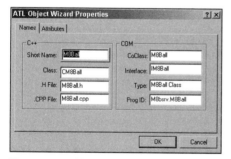

Figure 10-3: Selecting names for a new ATL object
to expose the M8B

Once the ATL object has been inserted into the DLL, it's time to add interfaces and properties. The code in Listing 10-6 shows the results of using the Visual Studio tools to mimic a small portion of the M8B functionality that I exposed in the DLL version.

Listing 10-6: Exposing the M8B component as an ATL object

```
// project m8bsrv, file m8ball.h
#include "resource.h"        // main symbols

// the fortune array and the number of fortunes
static LPCTSTR s_arFortune[] =
{
    "My sources say No.","My reply is No.",
    "Don't count on it.","Outlook not so good.",
    "Better not tell you now.","Reply hazy, try again.",
    "Cannot predict now.","Concentrate and ask again.",
    "Ask again later.","Outlook good.","Signs point to Yes.",
    "As I see it, Yes.","It is decidedly so.","Most likely.",
    "Without a doubt.","You may rely on it.","It is certain.",
    "Yes, definitely.","Yes."
};
static const s_nFortuneCt =
    sizeof(s_arFortune)/sizeof(s_arFortune[0]);


/////////////////////////////////////////////////////////////////
/////////
// CM8Ball
class ATL_NO_VTABLE CM8Ball :
    public CComObjectRootEx<CComSingleThreadModel>,
    public CComCoClass<CM8Ball, &CLSID_M8Ball>,
    public IDispatchImpl<IM8Ball, &IID_IM8Ball, &LIBID_M8BSRVLib>
{
    // ATL setup of interfaces
public:
    DECLARE_REGISTRY_RESOURCEID(IDR_M8BALL)
    DECLARE_PROTECT_FINAL_CONSTRUCT()
    BEGIN_COM_MAP(CM8Ball)
        COM_INTERFACE_ENTRY(IM8Ball)
        COM_INTERFACE_ENTRY(IDispatch)
    END_COM_MAP()

    // class constructor
public:
    CM8Ball() : m_nCurrentFortune(0)
        // make sure the random number seed is new
        { ::srand(::GetTickCount()); }

    // IM8Ball interface
public:
```

```
    // new fortune method
    STDMETHOD(get_Fortune)(/*[out, retval]*/ BSTR *pVal)
    {
        // loop through, making sure to get a new value
        int nFortune = m_nCurrentFortune;
        while(nFortune==m_nCurrentFortune)
        {
            nFortune =
                (int)(::rand() * s_nFortuneCt / RAND_MAX);
        }

        // save the new fortune
        m_nCurrentFortune = nFortune;

        // get the fortune from the index
        LPCTSTR szFortune = s_arFortune[nFortune];
        CComBSTR bstr(szFortune);

        // create a new value to return
        *pVal = bstr.Copy();
        return S_OK;
    }


    // rating method
    STDMETHOD(get_Rating)(/*[out, retval]*/ short *pVal)
    {
        // calculate the percentage for the current fortune
        int nRating =
            (m_nCurrentFortune * 100)/ (s_nFortuneCt - 1);
        *pVal = nRating;

        return S_OK;
    }

protected:
    int m_nCurrentFortune;
};
```

The code shown in Listing 10-6 creates an oracle with exactly the same
functionality as the one from the previous five listings. Without diving into the
details of COM or ATL, the CM8Ball class is a single-threaded COM object that
exposes a single IDispatch interface called IM8Ball. Using IDispatch allows any
COM-aware development environment to use the object, including Visual Basic.
The interface simply exposes two properties for retrieval – fortune and rating –
with the get_Fortune() and get_Rating() methods.

The COM version of M8B allows a client to create an instance of the object by talking exclusively to the COM APIs, which then look up the DLL, load it, and give the client the proper function pointers. Further, the DLL does not expose its functions to the client using a header file. The build process attaches a resource called a COM *type library* to the DLL that contains all the definitions of the interfaces that it exposes. COM clients use this type library to understand what interfaces and objects the DLL has made available and how to consume them.

CREATING A CLIENT

Now it is quite simple to create a client to use this new COM object with Visual Studio C++ COM support and the information baked into the DLL that supplies the object (the type library). Listing 10-7 shows the fortune-telling application that consumes the M8B COM object. The logic of this application is much the same as the applications in Listings 10-4 and 10-5 – ask a new M8B object for predictions until it gives an acceptable (over 50% probability) one.

Listing 10-7: Using the ATL M8B object from a C++ console application

```
// project m8ball4
#include <windows.h>
#include <iostream>

// get the typelib from the published DLL (only needed at
//   compile time)
#import <m8bsrv.dll>

void main()
{
    // tell COM we are going to use it
    ::CoInitialize(NULL);

    // create a new M8B object using the smart ptr
    //   generated by the import statement
    {
        M8BSRVLib::IM8BallPtr
            pM8Ball(__uuidof(M8BSRVLib::M8Ball));

        // get fortunes until we find a good one
        int nRating = 0;
        while(nRating < 50)
        {
            // get the fortune and rating by simply calling
            //   the functions in the smart ptr class
            _bstr_t strFortune = pM8Ball->GetFortune();
            nRating = pM8Ball->GetRating();
```

```
            // report it
            std::cout << "The 8 ball says: "
                << (LPCTSTR)strFortune
                << " (probability " << nRating << "%)"
                << std::endl;
        }
    }   // make sure the M8B object is destroyed by scoping

    // release the COM DLLs
    ::CoUninitialize();
}
```

Listing 10-7 has a very important first statement: the #import directive. This directive tells the C++ compiler to find the DLL file specified, grab the COM-type library attached, and create C++ classes that map to each of the objects exposed in the DLL. Armed with these tools, the program is very simple.

First, COM is initialized with a call to the CoInitialize() API. Then, a smart-pointer class, IM8BallPtr, object is instantiated. The constructor requires the GUID of the M8B class; this GUID is a 128-bit number that is unique in the world to identifying this class. The constructor looks up the number using the compiler-specific __uuidof() directive. The class passes this unique number to COM, which then loads the server DLL, creates an object, and returns a pointer to it. Now the instantiated object is ready to be used through the created methods: GetFortune() and GetRating(). Finally, we tell COM that we are done with it by letting the smart-pointer object fall out and release COM by calling the CoUninitialize() API before exiting.

One of the benefits of using COM to deliver the M8B object is that you also can use the object from Visual Basic or VBScript. The simple HTML <object> tag lets you instantiate an object for the lifetime of a Web page. Listing 10-8 shows a simple Web page that does just this and duplicates the logic of Listings 10-4, 10-5, and 10-7 with very few lines of code.

Listing 10-8: Using the ATL M8B object from VBScript in a Web page

```
<html>
<!-- project m8ball4, file m8ball4.htm -->
<title>Project m8ball4</title>
<body>

<!-- create an M8B object -->
<object
    classid="clsid:64C65771-46F5-11D3-BDCA-005004A1D3EE"
    id="m8b">
</object>
```

```
<!-- tell a good fortune -->
<script language="VBScript">

    ' loop through ratings until we find a good one
    Dim nRating
    nRating = 0
    While nRating < 50

        ' grab the fortune and rating
        Dim strFortune
        strFortune = m8b.Fortune
        nRating = m8b.Rating

        ' create a line to send to the browser
        Dim strLine
        strLine = "<br>The 8 ball says: " + strFortune + _
            " (" + CStr(nRating) + "%)"
        document.write strLine
    Wend
</script>
</body>
</html>
```

The page in Listing 10-8, named M8Ball4.HTM, simply creates an object named m8b using the <object> tag and the unique ID that I referred to earlier. The new object is accessible to all scripts on the page, and the one I created in the <script> section simply replicates the logic of the other fortune-telling applications. It asks for a new fortune and displays it on the page until it finds one that is non-pessimistic (at least 50% probability). The resulting Web page, shown in Figure 10-4, is not very interesting but it shows the power of scripting objects into Web pages.

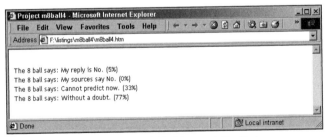

Figure 10-4: Using the M8B COM object to tell a fortune on a Web page

That's it. You now have the tools to share your code with raw DLLs or with simple COM objects. You also can use those DLLs and COM objects – or anyone else's from C++ or BASIC clients. Sharing code is the cornerstone of creating great applications.

Programming Services

There is another set of tools that Windows 2000 provides you to build applications. I loosely group these tools as *programming services*. These services give you some of the necessities for constructing applications. Examples are large (64-bit) integer support, string manipulation, time stamps with a real time clock, and a registry for storing configuration data. This section looks at a couple of these services, in particular large integer and time support.

Large integers

Windows 2000 is a 32-bit operating system that knows hardware is moving to 64 bits. One service added to the operating system in evidence of this is 64-bit integer support. You can find these long, long integers in the time, timer, virtual memory, and file I/O APIs. Sometimes they are typed LARGE_INTERGER or ULARGE_INTEGER, and sometimes they are typed ULONGLONG or LONGLONG.

The Visual C++ compiler supplies native 64-bit integer support with the __int64 type. Of course, this means that the compiler also supports the unsigned __int64 type for integers that cannot be negative. This compiler also has sized integer native types for 8-, 16-, and 32-bit sizes for consistency – the __int8, __int16, and __int32 types.

The leading double underscore, "__", on these types indicates that these are compiler-specific.

The Windows.H header file will alias the __int64 value as INT64 and its unsigned version as UINT64 when you include it. Values of this type are interchangeable with LONGLONG and ULONGLONG. Further, the LARGE_INTEGER type that is interchangeable with the FILETIME type is a union that includes a LONGLONG as its QuadPart member. Table 10-1 sums up the 64-bit data types that you will encounter in Windows 2000.

I introduce the FILETIME data type in the following section, "Time Support."

TABLE 10-1 64-BIT DATA TYPES

Signed Type	Unsigned Type	Generator
__int64	unsigned __int64	Visual C++ compiler
LONGLONG	ULONGLONG	WinNT.H (included by Windows.H)
LARGE_INTEGER. QuadPart	ULARGE_INTERGER. QuadPart	WinNT.H (included by Windows.H)
INT64	UINT64	BaseTsd.H (included by WinNT.H and Windows.H)

Before 64-bit support was added to the compiler, Windows recognized that a common operation that applications required was the ability to multiply two 32-bit numbers together and divide by another, allowing the intermediate result to exceed 32-bit precision. The MulDiv() API from the kernel was an early programming service that supplied this tool. Listing 10-9 shows some examples of using 64-bit arithmetic.

Listing 10-9: Some uses of 64-bit arithmetic

```
// project longlong
#include <windows.h>
#include <iostream>
#include <iomanip>


//
// reporting functions, accessed with the SHOW macro to
//  display the name in addition to the value
//
void ShowValue(const __int64& n64Value)
{
    // assign to a LARGE_INTEGER so that we can break it up
```

```
    ULARGE_INTEGER liValue;
    liValue.QuadPart = (unsigned __int64)n64Value;

    // show the leading 0s then the high and low parts in hex
    std::cout.fill('0');
    std::cout << "0x"
        << std::hex << std::setw(8) << liValue.HighPart
        << std::hex << std::setw(8) << liValue.LowPart
        << std::endl;
}
void ShowValue(const DWORD& dwValue)
{
    // show the leading 0s then the value in hex
    std::cout.fill('0');
    std::cout << "0x" << std::hex << std::setw(8) << dwValue
        << std::endl;
}
#define SHOW(var) { std::cout << #var " = "; ShowValue(var); }

void main()
{
    //
    // use the compiler's intrinsic support for 64-bit numbers
    //
    __int64 n64Value1 = 0x123456789ABCDEF0;
    SHOW(n64Value1);

    __int64 n64Value2 = 0x0FEDCBA987654321;
    SHOW(n64Value2);

    // add the two, should get 0x2222222222222211
    __int64 n64Value3 = n64Value1 + n64Value2;
    SHOW(n64Value3);

    // shift right some, should get 0x001111111111111
    __int64 n64Value4 = n64Value3 > 9;
    SHOW(n64Value4);

    // square a large DWORD, should get 0x00362594b58b57e1,
    //   would not fit in a DWORD
    DWORD dwValue1 = 123454321;
    __int64 n64Value5 = (__int64)dwValue1 * dwValue1;
    SHOW(n64Value5);
```

```
    // divide the 64-bit value by a large DWORD,
    //  should get 0x00e88f09
    DWORD dwValue2 = 999999999;
    DWORD dwValue3 = n64Value5 / dwValue2;
    SHOW(dwValue3);

    //
    // use Windows 64-bit support
    //

    // use the multiply/divide method to remain in the 32-bit
    //  world while arriving at the same value as dwValue3
    DWORD dwValue4 = ::MulDiv(dwValue1, dwValue1, dwValue2);
    SHOW(dwValue4);
}
```

The code in Listing 10-9 is mostly simple adding, multiplying, shifting, etc. on 64-bit quantities. One interesting snippet is the reporting of 64-bit values that assigns the integer to a LARGE_INTEGER union, then picks it apart for use in the stream output. I did this since the streams only accept 32-bit integers. Also, the MulDiv() API does produce a result identical to the 64-bit arithmetic, without requiring compiler support.

Time support

Windows 2000 supplies applications with a number of services for time; most involve finding the current system time and manipulating time stamps on disk files. The system also supplies APIs for converting old DOS times, moving times through time zones, and measuring time since system start.

SYSTEM TIMES

There are two native formats for times in Windows 2000. The first, SYSTEMTIME, is very much like the standard C struct tm. It is the broken-down representation of an absolute time, holding year, month, day, day of week, hour, minute, second, and millisecond.

Likewise, the other principal Windows time format, FILETIME, is very much like the standard C time_t. It is the linear representation of an absolute time, holding the number of tenth-milliseconds since the beginning of the year 1601.

You can use the GetSystemTime() and GetSystemTimeAsFileTime() APIs that return the current *Universal Time, Coordinated (UTC)* in each of the principal formats. In order to get the current time normalized for the time zone of the system, call the GetLocalTime() API. This call returns data in a SYSTEMTIME structure. Listing 10-10 shows a simple std::cout clock using these calls.

Listing 10-10: Using the Windows 2000 Time APIs

```cpp
// project systime
#include <windows.h>
#include <iostream>
#include <iomanip>
#include <conio.h>


// helper constants:
//   filetime units per sec = 1/100 ns = 10^7
static const __int64 c_nFtuPerSec = 10000000;
//   filetime units per min = 60 sec per min * ftu per sec
static const __int64 c_nFtuPerMin = 60 * c_nFtuPerSec;

// simple conversion from a filetime structure to a large int
__int64 FT2I64(const FILETIME& ft)
{
    LARGE_INTEGER li;
    li.HighPart = ft.dwHighDateTime;
    li.LowPart = ft.dwLowDateTime;
    __int64 n64 = (__int64)li.QuadPart;
    return(n64);
}
FILETIME I642FT(const __int64& n64)
{
    LARGE_INTEGER li;
    li.QuadPart = n64;
    FILETIME ft;
    ft.dwHighDateTime = li.HighPart;
    ft.dwLowDateTime = li.LowPart;
    return(ft);
}


// display the passed system (broken-down) time
void ShowTime(const SYSTEMTIME& st)
{
    std::cout.fill('0');
    std::cout << "Date: " << st.wYear
        << "/" << st.wMonth
        << "/" << st.wDay
        << " Time: " << st.wHour
        << ":" << std::setw(2) << st.wMinute
        << ":" << std::setw(2) << st.wSecond
        << "." << std::setw(3) << st.wMilliseconds << " ";
}
```

```
// display the passed file (linear) time
void ShowTime(const FILETIME& ft)
{
    __int64 n64Time = FT2I64(ft);
    std::cout << "1600+: "
        << (int)(n64Time / 1000000000)
        << std::setw(2)
        << (int)((n64Time% 1000000000)/ 10000000)
        << "." << std::setw(7) << (int)(n64Time % 10000000)
        << "sec ";
}

void main()
{
    // loop until the keyboard is hit
    while(!::_kbhit())
    {
        // fetch the system time broken-down in local time zone
        SYSTEMTIME st;
        ::ZeroMemory(&st, sizeof(st));
        ::GetLocalTime(&st);
        ::ShowTime(st);

        // fetch the system time as linear in UTC
        FILETIME ft;
        ::ZeroMemory(&ft, sizeof(ft));
        ::GetSystemTimeAsFileTime(&ft);

        // fetch the current time zone information
        TIME_ZONE_INFORMATION tzinfo;
        DWORD dwTZInfo = ::GetTimeZoneInformation(&tzinfo);
        if(dwTZInfo!=TIME_ZONE_ID_UNKNOWN)
        {
            // construct the local time as the filetime
            //  less the bias
            __int64 nTime = ::FT2I64(ft) -
                tzinfo.Bias * c_nFtuPerMin;
            ::ShowTime(::I642FT(nTime));
        }

        // start over at the beginning of the line and flush
        //  the stream
        std::cout << "\r";
        std::cout.flush();
```

```
        }
}
```

The code in Listing 10-10 illustrates the simplicity of using the SYSTEMTIME structure. In the example, the GetLocalTime() API is used to grab time for the local system, and the GetTimeZoneInformation() API is used to calculate the proper FILETIME for the system time retrieved in the GetSystemTimeAsFileTime() API.

The GetTimeZoneInformation() API returns a chunk of data in a TIME_ZONE_INFORMATION structure that tells you the minutes that the system is currently offset from UTC. In addition, the API sends back whether it is in standard or daylight saving time, the names of those zones, and the dates the transitions between the two are made. Windows also supplies a helper API, SystemTimeToTzSpecificLocalTime(), that converts a UTC system time into the current time zone for you.

FILE TIMES

The Windows 2000 file systems store a number of times associated with each file object. The file systems store time stamps for operations such as creation, last access, and last write in the best resolution possible. You can retrieve these times using the GetFileTime() API when you have a handle to a kernel file object, or by inspecting the results of a FindFirstFile() API in the WIN32_FIND_DATA structure.

As you saw in the previous section and in Listing 10-10, the FILETIME structure is a 64-bit, unsigned integer that represents hundreds of nanoseconds since the first day of 1601. To use the FILETIME data, you could convert it to broken-down time using the FileTimeToSystemTime() API. However, the system always stores file times as UTC; so to get a displayable time for the user, you should use the FileTimeToLocalTime() API, which takes care of adjusting for the current time zone of the system. To reverse the process, Windows supplies the helper APIs SystemTimeToFileTime() and LocalFileTimeToFileTime() and, of course, SetFileTime() to change one or all of a file object's time stamps.

To compare file times, the CompareFileTime() API gives you a simple greater, equal, or less result. The example in Listing 10-11 uses this API to find the oldest and newest file on the C: drive.

Listing 10-11: Finding the oldest and newest files

```
// project oldnewft
#include <windows.h>
#include <iostream>
#include <iomanip>

// display the passed filetime as system (broken-down) time
void ShowTime(const FILETIME& ft)
{
    // first, convert to local time
```

```
        FILETIME ftLocal;
        ::FileTimeToLocalFileTime(&ft, &ftLocal);

        // now convert to broken-down time
        SYSTEMTIME st;
        ::FileTimeToSystemTime(&ftLocal, &st);

        // finally, display it
        std::cout.fill('0');
        std::cout << " " << st.wYear
            << "/" << st.wMonth
            << "/" << st.wDay
            << " " << st.wHour
            << ":" << std::setw(2) << st.wMinute
            << ":" << std::setw(2) << st.wSecond
            << "." << std::setw(3) << st.wMilliseconds << " ";
    }


    // show the create time for a find data result
    void ShowTime(const WIN32_FIND_DATA& fd)
    {
        std::cout << fd.cFileName << " ";
        ::ShowTime(fd.ftCreationTime);
    }


    // find the oldest or newest file by passed wildcard in the
    //   passed root recursively, storing the result in the
    //   referred-to structure
    void RecurseFind(LPCTSTR szRoot, LPCTSTR szWildcard,
                        WIN32_FIND_DATA& fdResult, BOOL bFindOldest)
    {
        //
        // first let's look in the passed directory
        //
        TCHAR szSearch[MAX_PATH];
        ::strcpy(szSearch, szRoot);
        ::strcat(szSearch, "\\");
        ::strcat(szSearch, szWildcard);

        // start looping through all of the files in the dir
        WIN32_FIND_DATA fd;
        HANDLE hFind = ::FindFirstFile(szSearch, &fd);
        while(hFind!=INVALID_HANDLE_VALUE)
        {
            // do the file time comparison
```

```
    LONG nCompare = ::CompareFileTime(
        &fd.ftCreationTime,              // new file
        &fdResult.ftCreationTime);  // current high/low

    // save the result if we've moved higher or lower and
    //  that was the direction we were searching
    if((nCompare<0 && bFindOldest) ||
        (nCompare>0 && !bFindOldest))
    {
        fdResult = fd;

        // show the user the progress
        std::cout << szRoot << "\\" << fd.cFileName;
        ::ShowTime(fd.ftCreationTime);
        std::cout << std::endl;
    }

    // move to the next file
    if(!::FindNextFile(hFind, &fd))
    {
        ::FindClose(hFind);
        hFind = INVALID_HANDLE_VALUE;
    }
}


//
// now, look for all subdirs and do the same to them
//
// add the full wildcard to search for all directories
::strcpy(szSearch, szRoot);
::strcat(szSearch, "\\*");

// start looping through all of the files in the dir
hFind = ::FindFirstFile(szSearch, &fd);
while(hFind!=INVALID_HANDLE_VALUE)
{
    // for directories, count all files there
    if((fd.dwFileAttributes &
        FILE_ATTRIBUTE_DIRECTORY)!=0)
    {
        // ignore the . and .. dirs
        if(fd.cFileName[0]!='.')
        {
            // create the full path
            TCHAR szDir[MAX_PATH];
```

```
                    ::strcpy(szDir, szRoot);
                    ::strcat(szDir, "\\");
                    ::strcat(szDir, fd.cFileName);

                    // search the new dir first, passing the same
                    //  params
                    RecurseFind(szDir, szWildcard,
                        fdResult, bFindOldest);
                }
            }

            // move to the next file
            if(!::FindNextFile(hFind, &fd))
            {
                ::FindClose(hFind);
                hFind = INVALID_HANDLE_VALUE;
            }
        }
    }
}

void main()
{
    // initialize a find data to have a creation time of now
    //  (cannot possibly be the oldest file)
    FILETIME ftNow;
    ::GetSystemTimeAsFileTime(&ftNow);
    WIN32_FIND_DATA fd;
    fd.ftCreationTime = ftNow;

    // find the oldest file created on the c: drive
    RecurseFind("c:","*", fd, TRUE);
    WIN32_FIND_DATA fdOldest = fd;

    // now that we have the oldest, use it as the beginning
    //  point to find the newest
    RecurseFind("c:","*", fd, FALSE);
    WIN32_FIND_DATA fdNewest = fd;

    // show the user
    std::cout << "\nOldest - ";
    ::ShowTime(fdOldest);
    std::cout << "\nNewest - ";
    ::ShowTime(fdNewest);
    std::cout << std::endl;
}
```

The example in Listing 10-11 shows you how simple it is to use the CompareFileTime() API on results of a file find. The code uses the recursive directory descent that I first showed you in Listing 4-4 (in Chapter 4) to scan through the drive looking for files created before or after a passed time stamp. To start with, I use the current time as a high bar to find the oldest file, and then I use that oldest time as a low bar to find the newest file. The utility function for showing a file time uses the FileTimeToLocalFileTime() API to move from UTC to local time. Then it uses the FileTimeToSystemTime() API to break the time apart into useful chunks for display. The output shows you progressively older files then progressively newer files displayed; the end of the display is shown in Figure 10-5.

Figure 10-5: Locating the oldest and newest files on a drive

SYSTEM TICKERS

Often, when diagnosing performance bottlenecks in your software, you need to get the elapsed time of an operation. To support this, Windows supplies two APIs: GetTickCount() and QueryPerformanceCounter(). These APIs reference classic system *tickers* that simply tick away time at some frequency and store the number of ticks that have occurred thus far. The former API is backward compatible with old 16-bit systems and supplies the time since the system started in roughly 10-millisecond chunks, rolling over every 50 days or so. Not all hardware that runs Windows 2000 implements the latter API; but when implemented, it gives you access to the fastest timer running on the system – typically in the microsecond range.

In order to use these tickers, I like to wrap them up in simple classes that use scoping to control their start and stop. I do this because the actual value of the ticker is never important, only its change in value, and the simplest way to mark starts and stops in C++ is scoping. The example in Listing 10-12 shows you how to do this using the classes CTicker and CHResTicker. Both ticker classes follow the same logic: at object instantiation grab the ticker count and at destruction grab it again, calculate the elapsed time, and dump it to the console output.

Listing 10-12: Using the system tickers with scoped objects

```cpp
// project ticks
#include <windows.h>
#include <iostream>
#include <iomanip>

// simple class to display the time it takes to travel its
//   scope
class CTicker
{
public:

    // constructor simply saves the value of the tick
    //   count
    CTicker() :
      m_dwTicker(::GetTickCount())
    {
    }

    // destructor simply displays the elapsed values
    ~CTicker()
    {
        PrintElapsed();
    }

    // helper function to retrieve the tick of start
    DWORD GetStart() const
    {
        return(m_dwTicker);
    }

    // helper function to display the elapsed time
    void PrintElapsed()
    {
        DWORD dwElapsedMs = ::GetTickCount() - GetStart();
        std::cout << dwElapsedMs << " ms" << std::endl;
    }

    // method to determine the resolution of the ms timer
    static void PrintResolution()
    {
        DWORD dwAdjust(0);
        DWORD dwIncr(0);
        BOOL bAdjustDisabled(FALSE);
```

```
        ::GetSystemTimeAdjustment(
            &dwAdjust,  // size of adjustment
            &dwIncr,    // frequency of adjustments
            &bAdjustDisabled);  // adjustments disabled

        std::cout.fill('0');
        std::cout << "Ticker resolution: "
            << (dwIncr/10000) << "." << std::setw(4)
            << (dwIncr%10000) << " ms " << std::endl;
    }
protected:
    DWORD m_dwTicker;
};

// simple class to display the time it takes to travel its
//  scope
class CHResTicker
{
public:

    // constructor simply saves the value of the tick
    //  count
    CHResTicker() :
      m_nTicker()
    {
      ::QueryPerformanceCounter(&m_nTicker);
    }

    // destructor simply displays the elapsed values
    ~CHResTicker()
    {
        PrintElapsed();
    }

    // helper function to retrieve the tick of start
    LARGE_INTEGER GetStart() const
    {
        return(m_nTicker);
    }

    // helper function to display the elapsed time
    void PrintElapsed()
    {
        // grab the current value of the counter and grab the
        //  elapsed ticks
```

```
            LARGE_INTEGER nTickNow;
            ::QueryPerformanceCounter(&nTickNow);
            __int64 nElapsedTix = nTickNow.QuadPart -
                GetStart().QuadPart;

            // find the tick resolution and calculate the elapsed
            //   milliseconds
            LARGE_INTEGER nTickRes;
            ::QueryPerformanceFrequency(&nTickRes);
            double dblMs = (double)1000 * nElapsedTix
                / nTickRes.QuadPart;
            std::cout << dblMs << " ms" << std::endl;
        }

        // find the resolution of the high-res timer
        static void PrintResolution()
        {
            // get the resolution as number of ticks per second
            LARGE_INTEGER nTickRes;
            ::QueryPerformanceFrequency(&nTickRes);
            double dblRes = (double)1000000/nTickRes.QuadPart;
            std::cout << "High-res ticker resolution: "
                << dblRes << " microsecs" << std::endl;
        }
protected:
    LARGE_INTEGER m_nTicker;
};

void main()
{
    // run a simple test with the ms ticker
    CTicker::PrintResolution();
    {
        CTicker ticker;
        for(int n=0;n<10000000;n++)
            ;
    }

    // rerun the test with the high-res ticker
    CHResTicker::PrintResolution();
    {
        CHResTicker ticker;
        for(int n=0;n<10000000;n++)
            ;
```

```
    }
}
```

The two classes shown in Listing 10-12 demonstrate how to use instance variables to time an operation. When the program creates an instance of each class, the instance queries the backing ticker and stores the value. The classes are implemented in-line, making the wasted execution time minimal in addition to the system call. At the end of the scope, the instance destructor is called, which flows through the `PrintElapsed()` method, emitting the time to `std::cout`. Usually, the classes send their timings to the debugging log. You can modify the classes easily for this. In addition, you can extend the classes to reset the timer and grab the elapsed time at any point.

 Chapter 18, "Development Support," covers the debugging logs in detail.

System Services

There is another set of services for interacting with the Windows 2000 system from your applications. I loosely call these *system services*. They include the Windows registry, system policies, system information, user profiles, and system lifetime APIs. This section covers some of these services, in particular the registry, system information, and system lifetime.

Windows registry

Windows 2000 provides all applications with a database for storing configuration data – it's called the *registry*. You access the registry to create, modify, and retrieve data using objects from `AdvAPI32.DLL` that are much like kernel objects. The registry provides a single place to go for all configuration information for all applications and services on the system. It replaces the scattered `.INI` file paradigm found on other operating systems, including earlier Windows systems.

REGISTRY STRUCTURE

The structure of the registry is much like the file system. It contains a hierarchy of keys (folders) that each can contain subkeys and values (files). These keys are all rooted in several system-defined hives (drives). The values are the important pieces; they contain the information that your application and the system look for.

All values are named uniquely within a key and restricted to a limited set of types (for example strings, integers, and raw binary). Since this is configuration data, Windows's intention is that the size of the data should be kept small – say less than 2KB. Larger data should be stored externally and referenced from a registry value.

Windows supplies a set of predefined root keys, also known as *hives*. These hives help Windows organize the content of the registry by its purpose. The principal two hives are HKEY_CURRENT_USER (often referred to as *HKCU*) and HKEY_LOCAL_MACHINE (often referred to as *HKLM*). They store configuration data specific to the currently logged on user and the entire machine respectively. The HKEY_CLASSES_ROOT and HKEY_CURRENT_CONFIG hives actually are mirrors of keys under HKCU and HKLM – much like directory links in a file system.

Completing the file system analogy, keys and values even are addressed just like Windows directories and files. For example, on your machine you have a key called "My Computer\HKCU\Software\Microsoft\Notepad." In that key is the string value "My Computer\HKCU\Software\Microsoft\Notepad\lfFaceName" that specifies the presentation font whenever you run Notepad.EXE.

CORE APIS

Now that you have a bit of background on how the registry works, let's look at the APIs you need. I've summarized these in Table 10-2. First, you must open a key to use any of its values or subkeys and like any other pseudo-kernel object, you must close it when you are finished. Since you must have an open object to use any subkeys, use one of the predefined hives. For example, HKLM and HKCU are open and available to you always. The RegOpenKeyEx() API is a starting point for most read registry operations. It requires a handle to an open key, the string name of the key you wish to open, and a bitmask of operations that you may wish to perform on the key; it returns you the newly opened key when successful. When you are finished with a key that you opened, you must call the RegCloseKey() API to free the resource.

TABLE 10-2 CORE REGISTRY APIS

API Name	Description
RegOpenKeyEx()	Creates a handle to an existing registry key under a currently open key. Requires the name of the key and desired access.
RegCreateKeyEx()	Makes a new registry key beneath an existing key and returns a handle to it. Requires the name of the new key, security attributes, desired access, and some special flags. This will open a key if it already exists.
RegCloseKey()	Analog of the CloseHandle() API for registry objects; releases reference to the underlying object.

`RegSetValueEx()`	Creates or changes a named value under the supplied registry key. Requires the name, type, and size of the supplied data to store.
`RegQueryValueEx()`	Retrieves the current value for a named entry in a registry key. Requires the name and buffers to hold the type of data, size of the data, and the data itself.
`RegDeleteValue()`	Removes a value, by name, from a registry key.
`RegDeleteKey()`	Removes a subkey, by name, for a parent registry key.
`RegEnumKeyEx()`	Steps through all subkeys of the passed parent registry key, returning some details of the key's configuration.
`RegEnumValue()`	Steps through all values in the passed registry key, returning details of the value such as its name, type, and size.
`RegQueryInfoKey()`	Takes the handle to an opened key and retrieves all details about the key's current state. Values include the sizes of the longest subkey name, longest value name, and largest value data in the key.

`RegOpenKeyEx()` gives you access to existing keys, but you must use the `RegCreateKeyEx()` API to create keys in the registry. In fact, the creation API opens the requested key if it already exists, but its parameter list is a bit more complicated. In addition to the parameters passed when opening a key, in creating a key you must pass a flag indicating special options such as persistent, temporary, or for backing up/restoring; and a security attributes parameter as required in kernel object creation. The create method returns the key and a flag telling you whether it was just created or it already existed.

With an open key, you can use the `RegSetValueEx()` and `RegQueryValueEx()` APIs to store and retrieve data into the registry. These functions both take the open key, the string name of the value, and a buffer for the data. The set function also takes a type for the data and its size while the query function returns those parameters.

Listing 10-13 shows a quick example of how to use these APIs. The application will simply store a value in the registry then retrieve it, displaying the steps along the way at the console window.

Listing 10-13: Using the set and get APIs for values in the registry

```
// project reggetset
#include <windows.h>
#include <iostream>

// the string naming the test key
```

```
static LPCTSTR g_szTestKey = "Software\\IDG Books\\"
    "Windows 2000 Developer's Guide\\1.0\\RegGetSet";

// helper method to open this program's key
HKEY OpenKey()
{
    // return buffers
    HKEY hkeyTest = NULL;
    DWORD dwDisposition(0);

    // create or open the key
    LONG nResult = ::RegCreateKeyEx(
        HKEY_CURRENT_USER,      // open the key under HKCU
        g_szTestKey,            // the name of the key
        0,                      // reserved, must be 0
        NULL,                   // class, should be NULL
        REG_OPTION_NON_VOLATILE,// persist this key
        KEY_ALL_ACCESS,         // give the owner all access
        NULL,                   // default security
        &hkeyTest,              // the resulting key
        &dwDisposition);        // created or opened
    if(nResult==ERROR_SUCCESS)
    {
        // reflect the current state (open and maybe created)
        if(dwDisposition==REG_CREATED_NEW_KEY)
        {
            std::cout << "Created new key." << std::endl;
        }
        std::cout << "Key 'HKCU\\" << g_szTestKey
            << "' now open." << std::endl;
    }
    else
    {
        hkeyTest = NULL;
    }
    return(hkeyTest);
}

// helper method to save a string value to this program's key
void SaveValue(LPCTSTR szName, LPCTSTR szValue)
{
    // open up the key and validate the passed params
    HKEY hkeyTest = ::OpenKey();
    if(hkeyTest!=NULL && szName!=NULL && szValue!=NULL)
```

```
    {
        // save the passed value
        LONG nResult = ::RegSetValueEx(
            hkeyTest,            // key to add under
            szName,              // name of the value
            0,                   // reserved, must be 0
            REG_SZ,              // type - string
            reinterpret_cast<CONST BYTE*>(szValue),// the value
            ::strlen(szValue)); // size of the data
        if(nResult==ERROR_SUCCESS)
        {
            std::cout << "Saved value: " << szName << "="
                << szValue << std::endl;
        }

        // close up the key
        ::RegCloseKey(hkeyTest);
        hkeyTest = NULL;
    }
}

// helper method to display values from this program's key
void ShowValue(LPCTSTR szName)
{
    HKEY hkeyTest = ::OpenKey();
    if(hkeyTest!=NULL && szName!=NULL)
    {
        // find the size and type of the value
        DWORD dwType(0), dwSize(0);
        LONG nResult = ::RegQueryValueEx(
            hkeyTest,            // the key to query under
            szName,              // the value to find
            0,                   // reserved, must be 0
            &dwType,             // the type of the value
            NULL,                // don't supply a buffer
            &dwSize);            // size of the required buffer

        // create the buffer
        if(nResult==ERROR_SUCCESS)
        {
            BYTE* pVal = new BYTE[dwSize];

            // re-query supplying the buffer to save to
            nResult = ::RegQueryValueEx(
```

```
                    hkeyTest,           // the key to query under
                    szName,             // the value to find
                    0,                  // reserved, must be 0
                    &dwType,            // the type of the value
                    pVal,               // buffer to save in
                    &dwSize);           // size of required buffer

          // report the value (string only)
          if(nResult==ERROR_SUCCESS && dwType==REG_SZ)
          {
               std::cout << "Found value: " << szName << "="
                    << reinterpret_cast<LPCTSTR>(pVal)
                    << std::endl;
          }

          // clean up the array
          delete [] pVal;
          pVal = NULL;
     }

     // close up the key
     ::RegCloseKey(hkeyTest);
     hkeyTest = NULL;
     }
}

void main()
{
     // first, save the value
     ::SaveValue("CEO", "Pierre de Fermat");

     // now, report the value
     ::ShowValue("CEO");
}
```

The example in Listing 10-13 shows you how to open, write, read, and close keys and values in the registry. The OpenKey() helper method simply opens or creates the key the program uses, making sure to return NULL when it fails. The caller must close this key when it no longer needs access to the registry. The SaveValue() function simply takes a string name and value to write under the key; this can be overloaded to take other types such as REG_DWORD or REG_BINARY. The ShowValue() function is interesting in that it first calls RegQueryValueEx() to find the type and size of the buffer required to hold the value. When it finds the value is a string, the function then allocates a buffer large enough to hold it and queries again for the actual value to show it off. When using the registry, it's often useful to list all of the values or subkeys in a key. The `RegEnumKeyEx()` and `RegEnumValue()` APIs loop through all keys or values in a key. They take the handle to the open key and the index of the key or value in which you are interested; you simply increment the index until the function returns `ERROR_NO_MORE_ ENTRIES`. You should call the functions with a large enough buffer to hold the largest value or subkey name under the key; you can find these values by calling the `RegQueryInfoKey()` API. Listing 9-15 shows a depth-first recursion of a key in the registry, displaying all subkeys and value names.

Listing 10-14: Using the registry subkey and value enumerator APIs

```
// project regenum
#include <windows.h>
#include <iostream>

// helper method to open the root key
HKEY OpenKey(HKEY hkeyOpen, LPCTSTR szKey)
{
    // return buffers
    HKEY hkey = NULL;
    DWORD dwDisposition(0);

    // create or open the key
    LONG nResult = ::RegCreateKeyEx(
        hkeyOpen,                   // open the key under
        szKey,                      // the name of the key
        0,                          // reserved, must be 0
        NULL,                       // class, should be NULL
        REG_OPTION_NON_VOLATILE,    // persist this key
        KEY_ALL_ACCESS,             // give the owner all access
        NULL,                       // default security
        &hkey,                      // the resulting key
        &dwDisposition);            // created or opened
    if(nResult!=ERROR_SUCCESS)
    {
        hkey = NULL;
    }
    return(hkey);
}

// helper method to display value names from the passed key
void ShowValueNames(HKEY hkey)
{
    // validate the input
```

```
if(hkey!=NULL)
{
    DWORD dwIndex(0);
    LONG nResult = ERROR_SUCCESS;
    while(nResult==ERROR_SUCCESS)
    {
        // get the name
        CHAR szName[1024];
        DWORD dwSize(sizeof(szName));
        nResult = ::RegEnumValue(
            hkey,         // open root to enumerate
            dwIndex,      // current index
            szName,       // name buffer
            &dwSize,      // size of the required buffer
            NULL,         // reserved - NULL
            NULL,         // don't need type info
            NULL,         // don't need value data
            NULL);        // don't need value size

        // show it
        if(nResult==ERROR_SUCCESS)
        {
            std::cout << "\tValue: " << szName
                << std::endl;
        }

        // bump the index
        ++dwIndex;
    }
}

// helper method to save a string value to this program's key
void RecurseKey(HKEY hkey)
{
    DWORD dwIndex(0);
    LONG nResult = ERROR_SUCCESS;
    while(nResult==ERROR_SUCCESS)
    {
        // get the key name
        CHAR szName[1024];
        DWORD dwSize(sizeof(szName));
        FILETIME ft;
        nResult = ::RegEnumKeyEx(
```

```
            hkey,        // open key to enumerate
            dwIndex,     // current index
            szName,      // name buffer
            &dwSize,     // size of name buffer
            NULL,        // reserved - NULL
            NULL,        // don't need class name
            NULL,        // don't need class size
            &ft);        // last write time

        // show the name
        if(nResult==ERROR_SUCCESS)
        {
            std::cout << "Subkey: " << szName << std::endl;

            // open the new key
            HKEY hkeyChild = ::OpenKey(hkey, szName);
            if(hkeyChild!=NULL)
            {
                // show the child's name then recurse it
                ::ShowValueNames(hkeyChild);
                ::RecurseKey(hkeyChild);

                // close it up
                ::RegCloseKey(hkeyChild);
                hkeyChild = NULL;
            }
        }

        // move to the next key
        ++dwIndex;
    }
}


void main()
{
    // open the root, recurse from there showing all keys and
    //  value names
    HKEY hkeyRoot = ::OpenKey(
        HKEY_CURRENT_USER,      // open key
        "Software\\IDG Books"); // subkey name
    if(hkeyRoot!=NULL)
    {
        ::RecurseKey(hkeyRoot);
    }
```

```
// cleanup
::RegCloseKey(hkeyRoot);
hkeyRoot = NULL;
}
```

The program simply opens the top-level key for this product and begins recursing it. The new open method is generic enough to simply take an open key and the name of the subkey to open. The recursion starts by calling RegEnumKeyEx() to find the name of the first subkey. The program then opens this subkey, shows its value names, then recurses it. The function to show the value names simply calls RegEnumValue() until it fails, displaying each name in turn. Figure 10-6 shows typical results of execution of Listing 10-14.

Figure 10-6: Recursively displaying the subkeys and values under a known key

Windows provides an entire set of utility functions for the registry. You can connect to the registry on another computer using the RegConnectRegistry() API, specifying the name and hive in which you are interested. You can back up and restore keys (including their subkeys and all values) using the RegSaveKey() and RegRestoreKey() APIs. Finally, you can delete a key or a value using the RegDeleteKey() and RegDeleteValue() APIs.

REGISTRY PRACTICES
In addition to the APIs that I have just shown, you need to know how and where to store data in the registry. There are only a couple of hard and fast rules for this. I present them in this section.

When using the registry, you need to separate user-specific data for your application from data shared across all users for the installation. You should reflect this separation of data in the registry by placing user-specific configuration in HKEY_CURRENT_USER (also known as HKCU) and machine-wide configuration in HKEY_LOCAL_MACHINE (also known as HKLM).

When choosing key names for your application, use the Windows convention. The convention places all application data under the Software key followed by the name of the originating organization, the product name, and its version number. Only after these four subkeys should your application begin creating configuration groups. An example of a data group, possibly "HKCU\Software\IDG\Win2k Dev Guide\1.0\Chapters," may contain a subkey for every chapter in the book. Also, be aware that keys are more space-intensive than values so group your data under keys.

System information

Often you will want your application to be aware of the system that is running it. This may cause you to execute conditional code, such as spawning more threads on a multiprocessor box. Windows is gracious enough to supply a set of APIs that enable you to gather almost any information that you might need to make such decisions.

There are several dimensions of system information: network names, hardware information, operating system version and configuration (or software), and GUI metrics. Let's briefly look at all of these – except the last.

GUI metrics are found with the `GetSystemMetrics()` API. Chapter 5, "The GDI API," covers this material.

NAMES

One of the first things you usually want to know when you meet a new machine is its name. Windows provides the `GetComputerName()` and `GetComputerNameEx()` APIs for determining how the computer is identified on the network. The former API supplies the NetBIOS name and only requires a buffer for holding it. The latter API subsumes the former and enables you to request any of the computer's possible known names on the network.

Another name that you might want is the name of the logged-in user. The `GetUserName()` locates this for you. Listing 10-15 blasts some of these names at you.

Listing 10-15: Using the naming information APIs

```
// project naming
#define _WIN32_WINNT 0x0500
#define WINVER 0x0500
#include <windows.h>
#include <iostream>

void main()
{
    // helper buffer
    const DWORD c_dwNameSize = 1024;
    CHAR szName[c_dwNameSize];
    DWORD dwSize(sizeof(szName));

    // show the NetBIOS name of the computer
    dwSize = c_dwNameSize;
```

```
if(::GetComputerName(szName, &dwSize))
{
    std::cout << "Computer (NetBIOS): " << szName
        << std::endl;
}

// show the fully qualified dns (FQDNS) name
dwSize = c_dwNameSize;
if(::GetComputerNameEx(
    ComputerNameDnsFullyQualified,  // get the FQDNS
    szName,                          // name buffer
    &dwSize))                        // size buffer
{
    std::cout << "Computer (FQDNS): " << szName
        << std::endl;
}

// show the user name
if(::GetUserName(szName, &dwSize))
{
    std::cout << "Current user: " << szName << std::endl;
}
}
```

Listing 10-15 is straightforward code. The program allocates a buffer that typically is large enough for any name and then queries for a few of them. The GetComputerName() API requires only the buffer to fill while theGetComputerNameEx() API requires the buffer plus an enumerated type, COMPUTER_NAME_FORMAT, that describes the type of name you want. Finally, the GetUserName() API again only requires the buffer to fill and its size. You immediately should recognize all of the results.

HARDWARE

The next thing you may want to know about the machine is the type of hardware running your operating system. In order to get most of this information, use the GetSystemInfo() API. This method fills a SYSTEM_INFO structure that mostly tells you details about the CPU configuration. Data such as number of processors and the revision of the processor are presented. Further, in order to support minor CPU differences, the IsProcessorFeaturePresent() API checks for things such as a floating point coprocessor or the MMX instruction set.

Windows supports hardware profiles for machines that have *docked* and *undocked* states – these states typically apply to portable computers (e.g., laptops) and indicate whether the machine has been plugged into immobile companion hardware. To determine the current hardware profile and whether it is docked, use the GetCurrentHwProfile() API. Finally, you can find other hardware information using the `GetKeyboardType()` API; it tells you what type of keyboard the user is using.

SOFTWARE

The final dimension of system information that you need is the configuration of the software running the application. First, you want the version of the operating system, which is available through the `GetVersionEx()` API. This function produces a data structure, `OSVERSIONINFOEX`, detailed in Table 10-3, containing version, build, and service pack numbers as well as platform, product, and suite types. Since so much information is presented in the `OSVERSIONINFOEX` structure, Windows supplies the `VerifyVersionInfo()` helper API to help you compare the data to your requirements.

TABLE **10-3** MEMBERS OF THE OSVERSIONINFOEX STRUCTURE

Member Name	Intention
DWORD dwMajorVersion	The most significant number in the system's version. Windows 2000 has a value of 5.
DWORD dwMinorVersion	The minor version of the system. Windows 2000 has a value of 0.
DWORD dwBuildNumber	The build number of the system.
DWORD dwPlatformId	The platform of the system – must be VER_PLATFORM_WIN32_NT.
TCHAR szCSDVersion[128]	A null-terminated string indicating the installed service pack, if any.
WORD wServicePackMajor	The major version of the installed service pack, if any.
WORD wServicePackMinor	The minor version of the installed service pack, if any.
WORD wSuiteMask	Flags indicating product suites installed on the machine, for example BackOffice or Terminal Services.
WORD wProductType	Type of system: workstation, server, or domain controller.

Windows also helps you find where it lives on the files system by providing the `GetWindowsDirectory()` and `GetSystemDirectory()` APIs. These functions tell you where to look for helper DLLs, fonts, or data files that you know must live there. The Windows directory is often `c:\winnt`, while the system directory is often c:\winnt\system32. The program in Listing 10-16 shows you some of the operating system configuration data.

Listing 10-16: Using the operating system information APIs

```
// project osinfo
#define _WIN32_WINNT 0x0500
#define WINVER 0x0500
#include <windows.h>
#include <iostream>

void main()
{
    // set up a version info data structure to hold the version
    //  of the operating system
    OSVERSIONINFOEX osvix;
    ::ZeroMemory(&osvix, sizeof(osvix));
    osvix.dwOSVersionInfoSize = sizeof(osvix);

    // fetch the version information and report
    ::GetVersionEx(reinterpret_cast<LPOSVERSIONINFO>(&osvix));

    // check for Win2k
    if(osvix.dwPlatformId==VER_PLATFORM_WIN32_NT &&
        osvix.dwMajorVersion==5)
    {
        std::cout << "Running Windows 2000 " ;

        if(osvix.wProductType==VER_NT_SERVER)
        {
            std::cout << "Server" << std::endl;
        }
        else
        {
            std::cout << "Professional" << std::endl;
        }
    }

    // build number
    std::cout << "Build: " << osvix.dwBuildNumber << std::endl;

    // show service pack
    std::cout << "Service Pack: " << osvix.szCSDVersion
        << std::endl;

    // the windows and system dirs
```

```
CHAR szWinDir[MAX_PATH], szSysDir[MAX_PATH];
::GetWindowsDirectory(szWinDir, MAX_PATH);
::GetSystemDirectory(szSysDir,MAX_PATH);

std::cout << "Windows dir: " << szWinDir
    << "\nSystem dir: " << szSysDir << std::endl;
}
```

Listing 10-16 demonstrates a simple call to get the version information. Windows 2000 shows up as NT, major version 5. The build number also is accessible in the new version information structure, along with a string version of the service pack label. Finally, the program displays the paths to the two principal folders for the operating system; Figure 10-7 shows the results.

Figure 10-7: Gathering information about the system

System lifetime APIs

Windows 2000 enables you to lock the workstation programmatically, log off the current user, and shut it down. You probably won't need to do this very often, but when you do, the following APIs can do the trick:

- ◆ LockWorkStation()
- ◆ ExitWindowsEx()
- ◆ InitiateSystemShutdownEx()

The first operation, locking the workstation, prevents anyone other than the currently logged on user, or an administrator, from using the computer. The LockWorkStation() API takes no parameters and can fail if not executed in the context of the current user.

The next operation, logging off the current user, shuts down all current applications as if the system is shutting down and returns the user to the log-in dialog box. You can start this procedure with the ExitWindowsEx() API by supplying a flag, EWX_LOGOFF.

The ExitWindowsEx() API also initiates the standard shutdown procedure with the EWX_SHUTDOWN flag in which Windows notifies all running applications with windows that it is about to exit; if none objects, it proceeds. The API takes a series of flags that enable you to log only the current user off, shut down and allow the user to power down, shut down and power off, or reboot the machine. Also, the API lets the caller specify whether Windows should disallow shutdown objections or not query hung applications about shutdown objections.

Finally, shutting down a system enables you to cease operations on the local system or a remote system over the network when you have administrator access to it. The InitiateSystemShutdownEx() API allows you to shut down a system forcibly, warning anyone logged in, and aborting if necessary. The API reboots the system, if directed, and emits a message to the system event log. In order to abort a system shutdown in progress, use the AbortSystemShutdown() helper API.

The only API that's benign enough to demonstrate is LockWorkstation(). The example in Listing 10-17 shows a quick application to lock up the Windows desktop.

Listing 10-17: Locking the workstation

```
// project lockws
#define _WIN32_WINNT 0x0500
#define WINVER 0x0500
#include <windows.h>

void main()
{
    // simple call to shut out all users from the desktop
    ::LockWorkStation();
}
```

The logic in Listing 10-17 doesn't require much explanation. The API call is specific to Windows 2000. When it is complete, the program ends. It doesn't block for an unlock of the workstation.

Summary

I have covered a lot of ground in this chapter. I showed you how to share unique code that you write using either Windows DLL support or COM objects. I also showed you how to use some of the native programming services that Windows gives you to write great applications like large integer and time support. Finally, you learned about the system services that you can take advantage of such as the registry, system information, and shutdown methods. These tools help you create world-class applications in Windows.

The next chapter covers the special set of processes called services. Services are applications the system runs for you – possibly whenever it is running – so that you can provide data and logic to other applications or users without interruption.

Chapter 11

Service Applications

THIS CHAPTER covers Windows 2000 services. Service applications are special derivatives of standard applications that are run by the system rather than by a user logged in at the desktop. Since the system itself runs service applications, you have the opportunity to add system facilities and capabilities that are available whenever the host machine is running. Consumers typically demand high levels of reliability and scalability out of service applications. Windows provides service tools to satisfy these demands.

I will lead you through working with service applications installed in the system and how to create a simple service for the system. I will also show you how to use some more advanced facilities in Windows 2000 from event logging to performance monitoring. Finally, I will cover security settings for services and the standard tools for administering them.

How to Interact with Services

A service EXE is very similar to a console or windowing application, but it is only managed and executed by the system's service control manager. The choreography of running a service application is a bit unusual but easily understood and easy to consume from a boilerplate or framework. The primary difference between a service application and other application types is the lack of an interactive interface; all communication between the administrator or a client and a service application is through programming interfaces the service exposes.

Service control manager

Only the Windows 2000 kernel can start up, shut down, pause, or otherwise control a service application. More specifically, a component of the kernel called the *service control manager (SCM)* is responsible for the registration and operation of all services on the machine. The SCM exposes a set of programmatic interfaces for maintaining the database of available services, starting and controlling services, querying service configurations, and obtaining the status of all running services.

You can see most of the facilities provided by the SCM in action by using the Computer Management snap-in for the *Microsoft Management Console (MMC)*. Right-clicking the My Computer desktop icon gives you the `Manage` command, which launches the snap-in, and then you can expand into Service and Applications and select the Services node. This tool lists, on the right-hand side, all of the available services on the machine with a description, status, and some interesting configuration data.

In addition to the Computer Management snap-in, the MMC runs other snap-ins to help you configure services. I discuss this later in the chapter.

Figure 11-1 shows you the snap-in running under MMC. Pay close attention to the column names and data — they represent the main configuration information of each service.

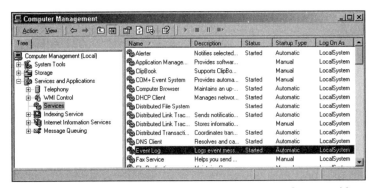

Figure 11-1: Using the services tree of the Windows 2000 Computer Management snap-in

One important piece of configuration data that the SCM maintains is its startup mode. The SCM can run a service automatically when the machine starts or automatically on demand from another, dependent service. You also can mark a service as manual startup, or as disabled. Another piece of configuration data in the SCM database is the running account. The SCM uses this account configuration as the owner of the process when the service starts up in order to authenticate against other services for such things as file or network access. Typically, services run under the Local System account, which gains access to most objects on the local machine – but almost none on networked machines.

The snap-in enables you to start, pause, resume, stop, and restart any service that is not disabled and has the command available. These commands are implemented as simple calls into the SCM APIs StartService() and ControlService(). Each service also can receive command-line parameters set in the General tab of the service's Properties dialog box.

The service's Properties dialog box features a Dependencies tab, which can be used to define other services on which a particular service is dependent. A service's dependency list allows the SCM to begin all other service applications that the target requires to be running before the SCM starts it. This helps the designer of a service guarantee that required applications are already running before a particular service is run. When shutting down a service, the SCM also shuts down all services that are dependent on the victim, preventing unexpected consequences such as a crash.

Managing services

Windows exposes the SCM to you as a singleton pseudo-kernel object from the AdvAPI32.DLL library. In order to manage services, you need to use the SCM starting with the OpenSCManager() API, which returns you a handle to the object. Table 11-1 summarizes the other SCM APIs that you will need to use.

TABLE 11-1 SERVICE CONTROL MANAGER APIS

API Name	Description
OpenSCManager()	Retrieves a handle to the singleton pseudo-kernel object. Requires an access level request; can accept the name of a remote machine to connect to its SCM.
CreateService()	Adds a new service to the SCM database, returning a handle to the service's kernel object.
OpenService()	Retrieves a handle to a singleton pseudo-kernel object that represents a service in the SCM database. Requires an access level request and the proper name of the service.
CloseServiceHandle()	Releases a reference to the singleton SCM or service object.
EnumServiceStatus()	Iterates through the service objects in the SCM database, returning the proper name and status of each service.

Continued

TABLE 11-1 SERVICE CONTROL MANAGER APIS *(Continued)*

API Name	Description
GetServiceDisplay Name()	Retrieves the display name for a service in the SCM database when supplied the proper name of the service.
GetServiceKeyName()	Retrieves the proper name of a service in the SCM database when supplied the display name of the service.
LockServiceDatabase()	Prevents other processes from modifying the SCM database, returning a handle to a lock object.
UnlockService Database()	Releases a lock on the SCM database.
QueryLockService Database()	Determines if the SCM database is currently locked.

When you create a handle to the SCM with the OpenSCManager() API, you must specify the type of access needed. The access type can range from simple GENERIC _READ, which enables you to enumerate services to SC_MANAGER_ALL_ACCESS, which enables you to lock the database and create new services. In addition, this call enables you to connect to another machine and open its services database, and it provides the ability to open an alternate services database even though none are currently available. When you are finished with the SCM object, you must release it with the Close ServiceHandle() API.

Connecting to the service control manager on a remote machine requires that you have administrative access to that machine.

Once you have a handle to the singleton SCM object, you can perform operations on the service database. One of the main facilities the SCM provides you is access to a particular service's entry in the database using the OpenService() API. Like the OpenSCManager() API, you must tell the system the access you are demanding to that service's entry in the database; possible access levels range from SERVICE_ QUERY_STATUS to SERVICE_ALL_ACCESS. To locate a service with OpenService(), you must supply its *proper* name. Listing 11-1 shows a simple program to grab the name and status of a service.

Listing 11-1: Fetching the status of a service

```cpp
// project svcstatus
#include <windows.h>
#include <iostream>
#include <string>

// simple helper method to show current status of the service
//   passed in by name
bool ShowServiceStatus(SC_HANDLE hSCM,
                       const std::string& strName)
{
    bool bFound(false);

    // open up the service
    SC_HANDLE hService = ::OpenService(
        hSCM,                  // the SCM
        strName.c_str(),       // name of the service
        SERVICE_QUERY_STATUS); // only need status
    if(hService!=NULL)
    {
        // get the current status
        SERVICE_STATUS ss;
        if(::QueryServiceStatus(hService, &ss))
        {
            // mark the return flag
            bFound = true;

            // show the current status
            std::cout << "Service '" << strName;
            if(ss.dwCurrentState==SERVICE_RUNNING)
            {
                std::cout << "' running." << std::endl;
            }
            else
            {
                std::cout << "' not running." << std::endl;
            }
        }

        // clean up the service handle
        ::CloseServiceHandle(hService);
        hService = NULL;
    }
    return(bFound);
}
```

```
void main()
{
    // open up the SCM
    SC_HANDLE hSCM = ::OpenSCManager(
        NULL,    // open the SCM on the current machine
        SERVICES_ACTIVE_DATABASE,    // use the current db
        GENERIC_READ);  // simple read access
    if(hSCM!=NULL)
    {
        // fetch the string from the user
        std::string strService;
        std::cout << "Enter name of service to query: "
            << std::endl;
        std::cin >> strService;

        // make sure we have a name
        if(!strService.empty())
        {
            // try the passed name
            if(!::ShowServiceStatus(hSCM, strService))
            {
                // often the user enters the display name, try
                //  to get the key name
                TCHAR szName[MAX_PATH];
                DWORD dwSize(sizeof(szName));
                if(::GetServiceKeyName(
                    hSCM,                // database owner
                    strService.c_str(), // display name
                    szName,              // service name
                    &dwSize))            // size of buffer
                {
                    // try again
                    strService = szName;
                    ::ShowServiceStatus(hSCM, strService);
                }
                else
                {
                    std::cout << "Could not locate '"
                        << strService << "' in the SCM."
                        << std::endl;
                }
            }
        }
    }
```

```
        // clean up the SCM
        ::CloseServiceHandle(hSCM);
        hSCM = NULL;
    }
}
```

Listing 11-1 shows you very simply how to open up the SCM (the acronym is often pronounced to rhyme with thumb) with read access. If you have permission to access the SCM, the example asks you for the name of a service to inspect. It attempts to display the status of that service, but you likely will pass it the service's display name as found in the Computer Management snap-in list view.

The example in Listing 11-1 then calls the GetServiceKeyName() API to translate a display name to a proper service name. For example, the service with display name ClipBook shown in Figure 11-1 has the proper name ClipSrv. With the proper service name, the example calls the status dumper again to show you whether it is currently running. The local ShowServiceStatus() function simply gets a SERVICE_STATUS structure for the service using the QueryServiceStatus() API and tests whether the service is currently in the running state. This data structure contains a bevy of other information about the service you're looking at, but the example only cares about the running state.

TIP   You also can find the real service name from the Properties dialog box in the snap-in. Just double-click the service's line in the list view and inspect the Service name text label.

In addition to opening a service for inspection or control, the SCM handle enables you to install a new service for the system using the CreateService() API. This function takes a whopping 13 parameters that make up the initial configuration of the service. I summarize these parameters in Table 11-2. Once you create a service, the function returns a handle to its service object and you are responsible for releasing the reference with the CloseServiceHandle() API.

TABLE 11-2 PARAMETERS OF THE CREATESERVICE() API

Parameter Name	Intention
SC_HANDLE hSCManager	The SCM database to own the new service object
LPCTSTR lpServiceName	The proper name for the service

Continued

TABLE 11-2 PARAMETERS OF THE CREATESERVICE() API *(Continued)*

Parameter Name	Intention
LPCTSTR lpDisplayName	The display name for the service
DWORD dwDesiredAccess	Access request to the new service object through the returned handle
DWORD dwServiceType	Type of service to create, can indicate a simple application or a driver
DWORD dwStartType	Startup conditions for the new service; examples are automatic, manual, and disabled
DWORD dwErrorControl	Flag that indicates the severity of a failure to start the new service
LPCTSTR lpBinaryPathName	The fully specified path to the service executable
LPCTSTR lpLoadOrderGroup	Name of the load ordering group that the service is a member of; can be NULL when not part of any group
LPDWORD lpdwTagId	When part of a load-ordering group, this returned flag will uniquely identify this service in that group
LPCTSTR lpDependencies	A null-string terminated list of null-terminated strings, which are proper names of service applications that the new service requires to be running before it runs
LPCTSTR lpServiceStartName	The name of the Windows account to run the service under for security privileges
LPCTSTR lpPassword	The authenticating password for the account in lpServiceStartName

---

Other database-read APIs that the SCM supplies are EnumServicesStatusEx() for walking the known services in the services database, and the display name helpers GetServiceDisplayName() and GetServiceKeyName(). Finally, for write operations to the database, the SCM requires that you lock out other processes to serialize access using the LockServiceDatabase() and UnlockServiceDatabase() APIs.

TIP To check if the service database is locked, and to determine who locked it and for how long it has been locked, use the `QueryServiceLockStatus()` API.

Service objects

The service handle that the `OpenService()` API returns to you is the gateway to all service interrogation, control, and configuration. I summarize the service object operations that the system makes available to you in Table 11-3.

TABLE 11-3 SERVICE OBJECT APIS

API Name	Description
QueryServiceConfig()	Fetches the current configuration parameters for the service in a QUERY_SERVICE_CONFIG structure. Each member of this structure corresponds to a parameter in the CreateService() API.
QueryServiceConfig2()	Fetches extended configuration information from the service object. This API returns either the description of the service, in a SERVICE_DESCRIPTION structure, or the actions the system should take on its failure, in a SERVICE_FAILURE_ACTIONS structure.
QueryServiceStatus()	Determines the current status of the service in a SERVICE_STATUS structure.
EnumDependentServices()	Iterates through each of the services that the sent service is dependent upon and returns the proper and display names as well as the status of those services in an ENUM_SERVICE_STATUS structure.
StartService()	Starts the passed service.
ControlService()	Sends a controlling command to the passed service, possible controls include start, pause, continue, and shut down.

Continued

TABLE 11-3 **SERVICE OBJECT APIS** *(Continued)*

API Name	Description
ChangeServiceConfig()	Modifies all of the data originally supplied in the CreateService() API except the proper and display names of the service.
ChangeServiceConfig2()	Modifies the description or failure actions that are retrieved in the QueryServiceConfig2() API.
QueryServiceObjectSecurity()	Retrieves a copy of the service object's Security Descriptor.
SetServiceObjectSecurity()	Changes the service object's Security Descriptor.
DeleteService()	Removes a service from the SCM database.

First, the system enables you to look up information on any installed service using the QueryServiceConfig(), QueryServiceConfig2(), and QueryService Status() APIs. The first configuration API, QueryServiceConfig(), returns 9 of the 13 parameters that the service creator supplied in the CreateService() API call; it does this with the QUERY_SERVICE_CONFIG structure. The second configuration API, QueryServiceConfig2(), supplies extended configuration information. Part of the extended information includes a description for the service and actions to take if the service terminates abnormally. Finally, the QueryServiceStatus() API retrieves the current status of the service in a SERVICE_STATUS_PROCESS structure, including the state, process identifier, and commands from the SCM that will be responded to by the service.

When opened with the appropriate access, the service object can be used to modify the configuration of a service through the ChangeServiceConfig() and Change ServiceConfig2() APIs. Like the interrogation APIs, QueryServiceXxx() that I just introduced, the first function enables you to modify the information supplied when creating the service. The second API, ChangeServiceConfig2(), is the only interface to set or change the description and failure actions for the service. (Currently, there is no CreateService2() API.)

One of the more interesting sets of configuration data for a service application is contained within the SERVICE_FAILURE_ACTIONS structure. This data instructs the system what actions to take if the service process terminates improperly. An improper termination occurs when the service does not tell the SCM it is exiting by sending the SERVICE_STOPPED value in the SetServiceStatus() API. You can specify a different action on each successive failure of the service. The SCM counts each failure occurrence of the service and takes the action you supply in an array of values in the data structure. Possible failure actions are as follows:

◆ Take no action and accept the failure silently

◆ Restart the service after a delay, using its current configuration

◆ Run another, different executable that might correct the problem
  or inform the administrator

◆ Reboot the machine, returning it to a known state

The Recovery tab of the service Properties dialog box enables you to explore the failure options. Listing 11-2 shows you an example of how to query that information. It's an extension of Listing 11-1.

Listing 11-2: Fetching the failure actions of a service

```
// project svcfailure
#define _WIN32_WINNT 0x0500
#define WINVER 0x0500
#include <windows.h>
#include <iostream>
#include <string>

// simple helper method to show current config of the service
//  passed in by handle
void ShowServiceConfig(SC_HANDLE hService,
                       const std::string& strName)
{
    // find the required size of the config struct by passing
    //  an empty buffer
    DWORD dwSize(0);
    ::QueryServiceConfig(
        hService,    // service of interest
        NULL,        // no return buffer
        0,           // width of return buffer
        &dwSize);    // actually required size

    // allocate the buffer and re-query
    QUERY_SERVICE_CONFIG* pQsc =
        (QUERY_SERVICE_CONFIG*)new BYTE[dwSize];
    if(::QueryServiceConfig(hService, pQsc, dwSize, &dwSize))
    {
        // show the service names
        std::cout << "Service '" << pQsc->lpDisplayName
            << " (" << strName << ")'"
            << std::endl;
    }
```

```cpp
// clean up the buffer
delete [] (BYTE*)pQsc;
pQsc = NULL;

// extended config info, again find the required size
::QueryServiceConfig2(
    hService,    // service of interest
    SERVICE_CONFIG_FAILURE_ACTIONS, // get failure actions
    NULL,        // no buffer, only want required size
    0,           // width of return buffer
    &dwSize);    // actually required size

// allocate the buffer and re-query
SERVICE_FAILURE_ACTIONS* pSfa =
    (SERVICE_FAILURE_ACTIONS*)new BYTE[dwSize];
if(::QueryServiceConfig2(hService,
    SERVICE_CONFIG_FAILURE_ACTIONS, (LPBYTE)pSfa,
    dwSize, &dwSize))
{
    // enumerate the actions
    for(DWORD nAction=0;nAction<pSfa->cActions;++nAction)
    {
        // show the action count and refer to the entry in
        //  the array
        std::cout << "Failure #" << nAction << ' ';
        SC_ACTION& action = pSfa->lpsaActions[nAction];

        // show a meaningful message for each action
        switch(action.Type)
        {
        case SC_ACTION_NONE:
            std::cout << "Take no action.";
            break;
        case SC_ACTION_REBOOT:
            std::cout << "Reboot the computer in "
                << action.Delay << " msec";
            if(pSfa->lpRebootMsg!=NULL)
            {
                std::cout << "\nReboot message: "
                    << pSfa->lpRebootMsg;
            }
            break;
        case SC_ACTION_RESTART:
            std::cout << "Restart the service in "
                << action.Delay << " msec";
```

```
                    break;
            case SC_ACTION_RUN_COMMAND:
                std::cout << "Run the file: "
                    << pSfa->lpCommand;
                break;
            }
            std::cout << std::endl;
        }
    }

    // clean up the SFA
    delete [] (BYTE*)pSfa;
    pSfa = NULL;
}

// helper method to locate a service in the SCM database by
//   passed name (display or system name)
SC_HANDLE LocateServiceByName(std::string& strName)
{
    // init the return buffer
    SC_HANDLE hService = NULL;

    // open up the SCM
    SC_HANDLE hSCM = ::OpenSCManager(
        NULL,                       // SCM on current machine
        SERVICES_ACTIVE_DATABASE,// use the current db
        GENERIC_READ);              // simple read access

        // make sure we have a name
    if(hSCM!=NULL && !strName.empty())
    {
        // try the passed name
        SC_HANDLE hTry1 = ::OpenService(
            hSCM,                   // the SCM
            strName.c_str(),        // name of the service
            SERVICE_ALL_ACCESS);// get all access
        if(hTry1!=NULL)
        {
            // found it
            hService = hTry1;
        }
        else
        {
            // often the user enters the display name, try
            //  to get the key name
```

```
                    TCHAR szName[MAX_PATH];
                    DWORD dwSize(sizeof(szName));
                    if(::GetServiceKeyName(
                        hSCM,                   // database owner
                        strName.c_str(),     // display name
                        szName,                 // service name
                        &dwSize))               // size of buffer
                    {
                        // try again
                        hService = ::OpenService(
                            hSCM,                   // the SCM
                            szName,                 // name of the service
                            SERVICE_ALL_ACCESS);// get all access
                        strName = szName;
                    }
                }
            }

        // clean up the SCM
        ::CloseServiceHandle(hSCM);
        hSCM = NULL;

        return(hService);
}

void main()
{
    // fetch the string from the user
    std::string strService;
    std::cout << "Enter name of service to query: "
        << std::endl;
    std::cin >> strService;

    // find the service and show its configuration
    SC_HANDLE hService = ::LocateServiceByName(strService);
    if(hService!=NULL)
    {
        ::ShowServiceConfig(hService, strService);

        // clean up the service
        ::CloseServiceHandle(hService);
        hService = NULL;
    }
}
```

You can see that Listing 11-2 has broken out the logic for looking up a service by name to its own function, LocateServiceByName(), which returns the handle to the service object when successful. The local ShowServiceConfig() function is the most interesting. It demonstrates how to find the required size of the configuration buffers by calling the QueryServiceConfig() API twice – the first time with a null buffer but a place to hold the buffer size. The extended API, QueryServiceConfig2(), fetches the failure actions data and my function walks through it. You should notice that most services do not have this information, which defaults to SC_ACTION_NONE for each failure. You can set the failure actions with the Computer Management snap-in before running the example. I suggest that you supply an innocuous, manual-start service such as ClipBook.

Yet another set of configuration data (not demonstrated in Listing 11-2) about the service that the system allows you to access through the service object is the dependent service list. *Dependent services* are services that the system must start before starting the supplied service. The EnumDependentServices() API walks through the names and current status of each service that the passed service requires to be running before it runs.

As you saw in Listing 11-1, the QueryServiceStatus() API tells you the current state of a particular service. In order to change this state, you must use the ControlService() API. This function sends a simple message to the service process if it is running; this message is an integer value telling it to stop, pause, continue, report its status, or shut down. In order to manually start a service executing, you must use yet another API, StartService(). The ControlService() API returns to you the same information you receive in the QueryServiceStatus() call.

To illustrate the ControlService() API, Listing 11-3 shows you how to stop and start a service. The program uses the custom LocateServiceByName() function from Listing 11-2 to get the service handle, then issues a SERVICE_CONTROL_STOP command. The program constantly queries the status while the service is stopping using a short loop, and then, when it has stopped, the program can restart it. Again, after issuing a call to StartService(), the program waits for the service to reach the running state.

Listing 11–3: Stopping and starting a service

```
// project svcrestart
#include <windows.h>
#include <iostream>
#include <string>

// ...
// function LookupServiceByName() implementation omitted
// ...

// helper method to restart a service
void Restart(SC_HANDLE hService, const std::string& strService)
{
```

```
std::cout << "Service '" << strService
    << "' stopping...";

// stop the service (whether it is started or not)
SERVICE_STATUS ss;
if(::ControlService(
    hService,                // target
    SERVICE_CONTROL_STOP,    // control code
    &ss))                    // returned status
{
    // check for stopping
    int nTry(0);
    while(ss.dwCurrentState==SERVICE_STOP_PENDING &&
        nTry++<80)
    {
        // let the user know we're in the process
        //  of stopping
        std::cout << ".";
        std::cout.flush();

        // pause 1/2 second
        Sleep(500);

        // get the new service state
        ::QueryServiceStatus(hService, &ss);
    }
}

// let user know the current state
if(ss.dwCurrentState==SERVICE_STOPPED)
{
    std::cout << "stopped." << std::endl;
}

// send the command
std::cout << "Service '" << strService
    << "' starting...";
if(::StartService(
    hService,   // target
    0,          // number of command-line args
    NULL))      // command-line args
{
    // check for starting
    int nTry(0);
```

```
        ::QueryServiceStatus(hService, &ss);
        while(ss.dwCurrentState==SERVICE_START_PENDING &&
            nTry++<80)
        {
            // let the user know we're in the process
            //   starting
            std::cout << ".";
            std::cout.flush();

            // pause 1/2 second
            Sleep(500);

            // get the new service state
            ::QueryServiceStatus(hService, &ss);
        }
    }

    // let user know the current state
    if(ss.dwCurrentState==SERVICE_RUNNING)
    {
        std::cout << "running." << std::endl;
    }
}

void main()
{
    // fetch the string from the user
    std::string strService;
    std::cout << "Enter name of service to restart: "
        << std::endl;
    std::cin >> strService;

    // find the service and show its configuration
    SC_HANDLE hService = ::LocateServiceByName(strService);
    if(hService!=NULL)
    {
        // restart the service
        ::Restart(hService, strService);

        // clean up the service
        ::CloseServiceHandle(hService);
        hService = NULL;
    }
}
```

Listing 11-3 adds the `Restart()` function that stops the passed service by sending the `SERVICE_CONTROL_STOP` command with the `ControlService()` API. After the command has been sent, the function enters a simple loop, checking the status of the stopping service with the `QueryServiceStatus()` API until the service appears to be stopped. The `Restart()` function then uses the `StartService()` API to run the service again. Before exiting, the function again enters a loop that waits for the `QueryServuceStatus()` API to indicate that the service is running.

In order to determine the security that the service creator gave the service object on installation, the system supplies the `QueryServiceObjectSecurity()` API. This enables you to get a copy of all or part of the service's `SECURITY_DESCRIPTOR` (SD). Once you have the SD, you can change it in the database using the `SetService ObjectSecurity()` API.

 Chapter 3, "Using Kernel Objects," covers security descriptors.

In order to uninstall a service, you must call the `DeleteService()` API. This function is very simple; it only requires that you successfully have created the service object with delete access. This function removes the service from the SCM database but does not stop that service if it is currently running.

Command line tools

In addition to the Computer Management MMC snap-in, Windows gives you a couple of tools to control services from the command prompt. The first is the long-time friend `Net.EXE`. Although the `Net` command's chief purpose is to manipulate networking services, you can supply any service name in the `start`, `pause`, `continue`, or `stop` commands. For example, the command `net start ClipSrv` begins the ClipBook service.

While the `Net` utility is useful, it's limited in service-related functionality. The `SC.EXE` program gives you almost complete access to the SCM. While developing a service, you can use the `SC` utility to install, control, configure, and delete that service's entry in the SCM database. When you get ready to deploy your service, you must use the programming interfaces I described earlier in this section to do the installation and configuration. Another nice feature of `SC.EXE` is that, unlike the snap-in or `Net.EXE`, it does not block by waiting for a response from the service when sending commands to that service.

The SC.EXE utility is part of the Microsoft Platform SDK; see the MSDN Website at http://msdn.microsoft.com to get a copy.

The Basics of Service Creation

Now that you know how to create, configure, and control services through the SCM, you probably want to know how to create a working service. The choreography of service execution is unique within Windows and is actually a little fun, as shown in the following section.

Lifetime of a service

When the SCM starts a service, it does so simply by loading the EXE file and running main() or WinMain() through the standard CreateProcess() route. In order to be a service, the program must give its main thread back to the SCM; it does this using the StartServiceCtrlDispatcher() API. A service executable must call this API as soon as possible after starting.

The sole parameter to StartServiceCtrlDispatcher() is an array of SERVICE_TABLE_ENTRY structures, each of which contain the proper name of a service and the address of its ServiceMain() function. Typically, this array contains only one entry and a terminating null structure. Before calling this StartServiceCtrl Dispatcher(), you should take care of whatever process-wide initialization that your service or services require, if you can do it quickly (in less than 30 seconds).

Within the call to StartServiceCtrlDispatcher(), the code inside the SCM spawns another thread for the process that jumps back into the service executable at the passed address. This callback function usually is called ServiceMain(); the SCM supplies this function with the command-line parameters that were passed by the caller to the StartService() API. The first parameter passed in to Service Main() is the proper name of the service.

This second thread that enters ServiceMain() is responsible for doing the work of the service either by itself or by starting other threads of execution. Once execution enters ServiceMain(), your code should take care of any service-specific initialization. The next thing that you must do in ServiceMain() is similar to the procedure in the main() function—you must call the RegisterServiceCtrlHandler() API. This API tells the SCM where to send control requests for stopping, pausing, and so on. The API takes the name of the service and the address to the Handler() callback. It returns to you a SERVICE_STATUS_HANDLE for reporting status back to the SCM.

It turns out that the main thread of the process actually makes the calls into your Handler() function. This thread is actually blocking inside the StartServiceCtrl Dispatcher() call, waiting for commands to send the service or for the Service Main() thread to terminate. When the ServiceMain() thread terminates, the main thread returns to your main() function and the process terminates.

SERVICE SKELETON

Listing 11-4 shows you the skeleton of a service application. It illustrates the actual
life of a simple service called ASimple. The skeleton process uses a little text file to
log the *thread identifiers (TIDs)* of the threads that run through the process.

Listing 11-4: Skeleton of a simple service application

```
// project simple
#include <windows.h>
#include <fstream>
#include <string>

// send a message to a file in the file system
void Log(LPCTSTR lpszFmt, ...)
{
    // construct the log file
    TCHAR szTempPath[MAX_PATH];
    ::GetTempPath(MAX_PATH, szTempPath);
    ::strcat(szTempPath, "simplesvc.log");

    // create the message
    va_list arglist;
    va_start(arglist, lpszFmt);
    TCHAR szMessage[2048];
    ::wvsprintf(szMessage, lpszFmt, arglist);
    va_end(arglist);

    // open up the temp file
    std::ofstream ofLogfile(szTempPath,
        std::ios::out|std::ios::app);

    // write out the message
    ofLogfile << "[TID " << ::GetCurrentThreadId()
        << "]: " << szMessage << std::endl;
}

// send status about the service to the SCM
void SetStatus(SERVICE_STATUS_HANDLE ssh, DWORD dwStatus)
{
    // start with basic status
    SERVICE_STATUS ss = {
        SERVICE_WIN32_OWN_PROCESS,  // service in the process
        SERVICE_STOPPED,            // currently stopped
        SERVICE_ACCEPT_STOP,        // allow stopping
        NO_ERROR,                   // exit code
        0,                          // exit code 2
```

```
        1,                          // checkpoint
        5000};                      // wait time for a start

    // pass the status on to the SCM
    ss.dwCurrentState = dwStatus;
    ::SetServiceStatus(ssh, &ss);
}


// handler for commands
VOID WINAPI Handler(DWORD dwCtl)
{
    ::Log("Service responding to control<%d>", dwCtl);
}


// the work function for the service
VOID WINAPI ServiceMain(DWORD dwArgc, LPTSTR* lpszArgv)
{
    ::Log("Beginning ServiceMain of service <%s>",
        lpszArgv[0]);

    // register the handler function
    SERVICE_STATUS_HANDLE ssh =
        ::RegisterServiceCtrlHandler(lpszArgv[0], Handler);

    // notify that we are starting, then running
    ::SetStatus(ssh, SERVICE_START_PENDING);
    ::Log("Service<%s> starting.", lpszArgv[0]);
    ::SetStatus(ssh, SERVICE_RUNNING);
    ::Log("Service<%s> running.", lpszArgv[0]);

    // do some work
    ::Sleep(15000);

    // notify that we are stopping, then stop
    ::SetStatus(ssh, SERVICE_STOP_PENDING);
    ::Log("Service<%s> stopping.", lpszArgv[0]);

    ::SetStatus(ssh, SERVICE_STOPPED);
    ::Log("Service<%s> stopped.", lpszArgv[0]);
}


// the process starter
void main()
{
```

```
::Log("Service process starting.");

// table of services
SERVICE_TABLE_ENTRY arSvc[] =
{
    { "AService", ServiceMain },
    { NULL, NULL }
};

// hand off the main thread to the SCM
if(!::StartServiceCtrlDispatcher(arSvc))
{
    ::Log("Error - Could not start dispatcher");
}

::Log("Service process terminating.");
}
```

In order to install the service from Listing 11-4, I used SC.EXE with the following syntax:

```
sc create ASimple binpath= c:\simple.exe
```

This command tells the SCM to recognize the new service called ASimple (so that it shows up early in the list) from the EXE file I copied to C:\ (to simplify my typing). I then used the Computer Management snap-in's Services node to start it and stop it immediately.

> The SC.EXE utility is very particular about its command line parameters. You must supply a space before and after each of its keywords, such as create and binpath=.

ASimple is actually a rather boring service. When the ServiceMain() function begins, it marks its status as start pending, logs that, then marks it as running and logs that. The service simply sleeps for 15 seconds to simulate real work and then sets its status as stopping and stops. That's it; clearly, instead of sleeping, the service should be doing something useful and will be when you write your own service.

One of the interesting functions in Listing 11-4 is the Log() function. This simple tracing method takes a printf-like syntax and outputs the results to a file in the temporary folder called SimpleSvc.LOG. The std::ofstream object constructor always begins writing at the end of the file and makes sure its contents get flushed to disk at the end through its destructor. The output in Listing 11-5 comprises the contents of SimpleSvc.LOG for a start-stop sequence of the service.

Listing 11-5: Contents of SimpleSvc.LOG

```
[TID 1736]: Service process starting.
[TID 1848]: Beginning ServiceMain of service <ASimple>
[TID 1848]: Service<ASimple> starting.
[TID 1848]: Service<ASimple> running.
[TID 1736]: Service responding to control<1>
[TID 1848]: Service<ASimple> stopping.
[TID 1736]: Service process terminating.
```

Listing 11-5 illustrates the threading that I talked about earlier, but it's slightly contrived. You can see the message from the handler come through with a control value of one, which is SERVICE_CONTROL_STOP, but the Handler() function never does anything other than log it – the service stops itself.

You should notice in Listing 11-5 that the thread that makes the call into the handler (TID 1736) is the process's main thread. The service choreography requires that the main thread of the process remains blocked in the SCM until another process calls into the SCM for control or status. Then the main thread of the process is allowed to call back into the Handler() function to send control requests to the service or fetch its status while running. The service in Listing 11-5 does not respond to any controls in its Handler() function. The next section will show what to do in that function.

FULLY CONTROLLED SERVICE

Implementing the Handler() function of a service application creates a *fully controlled service*. The service can tell the system that it is in any of the following seven states:

1. Stopped – no process object (or thread) exists for the service

2. Start pending – the service is completing its initialization and, when successful, will transition to the Running state

3. Running – the service is responding to requests from client applications

4. Pause pending – the service has been directed to suspend processing of client requests temporarily and it is transitioning into the Paused state

5. Paused – the service has suspended all processing of client requests, but is still running

6. Continue pending – the service has been directed to resume processing client requests and it is transitioning into the Running state from the Paused state

7. Stop pending – the service has been directed to stop and it is transitioning into that state

SCM rules govern the transitioning between these states. One such rule states that during a pending start or stop, no other controls are accepted. Connecting the `Handler()` function to the service such that it controls behavior properly requires the use of inter-thread communications primitives. Usually the thread initializes a set of anonymous event objects in the `ServiceMain()` function before calling the `RegisterServiceCtrlHandler()` API. Listing 11-6 is an example of a fully controlled service. It shows the use of an event object array to pass signals between the handler and the worker thread.

Listing 11-6: Fully controlled service with an event object array

```
// project eventhandler
#include <windows.h>
#include <fstream>
#include <string>


// ...
// function Log implementation omitted
// ...


//
// handles for pause, continue, and start
const int c_nEventCt = 3;
const int c_nEventIndexPause = 0;
const int c_nEventIndexContinue = 1;
const int c_nEventIndexStop = 2;
HANDLE  g_arEventControl[c_nEventCt];

// handle for setting service status
SERVICE_STATUS_HANDLE g_ssh = NULL;

// current status
DWORD g_dwStatus = SERVICE_STOPPED;

// send status about the service to the SCM
void SetStatus(DWORD dwStatus)
{
    // start with basic status
    SERVICE_STATUS ss = {
        SERVICE_WIN32_OWN_PROCESS,   // service in the process
        SERVICE_STOPPED,             // currently stopped
        SERVICE_ACCEPT_PAUSE_CONTINUE| // allow stopping and
            SERVICE_ACCEPT_STOP,     // pause-continue
        NO_ERROR,                    // exit code
        0,                           // exit code 2
```

```
        1,                          // checkpoint
        5000};                      // wait time for a response

    // pass the status on to the SCM
    ss.dwCurrentState = dwStatus;
    ::SetServiceStatus(g_ssh, &ss);

    // save the status internally
    g_dwStatus = dwStatus;
}


// handler for commands
VOID WINAPI Handler(DWORD dwCtl)
{
    // handle the controls we know how to
    switch(dwCtl)
    {
    case SERVICE_CONTROL_PAUSE:
        ::Log("Service received pause control.");
        ::SetEvent(g_arEventControl[c_nEventIndexPause]);
        break;
    case SERVICE_CONTROL_CONTINUE:
        ::Log("Service received continue control.");
        ::SetEvent(g_arEventControl[c_nEventIndexContinue]);
        break;
    case SERVICE_CONTROL_STOP:
        ::Log("Service received stop control.");
        ::SetEvent(g_arEventControl[c_nEventIndexStop]);
        break;

    // just reflect the current state to the SCM if we can't
    //   handle the control
    default:
        ::Log("Service received control<%d>", dwCtl);
        ::SetStatus(g_dwStatus);
        break;
    }
}


// logic for responding to a control signal, returns false when
//   the worker thread should end
bool HandleControl()
{
    bool bContinueRunning(true);
```

```
        // check for a pending event
        DWORD dwWait = ::WaitForMultipleObjects(
            c_nEventCt,           // events to poll
            g_arEventControl,     // the event array
            FALSE,                // wait for any of them to signal
            0);                   // just test and return the result

        // determine which event was signaled
        int nIndex = dwWait-WAIT_OBJECT_0;
        if(0<=nIndex && nIndex<c_nEventCt)
        {
            // clear the event
            ::ResetEvent(g_arEventControl[nIndex]);

            // act on it by setting the status and logging
            switch(nIndex)
            {
            case c_nEventIndexPause:
                ::SetStatus(SERVICE_PAUSED);
                ::Log("Service pausing...");
                break;
            case c_nEventIndexContinue:
                ::SetStatus(SERVICE_RUNNING);
                ::Log("Service continues...");
                break;
            case c_nEventIndexStop:
                ::SetStatus(SERVICE_STOP_PENDING);
                ::Log("Service stopping...");
                bContinueRunning = false;
                break;
            }

        }
    return(bContinueRunning);
}


// the work function for the service
VOID WINAPI ServiceMain(DWORD dwArgc, LPTSTR* lpszArgv)
{
    ::Log("Beginning ServiceMain of service <%s>",
        lpszArgv[0]);

    // initialize the handler events
    g_arEventControl[c_nEventIndexPause] =
```

```
        ::CreateEvent(NULL, TRUE, FALSE, NULL);
    g_arEventControl[c_nEventIndexContinue] =
        ::CreateEvent(NULL, TRUE, FALSE, NULL);
    g_arEventControl[c_nEventIndexStop] =
        ::CreateEvent(NULL, TRUE, FALSE, NULL);

    // register the handler function
    g_ssh = ::RegisterServiceCtrlHandler(lpszArgv[0], Handler);

    // notify that we are starting, then running
    ::SetStatus(SERVICE_START_PENDING);
    ::Log("Service<%s> starting.", lpszArgv[0]);
    ::SetStatus(SERVICE_RUNNING);
    ::Log("Service<%s> running.", lpszArgv[0]);

    // run through the loop, it only returns false when it is
    //   time to quit
    while(HandleControl())
    {
        // do some work while still running not if paused
        if(g_dwStatus==SERVICE_RUNNING)
        {
            ::Log("Doing some important work...");
            ::Sleep(1000);
        }
    }

    // clean up the handler event objects
    for(int nEvent=0;nEvent<c_nEventCt;++nEvent)
    {
        ::CloseHandle(g_arEventControl[nEvent]);
        g_arEventControl[nEvent] = INVALID_HANDLE_VALUE;
    }

    // tell the SCM that we've stopped
    ::SetStatus(SERVICE_STOPPED);
    ::Log("Service<%s> stopped.", lpszArgv[0]);
}

// the process starter
void main()
{
    ::Log("Service process starting.");
```

```
// table of services
SERVICE_TABLE_ENTRY arSvc[] =
{
    { "EventSimple", ServiceMain },
    { NULL, NULL }
};


// hand off the main thread to the SCM
if(!::StartServiceCtrlDispatcher(arSvc))
{
    ::Log("Error - Could not start dispatcher");
}


::Log("Service process terminating.");
}
```

Listing 11-6 shows the handler setting events and the new function, HandleControl(), governing the main work loop. The HandleControl() function returns success (true) until it receives the stop control. The body of the while loop that checks the events does no work if the service is in the paused state. Install this new service with the following command line:

```
sc create EventSimple binpath= c:\eventhandler.exe
```

Once installed, you can start, pause, continue, and stop the service. An example of a service control log for this fully controlled service is Listing 11-7.

Listing 11-7: Fully controlled service control log

```
[TID 1468]: Service process starting.
[TID 1432]: Beginning ServiceMain of service <EventSimple>
[TID 1432]: Service<EventSimple> starting.
[TID 1432]: Service<EventSimple> running.
[TID 1432]: Doing some important work...
[TID 1432]: Doing some important work...
[TID 1432]: Doing some important work...
[TID 1432]: Doing some important work...
[TID 1432]: Doing some important work...
[TID 1432]: Doing some important work...
[TID 1432]: Doing some important work...
[TID 1432]: Doing some important work...
[TID 1468]: Service received pause control.
[TID 1432]: Service pausing...
[TID 1468]: Service received continue control.
[TID 1432]: Service continues...
```

```
[TID 1432]: Doing some important work...
[TID 1432]: Doing some important work...
[TID 1432]: Doing some important work...
[TID 1432]: Doing some important work...
[TID 1432]: Doing some important work...
[TID 1468]: Service received stop control.
[TID 1432]: Service stopping...
[TID 1432]: Service<EventSimple> stopped.
[TID 1468]: Service process terminating.
```

You clearly can see the work being done in the log between the start and pause controls and then again between the continue and the stop control commands. The event objects are signaled on the main thread (TID 1468) while the worker thread (TID 1432) does its bidding.

Installing and configuring

In order to support configuration data storage and retrieval, the system grants the LocalSystem account access to the HKEY_LOCAL_MACHINE (also known as HKLM) registry hive. This account has no HKEY_CURRENT_USER (also known as HKCU) access since it is not a first-class user of Windows.

All of the configuration data for your service should be stored just as you would store it in HKCU, but with HKLM\Software\<company   name> \<product name>\<version number> as the root.

Often, production services are installed in the SCM using professional installers and should be configured using the Computer Management snap-in. To ease development and facilitate troubleshooting, engineers bake into the service EXE the ability to install and configure itself.

I usually do this by designing the service such that it does not require any command-line parameters from the SCM at startup time. When main() is executed with command-line arguments, the process knows that someone is installing or reconfiguring it and it should parse and respond. While this is not required, the effort required is minimal since you'll usually find usable source code in a free library or — at most — write it once and reuse it.

Supporting multiple services

The system makes it easy for you to design an EXE that actually exports more than one service. Looking back at Listing 11-4, you see that the parameter for the Start ServiceCtrlDispatcher() API tells the SCM the string name and address for the ServiceMain() using an array. This array of SERVICE_TABLE_ENTRY data has no predefined bounds and terminates with a null entry. This allows the SCM to start a thread for each name supplied (entering at the corresponding ServiceMain() function).

Each service from an EXE is addressed independently by the system in its specific Handler() method with the main thread of the process. All threads, and therefore services, exposed by an EXE share the process and process-wide variables.

In the multiple-service configuration, a single unhandled exception would crash not only the service in which it happens, but also all of the other services in the process. For this reason alone, I recommend against using this feature. One of the biggest reasons to wrap up an application as a service is to gain reliability (uptime), and you should give each process as good a chance as possible at delivering it. Delivering more than one EXE to the desktop or factoring your code out into shared libraries requires much less effort than fixing a problem in the field.

Event Logging and Performance

Now that you have the basic tools for creating services, you probably want to know what additional facilities you should interact with to create a first-class service. The two primary services are the event log and the performance monitor. A *secondary service* is the simple network management protocol that you can use for monitoring the state of your enterprise.

Event log

The event log is the central repository in the system for logging information, warnings, and errors that a service believes the administrator should be aware of in order to troubleshoot the service. Windows declares that you should use the event log to note things of interest that happen while your service is running – but it's up to you to decide what those things are.

First, let's look at the event log using the Event Viewer node of the MMC Computer Management snap-in (under System Tools). You can see that there are three separate logs. The first is for application-specific data; that's where your service will place messages. Another event log contains system security-related messages, while the last contains system-wide messages. The snapshot shows you where the Event Viewer lives in the computer management tree as well as some examples from my system log.

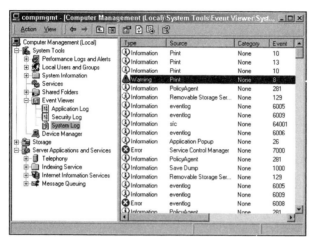

Figure 11-2: The event viewer of the Windows Computer Management snap-in

Figure 11-2 shows you that the event log classifies messages as information, warning, and error with each class having a distinctive icon. Next, the event viewer presents the source of event; this is where your service's application name goes. The viewer then presents the event's category, which each application defines specifically for its own purposes. Finally, the viewer presents the number of the event, as well as the date, time, user account running the process, and the computer on which the process ran in the list view.

The important information of a message in the event log is usually in its description. To get the description from the event viewer, simply double-click the entry or choose `Action...Properties...` from the menu bar. The Properties dialog box presents you with all of the information in the snap-in columns, plus a possibly long-winded explanation of what happened.

In order to add messages to the event log from your application, you must open an event log object with the `RegisterEventSource()` API. This function requires the name of the machine that owns the event log and the name of the application that is opening it. When you're finished with this object, you must call the `DeregisterEventSource()` API, handing it back the handle.

Once you have a valid handle to the event log, you can call the `ReportEvent()` API. This function takes all of the data displayed in the event viewer. Listing 11-8 shows you how to call this function and deliver data to the event log.

Listing 11-8: Writing a simple message into the event log

```
// project addevent
#include <windows.h>
```

```
#include <iostream>
#include <string>

void main()
{
    // get the string to log
    std::string strInfo;
    std::cout << "Enter something to place in the event log:"
        << std::endl;
    std::cin >> strInfo;

    // open up the event log for this application
    HANDLE hEventLog = ::RegisterEventSource(
        NULL,                   // no machine name - use the local
        "w2kdg.AddEvent");  // simple event source name
    if(hEventLog!=NULL)
    {
        // place the string from the user in a string array
        //  for the reporting function
        LPCTSTR arStr[2] = { NULL, NULL};
        arStr[0] = strInfo.c_str();

        // call the reporting function to deliver the string
        BOOL bReported = ::ReportEvent(
            hEventLog,  // the event log object
            EVENTLOG_INFORMATION_TYPE, // type of message
            0,      // no category
            0,      // no need to specify an ID
            NULL,   // no user SID
            1,      // strings sent
            0,      // additional data is zero length
            arStr,  // the single string
            NULL);  // no additional data

        // clean up the event log
        ::DeregisterEventSource(hEventLog);
        hEventLog = NULL;
    }
}
```

Listing 11-8 shows you how to register an event source, report an event, and then close up the event source. In the example, the reporting function takes mostly null parameters, which is perfectly acceptable for demonstration but not for production. In production service applications, you will create a MESSAGETABLE resource to attach to your executable that contains the strings that you write to the log. Internationalize this resource when you deliver the product to non-English platforms. You compile the resource with MC.EXE — the message compiler.

For more information on the message compiler, the message table resource, and the internationalization of application errors, see the MSDN library; search on "MESSAGETABLE".

The event log also supports access to administrator-level operations that you likely will never need. In order to gain access to the administrator functions, you need to access the singleton pseudo-kernel event log object with the OpenEventLog() API. I summarize the event log object APIs in Table 11-4. Of course, once you are finished with the event log object, you need to close it with the CloseEventLog() API.

TABLE 11-4 EVENT LOG OBJECT APIS

API Name	Description
OpenEventLog()	Creates a new handle to a singleton event log object on a machine; requires the name of the log of interest: Application, Service, or Security.
BackupEventLog()	Copies the current contents of the event log passed by handle to a disk file.
OpenBackupEventLog()	Creates a new handle to an event log object stored in a disk file.
ClearEventLog()	Erases the current contents of the passed event log after saving the content to a disk file.
GetNumberOfEventLog Records()	Retrieves the current count of records in the event log.
GetOldestEventLog Record()	Retrieves the 0-based index of the oldest record in the event log
ReadEventLog()	Fetches the details of an event log entry by 0-based index. It returns the data in an EVENTLOGRECORD structure.
GetEventLog Information()	Determines extra information about the event log; currently only supports a flag for whether the log is full or not.

Continued

TABLE **11-4 EVENT LOG OBJECT APIS** *(Continued)*

NotifyChangeEventLog()	Requires a handle to an event object. The system will signal this object when any process adds new event to the passed event log.
CloseEventLog()	Releases a reference to the passed event log object.

The event log APIs include OpenBackupEventLog(), BackupEventLog(), and ClearEventLog() for purging databases. The GetOldestEventLogRecord(), Get NumberOfEventLogRecords(), and ReadEventLog() APIs enable you to walk the event log database and examine its contents. A special API, GetEventLog Information(), lets you determine if the log is currently full. Finally, the NotifyChangeEventLog() API enables you to hand the system an event object to signal when a change is made to the event log object that you also hand it.

One word of caution when using the event log: It is not a substitute for internal tracing. Windows only expects your service to log events that could be useful when troubleshooting problems. Windows does not want you to use the event log for tracing out messages as I did in Listing 11-7.

Performance monitor

The next thing to add to your professional Windows service application is support for performance monitoring. The performance monitoring system provides a framework to report the status of an application without running it under the debugger. For example, an application might expose a count of consumed global resources (such as network sockets) or a count of unique resources (such as opened Web sessions). The performance monitoring application – either the MMC System Performance Monitor snap-in or the deprecated PerfMon.EXE – enumerates these counters in its GUI and enables the administrator to gather up logs of the values while displaying them in a graph.

In order to tell the performance monitor that you have values for it, you must tell it that your application has performance-monitoring counters. This information is stored in the system registry. For the system to collect this information, you must create a DLL to be loaded into the performance monitoring subsystem. That DLL communicates with your target application.

 I cover using the Windows registry Chapter 10, "Application Building Services."

The principal registry entries for your service are values in the `Performance` subkey under your service's hive:

```
HKLM\Software\CurrentControlSet\Services\<servicename>\Performance
```

The `Library` registry value under this key points to the DLL that the performance monitoring system connects to; this DLL exposes the open, collect, and close functions. These three main functions can be named anything you want – the `Open`, `Collect`, and `Close` registry values let the system know what the names are. Figure 11-3 shows you the contents of the `Performance` key for the `InetInfo` service.

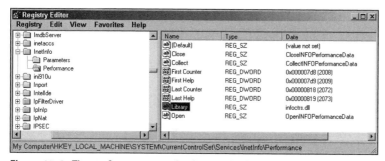

Figure 11-3: The performance monitoring entries in a service registry hive

The performance monitor DLL's open and close functions give your library the opportunity to initialize and shut down the interprocess communication that it uses to connect to the service. Typically, this is a named, memory-mapped file with a named mutex to guarantee thread synchronization. The DLL's collect function actually gathers the values from the performance counters.

In order to name the counters exposed by the performance monitor DLL's collect function, a bunch of complicated registry configuration must happen to select languages and store the data in Unicode. Luckily, the system supplies the `LodCtr.EXE` utility to reduce this task to a simple INI file creation. This mechanism delivers the names and descriptions to each counter that the performance monitor displays when you set up a log.

Setting up and collecting data from the application is an intricate task that involves filling a set of structures in the DLL's collect function. First, a `PERF_DATA_BLOCK` structure defines the signature of the performance data, including a version number and the number of performance objects contained. Next, the `PERF_OBJECT_TYPE` structure defines a named, described set of performance counters, including a default, a time stamp, and a code page. Along with the object type, a `PERF_COUNTER_DEFINITION` structure details the characteristics of the object's counters. Finally, the `PERF_COUNTER_BLOCK` actually contains the value of the count. Filling in this data for the performance monitor is a tedious exercise best left to boilerplate code, a template class library, or (at least) research on the *Microsoft Developer Network (MSDN)* library.

Chapter 17, "Delivering Applications," details the creation of a performance monitoring DLL.

Just as with event logging, the depth of support that you elect to add is a design choice. You can go to great lengths to support administration of your service with very detailed performance information, and some system administrator types will love using your service. On the other hand, you may choose to supply no performance information.

There is a performance penalty to collecting this information at runtime, but the benefits of the information usually far outweigh this usually minimal impact.

Simple Network Management Protocol

The *Simple Network Management Protocol (SNMP)* is a platform-neutral specification that creates an infrastructure for system administrators to monitor the state of their enterprises. Since Windows 2000 is focusing on being a great enterprise-level platform, it supplies a built-in SNMP agent service that starts at system boot.

For more information on the SNMP specification, you can begin with the Internet *Request For Comments (RFC)* that created it, RFC 1157. You can find this RFC and others online at http://www.cis.ohio-state.edu/hypertext/information/rfc.html.

The chief players in the SNMP architecture are *agents* and *managers* – and each is an individual process. Every SNMP-controlled system runs an SNMP agent that responds to requests from a manager. The administrator uses an SNMP system manager to interact with the SNMP agents. Currently, Windows does not supply a management console application for SNMP; you have to rely on third-party vendors.

The manager sends requests to an agent when it wants to effect a change on the part of the system that the agent is responsible for. Available verbs are limited to Get, Get-Next, and Set. These verbs should be sufficient to command and configure any application. This system enables administrators to control the entire enterprise from their SNMP management consoles.

Windows 2000 does not include an SNMP management application. To locate a commercial or free tool, see the "SNMP World" website at http://www. snmpworld.com/ for references.

Agent processes can send *alerts* to the manager when something interesting happens on the machine that it manages. Typically, the administrator filters these alerts, called *traps* in SNMP parlance, and passes some of them to a physical device such as a pager.

In order to participate in the SNMP system, you must create a special DLL that contains a *management information base (MIB)* describing the objects in your service to manage. You also must export a required set of functions from the DLL such as SnmpExtensionInit(), SnmpExtensionQuery(), and SnmpExtensionTrap() that allow the SNMP service to discover and use the MIB that describes management of your service. This DLL is simply added to the registry under the HKLM\ System\CurrentControlSet\Services\SNMP\Parameters\ExtensionAgents key with a numeric name one past the last integer found.

The details of creating and implementing an SNMP MIB are far beyond the scope of this book, and the actual work is complicated. When choosing whether to support SNMP in your service, you should consider the fact that it adds considerable ease of use to the administrator using its configuration support and it adds reliability with intelligent use of traps.

A great reference to get started using the Windows 2000 SNMP implementation and creating an SNMP MIB is *Managing Internetworks with SNMP*, 3rd Edition, by Mark A. Miller, P.E. (IDG Books Worldwide).

Security and Administration

Before concluding our discussion of service applications, you should be aware of a few more pieces of information. You need to choose the account that the service will run under carefully since it determines not only the resources that it has access to, but also the accounts that have access to it. Lastly, when creating a professional service, you'll need a way to configure it – the MMC snap-in architecture gives you the framework for doing just this.

I introduced the Microsoft Management Console (MMC) and snap-ins earlier this chapter, in the "How to Interact with Services" section.

Account security

When you create a system service application, one of the many parameters that you must specify in its configuration is the account name and password under which to run. The SCM uses this authentication information to make the kernel believe that it was that particular user who started the service process.

The system kernel has security very tightly integrated into every operation and uses the privileges token of the specified run-under account to gain access to all system resources. This means that when you specify the account of a member of the Administrators group, the service has the same access to files and network resources an administrator does. Likewise, when you specify an account that belongs only to the Guests group, the service only has access to resources that other guests do.

Chapter 3, "Using Kernel Objects," covers kernel object security.

This security architecture is a straightforward mechanism for controlling the access of a service application — but it is fraught with peril. An example of such peril is the classic *Internet Information Server (IIS)* problem: protecting the system against the whims of anonymous users. The IIS services run under an account that is typically the member of the Guests group. This choice for IIS gives first-time administrators headaches on a machine running the *NT File System (NTFS)*. This is because guests don't get Execute access throughout the machine automatically, rendering *Common Gateway Interface (CGI)* scripts useless until that privilege is manually granted to all guests or at least guests in the IIS script tree.

Running under the default account of LocalSystem grants the service all available privileges on the current machine. While LocalSystem does not grant network access permissions, it doesn't restrict the system from performing very damaging operations on that machine.

If you run your service under an account other than LocalSystem, especially an account with restricted privileges, any kernel or pseudo-kernel objects that you publish will need to properly set up security. This is a common problem when interacting with the IIS service for example; it usually runs under an account that is a member of the Guests group and has very few privileges. In order to expand the access that my objects grant other accounts and solve this problem, I have created the CGlobal AccessSA class.

Listing 11-9 shows you the simple `CGlobalAccessSA` definition and some test code. You can use an object of this class to grant all system accounts full access to a kernel object. This class replaces any reference to a `SECURITY_ATTRIBUTES` pointer in an object creation call with an instantiation.

Listing 11-9: Granting all access to a kernel object with a simple class

```cpp
// project easyaccess
#include <windows.h>
#include <iostream>
#include <string>

// Simple class to provide global access to a (psuedo-)kernel
//  object, simply instantiate one in any call requiring an
//  pointer to a SECURITY_ATTRIBUTES structure for setting
//  permissions. This class will grant all accounts full access
//  to the resulting object
class CGlobalAccessSA : public SECURITY_ATTRIBUTES
{
public:
    CGlobalAccessSA(bool _bInheritHandle=false)
    :
        SECURITY_ATTRIBUTES()
        ,m_pSD(NULL)
    {
        // create and initialize the SD
        m_pSD = static_cast<PSECURITY_DESCRIPTOR>
            (new BYTE[SECURITY_DESCRIPTOR_MIN_LENGTH]);
        ::InitializeSecurityDescriptor(
            m_pSD,                          // SD to initialize
            SECURITY_DESCRIPTOR_REVISION);  // current rev


        // set a NULL DACL for the security descriptor
        ::SetSecurityDescriptorDacl(
            m_pSD,    // SD to set a DACL
            TRUE,    // do want to present a DACL
            NULL,    // NULL DACL
            FALSE); // do not default the DACL

        // set internal members
        nLength = sizeof(SECURITY_ATTRIBUTES);
        lpSecurityDescriptor = m_pSD;
        bInheritHandle = _bInheritHandle!=0;
    }
```

```
~CGlobalAccessSA()
{
    // clean up our security descriptor
    delete [] m_pSD;
    m_pSD = NULL;
}

// casting to the base class, simply provide the this ptr
operator LPSECURITY_ATTRIBUTES()
{
    return(this);
}

protected:

    // security descriptor for global access
    PSECURITY_DESCRIPTOR m_pSD;
};

// class helper method to ensure that the class works, must be
//   run from an account with "Act as part of the Operating
//   System" privilege enabled
void TestGlobalAccessSA()
{
    // subkey to use for testing
    LPCTSTR c_strKey = "Software\\IDG Books\\"
        "Windows 2000 Developer's Guide\\GlobalSubkey";

    // create a new registry key with global access
    {
        HKEY hkeyNew(NULL);
        DWORD dwResult = ::RegCreateKeyEx(
            HKEY_LOCAL_MACHINE,     // hive to create under
            c_strKey,               // subkey name
            0,                      // reserved, must be 0
            NULL,                   // no class name
            REG_OPTION_NON_VOLATILE,// persist this
            KEY_ALL_ACCESS,         // returned handle access
            CGlobalAccessSA(),      // grant everyone access
            &hkeyNew,               // the result
            NULL);                  // don't need disposition

        // close it up if we created it
        if(dwResult==ERROR_SUCCESS)
        {
```

```
            std::cout << "Successfully opened global key: "
                "HKLM\\" << c_strKey << std::endl;
            ::RegCloseKey(hkeyNew);
            hkeyNew = NULL;
        }
    }


    // now, impersonate the machine's guest
    HANDLE hTokenGuest = NULL;
    if(::LogonUser(
        "Guest",      // account name
        ".",          // use the machine's database
        "",           // no password for guest
        LOGON32_LOGON_INTERACTIVE,  // simple type, guest can
        LOGON32_PROVIDER_DEFAULT,   // use the default provider
        &hTokenGuest))  // the resulting token
    {
        // impersonate the guest
        if(::ImpersonateLoggedOnUser(hTokenGuest))
        {
            // try to open the key
            HKEY hKeyOpen = NULL;
            DWORD dwResult = ::RegOpenKeyEx(
                HKEY_LOCAL_MACHINE,      // in HKLM
                c_strKey,                // key name
                REG_OPTION_NON_VOLATILE,// persistent
                KEY_ALL_ACCESS,          // get all access
                &hKeyOpen);              // result
            if(dwResult==ERROR_SUCCESS)
            {
                std::cout << "Opened key HKLM\\" << c_strKey
                    << " from Guest account" << std::endl;

                // clean up the key
                ::RegCloseKey(hKeyOpen);
                hKeyOpen = NULL;
            }

            // become ourself again
            ::RevertToSelf();
        }

        // clean up the token
        ::CloseHandle(hTokenGuest);
        hTokenGuest = NULL;
```

```
    }
}

void main()
{
    ::TestGlobalAccessSA();
}
```

You can see in Listing 11-9 that the actual class definition and implementation is quite straightforward. The constructor of the class simply initializes a *Discretionary Access Control List (DACL)* to NULL in a new *Security Descriptor (SD)* that is then set into the object's base *Security Attributes (SA)*. The conversion operator that casts instances of the class to SA pointers enables you to create an instance inline to the object's creating API call.

There is also interesting code in the local TestGlobalAccessSA() function. This function creates an object (a registry key in HKLM) then logs on as Guest and tries to open it. Guest users do not get access to the HKLM hive by default in Windows 2000 so this ensures that the class did its job.

 In order to successfully execute the LogonUser() API and then ImpersonateLoggedOnUser(),you must have the Act as part of the Operating System privilege enabled for your account.

MMC snap-in

Windows administration tools have come quite a long way since the old days of 16-bit Windows 3.1. A concerted effort to centralize administration in the Microsoft Management Console (MMC) is obvious in the Windows 2000 system. MMC is a simple document/view backbone that can run one or more snap-in modules to configure and administer a service or application.

The MMC application does little more than host these snap-ins for an administrator. When you run MMC, you can add and remove various available modules and then persist the configuration in a file with the .MSC extension. For example, in order to set the proper privileges for myself when constructing Listing 11-9, I created a new console with the Local Computer Policy snap-in.

Content in a snap-in appears first as nodes in the left-hand tree of the MMC, called the *scope pane*. When you begin expanding the nodes in the scope pane, the contents of the right-hand pane (called the *results pane*) change according to the snap-in logic.

Each snap-in module is an in-process COM server that implements a required set of interfaces, including IComponentData and IComponent. The former presents data in the scope pane, while the latter presents data in the results pane. These objects call back into MMC using the `IConsole2` and `IConsoleNameSpace2` interfaces to manage the user interface.

To let MMC know that you have a snap-in for it, simply add data under the `HKLM\Software\Microsoft\MMC\SnapIns` subkey. Placing a *Globally Unique Identifier (GUID)* for your `IComponent` lets the program know what COM (Component Object Model) object to create, using the `CoCreateInstance()` API, when it wants to access your snap-in.

Chapter 10, "Application Building Services," covers COM objects and GUIDs.

In addition to simple node enumeration and content filling, the snap-in architecture helps you provide a bunch of very powerful facilities to the administrator. In your snap-in, you can implement the `ISnapinAbout` and `ISnapinHelp` interfaces to let the MMC integrate your version information and help into its unified presentation to the user. The `IExtendContextMenu`, `IExtendControlBar`, and `IExtendPropertySheet2` interfaces enable you to add custom GUI components to the right-click menu, the toolbar, and the Properties dialog box for a data item. The `IResultOwnerData` and `IResultDataCompare` interfaces give you fine control over the sorting and contents of the results pane. Finally, the `IEnumTASK` interface interacts with the *taskpad*, which is a simplified version of MMC for quickly accessing operations you use often.

The MMC application provides you a myriad of helper interfaces – for example, `IToolbar`, `IHeaderCtrl`, `IMenuButton`, and `IControlBar` to add GUI components to the client area for manipulating your snap-in.

To simplify your snap-in experience, the *Active Template Library (ATL)* version 3.0 supplied with Visual C++ has an MMC snap-in object wizard. This takes most of the pain out of simple snap-in creation and makes the programming model straightforward. Listing 11-10 shows you the interesting code from a very simple ATL snap-in that simply walks the file system, beginning at the `C:` drive root.

Chapter 10, "Application Building Services," shows you how to use ATL to create COM objects.

Listing 11-10: ATL snap-in that walks the file system

```
// project snapsimple, file SnapSimple.h
#ifndef __SNAPSIMPLE_H_
```

```
#define __SNAPSIMPLE_H_
#include "resource.h"
#include <atlsnap.h>
#include <list>

class CSnapSimpleData : public CSnapInItemImpl<CSnapSimpleData>
{
    // ...
    // pointing the node to a folder
    void SetFolderName(const std::string& strFolderPath,
                       const std::string& strFolder);
    void SetFolderName(const std::string& strFolderPath);

    // expanding the node to find children
    void Expand();
    HRESULT OnExpand(CComQIPtr<IConsoleNameSpace,
        &IID_IConsoleNameSpace>& spConsoleNameSpace,
        long param);

    // custom data definitions for the folder snap-in
    std::string m_strFolder;
    typedef std::list<CSnapSimpleData*> CNodelist;
    CNodelist m_listFolder;
};

// project snapsimple, file SnapSimple.cpp
//
// Custom code
//

CSnapSimple::CSnapSimple()
{
    // when creating the root object, make sure the folder
    //  name gets set to the drive root
    CSnapSimpleData* pNode = new CSnapSimpleData;
    pNode->SetFolderName("c:");
    m_pNode = pNode;
    _ASSERTE(m_pNode != NULL);

    // Wizard generated...
    m_pComponentData = this;
}

// save the folder full path and name
```

```
void CSnapSimpleData::SetFolderName(
    const std::string& strFolderPath,
    const std::string& strFolder)
{
    m_strFolder = strFolderPath;
    m_bstrDisplayName = strFolder.c_str();
}
void CSnapSimpleData::SetFolderName(
    const std::string& strFolderPath)
{
    SetFolderName(strFolderPath, strFolderPath);
}


void CSnapSimpleData::Expand()
{
    // only fill up if not already done
    if(m_listFolder.empty())
    {
        // set up the search string
        std::string strSearch = m_strFolder;
        strSearch +="\\*";

        // loop through the found list
        WIN32_FIND_DATA fd;
        HANDLE hFind = ::FindFirstFile(strSearch.c_str(), &fd);
        bool bMore(true);
        while(bMore && hFind!=INVALID_HANDLE_VALUE)
        {
            // check for a folder and not (. or ..)
            if(fd.dwFileAttributes==FILE_ATTRIBUTE_DIRECTORY &&
                fd.cFileName[0]!='.')
            {
                // construct the full path
                std::string strFolderPath = m_strFolder;
                strFolderPath += "\\";
                strFolderPath += fd.cFileName;

                // create a new child node
                CSnapSimpleData* pNode = new CSnapSimpleData;
                pNode->SetFolderName(strFolderPath,
                    fd.cFileName);

                // add it to the list
                m_listFolder.push_back(pNode);
```

```
            }

                bMore = ::FindNextFile(hFind, &fd)!=0;
            }
        }
    }


    // this method responds to the user requesting the expansion
    //  of the node by creating the children and
    HRESULT CSnapSimpleData::OnExpand(CComQIPtr<IConsoleNameSpace,
            &IID_IConsoleNameSpace>& spConsoleNameSpace,
            long param)
    {
        HRESULT hr = S_OK;

        // make sure the child nodes are created
        Expand();

        // loop through the children
        CNodelist::const_iterator iter = m_listFolder.begin();
        while(iter!=m_listFolder.end() && SUCCEEDED(hr))
        {
            // create a backing data structure for the scope
            //  pane and call the base member function to fill
            SCOPEDATAITEM sdi;
            ::ZeroMemory(&sdi, sizeof(sdi));
            sdi.mask = SDI_STR|SDI_PARAM|SDI_IMAGE|
                SDI_OPENIMAGE|SDI_PARENT;
            (*iter)->GetScopePaneInfo(&sdi);

            // reset the display name and param for the callback
            sdi.displayname = MMC_CALLBACK;
            sdi.relativeID = param;

            // add the new item to the console scope
            hr = spConsoleNameSpace->InsertItem(&sdi);

            // move on
            ++iter;
        }
        return(hr);
    }
```

The example snap-in from Listing 11-10 uses the simplified programming model of the ATL classes to quickly create data items that represent the folders of the file system. The `CSnapSimpleData` class is firstly a node in the scope pane as implemented in ATL; secondly, it is the name of a file system directory. I simply add the full path name as a data member, then I wrap all child folders of that folder in the same class and hold them in a list. Figure 11-4 displays the results when you add the snap-in to a console.

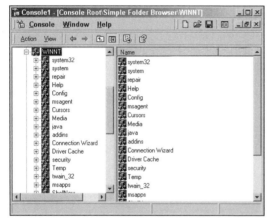

Figure 11–4: The simple folder browser snap-in hosted in the MMC

You can easily and quickly expand this example by adding commands for the administrator to execute on the folders and supplying additional data about the folders and files in the results pane. The amount of code to create the snap-in was minimal and it saved writing lots of mundane support software. The snap-in framework definitely simplifies the job of the administrator through its consistent interface; it simplifies your job by supplying a small set of interfaces for you to implement rather than requiring you to design and implement a full-blown administration application.

Summary

I've covered a lot of ground in this chapter. I showed you what service applications could do for you and how the SCM owns their configuration and manages their lifetime. I explained how to programmatically install, configure, and control a system service application, and then I showed you the basics of creating one along with an SDK tool, `SC.EXE`, which is an invaluable development aid. Next, I covered a couple of the main support facilities for service applications: the event log, the performance monitor, and SNMP. I wrapped up by covering some security issues and how to create snap-ins for the MMC application.

The next thing you need to know is the Windows memory management architecture. Chapter 12 walks you through how your application interacts with the system to store and retrieve temporary data.

Chapter 12

Memory Management

IN THIS CHAPTER

- ◆ Windows memory architecture
- ◆ Virtual memory
- ◆ Application heaps
- ◆ Memory extensions

THIS CHAPTER COVERS WINDOWS 2000's use of memory and shows you how you can manage memory in your application. Windows presentation of memory to your application is unique in its simplicity and protection. In addition, with most programming languages you won't even notice what the operating system is doing for you under the covers. You will just notice that your application works and that other applications don't prevent it from doing so.

The coverage begins with an overall look at the architecture of Windows 2000's memory, then dives into virtual memory management. Next, I examine process heaps along with some extensions that Windows provides for using the memory.

Windows Memory Architecture

Often, coverage of the Windows memory architecture – as based on Windows NT – gets wistful over how tough it was to work with memory over some size or how other systems let you crash them by writing over part of the executive. I won't look back here. You don't need to know all the work that Windows 2000 does for you behind the scenes; you just get to take advantage of it.

Windows 2000 is a 32-bit operating system. Beneath, the CPU natively uses 32-bit wide addresses to manipulate 32-bit wide chunks of memory. Each byte of memory is individually addressable using a 32-bit pointer – making the maximum possible memory size 2^{32} bytes or $4*2^{10}*2^{10}*2^{10}$ bytes or 4 *gigabytes (GB)*. Windows makes each application it runs think that it owns each byte of that possible 4GB.

The fact that the Windows 2000 operating system makes the application think it owns all of the possible 4GB makes the memory virtual. Few machines have 4GB of physical RAM, and even fewer have 4GB for each process. Windows maps *virtual memory (VM)* addresses into physical addresses transparently to each process. The big advantage that you, as the application programmer, get from virtual memory is that you never need to worry about impacting another application or the system – you can't. Windows maps your virtual memory address to its physical memory address behind the scenes for you and does not allow you to access another process's physical memory.

Physical memory is the RAM that the manufacturer installs in your system, plus the paging file that Windows allocates at the root of your drive. The system completely manages all physical memory; you have little control over what physical memory you use or when you use it. The system takes care of mapping a virtual memory address (e.g., 0x00400000) to a real byte in physical memory somewhere. In fact, most Windows EXE files get loaded into memory at the same virtual address of 0x00400000; since Windows is able to load many into memory simultaneously, the code for each must get mapped to a different physical memory location. Moreover, the system hides the fact that it is a virtual address and not an actual physical address from each application.

When a process needs to use memory for data or executable storage, it tells the system that it wants to use part of its virtual memory space. It also tells the system to back that part of its memory space with physical memory and how it intends to access the memory (read-only, read-write, and so on). This assignment of physical memory to your virtual address space is mostly out of your control – it just happens for you.

Windows makes sure it grabs exactly the memory that your application needs by allocating space in RAM, in the page file, or both. Windows moves your physical memory out of RAM and into the page file whenever it needs the (more precious) RAM for another virtual memory region.

When you attempt to access physical memory backing a virtual address that Windows has moved into the page file, it interrupts the access and moves it back into RAM (moving a region of memory from your process or another into the page file). This is an expensive operation in terms of execution time.

Windows gives you an API, `GetSystemInfo()`, that enables you to inspect some of the characteristics of virtual memory in your system. Listing 12-1 shows you how to call this function and displays the current memory values for your system.

Listing 12-1: Getting information about the system's memory settings

```
// project vmeminfo
#define _WIN32_WINNT 0x0500
#define WINVER 0x0500
#include <windows.h>
#include <iostream>
```

```
#include <shlwapi.h>
#include <iomanip>
#pragma comment(lib, "shlwapi.lib")

void main()
{
    // first, let's get the system information
    SYSTEM_INFO si;
    ::ZeroMemory(&si, sizeof(si));
    ::GetSystemInfo(&si);

    // format some sizes using the shell helper
    TCHAR szPageSize[MAX_PATH];
    ::StrFormatByteSize(si.dwPageSize, szPageSize, MAX_PATH);

    DWORD dwMemSize = (DWORD)si.lpMaximumApplicationAddress -
        (DWORD)si.lpMinimumApplicationAddress;
    TCHAR szMemSize[MAX_PATH];
    ::StrFormatByteSize(dwMemSize, szMemSize, MAX_PATH);

    // dump the memory info out
    std::cout << "Virtual memory page size: " << szPageSize
        << std::endl;

    std::cout.fill('0');
    std::cout << "Minimum application address: 0x"
        << std::hex << std::setw(8)
        << (DWORD)si.lpMinimumApplicationAddress
        << std::endl;
    std::cout << "Maximum application address: 0x"
        << std::hex << std::setw(8)
        << (DWORD)si.lpMaximumApplicationAddress
        << std::endl;

    std::cout << "Total available virtual memory : "
        << szMemSize << std::endl;
}
```

Listing 12-1 shows you that you have nearly 2GB available as memory to your applications (actually 2GB minus two 64KB guard sections at the top and bottom). It also shows you that the page size for virtual memory is 4KB, which means that any allocation of virtual memory actually happens in a multiple of 4096 bytes.

The 64KB guard sections in the virtual memory space are Windows way of protecting you from programming errors. Any attempt to access those portions of memory (read, write, or execute) generates an access violation, which raises an exception and stops execution. That is, if you have a NULL pointer (address 0) and attempt to de-reference an address some short distance after it, you most likely will attempt to read from or write to the lower guard block and generate an exception.

While the results I'm quoting for system information are typical, Windows is releasing a version of the operating system, Advanced Server, which gives applications 3GB of available virtual address space. Very large, data intensive server applications such as databases that have been constrained by the 2GB limit in most Windows systems welcome this extra space. In addition, the now-defunct versions of Windows written for non-Intel processors used different page sizes.

Windows also provides an API to gather general statistics about the current state of system memory. This API, GlobalMemoryStatusEx(), is shown in Listing 12-2 which examines the state of your system's memory.

Listing 12-2: Gathering general information about the state of the Windows memory

```
// project memstat
#define _WIN32_WINNT 0x0500
#define WINVER 0x0500
#include <windows.h>
#include <iostream>
#include <shlwapi.h>
#include <iomanip>
#pragma comment(lib, "shlwapi.lib")

// helper method to format and display memory stats
void DisplayMemory(DWORDLONG ullAvail, DWORDLONG ullTotal)
{
    TCHAR szAvail[MAX_PATH];
    ::StrFormatByteSize(ullAvail, szAvail, MAX_PATH);
    TCHAR szTotal[MAX_PATH];
    ::StrFormatByteSize(ullTotal, szTotal, MAX_PATH);

    std::cout << "available: " << szAvail
        << ", total: " << szTotal;
}

void main()
```

```
{
    // allocate and retrieve the memory status
    MEMORYSTATUSEX msx;
    ::ZeroMemory(&msx, sizeof(msx));
    msx.dwLength = sizeof(msx);
    if(::GlobalMemoryStatusEx(&msx))
    {
        // show current load
        std::cout << "Memory utilization: " << msx.dwMemoryLoad
            << "%" << std::endl;

        // show the virtual mem
        std::cout << "Virtual memory ";
        ::DisplayMemory(msx.ullAvailVirtual,
            msx.ullTotalVirtual);
        std::cout << std::endl;

        // show the physical memory
        std::cout << "Physical memory ";
        ::DisplayMemory(msx.ullAvailPhys, msx.ullTotalPhys);
        std::cout << std::endl;

        // show the page file memory
        std::cout << "Page file memory ";
        ::DisplayMemory(msx.ullAvailPageFile,
            msx.ullTotalPageFile);
        std::cout << std::endl;

        // show VLM stats
        TCHAR szVLM[MAX_PATH];
        ::StrFormatByteSize(msx.ullAvailExtendedVirtual,
            szVLM, MAX_PATH);
        std::cout << "VLM: " << szVLM << std::endl;
    }
}
```

The program in Listing 12-2 shows a very straightforward API. The call to Windows GlobalMemoryStatusEx() function is very simple and returns a MEMO-RYSTATUSEX structure that contains all of the information that you might want about the current state of memory. First, it gives you a loading of the system memory (0-100%). Then you get access to the currently unreserved portion of the virtual memory space and the total available space (slightly less than 2GB usually). The structure also gives you the used and available sizes of RAM and the page file. Finally, for systems with *very large memory (VLM)* available, it tells you exactly how much is unreserved.

Virtual Memory

The virtual address space of 4GB is broken into two main partitions: one for the process, covering the lower 2GB; and one for the system, covering the high 2GB. This means that your application's code, including DLLs, is loaded into the process address space (in the lower 2GB), and all of the data your process uses reside there.

The virtual address space of your process is broken into regions that are *free*, *committed*, or *reserved*:

◆ Committed regions of virtual memory have backing physical memory; you can write to, read from, or execute from these regions depending on access privileges.

◆ Reserved regions of virtual memory do not have backing physical memory, but do have associated access privilege.

◆ Free regions of virtual memory are not marked for any use and have the PAGE_NOACCESS privilege associated with them.

A privilege associated with a region of virtual memory tells the system what types of operations the process can perform on the memory. For example, you cannot write to or execute from a region with the PAGE_READONLY privilege. You also cannot write to or read from a region with the PAGE_EXECUTE privilege. The special PAGE_NOACCESS privilege means that the process should not attempt to use the address for any operation.

Just before a process is loaded, the entire virtual memory address space is marked as free with the PAGE_NOACCESS privilege. As the system loads the process's code and data, it marks regions of the address space as committed or reserved and associates privileges such as PAGE_EXECUTE, PAGE_READWRITE, and PAGE_READONLY with them.

Virtual memory inspection

The system provides a simple method for looking at the current state of a process's virtual memory, region by region — the VirtualQueryEx() API. This API enables you to inspect the size and attributes of any virtual memory address in a process that you specify. Listing 12-3 uses VirtualQueryEx() to walk its own virtual memory space.

Listing 12-3: Walking the virtual address space of a process

```
// project vmwalker
#define _WIN32_WINNT 0x0500
#define WINVER 0x0500
#include <windows.h>
#include <iostream>
```

```cpp
#include <shlwapi.h>
#include <iomanip>
#pragma comment(lib, "shlwapi.lib")

// helper methods to display the protection in human-readable
//  form for the user. The protection mask indicates what type
//  of access the application is allowed to make to the
//  memory and is enforced by the operating system
inline bool TestSet(DWORD dwTarget, DWORD dwMask)
{
    return((dwTarget & dwMask)==dwMask);
}
#define SHOWMASK(dwTarget, type) \
    if(TestSet(dwTarget, PAGE_##type))\
        {std::cout << "," << #type; }
void ShowProtection(DWORD dwTarget)
{
    SHOWMASK(dwTarget,READONLY);
    SHOWMASK(dwTarget,GUARD);
    SHOWMASK(dwTarget,NOCACHE);
    SHOWMASK(dwTarget,READWRITE);
    SHOWMASK(dwTarget,WRITECOPY);
    SHOWMASK(dwTarget,EXECUTE);
    SHOWMASK(dwTarget,EXECUTE_READ);
    SHOWMASK(dwTarget,EXECUTE_READWRITE);
    SHOWMASK(dwTarget,EXECUTE_WRITECOPY);
    SHOWMASK(dwTarget,NOACCESS);
}


// worker method to walk through virtual memory and display
//  its attributes for the user
void WalkVM(HANDLE hProcess)
{
    // first, let's get the system information
    SYSTEM_INFO si;
    ::ZeroMemory(&si, sizeof(si));
    ::GetSystemInfo(&si);

    // allocate a buffer to hold the information
    MEMORY_BASIC_INFORMATION mbi;
    ::ZeroMemory(&mbi, sizeof(mbi));

    // loop through the entire application address space
    LPCVOID pBlock = (LPVOID)si.lpMinimumApplicationAddress;
```

```
while(pBlock<si.lpMaximumApplicationAddress)
{
    // fetch the info for the next block of virtual memory
    if(::VirtualQueryEx(
        hProcess,                    // process of interest
        pBlock,                      // starting location
        &mbi,                        // buffer
        sizeof(mbi))==sizeof(mbi))   // size verification
    {
        // calculate the end of the block and its size
        LPCVOID pEnd = (PBYTE)pBlock + mbi.RegionSize;
        TCHAR szSize[MAX_PATH];
        ::StrFormatByteSize(mbi.RegionSize, szSize,
            MAX_PATH);

        // display the block address and size
        std::cout.fill('0');
        std::cout
            << std::hex << std::setw(8) << (DWORD)pBlock
            << " - "
            << std::hex << std::setw(8) << (DWORD)pEnd
            << (::strlen(szSize)==7?" (":" ( ") << szSize
            << ") ";

        // show the state of the block
        switch(mbi.State)
        {
        case MEM_COMMIT: std::cout << "Committed"; break;
        case MEM_FREE: std::cout << "Free"; break;
        case MEM_RESERVE: std::cout << "Reserved"; break;
        }

        // show the protection
        if(mbi.Protect==0 && mbi.State!=MEM_FREE)
        {
            mbi.Protect = PAGE_READONLY;
        }
        ShowProtection(mbi.Protect);

        // show the type
        switch(mbi.Type)
        {
        case MEM_IMAGE: std::cout << ",Image"; break;
        case MEM_MAPPED: std::cout << ",Mapped"; break;
```

```
        case MEM_PRIVATE: std::cout << ",Private"; break;
        }

        // check for an executable image
        TCHAR szFilename[MAX_PATH];
        if(::GetModuleFileName(
            (HMODULE)pBlock,// module handle actually vm
            szFilename,        // fully specified file name
            MAX_PATH)>0)      // buffer size actually used
        {
            // strip off the path and show
            ::PathStripPath(szFilename);
            std::cout << ",Module: " << szFilename;
        }

        std::cout << std::endl;

        // move the block pointer to get the next block
        pBlock = pEnd;
        }
    }
}


void main()
{
    // walk the virtual memory of the current process
    ::WalkVM(::GetCurrentProcess());
}
```

Listing 12-3 shows a very straightforward function, WalkVM(), that begins at the lowest virtual address available to a process and displays the characteristics of each block of virtual memory within it. A block of virtual memory is defined by the VirtualQueryEx() API as a contiguous block or memory with the same state (free, committed, and so on) and allocated with a uniform set of protection flags (read-only, execute, and so on).

The application in Listing 12-3 produces the results shown in Figure 12-1. Note the highlighted line that shows a 1.86GB free region with no access. Most of the virtual address space is never allocated from the system, and any attempt to read, write, or execute from the space generates a system exception.

Listing 12-3 also shows you how to interpret the MEMORY_BASIC_INFORMATION structure that the VirtualQueryEx() API fills; I detail the members of this structure in Table 12-1. This data describes the current state of a set of virtual memory pages in the process virtual memory space. The State field tells you if the region is free, committed, or reserved. The Protect field indicates what types of access protection Windows enforces on the region. The Type field tells you that the region is part of an executable image, a memory-mapped file, or simply private memory.

TABLE **12-1** MEMBERS OF THE MEMORY_BASIC_INFORMATION STRUCTURE

Member Name	Intention
PVOID BaseAddress	A pointer to the beginning of the virtual memory region.
PVOID AllocationBase	Pointer to the outside region of virtual memory if this particular region is a sub-allocation; otherwise this value is identical to BaseAddress.
DWORD AllocationProtect	Protection attributes on the originally allocated region of virtual memory. Possible values include PAGE_NOACCESS, PAGE_READONLY, PAGE_READWRITE, and PAGE_EXECUTE_READ.
DWORD RegionSize	The byte count for the region of virtual memory.
DWORD State	The current allocation state of the region. Possible values are MEM_COMMIT, MEM_FREE, and MEM_RESERVE.
DWORD Protect	Protection attributes for the current region of virtual memory. Possible values are the same as for the AllocationProtect member.
DWORD Type	Type of pages present in the region of virtual memory. Possible values are MEM_IMAGE, MEM_MAPPED, and MEM_PRIVATE.

The example in Listing 12-3 takes advantage of a well known, but unsupported, fact that an executable's module handle is actually the address of its image mapped into memory. The GetModuleFileName() API attempts to interpret the address that marks the beginning of each region of virtual memory and succeeds for the application EXE and each implicitly linked DLL module; this success is shown in the output Figure 12-1 as the readable module names.

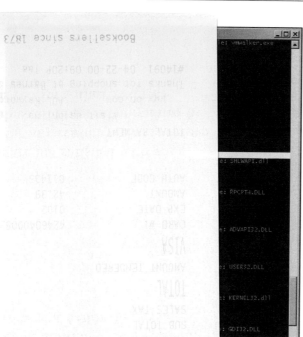

Listing 12-3 highlight the large free

...ation

...ry, I will show you how to manipulate it.
...ry APIs that let you finely control the vir-
...summarize these virtual memory manipu-
...

API Name	Description
VirtualQueryEx()	Inspects a region of virtual memory within a process by filling a MEMORY_BASIC_INFORMATION structure
VirtualAlloc()	Reserves or commits a portion of virtual memory for the process, setting allocation and protection flags

Continued

TABLE **12-2 VIRTUAL MEMORY APIS** *(Continued)*

API Name	Description
VirtualFree()	Releases or de-commits a portion of the virtual address space from application use
VirtualProtect()	Changes the protection specifications for a region of virtual memory
VirtualLock()	Protects the system from swapping a region of virtual memory into the page file by the system
VirtualUnlock()	Releases a locked region of virtual memory, permitting the system to swap it into the page file when necessary

The workhorse for virtual memory allocation is the VirtualAlloc() API. This API enables you to ask the system for new virtual memory or change the current state of already allocated memory. For new allocations, you can specify a desired starting address or let the system select one by passing NULL. The function also requires the size of the memory to be allocated or changed. The system rounds this size to the appropriate boundary of a virtual memory page. (I determined the size of a page in Listing 12-1.)

There are two modes that you can tell the system you want to use the virtual memory with VirtualAlloc(). One simply reserves memory in the address space; the other asks the system to back part of the address space with physical memory (space in RAM or the paging file). You specify these modes with the flAllocation Type parameter, which can have values such as *commit* and *reserve*. Finally, you must specify the access protection that you want Windows to enforce on the new region of virtual memory. You can tell Windows to treat the region as read-only, read-write, no-access, a variety of execute modes, or as a couple of special-purpose modes.

The companion API to VirtualAlloc() is, of course, VirtualFree(). This function enables you to release committed or reserved pages from the virtual memory space. You also can change committed pages to reserved pages with the dwFree Type parameter.

A helper API for VirtualAlloc() is VirtualProtect(). Use Virtual Protect() to alter the protection specification for a region of virtual memory. This can be very helpful if you temporarily want to guard a memory block from being written to, even from your own application – for instance, when you're tracking down a bug.

You typically won't use the direct virtual memory manipulation APIs in your application – only for operations involving very large size data. For example, when creating a database application, you may want to keep large portions of the database in memory to speed read operations and take advantage of large amounts of available RAM. Yet you probably don't want to spend the time up-front copying the entire database into memory. The example in Listing 12-4 shows you how to allocate a very large portion of memory, commit physical storage to a small portion of it (1/1000th), and then use that portion.

Listing 12-4: Allocating and using a large chunk of memory

```
// project largealloc
#define _WIN32_WINNT 0x0500
#define WINVER 0x0500
#include <windows.h>
#include <iostream>

// simple method to attempt to fill a block of memory with
//   zeros up to the length specified
void FillZero(LPVOID pBlock, DWORD dwSize)
{
    __try
    {
        BYTE* arFill = (BYTE*)pBlock;
        for(DWORD dwFill=0;dwFill<dwSize;++dwFill)
        {
            arFill[dwFill] = 0;
        }
        std::cout << "Memory zeroed." << std::endl;
    }
    __except(EXCEPTION_EXECUTE_HANDLER)
    {
        std::cout << "Could not zero memory." << std::endl;
    }
}


void main()
{
    // simple constants
    DWORD c_dwGigabyte = 1<<30;
    DWORD c_dwMegabyte = 1<<20;

    // use malloc to grab a 1GB chunk
    {
        LPVOID pBlock = ::malloc(c_dwGigabyte);
        ::FillZero(pBlock, c_dwMegabyte);
        ::free(pBlock);
```

```
    }

    // use valloc to grab a physical 1GB chunk
    {
        LPVOID pBlock = ::VirtualAlloc(
            NULL,            // don't specify beginning address
            c_dwGigabyte,    // ask for 1GB
            MEM_COMMIT,      // ask to commit physical storage
            PAGE_READWRITE);// read-write to it
        ::FillZero(pBlock, c_dwMegabyte);
        ::VirtualFree(pBlock, 0, MEM_RELEASE);
    }

    // use valloc to grab a virtual 1GB chunk
    {
        LPVOID pBlock = ::VirtualAlloc(
            NULL,            // don't specify beginning address
            c_dwGigabyte,    // ask for 1GB
            MEM_RESERVE,     // don't commit physical storage
            PAGE_READWRITE);// read-write to it
        ::FillZero(pBlock, c_dwMegabyte);
        ::VirtualFree(pBlock, 0, MEM_RELEASE);
    }

    // use valloc to grab a virtual 1GB chunk and commit the
    //   beginning 1MB
    {
        LPVOID pBlock = ::VirtualAlloc(
            NULL,            // don't specify beginning address
            c_dwGigabyte,    // ask for 1GB
            MEM_RESERVE,     // don't commit physical storage
            PAGE_READWRITE);// read-write to it

        ::VirtualAlloc(
            pBlock,
            c_dwMegabyte,
            MEM_COMMIT,
            PAGE_READWRITE);

        ::FillZero(pBlock, c_dwMegabyte);
        ::VirtualFree(pBlock, 0, MEM_RELEASE);
    }
}
```

Listing 12-4 shows you that in order to reserve a 1GB segment of the address space for your database, you can't commit physical storage to the entire region up front. The listing shows four methods of memory allocation – one of which works. The first technique attempts to use the standard C malloc() function, which must grab memory from an already committed small pool and fails. The second technique attempts to allocate the entire chunk with the VirtualAlloc() API, again with physical backing, anywhere in the virtual address space. This technique works only on machines that have more than 1GB of RAM, plus paging file. The third technique uses the VirtualAlloc() API to grab a large chunk, which succeeds, but does not commit any physical memory into that chunk.

The final, successful method of allocation shown in Listing 12-4 reserves the 1GB region and then commits physical memory to a very small (1MB) portion of it. This is what you would do with the hypothetical database application that led into Listing 12-4 – reserve the entire chunk, then read in small portions of it on demand, letting the system page under-used regions out to disk for you.

One way that Windows enables you to control the behavior of the virtual memory in your process space is with the VirtualLock() API. This function and its companion API, VirtualUnlock(), prevent or permit a block of virtual memory from being paged out of physical RAM and into the page file. This lets you tell the system that a particular region of memory requires such high responsiveness to the user that the system should not remove it from RAM. Of course, if you were to mark all of your virtual address space as locked, the system would come to a standstill in attempting to page every other piece of working memory in the system to disk.

Application Heaps

Since virtual memory allocations must occur on system page boundaries (typically 4KB), it is not practical to use if for fine-grained allocations. That is, using this scheme to allocate and free small chunks of memory (e.g., a simple 10-member integer array) is quite wasteful and chews up lots of extra physical backing for virtual memory that the system could give to another process. Worse, allocating space with the virtual allocator (the VirtualAlloc() API) frequently causes Windows 2000 to move other physical memory to the page file (often at the most inopportune times) causing a serious system performance slowdown.

Windows provides processes with the facility to dynamically allocate and free memory in very small chunks. Windows calls this facility an *application heap*. A heap handles this memory management in an efficient manner in terms of resources and performance.

A heap is a large chunk of physical memory that you get to reserve small portions by using a simple set of APIs. These APIs place what amounts to a linked list of structures that span the large chunk of memory. Each structure points to the next structure, has a flag marking it as in use or not, and owns a portion of the memory starting at a specific address with a specific number of bytes. There is always at least one member of the linked list that is not in use and holds all of the memory from the last in-use block to the end of the heap space. When the heap creates a new in-use member of the list of allocations, it tries to find a member of sufficient size already in the list; but it may have to extract a new in-use member from the anchor member.

Typically, an application allocates and frees chunks of memory thousands or millions of times during its lifetime. The heap takes care of handing out this memory to the process by reusing as much of the original backing physical memory as possible. The application must be sure to release each block that it allocates; otherwise, it may begin demanding physical memory from the system and degrading overall performance.

Heap life cycle

A Windows 2000 heap is a kernel object that is manipulated with the APIs that I summarize in Table 12-3. You instantiate it from the system with the `Heap Create()` API. `HeapCreate()` takes an options parameter and boundaries for the initial and maximum sizes and returns a handle to the object. When finished with the heap, you destroy it with the `HeapDestory()` API.

Chapter 3, "Using Kernel Objects," introduces kernel objects.

TABLE **12-3** APPLICATION HEAP APIS

API Name	Description
HeapCreate()	Creates a new heap object with an initial and maximum size, returning a handle.
HeapDestroy()	Releases the heap object and returns its resources to the system.
HeapAlloc()	Reserves a block of memory from the heap, returning a pointer to the memory.
HeapRealloc()	Resizes a block of memory in the heap, returning a pointer to the new block.
HeapFree()	Releases a block of memory reserved with HeapAlloc() to the heap for reuse.

API Name	Description
HeapSize()	Retrieves the size of a block from the heap when supplied the pointer to the beginning of that block.
HeapCompact()	Attempts to coalesce adjacent free blocks of memory within the heap in order to facilitate faster allocations.
HeapValidate()	Walks through the heap to verify that no corruption has occurred.
HeapWalk()	Iterates through each block in the heap, allowing you to inspect its contents.
HeapLock()	Prevents other threads in the process from allocating or freeing blocks in the heap. Used during setup for operations such as HeapWalk().
HeapUnlock()	Releases an inter-thread lock on a heap.

During normal application development, the C++ runtime library takes care of managing the lifetime of a central heap for you. Before the process's main thread enters the application's main(), WinMain(), or ServiceMain() function, the heap is created. It is destroyed once execution leaves the prime entry point.

During the life of the heap, you call the HeapAlloc() and HeapFree() APIs to grab and release chunks of memory. Typically, the C/C++ code maps the standard malloc()/new() methods to the former API and the free()/delete() methods to the latter API. This enables you to use your familiar, platform-independent coding tools to take advantage of the operating system's heap manager.

The Visual C++ compiler ships the source code to the C++ runtime library. Feel free to browse into the memory management implementation. You'll find that files, such as Malloc.C and Free.C, make very interesting reading.

In addition to the standard allocate and free methods, the heap enables you to reallocate memory from the heap. That is, like the realloc() C function, you can grow or shrink the size of a chunk of memory dynamically. This is something that none of the virtual memory APIs let you do. In order to resize a chunk of memory, use the HeapRealloc() API and make sure to use the returned pointer in place of the sent one even when shrinking the memory—Windows will feel free to move your block rather than just trim its size down. Of course, the C realloc() function typically is mapped to this API in the runtime library.

While you have memory allocated from the heap, you can take advantage of a couple of heap management facilities that Windows 2000 provides. First, the HeapCompact() API attempts to speed up heap operations by joining together fragmented free space within the heap. The HeapValidate() API walks through each block in the heap (whether in use or free) and makes sure that each is consistent. This function typically catches block overruns that happen when an application writes past the end of an allocated block. HeapValidate() also can check a single block, but that's seldom done. Finally, the HeapWalk() API enables you to scan through the heap block by block and inspect its contents.

Listing 12-5 is a simple heap-walker application that demonstrates the lifetime of a heap. It shows you how to create, allocate from, and walk a heap with the use of the HeapCreate(), HeapAlloc(), and HeapWalk() APIs.

Listing 12-5: The full lifetime of a process heap and its internals

```
// project walkheap
#define _WIN32_WINNT 0x0500
#define WINVER 0x0500
#include <windows.h>
#include <iostream>
#include <shlwapi.h>
#include <iomanip>
#pragma comment(lib, "shlwapi.lib")

// ShowBlock() is a helper function to display the contents
//  of a PROCESS_HEAP_ENTRY block from a process heap
inline bool TestSet(DWORD dwTarget, DWORD dwMask)
{
    return((dwTarget & dwMask)==dwMask);
}
#define SHOWMASK(dwTarget, type) \
    if(TestSet(dwTarget, PROCESS_HEAP_##type))\
        {std::cout << #type << " "; }
void ShowBlock(const PROCESS_HEAP_ENTRY& phe)
{
    // show the address
    std::cout.fill('0');
    std::cout <<"\tData:\t\t"
        << std::hex << std::setw(8)
        << (DWORD)phe.lpData << std::endl;

    // format the sizes
    TCHAR szSize[MAX_PATH];
    ::StrFormatByteSize(phe.cbData, szSize, MAX_PATH);
    TCHAR szOverhead[MAX_PATH];
```

```
    ::StrFormatByteSize(phe.cbOverhead, szOverhead, MAX_PATH);

// show the simple data
std::cout
    << "\tBlock size:\t" << szSize  << std::endl
    << "\tOverhead:\t"   << szOverhead << std::endl
    << "\tRegion #:\t"   << (int)phe.iRegionIndex
        << std::endl;

// show the flags
std::cout << "\tFlags:\t\t";
if(phe.wFlags==0)
{
    std::cout << "FREE";
}
else
{
    SHOWMASK(phe.wFlags, REGION);
    SHOWMASK(phe.wFlags, UNCOMMITTED_RANGE);
    SHOWMASK(phe.wFlags, ENTRY_BUSY);
    SHOWMASK(phe.wFlags, ENTRY_MOVEABLE);
    SHOWMASK(phe.wFlags, ENTRY_DDESHARE);
}
std::cout << std::endl;

// handle a region entry
if(TestSet(phe.wFlags, PROCESS_HEAP_REGION))
{
    // show the used and free space in the heap
    TCHAR szCommitted[MAX_PATH];
    ::StrFormatByteSize(phe.Region.dwCommittedSize,
        szCommitted, MAX_PATH);
    TCHAR szFree[MAX_PATH];
    ::StrFormatByteSize(phe.Region.dwUnCommittedSize,
        szFree, MAX_PATH);
    std::cout
        << "\tUsed:\t\t" << szCommitted << std::endl
        << "\tFree:\t\t" << szFree << std::endl;

    // show the addresses of the first and last blocks
    std::cout.fill('0');
    std::cout <<"\tFirst block:\t"
        << std::hex << std::setw(8)
        << (DWORD)phe.Region.lpFirstBlock << std::endl;
```

```
                std::cout << "\tLast block:\t"
                    << std::hex << std::setw(8)
                    << (DWORD)phe.Region.lpLastBlock << std::endl;
        }
    }


void main()
{
    // first, grab the handle to the current heap
    HANDLE hHeap = ::HeapCreate(
        HEAP_GENERATE_EXCEPTIONS,    // throw exceptions
        10 << 10,                    // start with 10kb
        10 << 20);                   // stop at 10Mb
    if(hHeap!=NULL)
    {
        // allocate a large and small block
        LPVOID pLarge = ::HeapAlloc(
            hHeap,                  // heap to grab from
            HEAP_ZERO_MEMORY,       // initialize the block
            1024);                  // grab 1k
        LPVOID pSmall = ::HeapAlloc(
            hHeap,                  // heap to grab from
            HEAP_ZERO_MEMORY,       // initialize the block
            1);                     // grab 1 byte

        // now, walk the heap
        PROCESS_HEAP_ENTRY phe;
        ::ZeroMemory(&phe, sizeof(phe));
        while(::HeapWalk(hHeap, &phe))
        {
            // check for matches
            if(phe.lpData==pLarge)
            {
                std::cout << "Found large block" << std::endl;
                ::ShowBlock(phe);
            }
            else if(phe.lpData==pSmall)
            {
                std::cout << "Found small block" << std::endl;
                ::ShowBlock(phe);
            }
            else
            {
                std::cout << "Anonymous block" << std::endl;
```

```
        ::ShowBlock(phe);
      }
   }

   // clean up the blocks
   ::HeapFree(hHeap, 0, pLarge);
   pLarge = NULL;
   ::HeapFree(hHeap, 0, pSmall);
   pSmall = NULL;
}

   // clean up the heap
   ::HeapDestroy(hHeap);
}
```

The simple heap walker in Listing 12-5 goes through the work of creating its own heap, allocating a couple of blocks, then displaying the results. The code is straightforward — HeapCreate() makes the heap that initially asks for 10KB from the system and may grow to 10MB. Next, a 1KB and a 1-byte block are reserved with HeapAlloc(). The HeapWalk() API begins at the start of the heap when it sees a null PROCESS_HEAP_ENTRY and runs through the entire heap. (It turns out there are only five entries.) Each entry in the heap is detailed to std::cout with the ShowBlock() helper function. The results are shown in Figure 12-2.

Figure 12-2: Heap block internals from the heap created in Listing 12-5

You can see the five entries in the heap from Listing 12-5 in Figure 12-2. The first entry is the header, called a *region block*, which gives statistics on the current heap utilization and its location in the virtual address space. You should see that 12KB are used. That's the specified initial size (10KB) rounded up to the next 4KB virtual memory page, while nearly the rest of the maximum size (10MB) is free. The next two blocks are the ones that I allocated. The first is the 1KB and the second is the 1-byte block. After the blocks that the program allocated is a free block with the remaining unused memory from the heap's 12KB. Last in the list is the block that holds the remaining reserved virtual memory that does not have physical memory committed to it.

Heap internals

There are remaining details about the heap that you might find interesting, but those details are beyond the scope of this book. I've shown you the tools to inspect virtual memory. The `Heap32ListFirst()` and `Heap32First()`APIs from the tool help library, `TlHelp32.DLL`, can give you some additional information about the makeup of the heap. The program in Listing 12-6 shows you how to look at the heaps in a process with the use of these two APIs.

Chapter 18, "Development Support," covers the tool help library in detail.

Listing 12-6: Examining heaps in a process

```
// project heaplist
#define _WIN32_WINNT 0x0500
#define WINVER 0x0500
#include <windows.h>
#include <iostream>
#include <shlwapi.h>
#include <iomanip>
#include <tlhelp32.h>
#pragma comment(lib, "shlwapi.lib")

DWORD GetHeapSize(HANDLE hHeap)
{
    // walk the heap and find the region block
    BOOL bFound(FALSE);
    PROCESS_HEAP_ENTRY phe;
    ::ZeroMemory(&phe, sizeof(phe));
    while(::HeapWalk(hHeap, &phe) && !bFound)
    {
        bFound = (phe.wFlags & PROCESS_HEAP_REGION)!=0;
```

```
    }

    // use the region block's statistics for the size
    DWORD dwSize(0);
    if(bFound)
    {
        dwSize = phe.Region.dwCommittedSize;
    }
    return(dwSize);
}

void main()
{
    // first, get the current heaps in the process
    HANDLE hSnapshot = ::CreateToolhelp32Snapshot(
        TH32CS_SNAPHEAPLIST, 0);
    if(hSnapshot!=NULL)
    {
        // buffer to hold heap info
        HEAPLIST32 hl;
        ::ZeroMemory(&hl, sizeof(hl));
        hl.dwSize = sizeof(hl);

        // loop through the heaps
        BOOL bFound = ::Heap32ListFirst(hSnapshot, &hl);
        while(bFound)
        {
            // list details of the heap
            std::cout << "Heap ID: " << hl.th32HeapID;
            if((hl.dwFlags & HF32_DEFAULT)!=0)
            {
                std::cout << " (default)";
            }

            // get the heap handle
            HEAPENTRY32 he;
            ::ZeroMemory(&he, sizeof(he));
            he.dwSize = sizeof(he);
            BOOL bMoreEntries = ::Heap32First(&he,
                hl.th32ProcessID, hl.th32HeapID);
            if(bMoreEntries)
            {
                // look up the size of the heap and report it
                DWORD dwSize = ::GetHeapSize(he.hHandle);
```

```
            TCHAR szSize[MAX_PATH];
            ::StrFormatByteSize(dwSize, szSize, MAX_PATH);
            std::cout << " size: " << szSize;
        }
        std::cout << std::endl;

        // move to the next heap
        bFound = ::Heap32ListNext(hSnapshot, &hl);
    }
    }
}
```

The code in Listing 12-6 shows you how to use the tool help library to take a snapshot of the heaps in a process, then walk through that list with the Heap32 ListNext() API. The list indicates which one is the default and assigns each a *heap identifier (HeapID)*. The Heap32First() API retrieves information on each heap in the process wrapped in a HEAPENTRY32 structure. The program then takes the handle from the HEAPENTRY32 structure and finds the size of the heap by calling into the GetHeapSize() helper function which in turn calls into the HeapWalk() API to find the block in the heap that contains the pertinent information. When you run this program, you find that this simple process has three different heaps — one allocated by the EXE and two from the linked system DLLs.

Windows also supplies some helper APIs for managing heaps. A process heap supplies an API called HeapSize() that retrieves the allocated size for a block of memory when you supply it with the pointer to the beginning. The HeapLock() and HeapUnlock() APIs prevent other threads from accessing the heap while the calling thread is accessing it. This prevents other threads from allocating or freeing memory and blocks them until the locking thread releases. Heaps are intrinsically thread-safe, but you can turn off the protection at create time if you know that only one thread can possibly access a heap and you need the additional performance of not testing a guarding critical section object on each allocation.

 Chapter 4, "Commonly Used Kernel Objects," covers critical section objects.

In the past, you as the application designer had to be very cautious about heap management since all processes on the system shared the memory space. This is not the case in Windows 2000. You have your own memory space, and while the system does give it to you from a shared source, only very severe memory leaks impact other processes. Also, since heaps and the virtual memory space are kernel objects, when the owning process terminates, all of those objects are released and all of the resources are returned to the shared pool. All memory and other resource use ends with the process termination.

Memory Extensions

In addition to the core virtual memory management and heap facilities that every application uses, Windows supplies some interesting memory management extensions. These extensions include utility functions, file mappings, and address windowing extensions (AWE). I will cover these topics briefly in this section.

Utility functions

Windows provides just a few utilities for working with memory within your process. You've already seen some of them used in various examples in the book, so let's go over them:

- `ZeroMemory()` API: This API runs through and clears out a block of memory. You must supply the pointer to the start and the number of bytes to zero.

- `FillMemory()` API: This API is very similar to the `ZeroMemory()` API except it loads a block of memory with a supplied byte-wide value, usually other than zero.

- `CopyMemory()` API: The `CopyMemory()` API duplicates a block of memory from one location to another, but the blocks cannot overlap. This API simply takes the pointers to the source and destination blocks along with the size.

- `MoveMemory()` API: The `MoverMemory()` API, like the `CopyMemory()` API, duplicates a block of memory from one location to another. In this case, the memory blocks can be overlapping. This API also requires pointers to the source and destination blocks along with the block size.

Windows also provides some useful helper routines for avoiding access violations. Access violations occur when you attempt to perform an operation on memory that your process has disallowed when it specified protection rights on that region of virtual memory. For example, writing to the 0x00400000 address, which typically is the beginning of the EXE code segment, generates an access violation. The helper utilities are as follows:

- `IsBadReadPtr()` API: This API takes the address and size of a memory block and makes sure that read access is available to the process throughout the block.

◆ `IsBadWritePtr()` API: In a similar fashion to the `IsBadReadPtr()` API, this API makes sure that write access is available to an entire block..

◆ `IsBadStringPtr()` API: This API makes sure that read access is available to a memory block, terminating either at the end of the block size specified or at a string terminator (null byte).

◆ `IsBadCodePtr()` API: This API checks for execute privileges at the passed address (no block size is required).

File mappings

In Chapter 4, I showed you the basics of memory-mapped files. Now that you have a good understanding of the virtual memory architecture of Windows, let's revisit the mechanism.

To refresh your memory, a file mapping is a kernel object created with the `CreateFileMapping()` API that enables you to access the contents of a permanent or temporary file as a block of memory in your virtual address space. That is, Windows 2000 matches up data from your address space to data on the disk, then lets you read or write it as if it were RAM. This mechanism is intrinsic to Windows since it is identical to using the page file to extend virtual memory.

In order to use a file mapping, you must specify the file. You can specify a file kernel object from the `CreateFile()` API, which requires a persistent file to back it. You also can ask the system to commit some physical memory to your mapping object. Think of this as a temporary or RAM file. To create a temporary file, simply specify `INVALID_HANDLE_VALUE` to the `CreateFileMapping()` API in place of a real file handle.

The file mapping backed by a temporary file is much the same as simply calling `VirtualAlloc()` API and committing storage to the region — except for the ability to give this mapping a name. Naming the file-mapping object allows another process to open it up when security permits and gives you the ability to exchange data with that process. This memory-mapped file mechanism is one of the more common ways for processes to communicate since it is so simple.

In order to begin accessing data within the file mapping object, you simply call the `MapViewOfFile()` API, which commits physical memory to the process and copies data from the backing file to it. This data represents the current values on the disk and, if modified, becomes the future values on the disk. If you have proper access to the memory-mapped file view, you can treat it just like any other block of memory and read or write to it randomly.

When you release the mapping with the `UnmapViewOfFile()` API, the data writes to the backing file. You also can force this to happen with the `FlushView OfFile()` API. If the file is temporary, the data gets written to the page file. Closing the file mapping with the `CloseHandle()` API releases the committed physical memory.

Address windowing extensions

Hardware is quickly evolving from 32-bit architectures to 64-bit architectures, and manufacturers are building systems that have very large physical memory spaces. In order to support systems with more than 2GB of physical memory, Windows 2000 now supports a transitional API called *address windowing extensions (AWE)*.

AWE creates views on the 64-bit wide memory and maps them to 32-bit memory to give you access from within your application. This technique is not new to 32-bit Windows; it was used during the transition from 8-bit to 16-bit and 16-bit to 32-bit architectures.

The basic premise behind AWE is that your application can request Windows to map some of the physical RAM above the 2GB mark into its virtual address space. This bypasses the traditional hands-off approach to committing physical memory to a process that Windows enforces.

Currently, there is no API that returns a 64-bit size for the available physical RAM. However, AWE works no matter how much RAM your system has. You can use the `GlobalMemoryStatusEx()` API to determine that the available physical memory is 2GB or more and use AWE.

To use the additional physical memory, you must first tell Windows to set aside part of your virtual address space for it. This is magic. Windows translates calls that reference memory in this newly allocated address space to calls to the higher-than-2GB RAM using the AWE device driver for the system without you knowing. The allocation uses the same `VirtualAlloc()` call that you used in the earlier section on virtual memory, but adds the `MEM_PHYSICAL` flag to the `MEM_RESERVE` flag to tell Windows that you will commit the memory to the region manually.

Next, you must tell Windows to set aside part of the high memory for your application. The `MapUserPhysicalPages()` API commits the memory for you. You must supply this function with the address of the virtual memory to fill, the number of pages within that region, and an array of page handles to fill. You also must calculate the number of virtual memory pages you are mapping manually, using the `GetSysteminfo()` API to find the page size discussed earlier. Windows fills the array of handles for you so that you can free them later.

When the mapping succeeds, you can use the memory as if it were any other memory in the system — Windows takes care of mapping it to the higher region for you. When you are finished with it, you must call the `FreeUserPhysicalPages()` API to return the RAM to the system. Of course, you also need to call the `VirtualFree()` API on the region to reclaim it in your address space.

The AWE API turns out to be very small and reasonably powerful since you get to lock RAM into your application in large chunks when it is available. Of course, there are some restrictions. You cannot share the memory with another process or set protection flags on it yourself — it's always read/write. Also, even though you don't have a way to know how many pages of RAM are available in the system, you don't want to lock down too many of them with the `MapUserPhysicalPages()` API — the system cannot give non-AWE applications virtual memory.

Summary

I've shown you a lot of fun stuff in this chapter. You now have a good understanding of the way Windows 2000 looks at memory from the architecture section and of how to use virtual memory for large allocations. You also should be familiar with the heaps from which a process can allocate small chunks of memory for use. Finally, you now have an idea of some of the extensions of the memory architecture that Windows offers to you: utility functions, file mappings, and address windowing.

The next thing you need to know about creating great applications for Windows is the file system. Chapter 13 gives you the tools you need to get the most out of the Windows file system.

Chapter 13

The File System

IN THIS CHAPTER

- ◆ File input/output APIs
- ◆ Windows 2000 file systems
- ◆ NTS features

THE FILE SYSTEM IN WINDOWS 2000 manages the information stored on disk drives. The operating system supplies many APIs that enable applications to access files in the file system. In this chapter, I first review some of the basic Win32 file input/output APIs and then describe how you can take advantage of some of the file-system features that Windows 2000 provides.

File Input/Output APIs

The Win32 API provides many API functions for file *input/output (I/O)*. It provides API functions that allow an application to create, open, read from, write to, and delete files. It also provides functions for searching and monitoring the file system. Table 13-1 lists and describes some of the common file I/O APIs. The following sections will describe these APIs in detail.

TABLE 13-1 COMMON FILE I/O APIS

File I/O API Function	Description
CreateFile()	Creates or opens a file, console, communication port, directory, disk device, mailslot, or pipe kernel object, and returns the handle to that object
DeleteFile()	Deletes the existing file passed by a string filename

Continued

TABLE 13-1 COMMON FILE I/O APIS *(Continued)*

File I/O API Function	Description
GetFileSize()	Returns the 32-bit (less than 4GB) size of the file specified by the passed object handle
GetFileSizeEx()	Returns the 64-bit size of the file specified by the passed object handle
GetTempFileName()	Creates a name for a temporary file
GetTempPath()	Returns the path used to store temporary files
FindFirstFile()	Searches a directory for a file that matches the specified name; returns a handle to the result set kernel object
FindFirstFileEx()	Searches a directory for a file that matches the specified name and attributes; returns a handle to the result set kernel object
FindNextFile()	Searches a directory for the next file in the passed result set kernel object that matches the search criteria
FindClose()	Closes the specified file search kernel object handle
FindFirstChangeNotification()	Creates a change notification kernel object for the specified change filter conditions and returns its handle
FindNextChangeNotification()	Tells the system to continue monitoring change notifications with the kernel object passed by handle
FindCloseChangeNotification()	Stops monitoring change notification and closes the kernel object handle
ReadFile()	Reads the specified number of bytes from a file passed by an object handle synchronously or asynchronously
ReadFileEx()	Reads the specified number of bytes from a file passed by an object handle asynchronously

File I/O API Function	Description
WriteFile()	Writes the specified data to a file passed by an object handle synchronously or asynchronously
WriteFileEx()	Writes the specified data to a file passed by an object handle asynchronously

Chapter 3, "Using Kernel Objects," covers creating and manipulating kernel objects such as files, file finds, and file change notifications.

Creating and opening files

The CreateFile() API creates or opens a file and a kernel object that represents that file. The CreateFile() API takes a file name, the desired access, the share mode, the security attributes, the creation flags, the file attributes, and a template file. I detail these parameters in Table 13-2. In addition to files, you can use the CreateFile() API to create and/or open the following kernel objects: consoles, communication ports, directories, disk devices, mailslots, and pipes. When you are finished using a file, you call the CloseHandle() API to free the resources associated with the file handle.

Chapter 15, "Additional System Services," covers consoles, mailslots, and pipes in more detail.

The following code snippets show several different ways to use the CreateFile() API. For example, the following code snippet opens an existing file for synchronous reading:

```
HANDLE hFile = CreateFile(strFileName, GENERIC_READ, 0,
    NULL, OPEN_EXISTING, 0, NULL);
```

The following code creates a new file, ready synchronous writing:

```
HANDLE hFile = CreateFile(strFileName, GENERIC_WRITE, 0,
    NULL, CREATE_NEW, FILE_ATTRIBUTE_NORMAL, NULL);
```

The following code opens an existing file for asynchronous reading:

```
HANDLE hFile = CreateFile(strFileName, GENERIC_READ, 0,
    NULL, OPEN_EXISTING, FILE_FLAG_OVERLAPPED, NULL);
```

Finally, the following code shows how to open a communications (COM) port for reading and writing:

```
HANDLE hComPort = CreateFile( "COM1", GENERIC_READ | GENERIC_WRITE,
    0, NULL, OPEN_EXISTING, 0, NULL );
```

As shown in the above code snippets, the `CreateFile()` API takes several parameters. Table 13-2 describes each of these parameters.

TABLE 13-2 CREATEFILE() PARAMETERS

Parameter	Description
`LPCTSTR lpFileName`	Specifies the name of the object to create or open. This name is dependant on the type of object; it can be a file name, communications port, pipe name, or other identifier.
`DWORD dwDesiredAccess`	Specifies the type of access for the file handle. This parameter can be 0, `GENERIC_READ`, or `GENERIC_WRITE`, or any combination of these values. A value of zero indicates that you just want to obtain device attributes, such as the file size; this information can be obtained without actually opening the file or device.
`DWORD dwShareMode`	Specifies the share mode for the handle. You can specify no sharing, read-only sharing, write-only sharing, and delete sharing — or any combination of these values.
`LPSECURITY_ATTRIBUTES lpSecurityAttributes`	Specifies the security descriptor for the object. If you specify `NULL` for this parameter, the object gets the default security descriptor.

Parameter	Description
DWORD dwCreationDisposition	Specifies how CreateFile() resolves creation issues. Table 13-3 lists the possible values for this parameter.
DWORD dwFlagsAndAttributes	Specifies the file attributes. Table 13-4 lists the possible values for this parameter.
HANDLE hTemplateFile	Specifies a file handle that supplies the file attributes for the file that is created.

The dwCreationDisposition parameter allows you to specify what action the CreateFile() API should take on files that already exist or on files that do not exist. Table 13-3 lists the possible values you can specify for this parameter.

TABLE 13-3 POSSIBLE DWCREATIONDISPOSITION VALUES FOR THE
CREATEFILE() API

Value	Description
CREATE_NEW	Creates a new file. CreateFile() fails if the file already exists.
CREATE_ALWAYS	Creates a new file. CreateFile() overwirtes the existing file if it already exists.
OPEN_EXISTING	Opens an existing file. CreateFile() fails if the file does not exist.
OPEN_ALWAYS	Opens the file if it exists; creates a new file if it does not.
TRUNCATE_EXISTING	Opens and truncates the size of the file to 0. CreateFile() fails if the file does not exist.

For additional information about values for the dwCreateDisposition parameter, see the documentation for the CreateFile() API on the MSDN.

The `dwFlagsAndAttributes` parameter allows you to specify the attributes for a file in the `CreateFile()` API. Table 13-4 lists the most commonly used values for this parameter.

TABLE 13-4 POSSIBLE DWFLAGSANDATTRIBUTES VALUES FOR THE CREATEFILE() API

Value	Description
`FILE_ATTRIBUTE_ARCHIVE`	Specifies that the file be archived
`FILE_ATTRIBUTE_ENCRYPTED`	Specifies that the file or directory be encrypted
`FILE_ATTRIBUTE_HIDDEN`	Specifies that the file is hidden
`FILE_ATTRIBUTE_NORMAL`	Specifies that the file has no other attributes set
`FILE_ATTRIBUTE_NOT_CONTENT_INDEXED`	Specifies that the file not be indexed by the indexing service
`FILE_ATTRIBUTE_READONLY`	Specifies that the file is read only
`FILE_ATTRIBUTE_SYSTEM`	Specifies that the file is used by the operating system
`FILE_ATTRIBUTE_TEMPORARY`	Specifies that the file is used for temporary storage
`FILE_FLAG_WRITE_THROUGH`	Specifies that the system write through any caching and go directly to disk.
`FILE_FLAG_OVERLAPPED`	Specifies that file operations be performed asynchronously
`FILE_FLAG_NO_BUFFERING`	Specifies that the system open the file with no buffering or caching
`FILE_FLAG_RANDOM_ACCESS`	Specifies that the file will be accessed randomly
`FILE_FLAG_SEQUENTIAL_SCAN`	Specifies that the file will be accessed from beginning to end
`FILE_FLAG_DELETE_ON_CLOSE`	Specifies that the system delete the file after its handles are closed
`FILE_FLAG_BACKUP_SEMANTICS`	Specifies that the file be accessed for a backup or restore operation

If the CreateFile() API succeeds, it returns a handle to a kernel object that represents the specified disk file. If the function fails, it returns INVALID_HANDLE_VALUE. You can use the GetLastError() API to receive more detailed error information.

Chapter 18,"Development Support," covers using the GetLastError() API.

Reading from and writing to files

Once you have created a new file or opened an existing file, use the ReadFile() and WriteFile() APIs to read and write to the file. The ReadFile() API reads a specified number of bytes starting from the current file position. The WriteFile() API writes the specified data to the file beginning at the current position.

The ReadFile() and WriteFile() APIs can be used for both synchronous and asynchronous file operations. In addition, the kernel provides the ReadFileEx() and WriteFileEx() APIs that are designed specifically for asynchronous I/O operations. I cover these APIs in the "Reading from and writing to a file asynchronously" discussion later in this section.

Listing 13-1 shows a code snippet for reading from a file. Listing 13-2 shows a code snippet for writing to a file.

Listing 13-1: Reading from a file

```
long nFileSize = GetFileSize(hFile, NULL);
DWORD nBytesRead(0);

BOOL bResult = ReadFile(hFile,
    m_strFileContents.GetBuffer(nFileSize),
    nFileSize, &nBytesRead, NULL);
m_strFileContents.ReleaseBuffer(-1);
```

Listing 13-2: Writing to a file

```
long nFileSize = m_strFileContents.GetLength();
DWORD nBytesWritten(0);

BOOL bResult = WriteFile(hFile,
    m_strFileContents, nFileSize, &nBytesWritten, NULL);
```

The ReadFile() API in Listing 13-1 takes an object handle to read from, a pointer to a buffer to receive the data, the size of the buffer and the number of bytes actually read, and a pointer to an overlapped structure that is used for asynchronous file operations. The API returns a nonzero value if the operation succeeds and zero if it fails. The example uses the `GetFileSize()` API to retrieve the size of the file. It then passes that value to the `ReadFile()` in order to read the entire contents of the file.

Windows 2000 provides the `GetFileSizeEx()` API to allow you to retrieve the size of files greater than 4GB.

The `WriteFile()` API in Listing 13-2 takes an object handle, a buffer to write to the object, the number of bytes to write, a buffer to receive the number of bytes actually written, and a pointer to an overlapped structure that is used for asynchronous file operations. The API returns a nonzero value if the operation succeeds and zero if it fails.

When reading from and writing to a file, you can use the `GetLastError()` API to obtain more detailed error information if either operation fails.

Creating and using temporary files

Often it is useful to create a temporary file to store data while your application is running. You can use the `GetTempPath()` API to obtain the Windows temporary directory. Windows 2000 enables a user to specify where the system should store temporary files using the `TMP` and `TEMP` environment variables. The path returned by the `GetTempPath()` API is the path specified by the `TMP` environment variable (if one is defined). If no `TMP` variable is defined, then the API uses the path defined by the `TEMP` variable. If neither environment variable is specified, it returns the Windows directory.

To create a temporary file name, you use the `GetTempFileName()` API. The `GetTempFileName()` API enables you to specify a prefix string for the temporary file name. The `GetTempFileName()` API uses the first three characters from this string as the first characters of the temporary file name. You also specify a unique number that the API converts to hexadecimal and uses for the remainder of the file name. Generally, specify zero for this value. In this case, the system generates a number based on the current system time and keeps generating file names until it finds a name that does not exist already, and then it creates the file. If you specify a nonzero value, the system does not check to see if a file with the same name exists and does not create a new file.

Chapter 17, "Delivering Applications," covers the use of temporary files.

Figure 13-1 shows a sample application that presents a dialog box you can use to generate temporary file names. The application allows you to enter a prefix string and a unique number. When you click the "Generate Temp File" button, the application will display the resulting temporary file name. Listing 13-3 shows the code used to generate the temporary file names with the `GetTempPath()` and `GetTempFileName()` APIs.

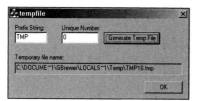

Figure 13-1: Temporary file name sample application

Listing 13-3: Creating a temporary file

```
//
// void CTempfileDlg::OnGenerateTemp(): called to generate a
//      temporary file name
//
void CTempfileDlg::OnGenerateTemp()
{
    // get the data fields
    UpdateData(TRUE);

    // get the temporary path
    CString strTempPath;
    DWORD nPathSize = GetTempPath(
        MAX_PATH, strTempPath.GetBuffer(MAX_PATH));
    strTempPath.ReleaseBuffer(nPathSize);

    // get the temporary name
    CString strTempName;
    GetTempFileName(strTempPath, m_strPrefix, m_nUnique,
        m_strTempFullName.GetBuffer(MAX_PATH));
    m_strTempFullName.ReleaseBuffer(-1);
```

```
// delete the temporary file if one is created
if (m_nUnique == 0)
{
    DeleteFile(m_strTempFullName);
}

UpdateData(FALSE);
}
```

In Listing 13-3, the `OnGenerateTemp()` function generates a temporary file using the parameters entered by the user. The function first retrieves the values the user enters. It then calls the `GetTempPath()` API to retrieve the temporary path. Next, it passes the temporary path, prefix, and unique number to the `GetTempFileName()` API to get the temporary file name. If the user specifies zero for the unique ID, the function deletes the created file. Finally, the function updates the dialog box with the generated, temporary file name.

Searching for files

The Windows 2000 kernel also provides functions for searching for files in a directory. The `FindFirstFile()` and `FindFirstFileEx()` APIs enable you to specify the criteria to search for a file. These APIs both return a handle to a file find kernel object that you can use to enumerate the files that match your search criteria.

Chapter 4, "Commonly Used Kernel Objects," covers the file find and other find objects from the Windows 2000 kernel.

Currently, the `FindFirstFileEx()` API only supports a limited set of additional options, but this may be extended in the future to allow for more flexibility in searches. The only additional functionality the `FindFirstFileEx()` API provides now is the ability to limit searches to directories and to perform case-sensitive searches.

Once you have the handle to the find object, you can use the `FindNextFile()` API to retrieve the files that match your criteria. The API returns discovered file information in a WIN32_FIND_DATA structure. This structure holds the file attributes, the creation time, the last access times, the last write time, the file size, and the file names. Table 13-5 describes these members. The FindNextFile() returns TRUE while there still are files that match your criteria. If it fails for any reason, it returns FALSE. The GetLastError() API returns ERROR_NO_MORE_FILES when there are no more files that match your criteria. Once you are finished with the file find object, call the FindClose() API; this frees all resources associated with the object.

TABLE 13-5 MEMBERS OF THE WIN32_FIND_DATA STRUCTURE

Member	Description
DWORD dwFileAttributes	Specifies the attributes for the file
FILETIME ftCreationTime	Specifies the time the file was created in Coordinated Universal Time (UTC) format
FILETIME ftLastAccessTime	Specifies the time the file was last accessed in UTC format
FILETIME ftLastWriteTime	Specifies the time the file was last written to in UTC format
DWORD nFileSizeHigh	Specifies the high-order 32-bits of the file size in bytes if the file is larger than 4GB
DWORD nFileSizeLow	Specifies the low-order 32-bits of the file size in bytes
DWORD dwReserved0	Reserved for future use
DWORD dwReserved1	Reserved for future use
TCHAR cFileName[MAX_PATH]	The full, long name of the file
TCHAR cAlternateFileName[14]	The short (8.3) name of the file

Figure 13-2 shows a sample application that searches the selected directory for files that match the specified search string. Listing 13-4 shows the code the sample uses to search for the files that match the selected criteria.

Figure 13-2: Find files sample application

Listing 13-4: Finding files with FindFirstFile() and FindNextFile()

```
//
//  CFileSearchDlg::OnFind() :
//
void CFileSearchDlg::OnFind()
{
    // clear list box
    m_lbFiles.ResetContent();

    // get the directory and search string
    UpdateData(TRUE);

    CString strFileSearch = m_strDirectory + "\\\\" + m_strSearch;

    // find all of the files that match the criteria

    // find the first file that matches the search criteria
    WIN32_FIND_DATA fileData;
    HANDLE hFileSearch = FindFirstFile(strFileSearch, &fileData);
    if (hFileSearch != INVALID_HANDLE_VALUE)
    {
        // add the file name to the list box
        m_lbFiles.AddString(fileData.cFileName);

        // get the next file that matches
        while(FindNextFile(hFileSearch, &fileData))
        {
            // add the file name to the list box
```

```
        m_lbFiles.AddString(fileData.cFileName);
    }

    // close the search handle
    FindClose(hFileSearch);
  }
}
```

The OnFind() method in Listing 13-4 searches a directory for all files that match a search pattern that the user specifies. The function first resets the list box to empty and then retrieves the information the user entered and builds a search string. It calls the FindFirstFile() API to retrieve the first file that matches the search criteria and adds it to the list box. Next, it loops through the rest of the files using the FindNextFile() API. After all of the files are retrieved, the method calls the FindClose() API to free the resources associated with the find object.

Monitoring changes in a directory

It is often useful to monitor a directory for changes. You can use the monitoring to notify a service, application, or user when the contents of a directory change. For example, a backup program can use change monitoring to dynamically maintain a list of files that it needs to back up. Alternatively, an indexing application might use change monitoring to keep its index updated.

You can watch for changes in a directory using the FindFirstChange Notification() API. This API enables you to specify a directory to monitor and what types of changes are interesting. Table 13-6 lists the change filter values that are available. The API returns a kernel object handle on which you can use any of the Windows 2000 waiting APIs to block a thread until a new change occurs. Once a change happens that meets your criteria, the wait condition is satisfied and the worker thread can process the change. To wait for another change, call the FindNextChangeNotification() and wait for the next change. When you are finished using the change notification object, call the FindCloseChange Notification() API to free all of the resources associated with the object.

Chapter 3, "Using Kernel Objects," covers the kernel waiting functions in detail. Chapter 4, "Commonly Used Kernel Objects," covers the change notification kernel object.

TABLE **13-6 CHANGE FILTER VALUES FOR THE FINDFIRSTCHANGENOTIFICATION() API**

Value	Description
FILE_NOTIFY_CHANGE_FILE_NAME	Monitors file name changes, including renaming, creating, and deleting file names
FILE_NOTIFY_CHANGE_DIR_NAME	Monitors directory name changes; includes renaming, creating, and deleting directories
FILE_NOTIFY_CHANGE_ATTRIBUTES	Monitors file and directory attributes changes
FILE_NOTIFY_CHANGE_SIZE	Monitors changes in file size; the system only detects the changes when the file is actually written to disk; if the write is cached then the notification occurs when the cache is flushed
FILE_NOTIFY_CHANGE_LAST_WRITE	Monitors the last write time of files; the system only detects the changes when the file is actually written to disk; if the write is cached the notification occurs when the cache is flushed
FILE_NOTIFY_CHANGE_SECURITY	Monitors the security descriptor for changes

Figure 13-3 shows a sample application that enables users to choose a directory to monitor and what changes they want to monitor. When you click the "Start Monitoring" button the application creates the find notification handles with the FindFirstChangeNotification() API and starts a thread to receive the change notifications. The change window displays any changes to the specified directory. When you click the "Stop Monitoring" button, the application frees the notification handles with the FindCloseChangeNotification() API. Listing 13-5 shows the sample code for the starting, stopping, and processing the change notifications.

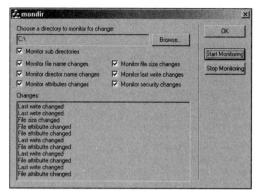

Figure 13-3: Directory monitoring sample application

Listing 13-5: Monitoring directory changes

```
//
// void CMondirDlg::OnStartMonitoring() : called to start
// monitoring a directory
//
void CMondirDlg::OnStartMonitoring()
{
    // retrieve user data
    UpdateData(TRUE);

    int nHandleIndex(0);

    // reset the handles
    memset(&m_arhChange, 0x00, sizeof(m_arhChange));

    // monitor the directory name changes
    if (m_bDirNameChange)
    {
        m_arhChange[nHandleIndex] = FindFirstChangeNotification(
            m_strDirectory, m_bSubDir, FILE_NOTIFY_CHANGE_DIR_NAME);
        ++nHandleIndex;
    }

    // monitor the file name changes
    if (m_bFileNameChange)
    {
```

```
        m_arhChange[nHandleIndex] = FindFirstChangeNotification(
            m_strDirectory, m_bSubDir,
            FILE_NOTIFY_CHANGE_FILE_NAME);
        ++nHandleIndex;
    }

    // monitor the file attribute changes
    if (m_bAttributeChange)
    {
        m_arhChange[nHandleIndex] = FindFirstChangeNotification(
            m_strDirectory, m_bSubDir,
            FILE_NOTIFY_CHANGE_ATTRIBUTES);
        ++nHandleIndex;
    }

    // monitor the file size changes
    if (m_bFileSizeChange)
    {
        m_arhChange[nHandleIndex] = FindFirstChangeNotification(
            m_strDirectory, m_bSubDir, FILE_NOTIFY_CHANGE_SIZE);
        ++nHandleIndex;
    }

    // monitor the last write changes
    if (m_bLastWriteChange)
    {
        m_arhChange[nHandleIndex] = FindFirstChangeNotification(
            m_strDirectory, m_bSubDir,
            FILE_NOTIFY_CHANGE_LAST_WRITE);
        ++nHandleIndex;
    }

    // monitor the security changes
    if (m_bSecurityChange)
    {
        m_arhChange[nHandleIndex] = FindFirstChangeNotification(
            m_strDirectory, m_bSubDir, FILE_NOTIFY_CHANGE_SECURITY);
        ++nHandleIndex;
    }

    // set number of valid handles
    m_pChange->m_numCount = nHandleIndex;

    // set exit to false
    m_pChange->m_bExit = FALSE;
```

```
    // start worker thread
    AfxBeginThread(ChangeNotification, m_pChange);
}


//
//   void CMondirDlg::OnStopMonitoring() : called to stop monitoring
//
void CMondirDlg::OnStopMonitoring()
{
    // if we are monitoring close the change handles
    if (m_pChange->m_bExit = FALSE)
    {
        // set the exit variable so the worker thread exits
        m_pChange->m_bExit = TRUE;

        for(
            int nIndex = 0;
            nIndex < m_pChange->m_numCount;
            ++nIndex
            )
        {
            FindCloseChangeNotification(m_arhChange[nIndex]);
        }
    }
}


//
// void CMondirDlg::AddStringToList : called by the worker thread
//      to add strings to the beginning of the edit control
//
void CMondirDlg::AddStringToList(LPCSTR lpszString)
{
    CString strEdit;
    m_editChanges.GetWindowText(strEdit);

    strEdit = lpszString + strEdit;

    m_editChanges.SetWindowText(strEdit);
}



//
//   ChangeNotification : the change notification thread proc
//
```

```
UINT ChangeNotification(LPVOID pParam)
{
    // get the thread information
    SChangeNotification* pChange = (SChangeNotification*)pParam;

    // while still monitoring
    while(!pChange->m_bExit)
    {
        // wait on the change handles
        DWORD nObjectWait = WaitForMultipleObjects(
            pChange->m_numCount, pChange->m_pChange,
            FALSE, INFINITE);

        // get the object that caused the wait to exit
        int nIndex = nObjectWait - WAIT_OBJECT_0;

        switch(nObjectWait - WAIT_OBJECT_0)
        {
            case 0:
                (pChange->m_pDlg)->AddStringToList(
                    "Directory named changed\r\n");
                break;

            case 1:
                (pChange->m_pDlg)->AddStringToList(
                    "File named changed\r\n");
                break;

            case 2:
                (pChange->m_pDlg)->AddStringToList(
                    "File attribute changed\r\n");
                break;

            case 3:
                (pChange->m_pDlg)->AddStringToList(
                    "File size changed\r\n");
                break;

            case 4:
                (pChange->m_pDlg)->AddStringToList(
                    "Last write changed\r\n");
                break;
```

```
            case 5:
                (pChange->m_pDlg)->AddStringToList(
                    "Security changed\r\n");
                break;
        }

        // continue monitoring
        FindNextChangeNotification(pChange->m_pChange[nObjectWait]);
    }

    return 0;
}
```

The `OnStartMonitoring()` method in Listing 13-5 is called when the user clicks to start monitoring directory changes. It first retrieves the information the user enters and initializes the change notification array. Then, for every item the user selects to monitor, the function calls the `FindFirstChangeNotification()` to start monitoring for changes. It stores the resulting notification handles in an array, then passes them to the worker thread to wait for the changes.

The `OnStopMonitoring()` method is called when the user chooses to stop monitoring directory changes or exits the application. The function first checks the exit flag to see if the application is monitoring changes currently and then sets the exit flag to true, so the worker thread exits. It then loops through the notification handles and calls the `FindCloseChangeNotification()` function to free the resources associated with the handles.

The `AddStringToList()` method is used by the worker thread to add strings to the beginning of the Edit control. The function first retrieves the text currently in the Edit control and then prepends the text to add. Then, the text in the Edit control is set to the new string.

The `ChangeNotification()` method is the worker thread procedure that waits for the directory change notifications. When it receives one, it figures out when notification happened and adds the appropriate text to the Edit control. Then it calls the `FindNextChangeNotification()` to wait for the new change.

Reading from and writing to files asynchronously

To read from or write to an object asynchronously, Windows 2000 provides the *overlapped* file operations. The `ReadFile()` and `WriteFile()` APIs enable you to specify an overlapped structure that tells them where to begin reading from or writing to. This structure also enables you to specify an event to wait for to synchronize your input and output. While the `ReadFile()` and `WriteFile()` APIs support both synchronous and asynchronous operations, the `ReadFileEx()` and `WriteFileEx()` APIs only support asynchronous operations. They also enable you to specify a completion function that is executed when the input/output operation completes.

Figure 13-4 shows a sample application that reads data from a file asynchronously. It allows you to select a file to open, then reads the contents of the file asynchronously with the `ReadFileEx()` API. Listing 13-6 shows the code for opening the file and reading it with the overlapped file operation. It also shows the completion function that the system calls when the read operation is complete.

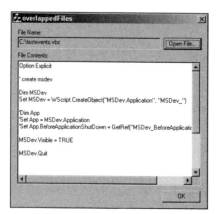

Figure 13-4: Overlapped file reading sample application

Listing 13-6: Reading a file asynchronously

```
//
// COverlappedFilesDlg::OnOpen() : called to open a file
//
void COverlappedFilesDlg::OnOpen()
{
    // display the file open dialog
    CFileDialog dlgFile(TRUE);
    if (dlgFile.DoModal() == IDOK)
    {
        // get selected file path
        m_strFileName = dlgFile.GetPathName();
        UpdateData(FALSE);

        // read the file asynchronously
        ReadFileContents();
    }
}


//
//  COverlappedFilesDlg::ReadFileContents() : read a file
```

```
//      asynchronously
//
void COverlappedFilesDlg::ReadFileContents()
{
    CString strFileContents;

    // open the file for asynchronous reading
    HANDLE hFile = CreateFile(m_strFileName, GENERIC_READ, 0,
        NULL, OPEN_EXISTING,
        FILE_FLAG_OVERLAPPED, NULL);
    if (hFile != INVALID_HANDLE_VALUE)
    {
        // get the size of the file
        long nFileSize = GetFileSize(hFile, NULL);

        // allocate a buffer the size of the file
        s_lpBuffer = new BYTE[nFileSize];

        // set up the overlapped struct
        s_overlapped.Internal = 0;
        s_overlapped.InternalHigh = 0;
        s_overlapped.Offset = 0;
        s_overlapped.OffsetHigh = 0;
        s_overlapped.hEvent = NULL;

        // read the file asynchronously
        BOOL bResult = ReadFileEx(
            hFile, s_lpBuffer, nFileSize, &s_overlapped,
            ReadComplete);
        if (bResult)
        {
            // create an event to wait on
            HANDLE hEvent = CreateEvent(NULL, FALSE, FALSE, NULL);

            while(TRUE)
            {
                // wait for the read operation to finish
                DWORD nCompletionStatus = WaitForMultipleObjectsEx(
                    1, &hEvent, FALSE, INFINITE, TRUE);
                if (nCompletionStatus == WAIT_IO_COMPLETION)
                {
                    break;
                }
            }
        }
```

```
              // close handle
              CloseHandle(hEvent);
        }
    }
}


//
// asynchronous completion routine
//
void CALLBACK ReadComplete
(
  DWORD dwErrorCode,
  DWORD dwNumberOfBytesTransfered,
  LPOVERLAPPED lpOverlapped

)
{

    // update the dialog
    m_pDialog->m_strFileContents += s_lpBuffer;
    m_pDialog->UpdateData(FALSE);

    delete s_lpBuffer;
    s_lpBuffer = NULL;
}
```

The OnOpen() method in Listing 13-6 is called to let the user choose a file to read. It displays a File Open common dialog box and—if the user selects a file—gets the path name, updates the dialog box, and calls ReadFileContents() to read the file asynchronously.

The ReadFileContents() function first opens the file for reading using the CreateFile() API, which uses the FILE_FLAG_OVERLAPPED flag. This flag specifies that the function reads the file asynchronously. It then gets the size of the file, allocates a buffer big enough to hold the file, and sets up the overlapped structure to begin reading from the beginning.

 Since the ReadFileContents() method uses the ReadFileEx() API to read the file, it does not need to specify an event on which to wait. Instead, it specifies a completion routine that the system calls when the read operation is complete.

The `ReadFileContents()` method then calls the `ReadFileEx()` API to read the file. It creates a dummy event and calls the `WaitForMultipleObjectsEx()` API to wait for the I/O operation to complete. The `WaitForMultipleObjectsEx()` API returns if either the event is signaled or the I/O operation completes.

The `ReadComplete()` function is the completion routine for the `ReadFileEx()` call. It adds the string to the buffer and updates the dialog box using a static pointer to the dialog box. Finally, it frees the input buffer.

Windows 2000 File Systems

Windows 2000 supports three different file systems:

1. File Allocation Table (FAT) file system

2. Protected-mode FAT file system

3. Windows NT file system (NTFS)

The FAT file system is the original file system used by MS-DOS. It is designed to handle disks that are now considered small and a simple folder organization. The FAT file system stores file information in a file allocation table located at the beginning of the volume. Two copies of the file allocation table are kept in case one is damaged.

The main advantage of the FAT file system is that MS-DOS, Windows 95 and 98, and even OS/2 can access FAT volumes. Its big disadvantage is that as the size of a FAT volume grows, the minimum cluster size grows. For hard drives larger than 512MB, the minimum cluster size is 16KB. For drives larger then 2GB, the minimum cluster size is 64KB. This leads to a large amount of wasted disk space, since a file must occupy a integral number of clusters. Thus a 1KB file on a 2GB drive will occupy 64KB of disk space. The FAT file system does not support volumes greater than 4GB in size.

The protected-mode FAT file system extends the FAT file system by providing support for long file names. The protected-mode FAT file system is compatible with the FAT file system. It stores the long file name information within the FAT structures. The FAT file system and the protected-mode FAT file system are the only file systems that are supported on removable media such as floppy disks.

The Windows NT File System (NTFS) provides all of the functionality of the FAT file system, while providing support for advanced file system features, such as security, compression, and encryption. It is designed to perform common file operations efficiently on very large disks. Unlike the FAT and protected-mode FAT file systems the minimum cluster size never grows greater than 4KB. However, NTFS volumes are only accessed by a Windows NT or Windows 2000 operating system.

NTFS version 5.0 (part of Windows 2000) provides new features that are designed to make the file system more secure and reliable and to better support distributed computing than in previous versions of Windows. I will discuss these new features in the next section.

NTFS Features

The Windows NT File System (NTFS) provides many advanced file system features not found in the FAT file system. NTFS supports file level security, Unicode file names, file compression, and file system recovery.

Version 5.0 of NTFS introduces even more file system features. To provide additional security, NTFS provides the ability to encrypt individual files using a public key system. To provide a more reliable file system, NTFS 5.0 provides Disk Quotas, Volume Mount Points, Reparse Points, Distributed Link Tracking, and support for sparse files. The following sections will discuss these NTFS features in detail.

Compressing files and directories

File compression is the mechanism that maps data from its original value to a new value that takes up less space on the disk. Whenever the data is required again, this compressed file must be decompressed to retrieve the original contents. Windows 2000 provides file compression at the file system level. The administrator simply enables compression on a disk volume, and all subsequent file I/O uses it. The Windows 2000 kernel supplies this facility, and it provides the APIs summarized in Table 13-7.

TABLE **13-7 FILE SYSTEM COMPRESSION APIS**

API	Description
GetVolumeInformation()	Retrieves information about a volume in the file system, including the FS_FILE_COMPRESSION and FS_VOL_IS_COMPRESSED attributes
DeviceIOControl()	Sends a control code to the file system device driver, including FSCTL_GET_COMPRESSION
GetFileAttributes()	Fetches the current file system attributes for the file or directory passed by the string name, including FILE_ATTRIBUTE_COMPRESSED
GetCompressedFileSize()	Determines the actual number of bytes required to store the file on the file system passed by name
GetFileSize()	Looks up the uncompressed size of the file passed by name

---

NTFS enables you to compress individual files in a directory. Other Windows 2000 file systems also may support file compression. You can determine if a file system supports compression by using the `GetVolumeInformation()` API and checking the `FS_FILE_COMPRESSION` flag.

Every file and directory in the NTFS and other file systems that support compression has a compression state. The compression state specifies how the data in a file or directory is compressed. You can set and retrieve the compression state using the `DeviceIOControl()` API. The `COMPRESSION_FORMAT_NONE` state indicates that the file or directory be uncompressed or is not compressed. The `COMPRESSION_FORMAT_LZNT1` specifies that the file or directory should be compressed with the `LZNT1` algorithm or is compressed with the `LZNT1` algorithm. These are the only two compression states currently supported by NTFS. If you set the compression state of a directory, the files that currently exist in the directory are not compressed or are uncompressed. However, any new file inherits the compression state of the directory.

> **NOTE** Other file systems, including NTFS, may support other compression state values in the future.

If you just want to check to see if a file or directory is compressed, you can check the file attribute of the file using the `GetFileAttributes()` or `GetFileAttributesEx()` APIs. If the compression attribute is set on a directory, any files or directories that are created in the directory inherit the compression settings from its parent.

To get the file size of a compressed file, you can use the `GetCompressed FileSize()` API. This API returns the compressed size of the file if the file is compressed. If the file is not compressed, the value returned will match the file size returned by `GetFileSize()` API.

Figure 13-5 shows the compression sample application that retrieves the compression information about a file and enables you to change the compression state. Listing 13-7 shows the code that the compression application uses for retrieving the compression information about a file.

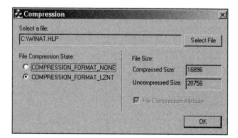

Figure 13-5: The file compression sample application

Listing 13-7: Retrieving file compression information

```
//
// GetFileInfo() called to get the
//     compression information for the file
//
void CCompressionDlg::GetFileInfo()
{
    //
    // Get Compression state
    //

    // Open the file
    HANDLE hFile = CreateFile(m_strFilePath, 0,
        FILE_SHARE_READ, NULL, OPEN_EXISTING, 0, NULL);
    if (hFile != INVALID_HANDLE_VALUE)
    {
        // get the compression state
        USHORT nState(0);
        DWORD nSize = sizeof(nState);
        DWORD nReturned;

        VERIFY(DeviceIoControl(hFile, FSCTL_GET_COMPRESSION,
            NULL, 0, &nState, nSize, &nReturned, NULL));

        switch(nState)
        {
            case COMPRESSION_FORMAT_NONE:
                m_nCompressionType = 0;
            break;

            case COMPRESSION_FORMAT_LZNT1:
                m_nCompressionType = 1;
            break;
        }

        // get the uncompressed file size
        m_nUncompressedSize = GetFileSize(hFile, NULL);

        CloseHandle(hFile);
    }

    // Get the compression attribute
    WIN32_FILE_ATTRIBUTE_DATA fileData;
    VERIFY(GetFileAttributesEx(m_strFilePath,
```

```
          GetFileExInfoStandard, &fileData));
    m_bFileCompression =
        ((fileData.dwFileAttributes & FILE_ATTRIBUTE_COMPRESSED) ==
            FILE_ATTRIBUTE_COMPRESSED);

    // get the compressed file sizes
    m_nCompressedSize = GetCompressedFileSize(
        m_strFilePath, NULL);

    UpdateData(FALSE);
}
```

In Listing 13-7, the GetFileInfo() method retrieves compression information about a file. It first opens the file, using zero instead of GENERIC_READ or GENERIC_WRITE since we are just going to retrieve attributes of the file. Then it calls the DeviceIOControl() API to get the compression state of the file. Next, it retrieves the uncompressed file size. It then uses the GetFileAttributesEx() API to retrieve the compression attribute of the file and the GetCompressedFileSize() to retrieve its compressed size. Finally, it updates the dialog box.

Listing 13-8 shows the code that the compression application uses to set the compression state of a file. The code uses the DeviceIOControl() API to set the compression type.

Listing 13-8: Setting a file's compression state

```
//
//  CompressFile: called to compress a file
//
void CCompressionDlg::CompressFile(USHORT nCompressionType)
{
    // Open the file
    HANDLE hFile = CreateFile(m_strFilePath,
        GENERIC_READ | GENERIC_WRITE, FILE_SHARE_READ,
        NULL, OPEN_EXISTING, 0, NULL);
    if (hFile != INVALID_HANDLE_VALUE)
    {
        // get the compression state
        DWORD nReturned;

        VERIFY(DeviceIoControl(hFile, FSCTL_SET_COMPRESSION,
            &nCompressionType, sizeof(nCompressionType),
            NULL, 0, &nReturned, NULL));

        CloseHandle(hFile);
    }
```

```
        GetFileInfo();
}
```

In Listing 13-8, the `CompressFile()` method first opens the file for input and output. It uses the `DeviceIoControl()` API with the `FSCTL_SET_COMPRESSION` control code to set the compression to the specified type and closes the handle. Then it calls the `GetFileInfo()` function to get the new information about the file.

Encrypting and decrypting files and directories

File encryption is the mechanism that maps data from its original value to a new value that is apparently unrelated: it maps a *plain text* file to an *encrypted* file. Whenever the data is required again, the encrypted file must be decrypted. Windows 2000 provides file encryption at the file system level much like it provides file compression that I covered in the previous section. The Windows 2000 kernel supplies file encryption and the APIs summarized in Table 13-8 to manage it.

TABLE **13-8 FILE SYSTEM ENCRYPTION APIS**

API	Description
`GetVolumeInformation()`	Retrieves information about a volume in the file system, including the `FS_FILE_SUPPORTS_ENCRYPTION` attribute.
`DeviceIOControl()`	Sends a control code to the file system device driver, including `FSCTL_GET_COMPRESSION`.
`GetFileAttributes()`	Fetches the current file system attributes for the file or directory passed by string name, including `FILE_ATTRIBUTE_ENCRYPTED`.
`EncryptFile()`	Encrypts the file or directory passed by the string name that uses the current account's encryption certificate. The file or directory has all of its plain text contents replaced with encrypted data.
`DecryptFile()`	Reverses the encryption for a file, replacing the file or directory passed by name with the original data.
`FileEncryptionStatus()`	Retrieves the current encryption state of the file or directory passed by name. The values returned by this function are summarized in Table 13-9.
`EncryptionDisable()`	Enables or disables the ability to encrypt files in the directory passed by string name.

Windows 2000 supports encrypting files using the *Encrypted File System (EFS)*. Currently, only NTFS volumes support the EFS, but others may in the future. You can check to see if a volume supports file encryption using the GetVolume Information() API and checking to see if the FILE_SUPPORTS_ENCRYPTION flag is set.

Chapter 15, "Additional System Services," introduces cryptography, encryption, and the CryptoAPI library.

You can encrypt a file or a directory. Like file compression, if you encrypt a directory, the files that currently exist in the directory are not encrypted; but any new file inherits the encryption values of the directory. You can encrypt a file when you create a new file by specifying the FILE_ATTRIBUTE_ENCRYPTED flag when you call the CreateFile() API. You also can encrypt an existing file using the EncryptFile() API.

You cannot compress and encrypt a file. If you try to encrypt a compressed file, Windows uncompresses the file before encrypting it. However, the size of most encrypted files is already reduced due to the encryption algorithm.

You can retrieve encryption information about files using the FileEncryption Status() API. You also can use the GetFileAttributes() and check the FILE_ ATTRIBUTE_ENCRYPTED flag. However, the FileEncryptionStatus() API gives you much more detail; it returns one of the values in Table 13-9.

TABLE 13-9 RETURN VALUES FROM THE FILEENCRYPTIONSTATUS() API

Value	Description
FILE_ENCRYPTABLE	The file is ready to be encrypted
FILE_IS_ENCRYPTED	The file is already encrypted
FILE_SYSTEM_ATTR	The file has the system file attribute enabled; these cannot be encrypted
FILE_ROOT_DIR	The passed directory is a root directory on a disk volume; these cannot be encrypted

Continued

TABLE **13-9** RETURN VALUES FROM THE FILEENCRYPTIONSTATUS() API *(Continued)*

Value	Description
FILE_SYSTEM_DIR	The passed directory is a system directory; these cannot be encrypted
FILE_UNKNOWN	The passed file may or may not be encrypted
FILE_SYSTEM_NOT_SUPPORT	The file system on which the file resides does not support encryption
FILE_READ_ONLY	The file is read only; these cannot be encrypted

Figure 13-6 shows a sample application that allows you to open a file, decrypt a file, save a file, and save an encrypted file. Listing 13-9 shows the code that the application uses to encrypt a file.

Figure 13-6: The file encryption sample application

Listing 13-9: Encrypting a file

```
//
// CEncryptDlg::OnEncryptFile()  : called to encrypt a file
//
void CEncryptDlg::OnEncryptFile()
{
    // display save dialog
    CFileDialog dlgFile(FALSE);
```

```
    if (dlgFile.DoModal() == IDOK)
    {
        // get selected file path
        CString strFileName = dlgFile.GetPathName();
        UpdateData(FALSE);

        // create a new file for writing
        HANDLE hFile = CreateFile(strFileName, GENERIC_WRITE, 0,
            NULL, CREATE_NEW, FILE_ATTRIBUTE_ENCRYPTED, NULL);
        if (hFile != INVALID_HANDLE_VALUE)
        {
            // update the variable
            UpdateData(TRUE);

            // get the length of the text in the edit control
            long nFileSize = m_strFileContents.GetLength();
            DWORD nBytesWritten(0);

            // write the file
            BOOL bResult = WriteFile(hFile,
                m_strFileContents, nFileSize, &nBytesWritten, NULL);

            // close the file
            CloseHandle(hFile);
        }
    }
}
```

In Listing 13-9, the OnEncryptFile() method enables the user to save the contents of the Edit control in an encrypted file. First, the function prompts the user for the file name to save the encrypted file. Then, it creates the file by passing the FILE_ATTRIBUTE_ENCRYPTED flag to the CreateFile() API. Finally, it writes the contexts of the Edit control to the file and closes the file handle.

Listing 13-10 shows the code to decrypt and open the file. The function uses the DecryptFile() API to decrypt the file and then opens and reads the file as if it were any other file in the file system.

Listing 13-10: Decrypting a file

```
//
// CEncryptDlg::OnDecryptFile() : called to decrypt a file
//
void CEncryptDlg::OnDecryptFile()
{
```

```
// display open dialog
CFileDialog dlgFile(TRUE);
if (dlgFile.DoModal() == IDOK)
{
    // get selected file path
    CString strFileName = dlgFile.GetPathName();
    UpdateData(FALSE);

    // decrypt the file
    BOOL bResult = DecryptFile(strFileName, 0);
    if (bResult)
    {
        // open the file for reading
        HANDLE hFile = CreateFile(strFileName, GENERIC_READ, 0,
        NULL, OPEN_EXISTING, 0, NULL);
        if (hFile != INVALID_HANDLE_VALUE)
        {
            // get the file size
            long nFileSize = GetFileSize(hFile, NULL);
            DWORD nBytesRead(0);

            // read the file
            BOOL bResult = ReadFile(hFile,
                m_strFileContents.GetBuffer(nFileSize),
                nFileSize, &nBytesRead, NULL);
            m_strFileContents.ReleaseBuffer(-1);
            if (bResult)
            {
                // update the dialog
                UpdateData(FALSE);
            }

            // close the handle
            CloseHandle(hFile);
        }
    }
}
```

In Listing 13-10, the `OnDecryptFile()` method opens and decrypts the file and then displays the decrypted file contents. The function first displays a File Open common dialog box, enabling users to select what file they want to open. After a user selects a file, the `OnDecryptFile()` method then calls the `DecryptFile()` API to decrypt it. The function then opens the file, reads the contents, and displays the data in the dialog box.

Specifying disk quotas

Windows 2000 enables you to specify *disk quotas* that limit the amount of storage space a user can store on an NTFS 5.0 volume. You can specify whether to issue a warning when users exceed their limit or whether to deny additional disk space for users.

Disk quotas provide administrators a way to manage their network disk space and generate warnings of potential problems before they result in network problems. This can lead to more reliable networks, resulting in more available systems with less downtime.

Windows 2000 provides several COM interfaces to facilitate the use of disk quotas. Table 13-10 lists the interfaces that are provided and their uses.

TABLE **13-10** DISK QUOTA COM INTERFACES

Interface	Use
IDiskQuotaControl	Controls disk quotas for an NTFS volume.
IDiskQuotaEvents	Receives quota-related information. Currently, only `OnUserNameChanged()` is implemented.
IDiskQuotaUser	Accesses quota user information.
IDiskQuotaUserBatch	Adds multiple users to a volume in one call.
IEnumDiskQuotaUsers	Enumerates users on a volume.

Figure 13-7shows the local disk property sheet. The Quota page allows an administrator to set the disk quota limits. In this example, the administrator enables disk quota management and denies additional space to users that exceed their limit. Each user is limited to 10MB of disk space and will be warned when they have used 8MB. The system will log each warning and attempt to allocate disk space that fails.

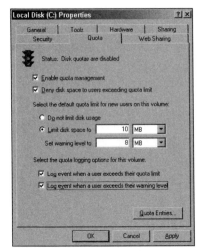

Figure 13-7: Specifying a disk quota

Volume mount points

NFTS 5.0 introduces *volume mount points*. A volume mount point is a directory that allows you to mount and access a different volume. By using volume mounting points, you can access different file systems as one volume. This allows applications and users to locate information across multiple volumes without having to know there are multiple volumes. Volume mount points are implemented by the system using *reparse* points. Reparse points are discussed further in the next section.

You can combine NTFS, FAT, and even CD-ROM volumes using volume mounting points. You can make any directory except the root directory a volume mount point. You can mount any drive to these volume mount points. For example, if you have volumes C, D, and R that represent your root drive, your CD-ROM drive, and a removeable media drive, you could mount volumes D and R to volume mount points on the C volume, as shown in Table 13-11

TABLE 13-11 MOUNTING VOLUMES TO VOLUME MOUNT POINTS

Volume Mount Point	Volume Mounted
C:\Mount\CDROM	D
C:\Mount\Rremoveable	R

To mount a volume, you use the SetVolumeMountPoint() API. This API mounts a specified volume at the specified mount point. The volume mount point is a traditional file system path name that ends with a backslash. The function also requires a unique name in a particular form, \\?\Volume{GUID}, not simply a file system path name. Drive letters are not a reliable method to identify a volume, since they may change when the system is restarted or the network configuration changes. To solve this problem the system assigns a unique volume name the first time the system accesses the volume. To retrieve the unique volume name you use the GetVolumeNameForVolumeMountPoint() API. This API takes a volume name and an output buffer and size and returns the unique volume name. Table 13-12 lists and describes all of the APIs that you can use with volume mount points.

For more information on volume mount points, refer to the MSDN.

TABLE 13-12 VOLUME MOUNT POINT APIS

API	Description
SetVolumeMountPoint()	Mounts the specified volume at the specified volume mount point
GetVolumeNameForVolumeMountPoint()	Returns the unique volume name for the specified volume mount point or root directory
GetVolumePathName()	Returns the volume mount point where a directory is mounted
DeleteVolumeMountPoint()	Removes a volume from a volume mount point
FindFirstVolume()	Locates a volume on the system
FindNextVolume()	Locates the next volume on the system
FindVolumeClose()	Closes the volume search handle
FindFirstVolumeMountPoint()	Locates the name of the volume mount point on the system

Continued

TABLE **13-12** VOLUME MOUNT POINT APIS *(Continued)*

API	Description
FindNextVolumeMountPoint()	Locates the next volume mount point on the system
FindVolumeMountPointClose()	Closes the volume mount point search handle

The following code snippet shows how to mount volume D at the volume mount point C:\Mount\CDROM:

```
bOK = GetVolumeNameForVolumeMountPoint(
    "D:\\", szUniqueName, NAME_SIZE);

if (bOK)
{
    bOK = SetVolumeMountPoint(
        "C:\\mount\\cdrom\\", szUniqueName);
}
```

The first parameter to the GetVolumeNameForVolumeMountPoint() API is the root directory to mount, "D:\\". This parameter must have a trailing backslash character. The second parameter and third parameters are a buffer that receives the unique name and the size of the buffer. The size of the buffer should be the maximum size for the unique name, which is 50. The SetVolumeMountPoint() API then mounts this unique volume at the "C:\\Mount\\CDROM\\" volume mounting point. The volume mounting parameter must also have a trailing backslash character.

Using reparse points

Reparse points are another new feature that NTFS 5.0 introduces. They allow application-defined data to be stored with a file or directory. When a file is opened with a reparse point set, the system searches for an appropriate file system filter. If an appropriate filter is found, that filter process the data. If one is not found, the open operation fails. Windows 2000 implements volume-mounting points using reparse points.

To work with reparse points, use the DeviceIOControl() API. To set a reparse point, use the FSCTL_SET_REPARSE_POINT operation flag. To retrieve the reparse point information, use the FSCTL_GET_REPARSE_POINT flag, and to remove a reparse point, use the FSCTL_DELETE_REPARSE_POINT flag.

When you set a reparse point, part of the reparse data identified is the reparse tag. This tag identifies which file system filter to use to process the reparse data. The remainder of the data can be used for whatever purpose the file system filter requires. However, this data is limited to 16KB. If more data is specified the reparse operation will fail.

You will generally not have any reason to use reparse points directly, since they only work with file system filters. You will use them indirectly through other file system features such as volume mounting points.

 For more information on reparse points, refer to the MSDN Platform SDK documentation on the NTFS and Reparse Points.

Distributed link-tracking

Windows 2000 provides *distributed link-tracking* to maintain the integrity of client links. The distributed link-tracking service tracks shell shortcuts and OLE links on NTFS 5.0 volumes. If a link is made on an NTFS volume and then later moved to another NTFS volume, the link will be found by the tracking service.

In previous versions of Windows, you would search for relocated links using a search methodology that would probably eventually yield results if the link were relocated on the same system. However, this method could be very time consuming and would not work across volumes.

Distributed link-tracking is implemented as two system services, one on each system (Tracking Service) and one that runs on each domain controller (Server Tracking Service). The Tracking Service that runs on each system tracks and maintains the links on that system. It is also responsible for exchanging information with the server tracking service. The Server Tracking Service listens to the various Tracking Services in the domain for notifications of file or volume moves; it then stores that information for later retrieval.

The link-tracking services are provided automatically by the system. The shell shortcut interface (IShellLink) and the OLE link interface (IOleLink) will automatically use the tacking services. Your applications do not have to take any steps to take advantage of distributed link-tracking.

Supporting sparse files

NTFS 5.0 provides a solution to the disk-storage waste problem that is caused by programs that use large files with little data in them. For example, programs that need very fast access to data often have large, indexed files with large portions of the file unused. These unused portions use up valuable disk space. NTFS provides support for *sparse files* to solve this problem. Sparse files only allocate disk space to the portions of the file that have data. To determine if a file system supports sparse files, call the `GetVolumeInformation()` API and check if the `FILE_SUPPORTS_SPARSE_FILES` flag is set.

To specify that a file is a sparse file, you use the `DeviceIoControl()` API with the `FSCTL_SET_SPARSE` control code. This specifies that large ranges of zero bytes in the file do not require a disk allocation. The system only allocates disk space for nonzero data.

After you specify a file as sparse, you can use the `FSCTL_SET_ZERO_DATA` control code of the `DeviceIoControl()` API to set regions of the file that should not be allocated. This call is the only way to set the non-allocated area of a file. If you write a range of zeros using another function, the system allocates the disk space required by the zeros.

You can use the `FSCTL_QUERY_ALLOCATED_RANGES` control code in the `DeviceIoControl()` API to search for ranges of available data. This API retrieves an array of ranges of areas that might contain data.

Summary

In this chapter, I covered the basic Win32 file APIs and took a look at some of the features that Windows 2000 provides. The new version of NTFS introduces new features that make the file system more reliable and more secure. These new features also provide more support for distributed computing — which will be needed as applications move beyond the desktop.

In the next chapter, I will provide an overview of the Active Directory and the ADSI API. I will describe how administrators and users can use the Active Directory to access and manage network resources. I will describe how to access the Active Directory object and show how to manage users and groups.

Chapter 14

The Active Directory

IN THIS CHAPTER

◆ Active Directory overview

◆ How to access Active Directory objects

◆ How to manage users and groups

IN THIS CHAPTER, I cover the Active Directory, which Windows 2000 uses for its directory service. I describe how you can use the ADSI API to access and manage active directory objects. I also provide examples of how to manage users and groups.

Many of the examples in this chapter use the COM interfaces that the ADSI API provides. I have used Visual Basic (VB) in some of the examples to make the code easier to understand. LDAP is an extremely important standard, one that is supported by Active Directory, and so that too is discussed in this chapter.

The samples in this chapter require that the computer you are running the samples on is part of an Active Directory domain.

An Overview of the Active Directory

A directory service manages network resources. It enables administrators to manage and users to access information about the users, groups, services, and resources that are available on the network. The directory service also allows administrators to restrict access to different network resources.

The *Active Directory* is the Windows 2000 directory service. The Active Directory is responsible for managing every object on the network. It is designed to scale from a single computer to an entire international network. The Active Directory provides services that allow users and administrators access and to manage large amounts of information easily.

The Active Directory is a collection of objects. Each object contains a set of attributes that represent a network resource such as a user, domain, printer, or an application. The Active Directory manages security for – and replicates these objects across – the network.

Active Directory domain objects represent Windows 2000 domains. They describe a security boundary of a Windows 2000 network. Multiple domain objects that are related make up an *Active Directory tree.* Multiple trees that share a common schema are contained in a *forest.* The global catalog is a domain controller that enables users and administrators to find an object in a forest without having to know exactly where it exists. The global catalog contains a complete replica of every domain in a forest.

The *ADSI (Active Directory Service Interfaces)* API provides an object-oriented API for accessing the Active Directory – the subject of the next section in this chapter. It also enables you to access other directories, such as Netware, Novell Directory Services, and Windows NT 4. The Active Directory is also a *Lightweight Directory Access Protocol (LDAP)* compliant directory so you can use the LDAP API to access the Active Directory. The LDAP is explained further in the sidebar.

For more information on the LDAP protocol, please visit the University of Michigan's LDAP page at `http://www.umich.edu/~dirsvcs/ldap/ldap.html`.

The Lightweight Directory Access Protocol

The LDAP is a protocol, initially developed at the University of Michigan, for accessing directory information. The LDAP runs over TCP/IP networks. This LDAP protocol was derived from the ISO X.500 Directory Access protocol and adapted to work over the Internet X.500. It's been around for a while, but its complexity (both in configuration and deployment, and in its use) greatly hindered its mass adoption. LDAP seeks to overcome these problems by providing a greatly simplified interface to directory services.

The LDAP organizes directory information in entries. An entry consists of a set of attributes that define the entry. A distinguished name (DN) uniquely identifies each entry.

Further, a tree style hierarchical structure organizes the entries. This structure defines the relationships between objects and makes it easy to manage large amounts of data.

To access and manipulate an LDAP directory service and its entries, the LDAP API is used. This API provides functions for creating, deleting, and modifying entries. It also provides functions for searching the directory.

How to Access Active Directory Objects

The ADSI is a set of Component Object Model (COM) objects and interfaces that you can use to access a directory. These interfaces provide a single API – called the ADSI API – to access directory services from a variety of providers. This frees your application to concentrate on the task at hand, managing network resources, instead of having to worry about the intricate details of how to access every type of directory that may exist in your network.

Chapter 10, "Application Building Services," introduces COM as a code packaging service.

ADSI provides a large set of interfaces to access the active directory. Table 14-1 lists some of the more commonly used ADSI interfaces. Every Active Directory object must support the `IADs` and `IDirectoryObject` interfaces and can expose other ADSI interfaces as necessary. ADSI also provides a number of helper API functions for clients that are not using OLE Automation (a facility of COM). Table 14-2 lists the helper functions that ADSI provides.

Refer to the MSDN for a more complete list and description of these interfaces and helper functions. Begin with the Platform SDK documentation on "Networking and Directory Services."

TABLE 14-1 COMMON ADSI INTERFACES

Interface	Description
IADs	The basic ADSI interface. Allows an application to access the properties and methods of an ADSI object. It also provides a way to identify the object, retrieve the object's schema definition, and manage the property cache.
IADsComputer	Manages information about a computer on a network.

Continued

TABLE 14-1 COMMON ADSI INTERFACES *(Continued)*

Interface	Description
IADsContainer	Creates, deletes, and manages ADSI objects. You also can use this interface to enumerate the objects that the container holds.
IADsDomain	Manages domain password policies.
IADsFileShare	Manages file share information.
IADsGroup	Manages group membership.
IADsMembers	Manages a list of active directory objects.
IADsNamespaces	Accesses the root node of a directory tree.
IADsOpenDSObject	Binds to an active directory object using the specified users credentials and binding options.
IADsPrintJob	Manages a print job.
IADsPrintQueue	Manages a print queue.
IADsPropertyList	Manages an object's data in the property cache.
IADsService	Manages information about the system services that run on a computer.
IADsUser	Manages user objects.
IDirectoryObject	Provides low-level access to Active Directory objects for early binding clients.
IDirectorySearch	Provides low-level searching interface for early binding clients.

TABLE 14-2 COMMON ADSI HELPER API FUNCTIONS

API Function	Description
ADsGetObject()	Binds to an active directory object that uses the current user's credentials and binding options
ADsOpenObject()	Binds to an active directory object that uses the specified users credentials and binding options
ADsGetLastError()	Returns the last error recorded in the calling thread

API Function	Description
`ADsSetLastError()`	Sets the last error code for the calling thread
`ADsBuildEnumerator()`	Obtains an enumerator for the specified active directory container
`ADsEnumerateNext()`	Enumerates the object, using the specified enumerator obtained with the `AdsBuildEnumerator()` API function
`ADsFreeEnumerator()`	Frees the specified enumerator
`ADsBuildVarArrayInt()`	Builds a variant array of integers
`ADSBuildVarArrayStr()`	Builds a variant array of strings
`AllocADsMem()`	Allocates the specified number of bytes
`FreeADsMem()`	Frees the specified memory block allocated with `AllocADsMem()`
`ReallocADsMem()`	Resizes the specified memory block allocated with `AllocADsMem()`
`AllocADsStr()`	Allocates memory to hold a copy of the specified string and copies the string to the allocated memory
`FreeADsStr()`	Frees the string allocated with `AllocADsStr()`
`ReallocADsStr()`	Replaces a sting allocated with `AllocADsStr()` with a new string
`ADsEncodeBinaryData()`	Converts binary data to a Unicode string which can be used as an ADSI search filter

In the following sections I describe how you can connect an Active Directory object by binding to it. I also describe how to enumerate a collection of Active Directory objects. As an alternative to navigating through the Active Directory tree to find an object, I also discuss how to search the directory to find objects that meet a specified criteria.

Binding

To access an object in the Active Directory, you must provide a string that uniquely identifies the object and then call an API function or method that returns a COM object that represents the directory object. This is called *binding* to the object, and the string that uniquely identifies the object is the binding string (also called an

AdsPath). The binding string consists of the progID of the directory provider, followed by ":", and then whatever syntax the provider requires. For example, if your directory provider is Windows NT 4.0, your provider name is WinNT and the provider syntax is as follows:

```
WinNT:[//DomainName[/ComputerName[/ObjectName[,className]]]]
WinNT:[//DomainName[/ObjectName[,className]]]
WinNT:[//ComputerName,computer]
```

Another example is the LDAP API. The LDAP provider syntax is as follows:

```
LDAP://HostName[:PortNumber][/DistinguishedName]
```

The way you use the binding string to bind to an object depends on the language you are using. If you use C/C++, you can use the ADsGetObject() API or the ADsOpenObject() API. If you use Visual Basic (VB) or VB Script, you can use either the GetObject() method or the OpenDSObject() method of the IADsOpen DSObject interface. The ADsGetObject() API and the GetObject() method use the current user's credentials and default binding options, whereas the ADsOpen Object() API and OpenDSObject() methods enable you to specify this information. Listing 14-1 shows a Visual Basic code snippet that uses the GetObject() method to bind to the "Villains" Windows domain. Listing 14-2 shows the equivalent C++ code snippet that uses the ADsGetObject() API to bind to the same "Villains" Windows domain.

Listing 14-1: Using the GetObject function in VB to bind to a domain

```
Dim domain As ActiveDs.IADs
Set domain = GetObject("WinNT://Villains")
```

Listing 14-2: Using the ADsGetObject API in C++ to bind to a domain

```
IADsDomain* pDomain;
HRESULT result;

result = ADsGetObject(L"WinNT://Villians", IID_IADsDomain,
    (void**)&pDomain);
```

The IADsDomain interface is a dual interface that derives from IADs and provides services for managing a network domain. In Listing 14-2, the ADsGet Object() API binds to the "Villains" Windows 2000 domain. The first parameter specifies the WinNT provider binding string that identifies the "Villains" domain. The second parameter specifies that a pointer to an IADsDomain interface be returned. The third parameter receives a pointer to the IADsDomain interface of the domain object, if the domain is found.

Listing 14-3 shows an example of using the `OpenDSObject()` method of the `IADsOpenDSObject` interface to bind to the "Villains" domain. Visual Basic is used in this code listing.

Listing 14-3: Using the OpenDSObject function in VB to bind to a domain

```
Dim openDS As IADsOpenDSObject
Dim domain As IADs

Set openDS = GetObject("WinNT:")

' supply full credentials to initiate a connection to a server.
Set domain = openDS.OpenDSObject( _
    "WinNT://Villains", _
    "testUser", _
    "password", _
    ADS_SECURE_AUTHENTICATION)
```

The `IADsOpenDSObject` interface enables you to specify a security context for binding to an object. The `OpenDSObject()` method enables you to specify the user name, password, and authentication options. In Listing 14-3, the code binds to the "Villains" domain using the security context of the `testUser` user object.

Listing 14-4 shows an example of using the `ADsOpenObject()` API to bind to the "Villains" domain using the same `testUser`. C++ is used in this code listing. This code is the functional equivalent to Listing 14-3.

Listing 14-4: Using the ADsOpenObject API in C++ to bind to a domain

```
IADs* pDomain;
HRESULT result;
result = ADsOpenObject(
    L"WinNT://Villains", "testUser", "password",
    ADS_SECURE_AUTHENTICATION, IID_IADs, (void**)&pDomain);
```

Enumeration

Once you have accessed a collection object in the active directory, you can use enumeration to retrieve the members of the collection. If you use an OLE Automation-compatible language, you can use the standard automation container methods to enumerate the collection.

Figure 14-1 shows the `EnumUsers` sample application. The sample allows you to specify a domain name to enumerate. When you click the "Enumerate" button, the sample application fills the list control with the names of all the users in the specified domain. In Figure 14-1, the user has enumerated the "Villains" domain. Listing 14-5 shows the Visual Basic code for the `EnumUsers` sample application.

Figure 14-1: The EnumUsers sample application

Listing 14-5: Enumerating users in a domain

```
Private Sub btnEnumerate_Click()

    Dim domain As IADsContainer
    Dim user As IADsUser

    ' get the domain name from the edit control
    Dim sDomain As String
    sDomain = editDomain.Text

    ' build the ADsPath
    Dim sBind As String
    sBind = "WinNT://" + sDomain

    ' bind to the container
    Set domain = GetObject(sBind)

    ' get all the user names
    listUsers.Clear

    domain.Filter = Array("user")
    For Each user In domain
        listUsers.AddItem user.Name
    Next

End Sub
```

The btnEnumerate_Click() function first creates a path to the specified domain and binds to the domain object. Then it clears the list box of any strings. The function also sets the Filter property to just enumerate user objects. It then enumerates all the users for the domain and adds their names to the list control.

The ADSI also provides enumeration APIs to assist you in using the enumeration interfaces if you use C or C++. The ADsBuildEnumerator(), ADsEnumerateNext(), and `ADsFreeEnumerator()` APIs handle obtaining an enumerator, enumerating objects, and freeing an enumerator, respectively. Listing 14-6 shows the C++ code to enumerate the users in a domain. This code is functionally equivalent to Listing 14-5.

Listing 14-6: Enumerating users in a domain in C++

```
//
//  CCenumusersDlg::OnEnumerate: called to enumerate the users
//
void CCenumusersDlg::OnEnumerate()
{
    USES_CONVERSION;

    IADsContainer* pContainer = NULL;
    HRESULT result(E_FAIL);;

    CString strBind;
    GetDlgItemText(IDC_DOMAIN, strBind);
    strBind = _T("WinNT://") + strBind;

    result = ADsGetObject(T2W(strBind), IID_IADsContainer,
        (void**)&pContainer);

    if (SUCCEEDED(result))
    {
        // clear list control
        m_lcUsers.ResetContent();

        // set the filter
        COleVariant varFilter;
        int num(0);
        LPWSTR lpwUsers = {L"user"};
        num = sizeof(lpwUsers)/sizeof(lpwUsers[0]);
        result = ADsBuildVarArrayStr(&lpwUsers, num, &varFilter);
        result = pContainer->put_Filter(varFilter);

        // obtain an enumerator
        IEnumVARIANT* pEnumVariant = NULL;
        result = ADsBuildEnumerator(pContainer, &pEnumVariant);
        if (SUCCEEDED(result))
        {
            COleVariant varItem;
            ULONG numRetrieved(0);
```

```
                LPDISPATCH lpDispatch = NULL;
                IADs* pADs = NULL;

                BSTR bstrName = NULL;

                result = ADsEnumerateNext(
                    pEnumVariant, 1, &varItem, &numRetrieved);
                while (result == S_OK)
                {
                    lpDispatch = V_DISPATCH(&varItem);
                    result = lpDispatch->QueryInterface(
                        IID_IADs, (void**)&pADs);
                    if (SUCCEEDED(result))
                    {
                        result = pADs->get_Name(&bstrName);
                        if (SUCCEEDED(result))
                        {
                            m_lcUsers.AddString(OLE2T(bstrName));
                            SysFreeString(bstrName);
                        }

                        pADs->Release();
                        pADs = NULL;
                    }

                    varItem.Clear();
                    result = ADsEnumerateNext(
                        pEnumVariant, 1, &varItem, &numRetrieved);
                }

                result = ADsFreeEnumerator(pEnumVariant);
                pEnumVariant = NULL;
            }

        pContainer->Release();
        pContainer = NULL;
    }
}
```

The OnEnumerate() function in Listing 14-6 performs the same steps as the btnEnumerate_Click() function from Listing 14-5. It first creates a path to the specified domain and binds to the domain object. Then it clears the list box of any strings. This function then sets the Filter property to enumerate user objects. The ADsBuildVarArrayStr() helper API is used to build the array of strings. It then enumerates all the users for the domain and adds their names to the list control.

Searching

In addition to navigating through the Active Directory hierarchy, the Active Directory also enables you to search the directory for objects, such as users or machines. The Active Directory provides three interfaces for you to use in querying the directory:

1. IDirectorySearch: This is a non-automation compatible COM interface. This interface provides a very high level, low overhead way to search the active directory. You use this interface if you need to perform simple directory searches in C++.

2. ActiveX Data Objects (ADO): The ADO interfaces use the OLE DB provider that ships with the Active Directory. ADO makes it simple to search the active directory from languages that utilize OLE Automation.

3. Object Linking and Embedding for Databases (OLE DB): You can also directly access the OLE DB provider to search the active directory. This provides access to all of the OLD DB functionality.

Listing 14-7 shows an example of using the IDirecorySearch interface to search for all the users in a domain using C++. The IDirectorySearch application uses this code to enumerate the users of the "Villains" domain.

Listing 14-7: Using IDirectorySearch in C++ to search for domain users

```
Au: Some of the code lines seem long. Please break them up. TV
changed to code 80 GB fixed. pf
//
//  CIDirectorySearchDlg::OnSearch(): called to search for a
//    user
//
void CIDirectorySearchDlg::OnSearch()
{
    HRESULT result(E_FAIL);

    USES_CONVERSION;

    IDirectorySearch* pDirSearch = NULL;

    // Open a connection with server

    result = ADsGetObject(L"LDAP://DC=Villains",
        IID_IDirectorySearch, (void**)&pDirSearch);
    if (SUCCEEDED(result))
    {
```

```
LPWSTR arAttr[] =
    { L"ADsPath", L"Name", L"samAccountName" };
ADS_SEARCH_HANDLE hSearch;

DWORD dwCount = sizeof(arAttr)/sizeof(arAttr[0]);

// Search for all users
CString strSearch ("(objectClass=user)");

result = pDirSearch->ExecuteSearch(T2W(strSearch),
    arAttr, dwCount, &hSearch );
if (SUCCEEDED(result))
{
    ADS_SEARCH_COLUMN col;
    while (pDirSearch->GetNextRow(hSearch) !=
        S_ADS_NOMORE_ROWS)
    {
        // Get the property
        result = pDirSearch->GetColumn(
            hSearch, L"name", &col);

        if (SUCCEEDED(result))
        {
            m_lcUsers.AddString(
                W2T(col.pADsValues->PrintableString));
            pDirSearch->FreeColumn(&col);
        }
    }

    pDirSearch->CloseSearchHandle(hSearch);
}
}
}
```

The OnSearch() function, in Listing 14-7, first binds to the "Villains" domain controller obtaining a pointer to the IDirectorySearch interface. If this succeeds, it then calls the ExecuteSearch() method to search for the users. The search string needs to be defined using the LDAP syntax. After the search returns, the function uses the GetNextRow() method to iterate through the result set adding the users names to the list control.

Listing 14-8 shows the same application as in Listing 14-7, but written in Visual Basic. It uses ADO to search the Active Directory. It uses the ADO connection, and command objects to search for the users in the "Villains" domain.

Listing 14-8: Using ADO in VB to search the directory

```
Private Sub btnSearch_Click()
    Dim Connection As New Connection
    Connection.Provider = "ADsDSOObject"
    Connection.Open "Active Directory Provider"

    Dim command As New command
    Set command.ActiveConnection = Connection
    command.CommandText = _
        "<LDAP://DC=Villains>;(objectClass=user); " + _
        "AdsPath, cn; subTree"

    Dim User As IADsUser

    Set rs = command.Execute
    While Not rs.EOF
        Set User = GetObject(rs.Fields(0).Value)
        listUsers.AddItem User.Name
        rs.MoveNext
    Wend

End Sub
```

The `btnSearch_Click()` function first creates an ADO connection object and connects to the Active Directory. It then creates a command object that is used to perform the search. The command text specifies the LDAP syntax for the query string. After the query is executed, the function iterates through the result set, obtaining references to the user objects from the ADS path returned from the query. From the user object, the function gets the name and adds it to the list.

Managing Users and Groups

One of the most common uses of a directory service is to manage user accounts. In this section, I show you how to add and remove users from a domain. I also briefly discuss how to retrieve and modify the properties for a user.

Active Directory group objects allow an administrator to manage a group of users as a whole. An administrator can use groups to control access to shared network resources, manage e-mail lists, or set network policies. I demonstrate how to create a new group object. In addition, I show how to add and remove users from a group.

Users

The Active Directory uses *user objects* to represent users and computers. The system uses the information contained in the user object to verify a user's password when the user logs on. The system also uses user objects to provide a specific security context for an application or service. User objects can be used to manage access to shared resources.

The user object contains many properties, including its name, security properties, and address properties. Most of these properties are stored in the directory and replicated to all other domain controllers within a domain. The system also replicates some of these properties to the global catalog. Other properties, such as lastLogon, lastLogoff, and logonCount, are specific to a particular domain controller and are not replicated. Still, the domain controller calculates other properties. Not all Active Directory providers support all of the possible properties of the IADsUser interface. Table 14-3 describes the properties for the WinNT providers' user object.

TABLE 14–3 WINNT USER PROPERTIES

Property	Access	Description
AccountDisabled	Read/Write	Specifies that the account is disabled
AccountExpirationDate	Read/Write	Specifies the date and time the users account is disabled, and the system does not permit the user to log in
BadLoginCount	Read only	Specifies the number of failed login attempts for the user
Description	Read/Write	Specifies the description for the user
FullName	Read/Write	Specifies the full name of the user
HomeDirectory	Read/Write	Specifies the home directory of the user
IsAccountLocked	Read/Write	Specifies that the user's account is locked
LastLogin	Read only	Specifies the date and time of the last log in for the user
LastLogoff	Read only	Specifies the date and time of the last log off for the user
LoginHours	Read/Write	Specifies the time periods that a user can log in

Property	Access	Description
LoginScript	Read/Write	Specifies the login script for the user
LoginWorkstations	Read/Write	Specifies the workstations users can log in from
MaxLogins	Read/Write	Specifies the number of simultaneous log in sessions the user can have
MaxStorage	Read/Write	Specifies the maximum amount of disk space the user is allowed
PasswordExpriationDate	Read/Write	Specifies the date and time the user's password expires
PasswordMinimumLength	Read/Write	Specifies the minimum number of characters the user's password can contain
PasswordRequired	Read/Write	Specifies whether a password is required
Profile	Read/Write	Specifies a path to the user's profile
Title	Read/Write	Specifies the title of the user

Figure 14-2 shows the CreateUser sample Visual Basic application that enables you to create and delete a user in the current domain. This sample allows you to enter a name of a user to add or delete. When you click the "Add User" button, the application tries to add the user to the current domain and sets the account password to the string "password." If you click the "Delete" button, the application tries to delete the user. Listing 14-9 shows the Visual Basic code to create a new user object and set the password for the user.

Figure 14–2: The CreateUser sample application

Listing 14–9: Creating a new user and setting a password for the user in VB

```
Private Sub btnAdd_Click()

    Dim container As IADsContainer
```

```
Dim user As IADsUser

' get the network object
Dim WshNetwork As IWshNetwork_Class
Set WshNetwork = CreateObject("Wscript.Network")

' get the domain name for the current user
Dim sDomain As String
sDomain = WshNetwork.UserDomain

' build the ADsPath
Dim sBind As String
sBind = "WinNT://" + sDomain

' bind to the container
Set container = GetObject(sBind)

' create the new user.
Dim sUser As String
sUser = edtName.Text
Set user = container.Create("user", sUser)

' update the directory
user.SetInfo

' Set the user's initial password
user.SetPassword ("password")

End Sub
```

This code in Listing 14-9 first obtains the Windows shell's network object to get the current domain name. It then builds an ADsPath string to bind to the domain object. The code then retrieves the user name to create from the edit control. It then creates the user and calls the SetInfo() method of the IADsUser interface to ensure the directory is updated.

Deleting users from the Active Directory is even easier. Listing 14-10 shows the Visual Basic code to delete users.

Listing 14-10: Deleting users from the Active Directory in VB

```
Private Sub btnDelete_Click()

    Dim container As IADsContainer
    Dim user As IADsUser
```

```
' get the network object
Dim WshNetwork As IWshNetwork_Class
Set WshNetwork = CreateObject("Wscript.Network")

' get the domain name for the current user
Dim sDomain As String
sDomain = WshNetwork.UserDomain

' get the user name
Dim sUser As String
sUser = edtName.Text

' build the ADsPath
Dim sBind As String
sBind = "WinNT://" + sDomain + "/" + sUser

' bind to the user
Set user = GetObject(sBind)

' get the container from the user
Set container = GetObject(user.Parent)

' delete the new user.
container.Delete "user", user.Name

Set user = Nothing
```

```
End Sub
```

This code first tries to bind to a user in the current domain. After it is bound to the user object, it obtains the container object that contains the object and calls the Delete() method on the IADsContainer interface, specifying which user should be deleted. It then frees its copy of the user object.

Groups

Groups are Active Directory objects that contain references to user objects and other groups. Groups provide a convenient way for administrators to organize users to manage access to shared resources.

Figure 14-3 shows a screen shot of the vbGroup sample application that enables you to manage groups of users on a domain. This application allows you to add and remove users from groups.

Figure 14-3: The vbGroup sample application

The application lists all of the groups on the current domain in the groups list box. If the user clicks the "Add New Group" button, the application displays a dialog box that allows the user to specify a name and a description for the new group.

When you select a group, the application enumerates all of the members of the selected group and displays its users in the "Users" list box. If you click the "Add..." button, the application displays a dialog box that allows you to select existing users to add to the selected group. Selecting a user and clicking the "Remove" button removes the user from the group. Listing 14-11 shows the Visual Basic code for the vbGroup sample application.

Listing 14-11: Managing groups in the directory in VB

```vb
Option Explicit

Dim sDomain As String
Dim domain As ActiveDs.IADsContainer

'
' Form_Load: initializes the form
'
Private Sub Form_Load()

    ' get the network object
    Dim WshNetwork As IWshNetwork_Class
    Set WshNetwork = CreateObject("Wscript.Network")

    ' get the domain name for the current user
    sDomain = WshNetwork.UserDomain

    ' build the ADsPath
    Dim sBind As String
```

```
    sBind = "WinNT://" + sDomain

    ' bind to the container
    Set domain = GetObject(sBind)

    LoadGroups

End Sub

'
' listGroups_Click: list the users for a group
'
Private Sub listGroups_Click()

    ' get the selected group
    Dim Group As IADsGroup

    Dim sGroup As String
    sGroup = listGroups.Text
    Dim sBind As String
    sBind = "WinNT://" + sDomain + "/" + sGroup
    Set Group = GetObject(sBind)

    ' clear list control
    listUsers.Clear

    'enumerate users
    Dim User As IADs

    For Each User In Group.Members
        listUsers.AddItem User.Name
    Next User

End Sub

'
' btnAddGroup_Click: creates a new group
'
Private Sub btnAddGroup_Click()

    ' Show new group dialog
    dlgNewGroup.Show vbModal

    ' create the new group
```

```
        Dim Group As IADsGroup
        Set Group = domain.Create("group", _
            dlgNewGroup.editGroupName.Text)
        Group.SetInfo

        ' add a description if one was provided
        Dim sDescription As String
        sDescription = dlgNewGroup.editDescription.Text
        If sDescription <> "" Then
            Group.Description = sDescription
            Group.SetInfo
        End If

        ' add added group
        listGroups.AddItem Group.Name

        ' select the newly added group
        listGroups.ListIndex = listGroups.NewIndex

        ' unload the dialog
        Unload dlgNewGroup
    End Sub

    '
    ' btnAdd_Click: adds a user to a group
    '
    Private Sub btnAdd_Click()

        ' show the user's dialog
        dlgUsers.Show vbModal

        ' get the group from the selected
        Dim Group As IADsGroup

        Dim sGroup As String
        sGroup = listGroups.Text
        Dim sBindGroup As String
        sBindGroup = "WinNT://" + sDomain + "/" + sGroup
        Set Group = GetObject(sBindGroup)

        ' build user string
        Dim sUser As String
        sUser = dlgUsers.listUsers.Text
        Dim sBindUser As String
```

```
    sBindUser = "WinNT://" + sDomain + "/" + sGroup + "/" + sUser

    ' add user
    Group.Add sBindUser

    ' refresh user list
    listGroups_Click

    ' unload dialog
    Unload dlgUsers

End Sub

'
' btnRemove_Click: removes a user from a group
'
Private Sub btnRemove_Click()

    ' get selected group
    Dim Group As IADsGroup

    Dim sGroup As String
    sGroup = listGroups.Text
    Dim sBindGroup As String
    sBindGroup = "WinNT://" + sDomain + "/" + sGroup
    Set Group = GetObject(sBindGroup)

    ' build user string
    Dim sUser As String
    sUser = listUsers.Text
    Dim sBindUser As String
    sBindUser = "WinNT://" + sDomain + "/" + sGroup + "/" + sUser

    ' remove user
    Group.Remove sBindUser

    ' refresh user list
    listGroups_Click

End Sub

'
' LoadGroups: loads the groups for the domain
'
```

```
Private Sub LoadGroups()

    ' Load groups on the domain
    domain.Filter = Array("group")

    ' clear lists
    listGroups.Clear

    ' enumerate groups
    Dim Group As IADsGroup

    For Each Group In domain
        listGroups.AddItem Group.Name
    Next Group

End Sub
```

The Form_Load() method for the VB form object in Listing 14-11 first gets the domain name for the current user and binds the global domain variable. It then calls the LoadGroups() method to fill the group list control with all of the groups for the domain.

The listGroups_Click() method retrieves the users from the selected group. The method first binds to the selected group. Then it clears the list box and enumerates the Group.Members collection adding the user name to the list control.

The btnAddGroup_Click() method enables a user to create a new group. The method first displays the Create group dialog box that enables users to specify the name and description of the group they want to create. It then creates the group using the domain object.

The btnAdd_Click() method adds a user to a group. The method first displays a dialog enabling you to select a user from all of the users on the domain. Then it binds to the selected group, builds the binding string for the user, and adds the user to the group. It then reloads the list of users and unloads the dialog's form.

The btnRemove_Click() method removes the selected user from a group. It first binds to the selected group, then builds a binding string for the user, removes the user, and reloads the list of users.

The LoadGroups() method is a helper method that enumerates the list of groups for a domain. As the method enumerates each group, it adds the group's name property to the listGroups list box.

Summary

In this chapter, I covered some of the basics of the Active Directory and the ADSI API. The Active Directory provides a way for administrators and users to access and manage network resources. The Active Directory is designed to be scalable, extensible, and distributed. ADSI provides many interfaces to enable you to manage network resources. It also allows an application to access different directory services without having to know about the details of each service.

In the next chapter, I cover a few Windows 2000 system services that did not quite fit into any of the previous chapters. You can take advantage of these services to simplify your application development.

Chapter 15

Additional System Services

IN THIS CHAPTER

- ◆ Character mode consoles
- ◆ Power management system
- ◆ Lightweight interprocess communication
- ◆ Internet integration
- ◆ Cryptography algorithms and protocols

IN THIS CHAPTER, I show you how to use a few Windows 2000 system services that did not quite fit in any of the previous chapters. These facilities come from both the Windows kernel itself and from other parts of the system. The kernel provides character mode consoles, a power management system, and lightweight communication objects (such as mailslots and pipes). The Internet Explorer shell provides the Internet API in the form of `WinInet.DLL`, and the system provides support for cryptography through `Crypt32.DLL`.

Character Mode Consoles

Character mode consoles in Windows 2000 are actually a bit of a throwback to the non-GUI days of software development. In the past, computers only supported display terminals of 25 lines of 80 characters through which users got all of their output. It turns out that the simplicity of this design is still useful today.

The character mode console typically is used from software through the C standard library `printf()` and `scanf()` functions. Although the C++ standard stream objects `std::cout` and `std::cin` have superceded these functions, you've used character mode input and output throughout your career as a professional programmer. Windows supplies the console kernel object so that you can write software that uses these old and familiar concepts.

The general consumer will no longer accept an application that uses the console as its primary means for user interaction. Great Windows applications must use compelling, rich GUI in order to succeed. You should use console mode for administration, utilities, and other such situations that favor function over form. In this section, I will first cover the basic characteristics of console applications; then I will show you how to use APIs for controlling their attributes and buffers; and finally, I will touch on interacting with the user.

Basic characteristics

Character mode applications use the concept of a standard input stream (stdin) and a standard output stream (stdout) to manage the flow of information from the keyboard to the terminal. Windows 2000 supplies applications with virtual keyboards and terminals through its *console kernel objects*. These objects appear as windows on the desktop but only support the display of characters in a two-dimensional array; graphic objects are not supported.

 Windows 2000 enables you to display the console window in full-screen mode. Press **Alt-Enter** from a command box to toggle full-screen mode on and off.

A Windows console kernel object consists of an input buffer and at least one screen buffer that the console window can display. The input buffer delivers keystrokes and mouse clicks from the user to the application, while the output buffer receives data from the application in a two-dimensional array.

As I stated early on in this book (Chapter 2), Windows does not have many preconceived notions about the nature of a process. Processes that begin as console applications can create GUI objects such as dialog boxes, and processes that begin as GUI applications can create consoles for character streaming. I summarize the high-level APIs that you will use to interact with console objects in Table 15-1.

TABLE **15-1 HIGH-LEVEL CONSOLE OBJECT APIS**

API	Description
AllocConsole()	Creates and attaches a new console object to a process that has no current console.
FreeConsole()	Detaches and possibly destroys the console object currently attached to the process.
GetStdHandle()	Retrieves a kernel object handle to one of the standard streams associated with the current console object. Possible handles include STD_INPUT_HANDLE, STD_OUTPUT_HANDLE, and STD_ERROR_HANDLE.
CloseHandle()	Releases a reference to console stream object.

There are two ways to create a console for an application. The first method is to mark the EXE as a console application, which tells Windows to execute the CreateProcess() API on the file with the valid handles to a console object set into the STARTUPINFO parameter; the system will either create a new console or supply the console of the creating process. The second method is to use the AllocConsole() API. You can detach and destroy the application's current console with the FreeConsole() API.

Chapter 2, "Basic Operating System Programming," covers process attributes and process creation in detail.

Console objects are unlike other kernel objects; they are not first-class securable objects like mutexes or events. The kernel does not permit a process to own more than one console object. In fact, the AllocConsole() and FreeConsole() APIs do not take any parameters because an application can disassociate itself only from the current console (if there is one) and only can receive a new console if it currently does not have one. Windows does destroy the console object when no current process references it. Listing 15-1 shows you a console application that changes consoles during execution by releasing the one given to it at startup and creating a new one.

Listing 15-1: Changing and creating a console

```
// project replacecons
#include <windows.h>

// helper method to pause for a keypress in the current
//   standard input stream
void WaitForKeypress()
{
    // fetch the standard input handle
    HANDLE hStdin = ::GetStdHandle(STD_INPUT_HANDLE);

    // save the console mode
    DWORD dwModeOrig(0);
    if(hStdin!=NULL && ::GetConsoleMode(hStdin, &dwModeOrig))
    {
        // disable all buffering of the input stream
        ::SetConsoleMode(hStdin, 0);

        // wait for a key to be pressed
```

```
        TCHAR szBuf[1];
        DWORD dwRead(0);
        ::ReadFile(
            hStdin, // read from standard input
            szBuf,  // save to our dummy (1 char) buffer
            1,      // only read a single char
            &dwRead,// throw away the bytes read
            NULL);  // no overlapped I/O

        // restore the console mode
        ::SetConsoleMode(hStdin, dwModeOrig);
    }

    // release the stream
    ::CloseHandle(hStdin);
    hStdin = NULL;
}

void main()
{
    // release the current console
    ::SetConsoleTitle("Original console");
    ::FreeConsole();

    // create a new console
    ::AllocConsole();
    ::SetConsoleTitle("New console");

    // pause for a keypress
    WaitForKeypress();
}
```

The application in Listing 15-1 sets the title of the original console with the SetConsoleTitle() API, then disassociates from it with the call to FreeConsole(). Next, the application creates a new console with the AllocConsole() call and sets its title appropriately. Finally, the application calls into a useful little helper function, WaitForKeypress(), which references the current input stream and uses the blocking ReadFile() API to stop the current thread until the user presses a key.

 You should make a note of where the helper function is in Listing 15-1 named WaitForKeypress(). You may want to use this again in your applications.

Like other kernel objects, you refer to the console through handles. A console has three distinct handles that actually specify three data streams. The *input handle* refers to the keyboard presses and mouse events from the user; it is standard input. The *output handle* refers to the data displayed directly on the console window; it is standard output. The third console handle is *standard error*; applications should use this data stream for reporting warnings or errors to the user rather than reporting them in the standard output stream. In order to gain access to these handles, use the GetStdHandle() API; this function simply takes a value indicating which handle you want and returns it to you when you have an associated console. To release your reference to the console stream, use the CloseHandle() API as you do for other kernel objects. The WaitForKeypress() function in Listing 15-1 demonstrates both of these APIs.

Using console attribute APIs

A process has some control over its console's window on the desktop — but not full control. You cannot change the location of the actual window that holds the console or force it to close unless you are the only process that is associated with it. You can affect some of the appearance using the console attribute APIs that I summarize in Table 15-2

TABLE **15-2 CONSOLE ATTRIBUTE APIS**

API	Description
GetConsoleTitle()	Retrieves the current title of the console's desktop window
SetConsoleTitle()	Changes the title of the console's desktop window
GetConsoleCP()	Retrieves the code page of the console input stream
SetConsoleCP()	Changes the code page of the console input stream
GetConsoleOutputCP()	Retrieves the code page of the console output stream
SetConsoleOutputCP()	Changes the code page of the console output stream

Continued

TABLE **15-2 CONSOLE ATTRIBUTE APIS** *(Continued)*

API	Description
`SetConsoleTextAttributes()`	Alters the foreground and background colors of new text written to or read from the console
`GetConsoleScreenBufferInfo()`	Fetches the attributes of the screen buffer associated with the output stream of the console in a `CONSOLE_SCREEN_BUFFER_INFO` structure

---

The example in Listing 15-1 shows you the `GetConsoleTitle()` and `SetConsoleTitle()` APIs; these reflect and affect the state of the title bar on the console's desktop window respectively. That is all that your application can use to modify the state of the window holding its console. You have no control over location, size, font, scroll bars, and so on.

The console's code page determines the character that each byte value input from or displayed to a user will be. That is, the code page maps keystrokes to byte values and byte values to display characters. It is simply a translation table between numbers and symbols. The code page for the input stream within the console can be queried and modified with the `GetConsoleCP()` and `SetConsoleCP()` APIs. Similarly, the output stream code page can be queried and modified with the `GetConsoleOutputCP()` and `SetConsoleOutputCP()` APIs.

In addition to the character that the console renders for the value of a byte output to the console, the console enables you to specify the coloring of the character. This is not the sexiest thing in Windows, but it does allow you to add some flash to console applications. The `SetConsoleTextAttribute()` API enables you to change the color in which the console displays characters. The attribute value is a bitmask containing values for the presence of red, green, and blue in the foreground or background; for example, `FOREGROUND_GREEN | BACKGROUND_RED | BACKGROUND_BLUE` produces green text on a purple background when the character is rendered.

To actually display data to the user, the console object uses a *buffer* and a *window*. The window is a portal that displays the data in the buffer. A window's size is controlled by the user and can have only as many rows and columns as the buffer that backs it. The buffer is the actual data for display and can have more rows or columns than the window. The window can be moved arbitrarily on top of the buffer. For example, if your buffer is 80 columns and 50 rows while the window is 80 columns by 25 rows, in the console window you might show the top 25 rows, the bottom 25 rows, or some in between.

You can query the size of the console window in characters using the GetConsoleScreenBufferInfo() API. This API takes a handle to the output stream and a reference to a data structure to fill.

Listing 15-2 shows you how to examine and change some of the attributes in a console's window. It uses some of the APIs described in the above paragraphs.

Listing 15-2: Examining and changing attributes in a console

```
// project attribcons
#include <windows.h>
#include <iostream>

void main()
{
    // look up the standard output handle
    HANDLE hStdout = ::GetStdHandle(STD_OUTPUT_HANDLE);

    // fetch the screen buffer information for stdout
    CONSOLE_SCREEN_BUFFER_INFO csbi;
    if(::GetConsoleScreenBufferInfo(hStdout, &csbi))
    {
        // current text attributes
        std::cout << "Text attributes: " << csbi.wAttributes
            << std::endl;
        ::SetConsoleTextAttribute(hStdout,
            FOREGROUND_BLUE|
            BACKGROUND_GREEN);

        // report the buffer size
        std::cout << "Output buffer height: " << csbi.dwSize.Y
            << " width: " << csbi.dwSize.X << std::endl;
        ::SetConsoleTextAttribute(hStdout,
            FOREGROUND_RED|FOREGROUND_GREEN|FOREGROUND_BLUE|
            BACKGROUND_RED);

        // report on the desktop window's attributes
        DWORD dwWinHeight = csbi.srWindow.Bottom -
            csbi.srWindow.Top + 1;
        DWORD dwWinWidth = csbi.srWindow.Right -
            csbi.srWindow.Left + 1;
        std::cout << "Window height: " << dwWinHeight
            << " width " << dwWinWidth << std::endl;
        ::SetConsoleTextAttribute(hStdout,
            FOREGROUND_BLUE|FOREGROUND_INTENSITY);
    }
```

```
    // clean up the output handle
    ::CloseHandle(hStdout);
    hStdout = NULL;

    // report the code page
    std::cout << "Code page: " << ::GetConsoleCP()
        << std::endl;
}
```

The simple example in Listing 15-2 runs through some of the APIs that I've discussed in this section. The output, as shown in Figure 15-1, illustrates the properties of the console that are available for inspection along with a simple toggling of color attributes. The application shows you the various attributes retrieved through the GetConsoleScreenBufferInfo() API one at a time, changing colors using the SetConsoleTextAttribute() API. The example finishes up by displaying the current input code page using the GetConsoleCP() API.

Figure 15-1: Using text attributes in console output

You can modify the window and buffer attributes of a console by right-clicking a console window and selecting Properties. Windows will pick up the settings next time it runs the application if you choose to save them. You should try different settings and rerun the application in Listing 15-2 to see the results.

Using console buffers

A *console buffer object* is a pseudo-kernel object that represents data area in the virtual memory space of your process that holds characters and attributes for display in its console. A console may have more than one console buffer, but can have only a single active buffer at any point in time, and that is the one that the desktop window displays. You will want to manually manage Windows console buffers when, for example, you have different, complicated presentations of data that the user needs to see sequentially – you calculate the new one in a new buffer, and then quickly swap it into the display. To manage these buffers, you will use the APIs in Table 15-3

TABLE 15-3 CONSOLE BUFFER MANAGEMENT APIS

API	Description
CreateConsoleScreenBuffer()	Allocates a new screen buffer object and returns a handle. Requires security attributes, a requested access, and a sharing mode.
SetConsoleScreenBufferSize()	Alters the size of the passed buffer object to a new count of rows and columns.
SetConsoleActiveScreenBuffer()	Changes the console buffer currently displayed to the one passed.
WriteConsoleOutput()	Copies data from a supplied byte array directly into a buffer object. Requires the starting column and row along with a height and width of the rectangle to write.
ReadConsoleInput()	Copies and removes data from the passed input buffer object into the passed byte array.
WriteConsoleOutputCharacter()	Sends characters from a passed byte array into a buffer object beginning at a specified row and column, wrapping at the current column width of the buffer.
ReadConsoleInputCharacter()	Copies characters out of the passed input buffer object into a passed byte array beginning at the passed row and column location.
WriteConsoleOutputAttribute()	Changes the foreground and background color attributes using a passed data array, beginning at a specified row and column then wrapping at the current column width of the buffer object.

Continued

TABLE 15-3 CONSOLE BUFFER MANAGEMENT APIS *(Continued)*

API	Description
`ReadConsoleInputAttribute()`	Copies foreground and background color attributes from the passed input buffer object into a new data array beginning at a specified row and column.
`FillConsoleOutputCharacter()`	Duplicates the passed character a specified number of times in the passed console output buffer, beginning at a desired row and column.
`FillConsoleOutputAttribute()`	Duplicates the passed foreground and background color attribute a specified number of times in the passed console output buffer, beginning at a desired row and column.
`GetConsoleMode()`	Retrieves flags that describe the behavior of the input or output console screen buffer.
`SetConsoleMode()`	Alters the behavior of the passed input or output screen buffer.
`GetConsoleCursorInfo()`	Retrieves the current size and visibility of the console screen buffer's cursor in a `CONSOLE_CURSOR_INFO` structure. Retrieves the position of the cursor with the `GetConsoleScreenBufferInfo()` API.
`SetConsoleCursorInfo()`	Alters the size and visibility of passed console screen buffer's cursor.
`SetConsoleCurorPosition()`	Moves the position of the cursor in the passed console buffer.

You can think of the console buffer as a two-dimensional array of `CHAR_INFO` structures, which simply are composed of a character and its color attribute. To create a new console buffer, use the `CreateConsoleScreenBuffer()` API. This creation API is similar to other kernel object creators — it requires an access mode and security attributes. The access mode sets read-only or read-write protection on the buffer, and the security attributes enable you to create an inheritable buffer. The creation API also requires a sharing mode when used in a multithreaded environment.

The result of a successful call to `CreateConsoleScreenBuffer()` is a handle to the new object. This handle is similar to the handles returned by the `GetStd Handle()` API—you must release your reference to the backing object with `CloseHandle()` when you're finished with it. Before manipulating the screen buffer, you should configure it. The `SetConsoleScreenBufferSize()` API enables you to specify the size in rows and columns of the buffer.

You can manipulate the buffer by directly writing to it with the `Write ConsoleOutput()` API. The write function copies a rectangular block of `CHAR_INFO` data into the specified screen buffer. In addition to this function, you can copy characters only with the `WriteConsoleOutputCharacter()` API, which copies a linear buffer to continuous cells in the screen buffer, wrapping at the end of each row. Finally, the `WriteConsoleOuputAttribute()` API behaves similarly to `WriteConsoleOutputCharacter()`, but it modifies the attributes of the screen buffer, not the characters.

For block filling a console screen buffer, the kernel offers the `FillConsole OutputCharacter()` API, which takes a single character and start location and copies that character into as many cells in the buffer as you specify. In similar fashion, the `FillConsoleOutputAttribute()` API floods a buffer with a single attribute value.

By default, the standard output buffer is the active buffer for a console. You can make a new buffer active in the console window at any time by calling the `SetConsoleActiveScreenBuffer()` API, which simply takes a handle to the activating buffer. Swapping buffers into the window enables you to make modifications to the data offline and then quickly display them to the user. Listing 15-3 shows the creation and use of a secondary buffer to execute this swap.

Listing 15-3: Creating and using a secondary console screen buffer

```
// project buffercons
#include <windows.h>

void main()
{
    // save the current standard output handle
    HANDLE hStdout = ::GetStdHandle(STD_OUTPUT_HANDLE);

    // fetch the attributes of the current output
    CONSOLE_SCREEN_BUFFER_INFO csbi;
    ::GetConsoleScreenBufferInfo(hStdout, &csbi);

    // create an offscreen buffer
    HANDLE hAltout = ::CreateConsoleScreenBuffer(
```

```
                    GENERIC_READ|GENERIC_WRITE,  // read-write access
                    0,                            // no sharing required
                    NULL,                         // default security
                    CONSOLE_TEXTMODE_BUFFER,      // must be text mode
                    NULL);                        // must be null
        if(hAltout!=NULL)
        {
            // size the new buffer the same as the current
            ::SetConsoleScreenBufferSize(hAltout, csbi.dwSize);

            // fill each buffer with its number
            DWORD dwLength = csbi.dwSize.X * csbi.dwSize.Y;
            DWORD dwCopied(0);
            COORD coStart = {0,0};
            ::FillConsoleOutputCharacter(
                hStdout,        // the buffer to set chars in
                '1',            // character to set
                dwLength,       // number of chars to set
                coStart,        // starting cell
                &dwCopied);     // cells copied
            ::FillConsoleOutputCharacter(hAltout, '2', dwLength,
                coStart, &dwCopied);

            // now, loop through flipping colors on the buffers
            for(int nAttrib=0xFF ; nAttrib>0 ; --nAttrib)
            {
                // change the offscreen buffer
                ::FillConsoleOutputAttribute(
                    hAltout,      // the new buffer
                    nAttrib,      // color to set the text
                    dwLength,     // number of colors to set
                    coStart,      // beginning point
                    &dwCopied); // return count of chars changed

                // flip to the new buffer and wait
                ::SetConsoleActiveScreenBuffer(hAltout);
                ::Sleep(100);

                // change the color and do the same operation to
                //  the other (original) buffer
                --nAttrib;
                ::FillConsoleOutputAttribute(hStdout, nAttrib,
                    dwLength, coStart, &dwCopied);
                ::SetConsoleActiveScreenBuffer(hStdout);
```

```
        ::Sleep(100);
      }
    }

    // clean up the new buffer
    ::CloseHandle(hAltout);
    hAltout = NULL;
  }
```

The example in Listing 15-3 creates a new console buffer and sets it to the same size as the one currently in the console window. The program then changes the characters in each buffer to be unique (ones and twos). Finally, the program loops through attribute values, sets the attributes of each buffer, and makes it active in the console window. The program also executes a little pause between buffer swaps so that you can see the change.

There are some other console buffer object APIs that I described in Table 15-3 but did not use in Listing 15-3 which you may find helpful. In addition to the data in the buffer, the screen buffer object has the concept of an active cursor. The cursor has a position that can be set with `SetConsoleCursorPosition()`; its location is queried with the `GetConsoleScreenBufferInfo()` API that is also used in Listing 15-2. In addition to position, the cursor has visibility and size that can be set and queried with the `SetConsoleCursorInfo()` and `GetConsoleCusorInfo()` APIs.

Finally, a console screen buffer has an output mode associated with it. The console's output mode, along with its code page and current text attributes, determines the behavior when certain characters are sent to it with the `WriteFile()` and `WriteConsole()` APIs. The output mode is queried and set with the `GetConsoleMode()` and `SetConsoleMode()` APIs. The output mode can be set with a bitmask that enables you to wrap and scroll the buffer in the window with the `ENABLE_WRAP_AT_EOL_OUTPUT` flag. You can tell the console to interpret escape sequences, such as the carriage return, with the `ENABLE_PROCESSED_OUTPUT` flag.

Handling console input and output

One last thing that you need to know when using the console object is how to read and write to it directly through using Windows APIs. To exchange data with the console, you have two choices: *high-level* and *low-level APIs*.

 The low-level APIs enable you to read and write data from the console streams one character at a time. However, they are beyond the scope of this text.

The high-level APIs for handling console *input/output (I/O)* also come in two flavors: *console-specific APIs* and *general kernel object APIs*:

◆ Console-specific APIs include the ReadConsole() and WriteConsole() APIs. These functions are supplied by Kernel32.DLL to work solely on console kernel objects and natively support Unicode characters.

◆ General kernel object APIs include the ReadFile() and WriteFile() APIs introduced in Chapter 4, "Commonly Used Kernel Objects." You can use these functions to read and write any file or console kernel object.

My recommendation is to use the standard kernel object APIs, ReadFile() and WriteFile(), when dealing with direct console I/O. They're simple to use once you've used them on disk files. Listing 15-4 shows you how to write directly to the console output.

Listing 15-4: Writing directly to the console output

```
// project writecons
#include <windows.h>
#include <string>

// helper method to send a string out to stdout
bool WriteOutDirect(const std::string& strOut)
{
    bool bWriteOK(false);

    // fetch the standard output stream
    HANDLE hStdout = ::GetStdHandle(STD_OUTPUT_HANDLE);
    if(hStdout!=INVALID_HANDLE_VALUE && !strOut.empty())
    {
        DWORD dwWritten(0);
        bWriteOK = ::WriteFile(
            hStdout,                  // send to standard output
            strOut.c_str(),           // the passed string
            (DWORD)strOut.length(),   // length of string
            &dwWritten,               // return of bytes written
            NULL)!=0;                 // not overlapped
    }
    return(bWriteOK);
}

void main()
{
    // dump the current environment to the output stream
```

```
LPTSTR pszEnvBlock = reinterpret_cast<LPTSTR>(
    ::GetEnvironmentStrings());
if(pszEnvBlock!=NULL)
{
    // when used as a CGI application, the application must
    //  signal the type of content it is generating
    WriteOutDirect("content-type: text/plain\n\n");

    // loop through the strings
    LPTSTR pszVar = pszEnvBlock;
    std::string strVar = pszVar;
    while(!strVar.empty())
    {
        // move the pointer to the next string
        pszVar += (strVar.length() + 1);

        // ignore hidden variables
        if(strVar[0]!='=' && strVar[0]!='_')
        {
            // add a CR and dump the string
            strVar += '\n';
            ::WriteOutDirect(strVar);
        }

        // grab the next string
        strVar = pszVar;
    }

    // release the environment strings
    ::FreeEnvironmentStrings(pszEnvBlock);
    pszEnvBlock = NULL;
}
}
```

Listing 15-4 shows you how to create a simple application that loops through the environment variables for a process and sends them to the console using the WriteFile() API. This application is actually intended to create a CGI application. For more information, see the sidebar "CGI Console Applications."

The example in Listing 15-4 simply retrieves the block of environment variables using the GetEnvironmentStringd() API and loops through each, sending them to the local helper function WriteOutDirect(). This helper function then retrieves the handle to the console output stream, using the GetStdHandle() API, and sends it the entire string using the WriteFile() API. This technique is the most direct method for sending data to the output stream – no runtime library is involved.

CGI Console Applications

A Web server uses a *Common Gateway Interface (CGI)* application to interact with other applications in the system and construct HTML pages that have dynamic (calculated on-the-fly) content rather than static (authored and stored) content. The CGI application uses console input and output exclusively for interchanging data with the Web server.

When writing a CGI application, make sure that the console stream handling is done as efficiently and correctly as possible; you may want to use the direct ReadFile() and WriteFile() APIs. The code example in Listing 15-4 constructs a helper method called WriteOutDirect() that dumps characters directly to the console standard output stream — which delivers the output bytes as cleanly as possible. No putchar() or iostream handling gets between the application and the console.

For more information on CGI applications, see the specification at http://hoohoo.ncsa.uiuc.edu/cgi/interface.html.

In CGI, the Web server uses environment variables to send information to your application. The simple CGI application in Listing 15-4 grabs this block of data and reflects it to the caller with a plain-text dump. The first line of output, the content-type header, tells the browser that the returned response will be text. The application then simply runs through each variable and dumps it to the stream. To use the application, you can copy the EXE file to your Web server's scripts directory — C:\InetPub\Scripts\ on my machine with Internet Information Server (IIS) version 5.0 — and use the address prefix http://localhost/scripts/ to see the output. The following figure shows you the results.

The figure shows the results of running the program from Listing 15-4 as a CGI application. If you inspect the results, you can see some variables that typically are not in a user's environment — namely the variables beginning with GATEWAY, HTTP, REMOTE, SCRIPT, and SERVER.

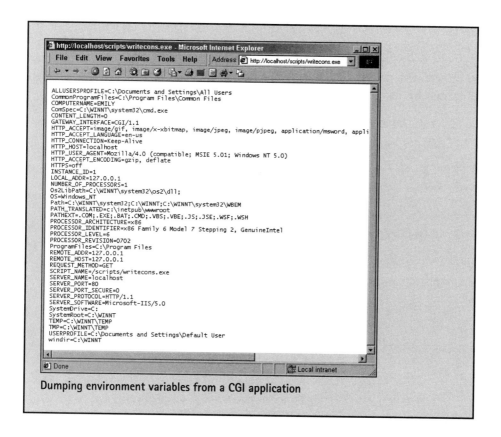

```
ALLUSERSPROFILE=C:\Documents and Settings\All Users
CommonProgramFiles=C:\Program Files\Common Files
COMPUTERNAME=EMILY
ComSpec=C:\WINNT\system32\cmd.exe
CONTENT_LENGTH=0
GATEWAY_INTERFACE=CGI/1.1
HTTP_ACCEPT=image/gif, image/x-xbitmap, image/jpeg, image/pjpeg, application/msword, appli
HTTP_ACCEPT_LANGUAGE=en-us
HTTP_CONNECTION=Keep-Alive
HTTP_HOST=localhost
HTTP_USER_AGENT=Mozilla/4.0 (compatible; MSIE 5.01; Windows NT 5.0)
HTTP_ACCEPT_ENCODING=gzip, deflate
HTTPS=off
INSTANCE_ID=1
LOCAL_ADDR=127.0.0.1
NUMBER_OF_PROCESSORS=1
Os2LibPath=C:\WINNT\system32\os2\dll;
OS=Windows_NT
Path=C:\WINNT\system32;C:\WINNT;C:\WINNT\system32\WBEM
PATH_TRANSLATED=c:\inetpub\wwwroot
PATHEXT=.COM;.EXE;.BAT;.CMD;.VBS;.VBE;.JS;.JSE;.WSF;.WSH
PROCESSOR_ARCHITECTURE=x86
PROCESSOR_IDENTIFIER=x86 Family 6 Model 7 Stepping 2, GenuineIntel
PROCESSOR_LEVEL=6
PROCESSOR_REVISION=0702
ProgramFiles=C:\Program Files
REMOTE_ADDR=127.0.0.1
REMOTE_HOST=127.0.0.1
REQUEST_METHOD=GET
SCRIPT_NAME=/scripts/writecons.exe
SERVER_NAME=localhost
SERVER_PORT=80
SERVER_PORT_SECURE=0
SERVER_PROTOCOL=HTTP/1.1
SERVER_SOFTWARE=Microsoft-IIS/5.0
SystemDrive=C:
SystemRoot=C:\WINNT
TEMP=C:\WINNT\TEMP
TMP=C:\WINNT\TEMP
USERPROFILE=C:\Documents and Settings\Default User
windir=C:\WINNT
```

Dumping environment variables from a CGI application

Finally, when dealing with applications that use console input and output, you probably want to handle the **Ctrl+C** and **Ctrl+Break** signals from the user. The SetConsoleCtrlHandler() API enables you to modify the behavior of these key presses by letting you supply a callback function. The default handlers for these signals call the ExitProcess() API, which is a harsh way to end your application. You also can respond to the user closing the console desktop window, logging off, and shutting down the machine in one of these handler routines. These APIs are not shown in Listing 15-4.

Power Management System

Windows 2000 includes support for managing the power consumption of the hardware with the *OnNow Design Initiative*. This specification lists guidelines for designing hardware and software that enables the computer to behave like an appliance:

instantly and always available when the user presses the on switch, while at the same time appearing to be off when not in use yet ready to respond to internal wake-up events. Most major PC manufacturers have designed their newest systems to comply with this specification. This section will show you how to take advantage of it from within your applications.

 For more information about the OnNow Design Initiative, see `http://www.microsoft.com/hwdev/onnow/default.htm`.

By integrating the hardware and software, Windows enables applications to keep the user informed of the hardware power state and the hardware informed of the system use state. This avoids problems from the past such as hardware thinking that the system was not in use because the user was not pressing keys or using the mouse.

The power management system allows the system to do the following:

1. Gracefully handle changes in hardware configuration, such as the introduction or removal of a docking station

2. Permit an application to schedule itself to wake up and perform an operation when the system otherwise would not be in use

3. Promote the always-on system, which enables you to create applications and services that work after hours

4. Help to extend battery life as compliant applications shut down non-critical operations when running on battery

Managing the power state

OnNow stipulates four power states for the system: *working, sleeping, soft off,* and *mechanical off.* The four states are described as follows:

1. The *working* state is fully powered and usable.

2. The *sleeping* state is the most interesting. The system appears to be off, but it consumes power at some level and responds to external communication and internal timer events.

3. In the *soft-off* state, the system appears to be off; but the working state can be resumed by restoring the context from persistent memory.

4. The *mechanical-off* state is a no-power state; the system requires a full boot to resume working.

You can manage these power states with the APIs shown in Table 15-4. You should note that the system's processor(s) are not running in any state other than the working state. The system exits the working state whenever the user leaves it idle for a period or requests it by pressing a switch or asking the shell. In order be a great Windows application, your software needs to be aware of the status of the power management system and may need to manage it.

TABLE 15-4 POWER STATE MANAGEMENT APIS

API	Description
GetSystemPowerStatus()	Retrieves the current power status for the system in a SYSTEM_POWER_STATUS structure.
IsSystemResumeAutomatic()	Determines if the system was restored to the working state through a wake-up event and not on user demand.
RequestWakeupLatency()	Specifies how quickly the computer should enter the working state when a wake-up event occurs. This determines what level of sleeping state the system should enter.
SetSystemPowerState()	Attempts to power down the system and enter a sleeping state. Requires two Boolean parameters: fSuspend indicates a request to suspend (TRUE) or hibernate (FALSE) and fForce indicates that applications will not (TRUE) or will (FALSE) get the opportunity to reject the operation.
SetThreadExecutionState()	Tells the system that it should not interrupt the current thread to sleep. Requires a single parameter indicating the reason that the thread should not be interrupted.

OnNow actually subdivides the sleeping state of the system into three levels that determine how much power the system consumes while sleeping. The lower the power consumption, the deeper the sleep — and the longer it takes to resume to the working state. The system attempts to use the lowest power consumption that all devices support by default. You can ask the system to use the lightest sleep with the RequestWakeupLatency() API, which takes a single parameter that suggests the sleep substate.

The system's final power state is soft off. This state also is called *hibernation* and, upon entering, saves the current operation context to disk so that it can resume later. The hibernation state takes the longest to enter and resume but it uses the least power; in fact, it sometimes uses none.

FINDING THE SYSTEM POWER STATE

The kernel exposes the `GetSystemPowerStatus()` API for you to determine the current state of the system power. The function takes a single parameter, an instance of the `SYSTEM_POWER_STATE` structure, which delivers the state of external or battery power. Listing 15-5 shows you how to interpret the data.

Listing 15-5: Inspecting the system's power state

```
// project powerstatus
#define _WIN32_WINNT 0x0500
#define WINVER 0x0500
#include <windows.h>
#include <iostream>
#include <string>


void main()
{
    // initialize the structure and fetch the power status
    SYSTEM_POWER_STATUS sps;
    ::ZeroMemory(&sps, sizeof(sps));
    if(::GetSystemPowerStatus(&sps))
    {
        // check for battery of AC power
        {
            std::string strState;

            switch(sps.ACLineStatus)
            {
            case AC_LINE_OFFLINE:
                strState = "Offline";
                break;
            case AC_LINE_ONLINE:
                strState = "Online";
                break;
            case AC_LINE_BACKUP_POWER:
                strState = "Backup";
                break;
            default:
                strState = "Unknown";
                break;
```

```
        }
        std::cout << "AC power: " << strState << std::endl;
    }

    // look for a battery
    {
        std::string strState;
        switch(sps.BatteryFlag)
        {
        case BATTERY_FLAG_HIGH:
            strState = "High";
            break;
        case BATTERY_FLAG_LOW:
            strState = "Low";
            break;
        case BATTERY_FLAG_CRITICAL:
            strState = "Critical";
            break;
        case BATTERY_FLAG_CHARGING:
            strState = "Charging";
            break;
        case BATTERY_FLAG_NO_BATTERY:
            strState = "Not present";
            break;
        default:
            strState = "Unknown";
            break;
        }
        std::cout << "Battery state: " << strState
            << std::endl;
    }

    // report on the battery if we have one
    if(sps.BatteryFlag!=128)
    {
        // battery possible (time)
        std::cout << "Battery life: ";
        if(sps.BatteryFullLifeTime!=BATTERY_LIFE_UNKNOWN)
        {
            std::cout << sps.BatteryFullLifeTime << " sec"
                << std::endl;
        }
        else
        {
```

```
            std::cout << "Unknown" << std::endl;
        }

        // battery left (percentage)
        std::cout << "Battery charge: ";
        if(sps.BatteryLifePercent!=
            BATTERY_PERCENTAGE_UNKNOWN)
        {
            std::cout << sps.BatteryLifePercent << "%"
                << std::endl;
        }
        else
        {
            std::cout << "Unknown" << std::endl;
        }

        // battery left (time)
        std::cout << "Battery charge: ";
        if(sps.BatteryLifeTime!=BATTERY_LIFE_UNKNOWN)
        {
            std::cout << sps.BatteryLifeTime << " sec"
                << std::endl;
        }
        else
        {
            std::cout << "Unknown" << std::endl;
        }
    }
  }
}
```

The simple example in Listing 15-5 fetches the current status of power for the system with the GetSystemPowerStatus() API and reports it. The most important field for your applications is ACLineStatus, which tells you whether you should run threads that may consume battery power but are not critical to, or demanded by, the user.

SUSPENDING THE SYSTEM POWER STATE

You can affect the power management state of the system with the SetSystem PowerState() API. This API has two Boolean flags; one flag, fSuspend, moves to suspend or hibernate mode, and the other flag, fForce, lets other applications reject the request to suspend. The example in Listing 15-6 shows you one way to use this API.

Listing 15-6: Suspending a system

```
// project suspend
#define _WIN32_WINNT 0x0500
#define WINVER 0x0500
#include <windows.h>
#include <iostream>

// helper method to dump the last encountered error to the
// output stream
void ReportLastError()
{
    // fetch the last error code
    DWORD dwLastError = ::GetLastError();

    // get the system to create a descriptive error string
    LPCTSTR szError;
    ::FormatMessage(
        FORMAT_MESSAGE_FROM_SYSTEM |    // system error
        FORMAT_MESSAGE_ALLOCATE_BUFFER, // create a buffer
        NULL,          // no source string
        dwLastError,// error to describe
        0,             // use system language
        (LPTSTR)&szError,   // buffer to return
        0,             // ignored
        NULL);         // ignored

    // report it
    std::cerr << "Last error: " << szError << std::endl;
}


// helper method to give the current thread the ability to
// shut down/suspend the machine if possible
void EnableShutdownPrivilege()
{
    // grab this process's account token
    HANDLE hToken = INVALID_HANDLE_VALUE;
    if(::OpenProcessToken(
        GetCurrentProcess(),        // this process
        TOKEN_ADJUST_PRIVILEGES,    // need to change
        &hToken))                   // return buffer
    {
        // find the LUID for shutdown
        TOKEN_PRIVILEGES tkp;
```

```
        if(::LookupPrivilegeValue(
            NULL,                    // this system
            SE_SHUTDOWN_NAME,        // required priv
            &tkp.Privileges[0].Luid))// dest buffer
        {
            // set the params for adjustment
            tkp.PrivilegeCount = 1;
            tkp.Privileges[0].Attributes = SE_PRIVILEGE_ENABLED;

            // try to adjust the privileges
            ::AdjustTokenPrivileges(
                hToken,     // token to change
                FALSE,      // not disabling all others
                &tkp,       // new privilege
                0,          // don't want previous state
                NULL,       // don't want previous state
                0);         // don't want previous state
        }
    }
}


void main()
{
    // first, we need the shutdown privilege
    ::EnableShutdownPrivilege();

    // change the system to the suspended state
    if(!::SetSystemPowerState(
        TRUE,    // suspend, not hibernate state
        FALSE)) // allow other applications to object and abort
    {
        std::cout << "Unable to suspend machine." << std::endl;
        ::ReportLastError();
    }
}
```

In order to place the system in a low-power state with the SetSystem
PowerState() API, the executing thread must have the SE_SHUTDOWN_NAME privilege. In order to ensure the account has this, the example in Listing 15-6 supplies a
helper function called EnableShutdownPrivilege(), which gets the account
token, finds the identifier of the required privilege, and enables it. The main execution path then attempts to suspend the machine. If the suspension is unsuccessful,
the helper method ReportLastError() is called to explain why.

You will use the helper functions in Listing 15-6, `ReportLastError()` and `EnableShutdownPrivilege()`, time and again when writing applications that use the Windows API directly. You'll want the first one for logging problems when and where they occur, rather than looking them up manually. You'll want the second so that you don't have to rely on manual configuration of the running account before your application can be successful.

PERFORMING OTHER POWER STATE MANAGEMENT TECHNIQUES

In order to tell Windows that your application should not be suspended, the kernel supplies the `SetThreadExecutionState()` API. This function takes a single parameter that tells the system why it should not suspend the computer until the thread exits or resets the execution state. Flag values include `ES_DISPLAY_REQUIRED`, which tells the system that the thread is affecting the display, and `ES_USER_PRESENT`, which tells the system that a user has asked to avoid suspend operations.

You should call the `SetThreadExecutionState()` API whenever your application runs a job at the request of the user that the system should not suspend. The typical example of such an operation is a PowerPoint presentation; this API avoids the laptop suspending and screen going blank while the presenter describes the contents of a slide.

The last thing that you should do to manage the power state of a Windows system is to take advantage of the resume flag in the waitable timer. The `SetWaitableTimer()` API supplies a flag that enables you to tell the system to resume from the sleep state when the timer expires. You should take advantage of this flag by resuming the system when the operation is one that the user actually does want to happen even if the system is sleeping, such as downloading a large file or defragmenting a disk.

Chapter 4, "Commonly Used Kernel Objects," introduces waitable timers.

Responding to power state changes

Now that you're aware of the power management states in the system, your applications should be aware that they can be suspended or resumed at any time. The system notifies you of these power state changes using a Windows message, `WM_POWERBROADCAST`. The system delivers this message to your application when entering and exiting the sleep state, and when the power source is switched or falls to a preselected level.

The reason for the WM_POWERBROADCAST message is contained in the message's WPARAM; the codes begin with PBT_ and usually don't involve the LPARAM. I describe these codes in Table 15-5.

TABLE 15-5 WM_POWERBROADCAST NOTIFICATION CODES

Notification Code	Intention
PBT_APMBATTERYLOW	The battery currently driving the system is failing.
PBT_APMPOWERSTATUSCHANGE	The power has been changed from AC to battery or vice-versa, or the battery life remaining has fallen through a level defined by the user.
PBT_APMQUERYSUSPEND	Requests permission from all applications to enter the suspended state; each application may return TRUE to permit the suspension or BROADCAST_QUERY_DENY to prevent it.
PBT_APMQUERYSUSPENDFAILED	Informs all applications that an attempt to transition to the suspended state was denied by another application in the system.
PBT_APMRESUMEAUTOMATIC	Indicates that the system has resumed working due to a wake-up event such as a waitable timer.
PBT_APMRESUMECRITICAL	Indicates that the system has resumed working after suspending due to battery failure. This indicates that the application was suspended without any prior warning.
PBT_APMRESUMESUSPEND	Indicates that the system has resumed working due to a user demand.
PBT_APMSUSPEND	Informs all running applications that the system is about to enter the suspended state.

The first power status message that your application may care about is the PBT_APMPOWERSTATUSCHANGE. This message indicates that the system has switched from battery to AC power or vice-versa. To determine the direction of the switch, you should call the GetSystemPowerStatus() API, then enable or disable appropriate operations (threads) in your application. This enables you to run only power-intensive, low-value operations when plugged into the AC power.

The next notification that your application may be interested in is the PBT_ APMBATTERYLOW. When the battery is low, your application may want to close up unused files or perform other operations that it otherwise would wait to do until shutdown so that if power suddenly is lost, bad things don't happen.

The system sends the PBT_APMQUERYSUSPEND notification when the user wants to suspend the system. This enables your application to clean up network connections and close down anything else that may not return from the sleep mode properly. You have the option of telling the system that your application does not want to suspend by returning BROADCAST_QUERY_DENY. If the user asks for sleep mode, you should deny the operation only when you require intervention from the user, such as inserting a disk or choosing a file name. The message LPARAM indicates whether you have permission to ask the user; if you don't, you simply must fail the query. If you permit the system to suspend, the next power message that you receive likely is PBT_APMSUSPEND, which indicates that system is about to suspend.

A good way to handle the suspend and resume cycle is to close everything down, log what you did, and wait for the PBT_APMRESUMESUSPEND notification. Once the resume message comes, your application can reverse the shutdown log, opening files and network connections with error handling. This enables you to provide an application that continues to run seamlessly through sleep stages.

There are cases when the system does not send the PBT_APMSUSPEND message, such as when the battery simply cuts out. In this case, applications receive the PBT_APMRESUMECRITICAL notification when the system moves to the working state again. Also, if the suspend fails because another application denies the request, the system sends the PBT_APMQUERYSUSPENDFAILED notification and you should undo any preparation for suspension that your application already completed.

Lightweight Interprocess Communications

The Windows 2000 kernel provides two forms of lightweight interprocess communication that I haven't discussed yet: mailslots and pipes. A *mailslot* is a one-way mechanism in which one process drops off a message for another to pick up. A *pipe* can be a one-way or bidirectional stream of data from one process to another. This section introduces the basics of these communication mechanisms and shows you some simple applications for them.

You should be aware that both of these mechanisms are specific to Windows. Although the implementation details are not important for our purposes, these objects are not cross-platform and operate only between Windows machines within the networking enterprise.

Using mailslots

As I stated earlier, a mailslot enables processes to communicate with one another. Mailslots are first-class kernel objects; they are nameable and securable. The creator/owner of a mailslot is the server – it is the only process that may read data from the mailslot. Only the addressee can open its mail. The process that sends messages to that mailslot is a client. It just dumps messages into the slot and continues processing. The server will read the message and take appropriate action. Mailslots are a one-way communication mechanism. The sender receives no feedback that the message arrived or that the receiver acted upon it.

A mailslot actually behaves much like a file object; in fact, you use the standard kernel `ReadFile()` and `WriteFile()` APIs to access the data in a mailslot. The kernel allocates volatile memory to back each mailslot and restricts the size of the slot to 64KB, so use mailslots for short message passing and place larger chunks of data in supporting temporary disk files or some other mechanism. I describe the APIs specific to creating and using mailslots in Table 15-6.

TABLE 15-6 MAILSLOT OBJECT SERVER APIS

API	Description
`CreateMailslot()`	Creates a new mailslot kernel object, returning a handle to it. Requires a name, maximum message size, timeout for read operations, and security attributes.
`GetMailslotInfo()`	Inspects the current state of the mailslot passed by handle. Retrieves total number of messages in queue and the size of the next message to read.
`SetMailslotInfo()`	Changes the read timeout for the passed mailslot.

To create a new mailslot, use the `CreateMailslot()` API. This function, like other kernel object creators, requires a name and security attributes. Names for mailslots must begin with the string `\\.\mailslot\` during creation and should continue on with `CompanyName\Application\SlotName` in order to guarantee uniqueness.

Mailslot names are similar to the names of shares in the file system, but they must all begin with `\\<hostname>\mailslot\`; `<hostname>` can be "." for the current machine, "*" for all machines in the primary domain, a specific domain name for all machines in that domain, or the name of a specific machine.

Further, the `CreateMailslot()` API takes a maximum message length and write timeout threshold. Usually, a maximum message length is not chosen because the hard maximum of 64KB is so small that trimming out any more seems fruitless. Often the write timeout is set to `MAILSLOT_WAIT_FOREVER` rather than a calculated duration, in milliseconds. This allows threads to block on data appearing in the mailslot. The server process can alter this timeout threshold at any point using the `SetMailslotInfo()` API, which takes the handle of the mailslot and the new timeout value. The simple example in Listing 15-7 creates a mailslot.

Listing 15-7: Creating a mailslot

```
// project createslot
#include <windows.h>
#include <iostream>

void main()
{
    // unique name the for mailslot from this app
    static LPCTSTR c_szSlotName =
        "\\\\.\\mailslot\\w2kdg\\createslot\\simple";

    HANDLE hSlot = ::CreateMailslot(
        c_szSlotName,            // unique name
        0,                       // no max message size
        MAILSLOT_WAIT_FOREVER,   // no timeout
        0);                      // default security
    if(hSlot!=INVALID_HANDLE_VALUE)
    {
        // look at the profile of the slot
        DWORD dwMaxSize(0), dwNextSize(0), dwMsgCount(0),
            dwReadTimeout(0);
        if(::GetMailslotInfo(
            hSlot,               // our simple slot
            &dwMaxSize,          // possible size
            &dwNextSize,         // size of next message
            &dwMsgCount,         // messages waiting
            &dwReadTimeout))     // millisec til timeout
        {
            // dump the waiting count to the console
            std::cout << "Messages waiting: " << dwMsgCount
                << std::endl;
        }
    }

    // clean up the object
```

```
    ::CloseHandle(hSlot);
    hSlot = INVALID_HANDLE_VALUE;
}
```

The simple example in Listing 15-7 creates a well-named mailslot and looks at the information that the system maintains about it. This application is a *mailslot server* because it creates the slot. Once the server closes its last reference to the slot, the system destroys the backing object.

Once your server application successfully creates a mailslot, you need to publish its name so clients may use it. In order for a client process to open and use your mailslot, it must use the CreateFile() API, supplying the name of the mailslot as the file to open. With a successfully created file kernel object, the client may call the WriteFile() API to dump messages into the slot.

As messages arrive in the mailslot, the server process must remove and process them. A process usually creates a worker thread that monitors the mailslot and passes messages from other processes to the proper destination thread. In order to discover a message waiting in the mailslot, the server application calls the GetMailslotInfo() API. The GetMailslotInfo() API requires the handle to the kernel object as returned from CreateMailslot() and sends back the maximum message size, the size of the next message waiting, the number of messages waiting, and the read timeout period.

Since mailslots restrict the data to something small, they're very simple to deal with inside your application. The example in Listing 15-8 shows you a simple server application that reports any messages it receives until you stop it.

Listing 15-8: Running a mailslot server

```
// project slotwatcher
#include <windows.h>
#include <iostream>

void main()
{
    // unique name for the mailslot from this app
    static LPCTSTR c_szSlotName =
        "\\\\.\\mailslot\\w2kdg\\ch15\\timeslot";

    // create the new mailslot
    HANDLE hSlot = ::CreateMailslot(
        c_szSlotName,            // unique name
        0,                       // no max message size
        MAILSLOT_WAIT_FOREVER,   // no timeout
        0);                      // default security
    if(hSlot!=INVALID_HANDLE_VALUE)
    {
```

```
while(true)
{
    // look at the profile of the slot
    DWORD dwNextSize(0), dwMsgCount(0);
    if(::GetMailslotInfo(
        hSlot,              // our simple slot
        NULL,               // don't need possible size
        &dwNextSize,        // size of next message
        &dwMsgCount,        // messages waiting
        NULL))              // don't need timeout
    {
        // check for a new message
        if(dwMsgCount>0)
        {
            // create a new buffer
            char* szBuffer = new char[dwNextSize + 1];

            // read in the data from the slot
            DWORD dwRead(0);
            if(::ReadFile(
                hSlot,          // slot to read from
                szBuffer,       // buffer
                dwNextSize,     // buffer size
                &dwRead,        // size received
                NULL))          // not overlapped
            {
                // terminate the buffer and dump it out
                szBuffer[dwRead] = '\0';
                std::cout << szBuffer << std::endl;
            }

            // clean up the buffer
            delete [] szBuffer;
            szBuffer = NULL;
        }
        else
        {
            // pause for a bit
            ::Sleep(100);
        }
    }
}
}
```

```
    // clean up the object
    ::CloseHandle(hSlot);
    hSlot = INVALID_HANDLE_VALUE;
}
```

The program in Listing 15-8 simply creates a uniquely named mailslot at startup. The program immediately enters a *forever loop* that looks at the current state of the mailslot with GetMailslotInfo(). Next, if there is a message waiting, the example creates a buffer to hold it and uses ReadFile() to grab it. The act of reading the data clears the message from the queue. If no message is waiting, the program pauses for a short time so that it doesn't chew up the CPU looking for new messages. Unfortunately, a mailslot kernel object cannot be used with the kernel waiting functions.

The program then null-terminates and dumps the message — assumed to be a text string — to the console output. In order to create messages for the server to watch, the program in Listing 15-9 sends the current time as a mailslot client.

Listing 15-9: Running a mailslot client

```
// project slotwriter
#include <windows.h>
#include <iostream>
#include <time.h>

void main()
{
    // save the name of this system
    TCHAR szComputerName[MAX_COMPUTERNAME_LENGTH+1];
    DWORD dwNameSize(MAX_COMPUTERNAME_LENGTH);
    ::GetComputerName(szComputerName, &dwNameSize);

    // broadcast to all mailslots of this name in the domain
    static LPCTSTR c_szSlotName =
        "\\\\*\\mailslot\\w2kdg\\ch15\\timeslot";

    // create the new mailslot
    HANDLE hSlot = ::CreateFile(
        c_szSlotName,           // unique name
        GENERIC_WRITE,          // writeaccess
        FILE_SHARE_READ,        // must allow reading
        NULL,                   // default security
        OPEN_EXISTING,          // must exist
        FILE_ATTRIBUTE_NORMAL,  // standard file
        NULL);                  // no template
    if(hSlot!=INVALID_HANDLE_VALUE)
```

```
    {
        // write stuff forever
        while(true)
        {
            // get the current time
            time_t timeNow;
            time(&timeNow);

            // convert to local time
            struct tm* ptmLocal = localtime(&timeNow);

            // create a time message
            TCHAR szTime[1024];
            ::strcpy(szTime, szComputerName);
            ::strcat(szTime, "'s SlotWriter time is: ");
            ::strcat(szTime, asctime(ptmLocal));

            // send the time to the file
            DWORD dwWritten(0);
            ::WriteFile(
                hSlot,                // write to the slot
                szTime,               // send the time string
                ::strlen(szTime)+1,   // add the null string
                &dwWritten,           // grab the bytes written
                NULL);                // not overlapped

            // pause while the time changes
            ::Sleep(1000);
        }
    }

    // clean up the object
    ::CloseHandle(hSlot);
    hSlot = INVALID_HANDLE_VALUE;
}
```

The mailslot client application shown in Listing 15-9 first opens the kernel file object that represents all mailslots of the appropriate name in the primary domain. With the handle to the mailslot(s), the client enters an infinite loop to fetch the time as a string, label it, and send it to the mailslot(s). Afterwards, the client pauses until it knows that the time has changed (1 second) and then does it again. When you run the mailslot client, SlotWriter.EXE, you must have at least one server (SlotWatcher.EXE) running in the domain; otherwise it exits immediately.

You should notice that the name of the mailslot is very similar to the *Universal Naming Convention (UNC)* format. In fact, by interpreting the "." of the name as the name of the computer that owns the mailslot, you can think of the "mailslot" field of the name as a network share. This analogy is exactly what the designers intended. Your application can access a mailslot on another machine using `\\<computername>\mailslot\` as the beginning of the file name in the call to `CreateFile()`.

This convention goes even further and allows some powerful operations. Using `\\<domainname>\mailslot\` as the prefix for the file name in `CreateFile()` retrieves the handle to all mailslots on all machines in the specified domain that have the same name (following `mailslot\`). Supplying `\\*\mailslot\` opens all mailslots on all machines within the primary domain that share the same name. This enables you to create applications that can broadcast data throughout the domain using simple `CreateFile()` and `WriteFile()` calls—once you distribute a mailslot server to each.

Using pipes

Pipes are another lightweight interprocess communication device that the Windows 2000 kernel supplies your applications. Like the mailslot metaphor, the pipe metaphor was selected carefully. It implies a connection between the client and server application to exchange data.

The basics of pipes are very similar to mailslots. They allow applications on Windows machines within the enterprise to have simple, direct communication with one another using file object read and write APIs. The operating system mercifully hides the intricacies of connecting the processes whether they're on the same machine or connected by a *wide area network (WAN)*.

Your application can use pipes for one-way or two-way communication. A one-way pipe either contains inbound or outbound data; a two-way pipe contains both and is called *duplex*.

Pipes can be *anonymous* or *named*. Named pipes have many more capabilities than anonymous pipes, such as the ability to communicate over the network.

ANONYMOUS PIPES

An anonymous pipe, as you might expect, has no name like other first-class kernel objects. It is created with the `CreatePipe()` API, which sends back a kernel object handle to the inbound and outbound sides of the pipe. All anonymous pipes are one-way, and it is the responsibility of your server to get one of those handles to the other process.

Sharing handles means that there already must be a channel for communication between the two processes. The send or receive handle is sent after creating a new one using the `DuplicateHandle()` API. This new channel of communication is one-way—it either broadcasts from the server or for the server. To establish bidirectional communication, you need only repeat the procedure.

Once both parties have handles to the pipe, one side calls the `WriteFile()` API on the pipe handle when it has data, while the other calls the `ReadFile()` API to wait for the receive data. The `ReadFile()` operation does not return until the `WriteFile()` on the other end completes or the supplied buffer is filled. The two processes have threads that are very tightly coupled once they start using the anonymous pipe.

To complete use of the pipes, both sides must agree that no more data will be sent. Once each side releases its reference to the underlying kernel object with the `CloseHandle()` API, the system destroys the pipe and reclaims its resources.

NAMED PIPES

Named pipes differ from anonymous pipes in that they have a unique name. Their name format is much the same as the mailslot: `\\.\pipe\` as a prefix and `CompanyName\Application\PipeName` as the suffix. This naming allows two processes to use the named pipe whether or not they are on the same machine. The named pipe also can be used as the first means of communication between processes.

The creation of a named pipe, along with its use, is slightly more complicated. However, the general purpose is the same: enable two processes to communicate using the file APIs they should be familiar with already.

Please see the MSDN Platform SDK documentation on Interprocess Communication and Pipes for more details about the creation and use of a named pipe.

Internet Integration

The Windows 2000 operating system expects that most users will connect it to the Internet. In order to help your application take advantage of this very large network and fulfill *Metcalfe's law*, Windows supplies the *WinInet library* so that you can perform Internet operations easily. This library is very tightly coupled with the Internet Explorer application and essentially provides you with a way to command the browser and receive its output with your application. This section shows you how to leverage the facilities that WinInet provides.

Metcalfe's law, named after Robert M. Metcalfe of 3Com Corporation, states that the value of a network increases with the square of the number of connections.

Configuring and using the Internet

The WinInet library, delivered by `WinInet.DLL`, lets your application act as an Internet client and connect to services on machines regardless of their physical location. The library enables you to use the high-level *Hypertext Transfer Protocol (HTTP)* and the *File Transfer Protocol (FTP)* over TCP/IP with simple-to-write code.

DIALING INTO THE INTERNET

Windows gives you the tools necessary to establish a connection with your local *Internet Service Provider (ISP)* in the WinInet library. I summarize the connection APIs that you will need in Table 15-7.

TABLE 15-7 INTERNET CONNECTION APIS

API	Description
`InternetGetConnectedStateEx()`	Determines the current state of any connection to the Internet and the name of that connection
`InternetAttemptConnect()`	Tries to connect to the Internet using the default connection, prompting the user if necessary
`InernetAutodial()`	Starts the modem dialing the default Internet connection, suppressing user interaction if requested
`InernetDial()`	Similar to `InternetAutodial()`; begins a modem connection to the Internet using a specific connection
`InternetCheckConnection()`	Attempts to connect to the passed URL
`InternetGoOnline()`	Prompts the user for permission to connect to the passed URL
`InternetHangUp()`	Disconnects the passed connection to the Internet
`InternetAutodialHangup()`	Disconnects the automatically dialed connection to the Internet

You can query and modify the system's Internet configuration through the WinInet library. First, the system's current connection state is available through the

InternetGetConnectedStateEx() API. This function tells you if there is an available connection to the Internet and the type of connection. Then the system administrator establishes a connection with the Internet Connection Wizard application, available through the shell. Listing 15-10 shows you how to use this API to determine the current state of connectivity.

Listing 15-10: Determining the current state of Internet connectivity

```
// project inetconntype
#define _WIN32_WINNT 0x0500
#define WINVER 0x0500
#include <windows.h>
#include <iostream>
#include <string>
#include <wininet.h>
#pragma comment(lib, "wininet.lib")

inline bool TestFlag(DWORD dwValue, DWORD dwFlag)
{
    bool bSet = (dwValue & dwFlag)!=0;
    return(bSet);
}


void main()
{
    // get the current connection status
    DWORD dwFlags(0);
    TCHAR szName[MAX_PATH];
    if(::InternetGetConnectedStateEx(
        &dwFlags,    // buffer to hold the flags
        szName,      // the name of the connection
        MAX_PATH,    // size of the name buffer
        0))          // must be 0
    {
        // dump the connection name
        std::cout << "Using connection named: " << szName
            << std::endl;

        // current hook-up state
        std::cout << "Internet connection is "
            << (TestFlag(dwFlags, INTERNET_CONNECTION_OFFLINE)
                ? "OffLine" : "OnLine")
            << std::endl;

        // dump out other flags
```

```
        if(TestFlag(dwFlags, INTERNET_CONNECTION_MODEM))
        {
            std::cout << "Modem used to connect." << std::endl;
        }
        if(TestFlag(dwFlags, INTERNET_CONNECTION_LAN))
        {
            std::cout << "LAN used to connect." << std::endl;
        }
        if(TestFlag(dwFlags, INTERNET_CONNECTION_PROXY))
        {
            std::cout << "Proxy server used to connect."
                << std::endl;
        }
        if(TestFlag(dwFlags, INTERNET_RAS_INSTALLED))
        {
            std::cout << "RAS is available." << std::endl;
        }
    }
    else
    {
        // can't use the Internet
        std::cout << "No Internet connection available."
            << std::endl;
    }
}
```

The simple example in Listing 15-10 illustrates the data that the `InternetGet ConnectionStateEx()` API returns. The example checks for any connection with the return value from the function, then uses the returned name and flags to interpret and report its current state.

In order to change the current state of the connection, you can call one of the WinInet connecting APIs. First, the `InternetAttemptConnect()` API directs the system to try to establish a connection if one doesn't already exist. This function interacts with the user if need be to make the connection. If `InternetAttemptConnect()` fails, the user does not wish to go online, and your application should accept the news gracefully and operate in an offline mode.

The `InternetAutodial()` API tells the system to connect to the Internet using the default connection. You can tell the system to attempt this connection in *unattended mode* (no user intervention required) with the first of two flags. The second flag specifies a parent window for any dialog boxes the system may pop up for the user.

The `InternetDial()` API is much like `InternetAutodial()`, except that it requires the name of a connection to dial. Connections are stored in the *remote access service (RAS)* phone book. Use the `RasEnumEntries()` API and other RAS functions to select one. The `InternetDial()` API also enables you to supply some additional configuration options for any dialog boxes the system may wish to display.

CHECKING A URL CONNECTION

One of the basic elements of the Internet is the *Uniform Resource Locator (URL)*. A URL describes the location of data or a service precisely on any machine connected to the Internet, much like a fully specified telephone number. Once you have a URL, you can retrieve the content behind it. In order to determine whether the machine running your application has access to the data behind a URL, WinInet supplies the `InternetCheckConnection()` API. This function takes a URL, attempts to establish a connection to it over the Internet, and returns success or failure to you. Listing 15-11 shows you the simplicity of this function.

Listing 15-11: Checking a connection to a URL

```
// project inetcheck
#define _WIN32_WINNT 0x0500
#define WINVER 0x0500
#include <windows.h>
#include <iostream>
#include <wininet.h>
#pragma comment(lib, "wininet.lib")

void main()
{
    // check the connection
    static LPCTSTR c_szUrl = "http://www.idg.com";
    if(::InternetCheckConnection(
        c_szUrl,                       // check a known location
        FLAG_ICC_FORCE_CONNECTION,     // make the connection
        0))                            // must be 0
    {
        std::cout << "Connection to " << c_szUrl
            << " is currently available." << std::endl;
    }
    else
    {
        std::cout << "Connection not responding." << std::endl;
    }
}
```

The example in Listing 15-11 makes sure that the system you run it on currently has access to the IDG Books Worldwide Web site. If the system is not online, you can use the final connection API, `InternetGoOnline()`, to ask the system to establish it and attempt to access the passed URL.

When your application is finished with the Internet connection, you should call the `InternetHangUp()` or `InternetAutodialHangUp()` API, depending on the method you used to connect. You need not disconnect from the Internet if the system already is connected.

MANIPULATING URLS

The WinInet library adds some helper methods for you to manipulate URLs. I summarize these helper functions in Table 15-8.

TABLE 15-8 URL HELPER APIS

API	Description
InternetCanonicalizeUrl()	Creates a new URL that replaces all unsafe characters and spaces with escape sequences
InternetCombineUrl()	Takes a base and relative URL and creates a new, fully specified URL
InternetCreateUrl()	Creates a new URL from its component parts in the URL_COMPONENTS structure
InternetCrackUrl()	Fills a URL_COMPONENTS structure with the pieces from a URL string

First, the InternetCanonicalizeUrl() API takes a URL that a user enters and prepares it for use within other APIs that require a URL. URL canonicalization includes such things as escaping spaces, removing "." and ".." relative paths, and encoding non-ASCII as well as reserved characters. The InternetCombineUrl() API takes a base URL and appends the relative location of a resource on the server.

To create a URL from component parts, use the InternetCreateUrl() API. This function takes a URL_COMPONENTS structure that breaks the URL into smaller pieces. The function's companion API is InternetCrackUrl(), which breaks a URL from string form apart into components. The example in Listing 15-12 shows you how to use these two APIs on URLs.

Listing 15-12: Creating and cracking URLs

```
// project urls
#define _WIN32_WINNT 0x0500
#define WINVER 0x0500
#include <windows.h>
#include <iostream>
#include <wininet.h>
#pragma comment(lib, "wininet.lib")

void main()
{
```

```cpp
// construct an url from basic components
URL_COMPONENTS urlcmp;
::ZeroMemory(&urlcmp, sizeof(urlcmp));
urlcmp.dwStructSize = sizeof(urlcmp);

// create http://www.idg.com/
urlcmp.nScheme = INTERNET_SCHEME_HTTP;
urlcmp.nPort = INTERNET_DEFAULT_HTTP_PORT;
urlcmp.lpszHostName = "www.idg.com";
urlcmp.lpszUrlPath = "/";

// assemble the output
DWORD dwLength(1024);
TCHAR szUrl[1024];
if(::InternetCreateUrl(
    &urlcmp,         // the component version
    ICU_ESCAPE,      // escape the output properly
    szUrl,           // the output buffer
    &dwLength))      // length of the buffer/result
{
    std::cout << "Assembled URL: " << szUrl << std::endl;
}

// before cracking an url, reset the URL_COMPONENTS struct
//  and tell the API which fields to fill by setting the
//  lengths to 1 after setting the fields to NULL
::ZeroMemory(&urlcmp, sizeof(urlcmp));
urlcmp.dwStructSize = sizeof(urlcmp);
urlcmp.dwHostNameLength = 1;
urlcmp.dwSchemeLength = 1;
urlcmp.dwUrlPathLength = 1;

// now, crack apart the URL
if(::InternetCrackUrl(
    szUrl,      // the candidate URL
    0,          // the URL is 0-terminated
    0,          // no flags
    &urlcmp))   // output buffer
{
    // copy the chunks of the url
    TCHAR szScheme[1024];
    ::strncpy(szScheme, urlcmp.lpszScheme,
        urlcmp.dwSchemeLength);
    szScheme[urlcmp.dwSchemeLength] = '\0';
```

```
TCHAR szHostname[1024];
::strncpy(szHostname, urlcmp.lpszHostName,
    urlcmp.dwHostNameLength);
szHostname[urlcmp.dwHostNameLength] = '\0';
TCHAR szPath[1024];
::strncpy(szPath, urlcmp.lpszUrlPath,
    urlcmp.dwUrlPathLength);
szPath[urlcmp.dwUrlPathLength] = '\0';

// show the results
std::cout << "Scheme: " << szScheme
    << "\nHostname: " << szHostname
    << "\nPath: " << szPath
    << std::endl;
    }
}
```

The program in Listing 15-12 first creates a new URL from its component pieces. The program sets the scheme and port to the defaults for the HTTP protocol, the host's name to the IDG Books Worldwide Web site, and the path to the root, "/". The resulting string looks like one that you type into a browser's Open dialog box (click on the File menu and choose Open...). The program then takes the constructed URL and breaks it back up into its component parts. The URL_COMPONENTS structure must be zeroed out where you want the InternetCrackUrl() API to fill data, and the length there must be set to a nonzero value.

Getting Internet content

The WinInet library main purpose is, of course, to facilitate the delivery and retrieval of content across the Internet. To accomplish this, the library supplies two families of APIs: one generic family for accessing any content on any server using the TCP/IP networking protocol and one family that has specific support for accessing content over the most popular protocols built on top of TCP/IP. This section will look at retrieving content using both families: the basic Internet*Xxx*() APIs and the HTTP-specific Http*Xxx*() APIs.

INTERNET WININET APIS
The first pseudo-object that you need from the library is the Internet *object*, referenced through the HINTERNET handle. I summarize the APIs that you will need to manipulate it in Table 15-9. In order to create an Internet object, use the InternetOpen() API. The function requires a string to describe the Internet-using program and configuration for the access, which can take the form of a proxy server – direct or as configured by the user. When you are finished with the Internet object, use the InternetCloseHandle() API to let the system know.

TABLE 15-9 INTERNET OBJECT APIS

API	Description
InternetOpen()	Creates a new object representing a connection to the Internet
InternetOpenUrl()	Creates an object that represents a connection to a specific URL on a specific Internet server
InternetReadFile()	Retrieves data from an Internet connection object
InternetCloseHandle()	Releases a reference to a connection object for a specific Internet server or the Internet in general

With an HINTERNET handle, the next function you need is the Internet OpenUrl() API. This function creates a new Internet object that represents the file the supplied URL returns an HINTERNET handle to. When using Internet OpenUrl(), you must specify the session and URL, and you may specify headers to send in the request or extended options, such as not to use Internet cookies during the request.

The handle returned from the open function is very similar to a file handle. You use a read and write API to transfer data through the handle. Release the associated resources when you are finished with it using the InternetCloseHandle() API.

Once you open a URL with InternetOpenUrl(), you may want to read the data at the location. The simple InternetReadFile() API takes the handle from the open function and retrieves the data from it. The function grabs data from the URL one chunk at a time, returning the number of bytes read. The simple example in Listing 15-13 shows you how to get a Web page over the Internet.

Listing 15-13: Retrieving a Web page generically over the Internet

```
// project readwebpage
#define _WIN32_WINNT 0x0500
#define WINVER 0x0500
#include <windows.h>
#include <iostream>
#include <wininet.h>
#pragma comment(lib, "wininet.lib")

void main()
{
    // open up the Internet
    HINTERNET hInet = ::InternetOpen(
```

```
            "w2kdg readwebpage",        // the name of this agent
            INTERNET_OPEN_TYPE_PRECONFIG,// use present config
            NULL,                       // no proxy name
            NULL,                       // no proxy bypass
            0);                         // no special flags
    if(hInet!=NULL)
    {
        // open up the URL
        HINTERNET hUrlIdg = ::InternetOpenUrl(
            hInet,                  // use the internet
            "http://www.idg.com/",  // the url to get
            NULL,                   // no headers
            0,                      // no headers
            INTERNET_FLAG_RELOAD,   // make sure to get fresh
            0);                     // no context to supply
        if(hUrlIdg!=NULL)
        {
            // create a 20kb buffer
            TCHAR szBuffer[20 << 10];
            DWORD dwRead(0);
            if(::InternetReadFile(
                hUrlIdg,            // url to read from
                szBuffer,           // destination
                20<<10 - 1,         // size of buffer
                &dwRead))           // bytes read
            {
                // dump the buffer to the output stream
                szBuffer[dwRead] = '\0';
                std::cout << szBuffer << std::endl;
            }

            // close the handle
            ::InternetCloseHandle(hUrlIdg);
            hUrlIdg = NULL;
        }

        // close the handle
        ::InternetCloseHandle(hInet);
        hInet = NULL;
    }
}
```

The program in Listing 15-13 retrieves the contents of the IDG Books Worldwide default Web page. First, it opens up the Internet using the current Internet configuration.

Then it opens up an object that represents the URL, making sure to get it freshly and not from the Internet files cache. Finally, the example reads the data using the `Internet ReadFile()` API and dumps it out to the console.

Thus far, we've dealt with WinInet APIs that begin with the prefix `Internet`. You can use these functions for URLs that reference resources behind HTTP or FTP servers. In addition to the APIs that I've shown you already, there are functions to customize almost every aspect of the communication between the system that your application is running on and the server. For instance, the `InternetSetOption()` and `InternetSetStatusCallback()` APIs enable you to program the connection at a very low level.

HTTP/FTP WININET APIS

To bring the abstraction level up, use the WinInet functions that are prefixed with `Http` and `Ftp`. These functions are meant for communicating with these servers and are tailored to expose everything you need for HTTP and FTP configuration. You can notice the first difference after the call to `InternetOpen()`. I summarize some of these more abstract APIs in Table 15-10.

The WinInet APIs also enable you to communicate at a high level with Gopher servers. However, the Gopher protocol effectively is obsolete as I write.

TABLE 15-10 HTTP OBJECT APIS

API	Description
`InternetConnect()`	Creates a protocol-specific connection to a particular URL on a known type of Internet server (HTTP or FTP)
`HttpOpenRequest()`	Creates a new request object to send to an HTTP server
`HttpAddRequestHeaders()`	Appends information to the request to be sent to the HTTP server

Continued

TABLE 15-10 HTTP OBJECT APIS *(Continued)*

API	Description
HttpSendRequest()	Transmits the request object to the destination HTTP server
HttpQueryInfo()	Inspects the header information in a response from an HTTP server

The `InternetConnect()` API breaks apart the `InternetOpenUrl()` parameter list to make it simpler for you to specify the components of an HTTP or FTP URL. It connects to a machine rather than a URL on that machine. It first requires the *domain name system (DNS)* name or *Internet Protocol (IP)* address of the server to which you want to connect. Next, the type of service (HTTP or FTP) and the port that the service is listening on is required; the WinInet header file defines the default and well-known ports for you. Finally, you can supply a user name and password for sites that require them.

 I use HTTP as the protocol of choice for the rest of this section because it is more common. Most everything I cover has an FTP equivalent.

Once you establish a connection with the target machine, use the `Http OpenRequest()` API to prepare the request. The HTTP request requires a verb, usually either `GET` or `POST`, which tells the server what action you are taking. Next, supply the resource you are interested in – a file, an executable, or data for which you want a response. You also can specify details of the HTTP header that are beyond the scope of this text.

The return from `HttpOpenRequest()` is an `HINTERNET` handle; use this handle just like a handle from `InternetOpenUrl()` earlier. You can add more header information to the request with the `HttpAddRequestHeaders()` API. This function enables you to add, replace, and merge any header data that you eventually will send to the Web server.

To execute the request, you must send it to the server. The `HttpSendRequest()` API does the work of communicating your request to the service. It enables you to add even more header information and supply data for commands, such as `POST` and `PUT`, that may take large quantities. This function blocks the calling thread while it sends the request and waits for the response. If something goes wrong, use the GetLastError() API to find out why and the ReportLastError() helper method from Listing 15-6 to report it if you cannot correct the problem in your application.

Once you send the request to the Web server, you can look at the response. The HttpQueryInfo() API enables you to examine the header information of the response from the Web server. This function takes a parameter that specifies the header that you are interested in and a buffer to hold the results. WinInet supplies all headers as strings so that when you want the length of the return, usually in HTTP_QUERY_CONTENT_LENGTH, you have to convert the return from a string to an integer.

Once you send the request, you also can use the same InternetReadFile() API to fetch the body of the results that you did in Listing 15-13. Listing 15-14 puts the steps together for accessing a Web page using the WinInet Http functions.

Listing 15-14: Retrieving a Web page through HTTP over the Internet

```
// project httpget
#define _WIN32_WINNT 0x0500
#define WINVER 0x0500
#include <windows.h>
#include <iostream>
#include <wininet.h>
#pragma comment(lib, "wininet.lib")

void main()
{
    // open up the Internet
    HINTERNET hInet = ::InternetOpen(
        "w2kdg readwebpage",            // the name of this agent
        INTERNET_OPEN_TYPE_PRECONFIG,// use present config
        NULL,                           // no proxy name
        NULL,                           // no proxy bypass
        0);                             // no special flags
    if(hInet!=NULL)
    {
        // open up the server
        HINTERNET hServer = ::InternetConnect(
            hInet,                      // Internet connection
            "www.idg.com",              // server name
            INTERNET_INVALID_PORT_NUMBER,// use the default
            NULL,                       // no username
            NULL,                       // no password
            INTERNET_SERVICE_HTTP,      // the web server
```

```
        0,                        // no flags
        0);                       // no context
    if(hServer!=NULL)
    {
        // create the HTTP request
        HINTERNET hRequest = ::HttpOpenRequest(
            hServer,                   // server connecting to
            "GET",                     // get the page
            "/",                       // default page
            HTTP_VERSION,              // default version
            NULL,                      // no referrer
            NULL,                      // accept all content
            INTERNET_FLAG_RELOAD,      // get a fresh version
            0);                        // no context
        if(hRequest!=NULL)
        {
            // send the request
            if(::HttpSendRequest(
                hRequest,              // request to send
                NULL,                  // no extra headers
                0,                     // no extra headers
                NULL,                  // no optional data
                0))                    // no optional data
            {
                // reflect the headers from the response
                TCHAR szHeaders[10 << 10];
                DWORD dwLength(10<<10);
                DWORD dwIndex(0);
                if(::HttpQueryInfo(
                    hRequest,
                    HTTP_QUERY_RAW_HEADERS_CRLF,
                    szHeaders,
                    &dwLength,
                    &dwIndex))
                {
                    szHeaders[dwLength] = '\0';
                    std::cout << szHeaders;
                }

                // reflect the body of the response
                TCHAR szBody[20 << 10];
                DWORD dwRead(0);
```

```
                if(::InternetReadFile(
                    hRequest,               // response
                    szBody,                 // destination
                    20<<10 - 1,             // size of buffer
                    &dwRead))               // bytes read
                {
                    // dump the buffer to the output stream
                    szBody[dwRead] = '\0';
                    std::cout << szBody << std::endl;
                }

            }

            // close the handle
            ::InternetCloseHandle(hRequest);
            hRequest = NULL;
        }

        // close the handle
        ::InternetCloseHandle(hServer);
        hServer = NULL;
    }

    // close the handle
    ::InternetCloseHandle(hInet);
    hInet = NULL;
    }
}
```

The program in Listing 15-14 simply runs through the steps that I've discussed to send a request to an HTTP server and collect the response. First, it opens the Internet with InternetOpen() and a connection to the IDG Books Worldwide Web server with InternetConnect(). It constructs a GET request for the default or root page of the server, addressed with the single forward slash, "/" using the HttpOpenRequest() API.

Next, the example sends the new request to the server with the Http SendRequest() API and waits for the response. Once the response is available, the example retrieves the HTTP response headers from the server using the HttpQueryInfo() API and dumps them out to the console. Finally, it fetches the body of the Web page using InternetReadFile(). Figure 15-2 shows the resulting console display, which is exactly what you would expect.

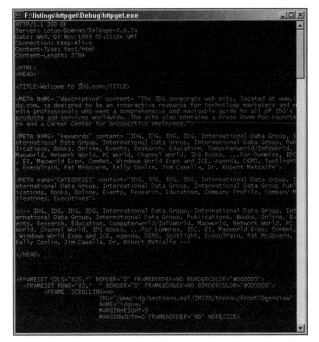

Figure 15-2: The HTML source for the Web page retrieved in
Listing 15-14

Cryptography Algorithms and Protocol

The branch of computer science that solves problems related to the privacy, authenticity, and integrity of data is *cryptography*. This broad field has devised many different algorithms and protocols over time to fend off those who want to corrupt or co-opt the communication between two parties. Leaders in this field often call it both an art and a science; it is full of obtuse, theoretical mathematics and complicated procedures. The end goal is to give you the tools to thwart lurking foes that want to inspect the very valuable data that you create and use it for ill purposes.

For those of you interested in the actual theories and implementation of cryptographic algorithms and protocols, I highly recommend the text *Applied Cryptography* by Bruce Schneier published by John Wiley & Sons, Inc. This is a seminal work in the area, and it's a whole lot of fun to read.

CryptoAPI basics

Windows 2000 gives your applications access to a small part of this world through its CryptoAPI library, delivered in `Crypt32.DLL`. This library delivers algorithms and procedures that are very complex and difficult to implement from scratch. You should use the CryptoAPI whenever you need to secure data outside the standard Windows-supplied mechanisms, such as account/domain security or the *encrypting file system (EFS)*.

 Chapter 13,"The File System," covers EFS in detail.

Since cryptographic algorithms are complicated, rapidly changing, and often proprietary, the CryptoAPI is built on a modular architecture that uses a *cryptographic service providers (CSP)* module to deliver services to calling applications. By default, Windows ships you the Microsoft RSA Base Provider. You can install others that you purchase or even write. They plug in beneath the API, and you can access them in the same manner from your application. Use the APIs in Table 15-11 to access the CSP

TABLE 15-11 CRYPTOGRAPHIC SERVICE PROVIDER APIS

API	Description
`CryptAcquireContext()`	Creates a reference to an installed CSP object and a container of cryptographic keys that it manages
`CryptGetProvParam()`	Inspects configuration and parameters from a CSP object
`CryptReleaseContext()`	Releases a reference to a CSP object
`CryptGetDefaultProvider()`	Retrieves a handle to the default installed CSP object
`CryptEnumProviders()`	Scans through the list of installed CSP modules
`CryptEnumProviderTypes()`	Lists the available CSP types installed on the system

In addition to supplying algorithms and implementations of the CryptoAPI that are new and exciting, each CSP is responsible for maintaining keys for users. *Cryptographic keys* are small chunks of data that the cryptographic algorithms require to transform data successfully from a plain message to something nobody else can read and back again. These keys are critical to recovering data once you've used the CryptoAPI to hide it.

To access a CSP, use the `CryptAcquireContext()` API. This function creates a CSP object and returns a handle to it as an `HCRYPTPROV`. You can choose which CSP to access by name or by using one of the predefined types of providers; often you may choose the system-supplied provider by selecting the `PROV_RSA_FULL` type.

When getting a CSP, you also can select the container to hold any cryptographic keys that you generate. Typically, let the provider choose this container by supplying `NULL`. The CSP will select the key container based on the account that is running your application.

Once you have a CSP object, you can inspect its configuration using the `CryptGetProvParam()` API. When you're finished with the object, you should release it with the `CryptReleaseContext()` API. Listing 15-15 shows you a simple example of setting up a CSP for use.

Listing 15-15: Initializing a CSP

```
// project cspuse
#define _WIN32_WINNT 0x0500
#define WINVER 0x0500
#include <windows.h>
#include <wincrypt.h>
#include <iostream>
#pragma comment(lib, "crypt32.lib")

void main()
{
    // fetch the CSP
    HCRYPTPROV hCSP = NULL;
    if(::CryptAcquireContext(
        &hCSP,            // handle to the new object
        NULL,             // use default key container
        NULL,             // use default provider for type
        PROV_RSA_FULL,    // get RSA provider, MS Base
        0))               // no special flags
    {
        // get the name of the CSP
        BYTE szName[MAX_PATH];
        DWORD dwLength(MAX_PATH);
        if(::CryptGetProvParam(
```

```
        hCSP,        // object to inspect
        PP_NAME,     // grab the name
        szName,      // buffer to hold data
        &dwLength,   // length of buffer/copied
        0))          // no special flags
    {
        std::cout << "CSP name: " << szName << std::endl;
    }

    // get the name of the key container
    BYTE szCtr[MAX_PATH];
    dwLength = MAX_PATH;
    if(::CryptGetProvParam(
        hCSP,        // object to inspect
        PP_CONTAINER,// grab the container name
        szCtr,       // buffer to hold data
        &dwLength,   // length of buffer/copied
        0))          // no special flags
    {
        std::cout << "Key container: " << szCtr
            << std::endl;
    }

    // release the CSP
    ::CryptReleaseContext(
        hCSP,        // object to release
        0);          // must be 0
    hCSP = NULL;
    }
}
```

The application in Listing 15-15 simply creates an object for the CSP and inspects a couple of its configuration parameters. On a fresh installation of Windows 2000, when you run the example, you should see that the provider is the Microsoft Base Cryptographic Provider and the key container is actually your login name.

You can perform other operations on the CSP object. You can inspect additional parameters, set some parameters, and add references to the handle to pass it on. For our purposes, all we need is access to it. Other operations are beyond our scope and restricted to system administration applications.

Encryption

In order to transmit a message from a sender to a receiver without anyone else reading its contents en route, the sender often disguises the content. *Encryption* is the process of transforming data from its original form to something that is difficult to retrieve without the exact knowledge of how you transformed it.

Modern cryptography enables you to select from a wide variety of algorithms to encode data in order to keep it secret. You probably have heard of the *data encryption standard (DES)* and the *Rivest-Sahmir-Adleman (RSA)* encryption that use secret numbers, called *keys*, to transform your data. The goal of these encryption algorithms is not to make it impossible to take the resulting, transformed, data and retrieve the original; the goal is to make it take more time and effort than a foe could spend.

The default CSP supplies the RSA encryption algorithm, which is a flavor of a *public-key algorithm*. The details of the public-key algorithms are unimportant, but you should be aware that they work on a pair of keys: one private and the other, of course, public. The private key is the only key that can undo encryption done with the public key and the public key is the only key that can recover data encrypted with the private key.

The CryptoAPI libray's main focus is, of course, the implementation of algorithms such as these. Table 15-12 shows you some of the APIs that you will use from the library.

TABLE 15-12 ENCRYPTION APIS

API	Description
CryptEncrypt()	Maps plain text to cipher text using the key object supplied by handle.
CryptDecrypt()	Maps cipher text to plain text using the key object supplied by handle.
CryptProtectData()	Simple function that encrypts a passed chunk of data for use only by the logged in user on the same machine.
CryptUnprotectData()	Decrypts data that was encrypted with the companion CryptProtectData() function.
CryptGenKey()	Creates a new cryptographic key or public/private key pair for the passed algorithm.
CryptDuplicateKey()	Makes a copy of a source key.

API	Description
CryptExportKey()	Creates a data block that represents the passed key object and can be passed to another process for use. This is typically done with public keys.
CryptImportKey()	Interprets a data block created by the companion CryptExportKey() function and creates a new key object in its process space.

The CryptoAPI library supplies encryption facilities through its CryptEncrypt() API. The parameter list to this function only has three interesting members: the data to encrypt, the result buffer, and the encryption key. The encryption key is an object that specifies the method of encryption and any special algorithmic setup the key creator wants. You generate an encryption key with the CryptGenKey() API. To show you how to use the CryptEncrypt() function, Listing 15-16 encrypts a string buffer and dumps it to the console.

Listing 15-16: Encrypting a string buffer

```
// project encrypt
#define _WIN32_WINNT 0x0500
#define WINVER 0x0500
#include <windows.h>
#include <wincrypt.h>
#include <iostream>
#pragma comment(lib, "crypt32.lib")

PBYTE EncryptBuffer(HCRYPTKEY hKey, const PBYTE pPlain,
                    size_t nSrcLen)
{
    // get chunk size of buffer
    DWORD dwChunkLen(0);
    ::CryptEncrypt(
        hKey,    // encryption key
        NULL,    // no additional hash key
        TRUE,    // only encrypt one block
        0,       // no special flags
        NULL,    // no data, just want size
        &dwChunkLen,// chunk size
        nSrcLen); // size of input
```

```
        // use chunk size to allocate buffer
        DWORD dwBufferLen = dwChunkLen + nSrcLen;
        PBYTE pEncrypted = new BYTE[dwBufferLen];
        ::ZeroMemory(pEncrypted, dwBufferLen);
        ::memcpy(pEncrypted, pPlain, nSrcLen);

        // encrypt one chunk at a time
        for(DWORD dwComplete=0;
            dwComplete<dwBufferLen;
            dwComplete += dwChunkLen)
        {
            // set up the next chunk
            PBYTE pBuffer = pEncrypted + dwComplete;
            DWORD dwEnc(dwChunkLen);
            BOOL bLast = dwComplete + dwChunkLen >= dwBufferLen;

            // encrypt the next chunk
            ::CryptEncrypt(
                hKey,   // encryption key
                NULL,   // no additional hash key
                bLast,  // flag for last block
                0,      // no special flags
                pBuffer,// pointer to next chunk
                &dwEnc, // bytes encrypted
                dwChunkLen); // size of input
        }
        return(pEncrypted);
    }

void main()
{
    // fetch the CSP
    HCRYPTPROV hCSP = NULL;
    if(::CryptAcquireContext(
        &hCSP,          // handle to the new object
        NULL,           // use default key container
        NULL,           // use default provider for type
        PROV_RSA_FULL,  // get RSA provider, MS Base
        0))             // no special flags
    {
        // create a new key
        HCRYPTKEY hKey = NULL;
        if(::CryptGenKey(
            hCSP,       // provider
```

```
            CALG_RC2,     // use symmetric algorithm
            0,            // no special flags
            &hKey))       // new key
    {
        // data to encrypt
        LPCTSTR szPlainText =
            "The quick brown fox jumped over the lazy dog.";
        size_t nPlainSize = ::strlen(szPlainText) + 1;

        // send the buffer to the encrypter
        PBYTE pCipherText = EncryptBuffer(hKey,
            (const PBYTE)szPlainText, nPlainSize);
        std::cout << "Plain: " << szPlainText
            << "\nCipher: " << pCipherText << std::endl;

        // clean up the buffer
        delete [] pCipherText;
        pCipherText = NULL;

        // release the key
        ::CryptDestroyKey(hKey);
        hKey = NULL;

    }

    // release the CSP
    ::CryptReleaseContext(
        hCSP,         // object to release
        0);           // must be 0
    hCSP = NULL;
    }
}
```

The application in Listing 15-16 creates a helper function, EncryptBuffer(), that takes an encryption key and a buffer, uses the former on the latter, and returns the results. The example uses the *Rivest Cipher 2 (RC2)* algorithm, which is symmetric. The cipher text can be reversed to find the plain text with the key. The CryptEncrypt() API can work only on 8-byte chunks when running RC2 (defined as part of the algorithm), and the helper method finds this out in order to break the input buffer up into suitable chunks and call the function over and again with them.

The call to CryptGenKey() API is very straightforward in Listing 15-16. It asks for a RC2 key from the CSP. This turns out to be of little use because the key cannot be shared outside the current account and process. In order to create keys for sharing with processes that want the data you generate, you must create exportable keys. Each container has a public-private key pair called the key exchange pair that you use to encrypt the actual exportable key for use by the other process. The other process then decrypts and uses the original key when it needs the data.

This coverage of encryption barely scratches the surface of the capabilities provided by the CryptoAPI. I recommend that you consult the MSDN for detailed, expansive documentation on encryption; begin with the Platform SDK documentation on security and cryptography. It includes the CryptoAPI reference.

The companion function to `CryptEncrypt()` is the `CryptDecrypt()` API. This function takes many of the same parameters and performs the reverse operation.

You should note that you must have a copy of the original key when decrypting because state information gets stored into the object by the encryption engine. The `CryptDuplicateKey()` API takes care of this for you.

Authentication and data integrity

In addition to encryption, cryptography provides authentication and data integrity to rebuff attacks. By applying a digital signature to a document, you are authenticating that it came from you. Also, the digital signature contains an integrity check that guarantees the bits of data you encrypt and takes responsibility for actually making it to the destination.

The cryptography world implements the integrity check for a data in a *hash value*. A hashing algorithm generates the hash value for the data. The algorithm is constructed in such a way that altering any bit produces a different value, and there is virtually no way to return to the original value. That is, it is very, very unlikely that any two documents could contain data that hashes identically.

In order to check integrity, the consumer of the data attempts to produce the same hash value using the same algorithm. If the two values match and the data is sensible, it is highly unlikely that any attacker replaced your original data with his own.

In order to authenticate that the data and hash value came from you, as opposed to someone else, you must have a public-private key pair that you use for signing. Then you simply take your private key and encrypt the hash value (and maybe some other data that accompanies the document). The consumer of the data then takes your public key and unwraps the hash value to verify it is the same data you sent.

To make sure that you are you in the digital signature, however, is more difficult. The current solution is the rather informal *public key infrastructure (PKI)* of the Internet. You first convince a trusted third party called a *certificate authority (CA)* that you are you, and this authority digitally signs a statement that your public key represents you. The user of your data then must believe this third party.

The CryptoAPI has a large section dedicated to creating hash values for data, signing data, and communicating with CAs. Exploring these functions falls outside the scope of this text.

I encourage you to use the MSDN CryptoAPI documentation for more information on creating hash values.

Summary

This chapter covered five distinct technologies that are important, but that had no real home anywhere else in this book. I know you appreciate the extent of console programming that Windows provides you, especially if you're from a UNIX background. You must embrace the power-management features of Windows in order to have your application certified with the Windows logo. (More details about this are in Chapter 17, "Delivering Applications.") The lightweight communication that I showed you is Windows-only, but it is very powerful. The integration of the Internet into your application will prove to be a powerful, compelling feature when done right. Finally, the use of cryptography where required will be easier to get correct thanks to the CryptoAPI.

Next, I'll show you what's new in COM. COM+ is the subject of Chapter 16, and it is one of the core technologies that lies just under the surface of almost everything within the operating system. Not only do you need it, but you'll really enjoy it, too.

Chapter 16

Working with COM+

IN THIS CHAPTER

- ◆ An overview of COM+
- ◆ COM+ services
- ◆ COM+ application deployment

THIS CHAPTER COVERS COM+, which provides a runtime environment to develop component-based applications. It is the evolution of the Component Object Model (COM) and the Microsoft Transaction Server (MTS), and, as such, extends the COM.

COM+ is a new service of Windows 2000. In this chapter, I provide an overview of COM+ and describe the services COM+ provides for your components. I finish the chapter by showing you how to deploy your COM+ applications.

An Overview of COM+

As noted above, *COM+* provides a runtime environment to develop component-based applications. COM+ extends the COM by providing additional services for scalability, robustness, and security.

COM provides developers a way to share code as binary components. The developer defines some interfaces for their component and provides implementations for these interfaces in a COM object. Multiple COM objects can be combined into a COM component. The component can be packaged as an in-process DLL or an out-of-process EXE. A client application does not need to have any knowledge of how the object is packaged or even where it resides. When a client application accesses the component, the COM subsystem loads the component and handles the communication between the client and the object.

Chapter 10, "Application Building Services," provides more information on COM components.

The COM model works well for providing clients with access to these components. However, it places the burden on the component to handle resource management and security. The COM+ runtime provides these services automatically for COM+ components. This frees the component to concentrate on performing its work, letting the system handle the mundane tasks of resource management and security.

The COM+ environment provides support for just-in-time activation, transaction processing, queued components, object pooling, and role-based security. Just-in-time activation allows the system to manage resources more efficiently, by allowing the system to deactivate a component that is not currently in use. Transaction processing provides for robust, recoverable operations. Queued components allow for greater system availability, by queuing requests to be processed later. Object pooling provides a way to manage components that are expensive to create. And role-based security allows access control to be set for at the COM+ application level. I will discuss these services in detail in the "COM+ Services" section of this chapter.

All COM+ components are DLLs that the COM+ environment manages. These DLLs are all loaded into the COM+ environment. This allows the environment to interact with, and provide services for, all components.

A COM+ component can be either *configured* or *unconfigured*. In order to take advantage of COM+ services, the component must be configured. To configure a component, add it to a COM+ application. An *unconfigured* component is a component that is not part of a COM+ application.

 I demonstrate configuring a component later in Listing 16-1.

In the rest of this section, I describe COM+ applications. I also introduce COM+ interceptors and contexts, and provide an example of how to configure a COM+ component.

COM+ applications

A *COM+ application* is a group of related COM+ components that share compatible attributes. COM+ uses the catalog manager to manage the applications and attributes. Each configured component belongs to one application.

There are two main types of COM+ applications: server applications and library applications.

◆ **Server applications:** These are the most common COM+ applications. They run in their own processes and can support all of the COM+ component services.

◆ **Library applications:** These applications run in the client process that creates them; they do not support pooling, queuing, or remote access.

There are two additional types of COM+ applications: application proxies and COM+ preinstalled system applications:

◆ **Application proxy applications:** These COM+ applications allow your client applications to remotely access the server application.

◆ **COM+ preinstalled system applications:** The COM+ environment preinstalls several system applications to implement internal services. These applications include the COM+ system application, and the COM+ utilities.

Interceptors and contexts

COM+ uses interceptors and contexts to provide services to components. When you create an object, COM+ returns an interceptor to the object instead of a reference to the object itself. The client applications no longer access the object's interfaces directly. This may seem like just adding another layer between clients and servers, but it allows COM+ to provide all of its services without your components having to do much. The interceptor does all of the work.

The interceptor returned is responsible for setting up the runtime environment in which the object lives. Interceptors examine every call to your component and make system calls to provide any services needed.

The runtime environment that is set up by the interceptor is called a *context*. A context is a group of objects within a process that share compatible attributes. Every component belongs to one context, but there can be many contexts within a process. The COM+ environment creates a proxy to handle the cross-context call.

A simple COM+ application

Now, let's create a simple COM+ application. This component takes advantage of COM+ object constructor strings. You can use object constructor strings to enable an administrator to configure a component. The COM+ environment passes the specified string to the component at creation time.

This example shows you how to create a COM+ application, add a COM+ component to it, and demonstrate how to configure the component. Listing 16-1 shows the code for the Simplecomplus component. This component is a simple Active Template Library (ATL) component with one method that displays a dialog box.

Listing 16-1: A simple COM+ component

```cpp
// Simple.h : Declaration of the CSimple Application

#ifndef __SIMPLE_H_
#define __SIMPLE_H_

#include "resource.h"       // main symbols

const int MAX_CONSTRUCT_SIZE = 255;

/////////////////////////////////////////////////////////////////
// CSimple
class ATL_NO_VTABLE CSimple :
    public CComObjectRootEx<CComSingleThreadModel>,
    public CComCoClass<CSimple, &CLSID_Simple>,
    public IDispatchImpl<ISimple, &IID_ISimple,
        &LIBID_SIMPLECOMPLUSLib>,
    public IObjectConstruct
{
public:
    CSimple();

DECLARE_REGISTRY_RESOURCEID(IDR_SIMPLE)

DECLARE_PROTECT_FINAL_CONSTRUCT()

BEGIN_COM_MAP(CSimple)
    COM_INTERFACE_ENTRY(ISimple)
    COM_INTERFACE_ENTRY(IDispatch)
    COM_INTERFACE_ENTRY(IObjectConstruct)
END_COM_MAP()

// ISimple
public:
    STDMETHOD(ShowDialog)();

// IObjectConstruct
public:
    STDMETHOD(Construct)(IDispatch* pCtorObj);

// members
protected:
    TCHAR m_szConstruct[MAX_CONSTRUCT_SIZE + 1];
};
```

```
#endif //__SIMPLE_H_

// Simple.cpp : Implementation of CSimple
#include "stdafx.h"
#include "Simplecomplus.h"
#include "Simple.h"
#include "dlgConstruct.h"

///////////////////////////////////////////////////////////////
// CSimple

//
//   CSimple::CSimple : constructor
//
CSimple::CSimple()
:    m_szConstruct()
{
    m_szConstruct[0] = NULL;
}


//
//   CSimple::ShowDialog() : shows the dialog
//
STDMETHODIMP CSimple::ShowDialog()
{
    // create the dialog and set the construction string
    CConstructDialog dlg;
    dlg.SetConstructString(m_szConstruct);

    // display the dialog
    dlg.DoModal();

    return S_OK;
}


//
//   CSimple::Construct : initialize the object instance
//
STDMETHODIMP CSimple::Construct(IDispatch* pCtorObj)
{
    HRESULT hr(E_FAIL);
    BSTR bstrConstruct(NULL);
```

```
// get the IObjectConstructString interface
IObjectConstructString* pConstructString = NULL;
hr = pCtorObj->QueryInterface(IID_IObjectConstructString,
    (void**)&pConstructString);
if (SUCCEEDED(hr))
{
    // get the object constructor string
    hr = pConstructString->get_ConstructString(
        &bstrConstruct);
}

if (SUCCEEDED(hr))
{
    // save the object constructor string
    USES_CONVERSION;
    strncpy(m_szConstruct, OLE2T(bstrConstruct),
        MAX_CONSTRUCT_SIZE);



    m_szConstruct[MAX_CONSTRUCT_SIZE] = NULL;
}

return hr;
}
```

Listing 16-1 shows a simple in-process COM object implementing two interfaces: the ISimple dual interface and the IObjectContruct interface. The ISimple interface provides the ShowDialog() method that displays a dialog, which displays the object constructor string. The CConstructDialog class is a simple class, derived from the CAxDialogImpl class, that displays the string—set with the SetConstructString() function—in a static control.

 The code for the CConstructDialog class is not shown in the above code sample.

The COM+ environment uses the IObjectConstruct interface to allow an object access to the constructor string. COM+ passes a pointer to the IObjectConstruct String interface, which contains the constructor string as a property.

CONFIGURING THE COMPONENT

After you build and register this component, you can configure it by adding it to a COM+ application. You can add it to an already existing COM+ application or create a new application. In this example, you create a new COM+ application.

To create a new COM+ application, use the Component Services administration tool, which is part of the Administrative Tools control panel applet. Figure 16-1 shows the Component Services administration tool with the local computer's COM+ applications node expanded.

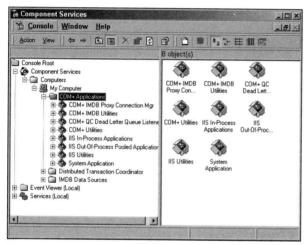

Figure 16-1: Component Services Administration Tool

From here, you can create a new application using the COM Application Install Wizard. To start the wizard, chose "to create a new application" from the Action toolbar menu. This wizard enables you to install an existing application or create an empty application. I will cover installing an existing application later in the chapter. When you choose to create an empty application, you can specify the name for the application and whether the application is a server or library application. Figure 16-2 shows the initial Create Application Wizard page. In this example, I create an application called the "Sample COM+ Application."

The next wizard page is the Application Identity Wizard page. It enables you to specify the identity the applicant assumes. You can set this identity to the interactive user or a specific user. Figure 16-3 shows the Application Identity Wizard page with the interactive user selected.

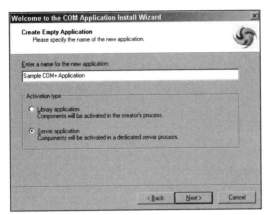

Figure 16-2: Initial Create Application Wizard page

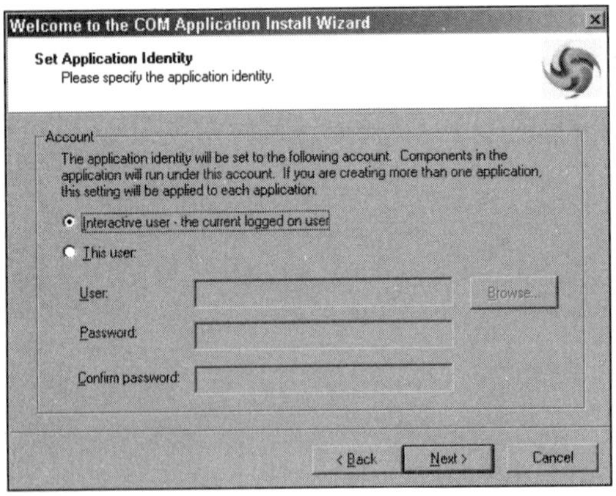

Figure 16-3: Application Identity Wizard page

From the newly created application, you can add your component to it using the COM Component Install Wizard. This wizard enables you to install new components or import components that are already registered.

To start the wizard, open the COM+ application that you just created and select the "Components" folder. Then chose "to create a new component" from the action toolbar button. In the wizard, choose to either "Install component(s) that are already registered" or "Install new component(s)."

If you choose "Install component(s) that are already registered," you are presented with a list of already registered components to select from. Select the component you wish to add and the wizard will add the component to the application.

If you choose "Install new component(s)," you are presented with a File Open dialog box that allows you to select the file to install. After you select the file that contains the component you wish to add, you are presented with the wizard page shown in Figure 16-4. This page enables you to view the components you are about to install and/or change your selection. If you choose the "Next" wizard button, the wizard displays a final page. The final page tells you if the wizard has everything it needs to add the component to the application. When you chose finish, the wizard adds the component to the application.

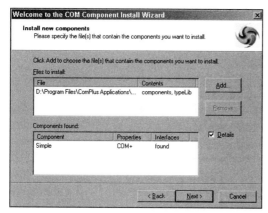

Figure 16-4: The COM Component Install Wizard enables you to install new components

Now that the component is added to the application, you can specify the object constructor string. To specify the object constructor string, select properties for the component you want to configure and go to the activation page. To display the properties for the application, first select the application and then select properties from the Action toolbar button menu. Figure 16-5 shows the activation page. First check the Enable Object Construction check box and then set the object constructor string.

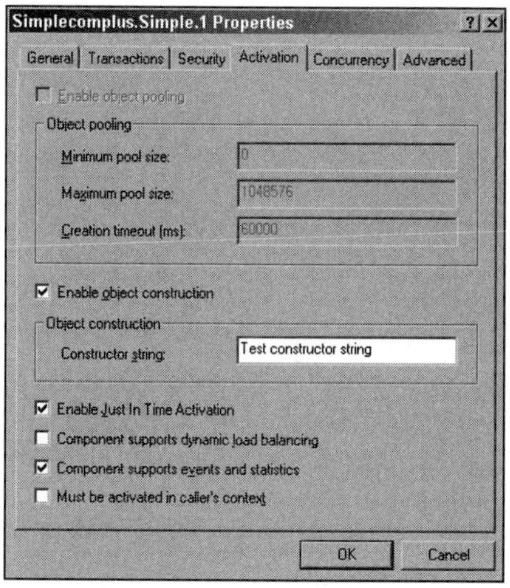

Figure 16-5: The activation page

CREATING AND INTERACTING WITH THE COMPONENT

Now that the component is configured, clients can create and interact with the object. Listing 16-2 shows a small Visual Basic script that creates an instance of the `Simplecomplus` object and calls the `ShowDialog()` method.

Listing 16-2: Visual Basic script

```
Dim objSimple
Set objSimple = CreateObject("Simplecomplus.Simple")
objSimple.ShowDialog
```

If the component is not part of a COM+ application, everything works the same as it did with COM. The `CreateObject()` API call creates the instance of the `Simplecomplus` object in the scripting host EXE's process and then calls the `ShowDialog()` method. The `Simplecomplus` object has no knowledge of any object constructor string.

With the component configured in a COM+ application, the process is a bit more involved. The COM+ environment intercepts the `CreateObject()` API calls and determines that the `Simplecomplus` component is part of the `Sample` COM+ application — which is a server application. Therefore, the environment creates a surrogate process, `Dllhost.exe`, to load the component. After the component is loaded into the surrogate process, the environment calls the `Construct()` method of the `IObjectConstruct` interface object, passing a pointer to the `IObjectConstructString` interface. After the object is created, the VB script calls the `ShowDialog()` method — now across processes.

COM+ Services

COM+ provides services that provide additional robustness, scalability, and security. These services include just-in-time activation, transaction processing, queued components, object pooling, and role-based security. In this section, I describe the various services that COM+ provides.

Just-in-Time activation

COM+ provides Just-in-Time (JIT) activation to help manage resources efficiently and promote scalability. If you specify that a component supports JIT, the COM+ environment deactivates the component even if a client has an outstanding reference to the object. The client application does not have any knowledge of this and continues to think that the object is active. When the client calls the object, COM+ activates the object "Just-in-Time."

Using JIT activation frees clients from having to worry about how they use potentially expensive server objects. Before the advent of JIT activation, client applications had to balance the cost of obtaining and releasing a server object versus the cost of keeping the server object alive. Now the COM+ environment can make this determination without the client application doing anything.

There are a couple of requirements that an object must satisfy to be able to support Just-in-Time activation:

◆ The object must synchronize access to it methods. This prevents two clients from accessing the object at the same time, then one of them returning and deactivating the object out from underneath the other client.

◆ The object must not hold onto its state. Any state will be lost when the object is deactivated.

The COM+ environment deactivates an object based on the done bit property. When the done bit property is set, the COM+ interceptor deactivates the object when the current method call returns. If the done bit is not set, then the object remains active after the current method call returns. When COM+ creates an object and initializes its context, the done bit is set to FALSE. COM+ creates every object that supports JIT activation in its own context.

You can set the done bit in three ways:

1. You can use the IContextState interface

2. You can use the IObjectState

3. You can set the auto done property of a method

The SetDeactivateOnReturn() method of the IContextState interface can set or clear the done bit property for the context. The SetComplete() and SetAbort() methods of the IObjectState interface also set and clear the done bit respectively. I cover the SetComplete() and SetAbort() methods more thoroughly in the transaction section that follows. You set the auto done property administratively on a method-by-method basis.

Transactions

The COM+ environment integrates MTS transaction support so that your components can provide robust, controlled set of actions – usually multiple database operations. A transaction is a set of actions that preserve the integrity of the data that it updates. Transactions are an all or nothing proposal; either all of the operations that make up the transaction are committed or they are all aborted.

The functionality of the Microsoft Transaction Server (MTS) was incorporated into COM+. Any MTS packages are converted to COM+ applications during the Windows 2000 setup. This allows you to take advantage of the new services that COM+ provides in addition to transactions.

The COM+ environment ensures that if a transaction is committed, it is recoverable even if the system crashes immediately after the commit operation.

COM+ components can take advantage of the transaction support offered by the COM+ environment by setting one of the transactional attributes. A component can support transactions, require a transaction, or require a new transaction. Components that support transactions participate in a transaction if the client provides one. If a component requires a transaction, it participates in its client's transaction if it has one; otherwise COM+ creates a transaction for it. If the component requires a new transaction, COM+ always creates a new transaction. A component also can disable transaction support altogether, which can be used to save the overhead of creating a context for the component. The default is set to not supported, which specifies that the component does not participate or vote in its client's transaction.

The COM+ environment always creates a new context when it activates a transactional object. This context holds object-related information such as the transaction identifier. It also holds the consistency and done bits. The consistency bit indicates whether the object is in a consistent state or not. The requirements for an object being in a consistent state are up to each individual object.

When a component sets the consistency bit, it casts a vote to commit or abort the transaction in which it is executing. When it sets the done bit, it finalizes the vote. A component can change the consistency bit many times during a method call, but only the last one counts. COM+ only checks the consistency bit when a method call returns and the done bit is set to TRUE.

COM+ looks at the *transaction flag* to determine if a transaction should be committed or aborted. The transaction flag manages the state of an entire transaction. COM+ sets the transaction flag to FALSE when it starts a transaction. When the transaction flag is set to FALSE, it indicates everything is fine with the transaction and the transaction should be committed. When the transaction flag is set to TRUE, something is wrong and COM+ aborts the transaction. Because of the negative nature of the transaction flag, it is often called the "doomed" flag. COM+ sets the transaction flag to TRUE when an object executing in the transaction is deactivated in an inconsistent state. Once any object votes to "doom" the transaction, the transaction can never be committed.

Listing 16-3 shows a very simple transaction-based component. The component provides the AddAddress() method that is supposed to add an address to the database. For this example, I removed the database calls so you can see the transaction calls better.

Listing 16-3: Simple transaction-based component

```cpp
// Transaction.h : Declaration of the CTransaction Application

#ifndef __TRANSACTION_H_
#define __TRANSACTION_H_

#include "resource.h"       // main symbols
#include <comsvcs.h>

/////////////////////////////////////////////////////////////////
// CTransaction
class ATL_NO_VTABLE CTransaction :
    public CComObjectRootEx<CComSingleThreadModel>,
    public CComCoClass<CTransaction, &CLSID_Transaction>,
    public IDispatchImpl<ITransaction, &IID_ITransaction,
        &LIBID_SIMPLETRANSACTIONLib>
{
public:
    CTransaction()
    {
    }


DECLARE_REGISTRY_RESOURCEID(IDR_TRANSACTION)

DECLARE_PROTECT_FINAL_CONSTRUCT()

DECLARE_NOT_AGGREGATABLE(CTransaction)

BEGIN_COM_MAP(CTransaction)
    COM_INTERFACE_ENTRY(ITransaction)
    COM_INTERFACE_ENTRY(IDispatch)
END_COM_MAP()

// ITransaction
public:
    STDMETHOD(AddAddress)(BSTR Name, BSTR Address, BSTR City,
        BSTR State, BSTR Zip, BSTR Phone);
};

#endif //__TRANSACTION_H_
```

```
// Transaction.cpp : Implementation of CTransaction
#include "stdafx.h"
#include "Simpletransaction.h"
#include "Transaction.h"


/////////////////////////////////////////////////////////////////////
// CTransaction


//
//  CTransaction::AddAddress: called to add an address to the database
//
STDMETHODIMP CTransaction::AddAddress
(
    BSTR /*Name*/
    ,BSTR /*Address*/
    ,BSTR /*City*/
    ,BSTR /*State*/
    ,BSTR /*Zip*/
    ,BSTR /*Phone*/
)
{
    HRESULT hr(E_FAIL);

    CComPtr<IObjectContext> pObjectContext;

    try
    {
        // get the object context
        hr = GetObjectContext(&pObjectContext);

        if (SUCCEEDED(hr))
        {
            // add record to database
            //
            MessageBox(NULL, _T("Add record to database"),
                _T("Simple Transaction"), MB_OK);
            //
```

```
            if (SUCCEEDED(hr))
            {
                // mark the transaction as done
                hr = pObjectContext->SetComplete();
            }
            else
            {
                // if something happened abort the transaction
                (void)pObjectContext->SetAbort();
            }
        }
    }
    catch(...)
    {
        // if something happened abort the transaction
        if (pObjectContext != NULL)
        {
            (void)pObjectContext->SetAbort();
            hr = E_FAIL;
        }
    }

    return hr;
}
```

The AddAddress() method first obtains a reference to the object's context, which it uses to set the transaction state. It then tries to add the record to the database. If the record is added successfully, then the method calls the SetComplete() method of the object context to inform COM+ that everything went OK and it should try to commit the transaction. If the database operation fails, or an exception is thrown, the method calls the SetAbort() method to tell COM+ that something went wrong and the operation should be aborted.

To configure this component, you create a COM+ application and add the component to the application. I added the component to the sample COM+ application that I created in the previous sample. After adding the component to an application, you need to set the transaction attribute. Figure 16-6 shows the Transaction property page for the component. For this component, I set the transaction property to required, which specifies that COM+ will create a transaction in which to execute the component if the caller does not provide one.

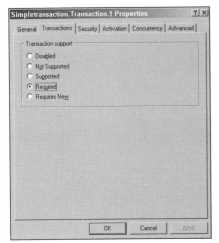

Figure 16-6: The Transaction property page for the component

Listing 16-4 shows a small Visual Basic scriptlet that creates an instance of the component and calls the AddAddress() method.

Listing 16-4: Creating the transaction component

```
Dim objSimpleTrans
Set objSimpleTrans = CreateObject("Simpletransaction.Transaction")
objSimpleTrans.AddAddress "Name", "Address", "City", "State", "Zip",
    "Phone"
```

When the Visual Basic script creates the component, the COM+ environment creates a surrogate process and loads the component into it. It then creates a new context for the component, setting the consistent bit to TRUE and the done bit to FALSE. The script then calls the AddAddress() method to add the record.

The transaction support that COM+ provides enables you to make your components more robust by ensuring that your applications are always in a consistent state. If any part of a transaction fails, COM+ rolls back the transaction for you.

Queued components

Queued components provide a way for you to make COM calls asynchronously. This enables you to develop your components without worrying about the availability or accessibility of the sender or receiver. This also enables you to provide much greater reliability and accessibility for your components. If a component is currently not available – whether it crashed, the client computer is not connected to the network, or any other reason – the request is delivered when the component becomes available. This is known as *guaranteed delivery*.

There are several different components involved in resolving a client's call to a queued component. The queued component's recorder intercepts all calls a client makes to a queued component, then packages the call as a message for the server. The queued component listener is responsible for retrieving messages from the queue and sending them to the queued components' player. The queued components' player then calls the method of the queued component.

To allow a client to obtain an instance of a queued component, the system provides two monikers: the new moniker and the queue moniker.

The *new moniker* enables you to activate a component directly. The new moniker takes a program (PROGID) or class (CLSID) identifier for the component to be activated as a parameter. For example

```
CoGetObject(L"new: Queued.QueuedDialog", NULL, IID_ IQueuedDialog,
    (void**)&pDialog);
```

You can use the new moniker with any component that supports the IClassFactory interface — not just queued components.

You use the *queue moniker* in conjunction with the new moniker to activate a queued component. The queue moniker receives the CLSID from the new moniker to the right of it. For example

```
CoGetObject(L"queue:/new: Queued.QueuedDialog", NULL, IID_
    IQueuedDialog, (void**)&pDialog);
```

You can pass optional parameters to control how the system passes messages to the message queue service. You can modify the destination computer name, the destination queue name, the delivery mechanism, the message priority, and the privacy level among other parameters. For example

```
CoGetObject(L"queue:Priority=6,ComputerName=TestMachine/new:
    Queued.QueuedDialog ", NULL, IQueuedDialog, (void**)&pDialog);
```

Listing 16-5 shows the code for the queued sample component that displays a dialog box. The CQueuedDialog component exposes only one method: AddDialog().

Listing 16-5: Simple queued component example

```cpp
// QueuedDialog.h : Declaration of the CQueuedDialog

#ifndef __QUEUEDDIALOG_H_
#define __QUEUEDDIALOG_H_

#include "resource.h"        // main symbols

/////////////////////////////////////////////////////////////////////
/////////
// CQueuedDialog
class ATL_NO_VTABLE CQueuedDialog :
    public CComObjectRootEx<CComSingleThreadModel>,
    public CComCoClass<CQueuedDialog, &CLSID_QueuedDialog>,
    public IDispatchImpl<IQueuedDialog, &IID_IQueuedDialog,
&LIBID_QUEUEDLib>
{
public:
    CQueuedDialog()
    {
    }

DECLARE_REGISTRY_RESOURCEID(IDR_QUEUEDDIALOG)

DECLARE_PROTECT_FINAL_CONSTRUCT()

BEGIN_COM_MAP(CQueuedDialog)
    COM_INTERFACE_ENTRY(IQueuedDialog)
    COM_INTERFACE_ENTRY(IDispatch)
END_COM_MAP()

// IQueuedDialog
public:
    STDMETHOD(AddDialog)(BSTR Text);
};

#endif //__QUEUEDDIALOG_H_


// QueuedDialog.cpp : Implementation of CQueuedDialog
#include "stdafx.h"
#include "Queued.h"
#include "QueuedDialog.h"
```

```
///////////////////////////////////////////////////////////////////
/////////
// CQueuedDialog

//
//   AddDialog: called to display a dialog
//
STDMETHODIMP CQueuedDialog::AddDialog(BSTR Text)
{
    USES_CONVERSION;
    MessageBox(NULL, OLE2T(Text), "Queued Dialog", MB_OK);
    return S_OK;
}
```

The CQueuedDialog() class implements a pretty simple COM component that implements one dual interface: IQueuedDialog. The IQueuedDialog interface provides the AddDialog() method that takes a string parameter. This method displays this string in a message box. This is pretty straightforward, right?

However, when this component is configured as a queued component, this simple component becomes much more powerful. To configure the Queued dialog component as a queued component, first create a new COM+ application, "Sample Queued Application," following the same steps used to create the "Sample COM+ Application." After the application is created, the Queued dialog component is added to the application.

Now I have a COM+ application, with the queued dialog component as a component. The next step is to view the properties for the "Sample Queued Application" and check the queued and listen check boxes on the "Queuing" tab. This configures the application as supporting queuing. Then, view the properties for the IQueued Dialog interface in the interface folder under the queued dialog component and check the queued property of the interface. This tells the system that this interface supports queuing.

The Queued Dialog component is now configured so that it supports queuing. Now use the following Visual Basic script code to launch the component:

```
Dim objSimple
Set objSimple = GetObject("queue:/new:Queued.QueuedDialog.1")
objSimple.AddDialog "Hi"
```

This code uses the queue moniker to create the Queued dialog component. Now, if for some reason our simple little COM component cannot respond to a request, it resides on a machine that is currently unavailable, or it has crashed, the requests are queued for it and processed when the component becomes available. This is all accomplished without changing one line in the component.

COM+ events

The COM+ events service provides support for a publish-and-subscribe event system. This system enables publishers to provide information about what events they are making available and enables subscribers to find out what events are available for them.

This allows the COM+ environment to handle much of the dirty work for the components. The components themselves do not have any knowledge of the subscriptions. The COM+ environment maintains the subscriptions.

PUBLISHING EVENTS

If you want to publish an event, you first need to create an `EventClass` that describes the event you want to publish. The `EventClass` contains the event's `CLSID`, class name, type library, and publication attributes. You need to create a DLL that provides the interfaces for the events. The methods for your interfaces can contain only input parameters and return an `HRESULT`. You do not need to implement the methods; you just need to create a type library and export the `DllRegisterServer()` function to register the component just like any other COM component. The component's `CLSID` and `ProgID` become the event's `CLSID` and name. Once this component is created, you can use the `InstallEventClass()` or `InstallMultipleEventClasses()` methods of the `ICOMAdminCatalog` interface or the Component Services administration tool to add the component to a COM+ application. Because the `EventClass` is a configured component, it can take advantage of all the other COM+ services.

After you create and configure the `EventClass`, you can publish an event by instantiating an event object, getting the event interface, and calling a method. COM+ associates the appropriate subscriptions with the `EventClass` when the `EventClass` is instantiated. The event system creates the `EventClass` and is responsible for delivering the events to the subscribers.

Listing 16-6 shows the definition of the SampleEvents `EventClass`. This EventClass defines the `ISampleEvents` interface with two event methods: `Event1()` and `Event2()`.

Listing 16-6: The SampleEvent EventClass

```
// eventdll.idl : IDL source for eventdll.dll
//

// This file will be processed by the MIDL tool to
// produce the type library (eventdll.tlb) and marshalling code.

import "oaidl.idl";
import "ocidl.idl";
    [
        object,
        uuid(0792D140-7603-11D3-9C6A-0010A4F3A21C),
```

```
    dual,
    helpstring("ISampleEvents Interface"),
    pointer_default(unique)
]
interface ISampleEvents : IDispatch
{
    [id(1), helpstring("method Event1")] HRESULT Event1([in] long Param);
    [id(2), helpstring("method Event2")] HRESULT Event2([in] BSTR Param2);
};


[
    uuid(188814F0-7603-11D3-9C6A-0010A4F3A21C),
    helpstring("SampleEvents Class")
]
coclass SampleEvents
{
    [default] interface ISampleEvents;
};
```

The `Event1()` method takes a long value as a parameter. The `Event2()` method takes a string value as a parameter. Only the definition of the event interface is defined in the event class. This definition needs to be compiled into a self-registering DLL and installed into a COM+ application. First, create a COM+ application to hold the event class. Then chose the "Install New Event Class" and specify the path to your event class DLL. This publishes the event with the system and allows the creation of subscriptions to the event.

SUBSCRIBING TO EVENTS

To subscribe to an event, you create a subscription object and add it to an application. You use the `InstallComponent` method of the `ICOMAdminCatalog` interface to create the subscription object. The subscription object contains the identity and location of the subscriber, the delivery method, the methods to subscribe, and the event class that the subscriber wants to receive.

You can subscribe to an event in three different ways. You can create a persistent, transient, or per-user subscription:

1. Persistent subscriptions: These are not tied to a particular instance of an object. Every time an event is published, the COM+ environment creates a new instance of an object for each persistent subscription.

2. Transient subscriptions: These are tied to a specific object. When an event is published, the COM+ calls the instance of the object that subscribed. The COM+ event system holds a reference on the object until the event is unsubscribed.

3. Per-user subscriptions: With these subscriptions, COM+ only delivers an
event when the subscriber is logged in to the event service.

Listing 16-7 shows the Visual Basic code for the vbEventSub sample application.
This sample application handles the two methods from the SampleEvent
EventClass published in the previous example.

Listing 16-7: Subscribing to an event

```
Implements EVENTDLLLib.SampleEvents

Private Sub SampleEvents_Event1(ByVal Param As Long)
    Dim str As String
    str = Param
    MsgBox str
End Sub


Private Sub SampleEvents_Event2(ByVal Param As String)
    MsgBox Param
End Sub
```

The vbEventSub sample application is implemented as a Visual Basic ActiveX
DLL. It implements the SampleEvents interface defined in the previous example.
The Event1() method converts the long parameter to a string and displays it in a
message box. The implementation for the Event2() method simply displays the
string parameter in a message box.

Once this sample application is built, it is added to COM+ application. After it is
part of a COM+ application, you can subscribe to the event methods you wish to
handle. To subscribe to an event, select the subscriptions folder under the component in the component services application. Then select new subscription to start
the Component Services Event wizard. Then you select the EventClass you wish to
receive events from and specify a name for the subscription. Your component is
now subscribed to the events.

Now that the event is published and subscribed to, all that remains is to trigger
the event. Listing 16-8 shows the sample code for the vbPublisher sample application. This application provides a mechanism to trigger the two event methods.

Listing 16-8: Triggering the event

```
Private Sub btnFireEvent1_Click()
    Dim lParam As Long
    lParam = editParam1.Text
```

```
    Dim objEvent As Object
    Set objEvent = CreateObject("EventDll.SampleEvents")
    objEvent.Event1 lParam
End Sub

Private Sub btnFireEvent2_Click()
    Dim strParam As String
    strParam = editParam2.Text

    Dim objEvent As Object
    Set objEvent = CreateObject("EventDll.SampleEvents")
    objEvent.Event2 strParam
End Sub
```

The `btnFireEvent1_Click()` function creates an instance of the SampleEvents EventClass and calls the `Event1()` method with the contents of an numeric edit control. The `btnFireEvent2_Click()` is similar except the it calls the `Event2()` method with the contents of a text edit control. They will then notify each subscriber to the event that the event has occurred.

Object pooling

Using object pools, you can pre-create instances of objects. Applications can obtain an instance of a pooled object from this pool without having to create the object. When an application is done using a pooled object, it can be returned to the pool for reuse.

This is useful when you have an object that takes a long time to be created. For instance, take an object that connects to a database. You can create a pool of objects that a client application can access without having to pay the cost of connecting to the database every time.

In order for an object to be pooled, the object must satisfy several requirements. An object must

◆ Manage its state

◆ Be aggregatable

◆ Have no thread affinity

◆ Be context neutral

◆ Be configured as a pooled object

To manage its state, an object must implement the `IObjectControl()` interface. The `IObjectControl` interface has three methods: `Activate()`, `Deactivate()`, and `CanBePooled()`. The COM+ environment calls the `Activate()` method to activate a COM+ object that currently is not active. Then the object can perform any context-specific initialization that it needs to perform. After the Activate() method returns, there should not be any difference between a newly created object and a reused pool object. The COM+ environment calls the Deactivate() method when the object is deactivated. The environment deactivates an object after it calls SetComplete() or SetAbort(), or the last reference to the object is released. The Deactivate() method should return the object to its initial state so that the Activate() method can reactivate it when necessary. After the COM+ environment calls the Deactivate() method, it calls the CanBePooled() method to determine if the object should be released or returned to the object pool.

In order to be pooled, an object must run in either a multithreaded or thread-neutral apartment. COM+ introduces the thread-neutral apartment model to reduce the complexity of developing a thread-independent component. The thread-neutral model serializes access to the component, but allows it to be executed on any thread.

For more information on the apartment model, please refer to the "Process, Apartments, and Threads" topic in the Component Services section of the Platform SDK documentation on the MSDN.

The thread-neutral model is the preferred method for COM+ objects.

The code in Listing 16-9 implements the same component as does Listing 16-3, modified to support pooling the components All that is required is to provide an implementation of the IObjectControl interface.

Listing 16-9: Pooled object sample

```
// Transaction.h : Declaration of the CTransaction

#ifndef __TRANSACTION_H_
#define __TRANSACTION_H_

#include "resource.h"       // main symbols
#include <comsvcs.h>


/////////////////////////////////////////////////////////////////////////////
```

```
// CTransaction
class ATL_NO_VTABLE CTransaction :
    public CComObjectRootEx<CComSingleThreadModel>,
    public CComCoClass<CTransaction, &CLSID_PoolTransaction>,
    public IObjectControl,
    public IDispatchImpl<IPoolTransaction, &IID_IPoolTransaction,
        &LIBID_SIMPLETRANSACTIONLib>
{
public:
    CTransaction()
    {
    }


DECLARE_REGISTRY_RESOURCEID(IDR_TRANSACTION)


DECLARE_PROTECT_FINAL_CONSTRUCT()


DECLARE_NOT_AGGREGATABLE(CTransaction)


BEGIN_COM_MAP(CTransaction)
    COM_INTERFACE_ENTRY(IPoolTransaction)
    COM_INTERFACE_ENTRY(IObjectControl)
    COM_INTERFACE_ENTRY(IDispatch)
END_COM_MAP()

// IObjectControl
public:
    STDMETHOD(Activate)();
    STDMETHOD_(BOOL, CanBePooled)();
    STDMETHOD_(void, Deactivate)();

    CComPtr<IObjectContext> m_spObjectContext;

// ITransaction
public:
    STDMETHOD(AddAddress)(BSTR Name, BSTR Address, BSTR City,
        BSTR State, BSTR Zip, BSTR Phone);
};


#endif //__TRANSACTION_H_


// Transaction.cpp : Implementation of CTransaction
#include "stdafx.h"
#include "Simpletransaction.h"
```

```
#include "Transaction.h"

/////////////////////////////////////////////////////////////////////
// CTransaction

//
// CTransaction::Activate(): called when COM+ activates the component
//
HRESULT CTransaction::Activate()
{
    HRESULT hr = GetObjectContext(&m_spObjectContext);
    return hr;
}


//
// CTransaction::CanBePooled(): called to determine if the object can
// be pooled
//
BOOL CTransaction::CanBePooled()
{
    return TRUE;
}


//
// CTransaction::Deactivate(): called when COM+ deactivates the component
//
void CTransaction::Deactivate()
{
    m_spObjectContext.Release();
}



//
// CTransaction::AddAddress: called to add an address to the data base
//
STDMETHODIMP CTransaction::AddAddress
(
    BSTR /*Name*/
    ,BSTR /*Address*/
    ,BSTR /*City*/
    ,BSTR /*State*/
    ,BSTR /*Zip*/
    ,BSTR /*Phone*/
)
```

```
{
    HRESULT hr(S_OK);

    DebugBreak();

    try
    {
        // add record to database
        //
        // ...
        //

        if (SUCCEEDED(hr))
        {
            // mark the transaction as done
            hr = m_spObjectContext->SetComplete();
        }
        else
        {
            // if something happened abort the transaction
            hr = m_spObjectContext->SetAbort();
        }
    }
    catch(...)
    {
        // if something happened abort the transaction
        hr = m_spObjectContext->SetAbort();
    }

    return hr;
}
```

This code provides an implementation of the IObjectContol interface. The implementation of the Activate() method retrieves the object context for this instance of the object and stores it in the m_spObjectContext member. The CanBePooled() method returns TRUE indicating that the object supports object pooling. The DeactivateMethod() releases the objects context stored in the m_spObjectContext. The AddAddress() method is the same as before, except that it uses the context stored in the m_spObjectContext member instead of retrieving it every time the function is called. This can result in much more efficient operation of methods that are called often.

COM+ security

COM+ provides role-based security, authentication services, and impersonation and delegation to help you protect your COM+ applications from unauthorized access:

◆ Role-based security: This is the cornerstone of COM+ security. Role-based security allows you the flexibility to administratively configure which clients can access a component – down to the method level if necessary. I describe role-based security in detail below.

◆ Authentication services: The COM+ environment uses the authentication services to ensure that clients are who they claim to be.

◆ Impersonation: Clients are allowed to delegate tasks to components; the components then can carry out tasks as the client.

Keeping with the COM+ philosophy of automatically providing services for components, the COM+ environment automatically can provide role-based security for your component. A *role* is a group of users that share identical access rights. You can administratively declare what roles your component allows access using the Component Services administrative tool. You can assign roles on an application, an interface, or method granularity.

If your component needs even more control over its security, you can use role-based security programmatically. Use the `IsCallerInRole()` method of the `ISecurityCallContext` or `IObjectContext` interface to determine if the caller of a method is a member of a role. To get the `ISecurityCallContext`, you call the `CoGetCallContext()` API with `IID_ISecurityCallContext` for the `riid` parameter. Generally, you should use `ISecurityCallContext` instead of `IObjectContext`, since you can use the same interface to obtain the security properties as well.

When designing your components, you should keep in mind security considerations. Try to organize your interfaces and methods to take advantage of role-based security. This can simplify your component code greatly. Role-based security works best when you can divide users into groups that can perform certain operations. For example, backup operators have access to the backup application or interface. Role-based security does not work well when security is based on information passed into a method. For example, users can only access their own accounts.

 You should try to keep your roles as simple as possible. This makes it easier for administrators to assign users to roles. Also, the more roles there are, the longer it takes COM+ to look up the user. An increased number of roles can degrade performance.

The COM+ interface only checks security at COM+ application boundaries. Therefore, if two components are in the same application, COM+ does not perform a security check between components. If you want COM+ to perform a security check, you need to place the components in separate applications.

COM+ Application Deployment

Once you create and configure a COM+ application, you can package it up in a Windows installer package to distribute it. When you package the application, COM+ combines the required files in a `.cab` file and places the `.cab` file in the Windows installer file. Once you generate the installer file, you can install the COM+ application on another computer. The computer you install the application on must support COM+.

Figure 16-7 shows the Application Export Wizard page for exporting a server application. You specify the location where you want the Windows installer package created and whether you want to export a server application or an application proxy. If you choose to export a server application, you can also specify if the user identities should be exported with roles.

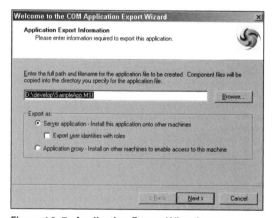

Figure 16–7: Application Export Wizard page

To run COM+ applications remotely, you can create an application proxy using the Component Services administration tool. The application proxy consists of the proxy/stub and type libraries that the system uses for DCOM remoting. When you create an application proxy, it is a good idea to create a type library that is separate from the implementation. This prevents server implementation code from being required in the application proxy. You can install application proxies on any platform that supports DCOM and the Windows installer. This provides for greater flexibility in distributing your COM+ applications.

Summary

COM+ extends COM by providing a powerful runtime environment. This environment allows COM+ to provide services that your components can use without having to worry too much about low-level distributed computing principals. COM+ will continue to evolve as new features are added through add-ons to Windows 2000.

The next chapter covers delivering applications. It will provide information on some development practices that you can use to produce better code as well as the measures you need to take to comply with the Microsoft Application Specification.

Part IV

The Finishing Touches

IN THIS PART

Chapter 17

Delivering Applications

IN THIS CHAPTER

◆ Programming practices

◆ Complying with the application specification

NOW THAT YOU'VE LEARNED about the services that Windows 2000 provides to make great applications, I want to show you some of the tools that you need to package and deliver those applications to your end users. This chapter covers some of the programming practices you need to adhere to when building your application. Further, I give you an overview of the features that your application will need in order to comply with the Windows 2000 Application Specification and be the best it can be.

Programming Practices

When creating an application, you will concentrate mostly on using the facilities from Windows 2000 that are required to implement your logic. You also will concentrate on getting your logic correct, providing a usable user interface, and avoiding bugs. You probably won't worry much about separating your data from that of other applications or a user with limited system privileges running your application, among other things. This section covers some practices that should become second nature so that you don't get caught by surprise when you ship your application.

Folders and paths

Most applications access the file system. When you need to read or write a file, you need to locate it in a folder. There is a simple order of preference for this:

◆ Ask the system where the folder is

◆ Prefer folders relative to a known folder

◆ Prefer Universal Naming Convention (UNC) paths

You also should be wary of a path changing during the lifetime of your process and always query for the location of a folder just before you use it.

WELL-KNOWN FOLDERS

Windows 2000 creates a standard set of folders that applications frequently use. Examples of these are the Windows folder (usually `C:\WinNT`) and the program files folder (usually `C:\Program Files`). In addition, each user account on the system receives a set of standard folders such as the start menu and Internet cache. In order to retrieve the location of these folders, the system provides the `SHGetFolder Path()` API.

Throughout this book, I've shown you instances of the `SHGetFolderPath()` API. This API is the best way to find a well-known folder in the system. As a refresher, Listing 17-1 shows you how to fetch the location of the Internet favorites for the current user.

Listing 17-1: Finding the Favorites folder

```
// project favorites
#define _WIN32_WINNT 0x0500
#define WINVER 0x0500
#include <windows.h>
#include <iostream>
#include <shlobj.h>

void main()
{
    // try looking up the location
    TCHAR szPath[MAX_PATH];
    if(SUCCEEDED(::SHGetFolderPath(
        NULL,              // use the desktop for the owner window
        CSIDL_FAVORITES,// grab the favorites
        NULL,              // use the token of the logged-in user
        SHGFP_TYPE_CURRENT, // get the current value
        szPath)))          // the buffer to hold the path
    {
        std::cout << "Favorites Path: " << szPath << std::endl;
    }
}
```

The simple application in Listing 17-1 calls the `SHGetFolderPath()` API to find the folder holding the current user's Internet favorites. This information is account-specific (notice the login name preceding the final folder) so you probably never would hard-code it anyway.

Chapter 9, "Shell Services," also covers CSIDLs.

A more common habit is to hard-code the path to a well-known folder, such as the Windows 2000 system folder (commonly named C:\WinNT\System32). An application that opens a file in this folder will work almost all of the time, but sometimes the correct location is C:\NT5\System32. This makes the habit of hard coding path names dangerous. In order to properly retrieve this well-known folder location all of the time, use the GetSystemDirectory() API or SHGetFolder Path() with CSIDL_SYSTEM. The simple application in Listing 17-2 shows you both ways.

Listing 17-2: Specifying the location of a log file

```
// project systemfolder
#define _WIN32_WINNT 0x0500
#define WINVER 0x0500
#include <windows.h>
#include <iostream>
#include <string>
#include <shlobj.h>
#include <shlwapi.h>
#pragma comment(lib, "shlwapi.lib")

// use the Shell API
std::string GetSystemFolder()
{
    std::string strPath;

    // try looking up the location
    TCHAR szPath[MAX_PATH];
    if(SUCCEEDED(::SHGetFolderPath(
        NULL,             // use the desktop for the owner window
        CSIDL_SYSTEM,     // grab the system folder
        NULL,             // use the token of the logged-in user
        SHGFP_TYPE_CURRENT, // get the current value
        szPath)))         // the buffer to hold the path
    {
        // convert to a std string and send it back
        strPath = szPath;
    }
```

```
    return(strPath);
}

// use the simple kernel API
std::string GetSystemPath()
{
    std::string strPath;

    // look up the location, supplying a char array
    TCHAR szPath[MAX_PATH];
    if(::GetSystemDirectory(szPath, MAX_PATH)>0)
    {
        // convert to a std string and send it back
        strPath = szPath;
    }
    return(strPath);
}

// helper function to retrieve the log file for the application
std::string GetLogFilename()
{
    TCHAR szFilename[MAX_PATH];
    ::PathCombine(
        szFilename,                   // result buffer
        ::GetSystemFolder().c_str(),// base folder
        "w2kdg.systemfolder.log");   // file

    // convert to a string object and return
    std::string strFilename = szFilename;
    return(strFilename);
}

void main()
{
    std::cout << "Path to log file: " << ::GetLogFilename()
        << std::endl;
}
```

The little application in Listing 17-2 creates a helper function to look up a file name for the application's log. The helper function, GetLogFilename(), simply finds the path to the system folder using another helper function, GetSystem Folder(). There are two different system calls that can get you the system folder; I've supplied wrapper functions that return a string object for each.

TEMPORARY FILES

In addition to CSIDL folders, you should be careful to place temporary files in the Windows 2000 temporary folder. This folder is available at all times using the GetTempPath() API. This function is very simple; it takes a buffer to hold the path, which can be up to MAX_PATH characters long. Only use this folder to hold temporary files for your application; that is, don't store your temporary files in any other location.

With the temporary folder, you can ask the system to help you create a name for a temporary file. The GetTempFileName() API takes a path, a prefix with which to group your temporary files, a serial number, and a buffer to hold the result. It's that simple. You should use this function whenever you want to make a temporary file — no matter in what folder you want to store it. The simple example in Listing 17-3 shows you how easy these APIs are to use.

Listing 17-3: Using the temporary path and file name functions

```
// project tempfile
#include <windows.h>
#include <string>
#include <iostream>

// simple function to create a throwaway, fully specified
//   temporary file name
std::string MakeTempFilename()
{
    std::string strFilename;

    // find the path
    TCHAR szPath[MAX_PATH];
    if(::GetTempPath(MAX_PATH, szPath)>0)
    {
        // ask for a new file in the path
        TCHAR szFilename[MAX_PATH];
        if(::GetTempFileName(
            szPath,         // path
            "TMP",          // prefix string
            0,              // let the system pick a number
            szFilename)>0)  // buffer
        {
            strFilename = szFilename;
        }
    }
    return(strFilename);
}
```

```
void main()
{
    std::cout << "Temporary file name: " << MakeTempFilename()
        << std::endl;
}
```

You can see that the `MakeTempFilename()` function in Listing 17-3 would be useful in almost any application. The function simply asks for the temporary file folder and requests a new, unique file name in that folder.

UNIVERSAL NAMES

The Windows operating system has supported long file name for several versions now. Use the pathing helpers in `ShLWApi.DLL` to manipulate paths in your application; they take into account all of the rules for pathing in Windows 2000.

You must support long file names, and you never should assume an 8.3 format or any of the restrictions that format imposed (for example, the absence of spaces in the path).

Chapter 9, "Shell Services," covers the Lightweight Shell API (`ShLWApi.DLL`) in detail.

I mentioned earlier that you should store paths as UNC names whenever possible. In order to do this, you need to use one of the networking API functions to turn a file name formatted as `<drive letter>:\path\file` into the `\\servername\share\path\file` of a UNC name. The `WNetGetUniversalName()` API lives in `Mpr.DLL` and simply takes a local file name and turns it into UNC. The example in Listing 17-4 uses the Open common dialog box to show you how this works.

Listing 17-4: Converting a local file name into a UNC

```
// project getunc
#define _WIN32_WINNT 0x0500
#define WINVER 0x0500
#include <windows.h>
#include <iostream>
#include <string>
#include <shlobj.h>
#include <shlwapi.h>
```

```
#pragma comment(lib, "shlwapi.lib")
#include <commdlg.h>
#pragma comment(lib, "mpr.lib")

// helper method to let the user select a network file
std::string GetNetworkFile()
{
    // initialize the structure for the Open common dialog
    OPENFILENAME ofn;
    ::ZeroMemory(&ofn, sizeof(ofn));
    ofn.lStructSize = sizeof(ofn);
    ofn.Flags = OFN_FILEMUSTEXIST | OFN_DONTADDTORECENT;

    // make a caption
    ofn.lpstrTitle = "Select a Network file";

    // pick an initial path
    TCHAR szInitPath[MAX_PATH];
    if(SUCCEEDED(::SHGetFolderPath(
        NULL,          // no parent window
        CSIDL_NETHOOD, // user's local network places
        NULL,          // user's security token
        SHGFP_TYPE_CURRENT,
        szInitPath)))
    {
        ofn.lpstrInitialDir = szInitPath;
    }

    // buffer to hold the file name
    TCHAR szFile[MAX_PATH] = "";
    ofn.lpstrFile = szFile;
    ofn.nMaxFile = MAX_PATH;

    // ask for the network file
    std::string strNetworkFile;
    if(::GetOpenFileName(&ofn))
    {
        // save it if the user found one
        strNetworkFile = ofn.lpstrFile;
    }
    return(strNetworkFile);
}

void main()
```

```
{
    // ask the user to fetch a network file and display it
    std::string strNetFile = GetNetworkFile();

    // convert to UNC if needed
    if(!::PathIsUNC(strNetFile.c_str()))
    {
        // allocate a buffer for the universal name
        DWORD dwSize(MAX_PATH * 2);
        PBYTE pbBuffer = new BYTE[dwSize];

        // ask the networking manager for the UNC version
        std::string strUNCName(strNetFile);
        if(::WNetGetUniversalName(
            strNetFile.c_str(),          // non-UNC name
            UNIVERSAL_NAME_INFO_LEVEL,   // get UNC
            reinterpret_cast<LPVOID>(pbBuffer),// buffer
            &dwSize)==NO_ERROR)          // buffer size
        {
            // reinterpret the buffer
            UNIVERSAL_NAME_INFO* pUni = reinterpret_cast<
                UNIVERSAL_NAME_INFO*>(pbBuffer);
            strUNCName = pUni->lpUniversalName;
        }

        // show the results
        std::string strMessage;
        strMessage += "Mapped local filename: ";
        strMessage += strNetFile;
        strMessage += "\nInto UNC filename: ";
        strMessage += strUNCName;
        ::MessageBox(NULL, strMessage.c_str(),
            "w2kdg.getunc", MB_OK);

        // clean up the buffer
        delete [] pbBuffer;
        pbBuffer = NULL;
    }
}
```

The example in Listing 17-4 shows you a few good things to do in your application. First, to pick a network file name, the program uses the Windows Open common dialog box through the `GetOpenFileName()` API located in `CommDlg.DLL`. This API takes an `OPENFILENAME` data structure to specify the behavior of the dialog box when the user interacts with it. You always should use the Open common dialog box whenever you want a file from the user. Figure 17-1 shows you the dialog box as created by Listing 17-4.

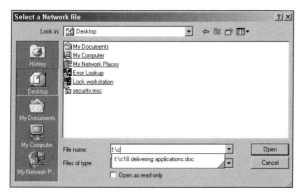

Figure 17-1: The Open common dialog box for selecting a network file name in Listing 17-4

The next thing that the program in Listing 17-4 shows you is how to initialize the Open common dialog box at a well-known place. You always should start the user in a tree beneath one of the CSIDL paths retrieved with the SHGetFolder Path() API. (We'll look at this in more detail later in the chapter.)

Finally, the code in Listing 17-4 takes the file name retrieved from the Open common dialog box and uses the PathIsUNC() API from ShLWApi.DLL. When it comes across a non-UNC file name, it uses WNetGetUniversalName() to reduce it to UNC. Figure 17-2 shows the results.

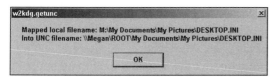

Figure 17-2: Listing 17-4's output shows a network file name expanded to a UNC file name.

You can see that the call to WNetGetUniversalName() is actually very straightforward; you should add it to any code you have that stores a file name or path selected by the user. This enables your application to work for the user even if the user remaps his or her drive, and it enables your application to work for another user on the machine without forcing an identical mapping. It's important that you do this immediately after you retrieve the file name or path because the user might disconnect that drive at any time, making the file name meaningless and ultimately causing the UNC mapping to fail.

Data storage

Windows 2000 has a set of well-known folders that you can reference from your application using the SHGetFolderLocation() API with CSIDLs — as seen throughout the text. Windows 2000 reserves some of these well-known locations along with the registry for you to store data for your application, depending on the nature of the data.

REGISTRY

First, remember that the primary purpose of the system registry is application configuration. The registry is not a general-purpose database for applications to use. You should keep the size of the data you write to it small, and you should not write any critical data to it.

Chapter 10, "Application Building Services," covers registry use in detail.

One thing to notice about data that you store in the registry is that you need to provide hard-coded default values for all of it. You must provide defaults in code, so you should not store the default values into the registry if the user does not set it specifically. That is, if the current value of a setting is its default, do not write it to the registry. If users do not choose something other than the default, they have no preference, so let future versions of the application know that. This practice enables you to upgrade the application and change the default value without interpreting the stored value as a user selection.

An interesting dilemma occurs when a user changes a preference from a non-default value back to the value of the default. It turns out that you should write that value to the registry, since the user now prefers it to any other available value. However, if you supply the ability to restore defaults, you should delete all registry values to indicate this.

Your application should store data in the HKEY_CURRENT_USER (HKCU) hive in most cases. In fact, you should use the standard \Software\CompanyName\ Application\Version path beneath HKCU for all of the user-specific settings for your application. You always will have write permission to this portion of the registry; when the administrator configures it, it will roam with users from machine to machine giving them a consistent experience with your application.

Occasionally, your application will need to store machine-specific configuration settings into the registry. Machine-wide settings should be stored with the same path as in HKCU under the HKEY_LOCAL_MACHINE (HKLM) hive. This can be done only when an account that has administrator-level privileges runs your application because only these accounts generally have write access to HKLM.

DATA FOLDERS

The next thing to pay attention to when you create an application for delivery is how you separate the application's data from the software. The main reason to do this is simple convenience for the users – they won't have to spend a lot of effort hunting down your data when they want to back it up or just look at it.

Windows has a simple solution for data separation: use the CSIDLs for application data (CSIDL_COMMON_APPDATA and CSIDL_APPDATA). These application data folders are much like the registry hives HKLM and HKCU, respectively. Use the common application data folder, CSIDL_COMMON_APPDATA, for machine-wide data storage and the user-specific application data folder, CSIDL_APPDATA, for user-specific data storage.

You generally place data in CSIDL_COMMON_APPDATA at installation time. The folder likely will be accessible only for writing by administrator-level accounts. By default, your application should place all newly constructed data in a user-specific application data folder because it is done in the context of a particular user.

Windows 2000 typically implements these folders, named Application Data, by storing the common folder under the \Documents and Setttings\All Users\ directory and the user-specific folder under the \Documents and Settings\ <username> directory. Figure 17-3 shows you where they live in a typical file system.

This is where you should store data files generated by your application for the user. When storing data in these folders, choose a naming convention much like that of the registry; append \CompanyName\Application\ to the real folder path and then subdivide the data when needed. This recommendation makes little sense without the standard Open and Save common dialog boxes and without the SHGetFolderPath() API. Listing 17-5 shows you how to use your application to make the storage location almost transparent to the user.

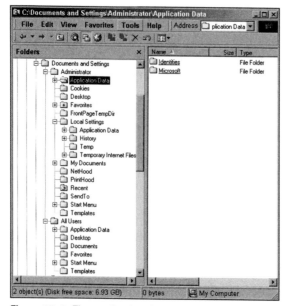

Figure 17-3: The application data folders in a typical Windows installation

Listing 17-5: Using the CSIDL_APPDATA folder as the default for application data storage

```
// project managedata
#define _WIN32_WINNT 0x0500
#define WINVER 0x0500
#include <windows.h>
#include <fstream>
#include <iostream>
#include <string>
#include <shlobj.h>
#include <shlwapi.h>
#pragma comment(lib, "shlwapi.lib")
#include <commdlg.h>

// helper method to construct the default data path
std::string GetDefaultDataPath()
{
    // the root of the data path for this application
    //   (under APPDATA, COMMON_APPDATA, or LOCAL_APPDATA)
    static LPCTSTR c_szDataPath = "w2kdg\\managedata\\";

    // the return buffer
    std::string strDefault;
```

```
    // find the application data
    TCHAR szPathRoot[MAX_PATH];
    if(SUCCEEDED(::SHGetFolderPath(
        NULL,                   // no parent window
        CSIDL_APPDATA,          // user's application data folder
        NULL,                   // user's security token
        SHGFP_TYPE_CURRENT,     // current value
        szPathRoot)))           // destination
    {
        // add our common data path and set it as the initial
        TCHAR szInitPath[MAX_PATH];
        ::PathCombine(szInitPath, szPathRoot, c_szDataPath);
        strDefault = szInitPath;
    }
    return(strDefault);
}

// recursively creates a directory, for use when the parent
//   folder does not exist
void RecurseCreateDir(const std::string& strDir)
{
    // try to create the directory
    if(!::CreateDirectory(strDir.c_str(), NULL) &&
        ::GetLastError()!=ERROR_ALREADY_EXISTS)
    {
        // copy and strip out the child-most dir
        TCHAR szParent[MAX_PATH];
        ::strcpy(szParent, strDir.c_str());
        ::PathRemoveBackslash(szParent);
        ::PathRemoveFileSpec(szParent);

        // create the parent
        RecurseCreateDir(szParent);

        // now, create the child
        ::CreateDirectory(strDir.c_str(), NULL);
    }
}

// helper method that fetches the save file name from the user
std::string GetSaveName(const std::string& strDefault)
{
    // default the save name to the passed value
    TCHAR szSave[MAX_PATH];
```

```
        ::PathCombine(szSave, GetDefaultDataPath().c_str(),
            strDefault.c_str());
        std::string strSave = szSave;

        // initialize the structure for the Open common dialog
        OPENFILENAME ofn;
        ::ZeroMemory(&ofn, sizeof(ofn));
        ofn.lStructSize = sizeof(ofn);
        ofn.Flags = OFN_DONTADDTORECENT;

        std::string strInit = GetDefaultDataPath();
        ofn.lpstrInitialDir = strInit.c_str();

        // buffer to hold the file name (defaulted to the save name)
        ofn.lpstrFile = szSave;
        ofn.nMaxFile = MAX_PATH;

        // ask for the file
        std::string strFilename;
        if(::GetSaveFileName(&ofn))
        {
            // save it if the user found one
            strSave = ofn.lpstrFile;
        }
        return(strSave);
    }


    // helper method to let the user select a network file
    std::string GetOpenDataFile()
    {
        // initialize the structure for the Open common dialog
        OPENFILENAME ofn;
        ::ZeroMemory(&ofn, sizeof(ofn));
        ofn.lStructSize = sizeof(ofn);
        ofn.Flags = OFN_FILEMUSTEXIST | OFN_DONTADDTORECENT;

        // set the starting point
        std::string strInit = GetDefaultDataPath();
        ofn.lpstrInitialDir = strInit.c_str();

        // buffer to hold the file name
        TCHAR szFile[MAX_PATH] = "";
        ofn.lpstrFile = szFile;
        ofn.nMaxFile = MAX_PATH;
```

```
    // ask for the file
    std::string strFilename;
    if(::GetOpenFileName(&ofn))
    {
        // save it if the user found one
        strFilename = ofn.lpstrFile;
    }
    return(strFilename);
}

void main()
{
    // make sure our data directory exists
    RecurseCreateDir(GetDefaultDataPath());

    // save a file into it
    {
        std::string strSave = GetSaveName("test.txt");
        std::ofstream ofSave(strSave.c_str());
        ofSave << "Test data";
    }

    // open a file from the folder
    std::string strOpen = GetOpenDataFile();
    if(!strOpen.empty())
    {
        std::ifstream ifRead(strOpen.c_str());

        TCHAR szLine[MAX_PATH];
        ifRead.getline(szLine, MAX_PATH);
        std::cout << szLine << std::endl;
    }
}
```

The example in Listing 17-5 shows you how to use the Windows 2000 application data folder as the parent for saving and opening data files for an application. The helper function GetDefaultDataPath() constructs the folder name that the application uses for data. Another helper function, RecurseCreateDir(), makes sure that the folder exists prior to interacting with the user.

Listing 17-5 then uses the Save common dialog box to enable users to pick their own name for a new data file. Figure 17-4 shows the dialog box pointing to CSIDL_APPDATA\w2kdg\managedata to suggest that the users simply place the new file in the application's folder. Then the Open common dialog box is started in the same folder, suggesting that the users get their data from the same place.

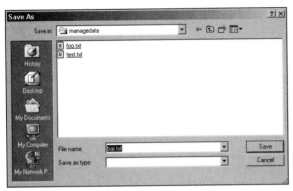

Figure 17-4: Pointing the user to the proper data folder for an application

Another dimension in the selection of the application data folder is roaming. Windows 2000 enables administrators to set up accounts to move easily among machines. This feature maps the CSIDL_APPDATA folder to a central location (not necessarily on the machine in use); when you use that folder for your data, you give the user a seamless experience.

In addition to the CSIDL_APPDATA folder, Windows 2000 creates a CSIDL_LOCAL_APPDATA folder for each account. The local application data folder is intended for noncritical data that either is machine-specific or, for some other reason, does not need to roam with the user from machine to machine.

Support for low-privileged accounts

One very common mistake that Windows 2000 application developers make is that they develop under an account with administrator-level privileges and don't test under low-privilege conditions. In fact, usually the application requires an administrator to install it and you don't find that it has problems until a true end-user runs it.

In order to minimize problems moving from administrator-level, privileged accounts to guest or other read-only accounts, follow these simple rules:

1. Open files, registry keys, and other kernel objects with the minimum access required for the operation.

2. Test for access-denied conditions and provide an alternate execution path when you cannot create or modify an object.

3. Provide hard-coded default values for all settings when the system might deny your application even read access.

Accounts that do not have write access to HKEY_LOCAL_MACHINE or CSIDL_COMMON_APPDATA often run your application. These accounts almost always have write access to CSIDL_APPDATA and the GetTempPath() folder.

To wrap up this section, Listing 17-6 shows you how to use the registry with only the required access levels. If the program cannot read from the registry, the settings revert to the defaults; if it cannot write the settings, it simply notes that and returns.

Listing 17-6: Handling application settings in restricted-access situations

```
// project regpref
#include <windows.h>
#include <iostream>

// simple class to demonstrate proper handling of restricted
//  access for application settings
class CPreferences
{
public:

    // ctor, simply initializes data to defaults
    CPreferences() : m_nWidth(c_nDefWidth),
        m_nHeight(c_nDefHeight) {}

    // save writes the data to the registry
    bool Save()
    {
        bool bSaveOK(true);

        // attempt the open with only set permission
        HKEY hkey = NULL;
        DWORD dwDisposition(0);
        DWORD dwResult = ::RegCreateKeyEx(
            HKEY_LOCAL_MACHINE,        // HKLM
            c_strKeyName.c_str(),      // our key
            0,                         // must be 0
            NULL,                      // no class specified
            REG_OPTION_NON_VOLATILE,// persistent values
            KEY_SET_VALUE,             // just want to change
            NULL,                      // default security
            &hkey,                     // result 1
            &dwDisposition);           // result 2
        if(dwResult==ERROR_SUCCESS)
        {
            // only set if it has changed
            if(m_nWidth!=c_nDefWidth)
            {
                ::RegSetValueEx(
```

```
                    hkey,                    // key to write under
                    "Width",                 // name of the value
                    0,                       // must be 0
                    REG_DWORD,               // it is a DWORD
                    (LPCBYTE)&m_nWidth,      // the value
                    sizeof(DWORD));          // buffer size
            }
            else
            {
                // clean out the previous value, the default
                //  is chosen
                ::RegDeleteValue(hkey, "Width");
            }

            // only set if it has changed
            if(m_nHeight!=c_nDefHeight)
            {
                ::RegSetValueEx(
                    hkey,                    // key to write under
                    "Height",                // name of the value
                    0,                       // must be 0
                    REG_DWORD,               // it is a DWORD
                    (LPCBYTE)&m_nHeight,     // the value
                    sizeof(DWORD));          // buffer size
            }
            else
            {
                // clean out the previous value, the default
                //  is chosen
                ::RegDeleteValue(hkey, "Height");
            }
        }
        else
        {
            bSaveOK = false;
        }
        return(bSaveOK);
    }

    // load fetches the data from the registry
    bool Load()
    {
        bool bLoadOK(true);
```

```
        // attempt the open with only query level
        HKEY hkey = NULL;
        DWORD dwResult = ::RegOpenKeyEx(
            HKEY_LOCAL_MACHINE,     // HKLM
            c_strKeyName.c_str(),   // our key
            NULL,                   // must be 0
            KEY_QUERY_VALUE,        // just want to look
            &hkey);                 // result
        if(dwResult==ERROR_SUCCESS)
        {
            DWORD dwSize(sizeof(DWORD));
            DWORD dwType(REG_DWORD);
            ::RegQueryValueEx(
                hkey,               // key to look under
                "Width",            // name of the value
                0,                  // must be 0
                &dwType,            // the type
                (LPBYTE)&m_nWidth,  // result buffer
                &dwSize);           // size of the data
            ::RegQueryValueEx(
                hkey,               // key to look under
                "Height",           // name of the value
                0,                  // must be 0
                &dwType,            // the type
                (LPBYTE)&m_nHeight, // result buffer
                &dwSize);           // size of the data
        }
        else
        {
            // revert to defaults
            *this = CPreferences();
            bLoadOK = false;
        }
        return(bLoadOK);
    }


    // the preference data and its defaults
public:
    DWORD m_nWidth;
    static const DWORD c_nDefWidth;
    DWORD m_nHeight;
    static const DWORD c_nDefHeight;

    // key name for the app
```

```cpp
protected:
    static const std::string c_strKeyName;
};

// static initialization
const DWORD CPreferences::c_nDefWidth  = 640;
const DWORD CPreferences::c_nDefHeight = 480;
const std::string CPreferences::c_strKeyName =
    "Software\\IDG Books\\Windows 2000 Developer's Guide"
    "\\regpref";

void main()
{
    CPreferences prefs;

    // fetch the preferences from the registry
    if(prefs.Load())
    {
        std::cout << "Width: " << prefs.m_nWidth <<
            " Height: " << prefs.m_nHeight << std::endl;
    }
    else
    {
        std::cout
            << "Could not load preferences, using defaults"
            << std::endl;
    }

    // swap the values of the preferences
    {
        DWORD dwSwap = prefs.m_nHeight;
        prefs.m_nHeight = prefs.m_nWidth;
        prefs.m_nWidth = dwSwap;
    }

    // now, save the values back
    if(!prefs.Save())
    {
        std::cout << "Could not save preferences."
            << std::endl;
    }
}
```

The class shown in Listing 17-6, `CPreferences`, uses the minimum permissions each time it attempts to load or save the values that it owns. It makes sure that if it cannot read the values from the registry, it writes over itself with a default object — a well-known state. When the object attempts to write its values to the registry, it guarantees to write only values that are not equivalent to the default values; when they are, it simply deletes the values from the registry (they provide no additional information).

Complying with the Application Specification

Once you have gone to the effort of ensuring that you are delivering a quality application, you will want to let your users know this. One attribute of a high-quality Windows application is that it complies with the application specification that Microsoft publishes. You can find The Application Specification for Windows 2000 at the following address:

`http://msdnisv.microsoft.com/msdnisv/win2000`

The application specification details the behavior that your application must exhibit in a number of situations. When you fully comply with the application specification, you are entitled to display a logo alongside your application packaging or advertisements that indicates to perceptive buyers that you have built a professional application. An application that complies with the specification provides a user experience consistent with Windows and allows the administrator wide latitude in configurations while easing deployment and reducing support times.

This section doesn't repeat the entire application specification for you, but it highlights the important rules and concepts that you typically have to build into your application from the get-go.

Specification fundamentals

The fundamentals section of the application specification details the simplest pieces that all applications must have in order to run well on Windows 2000. The following fundamentals should be second nature to all Windows developers.

◆ Avoid all throwback code construction. Use only 32-bit components. Don't use any of the old configuration mechanisms, such as `System.INI` or `AutoExec.BAT`.

◆ Apply the programming practices that I detailed in the last section. Support long file names and UNC pathing. Get folders from the shell, rather than assuming values, and use the system's temporary file name construction.

◆ Use the data and settings guidelines of placing data in an appropriate CSIDL-based folder. Classify and store your data appropriately; specify if it is meant for the user or the machine and if it should move along with the user. Provide hard-coded defaults for settings and use them when access to the storage is denied for any reason.

◆ Make sure that you support a low- or no-privilege account running your application. This also means providing or adhering to group policies instituted by the system or domain administrator.

◆ When you deliver an application that manipulates persisted data from files, you need to integrate the data type into the shell. This means you must provide icons, descriptions, and actions for the shell to serve up to the user in its explorer interface.

◆ Finally, use the Windows version checking intelligently. You should employ the `GetVersionEx()` and `VerifyVersionInfo()` APIs to enable features in your application that use the latest and greatest builds of the operating system. Ensure that your application runs well in the earliest version possible and runs greatly in the latest version.

Installation

Windows applications often fail during the initial user experience – at installation time. A big part of this problem has been the lack of operating system support for installation that would provide a consistent experience and a resilient result. The Windows *installer service* now solves this problem and is shipped to you as part of the Microsoft development environment. The Application Specification requires that you use the installer service to deliver your application.

The Windows installer service is part of the operating system and provides native support for data-driven installations. A data-driven installation begins with the end-result of the installation in mind and does whatever is necessary to reach that goal. In other words, you only need to design what components must be delivered to the end-user's machine, give them to the installer service, and let it place them where they belong. This differs greatly from the script-based installers that you find from add-on installers (run once).

The data that is installed on the machine includes the components (EXE files or DLLs), registry entries, supporting data files, and associations. Also, the installer service can place shortcuts – in any number of common or custom locations – to any of the files you place on the machine.

The installer service can do the following:

◆ The install is data-driven, so the installer service repairs a broken installation by comparing what it should have with what it does have and extracting anything required.

◆ It can remove all of the files that the application delivers simply by making sure the data is not there rather than following a script.

◆ It allows some interesting new features, such as application advertising, in which applications are installed on demand rather than by priority. Also, the user that installs a package from the installer service need not be an administrator.

The installer service uses installer packages to wrap up the image of where components belong and of the components themselves. Visual Studio 6.0 includes a user interface for creating these packages, usually .MSI files.

The *Visual Studio Installer* supplies editors that enable you to assemble files quickly, customize the user interface of the installer, set up the registry, and create associations in the system. To begin, simply launch the tool and create an empty installer as shown in Figure 17-5.

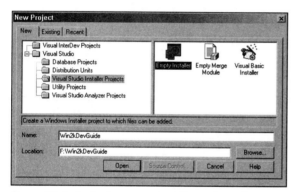

Figure 17–5: Beginning a new installer package for an example in this book

The appendix, "Using the Examples in This Book," shows you how to get and use the example shown in Figure 17-5.

The project started in Figure 17-5 delivers some of the example executables from code listings that I developed in this book. Once I select the location for the project, I add a single executable to the target machine's file system in the application's folder (likely C:\Program Files).

By telling the installer package where I want the EXE file, most of the work is done. Next, I add a shortcut to the EXE on the desktop and one in a newly created folder under user's Start...Programs... menu called Win2k Dev Guide. Figure 17-6 shows the installer user interface after the bulk of the work is completed.

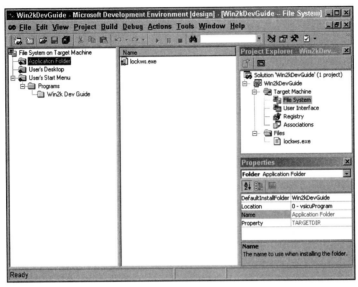

Figure 17-6: Installer project under development

Once I have all my files and shortcuts in place, I simply build the project and run it. It builds a fairly small-sized MSI file that contains everything I need to install, repair, and remove the software from a machine. When I execute the file, I am greeted by the pleasant interface shown in Figure 17-7.

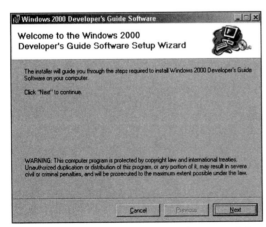

Figure 17-7: The installer executing for some of the example executables in this book

That is all I have to do to wrap up delivery of my very simple application that locks the workstation. Rather than place the raw EXE somewhere that my intended audience can copy it from, I now have a professional installer/remover that sets up the machine properly. In addition, I can add new files to the installation package at any time without worrying about how to script their delivery.

The installer service provides an easy route to making a professional-looking application. The fact that the application specification requires is only a detail – the installer service provides a very nice finishing touch on your application.

Side-by-side components

The tendency in application delivery is to componentize and deliver the executable as COM objects and other DLLs. This has proven problematic for applications that change interfaces over releases. The Application Specification for Windows 2000 requires that multiple versions of the same components can execute at the same time, side-by-side.

Chapter 10, "Application Building Services," introduces COM, and Chapter 16, "Working with COM+," explains its latest features.

EXECUTABLES

Component providers for applications (either in-house or out-of-house) get locked into interfaces when their component is shared by more than a single client. For example, suppose a library provider supplies A.DLL for application 1.EXE and places it in a shared location. Then, suppose another application, 2.EXE, comes along with its newer copy of A.DLL for the shared location. There can be no interface change in the A.DLL component without possibly breaking the first application.

Further, even if the interface remains constant, an application may depend on an undocumented side effect that changes in a new release and breaks it. Microsoft refers to this situation as "DLL Hell" for good reason.

To solve this problem for DLLs, the new recommendation is to avoid sharing them. That is, every application that uses a DLL should install its own private copy alongside its executable. The module search rules force Windows to load the private copy first – rather than any copy in the search path – and preserve the application's version and interface integrity.

This problem of shared components also happens for COM servers. In fact, COM servers may be worse off because they are shared system-wide by the GUID. An application cannot install another version of an existing COM server, even in a private location, without running the risk of breaking the original application.

To solve the COM server problem, you now can register the components with relative paths, making them very similar to DLLs. You also have to reference count the installation of the server though, because more than one application may reference it and you don't want to allow an uninstall until your application is uninstalled.

DATA AND OBJECTS

Separating the executable code by version turns out to be the easy part. The hard part is separating the data and interprocess kernel objects among application versions. This is much the same problem you may have experienced at some point when you converted a single-threaded application to a multithreaded one.

First, data that gets stored in the registry needs to be stored by version of the component. This is the reason behind the insistence on the format `HKCU(HKLM)\Software\CompanyName\ComponentName\Version` for the registry tree. Your components must allow different versions to pick up settings that are specific to each.

Data that you store in the file system must be managed the same way. Each component that looks for data in the file system must have a mechanism to distinguish data for its version from that of another version. Again, a simple convention for the naming of files or folders makes this a simple task.

Finally, shared interprocess kernel objects need to be separated by version number so that each version does not manipulate an object in a way that is incompatible with newer or older versions. Early on in this book, I demonstrated that a naming convention is required for these objects; you should extend it with a version number.

Chapter 3, "Using Kernel Objects," introduces the kernel object naming convention.

Look and feel

The final piece of the Application Specification for Windows 2000 is look and feel. Here is a short list of things you should do to comply with the Windows 2000 user interface guidelines:

- ◆ Support system-wide settings and respond to changes in the settings.

- ◆ Handle high-contrast and multi-monitor displays.

- ◆ Provide keyboard access to all features.

- ◆ Show the current keyboard focus location.

- ◆ Do not rely on sound for user notification.

- ◆ Properly use the Start menu.

Summary

You've seen a lot of fun stuff in this chapter, and you now have a list of significant improvements to your development process so you can produce better code. Now, you also are familiar with some of the additional steps you have to go through to comply with the Microsoft application specification – such as delivering a package for the installer service and supporting side-by-side versioning of your components.

The final thing you need to know about creating great applications for Windows is how to take advantage of the tools that are at your disposal to support your development. These tools include structured exception handling, the ToolHelp32 API, and the performance monitor. Chapter 18 details these for you.

Chapter 18

Development Support

IN THIS CHAPTER

- ◆ Errors and exceptions
- ◆ Process information
- ◆ Framework tools
- ◆ Performance monitoring
- ◆ Other tools

UP TO THIS POINT in the book, I've concentrated on showing you the facilities that Windows 2000 supplies you to make great applications for the user. In this chapter, I show you the Windows 2000 facilities that help you develop those applications. In general, these facilities aim to make your job of creating great applications easier. More specifically, they aim to give you control over the low-level interfacing between your application and the system.

The Windows API has a simple, consistent mechanism for your application to detect and report problems using the system. This error handling is baked right into the kernel, and the system enables you to extend it into your own application or APIs. In addition to error reporting, Windows 2000 provides structured exception handling that enables you to generate and react to execution problems that occur within your code or within a consumed code library.

Windows provides a pair of tools for examining the current state of the operating system and the state of processes running in the system. The ToolHelp32 API gives you a first-class set of tools for digging into the kernel objects a process owns. The *process status API (PSAPI)* looks at how the process uses system resources in general.

This chapter also shows you the great facilities that some of the standard application development frameworks give you to create great applications. The performance-monitoring framework enables you to instrument your application so system administrators can understand and watch its impact on their systems.

Finally, the chapter wraps up with a little grab bag of development and debugging stuff. This chapter is the last one in presentation, but not in content. You'll find yourself using some of the facilities that I present in almost every one of your applications.

Errors and Exceptions

The core Windows APIs rely on a simple and consistent error-reporting structure. You should be aware of this and use the errors reported by the APIs to make decisions in your application. This type of error reporting is rooted in the early implementations of the operating system; it was standard procedure in C programming.

In addition to simple error reporting, Windows has built-in error handling that is very similar to C++ exceptions. This *structured exception handling (SEH)* facility of Windows also is built from the very core of the system outward and is available to every application.

Using API error codes

When you look at the Windows *Platform SDK (software development kit)* documentation, you can see many functions that return a Boolean value for success. Most of the time, these methods do the job you ask of them and return success. Occasionally, however, an API fails. In order to determine why it fails, the documentation tells you to call the `GetLastError()` API. This and other APIs for dealing with system errors are summarized in Table 18-1.

TABLE 18-1 ERROR CODE APIS

API	Description
GetLastError()	Retrieves the last error code set by the calling thread
SetLastError()	Changes the error code value for the thread
FormatMessage()	Creates a human readable string for a system or application error code

The system maintains a result code for every thread in every process running. This single value represents additional information when a system or other API fails. You access this value with the `GetLastError()` or `SetLastError()` APIs. Most system APIs fill the last error value with a number that usually is defined in the SDK header file `WinError.H`.

Once you have the result code from `GetLastError()`, your application can take action to correct the error condition, report it to the user, ignore it, and so on. Windows gives you help to interpret this code with the `FormatMessage()` API. This function looks up strings that describe the error from the system DLLs. The program in Listing 18-1 shows you how to create, gather, and interpret an error code from the system.

Listing 18-1: Creating, gathering, and interpreting an error from a system API

```
// project reporterror
#define _WIN32_WINNT 0x0500
#define WINVER 0x0500
#include <windows.h>
#include <iostream>
#include <string>

// helper method to look up a string for the last error
//   generated by the system
std::string GetLastErrorString()
{
    // the return buffer
    std::string strError;

    // fetch the last error code
    DWORD dwLastError = ::GetLastError();

    // get the system to create a descriptive error string
    LPCTSTR szError;
    if(::FormatMessage(
        FORMAT_MESSAGE_FROM_SYSTEM |    // system error
        FORMAT_MESSAGE_ALLOCATE_BUFFER, // create a buffer
        NULL,                           // no source string
        dwLastError,                    // error to describe
        0,                              // use system language
        (LPTSTR)&szError,               // buffer to return
        0,                              // ignored
        NULL))                          // ignored
    {
        // save the string and free the buffer
        strError = szError;
        ::LocalFree((LPVOID)szError);
    }
    else
    {
        // format a default string if the system doesn't know
        //   about the result code
        TCHAR szUnknown[1024];
        ::sprintf(szUnknown, "Unknown(%d)", dwLastError);
        strError = szUnknown;
    }
    return(strError);
}
```

```
void main()
{
    // make a bad call to a system API, won't have access
    //  to process with ID 8
    HANDLE hProcess = ::OpenProcess(
        PROCESS_ALL_ACCESS,
        FALSE,
        8);
    if(hProcess==NULL)
    {
        std::cout << "Could not open process 8. Error: "
            << ::GetLastErrorString() << std::endl;
    }

    // handle an access denied error
    if(::GetLastError()==ERROR_ACCESS_DENIED)
    {
        // no-access handling
        std::cout << "No access to process, program will exit."
            << std::endl;
    }

    // reset the error code
    ::SetLastError(ERROR_SUCCESS);
    std::cout << "Error cleared, "
        << ::GetLastErrorString() << std::endl;
}
```

The simple example in Listing 18-1 attempts to create a process object with the
OpenProcess() API for a process that the system starts up; you likely will not have
sufficient rights to open the process for all access. The system returns a null handle
and sets the result code to ERROR_ACCESS_DENIED. The example then uses the
helper function GetLastErrorString() to retrieve the resulting code (in human-
readable string format) and dumps it to the console.

The GetLastErrorString() helper method calls the FormatMessage() API
and — because the result was set by a kernel API — the string is available. When the
string is not available to FormatMessage(), the helper function returns the numeric
value and a simple generic string. The program also can compare the result code
against a symbolic constant from WinError.H and act upon it. Finally, the example
resets the result code with a call to the SetLastError() API. This step is not
required since the next call to a system API replaces that code anyway.

When you create components that you deliver in the form of DLLs, one way to
communicate problems that occur inside your code is with the GetLastError()

mechanism. As you may expect, you have to tailor your return codes when you do this so that they do not conflict with Windows or other third-party result codes.

Chapter 10, "Application Building Services," introduces Dynamic Link Libraries (DLLs) as code sharing vehicles.

The 32-bit result code referenced by the GetLastError() API reserves bits for various attributes of the result. Bit 29 signals the user of the result code that it is a third-party (customer) result. The high two bits (Bit 31 and Bit 30) signal the severity (success, information, warning, or error) of the result.

When you construct error codes for your APIs, I encourage you to use the available high bits (Bit 27 through Bit 16) to describe the portion of your API (facility) that the result came from, and the low 16 bits (Bit 15 through Bit 0) to specify the error. In addition to just deciding on result codes, you can supply error strings for the API client to retrieve just as you retrieve error strings from the system. To support this, Windows 2000 supplies the message table facility.

A Windows *message table* is a resource attached to an EXE or DLL file much like a dialog box template or bitmap. You use the message compiler, MC.EXE, to create the MESSAGETABLE resource. This resource associates your result codes with strings from one or many languages. To access the result string, the message table client uses the same FormatMessage() API that I just introduced and specifies the FORMAT_MESSAGE_FROM_HMODULE flag. This flag, along with the handle to your DLL, tells Windows to grab the string for a result code from your resource.

Using structured exceptions

Structured exception handling (SEH) is the mechanism that Windows uses to communicate hardware or software problems – from anywhere in the operating system – to your application. A *structured exception* simply is an immediate change of execution to kernel mode in which the thread begins looking for a wrapping structured exception handler.

Wrapping SE handlers come in two flavors: *exception handlers* and *termination handlers*:

◆ Exception handlers: These attempt to react to, and possibly correct, the exception condition.

◆ Termination handlers: These simply react to and clean up in-use resources when an exception occurs.

Each time the system encounters a wrapping SE handler, it attempts to enter the exception handler code and always enters the termination handler code. If the system cannot find any SE handler in the system or in your code that reacts to the exception, it calls the unhandled exception handler. You can also extend this mechanism by creating your own exceptions to raise.

Structured exceptions are *thread-specific*. Every thread can generate and handle exceptions independent of other threads in the process. The default unhandled exception handler, however, stops all threads by calling the `ExitProcess()` API.

EXCEPTION HANDLERS

Structured exceptions are much like C++ exceptions – code within the system generates them in response to a programming or hardware error. The programmer calling into code that may or will generate a structured exception must wrap the code with an exception handler. (An exception handler is denoted by the compiler keywords __try, __except, and __finally summarized in Table 18-2.) An *access violation* is a type of structured exception, and Listing 18-2 shows an example of handling an access violation with _try and _except. I cover _finally a bit later.

TABLE 18-2 STRUCTURED EXCEPTION HANDLING COMPILER KEYWORDS

Keyword	Description
__try	Guards the following scoped section of code (between the braces) against structured exceptions.
__except	Decides whether to enter the following scoped section of code when an exception is raised. This code is the exception handler.
__finally	Guarantees that the following scoped section of code will always be executed, whether an exception occurs or not. This code is the termination handler.
__leave	Jumps out of a guarded section of code into the termination handler, if any.

Listing 18-2: Handling an access violation

```
// project eatgpf
#include <windows.h>
#include <iostream>
```

```
// simple method to create an access violation (applications
//   never have write access to memory location 0)
void GenerateAccessViolation()
{
    int* pNull = NULL;
    *pNull = 1;
}


void main()
{
    // the __try keyword begins the guarded block
    __try
    {
        ::GenerateAccessViolation();
    }
    // the __except keyword begins the handling block
    __except(EXCEPTION_EXECUTE_HANDLER)
    {
        std::cout << "Eating exception." << std::endl;
    }

    // execution will flow through here since all exceptions
    //   are eaten above
    std::cout << "Terminating normally." << std::endl;
}
```

The example in Listing 18-2 creates a virtual memory access violation by attempting to write to the virtual memory at address 0, and as you recall from Chapter 12, "Memory Management," Windows marks that section of virtual memory as no-access for all processes. The SEH block begins with the __try keyword; this instructs the compiler to notify the system that any exceptions generated by code executed between the braces should call into the corresponding __except block. This means that any exceptions not caught and suppressed by other code within the application, a third-party library, or the system end up here. The code within the __try braces is called *guarded code.*

You can think of the __except keyword as a function that takes a single parameter, the values of which I summarize in Table 18-3. That parameter instructs the system to enter the body of the handler (the code within the braces) or continue searching through other exception handlers that may be wrapping this one for one that can handle the condition. Listing 18-2 shows the code to use to enter the handler: EXCEPTION_EXECUTE_HANDLER.

TABLE **18-3** STRUCTURED EXCEPTION HANDLER DIRECTIVE VALUES

Value	Description
EXCEPTION_CONTINUE_EXECUTION	Ignore the exception and continue execution at the point of generation
EXCEPTION_CONTINUE_SEARCH	Pass the exception out to the next guarded block of code (marked with __try) for handling
EXCEPTION_EXECUTE_HANDLER	Enter the exception handling block of code following the __except keyword

---

Since the decision about whether the block should handle, pass on, or retry the exception is not always simple, Windows helps you out by supplying an exception context and enabling you to execute code in the __except call. You gather the context for the exception with the GetExceptionCode() and GetException Information() APIs. The former API simply returns the 32-bit code, which likely is one of the system errors (for example, EXCEPTION_ACCESS_VIOLATION or EXCEPTION_FLT_DIVIDE_BY_ZERO).

The second API to give you exception context, GetExceptionInformation(), returns to you an EXCEPTION_POINTERS structure that contains two more structures: the EXCEPTION_RECORD and the CONTEXT. The exception record contains the exception code, a flag revealing whether the code can be executed again, the memory address of the executing code, and some extended information. The context structure contains the state of the CPU when the exception was generated; the state of the CPU includes the values of all of its registers.

In order to pass the context information of the exception to the policy function, you must call either function within the __except construct. Often, the policy function is called a *filter function* because it passes through some exceptions and rejects others.

Even with the context of the exception, your application probably will decide on a policy for structured exceptions and simply log them. The application policy may be to suppress all access violations in a situation or to abort the application with the FatalAppExit() API on divide-by-zero errors. The example in Listing 18-3 shows you a simple method to log structured exceptions.

Listing 18-3: Logging structured exceptions

```
// project exceptinfo
#include <windows.h>
#include <iostream>
#include <iomanip>
```

```
// simple method to create an access violation (applications
//   never have write access to memory location 0)
void GenerateAccessViolation()
{
    int* pNull = NULL;
    *pNull = 1;
}


// helper method to log a structured exception, it is
//   incomplete as implemented here
void LogException(LPEXCEPTION_POINTERS pExceptPtrs)
{
    // save the data from the current exception information
    EXCEPTION_RECORD er = *(pExceptPtrs->ExceptionRecord);
    CONTEXT ctx = *(pExceptPtrs->ContextRecord);

    // show the exception code
    switch(er.ExceptionCode)
    {
    case EXCEPTION_ACCESS_VIOLATION:
        std::cerr << "Access violation";
        break;
    default:
        std::cerr << "Exception " << er.ExceptionCode;
        break;
    }

    // show the address and flags
    std::cerr.fill('0');
    std::cerr << " Address:"
        << std::hex << std::setw(8) << er.ExceptionAddress;
    std::cerr << " Flags:" << std::hex << er.ExceptionFlags;
    std::cerr << std::endl;
    // dump other fields here...

    // show the CPU context
    std::cerr << "CPU flags: "
        << std::hex << std::setw(8) << ctx.ContextFlags;
    std::cerr << " EAX: "
        << std::hex << std::setw(8) << ctx.Eax;
    std::cerr << std::endl;
    // dump the remaining context here
}
```

```
LONG AppExceptionPolicy(LPEXCEPTION_POINTERS pExceptPtrs)
{
    // log the exception
    ::LogException(pExceptPtrs);

    // the policy might do something interesting based on the
    //  exception code
    LONG nFilterCode(0);

    // grab the record and decide on an action
    EXCEPTION_RECORD er = *(pExceptPtrs->ExceptionRecord);
    switch(er.ExceptionCode)
    {
    default: nFilterCode = EXCEPTION_EXECUTE_HANDLER;
        break;
    }
    return(nFilterCode);
}


void main()
{
    // the __try keyword begins the guarded block
    __try
    {
        ::GenerateAccessViolation();
    }
    // the __except keyword begins the handling block
    __except(AppExceptionPolicy(GetExceptionInformation()))
    {
        std::cout << "Eating exception." << std::endl;
    }

    // execution will flow through here since all exceptions
    //  are eaten above
    std::cout << "Terminating normally." << std::endl;
}
```

The example in Listing 18-3 builds on Listing 18-2 by adding the helper function `AppExceptionPolicy()`, which requires the context for the exception as a parameter. The policy method first logs the exception information to the error stream in abbreviated form. You should augment this method with full logging in your own application. Near the end of the `AppExceptionPolicy()` function is a switch statement that looks at the exception codes and decides what the __except handler should do. It is this switch statement that actually implements the policy. The policy simply eats all exceptions, no matter the nature or generator.

TERMINATION HANDLERS

Another feature of SEH is the termination handler, as denoted by the __finally keyword. This block, like the __try and __except blocks, wraps a logical segment of code. The code within the termination handler braces is executed every time the guarded code is executed – whether or not an exception is generated. The termination handler should contain cleanup code that needs to be executed no matter how the execution through the __try block happens. Typically, you should place cleanup logic here. For example, a database application establishes a connection to the database in the __try block and attempts to execute an operation on that connection. That connection must be cleaned up whether the operation succeeds or fails, so the cleanup logic belongs within a __finally block. Listing 18-4 shows you a similar situation with a kernel event object.

Listing 18-4: Making sure an event object gets cleaned up

```
// project cleanupexcept
#include <windows.h>
#include <iostream>

// simple method to create an access violation (applications
//  never have write access to memory location 0)
void GenerateAccessViolation()
{
    int* pNull = NULL;
    *pNull = 1;
}


// helper method to test the signaled state of a kernel object
bool IsSignaled(HANDLE hObject)
{
    // call the wait method with a zero pause to test the state
    //  and exit, when it's signaled the return will be "OBJ0"
    bool bSignaled =
        ::WaitForSingleObject(hObject, 0)==WAIT_OBJECT_0;
    return(bSignaled);
}


// helper method to dump a string representing a bool value
LPCTSTR BOOLSTR(bool bValue){return(bValue ?"TRUE":"FALSE");}
LPCTSTR BOOLSTR(BOOL bValue){return(bValue ?"TRUE":"FALSE");}


// startup method for this exception-ridden application
```

```
void Start()
{
    // create the event to signal the active state
    HANDLE hEventActive = ::CreateEvent(
        NULL,                    // default security
        TRUE,                    // manual reset
        FALSE,                   // initially not signaled
        "w2kdg.cleanupexcept.event"); // unique name

    // the __try keyword begins the guarded block
    __try
    {
        // signal the active event and log it
        ::SetEvent(hEventActive);
        std::cout << "Active event signaled: "
            << BOOLSTR(IsSignaled(hEventActive)) << std::endl;

        // begin the application
        // ...
        ::GenerateAccessViolation();
    }
    // the __finally keyword begins the termination block
    __finally
    {
        // always reset the event to let others know the app is
        //  no longer active
        ::ResetEvent(hEventActive);
        std::cout << "Active event signaled: "
            << BOOLSTR(IsSignaled(hEventActive)) << std::endl;

        // note an abnormal termination
        std::cout << "Main loop terminating abnormally: "
            << BOOLSTR(AbnormalTermination()) << std::endl;
    }

    // clean up the active state event
    ::CloseHandle(hEventActive);
    hEventActive = INVALID_HANDLE_VALUE;
}

void main()
{
    // the application will eat any exceptions by supplying an
    //  empty handler block.
```

```
__try
{
    // begin the application
    ::Start();
}
__except(EXCEPTION_EXECUTE_HANDLER)
{
    // any exception will terminate the program
}
}
```

The application in Listing 18-4 has a main thread entry point that is embodied by the `Start()` function. This function creates a named event kernel object to signify to itself and other processes that it is running. Soon after signaling that it has become active, the application encounters a structured exception in the form of an access violation. To make sure that all concerned know that it no longer is active, the `SetEvent()` API and the main application thread are wrapped in a `__try/__finally` block. The code in the termination block ensures that the event is cleared when execution leaves the guarded code – either by design or because of a structured exception.

Although the event's signaled state always is cleared in Listing 18-4, the event object itself is not necessarily cleaned up because the call to the `CloseHandle()` API is made outside the `__finally` block. The helper function called `IsSignaled()` tests the signaled state of a kernel object, returning a `bool` to help with reflecting the signaled state to the user. The call to the `Start()` method also must be wrapped in a `__try/__except` block so that the `main()` function can eat the exception that the function generates.

 The Microsoft Visual C++ compiler adds the `__leave` keyword to SEH. This directive forces the execution to jump immediately to the end of the `__try` block and into the `__finally` block.

CUSTOM EXCEPTIONS

Custom exceptions are codes that you generate within your application or DLL to inform an internal or external client that something has gone wrong. In order to let the client know that an exception condition has occurred, you *raise* the exception. You can specify and generate exceptions from within your code using the `RaiseException()` API. This function requires an exception code that should be modeled after the result codes found using the `GetLastError()` API. Along with the result code, you can add exception context information as an array of 32-bit values of any length.

As a design issue, when you raise (generate) a custom exception, you probably want to keep it within code that you write. When a function generates an exception that there is no exception handler for, the system passes it to the unhandled exception filter. The unhandled exception filter is set for every thread of the process using the `SetUnhandledExceptionFilter()` API. This function has a signature identical to, and follows logic much like, the `AppExceptionPolicy()` function from Listing 18-3. This filter doesn't allow you to affect the response to an unhandled exception. However, it does enable you to log the exception.

I recommend installing this unhandled exception handler in all of your applications and executing exhaustive logging there. You can find much more complete implementations of SE logging functions on the MSDN.

Notifying the user of an error

There are Windows APIs that, by default, pop up error notices when your application calls and creates an error situation. Since this may not be the behavior that you want sometimes, the system lets you tune it with the `SetErrorMode()` API and the flags summarized in Table 18-4. This function allows you to (temporarily or permanently for the life of your process) enable or disable these dialog boxes. The simple program in Listing 18-5 shows you how to suppress an API error dialog box.

TABLE 18-4 PARAMETER FLAGS FOR THE SETERRORMODE() API

Flag	Description
SEM_FAILCRITICALERRORS	Suppresses the critical error dialog box from the system. The API call that would have produced an error dialog box fails and communicates the reason to the caller.
SEM_NOGPFAULTERRORBOX	Avoids the access violation dialog box from the system; however, the system does raise the structured exception.
SEM_NOOPENFILEERRORBOX	Silences the message box that indicates the system could not locate a requested file; the error is returned to the caller.

Listing 18-5: Suppressing API error dialog boxes

```
// project errormode
#include <windows.h>
#include <iostream>
#include <string>

void TestErrorMode(UINT nErrorMode)
{
    // set the new error mode
    UINT nOldErrorMode = ::SetErrorMode(nErrorMode);

    // this operation will cause a critical error if no
    //   floppy is in drive A: and ask the user to place a
    //   disk in the drive
    if(nErrorMode==SEM_FAILCRITICALERRORS)
    {
        ::LoadLibrary("a:Unknown.dll");
    }

    // this operation will generate a gp fault, which
    //   normally pops up a message for the user
    if(nErrorMode==SEM_NOGPFAULTERRORBOX)
    {
        int* pNull = NULL;
        *pNull = 1;
    }

    // restore the error mode
    ::SetErrorMode(nOldErrorMode);
}

void main()
{
    ::TestErrorMode(SEM_FAILCRITICALERRORS);
    ::TestErrorMode(SEM_NOGPFAULTERRORBOX);
}
```

The program in Listing 18-5 creates two simple error conditions and suppresses any notification to the user. The first situation looks for a file on a floppy drive; when there is no floppy in the drive, the system pops up a critical error dialog box as shown in Figure 18-1. Because this can happen to your application whenever it attempts to open a file that was opened last from a floppy, you might want to suppress it and look at the return code from the API or GetLastError(). To suppress the popup, you simply need to send the SEM_FAILCRITICALERRORS flag to

`SetErrorMode()`, remembering to restore the returned previous state when you don't need suppression any longer.

Figure 18-1: A critical error dialog box generated by Windows

Listing 18-5 also shows you how to suppress a similar popup with the `SEM_NOGPFAULTERRORBOX` flag for the `SetErrorMode()` API. When running the application from the command line, you won't see the familiar general protection fault dialog popup in Figure 18-2, as the program in Listing 18-5 de-references a null pointer. There is a final flag, `SEM_NOOPENFILEERRORBOX`, which suppresses a dialog box that the system displays when it cannot find a file (e.g., an implicitly linked DLL).

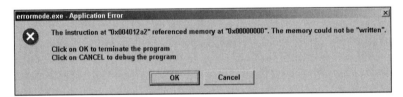

Figure 18-2: A general protection fault dialog box generated by Windows

In addition to suppressing or permitting error dialog boxes from the user, you can notify the user about error conditions yourself. The standard `MessageBox()` API enables you to select an error icon, like that in Figure 18-2, when displaying an error. Further, the `MessageBeep()` API enables you to play a tone that corresponds with an error or warning popup dialog box.

> Beeping the system speaker is rather boring but always works. If you want to be more flashy, you can use the `PlaySound()` API from the multimedia library, `WinMM.DLL`. For example, a call to `PlaySound("tada.wav", 0, 0)` will play the standard Windows 2000 startup tune.

Lastly, the `FlashWindowEx()` API enables you to visually notify the user of an error or exception condition when your application is not fully visible. This API also enables you to flash your application's task bar button or your caption a counted number of times, or continuously until you call it again to stop.

Process Information

Windows 2000 enables you inspect the internals of your process and other processes that you have access rights to by giving you two helpful sets of API calls: ToolHelp32 and PSAPI. The *ToolHelp32 library* (also known as the *Tool Help library*) gives you access to the lists of kernel objects that a process references. The *PSAPI library* examines the total system resources that a process uses while it runs.

Using the ToolHelp32 API

The ToolHelp32 library enables you to enumerate processes, threads, heaps, and modules in the system using the APIs summarized in Table 18-5. To do this, you can take an image of the system at any point in time. The library calls this image a *snapshot*; it is a kernel object that you create using the CreateToolhelp32 Snapshot() API.

Chapter 3, "Using Kernel Objects," explains how to use the snapshot and other kernel objects.

TABLE 18-5 TOOLHELP32 APIS

API	Description
CreateToolhelp32Snapshot()	Retrieves the current state of the system in a snapshot kernel object. Requires a flag to specify the contents of the snapshot and possibly the identifier of a process to inspect.
Process32First() / Process32Next()	Iterates through the current system processes listed in the snapshot object, filling a PROCESSENTRY32 structure with details about each.

Continued

TABLE **18-5 TOOLHELP32 APIS** *(Continued)*

API	Description
Thread32First() / Thread32Next()	Iterates through the current system threads listed in the snapshot object, filling a THREADENTRY32 structure with details about each.
Heap32ListFirst() / Heap32ListNext()	Iterates through the heaps retrieved for a specific process in the passed snapshot object. The heap is detailed in a HEAPLIST32 structure.
Heap32First() / Heap32Next()	Iterates through memory blocks in the heap passed by identifier from a HEAPLIST32 structure. The block details are returned in a HEAPENTRY32 structure.
Module32First() / Module32Next()	Iterates through the executable modules for a specific process in the passed snapshot object. Each module is detailed in a MODULEENTRY32 structure.

The ToolHelp32 library is implemented in Kernel32.DLL, and its definitions are in the header file TlHelp32.H.

To create a snapshot, you supply a bitmask that indicates which kernel object lists you want to include. If you ask for the module or heap list, you must supply the identifier of the process that owns them (which you want to explore). When you are finished with the Tool Help snapshot object, use the CloseHandle() API to release the resource.

PROCESSES

With a snapshot of processes, you can enumerate all processes running in the system. The Process32First() and Process32Next() APIs walk the list from the snapshot. Each API fills a PROCESSENTRY32 structure with the characteristics of a process in the snapshot, and the snapshot object maintains your position in the list.

Each process entry contains the system identifier for the process, the identifier of its parent, and the number of threads it currently owns. The entry also contains the name of the EXE file, the number of other processes referencing it, and the base priority for threads it spawns. Finally, the PROCESSENTRY32 structure contains a ToolHelp32-specific identifier for the default heap of the process and module that owns its code. Listing 18-6 shows you how to look up the entry for the current process.

Listing 18-6: Looking up a process's entry

```
// project thprocess
#define _WIN32_WINNT 0x0500
#define WINVER 0x0500
#include <windows.h>
#include <iostream>
#include <tlhelp32.h>

// helper method that fetches the process entry for the process
//   requested by system-wide ID
PROCESSENTRY32 LookupProcessEntry(DWORD dwProcessID)
{
    // create the process entry to return with zero size field
    PROCESSENTRY32 peTarget;
    ::ZeroMemory(&peTarget, sizeof(peTarget));

    // first, get the snapshot with all heaps
    HANDLE hSnapshot = ::CreateToolhelp32Snapshot(
        TH32CS_SNAPPROCESS,    // get processes
        0);                    // ignored
    if(hSnapshot!=NULL)
    {
        // initialize the test structure
        PROCESSENTRY32 pe;
        ::ZeroMemory(&pe, sizeof(pe));
        pe.dwSize = sizeof(pe);

        // start looping
        if(::Process32First(
            hSnapshot,         // snapshot to iterate
            &pe))              // return buffer
        {
            // check for a match and loop until we find one
            //   or run out of processes
            bool bFound = pe.th32ProcessID==dwProcessID;
            while(!bFound && ::Process32Next(hSnapshot, &pe))
```

```
            {
                bFound = pe.th32ProcessID==dwProcessID;
            }

            // save the entry
            if(bFound)
            {
                peTarget = pe;
            }
        }

        // release the snapshot
        ::CloseHandle(hSnapshot);
        hSnapshot = INVALID_HANDLE_VALUE;
    }
    return(peTarget);
}


// helper method to dump the contents of the process entry
//   to the output stream
void Show(const PROCESSENTRY32& pe)
{
    // dump the easy stuff
    std::cout << "Process ID: " << pe.th32ProcessID
        << ", EXE: " << pe.szExeFile
        << ", threads: " << pe.cntThreads
        << std::endl;

    // fetch the name of the parent process
    PROCESSENTRY32 peParent =
        ::LookupProcessEntry(pe.th32ParentProcessID);
    if(peParent.dwSize==sizeof(peParent))
    {
        std::cout << "Parent process: " << peParent.szExeFile;
    }
    else
    {
        std::cout << "Parent process ID: "
            << pe.th32ParentProcessID;
    }

    // other simple stuff
    std::cout << ", references: " << pe.cntUsage
        << ", thread priority: " << pe.pcPriClassBase
```

```
            << std::endl;

    // internal IDs for the heap and module
    std::cout << "Default heap ID: " << pe.th32DefaultHeapID
        << ", module ID: " << pe.th32ModuleID
        << std::endl;
}

void main()
{
    // look up the process entry for this process
    PROCESSENTRY32 peThis =
        ::LookupProcessEntry(::GetCurrentProcessId());
    if(peThis.dwSize==sizeof(peThis))
    {
        // dump out the contents
        ::Show(peThis);
    }
}
```

The example in Listing 18-6 creates a useful helper function, LookupProcess Entry(), that takes a system *process identifier (PID)*, a 32-bit value, and retrieves its PROCESSENTRY32 structure. This function creates a snapshot of the system's processes using CreateToolhelp32Snapshot() with the TH32CS_SNAPPROCESS flag to grab processes. Then it walks through its retrieving process entries until it finds the one with a matching PID. Before calling the Process32First(), the function must set the size field to the size of the structure; otherwise it will fail.

Once the entry for the current process is retrieved by passing the result from GetCurrentProcessId(), the main loop makes sure that it received a valid entry and dumps it to the output stream. The helper function ShowProcess() emits all of the fields of the entry. When it comes across the parent PID, it fetches the process entry for its EXE name rather than just emitting the number.

In addition to the simple dump of information shown in Listing 18-6, you can use the PIDs from the list of processes in the OpenProcess() API. When you create a process object for one of the processes you find with the Tool Help list, you should request PROCESS_QUERY_INFORMATION access to the process because most interesting processes deny you PROCESS_ALL_ACCESS unless the same account creates them.

Refer back to Chapter 2, "Basic Operating System Programming," for details about using the process objects and the OpenProcess() API.

THREADS

The next logical level of process information deals with the threads that it owns. You can create a Tool Help snapshot object containing a list of threads running in the system by supplying the TH32CS_SNAPTHREAD flag to the CreateToolhelp 32Snapshot() API.

The snapshot of threads is much like the list of processes I created in the last section. To run through the list, you must use the Thread32First() and Thread32 Next() APIs, which return a THREADENTRY32 structure. Each thread entry contains the system-wide *thread identifier (TID)* – a 32-bit value.

Just like the processes in the last section, once you have the thread's identifier, you can open a handle to that thread kernel object using the OpenThread() API. Also like the process object, if the owning process does not give you full security access, you need to request THREAD_QUERY_INFORMATION rights to the new thread object.

Once you have a thread, you can use any of the thread inspector APIs, such as GetThreadTimes() and GetThreadContext(), depending on your access. If you have full access to the thread, you may be able to use the SetThreadPriority(), SuspendThread(), and even TerminateThread() APIs. Listing 18-7 shows you how to fetch and iterate through the threads in the system.

Listing 18-7: Fetching and iterating through the threads in a process

```cpp
// project ththreads
#define _WIN32_WINNT 0x0500
#define WINVER 0x0500
#include <windows.h>
#include <iostream>
#include <tlhelp32.h>

// helper method to dump the contents of the thread entry
//  to the output stream
void Show(const THREADENTRY32& te)
{
    // dump the ID and use count
    std::cout << "Thread ID: " << te.th32ThreadID
        << ", references: " << te.cntUsage
        << ", base priority: " << te.tpBasePri
        << ", priority change: " << te.tpDeltaPri
        << std::endl;
}

// helper method to dump all threads for a process
void ShowThreads(DWORD dwProcessID)
{
    // header
```

```
        std::cout << "Process " << dwProcessID << " threads - "
            << std::endl;

        // first, get the snapshot with all threads
        HANDLE hSnapshot = ::CreateToolhelp32Snapshot(
            TH32CS_SNAPTHREAD,        // get threads
            0);                       // ignored
        if(hSnapshot!=NULL)
        {
            // initialize the thread structure
            THREADENTRY32 te;
            ::ZeroMemory(&te, sizeof(te));
            te.dwSize = sizeof(te);

            // loop while there are threads left
            bool bMore = ::Thread32First(
                hSnapshot,            // snapshot to iterate
                &te);                 // return buffer
            while(bMore)
            {
                // check for a matching process to dump
                if(te.th32OwnerProcessID==dwProcessID)
                {
                    ::Show(te);
                }

                // move on to the next thread
                bMore = ::Thread32Next(hSnapshot, &te);
            }

            // release the snapshot
            ::CloseHandle(hSnapshot);
            hSnapshot = INVALID_HANDLE_VALUE;
        }
}

void main()
{
    // dump all of the threads in the current process
    ::ShowThreads(::GetCurrentProcessId());
}
```

Listing 18-7 shows you how to call the `CreateToolhelp32Snapshot()` API to create a thread list and the `Thread32First()`/`Thread32Next()` APIs to walk through it. The helper function ShowThreads() loops through each thread in the system; every time it encounters one that belongs to the process, it dumps the thread entry to the console using the simple helper function.

HEAPS

Back in Chapter 12, I showed you how to use the Tool Help library to walk through heaps in a process. To review, you need to supply the process identifier and TH32CS_SNAPHEAPLIST in the CreateToolhelp32Snapshot() call. With the snapshot, you use the Heap32ListFirst() and Heap32ListNext() APIs to retrieve an entry for each heap the process owns.

Each entry in the heap list is a HEAPLIST32 structure. The process identifier and a Tool Help internal heap identifier describe a heap in the heap list entry, along with a flag indicating whether this heap is the default heap of the process. The default heap identifier in the process entry I showed you earlier corresponds to the internal heap identifier in the HEAPLIST32 structure.

Once you have the identifier of a heap in a process, you can use the Heap32First() and Heap32Next() APIs to iterate through blocks of memory in the heap. Each block of memory in the heap is described by a HEAPENTRY32 structure. The heap entry contains a starting memory address, a size, a flag describing its allocation state, and identifiers of the parent process and heap.

Listing 12-6 in Chapter 12, "Memory Management," shows an example of walking the Tool Help library heap list.

MODULES

The final object type that the Tool Help library makes available for your inspection is the executable module. A *module* is an EXE, DLL, or other file type that delivers executable code for the system to run. In a manner similar to the other available object types, you supply the TH32CS_SNAPMODULE to CreateToolhelp32Snaphot() and iterate the list with the Module32First() and Module32Next() APIs. Like the heap list, you must supply the process identifier from which you want modules because each process has a private set of loaded modules.

The entries in the module list are contained within MODULEENTRY32 structures. Each entry contains the name of the module and its executable file, the memory address that it was loaded into, and its size. Listing 18-8 shows you how to iterate and inspect this list.

Listing 18-8: Iterating and inspecting the modules in a process

```
// project thmodule
#define _WIN32_WINNT 0x0500
```

```cpp
#define WINVER 0x0500
#include <windows.h>
#include <iostream>
#include <iomanip>
#include <tlhelp32.h>
#include <shlwapi.h>
#pragma comment(lib, "shlwapi.lib")

// helper method to dump the contents of the module entry
//   to the output stream
void Show(const MODULEENTRY32& me)
{
    // dump the name and EXE
    std::cout << "Module: " << me.szModule
        << ", file: " << me.szExePath
        << std::endl;

    // create a string for the module size then dump its base
    //   address, module handle, and size
    TCHAR szSize[1024];
    ::StrFormatByteSize(me.modBaseSize, szSize, 1024);
    std::cout.fill('0');
    std::cout << "Address:"
        << std::hex << std::setw(8) << (DWORD)me.modBaseAddr
        << ", handle: "
        << std::hex << std::setw(8) << (DWORD)me.hModule
        << ", size: " << szSize << std::endl;
}

// helper method to dump all modules for a process
void ShowModules(DWORD dwProcessID)
{
    // header
    std::cout << "Process " << dwProcessID << " modules - "
        << std::endl;

    // first, get the snapshot with all modules
    HANDLE hSnapshot = ::CreateToolhelp32Snapshot(
        TH32CS_SNAPMODULE,        // get modules
        dwProcessID);             // process of interest
    if(hSnapshot!=NULL)
    {
        // initialize the thread structure
        MODULEENTRY32 me;
```

```
    ::ZeroMemory(&me, sizeof(me));
    me.dwSize = sizeof(me);

    // loop while there are modules left
    bool bMore = ::Module32First(
        hSnapshot,             // snapshot to iterate
        &me);                  // return buffer
    while(bMore)
    {
        // dump each module (with a blank line in between)
        ::Show(me);
        std::cout << std::endl;

        // move on to the next module
        bMore = ::Module32Next(hSnapshot, &me);
    }

    // release the snapshot
    ::CloseHandle(hSnapshot);
    hSnapshot = INVALID_HANDLE_VALUE;
    }
}

void main()
{
    // dump all of the modules in the current process
    ::ShowModules(::GetCurrentProcessId());
}
```

The code in Listing 18-8, similar to the other Tool Help code in this section, requires no explanation. Figure 18-3 shows the output from the program. You should notice that each module's handle is the same as its base address and, like other virtual memory addresses, is only useful within the owning process.

Using the PSAPI

Windows 2000 has replaced the most often used functionality of PSAPI with the Tool Help library. Previously, PSAPI was the only simple way to access the list of active processes and their modules. PSAPI remains the only easy access your application has to the list of active device drivers, as well as to information about the memory resources that a process consumes.

Figure 18-3: The list of modules loaded into the application in Listing 18-8

NOTE The list of device drivers for an application is beyond the scope of this text. To retrieve it from PSAPI, use the `EnumDeviceDrivers()` API. This function returns the list of base addresses for the device drivers in the system. You can send these values to APIs, such as `GetDeviceDriverBase Name()` and `GetDeviceDriverFileName()`, to get more information about the driver.

Windows delivers the PSAPI library as `PSAPI.DLL`. To use the library, you need the Platform SDK because the definitions live in the `PSAPI.H` header file that it delivers. Most of the PSAPI functions operate on process object handles that you can create by retrieving the identifier from the Tool Help library and using the `OpenProcess()` API with `PROCESS_VM_READ` and `PROCESS_QUERY_INFORMATION` access.

The first function that you may want from PSAPI is `GetProcessMemoryInfo()`. This function returns data in a `PROCESS_MEMORY_COUNTERS` structure that contains such things as page faults, working set sizes, and page file usage. Rather than interpret each of the fields for you, I direct you to the MSDN for more information and show you Listing 18-9.

Listing 18-9: Retrieving process memory information

```
// project meminfo
#include <windows.h>
#include <iostream>
#include <string>
#include <psapi.h>
#pragma comment(lib, "psapi.lib")
#include <shlwapi.h>
#pragma comment(lib, "shlwapi.lib")
```

```
// helper function to quickly transform a size to a size string
std::string SizeString(DWORD dwSize)
{
    TCHAR szSize[1024];
    ::StrFormatByteSize(dwSize, szSize, 1024);
    std::string strSize = szSize;
    return(szSize);
}

// displays memory stats
void Show(const PROCESS_MEMORY_COUNTERS& pmc)
{
    // page faults
    std::cout << "Page faults: " << pmc.PageFaultCount
        << std::endl;

    // working set stats
    std::cout
        << "Working set: " << SizeString(pmc.WorkingSetSize)
        << ", peak: " << SizeString(pmc.PeakWorkingSetSize)
        << std::endl;

    // page file use
    std::cout
        << "Page file: " << SizeString(pmc.PagefileUsage)
        << ", peak: " << SizeString(pmc.PeakPagefileUsage)
        << std::endl;
}

void main()
{
    // create a process memory stats buffer and fill it
    PROCESS_MEMORY_COUNTERS pmc;
    ::ZeroMemory(&pmc, sizeof(pmc));
    if(::GetProcessMemoryInfo(
        ::GetCurrentProcess(),    // this process
        &pmc,                     // return buffer
        sizeof(pmc)))             // size of buffer
    {
        Show(pmc);
    }
}
```

The program in Listing 18-9 just grabs the memory statistics for the current process and uses the `Show()` helper function to dump them to the console. I added a convenient helper function, `SizeString()`, to map memory sizes to human-readable strings while dumping to the output stream.

 TIP   You may want to copy the `SizeString()` function or at least its body to one of your common code libraries. It's one of those functions that you'll use all the time, especially in tracing code.

Windows defines the working set of a process as all of the physical memory that currently is mapped into the virtual memory space of the process. In addition to the statistics about the working set, the PSAPI library provides very detailed information on the current working set. The `QueryWorkingSet()` API takes a snapshot of all of the virtual memory pages that have physical memory behind them. The function returns a buffer of the page base addresses, along with the access (read-write, execute, and so on) that the process has to the page.

In addition to just walking the working set, the PSAPI library provides you with facilities to watch changes in the working set. The `InitializeProcessFor WsWatch()` and `GetWsChanges()` APIs enable you to gather up the changes as execution progresses. You can change the size of the working set manually with the kernel API `SetWorkingSetSize()`.

A final function that PSAPI offers is the `GetMappedFileName()` API. This API takes a virtual memory address and a process, then retrieves the name of a memory mapped into that region (if any). The Tool Help library has replaced the rest of the PSAPI library. The library offers information about modules that now are available through the `MODULEENTRY32` structure.

Framework Tools

Windows 2000 itself provides most of the facilities that I have presented so far in this chapter. This section will focus on the development support that the commonly used frameworks give you. The three frameworks discussed here provide debugging facilities:

1. The C++ Runtime Debug (CRTDBG) library from the Microsoft Visual C++ compiler: This custom implementation gives you a set of debugging facilities that enable you to watch memory allocations, emit traces, and embed coding assertions.

2. Microsoft Foundation Class Library (MFC): This library also offers the runtime debugging facilities, plus it meshes them into its object model.

3. Active Template Library (ATL): ATL also builds upon the C++ runtime in a different code stream and offers its own set of tools for debugging and developing great applications.

Using the C++ Runtime Debug library

The *C++ Runtime Debug (CRTDBG)* library contains facilities for memory use checking, memory leak checking, heap walking, reporting, and condition asserting. Unfortunately, most applications do not use any of it by default – even in debug mode. It comes mostly disabled.

To use the CRTDBG, include the header file CrtDbg.H. The compiler links its code with your application automatically according to the options you choose for C++ runtime support. The source code for the functions in the library lives in the CRT\SRC subfolder of your Visual C++ compiler installation. If you're really interested in the CRTDBG internals, you can browse through the source files there named DBG*.

MEMORY

The first option you have when you use the CRTDBG is to replace memory allocations in your application. To have the CRTDBG replace the standard new() and malloc() functions with instrumented versions, you must define the constant _CRTDBG_MAP_ALLOC before you include CrtDbg.H. These mapped allocator functions (along with their releasing counterparts) supply the source file and line number along with each call. The heap manager stores this information in the memory block.

Most of the function and macro names in the CRTDBG library contain a leading underscore, which signals that the identifier is specific to the compiler and library. This is not part of the standard C++ runtime library.

Just by hooking the heap functions, you alter your application dramatically. Each allocation from the heap reserves more memory than before so that the library can write extended information about the allocation. This extended information includes the location of the allocation in source code and its allocation number.

The allocation number isn't often useful as an absolute value; you typically use it to determine whether a particular allocation occurs before or after another so that you can infer program flow. Since most non-trivial applications allocate free memory based on user and system events, it's very unusual for an allocation to have the same number on successive runs.

The library also places guard blocks of memory before and after your data to ensure that you don't write past it or before it; the library calls these blocks *no man's land*. When you allocate memory, the library initializes the data in the memory block to a value you wouldn't expect to see in new memory (the value is 0xCD). This triggers bad behavior and even exceptions if you don't initialize the block properly before you use it. When you free the block of memory, the library writes over the data with a new nonsense value (the value is 0xDD) to help you find bugs that occur when you attempt to use an already-freed block of data.

There are a number of APIs that the CRTDBG library exposes for you to debug allocation problems. I summarize these APIs in Table 18-6.

TABLE 18-6 CRTDBG MEMORY APIS

API	Description
_CrtSetDbgFlag()	Changes the state of the debug allocator, retrieving the previous state. Flag values are summarized in Table 18-7.
_CrtCheckMemory()	Scans through the heap and verifies its integrity, returning TRUE if the heap is intact; otherwise it returns FALSE.
_CrtIsValidPointer()	Verifies that the passed memory block is ready for reading and writing by the thread.
_CrtIsValidHeapPointer()	Verifies that the passed address is within the application's heap.
_CrtIsMemoryBlock()	Verifies that the passed address is within the application's heap and retrieves debugging data about the allocation.
_CrtMemCheckpoint()	Retrieves the current state of the application's heap and fills a _CrtMemState structure.
_CrtMemDifference()	Compares checkpoint states, returning TRUE if there are any changes and dumping those differences to the reporting log.
_CrtMemDumpStatistics()	Turns a _CrtMemState structure into a human readable form and emits that to the reporting log.

Continued

TABLE 18-6 CRTDBG MEMORY APIS *(Continued)*

API	Description
_CrtDumpMemoryLeaks()	Called by the library at process exit to display all allocations that have not been freed since the beginning of execution.
_CrtSetBreakAlloc()	Stops execution just before executing a particular allocation, requires the number of the allocation.

Once you have the memory allocation and deallocation functions hooked, you must use the _CrtSetDbgFlag() API to enable memory-checking behavior. This function takes a single parameter that is a bitmask of the CRTDBG option flags summarized in Table 18-7. There are two flags that you should note: _CRTDBG_ALLOC_MEM_DF and _CRTDBG_LEAK_CHECK_DF. The former flag, enabled by default, turns on the heap allocation counter and enables debugging of new allocations. The latter flag instructs the library to look for dangling allocations when the application exits and report them to the debugger. Listing 18-10 shows you the basics of getting the CRTDBG into motion.

TABLE 18-7 CRTDBG DEBUG ALLOCATOR FLAGS

Flag	Default State	Description
_CRTDBG_ALLOC_MEM_DF	ON	Enables the debugging allocator
_CRTDBG_CHECK_ALWAYS_DF	OFF	Verifies the integrity of the heap before every allocation and free uses the _CrtCheckMemory() API
_CRTDBG_CHECK_CRT_DF	OFF	Includes allocations from within the runtime library in the debug heap
_CRTDBG_DELAY_FREE_MEM_DF	OFF	Keeps deallocated blocks of memory in the heap, but fills them with a known bad value, 0xDD
_CRTDBG_LEAK_CHECK_DF	OFF	Automatically checks for heap leaks when the application shuts down using a call to the _CrtDumpMemoryLeaks() API

Listing 18-10: Finding a heap leak with CRTDBG

```
// project leakcrtdbg
#include <windows.h>

#define _CRTDBG_MAP_ALLOC    // use the CRTDBG heap hooking
#include <crtdbg.h>

void main()
{
    // initialize the heap manager
#ifdef _DEBUG
    int nOldState = ::_CrtSetDbgFlag(
        _CRTDBG_ALLOC_MEM_DF |   // enable debug of allocations
        _CRTDBG_LEAK_CHECK_DF); // check application heap leaks
#endif

    // make an allocation
    PBYTE pLeak = new BYTE[1024];
}
```

The example in Listing 18-10 simply initializes the CRTDBG library as I outlined, creates a memory leak, and exits. The example, and all applications, must protect calls to the _CrtXxx() APIs with the #ifdef _DEBUG statement because the functions are not available in release mode. The output window of the debugger displays this leak as shown in Figure 18-4. You can see that the memory block is prefilled with the initialization value from the allocator, 0xCD.

Rumor has it that an old debugging heap allocator filled its memory with the more creative value, 0xDEADBEEF.

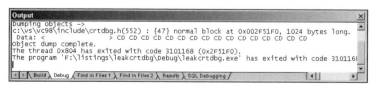

Figure 18-4: The report of a heap leak from Listing 18-10

Once the debugging heap is part of your application, you can choose to verify its integrity at any point of execution using the _CrtCheckMemory() API. This simple function returns a Boolean value indicating that the heap is still healthy. The heap check verifies that each block in the heap has valid allocation information, its guard blocks are intact, and (if a freed block) its data remains undisturbed (set to the freed value of 0xDD). You also can instruct the library to execute this check after each allocation and deallocation by passing the _CRTDBG_CHECK_ALWAYS_DF flag to the _CrtSetDbgFlag() API. However, that operation incurs a vast performance penalty and should be used only when debugging a specific problem — not as typical setup.

In addition to a full self-check, the debugging heap supplies functions to test individual pointers for use. The first API, _CrtIsValidPointer(), uses the system virtual memory APIs to verify that the starting address and length contains memory to which the calling process has read or read-write access. Next, _CrtIsValidHeapPointer() ensures that the passed memory address is located within the heap. Finally, _CrtIsMemoryBlock() tests that the passed starting address and length refer to a block within the heap. Listing 18-11 shows some simple uses of these functions.

Listing 18-11: Testing memory with CRTDBG helpers

```
// project testmem
#include <windows.h>
#include <iostream>
#include <iomanip>
#include <string>
#include <shlwapi.h>
#pragma comment(lib, "shlwapi.lib")

#define _CRTDBG_MAP_ALLOC    // use the CRTDBG heap hooking
#include <crtdbg.h>

// helper functions for output
LPCTSTR BoolStr(bool bValue){ return(bValue?"TRUE":"FALSE"); }
LPCTSTR BoolStr(BOOL bValue){ return(bValue?"TRUE":"FALSE"); }
std::string SizeString(size_t nSize)
{
    TCHAR szSize[1024];
    ::StrFormatByteSize(nSize, szSize, 1024);
    std::string strSize = szSize;
    return(szSize);
}

void ShowCheck(LPVOID pData, size_t nSize)
{
    // display the header
    std::cout.fill('0');
```

```
    std::cout << "Address:"
        << std::hex << std::setw(8) << (DWORD)pData
        << ", size: " << SizeString(nSize)
        << std::endl;

#ifdef _DEBUG
    // simple read access
    std::cout << "Read access: "
        << BoolStr(::_CrtIsValidPointer(pData, nSize, FALSE))
        << std::endl;

    // read/write access
    std::cout << "Write access: "
        << BoolStr(::_CrtIsValidPointer(pData, nSize, TRUE))
        << std::endl;

    // a heap pointer
    std::cout << "Within the heap: "
        << BoolStr(::_CrtIsValidHeapPointer(pData))
        << std::endl;

    // valid heap block
    LPTSTR szFile = NULL;
    int nLine(0);
    long nRequest(0);
    bool bHeapBlock = ::_CrtIsMemoryBlock(pData, nSize,
        &nRequest, &szFile, &nLine);
    std::cout << "A heap block: "
        << BoolStr(bHeapBlock);
    if(bHeapBlock)
    {
        std::cout << ", request: " << nRequest
            << ", File: " << szFile
            << ", Line: " << nLine;
    }
    std::cout << std::endl;
#endif

    // break up the output by sending another newline
    std::cout << std::endl;
}

void main()
{
```

```
    // initialize the heap manager
#ifdef _DEBUG
    int nOldState = ::_CrtSetDbgFlag(
        _CRTDBG_ALLOC_MEM_DF |  // enable debug of allocations
        _CRTDBG_LEAK_CHECK_DF); // check application heap leaks
#endif

    // make an allocation and test it
    {
        size_t nSizeMem = 1024;
        PBYTE pMemory = new BYTE[nSizeMem];
        ::ShowCheck(pMemory, nSizeMem);
        delete [] pMemory;
        pMemory = NULL;
    }

    // create a stack block
    {
        BYTE pMemory[1024];
        ::ShowCheck(pMemory, 1024);
    }

    // look at the EXE (cast the module handle to memory)
    {
        PBYTE pMemory = (PBYTE)::GetModuleHandle(NULL);
        ::ShowCheck(pMemory, 1024);
    }
}
```

The example in Listing 18-11 creates a helper method, ShowCheck(), which runs through the three memory validators that I discussed. It emits output according to the results of the tests, while the function tests four different scenarios: the pointer to a new heap block, a pointer a couple of bytes inside that same block, a block of memory created on the stack, and the execute-only code of the module. Figure 18-5 shows the results from Listing 18-11. You can see that the application has read access to all of the candidates and write access to the memory on the stack. The heap block shows the extended information that the manager carries around with it. The pointer just inside that block fails because it is not the pointer to the beginning of the block.

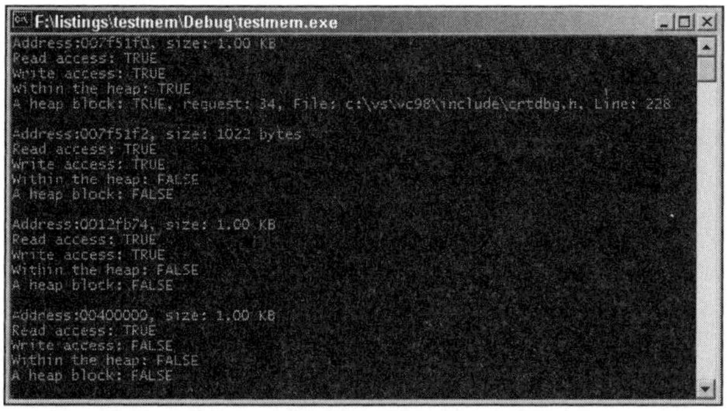

Figure 18-5: The results of testing memory using the CRTDBG functions

The library's memory management also contains functions to take a snapshot of the current state of the heap so it can show any changes later. The _CrtMem Checkpoint() API establishes a baseline for allocations at any point during execution; it returns a _CrtMemState object that contains the data. Once you have two memory allocation checkpoints, you can use the _CrtMemDifference() API to compare the new state of the heap to the old – returning a Boolean value indicating change.

Along with these functions comes the _CrtMemDumpStatistics() API, which takes a _CrtMemState object and dumps to the debugger data how many items were allocated, the total bytes allocated, the most allocated at one time, and the current allocation count. In place of using the debugger's output, you can supply your own function to dump memory data with the _CrtSetDumpClient() API.

The library also enables you to look at the difference between two memory states with the _CrtMemDifference() API, which returns a _CrtMemState structure. You can use a heap difference to give you hints about how much memory a particular part of your application is using. You view this by calling the _CrtMemDump Statistics() API.

To further facilitate debugging memory problems in your application, the CRT-DBG library enables you to instruct it to stop execution and break into the debugger on a particular allocation. You specify the allocation by number (the nth allocation) in the _CrtSetBreakAlloc() API. The library emits the ordinal value of the allocation in the heap-leak dump so you can supply this information back to the function.

In addition to simply breaking on a particular allocation, you can force the library to call into your code on every allocation with a hook function. To tell the library to use this hook function, call the _CrtSetAllocHook() API. It calls your function on every allocation, reallocation, and de-allocation with the size, request ordinal, and use-type, along with the file and line number of the call into the library. You can examine the contents of the memory request and decide to break into the debugger yourself, log the event, or ignore it.

REPORTING

The CRTDBG library offers you a reporting function for emitting log messages from your application and a set of APIs or Macros (which are summarized in Table 18-8) to control the reporting. You can use these log messages for debugging purposes, much like the old-style `printf()` debugging. The library supplies a set of reporting macros that are available only in debug mode, but you don't have to place #ifdef guards around them.

TABLE 18-8 CRTDBG REPORTING APIS AND MACROS

API or Macro	Description
_RPT*n*() / _RPTF*n*()	Generates a new message to the reporting log with _CrtDbgReport(). The _RPTF macros add the file name and line number; the *n* indicates the number of parameters after the format string that you must supply.
_CrtDbgReport()	Backs the _RPT macros by doing the actual work of sending the message to the reporting log.
_CrtSetReportMode()	Changes the destination for each type of report. Report types include _CRT_ERROR, _CRT_WARN, and _CRT_ASSERT. Destinations include _CRTDBG_MODE_DEBUG, _CRTDBG_MODE_FILE, and _CRTDBG_MODE_WNDW.
_CrtSetReportFile()	Specifies the backing file for reports that have a mode of _CRTDBG_MODE_FILE. Values include a valid file kernel object handle, _CRTDBG_FILE_STERR, and _CRTDBG_FILE_STDOUT.
_CrtSetReportHook()	Installs a hook function to receive all calls into the _CrtDbgReport() function for application-specific logging enhancements.

The reporting macros take a format string with a format identical to the standard C `printf()` function. You supply a template string and parameters to fill the format specifiers (such as %d or %s). The reporting macros have a prefix of _RPT or _RPTF and a number suffix indicating the number of parameters supplied. For example, the _RPTF2() macro requires two parameters after the format string. The _RPTF function produces identical output to the _RPT function, but adds the file and line number that generated the message.

In addition to the format string and parameters, the reporting macros require a reporting level to qualify the message. Available reporting levels include _CRT_ERROR, _CRT_WARN, and _CRT_ASSERT. The library enables you to choose where messages for each reporting level end up: the debugger output, a popup message box, a file, or any combination of the three using the _CrtSet ReportMode() API.

When you choose to send messages to a file, you can specify that file using the _CrtSetReportFile() API. You also can choose the standard output or standard error stream for the reports with the constants _CRTDBG_FILE_STDOUT and _CRT-DBG_FILE_STDERR, respectively.

Be aware that the _CrtSetReportFile() function takes a kernel object HANDLE from the CreateFile() API — **not** an HFILE reference from the deprecated OpenFile() API.

Each of the reporting macros uses the (debug-only) API, _CrtDbgReport(). The program in Listing 18-12 shows you how to initialize and use the reporting functions from the CRTDBG library.

Listing 18-12: Reporting an application process with the RPT macros

```
// project reporting
#include <windows.h>
#define _CRTDBG_MAP_ALLOC   // use the CRTDBG heap hooking
#include <crtdbg.h>

// helper method to dump the contents of a chunk of memory
void ReportMemory(const PBYTE pbMemory, size_t nSize)
{
    // show a header
    _RPT2(_CRT_WARN, "Dumping %d bytes from 0x%08x\n",
        nSize, (unsigned int)pbMemory);

    // dump the data in a single line
    for(size_t nByte=0; nByte<nSize; ++nByte)
    {
        BYTE bDump = pbMemory[nByte];
        _RPT1(_CRT_WARN, "%02x ", (unsigned int)bDump);
    }

    // terminate the line
    _RPT0(_CRT_WARN,"\n");
```

```
}

void main()
{
    // initialize the heap manager
#ifdef _DEBUG
    int nOldState = ::_CrtSetDbgFlag(
        _CRTDBG_ALLOC_MEM_DF |   // enable debug of allocations
        _CRTDBG_DELAY_FREE_MEM_DF | // clear out freed blocks
        _CRTDBG_LEAK_CHECK_DF); // check application heap leaks
#endif

    // set up the warning reporting mode, it should go to stdout
    //  and the debugger
#ifdef _DEBUG
    ::_CrtSetReportMode(
        _CRT_WARN,                  // set the mode of warnings
        _CRTDBG_MODE_FILE |         // send to a file
        _CRTDBG_MODE_DEBUG);        // also send to debugger
    ::_CrtSetReportFile(
        _CRT_WARN,                  // set the file for warning
        _CRTDBG_FILE_STDOUT);       // use stdout
#endif

    // create memory to leak
    {
        PBYTE pbLeak = new BYTE[1024];

        // show the programmer with location info and without
        _RPTF1(_CRT_WARN, "Allocated leak at address 0x%08x\n",
            (unsigned int)pbLeak);
        _RPT1(_CRT_WARN, "Allocated leak at address 0x%08x\n",
            (unsigned int)pbLeak);

        // dump the values of the first 16 bytes
        ::ReportMemory(pbLeak, 16);

        // do not free the memory
        //delete [] pbLeak;
        pbLeak = NULL;
    }

    // now, allocate and free a block
    {
```

```
    PBYTE pbPlugged = new BYTE[1024];
    delete [] pbPlugged;

    // dump the memory after the release
    ::ReportMemory(pbPlugged, 16);
    pbPlugged = NULL;
  }
}
```

The program in Listing 18-12 uses the _CrtSetReportMode() and _CrtSet
ReportFile() APIs to force the library to send _CRT_WARN log messages to both
the console's stdout stream and to the debugger's output window. Figure 18-6
shows the results of this program in the debugger's output window, which includes
the heap-leak detection. You can see in the results pane that the leaked memory is
filled with 0xCD values and the freed memory is filled with 0xDD as expected.

Listing 18-12 contains the helper function ReportMemory() that takes a byte
array and dumps it to the reporting stream, along with a header. You should notice
that I have to add the newline character at the end of the header and when the
function is finished reporting byte values. By forcing the consumer to emit the
newline, the library allows the creation of lines from pieces as in a memory dump.

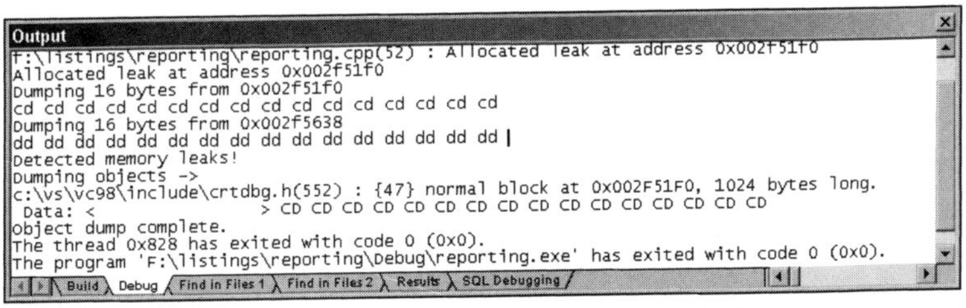

Figure 18-6: The debugger output from Listing 18-12, which shows traces and leak detection

A final, very powerful, feature of the reporting functionality of the library is the
reporting hook. You can force the library to call into your custom function each
time a message is emitted from the library. This function enables you to send the
data to a custom location, such as over a network, or integrate it with logs from
other parts of your application to create a master log.

To set the reporting callback function, use the _CrtSetReportHook() API. Your
function receives the report type, formatted string, and a slot to tell the library what
action it should take next. You can tell the reporting manager whether or not to
generate the standard trace and you also can tell it to break into the debugger.

By default, the reporting function sends warning messages to the debugger output; assertion failures and error messages cause it to display a message box for the
user. The default message boxes enable the user to break into the debugger, at

which point the library calls its _CrtDbgBreak() API. You also have access to this function in debug mode and can decide that debugging is required at runtime.

ASSERTIONS

A *coding assertion* simply is a verification of a condition that should occur at runtime. If a pointer is non-null when your function starts, you can place a line of code in the function that asserts that condition. Then each time the function executes, it tests that pointer's value, generating some sort of error for your response.

Coding assertions are one way to help raise the quality level of your code while you write it. They highlight any assumptions that you make in the code and bring violations of your assumptions to your attention. Even though you document and check for valid parameter values for your function, you should make sure that neither your own code nor someone else's violates those constraints. That's where the debug-only assertion comes in.

For more programming practices that can improve your effectiveness and the quality of your code (including detailed coverage on why assertions should be used always), see the books *Writing Solid Code* by Steve Maguire and *Code Complete* by Steve McConnell, both from Microsoft Press.

Even though assertions are traditionally used only during debug builds, there is a growing movement and strong motivation to leave the tests compiled into release code. It turns out that the size and runtime overhead of assertions is now trivial compared to the size and runtime of most business logic on modern computers. I recommend that you don't perform the assertion removal optimization until you prove that it is needed in your application.

The CRTDBG library delivers an assertion facility to you with the _ASSERT() and _ASSERTE() macros. Both of these macros are enabled during debug mode and compiled out in release mode (decided by the presence or absence of the _DEBUG define):

◆ The assertion macro requires a Boolean expression that it tests within a standard if statement for zero or nonzero results. When the Boolean expression fails, the macro calls the _RPTF() macro for the _CRT_ASSERT report to generate a message with file and line number.

♦ The _ASSERTE() macro adds the text of the expression that failed in addition to the other information from the _ASSERT() macro.

Standard handling of assertion failures displays a message box with Abort, Retry, and Ignore buttons. Clicking Abort stops execution of the application immediately. Clicking Retry starts the debugger up at the failure point. Finally, clicking Ignore continues execution. Listing 18-13 creates an assertion failure for you to see.

Listing 18-13: Reporting assertion failures

```
// project assert
#include <windows.h>
#include <crtdbg.h>

PBYTE ResetData(PBYTE pbMemory)
{
    // this function should be called only to replace a block,
    //   the original block is required
    _ASSERTE(pbMemory!=NULL);

    // make sure we have something to do
    if(pbMemory!=NULL)
    {
        delete [] pbMemory;
        pbMemory = new BYTE[1024];
    }

    // this function should always send back a valid block
    _ASSERT(pbMemory!=NULL);
    return(pbMemory);
}

void main()
{
    // set up the warning reporting mode, it should go to stdout
    //   and the debugger
#ifdef _DEBUG

    // grab the current assertion setup
    int nCurrentMode = ::_CrtSetReportMode(
        _CRT_ASSERT,                // the assert reports
        _CRTDBG_REPORT_MODE);       // just report the current mode

    // add the debugger to the current mode
```

```
    ::_CrtSetReportMode(
        _CRT_ASSERT,                // set the mode of asserts
        nCurrentMode |              // include the current mode
        _CRTDBG_MODE_DEBUG);        // also send to debugger
#endif

    // call the API nicely
    PBYTE pbMemOrig = new BYTE[1024];
    pbMemOrig = ::ResetData(pbMemOrig);

    // cleanup
    delete [] pbMemOrig;
    pbMemOrig = NULL;

    // cause the function to fail
    ::ResetData(NULL);
}
```

It's simple to write bugs, so Listing 18-13 looks like it goes too far. The program first makes sure that assertion failures are dumped to the debugger output in addition to the default handling (the dialog box). I prefer to have all of the reporting done to the same place, even if it is done elsewhere as well. My reason for this is so that I have as much context as possible when I go to fix a problem. Once the reporting is set up, the application executes the helper ResetData() method correctly and then incorrectly (in violation of the programming contract).

The first time through ResetData(), nothing happens. However, the second time through, an assertion-failure dialog box (like that in Figure 18-7) shows up immediately. Note the name of the executable, the file name/line number of the failure, and the text of the expression, just as I type it. The next exception dialog box is just like it, without the expression text.

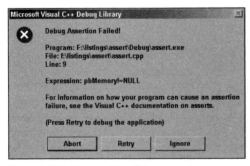

Figure 18-7: An assertion failure warning

To simplify my life, I often map the assertion macro — of whatever framework I am using — to ASSERT with a #define. This creates quick, uniform access to the assertion facilities. You'll see in the next sections why you may want to adopt this practice, too.

Using the Microsoft Foundation Class Library

The *Microsoft Foundation Class Library (MFC)* uses the CRTDBG for its debugging heap and integrates with its reporting. MFC has a predominant class hierarchy, so it has some built-in, extended features to simplify debugging your new classes.

I assume that you are familiar with MFC. This section is aimed at making the lives of MFC users a bit easier, not at introducing MFC.

For an introduction to MFC, pick up *Programming Visual C++* by David J. Kruglinski, Scot Wingo, and George Shepherd from Microsoft Press.

As I mentioned, MFC uses the CRTDBG library's debug heap almost directly. You must supply the line #define new DEBUG_NEW before using the new operator in order to capture the file name and line number information along with allocations in the MFC heap. To enable heap allocation tracking, MFC supplies the AfxEnable MemoryTracking() API. You should include a call to this in your (debug-only) application startup code.

MFC supplies the CMemoryState class for you to get access to allocation snapshots and statistics. It turns out that this class is identical in memory layout to the _CrtMemState structure — with the addition of all of the memory state manipulators as methods. I don't go over its use or layout because it is so simple. See the MSDN for exact syntax.

Like the runtime debug library, MFC supplies a reporting facility. However, the syntax for MFC tracing is a bit simpler. You can use the single TRACE() macro. This macro is available only in debug mode and takes a variable number of parameters. The first of these parameters is a format string; the rest are parameters for its printf()-like syntax. MFC sends all traces to the debugger.

MFC extends the `printf()`-like tracing with object dumping. In the MFC hierarchy, the `CObject` class is the base-most class for the majority of other classes. `CObject` defines a `Dump()` method for you to implement in your derived classes. This method takes a `CDumpContext` object as a parameter, which has `iostream`-like syntax for streaming in text.

TIP You should override this method in your derived classes to emit the current state of your object whenever the framework calls it.

The `CObject::Dump()` method is called whenever a heap leak is detected by the debug allocator. The allocator walks through all leaks in the heap, checks for an object derived from `CObject`, and attempts to call its `Dump()` method. This output then gives you a chance to examine the object's state while it is leaked, perhaps to identify and fix the leak. You also can force a dump of your object to the debugger at any time with the `AfxDump()` API.

In addition, like the runtime library, MFC supplies an assertion facility. In this case, you must use the single `ASSERT()` macro to test your condition. This macro emits the file name and line number of a failure, but not the text of the expression that failed. In addition to the simple assertion, MFC supplies the `VERIFY()` macro, which enables you to place code in the assertion that still executes in release mode. The expression's result is thrown away.

In similar fashion to the `Dump()` method, MFC integrates assertions into `CObject`-derived classes with the `AssertValid()` method. This method is intended to be a self-consistency check that any client of the object, or the object itself, can call at any point in execution. The self-consistency check should make sure that each data member conforms to valid values for some state. You can execute a self-consistency check at any time with the `ASSERT_VALID()` macro. This macro first ensures that the pointer you hand it points to a valid `CObject` before calling the object's `AssertValid()` method.

You can see that the debugging value that MFC adds is centered around its object model. Listing 18-14 shows you how to set up and use the debugging facilities that I have presented.

Listing 18-14: Using the MFC debugging features

```
// project mfcdebug, file mfcdebug.cpp
//
// ... other code precedes
//
// simple debug-enabled CObject-derived class
class CDebugObject : public CObject
```

```
{
public:
    CDebugObject(int nID) : m_nID(nID) {}
    virtual ~CDebugObject(){}

    // implementation
protected:
    int m_nID; // simple identifier

    // debugging
public:
#ifdef _DEBUG
    virtual void Dump(CDumpContext& dc) const
    {
        // first, dump the parent object
        CObject::Dump(dc);

        // dump our state
        dc << "\nA CDebugObject, m_nID=" << m_nID << "\n";
    }

    virtual void AssertValid() const
    {
        // first, check the base class
        CObject::AssertValid();

        // make sure the ID is nonzero
        ASSERT(m_nID!=0);
    }
#endif
};

// exhibition of debugging features
void DebuggingStuff()
{
    TRACE("Entering debugging demonstration.\n");

    // enable memory tracking for the application and set
    //  the heap-leak dump to be deep
    ::AfxEnableMemoryTracking(TRUE);
    afxDump.SetDepth(1);

    // create a debuggable object
    int nID = 42;
```

```
        CDebugObject* pDbgObj = new CDebugObject(nID);
        ASSERT_VALID(pDbgObj);

        // show the debuggable object
        ::AfxDump(pDbgObj);

        TRACE("Leaking debuggable object with id %d\n", nID);
}
//
// other code follows ...
//
```

The code snippet in Listing 18-14 creates a simple object that complies with the debugging profile by overriding the `AssertValid()` and `Dump()` methods. This `CDebugObject` class is very simple, with no methods and a single data member — its identifier. The `Dump()` method simply emits that identifier to the output stream, and the `AssertValid()` method simply ensures that the identifier is nonzero.

The `DebuggingStuff()` helper function initializes the debugging heap and the dump of the heap, then leaks one of the new objects. It also shows you how to call the `TRACE()` macro with and without parameters and how to use the `AfxDump()` API to show the current state of an object.

Using the Active Template Library

The *Active Template Library (ATL)* supplies debugging facilities also built on those of the CRTDBG library. It uses the debugging heap directly and does not attempt to wrap it in any way. ATL also directly maps its assertion macro, `ATLASSERT()`, to the `_ASSERTE()` macro from the runtime library.

I assume you are familiar with ATL. This section is aimed at making the lives of ATL users a bit easier, not at introducing ATL.

For an introduction to ATL, pick up a copy of *The Active Template Library: A Developer's Guide* by Tom Armstrong from IDG Books Worldwide.

ATL does provide a tracing facility that is independent of CRTDBG. It supplies the `ATLTRACE()` macro that, like the MFC `TRACE()` macro, takes a `printf()`-like format string and parameter list of the message you want to log. This output is sent to the debugger and nowhere else.

In addition to the simplistic ATLTRACE() macro, there is an ATLTRACE2() macro that primarily is used within the framework. This overload requires a category and level to qualify the trace you send. The category is a bitmask from the atlTrace Flags enumeration in AtlBase.H. Example values are atlTraceRefCount and atlTraceQI for reference count and query-interface operations, respectively. The value for the trace level describes its importance; zero is most important.

The framework enables all tracing categories by default. To alter that, you need to define the ATL_TRACE_CATEGORY macro to meet your needs before including AtlBase.H. The trace level is set to zero by default. To enable full tracing from the framework, you should define ATL_TRACE_LEVEL as 0xFFFFFFFF.

You can add traces with or without categorization at any point in the execution of your ATL objects with the ATLTRACE() or ATLTRACE2() macros. Another valuable helper that the framework gives you is the ATLTRACENOTIMPL() macro for not-yet-implemented interfaces. You simply supply a description of the function, or reason why the method is not implemented yet, and the framework sends an E_NOTIMPL to the caller while logging a message to the debugger.

Finally, the ATL library lets you enable some additional tracing with the _ATL_DEBUG_INTERFACES and _ATL_DEBUG_QI defines. You should make these two defines before you include AtlBase.H. They give you extended information about interface searching and use within your COM server. The search for a particular interface is detailed in the debugger output as is the reference counting of objects that you create. You should modify the inclusion of AtlBase.H to look like Listing 18-15.

Listing 18-15: Full-blown debugging of ATL

```
//
// ... other code precedes
//
#ifdef _DEBUG
    #define _ATL_DEBUG_INTERFACES
    #define _ATL_DEBUG_QI
    #define ATL_TRACE_LEVEL 0xFFFFFFFF
    #define ATL_TRACE_CATEGORY 0xFFFFFFFF
#endif
#include <atlbase.h>
//
// other code follows ...
//
```

Listing 18-15 shows you the best way to enable the debugging features that ATL offers. You should place this snippet in the central include of any ATL project in place of your include of the AtlBase.H header.

Performance Monitoring

The Windows 2000 performance-monitoring framework enables system administrators to monitor the impact that your service application has on system resources. Performance data enables administrators to tune the configuration parameters that your application exposes for their desired balance of resources and features.

 Developers typically only enable performance monitoring for service applications, as I state above, but that need not be the case. Any Windows 2000 application can integrate with the performance-monitoring framework, as is demonstrated by the example application in this section.

Further, by integrating performance monitoring into your service application, you can have a development facility that helps you optimize performance and track down subtle bugs. This section shows you how to design performance counters and objects that expose the important pieces of your application to the system. Then it shows you how to tell the system that the counters are there.

Delivering correct functionality

When you create a new service application, your first priority is to design and write the code that gets the job done. Initially, you shouldn't worry about execution speed or consuming system resources; you should worry about delivering correct functionality. As your project progresses, however, begin to turn your attention to how well your application behaves in the operating system. To illustrate the process, I created a short application in Listing 18-16 that fulfills a task and does it correctly.

Listing 18-16: Creating a correct and purposeful application

```cpp
// project perfapp, file perfapp.cpp
#include <windows.h>
#include <string>
#include <fstream>
#include <iostream>

// SBookStats maintains statistics on the book writing
struct SBookStats
{
    DWORD   m_dwCharacterCt;// total chars typed
    DWORD   m_dwWordCt;     // total words entered
    DWORD   m_dwSentenceCt; // total sentences entered
```

```cpp
    DWORD   m_dwPageCt;     // total pages written

    // simple ctor to clear out all of the counters
    SBookStats() : m_dwCharacterCt(0), m_dwWordCt(0),
        m_dwSentenceCt(0) {}

    // AddXxx() methods will take a word, sentence, and page
    //  and update the stats properly
    void AddWord(const std::string& strWord)
    {
        m_dwCharacterCt += strWord.length();
        ++m_dwWordCt;
    }
    void AddSentence(const std::string& /*strSentence*/)
    {
        ++m_dwSentenceCt;
    }
    void AddPage(const std::string& /*strPage*/)
    {
        ++m_dwPageCt;
    }
};
SBookStats  g_stats; // statistics about all books from app

// CBookWriter creates books to specification and emits them
//  disk in the passed file name
class CBookWriter
{
public:
    // method to create a new book
    void WriteBook(const std::string& strFilename,
        int nPageCt) const
    {
        std::ofstream ofBook(strFilename.c_str());

        // write as many pages as requested
        for(int nPage=0; nPage<nPageCt; ++nPage)
        {
            // create a page (about 40 sentences)
            std::string strPage;
            for(int nContent=0; nContent<40; ++nContent)
            {
                strPage += CreateSentence();
                strPage += "\n";
```

```cpp
        }

        // write the page & count the stats
        ofBook << strPage << "Page #" << nPage << "\n\n";
        g_stats.AddPage(strPage);

        // take a little time off after every page
        ::Sleep(100);
    }
}

// method to generate a sentence
std::string CreateSentence() const
{
    std::string strSentence;

    // sentences have 2-20 words and a period
    int nWords = 2 + (::rand()*21)/RAND_MAX;
    for(int nWord=0; nWord<nWords; ++nWord)
    {
        // add a new word
        if(!strSentence.empty())
        {
            strSentence += ' ';
        }

        std::string strWord;
        strSentence += CreateWord();

        // record the word for perf monitoring
        g_stats.AddWord(strWord);
    }

    // record the sentence for perf monitoring
    g_stats.AddSentence(strSentence);

    strSentence += '.';
    return(strSentence);
}

// method to generate a random word
std::string CreateWord() const
{
    std::string strWord;
```

```
        // words are a-z (capitalization and contractions
        //  ignored), length is 1-12 chars
        int nChars = 1 + (::rand()*12)/RAND_MAX;
        for(int nChar=0; nChar<nChars; ++nChar)
        {
            // add a new char
            int nAlpha = (::rand()*26)/RAND_MAX;
            char cAdd = 'a' + nAlpha;
            strWord += cAdd;
        }
        return(strWord);
    }


    // simple function to create a fully specified book name
    static std::string MakeBookFilename()
    {
        std::string strFilename;

        // find the path
        TCHAR szPath[MAX_PATH];
        if(::GetTempPath(MAX_PATH, szPath)>0)
        {
            // ask for a new file in the path
            TCHAR szFilename[MAX_PATH];
            if(::GetTempFileName(
                szPath,         // path
                "NOV",          // prefix string
                0,              // let the system pick a number
                szFilename)>0)  // buffer
            {
                strFilename = szFilename;
            }
        }
        return(strFilename);
    }
};

void main()
{
    // begin working, write a bunch of 1000 page books
    while(true)
    {
        // emit a little description of the task
```

```
        // (it takes some time)
        std::string strFilename =
            CBookWriter::MakeBookFilename();
        std::cout << "Writing book, filename: " << strFilename
            << std::endl;

        // create an author
        CBookWriter author;
        author.WriteBook(strFilename, 1000);
    }
}
```

The application in Listing 18-16 writes books on demand. The CBookWriter class accepts a file name and page count and fills the file with page after page of words assembled into sentences. This application gives up complexity for efficiency, creating words as random letter strings. Since the example is so efficient, it's likely to require many system resources in order to run.

In order to get a good picture of your application's behavior, you should add Windows performance counters and objects so that you can use the system's tools to monitor the internals of your application alongside the internals of Windows. Telling Windows about the performance counters and objects is as easy as making some registry entries.

A *performance object* is a set of one or more counters that describe some aspect of your application. Each counter in the object either should increase or not change every time the system samples it from your application. The system stores the counter values for you; the client application interprets them. The typical client application that you use is the management console snap-in contained in the file PerfMon.MSC and found in the Administrative Tools folder off the Start... Programs... menu.

Chapter 11, "Service Applications," introduces snap-in modules for the Microsoft Management Console (MMC).

Your application can expose as many performance object types and as many instances of each performance object as make sense. The performance monitor client enables the administrator to browse through all of the performance objects present in the system and each instance of each object. For each performance object instance, administrators can select any counter that they want to inspect. Figure 18-8 shows you the PerfMon.MSC counter selection dialog box. The figure shows the object, instance, and counter lists.

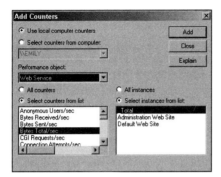

Figure 18-8: The counter selection dialog box from the performance monitor snap-in

The `PerfMon.MSC` snap-in enables you to graph, capture, and inspect data from any of the counters. It also derives instantaneous rates for any of the counters by querying the counter at a known frequency and dividing the change in value by that period.

Registering counters

In the program in Listing 18-16, it is clear that the generation of characters, words, sentences, and pages impacts the application's performance. To tell the system that those counters are available, the application must update the registry.

The system only expects to gather information from service applications and so it uses the service database in the registry at `HKLM\System\CurrentControlSet\Services` to locate those applications that want monitoring. Each service application has a namesake key under the `HKLM\...\Services` parent. Beneath the application's key you need to add a `Performance` key that contains values for the performance system to use when gathering your data.

To allow the system to gather performance data from you, supply it a DLL with three specific entry points: open, collect, and close. You can name this DLL and entry points anything you want, provided they have the required interface. To tell the system these names, you must add the `Library`, `Open`, `Collect`, and `Close` string values to the `Performance` key; the system executes `LoadLibrary()` and `GetProcAddress()` calls on each of the strings.

For details on dynamic linking, see Chapter 10, "Application Building Services."

Finally, you can tell the system what counters you have in your performance DLL using another location in the registry. This counter registration is very complicated so Windows supplies an API from the `LoadPerf.DLL` library called `LoadPerfCounterTextStrings()` that simplifies your job. It requests that you place definitions and descriptions for your counters in a text file that has the same format as an old INI file.

To fill out the INI file for counter definitions, you need to specify the application name, a language that you support, and the definitions of your objects and their counters. The counter registration also requires the name of a header file with C++ preprocessor constants for your objects and counters. The format is available on the MSDN, so I don't dive into it. However, I do show you how to configure all of the performance monitoring from your application in Listing 18-17.

Listing 18-17: Configuring performance monitoring

```cpp
// project perfapp, file regperf.cpp
#include <windows.h>
#include <iostream>
#include <fstream>
#include <string>
#include <loadperf.h>
#pragma comment(lib, "loadperf.lib")

#include "perfapp.h"

// The next two helper methods take care of registering the
//   application as a service that provides performance data.
//   This step is required in order to let the performance
//   monitoring system know that the app exists, the definals
//   should be moved to a header file for broad consumption.
#define APPNAME "W2KDGPerfApp"
#define REGSTR_APPKEY_PERF "System\\CurrentControlSet"\
    "\\Services\\" APPNAME "\\Performance"
#define PERFLIB_NAME "W2KDGPerf.DLL"
#define PERFLIB_FUNC_OPEN "OpenPerformanceData"
#define PERFLIB_FUNC_COLLECT "CollectPerformanceData"
#define PERFLIB_FUNC_CLOSE "ClosePerformanceData"

// helper method to write out a registry string value
DWORD SetRegString(HKEY hkey, const std::string& strName,
                   const std::string& strValue)
{
    return(::RegSetValueEx(
        hkey,                   // use the passed key
        strName.c_str(),        // value name
        0,                      // must be 0
        REG_SZ,                 // setting a string
```

```
        (PBYTE)strValue.c_str(),// value buffer
        strValue.length()+1));  // length (with room for null)
}


// workhorse to create all of the registry values
void RegisterPerformanceApp()
{
    // create the application performance key
    HKEY hkeyPerf = NULL;
    DWORD dwResult = ::RegCreateKeyEx(
        HKEY_LOCAL_MACHINE,     // create under HKLM
        REGSTR_APPKEY_PERF,     // application performance key
        0,                      // must be 0
        NULL,                   // no class required
        REG_OPTION_NON_VOLATILE,// save the key
        KEY_WRITE,              // need to write to it
        NULL,                   // default security
        &hkeyPerf,              // result
        NULL);                  // don't need the disposition
    if(dwResult==ERROR_SUCCESS && hkeyPerf!=NULL)
    {
        // set up the required performance values
        ::SetRegString(hkeyPerf, "Library", PERFLIB_NAME);
        ::SetRegString(hkeyPerf, "Open", PERFLIB_FUNC_OPEN);
        ::SetRegString(hkeyPerf, "Collect",
            PERFLIB_FUNC_COLLECT);
        ::SetRegString(hkeyPerf, "Close", PERFLIB_FUNC_CLOSE);

        // close up the key
        ::RegCloseKey(hkeyPerf);
        hkeyPerf = NULL;
    }
}


// The next set of definals and the helper method make sure
// that the performance monitoring system knows about the
// counters exposed by this application and associates
// human-readable strings with each counter for display to the
// administrator
#define SYMBOLS \
    "#define OBJ_AUTHOR        0\n"\
    "#define COUNTER_WORD      2\n"\
    "#define COUNTER_SENTENCE  4\n"
```

```
#define COUNTERS_1 \
    "[info]\n"\
    "drivername=" APPNAME "\n"\
    "symbolfile="
#define COUNTERS_2 \
    "\n\n"\
    "[languages]\n"\
    "009=English\n\n"\
    "[objects]\n"\
    "OBJ_AUTHOR_009_NAME=W2KDG Automated Author\n"\
    "[text]\n"\
    "OBJ_AUTHOR_009_NAME=W2KDG Automated Author\n"\
    "OBJ_AUTHOR_009_HELP=Statistics about W2KDG Author.\n"\
    "COUNTER_SENTENCE_009_NAME=Sentences written.\n"\
    "COUNTER_SENTENCE_009_HELP=Total sentences written.\n"\
    "COUNTER_WORD_009_NAME=Words written.\n"\
    "COUNTER_WORD_009_HELP=Total words written.\n"

void RegisterCounterStrings()
{
    // create the symbol file
    std::string strSymfile = ::MakeFilename("SYM");
    {
        std::ofstream ofSymfile(strSymfile.c_str());
        ofSymfile << SYMBOLS;
    }


    // create the counters file
    std::string strCounterfile = ::MakeFilename("CNT");
    {
        std::ofstream ofCounterfile(strCounterfile.c_str());
        ofCounterfile << COUNTERS_1 << strSymfile
            << COUNTERS_2;
    }


    // now, attempt to load the counters up. note that you must
    //  construct the command line that you would use
    //  to register the performance counters manually
    TCHAR szCmdLine[MAX_PATH];
    ::strcpy(szCmdLine, "lodctr ");
    ::strcat(szCmdLine, strCounterfile.c_str());
    DWORD dwResult = ::LoadPerfCounterTextStrings(
        szCmdLine,  // name of file to use
        FALSE);     // allow feedback
```

```
}

// Entry point for the application. It will call into here to
//  ensure that the performance monitoring is ready
void RegisterPerformanceCounters()
{
    // first, make sure the system recognizes the app
    RegisterPerformanceApp();

    // now, create the INI file and load the counters
    RegisterCounterStrings();
}
```

The code in Listing 18-17 adds on to the application in Listing 18-16 and creates the required keys in the registry to let the system know it has performance counters. The first helper function, `RegisterPerformanceApp()`, creates the required entries in the services database so that the system knows the application has performance counters. The next function, `RegisterCounterStrings()`, creates and loads the strings that describe the object and counters from the application. I recommend that you take this code and adapt it for your own application; getting it correct isn't easy.

 TIP   The Microsoft Platform SDK supplies a helper utility, `ExCtrLst.EXE`, which enumerates all of the performance-monitoring DLLs known to the system and the current state of each. Use it during development to verify that your counters are properly registered.

After the application runs the `RegisterPerformanceCounters()` function, the registry is updated with system-supplied helper data for counter and help indices as well as a list of performance objects supplied by the DLL. Figure 18-9 shows you the state of the registry after execution for the applications from Listings 18-16 through 18-17.

Gathering data

In Listing 18-16, I began to maintain statistics about the application in the helper `SBookStats` structure. The application creates a single instance of this structure and calls its methods each time it creates a new portion of the book. The data gathering is very efficient and should have little impact on the runtime (it's much faster than writing to disk), but it provides the basic instrumentation that I need to integrate the application into the performance-monitoring framework.

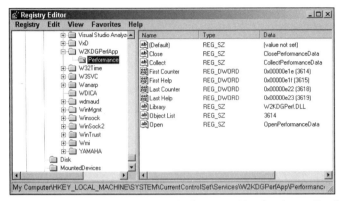

Figure 18-9: The services database Performance hive for the application

The impact that performance counters have on the runtime efficiency of an application is always a source of concern. You can, of course, provide an application preference to disable them, but I've never come across a case where that made a demonstrable difference.

As I explained earlier, the basic application that wants to expose data to the performance monitor must create a DLL that the system can load and retrieve data. Since a process other than the data generator loads this DLL, you have to create an interprocess communication (IPC) mechanism for the data. The most straightforward mechanism to use is the kernel memory-mapped file object.

The design for this IPC centers on simplicity and correctness. The data is a simple set of 32-bit values, the processor's native data size. First, I choose a name for the object that uniquely identifies it in the system. I do this by prefixing my company and project names to the name of the object. Next, I share a simple data structure between the two applications; it is available for reading and writing in the application and consumed in read-only mode by the DLL. I guard access to the memory-mapped file object with an interprocess kernel mutex object to ensure that the data remains consistent from the last update pass. Finally, I create a worker thread in the main application to populate the memory-mapped file with current data periodically.

Inter-thread kernel objects that you can share across processes are covered in detail in Chapter 4, "Commonly Used Kernel Objects."

Now that I have the design of the data gathering, it's time to modify the application to expose its data. Listing 18-18 shows you the resulting implementation.

Listing 18-18: Exposing performance data from the application

```
// project perfapp, file datagen.cpp
#define _WIN32_WINNT 0x0500
#define WINVER 0x0500
#include <windows.h>
#include <fstream>
#include <string>

#include "perfapp.h"

// helper data for sampling execution
static bool g_bSample = false;

// naming for interprocess synchronization objects
#define NAMESTR_MMF_STATS "W2KDG.PerfApp.Mmf.Statistics"
#define NAMESTR_MUTEX_STATS "W2KDG.PerfApp.Mutex.Statistics"

// helper function to create a memory-mapped file to transfer
//   statistics between processes
HANDLE InitializeTransferArea()
{
    // create a new memory-mapped file for sharing performance
    //   data
    HANDLE hMmfTransfer = ::CreateFileMapping(
        INVALID_HANDLE_VALUE,    // let the system find memory
        NULL,                    // default security
        PAGE_READWRITE,          // read-write access
        0,                       // less than 4GB
        sizeof(SBookStats),      // size to required structure
        NAMESTR_MMF_STATS);      // use the sharable name
    return(hMmfTransfer);
}

// helper method to create a lock for the transfer area
HANDLE InitializeTransferMutex()
{
    // create a new mutex object for guarding the transfer area
    HANDLE hMutexTransfer = ::CreateMutex(
        NULL,                    // default security
        TRUE,                    // initially own the mutex
        NAMESTR_MUTEX_STATS);    // use the sharable name
```

```
        return(hMutexTransfer);
}


// helper function to create and initialize a timer object to
//   govern the rate of sampling of the statistics
HANDLE InitializeSamplingTimer()
{
    // create a new waitable timer object for sampling stats
    HANDLE hTimerSample = ::CreateWaitableTimer(
        NULL,                   // default security
        FALSE,                  // auto-reset
        NULL);                  // not shared, no name
    if(hTimerSample!=NULL)
    {
        // try initializing the timer for 2 samples/sec
        LARGE_INTEGER liDueTime = {0,0};
        if(!::SetWaitableTimer(
            hTimerSample,       // timer to set
            &liDueTime,         // initial expiration time
            500,                // sample every 0.5 sec (in ms)
            NULL,               // no completion routine
            NULL,               // no arg to completion routine
            FALSE))             // do not resume from sleep
        {
            // close up the timer on failure to initialize
            ::CloseHandle(hTimerSample);
            hTimerSample = NULL;
        }
    }
    return(hTimerSample);
}


// simple sampling routing gets a copy of the data from the
//   main thread and dumps it to the transfer area, the consumer
//   will simply copy it into a new instance of the structure
void SampleData(LPVOID pView)
{
    SBookStats* pDest = static_cast<SBookStats*>(pView);
    *pDest = ::SnapStatistics();
}


// worker thread to place samples of the statistics in the
//   transfer area
DWORD WINAPI PerfThread(LPVOID /*lpParam*/)
```

```
{
    // create the memory-mapped file and its mutex
    HANDLE hMmfTransfer = ::InitializeTransferArea();
    HANDLE hMutexTransfer = ::InitializeTransferMutex();
    if(hMmfTransfer!=NULL && hMutexTransfer!=NULL)
    {
        // create the file-mapping view
        LPVOID pView = ::MapViewOfFile(
            hMmfTransfer,    // view from the sampling area
            FILE_MAP_WRITE,  // must write to it
            0,               // view from the beginning
            0,               // view from the beginning
            0);              // view the entire file

        // create the sampling timer
        HANDLE hTimerSample = ::InitializeSamplingTimer();
        if(pView!=NULL && hTimerSample!=NULL)
        {
            // enter a loop, sampling data until told to stop
            while(g_bSample)
            {
                // pause until the timer expires
                DWORD dwWaitResult = ::WaitForSingleObject(
                    hTimerSample,   // pause for sampling timer
                    INFINITE);      // block indefinitely
                if(dwWaitResult==WAIT_OBJECT_0)
                {
                    // now, wait until we can get the mutex
                    dwWaitResult = ::WaitForSingleObject(
                        hMutexTransfer, // pause for the mutex
                        INFINITE);      // block indefinitely
                    if(dwWaitResult==WAIT_OBJECT_0)
                    {
                        // sample the data and release the
                        //  mutex lock on the transfer area
                        ::SampleData(pView);
                        ::ReleaseMutex(hMutexTransfer);
                    }
                }
            }

            // clean up the file view
            ::UnmapViewOfFile(pView);
            pView = NULL;
```

```
        }

        // clean up the timer
        ::CloseHandle(hTimerSample);
        hTimerSample = NULL;
    }

    // clean up the mmf and mutex
    ::CloseHandle(hMmfTransfer);
    hMmfTransfer = NULL;
    ::CloseHandle(hMutexTransfer);
    hMutexTransfer = NULL;

    // simple exit code
    return(0);
}

// create the performance data generation infrastructure
void InitializePerformanceCounters()
{
    // signal that sampling can begin
    g_bSample = true;

    // start the worker thread
    HANDLE hThreadWorker = ::CreateThread(
        NULL,              // default security
        0,                 // default stack
        PerfThread,        // performance counter thread
        NULL,              // no parameters to thread
        0,                 // creation flags
        NULL);             // don't need the thread ID

    // release our reference to the thread
    ::CloseHandle(hThreadWorker);
    hThreadWorker = NULL;
}

// helper method to terminate the sampling
void ShutdownPerformanceCounters()
{
    g_bSample = false;
}
```

The module shown in Listing 18-18 simply adds a worker thread to the application that samples the application's statistics every half second. To do this, the module creates a named memory-mapped file object and a named mutex object to guard it. The thread relies on a waitable timer to trigger the sampling, waits for the guard mutex to become available, then copies the current values of the counters into the shared memory region.

> You should choose the frequency of sampling within the application to make sense for the application; it is independent of the sampling frequency that the performance-monitoring system will use on that data. The IPC mechanism de-couples the sampling rates.

The implementation in Listing 18-18 is very straightforward; both the server (application) and client (performance counter DLL) share definitions of the CBookStats structure to allow simple binary copies of the data from and into instances. The client application follows much of the same logic, but makes the sample on demand from the system rather than in response to a timer expiration.

Exporting data

Now that the main application is exporting data in a format that I can expose to the system, I need to implement the performance counter DLL. The system already designed the library for me. It has the three entry points I already mentioned: open, collect, and close.

The system calls my open method when it initializes the performance-monitoring system. During the open call, I must initialize whatever internals are required to fetch the data from the generating application. Next, the system calls the collect method whenever it wants to (I don't care). Each call to the collect method supplies the numeric values of the counter in which the system is interested and expects me to supply that data.

Finally, when the performance-monitoring system is finished with my performance counters, it calls the close method. I implemented the performance counters for the book-authoring application in Listing 18-19.

Listing 18-19: Implementing a performance counter DLL

```
// project W2KDGPerf
#include <windows.h>
#include <string>
#include <fstream>

// helper includes from the application which exposes the data
```

```
#include "..\\perfapp\\perfapp.h"
#include "..\\perfapp\\countersym.h"

// the following structures define and initialize the
//  performance object and its counters
struct SObjectDefinition
{
    PERF_OBJECT_TYPE        m_type;
    PERF_COUNTER_DEFINITION m_defWordCt;
    PERF_COUNTER_DEFINITION m_defSentenceCt;
};
struct SCounter
{
    PERF_COUNTER_BLOCK      m_block;
    DWORD                   m_dwWordCt;
    DWORD                   m_dwSentenceCt;
    DWORD                   m_dwBookCt;
};
static SObjectDefinition g_objdef =
{
    // object type
    {
        // sizes (total, then definition)
        (sizeof(SObjectDefinition) + sizeof(SCounter)),
        sizeof(SObjectDefinition),
        sizeof(PERF_OBJECT_TYPE),    // offset to first def
        OBJ_AUTHOR,                  // object title index
        NULL,                        // title string
        OBJ_AUTHOR,                  // object help index
        NULL,                        // help string
        PERF_DETAIL_NOVICE,          // for anyone
        ((sizeof(SObjectDefinition)-sizeof(PERF_OBJECT_TYPE))/
            sizeof(PERF_COUNTER_DEFINITION)), // # of counters
        0,                           // first is default counter
        PERF_NO_INSTANCES,           // no instances available
        0,                           // instance code page
        {0,0},                       // no starting time
        {0,0}                        // no starting frequency

    },
    // word counter definition
    {
        sizeof(PERF_COUNTER_DEFINITION),//size
        COUNTER_WORD,                    // counter title index
```

```
            NULL,                       // no title string
            COUNTER_WORD,               // counter help index
            NULL,                       // no help string
            -2,                         // in 100s of words per sec
            PERF_DETAIL_NOVICE,         // for anyone
            PERF_COUNTER_COUNTER,       // counter (rate)
            sizeof(DWORD),              // size of data
            offsetof(SCounter, m_dwWordCt)  // offset to data
      },
      // sentence counter
      {
            sizeof(PERF_COUNTER_DEFINITION),//size
            COUNTER_SENTENCE,           // counter title index
            NULL,                       // no title string
            COUNTER_SENTENCE,           // counter help index
            NULL,                       // no help string
            -1,                         // in 10s of sent/sec
            PERF_DETAIL_NOVICE,         // for anyone
            PERF_COUNTER_COUNTER,       // counter (rate)
            sizeof(DWORD),              // size of data
            offsetof(SCounter, m_dwSentenceCt)  // offset to data
      }
};

// configuration data
static HANDLE g_hMmfTransfer = NULL;
static HANDLE g_hMutexTransfer = NULL;
static LPVOID g_pTransferData = NULL;
static DWORD  g_dwCounterOffset = 0;
static DWORD  g_dwHelpOffset = 0;

void InitializeTransferData()
{
    // open the memory-mapped file for sharing performance data
    g_hMmfTransfer = ::OpenFileMapping(
        FILE_MAP_READ,          // open for reading
        FALSE,                  // don't need to inherit
        NAMESTR_MMF_STATS);     // use the sharable name

    // create the file-mapping view
    if(g_hMmfTransfer!=NULL)
    {
        g_pTransferData = ::MapViewOfFile(
            g_hMmfTransfer,     // the transfer area
```

```
            FILE_MAP_READ,        // read access
            0,                    // view from the beginning
            0,                    // view from the beginning
            0);                   // view the entire file
    }

    // open the mutex object for guarding the transfer area
    g_hMutexTransfer = ::OpenMutex(
        SYNCHRONIZE,              // open for synchronizing
        FALSE,                    // don't need to inherit
        NAMESTR_MUTEX_STATS);     // use the sharable name

    // open up the registry and fetch the counter and help
    //  offsets
    HKEY hkeyPerf = NULL;
    if(ERROR_SUCCESS==::RegOpenKeyEx(
        HKEY_LOCAL_MACHINE,       // perf data in HKLM
        REGSTR_APPKEY_PERF,       // perf key name
        0,                        // must be 0
        KEY_READ,                 // read access
        &hkeyPerf))               // return buffer
    {
        // get the counter offset
        DWORD dwType = REG_DWORD;
        DWORD dwSize = sizeof(DWORD);
        ::RegQueryValueEx(
            hkeyPerf,             // app key
            "First Counter",      // offset value name
            0,                    // must be 0
            &dwType,              // return type (starts dword)
            (LPBYTE)&g_dwCounterOffset, // buffer
            &dwSize);             // buffer size

        // repeat to get the help offset
        ::RegQueryValueEx(hkeyPerf, "First Help", 0, &dwType,
            (LPBYTE)&g_dwHelpOffset, &dwSize);

        // close up the registry
        ::RegCloseKey(hkeyPerf);
        hkeyPerf = NULL;
    }
}

// helper function to determine whether this library has
```

```
//  been initialized already (must be done only once per
//  process)
bool IsInitialized()
{
    return(g_pTransferData!=NULL && g_hMutexTransfer!=NULL);
}


extern "C" DWORD APIENTRY OpenPerformanceData(LPWSTR)
{
    DWORD dwResult = ERROR_SUCCESS;

    // set up the transfer objects
    if(!::IsInitialized())
    {
        // get the transfer data
        ::InitializeTransferData();

        // fix up the title indicies
        g_objdef.m_type.ObjectNameTitleIndex +=
            g_dwCounterOffset;
        g_objdef.m_type.ObjectHelpTitleIndex +=
            g_dwHelpOffset;

        g_objdef.m_defWordCt.CounterNameTitleIndex +=
            g_dwCounterOffset;
        g_objdef.m_defWordCt.CounterHelpTitleIndex +=
            g_dwHelpOffset;

        g_objdef.m_defSentenceCt.CounterNameTitleIndex +=
            g_dwCounterOffset;
        g_objdef.m_defSentenceCt.CounterHelpTitleIndex +=
            g_dwHelpOffset;
    }
    return(dwResult);
}


SBookStats LookupStatistics()
{
    SBookStats* pData =
        static_cast<SBookStats*>(g_pTransferData);
    SBookStats data = *pData;
    return(data);
}
```

```
extern "C" DWORD APIENTRY CollectPerformanceData(
    LPWSTR pwszValue,
    LPVOID* ppData,
    LPDWORD pdwBytes,
    LPDWORD pdwObjectTypes)
{
    // begin by initializing a result code
    DWORD dwResult = ERROR_SUCCESS;

    // check for proper initialization
    if(::IsInitialized())
    {
        // create the buffer
        SObjectDefinition* pDest =
            static_cast<SObjectDefinition*>(*ppData);

        // calculate the required size
        DWORD dwReqSize = sizeof(SObjectDefinition) +
            sizeof(SCounter);
        if(dwReqSize<*pdwBytes)
        {
            // begin with the data definition
            ::memcpy(pDest, &g_objdef, sizeof(g_objdef));

            // now, find the location to add the data
            SCounter* pCounter = reinterpret_cast<SCounter*>(
                reinterpret_cast<PBYTE>(pDest) +
                sizeof(g_objdef));
            pCounter->m_block.ByteLength = sizeof(SCounter);

            // copy the data
            SBookStats stats = ::LookupStatistics();
            pCounter->m_dwWordCt = stats.m_dwWordCt;
            pCounter->m_dwSentenceCt = stats.m_dwSentenceCt;

            // make sure the definition block is set correctly
            pDest->m_type.TotalByteLength = dwReqSize;
            pDest->m_type.NumInstances = PERF_NO_INSTANCES;

            // now, move the data pointer and save object count
            *ppData = reinterpret_cast<LPVOID>(
                reinterpret_cast<PBYTE>(pDest) + dwReqSize);
            *pdwBytes = dwReqSize;
            *pdwObjectTypes = 1;
```

```
        }
        else
        {
            // not enough room, ask for more
            *pdwBytes = 0;
            *pdwObjectTypes = 0;
            dwResult = ERROR_MORE_DATA;
        }
    }
    else
    {
        *pdwBytes = 0;
        *pdwObjectTypes = 0;
    }
    return(dwResult);
}


// the next two methods handle the cleanup of the DLL, the
// first does the work while the second interfaces with the
// system
void ShutdownTransferData()
{
    // clean up the data transfer area
    if(g_pTransferData!=NULL)
    {
        // clean up the view
        ::UnmapViewOfFile(g_pTransferData);
        g_pTransferData = NULL;

        // clean up the file mapping
        ::CloseHandle(g_hMmfTransfer);
        g_hMmfTransfer = NULL;
    }

    // clean up the mutex
    if(g_hMutexTransfer!=NULL)
    {
        ::CloseHandle(g_hMutexTransfer);
        g_hMutexTransfer = NULL;
    }
}


extern "C" DWORD APIENTRY ClosePerformanceData()
{
```

```
if(::IsInitialized())
{
    ::ShutdownTransferData();
}
return(ERROR_SUCCESS);
}
```

Listing 18-19 looks intimidating; but when you break it into pieces, you can see that it's not that difficult to create a performance counter DLL. The four main components of the implementation are the object/counter definition, initialization, collection, and shutdown.

The first piece, the performance object and counter definition section, creates a pair of cookbook structures. The collect function requires that a performance object have one PERF_OBJECT_TYPE structure and a PERF_COUNTER_DEFINITION for each counter it contains. This object definition tells the system what the data it collects from you means. You should look at the documentation for details on these structures. After the object definition, you need to supply the actual counter structure that holds the data. To create the counter structure, you need a PERF_COUNTER_BLOCK structure to lead in and then a data location for each of the counters you define.

The next logical section of the DLL is the initialization. Part of this initialization is standard: you need to look up the indices for the first counter and help descriptions. The performance counter string loading in Listing 18-17 generated these values. With the values for the counter and help descriptions, you need to fix up the data in the object definition. The custom part of the initialization section in Listing 18-19 is responsible for creating the IPC objects to gain access to the data from the server application. This construction is much the same as the generator code in Listing 18-18.

The workhorse method for the performance counter DLL is the collect method. The system supplies this method a buffer and size into which you copy your object definition and current counter data. The general procedure is to copy the seed object definition and the counter data one after the other. Just before copying the counter data, the DLL in Listing 18-19 fetches it from the application. The collection method can get complicated when you add instance data to your counters or when a client from another machine decides it wants data. These configurations are beyond the scope of this text, however.

The final phase of performance data collection is, of course, shutdown. This phase may or may not be executed by the client application. The library is responsible only for releasing any resources, such as the IPC objects in Listing 18-19. You can build the example and run the performance monitor snap-in, adding the counters from the W2KDG Automated Author object. Figure 18-9 shows the resulting chart. The chart represents the monitoring DLL built in Listing 18-16 through Listing 18-19.

You may find debugging a performance monitor DLL challenging until you build and use the PerfMon.EXE project from the Microsoft Platform SDK as your host application.

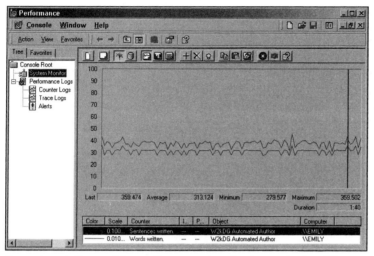

Figure 18-10: The resulting performance chart for the monitoring DLL

That's it. Creating the performance-monitoring DLL should be a simple matter of modifying the code in the last four listings when your application is ready to be fully integrated into the operating system. You should take care to design your performance objects and counters to be meaningful to you and the administrator and you should refer to the MSDN for details on each piece.

Other Tools

There are just a couple of minor notes that I want to make before finishing. Primarily, keep your eyes on the MSDN and the tools that Microsoft adds with every release and service pack for Windows. The developers that write the operating system also write tools for themselves that make it easy to test and develop new code. Keeping yourself informed about new tools is the most valuable tool in your box.

Debugger integration

There are a few debugging APIs that Windows provides to integrate with its Just-in-Time (JIT) debugging facility. The first is the famous DebugBreak() API. This function is exported by Kernel32.DLL and simply raises a debugging structured exception. If there is a debugger running the application, it takes control of the application. When a debugging structured exception is emitted while a debugger is not running, the system attempts to start it (if one is installed on the system). If there is no debugging application registered with the system as the JIT debugger, the system terminates the application just as it does for any other uncaught exception.

You should prefer the DebugBreak() API to any low-level interrupt (int 3 for you assembly programmers). It is the kernel-friendly way to stop execution. Commonly, you may use the function to give yourself the opportunity to attach a debugger to a service application.

 Chapter 11, "Service Applications," covers the details of creating services.

Another debugger-aware function is the IsDebuggerPresent() API. This facility enables you to detect the presence of an outer debugging application at runtime. You may use this function to hint at calling more heavyweight debugging features in your code – such as extended logging.

Finally, the kernel supplies the OutputDebugString() API for you to send messages to the debugger's output window. The CRTDBG library, in my opinion, has replaced this facility for the most part. It gives you finer control over the destination and typing of your debugging messages. You should prefer not to use OutputDebugString().

Portable executable image helper API

Only a few of you will ever require access to the internals of the file format for all EXE and DLL files. When you do need it though, you shouldn't parse through the specification and write the code yourself (no matter how much you want to). The *portable executable (PE)* format supports compiler and debugger vendors because it is an open standard that anyone can extract meta-data about the code within the file. Windows provides them, and you, with the *ImageHlp library* to examine almost all aspects of a PE file or files.

The MSDN thoroughly documents the ImageHlp library and, since it is beyond the scope of this book, I'll mention its facilities briefly. ImageHlp supplies a few utility functions for finding PE files, APIs for querying the debugging information in a file, and functions to extract debugging symbols including C++ name decorations. The library also provides general information about the contents of the EXE or DLL file and enables you to modify some of that information in creating altered applications or libraries.

Summary

Hopefully, this chapter filled in a lot of gaps in your toolkit for creating great Windows applications. I showed you how to use and leverage the Windows API error mechanism and how to deal with structured exceptions. I then showed you how to use the Tool Help API and PSAPI to examine the details of processes running in the system. Next, I covered the details of some of the facilities that the C++ runtime, MFC, and ATL libraries provide you to create and debug applications. Finally, I wrapped up with an implementation of a performance-monitored application, giving you boilerplate code to use in your applications.

As I explained in the preface, I designed the content in these 18 chapters so that it can be used to learn Windows 2000 development systematically and methodically or as a tutorial or reference. I suggested that you start at Chapter 1, "An Overview of Windows 2000," and then proceed one chapter at a time. More experienced developers, however, will find that the index in the back of this book provides rapid access to specific lessons, listings, and examples – all of which will be invaluable to you in your development efforts.

And there you have it. Back in Chapter 1, I promised that by the time you completed this book you'd be armed with enough information and experience to write and deploy world-class applications. I hope you agree that I kept my promise.

And with that, Happy Coding!

Appendix

Using the Examples in This Book

THROUGHOUT THIS BOOK, I've shown you example applications that demonstrate how to use portions of the Windows 2000 operating system. In order to make these examples easy to use, I've placed them online for you to retrieve.

This appendix shows you where to find the source code and what tools you need to build the example applications from it. I then show you how to build the examples and how to contact me if you run into problems.

Finding the Source Code

I placed all of the source code for this book at the following publicly accessible Web site:

`http://w2kdg.forta.com/`

You should point your browser to this URL and follow the download instructions there.

The source code is organized under a top-level folder called `W2kDGSrc`. You can download a single file, `W2kDGSrc.ZIP`, which creates the entire source hierarchy for you when you open it.

The source hierarchy has a folder for each chapter in the book beneath the top-level folder. Each chapter folder is named `CHxx`, in which `xx` is the number of the chapter; for example, `W2kDGSrc\CH09` holds the entire source code for Chapter 9. On the Web site, each folder has a single file, `Listings.ZIP`, which creates the source hierarchy for the listings in that chapter. Each listing folder contains a Visual Studio workspace at the root and a subfolder for most examples, each containing its own Visual Studio project.

Finally, the Web site contains the source code listings in fully expanded form. Under the top-level `W2kDGSrc\CHxx\` folder, you can browse into each subproject folder and download any file you wish.

Getting and Configuring Tools

To use the example source code that I created in this book, you need some development tools. This section details the specifications for these tools and tells you how to configure them.

Tool list

In order to build and run the examples presented in this book, you need an installation of Windows 2000. You can use either the Professional or the Server edition – as long as it is later than the RC2 release (build 2128).

 The listings in this book were built and tested with Windows 2000 RC3; they will be updated to build and run in the final release of Windows 2000. This may force changes to the code.

In addition to the operating system, you need the Microsoft Platform SDK for Windows 2000. The Platform SDK is available online from the Microsoft MSDN website at `http://msdn.microsoft.com/`. It also is available in CD-ROM form with an MSDN subscription.

Finally, you need the latest version of Visual Studio and the Visual C++ compiler. The listings in this book were built and tested with Visual C++ 6.0, Service Pack 3. You can purchase this software from Microsoft or a third party as an individual unit. However, I recommend you buy an MSDN subscription, which includes a license for Visual Studio.

 If you use a preview version of Windows 2000 to run the examples, you may need a *hotfix* for Visual Studio to avoid intermittent access violations. You can download this fix online at `http://windowsupdate.microsoft.com/`.

Tool configuration

In order to run some of the examples, you must have administrator access to the system you are using. This means that you probably want to run them on a system that you can afford to have reconfigured and not a system that performs a vital function for you.

In Listing 10-4, I mention a *publishing folder* that contains built and consumable headers, import libraries, and DLLs. I usually place this publishing folder somewhere off the root of the disk drive that I use to develop on and name it something easy like `pub`. For example, if you place the listings in the `D:\W2kDGSrc\` folder, you should create a `D:\pub` folder.

To use the publishing folder, you must set the path to it in your environment and in Visual Studio. To set the path in your environment, right-click the `My Computer` icon on your desktop and select `Properties` from the menu. Now, go to the Advanced page, click the Environment Variables button, and find the `path` variable in the User variables list box. You simply need to add your publishing folder to the value for the `path` variable, dismiss the dialog boxes, and restart any applications that you want to pick up the change.

To tell Visual Studio about your publishing folder, choose `Tools...Options...` from the main menu bar. Next, go to the Directories dialog page and add the folder name to the Directories list for include files and for library files.

Building the Listings

Each chapter in the book has a top-level Visual Studio workspace named `Listings.DSW`. This workspace is located in the chapter folder, usually `W2kDGSrc\CHxx\Listings.DSW`. The top-level workspace has a second-level project for every project named in the listings. You will find this name at the top of each listing.

You can build all of the listings at once by loading the workspace into Visual Studio and choosing `Build... Batch Build...` from the menu. You then select which projects you want to demonstrate in the list box and press the Build button.

I also made it easy to build the examples in each chapter using the Visual Studio command line. Simply open up a command window, change to the chapter directory (`W2kDGSrc\CHxx`), and use the following command:

```
msdev listings.dsw /make all
```

The Visual Studio environment starts up in noninteractive mode, loads the workspace, then builds, as a batch, all flavors of all projects in that chapter. This command line works for all chapters and creates both debug-mode and release-mode versions of most example applications.

Getting Help

I tried my best to make the listings as easy to retrieve, build, and use as I could, but you still may have problems. Once you decide that you need help or have a comment for me, please send an e-mail to `w2kdg@forta.com`. I will monitor this mailbox and respond to you as quickly as I can.

I will use comments and problems from readers to improve the quality and ease of use for the listings. As questions and answers occur, I will create a FAQ that you will find on the book's home page, `http://w2kdg.forta.com/`.

Index

Continued